The **Gun Digest**® Book Of
BERETTA
Pistols

Massad Ayoob

©2005 Gun Digest

Published by

Gun Digest® Books
An imprint of F+W Publications

Our toll-free number to place an order or obtain
a free catalog is (800) 258-0929.
All rights reserved. No portion of this publication may be reproduced or transmitted in any form or by any means, electronic or mechanical, including photocopy, recording, or any information storage and retrieval system, without permission in writing from the publisher, except by a reviewer who may quote brief passages in a critical article or review to be printed in a magazine or newspaper, or electronically transmitted on radio, television, or the Internet.

Library of Congress Catalog Number: 2005924818
ISBN: 0-87349-998-0

Edited by Kevin Michalowski
Designed by Sandi Morrison

Printed in the United States of America

Contents

About the Author 4
Acknowledgements 5
Introduction 6

1 Magnificent Mouse Guns: The Smallest Beretta 10
2 Beretta's .22 Caliber Fun Guns 19
3 The Beretta Tomcat 34
4 The Beretta .380's 42
5 Model 92: The Flagship of the Beretta Fleet 52
6 The Beretta 92/96 Combat Compacts 71
7 The Beretta Vertec 81
8 The Beretta 96 88
9 Beretta Cougar 8000 and 8048 94
10 Beretta's Big Blasters: The .357 and .45 101
11 The Beretta 9000 112
12 Beretta Oddities 117
13 Today's Beretta Revolver 127
14 Beretta Accessories 141
15 The Beretta Elite Series 170
16 Maintaining Your Beretta 180
17 Careful Customizing Can Make Your Beretta Better 195
18 Selecting Ammunition For Your Beretta 215
19 Beretta Field Performance: An Update 229
20 The Epiphany of the Beretta 233
21 Shooting the Beretta 239
22 Manipulating the Beretta 243
23 Drawing the Beretta 253
24 Mastering the Beretta 261
25 The Beretta in the Training Environment 277
26 La Finé 287

About the Author

Massad Ayoob got his first Beretta pistol at the age of 12 and has been shooting them ever since. He has shot them at local matches and at the Nationals at Camp Perry, and taught their use around the world. He is the developer of the StressFire shooting system incorporated into U.S. Army combat pistolcraft doctrine.

The long-time handgun editor of *Guns* magazine, law enforcement editor of *American Handgunner,* and associate editor of *Combat Handguns* and *Guns & Weapons for Law Enforcement,* Ayoob has served as a sworn police officer for more than 30 years and has been head of the firearms committee of the American Society of Law Enforcement Trainers since 1987. In 1998, he was named the Outstanding American Handgunner of the Year. He has won numerous state and regional handgun championships, and held two national titles, being one of only a handful of confirmed Four Gun Masters in IDPA. Ayoob currently divides his time between New Hampshire and Florida.

Massad Ayoob

Acknowledgments

Some information has been given to me "off the record," and therefore will not appear in this publication unless the verification comes from another source. For instance, I won't name the executives at other gun companies who privately admitted to me that they knew damn well that Beretta had won the U.S. military contract fair and square.

Some input has been given "not for attribution." This means a promise to the speaker that his or her identity will not be revealed. If that compromises credibility, so be it. Let the reader be the judge of the information.

I would like to thank the many executives at Beretta, past and present, who kindly shared information with me. They include Cathy Williams, PR manager *extraordinaire;* Gabriele de Plano, Jeff Reh, Todd Green and Brian Felter. And to the many I can't name, you who know who you are, I am also grateful.

I would like to thank Ernest Langdon, who knows more about winning combat pistol championships with Berettas than anyone else because he has done it more than anyone else. Ernest's work is also the gold standard for combat Beretta pistolsmithing, and his comments were invaluable to this effort.

Thanks also to master Beretta armorers Bill Pfeil and Rick Devoid. Their intimate knowledge of how Berettas work was particularly valuable to the chapter on maintenance. Huge thanks to the men of the U. S. Marine Corps RTU and the U.S. Army Marksmanship Training Unit for their insights into the accurizing of the Beretta M9 into a match-winning bull's-eye pistol.

And finally, thanks to my editorial assistants: Herman Gunter III, Anna Gunter, and Gail Pepin. Without their efforts, the unforgiving deadline never would have been met.

It is a monumental task to review all the modern Beretta pistols and not one that can be undertaken in short order. To that end, portions of a number of the reviews that appear within this book were first published as magazine articles when those guns were first brought to market. In all cases, my assessments of the pistols in question still stand as they did when I wrote the original reviews. We gratefully acknowledge and thank the publishers of *American Handgunner, Shotgun News, Combat Handguns, Gun World, Guns,* and *Guns and Weapons For Law Enforcement* for their permission to use that important material in this book.

Introduction

This is the author's first Beretta. He received it from his dad for his 12th birthday. Ayoob has appreciated Beretta quality ever since.

It is a good-shooting pistol, and I still have it. The previous owner had gotten tired of its awkward 180-degree safety and removed it. He replaced the safety with a plug of brass and apparently just used the half-cock notch for safety. Beretta ergonomics got a lot better later.

When my first-born was ready for pistol shooting at age 8, I started her with the littlest Beretta; the Minx .22 Short. With that gun, she learned the fundamentals of good handgunning. Eleven years later, she used another Beretta at the National Tactical Invitational, and her skillful use of that Model 92FC 9mm won her the women's championship. She still owns those guns. The 92FC is one of the carry pistols on her license.

It was a pleasure and an honor to be asked to write *The Gun Digest Book of Beretta Pistols*. I go back a ways with these fine handguns.

I got my first centerfire handgun "of my very own," when I was 12 years old. It was a Beretta Model 34. The gun was a World War II veteran and so was the man who gave it to my dad. The first owner had retrieved it from an Axis soldier who, in the words of the day, "… didn't need it any more." The day came when the vet wanted to avoid the memories the gun brought with it and he traded it to my dad who gave it to me for my birthday.

Cat Ayoob fondly reminisces with the Beretta 92FC she used to win her class at the National Tactical Invitational at the age of 19.

Over the years, I've tested a lot of Berettas for various gun magazines including *American Handgunner, Guns, Combat Handguns* and others. Seventeen years as head of the firearms committee for the American Society of Law Enforcement Trainers put me in touch with senior weapons instructors of many police departments that had adopted Berettas. In the late 1980s, I experienced the humbling honor of being asked to teach for the U.S. Army's Marksmanship Training Unit. Networking at various pistol championships has given me a chance to talk shop with the leading armorers of the Army and the Marine Corps, and over the years, I've also made the acquaintance of a number of Beretta's staff. This put me in a splendid position in terms of resources to put this book together. The source material is everything.

In the pages that follow, you'll meet many pistol champions who swear by the Beretta and use it by choice. You'll see for yourself the pros and the cons of the three primary fire control mechanisms Beretta offers on its modern fighting pistols: the F series with manual safety, the D series with decocker only, and the slick-slide, double-action-only D series that "shoots like a revolver."

Far more important than those who've won pistol championships with Berettas are those who have used them to win gunfights and cheat death. They've used all three types, including Model F pistols both on and off safe. Let me introduce you to a few of them now.

Greg Lee serves with the Nashville Metropolitan Police. He was carrying a privately owned, department-approved 9mm Beretta, on safe, when a suspect drew a revolver and brought it up on Greg and his partner. In one smooth, practiced movement, Greg cleared his 92F from his SS-III security holster, popped off the safety, and lit up the would-be cop-killer with a stream of 124-grain Federal HydraShok bullets. The bad guy went down dead, before he could hurt either Greg or his partner. Greg proved, among other things, that a Beretta carried on safe in a security holster could be operated fast enough and reflexively enough to win a quick-draw contest for the ultimate stakes.

Stacy Lim is a member of the LAPD. She was off duty and carrying her department-issue 92F when she experienced a carjacking by gang-bangers. When she identified herself, the point man of the bad guys shot her through the chest with a .357 Magnum. The bullet tore her spleen apart, pierced her heart, and punched a massive exit wound in her back. Her 92F had already been off safe, carried that way per department edict, and she brought it up and shot him a couple of times, chased him when he ran, and shot him twice more. All four of the 115-grain Remington hollowpoints she unleashed found vital flesh. He died. Stacy survived. She is, to my knowledge, the world's only known survivor of a .357 Magnum gunshot wound to the heart. Eight months later she returned to full patrol duty. Last I knew she still wore at her hip the trusty Beretta that had kept her assailant from finishing her off. The gun had saved her life.

Sgt. Marcus Young serves with Ukiah, Calif. Police. A man armed with a knife and a five-shot .38 Special ambushed him. He was shot in the face, chest, back and one arm, and had the other arm torn open. While the homicidal attacker was trying to get at an HK machine gun in the patrol car, Marcus managed to aim with his badly damaged weak hand, the other arm being paralyzed, and trigger four careful shots. Each of the .40 caliber bullets went exactly where he aimed his privately owned, department-approved Beretta 96G and the suspect slumped dying in the front seat, his orgy of violence permanently ended.

Author, left, with Sgt. Marcus Young, who won the NRA's Police Officer of the Year award and saved many lives when, despite multiple severe wounds, he killed a heavily armed criminal with his privately owned, department-approved Beretta 96 service pistol.

Marcus at this writing is still recovering from multiple surgeries, working light duty at the department, and very glad that he chose to carry a Beretta pistol that allowed him to shoot straight under some of the worst circumstances imaginable.

Then there is the armed citizen I don't have permission to name. This man got a permit and chose to carry concealed a Beretta 96D Centurion. In a road rage incident a man attacked and injured him severely. Realizing he was about to be beaten to death, he drew the Beretta and fired a single, accurate .40 caliber bullet into his antagonist's chest. The assailant reeled back, mortally wounded, and the fight was over. The shooting was ruled a justifiable homicide.

The Shape Of Pages To Come

Don't expect a puff piece. I don't work for Beretta, I work for you, and my job is to tell you the truth that I've investigated and experienced. You'll see why CCI may not be the best ammo for a customized 9mm Beretta, but why it is the best ammo you can put in your little Beretta Minx. I will point out where there were weaknesses with some of the guns and how to fix them if they haven't already been fixed. I will show you how and why the Model 92 has earned a reputation as one of the all-time great handguns and why the Model 9000 was the worst piece of crap that ever left a Beretta factory.

In some of the quotes and reprinted passages, reference will be made to the magazine ban. It lasted for ten years and definitely affected sales and purchasing patterns of pistols. The references are left in to be true to the times the words describe and reflect.

There will be some intentional repetition, but only when it is a point worth repeating. For example, there is the life-saving potential of the F-series Beretta pistol when carried "on safe." In the accounts rendered above, any number of quality handguns might have saved the lives of the brave men and women who wielded them. However, in studying the deaths and injuries of police officers in action I've seen again and again when the on safe pistol in general – and the on safe Beretta pistol in particular – saved the Good Guy's life when the Bad Guy gained control of it.

After seeing cases in which the Beretta had saved their deputies' lives in such incidents, the Los Angeles County Sheriff's Department made it mandatory for their thousands of armed personnel to carry their 92Fs on safe. Within just a few years of that policy change, according to that department's veteran trainer, Harold Flynt, four more saves were documented. The North Carolina Highway Patrol

Deputy sheriff David Maglio lowers his department-issue Beretta 92F after shooting a perfect score. Berettas have earned an impressive reputation in American police service.

has carried Beretta pistols on safe since 1983. The department progressed from the 92F 9mm to the 96F 9mm to their current Beretta Cougar Model 8357F in .357 SIG. One of their instructors told me that in 20 years of on safe carry, so many lives have been saved in gun grabs that the department has lost count. Yet LASD and NCHP have one more thing in common: No deputy or trooper in those departments has ever been hurt for failure to remember to disengage the safety on a Beretta during the draw to fire in self-defense.

That is a point that bears repeating. To say, "On safe carry saves lives" just once is to leave five words floating in the sea of a book that spans 130,000 words. It understates the huge importance of the documented information being imparted. On safe Beretta F pistols have saved many lives. While many other pistols have this feature – and many such saves have been documented with them – it is worth noting that no such pistol's slide-mounted safety lever is easier to operate than the Beretta's. The easier the safety catch is to operate the more likely the user is to employ it for its intended purpose.

The importance of keeping the finger off the trigger when not in the act of intentionally firing the weapon is likewise huge and is likewise repeated throughout the text that follows. Auto mechanics know how motorists drive cars and authors know how readers read books. Many jump from chapter to chapter. When talking about things that can save lives and prevent tragedy, the writer is irresponsible if he just mentions them once up front when he knows that many of his readers will dive into a book in the middle at a chapter heading that most interests them.

For the same reason the importance of proper care of the gun and using only proper magazines is emphasized again and again. The war in Afghanistan and Iraq reinforced the lesson that using cheap aftermarket magazines, even if the Government buys them on bid, can cause the finest pistols to jam. The advice is clear: Use *only* Beretta and MecGar brand magazines in these guns. Since MecGar of Italy is a primary vendor of magazines to Beretta, a MecGar magazine for a Beretta *is*, for all practical purposes, a Beretta magazine.

The history of the Beretta firearms company is huge and rich. It is worthy of a lavish book of its own and I won't cover it here because that book is already in print. It is *The World of Beretta: An International Legend* by the man who is probably the world's leading firearms historian, R.L. "Larry" Wilson. Larry has been both my teacher and my student, depending on the discipline involved. I'm proud to call him my friend. My respect for his work will be apparent in the following pages from the frequency with which I quote his exhaustive and scholarly work. This book will focus on the Beretta pistols currently in wide use, and how to use them. There is not room to do the company's history justice, and no one is ever going to beat Larry Wilson at that game in any case.

Magnificent Mouse Guns:
The Smallest Berettas

Small pistols with small bullets have a place. I don't want a small-caliber pistol for self-defense. If, after taking all things into consideration, you make the informed decision that *you* want a small-caliber pistol, I don't think you can do better than those made by Beretta.

I've heard it said, "If the Beretta .25 was good enough for James Bond it's good enough for me." Just remember that James Bond was a fictional character. Another scribe commented that he had read the Beretta .25 was the preferred handgun of the Boston mob, and they knew about killing people. Well, the Boston mob certainly knows about committing murder, but shooting helpless victims in the back of the head with a small-caliber pistol has nothing to do with defending yourself against a violent, aggressive creature that may come at you on two legs or four.

Fine accuracy and extreme reliability make the Beretta the .25 caliber pistol of choice in my book. A lot of these very small guns are prone to malfunction. The .25 Berettas are not. No more reliable pistol has ever been manufactured in the caliber. Beretta has produced the double-action Model 21, a.k.a. Beretta Bobcat, for many years. For almost half a century they made the Jetfire, which is perhaps the finest very small single-action .25 ever produced.

The Bobcat is also available in .22 Long Rifle. Whether the .22 LR or the .25 ACP is the more effective is a matter of debate. The ballistics tables give it to the .22, but the ballistics tables are calibrated on longer barreled pistols that produce more velocity and therefore more energy. When you chronograph the two calibers out of identical short-barrel pistols, the .25 is generally seen to be putting out a little bit more power.

The .22's big advantage is its cheap ammunition. If you need to defend yourself with a small cartridge you need to place the bullet with surgical accuracy. That sort of accuracy with a small pistol under stress comes only from constant practice that makes precise shooting a matter of autopilot. Because of its much lower cost, .22 LR ammunition is much more conducive to skill-building practice than even the cheapest .25 caliber ammo. Reliability, however, is a factor that cannot be compromised in a defensive firearm. The .22 LR is a

The tiny Beretta Jetfire may be the best vest-pocket size .25 auto in the world, says author.

The fixed sights of baby Berettas can't be compared to the fine ones on their larger cousins, but are better than most of the tiny pistols available.

Taurus PT-22 in .22 Long Rifle is a very good copy of the Beretta Model 21 Bobcat, rendered in double-action-only.

long, narrow cartridge with a proportionally wide rim that has given gun designers and engineers fits when they try to build a small pistol around it. I have seen some Beretta 21 series pistols that were 100 percent reliable in .22 LR, and some that were not. Every Beretta .25 ACP I have seen has been totally reliable.

The Bobcat is "drop safe." That is, can be carried with a round in the chamber without fear that it will discharge accidentally if dropped or struck.

"The Bobcat/Model 21 pistols have a light firing pin moving within a heavy firing pin spring," explains Gabriele de Plano of Beretta. "The gun is drop safe because the gun can't be hit with enough impact to make the firing pin move sufficiently inside its channel to cause a discharge. Only the hammer striking the firing pin will make it fire. This is why it passes the drop test."

A pistol with a round in the chamber is what you want in a gun of this type. With calibers this feeble, your only chance is to get the gun out quickly and place an accurate shot swiftly. There may well not be time to get a round into the chamber. The double-action first shot of the Bobcat/Model 21 series pistols makes most people more comfortable carrying them with a live round up the spout. While I, and I'm sure Beretta, would recommend that a gun in the pocket be carried in a pocket holster, we are both aware that some people are just going to drop the gun into the pocket or purse. When it is carried like that there is the potential for the manual safety to be "rubbed" into the "fire" position unintentionally. The double-action first shot is a safety fallback.

My best advice would be to get a .22 Bobcat and shoot the heck out of it. If after several hundred rounds it has not had a malfunction, it's probably good to go. Just keep it clean and properly lubricated and it should stay reliable. If you get any malfunctions after the first couple hundred break-in rounds, send it back to the factory, and when it is returned to you, repeat the process. If it still isn't working, swap it for the .25 caliber version. If you don't want to go through that hassle, just get the .25 caliber to start with.

Make sure you do a goodly amount of your practice in double-action firing mode. If that's how you carry it, that's how you should train with it. The first shot is the most important, in most cases. A long, heavy pull exerted against a short, light gun requires lots of experience working the trigger before the shooter can keep the muzzle on target as the index finger manages the double-action firing stroke at combat speed.

The Bobcat is basically a pocket pistol. Its key design feature is its double-action first-shot trigger mechanism. A long, heavy pull of the trigger for the first shot is seen by those people who have long experience in the investigation of unintentional firearms discharges as a bulwark against accidental

A short forward press on the thumb lever activates the tip-up barrel feature on small-frame Berettas produced since 1954.

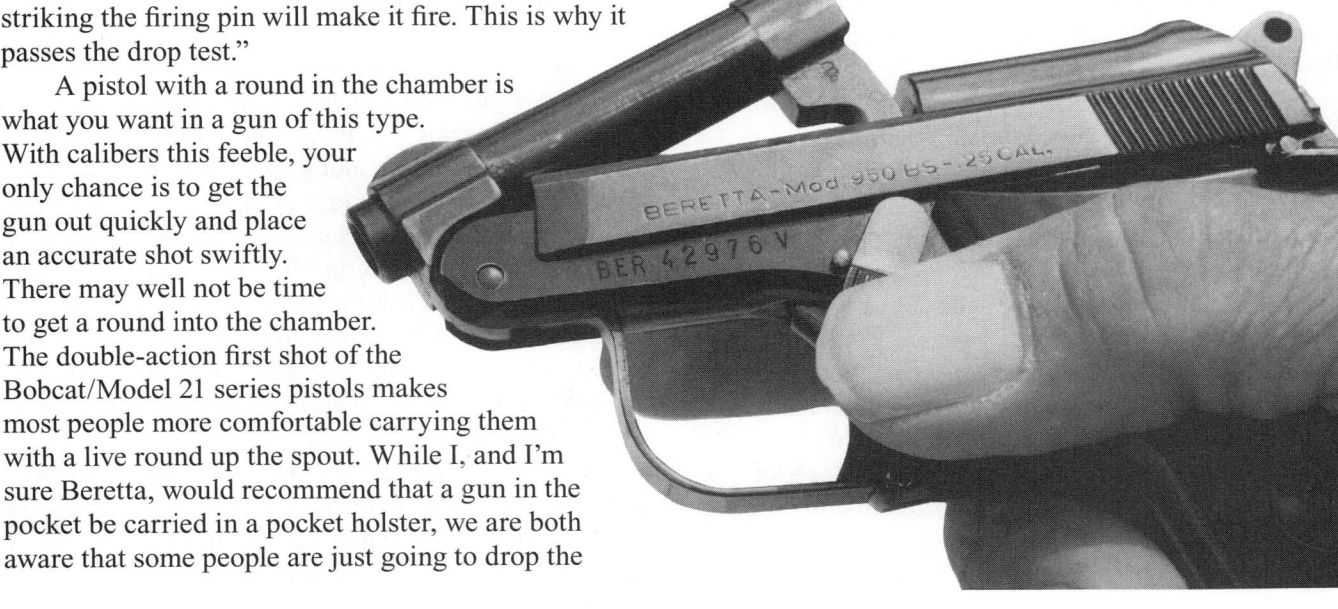

Here is a 950 BS Jetfire .25 shown cocked and locked with a live round in the chamber. What looks like a large, knurled screw at the lower rear of the grip panel is actually a push-button magazine release.

discharge under stress. The Bobcat/21 series also has a frame-mounted manual safety located in the same place, and operated in the same way, as the safety catch on the classic Colt 1911 and Browning Hi-Power pistols.

As is common, the sights on these little guns are small, but they're better than a lot of what the competition offers. Painting them a bright color may help your eye to pick them up. Use enamel from a hobby shop or refrigerator enamel from an appliance store.

The smallest of Beretta pistols is the 950/Jetfire series, which was produced for nearly 50 years beginning in 1954. The reliable, accurate Jetfire .25 will fit not just in your jacket pocket, but also in the little business card pocket most clothing manufacturers sew *inside* the pocket of a blazer or suit coat. If you need a really tiny backup gun, this is one to consider.

A variation of the Jetfire and its .22 Short companion gun is the Beretta Minx, with a 4-inch barrel. In perspective, the Jetfire made the little Minx look like a long-barreled miniature target gun. These fell out of favor and were dropped from the catalog because they were incongruous to the Model 950's function as a pocket pistol. However, for the person looking for a very small and light pistol to introduce shooters with very small hands to recreational handgun shooting, a .22 Short Minx with a 4-inch barrel is ideal.

The Minx and Jetfire are neat little guns. Toward the end of their epoch, they were produced in stainless steel, called Inox by Beretta. If the 950 series is ever brought back, which I hope one day it will be, I would like to see a 4-inch barrel .22 Short plinking version with larger front and rear sights that would be more amenable to the development of good shooting habits. A small adjustable sight like the ones found on Smith & Wesson's little Kit Guns, or on the smallest .22 revolvers produced by Taurus would be ideal.

The 950 series was so popular it is now widely available on the secondhand shelves of gun shops. I hope they are returned to the line eventually.

I wrote about these baby Berettas in an article in the 2000 edition of Harris Publications' *The Complete Book of Handguns*. Everything I said then still goes now.

The Littlest Beretta

The .22 pistol comes into its own as a recreational handgun. Plinking – informal target shooting at things like tin cans – is always more fun if you can bring one or more kids along and introduce them to the shooting sports. Because of that a pistol adaptable to small hands has particular value for recreational shooting. The little Beretta Minx in .22 Short fills this bill nicely. Its light weight, 10 to 11 ounces, made it a darling of those who wanted to carry a gun but didn't expect to need one, and that feathery weight makes it an ideal "fun gun" for people who don't have much upper body strength.

In his excellent book, *Modern Beretta Firearms* (Stoeger Publishing Company, 1994), gun expert Gene Gangarosa, Jr. notes that the first version had no manual safety. That original Model 950 was

Left: the .25 ACP Jetfire. Center: the .22 Short Minx. Right: A 950 EL, Beretta's deluxe version.

typically carried with the hammer at half-cock if a round was in the chamber. Many users simply carried it with the chamber empty. In 1978, when Beretta began assembling these guns in Maryland instead of Italy, a manual safety was added. Thus was born today's Model 950 BS, which can be carried cocked and locked. Because it was understood that when worn loaded the gun was likely to be carried loose in a pocket, the factory made sure there was a strong detent to hold the thumb latch in place. This has required firm pressure to engage or disengage the safety on every sample I've examined. (A source at Beretta once told me that while the 950 series has no designated internal, passive firing pin safety device, the nature of the firing pin spring was such that tests convinced the factory that the pistol was "drop safe" under all reasonable circumstances with a round in the chamber.)

When my first child was 8, she had been shooting a .22 rifle for two years and was ready for handguns. I started her with a Beretta 950. She was able to operate the controls, even though she needed her off hand to help sometimes with the safety catch. She quickly progressed to bigger guns, but not before she had acquired an S&S courtesy of famed gunsmith John Lawson. John likes kids, and the "S&S" stands for "Sugar and Spice." It was a 950 EL, the deluxe model with gold inlay. John eased up the trigger and made the safety a little lighter to operate since he knew she wouldn't be carrying the gun in a pocket. He even had the barrel ported, which was really cute. Ted Blocker made up one of his ISI competition rigs for it, right down to an itty-bitty double magazine pouch. He said it was the smallest dress gunbelt set he had ever made. Still, it was with this gun and rig that she learned quick draw. Eleven years later, using another Ted Blocker holster and a bigger Beretta, she would win High Woman honors at the National Tactical Invitational at Gunsite Ranch.

Many carried the Beretta 950BS with the hammer down on an empty chamber.

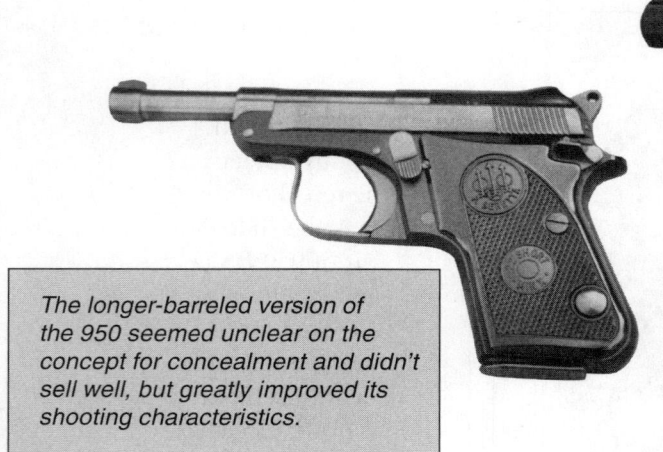

The longer-barreled version of the 950 seemed unclear on the concept for concealment and didn't sell well, but greatly improved its shooting characteristics.

The best very small plinking pistol ever, in the author's view, was this uncommon 4-inch variation of the Beretta Minx.

Handling The 950 BS

Though small, this pistol does not bite the hand with the edge of the slide as so many .25 through .380 pistols will do, when fired by average-size men. It doesn't seem to ding the hands of petite females or kids at all.

The trigger pull is surprisingly good for a pocket pistol. The 950 BS seems to average 5 to 6 pounds of pull weight. Lawson brings that down to an easy and crisp 4 pounds.

Like bigger Berettas of the mid-20th century, the 950 BS has a push-button magazine release located at the lower rear of the left grip panel. Some are of the opinion that's not the best place to put it. It looks to this writer as though the Italian designers simply bought into the German concept of the 1930s, where the thinking was it would be a good idea for weapons with removable magazines to have designs that forced the shooter to remove them by hand instead of ejecting them and leaving them behind on the battlefield. (You see this concept today with other German small arms, notably the HK series of submachine guns and battle rifles.)

The shooter used to pressing a button with his thumb to eject a magazine has a tendency to try to do this with the baby Beretta by flipping it upward in his hand. DON'T DO IT! This gives you a very tenuous grasp on the pistol, and creates an excellent chance that you'll drop it, with a round in the chamber, the hammer cocked and the safety off. You don't need me to tell you that this would be a bad thing.

The smoothest reload for the right-handed shooter is to bring the left palm down under the butt of the pistol. Now, as the left thumb pushes straight in on the button, the magazine drops cleanly into the palm of the hand to allow for a secure grasp. Take it out, put it away, reload and carry on.

That's the smoothest magazine removal, presuming casual plinking. The most efficient reload, which presumes a "need for speed," is the one I taught my little girl. Withdraw the fresh magazine, holding it between thumb and middle finger with the bullet noses toward the index finger, which is alongside the front of the mag. Extend your thumb and jab the mag release. The spent mag will fall away cleanly if you press in hard and the pistol's grip is perpendicular to the ground. Now, insert the fresh mag.

This pistol has no slide release lever and no slide lock. If it has been run completely dry, you have to "jack" the slide to the rear and let it fly forward.

A signature feature of the 950 pistol is the tip-up barrel. Beretta continued this concept with their double-action Model 21 .22 LR and their Model 86 .380

The author's daughter, Cat, looks back from adulthood at the .22 Short Beretta Minx pistols with which she started a distinguished pistol shooting career.

For comparison, here is a S&W Model 342 AirLite (top, with Crimson Trace LaserGrips) and "long-barrel" Beretta Minx.

ACP. Taurus applied it to their double-action-only clones of the Model 21, the PT-22 and PT-25. On the 950 there is a lever above the trigger guard on the left side of the frame that's pushed forward to cause the barrel to pop up with its breech in the air and the muzzle down. To allow for the tip-up feature, the 950's straight blow-back action has no extractor.

The tip-up design eliminates the need to jack a slide at all. Its mechanism is easily manipulated, and readily allows anyone to check a chamber, even if they have very little strength. This is one reason I really like this auto pistol for teaching handgun techniques to kids. It also makes enormous sense for adults whose physical strength in the hands or upper body is limited.

Many years ago, a very good friend of mine who was quadriplegic and had only very limited use of his hands asked my advice on a carry gun. He couldn't handle the recoil of even a .32 or .380, and he couldn't draw back the slide of his Walther PPK. I got him into a pair of 950 BS pistols: a Jetfire .25 for carry, and the functionally identical Minx .22 Short for practice. It worked for him, and until his death he was confident that he had a gun that would work to protect himself and his wife. He knew the limitations of the .25 auto cartridge, but he also knew his own limitations. I knew his determination, and I wouldn't have wanted to be the thug who tried to mug him or his wife.

Why a .25 for carry, and a .22 Short for practice? First, my friend didn't reload his own ammo, and .22 Short rimfire rounds were a whole lot cheaper. Second, while the .25 ACP is pretty pathetic as a self-defense round, the .22 Short is even weaker. Third, while the 950 pistol holds six rounds in the magazine and a seventh in the chamber in caliber .22 Short, it holds eight in the magazine and a ninth up the pipe when chambered in .25 ACP. Finally, while the Beretta 950 is unexcelled for reliability in the world of .25 autos, the 950 in .22 Short jams often enough that I wouldn't trust if for anything more serious than recreational shooting or small vermin eradication at close range.

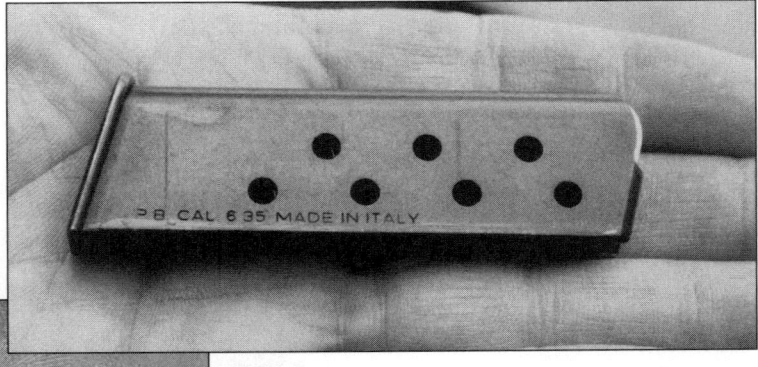

Left: The magazine for .22 Short Minx …

Above: … is distinctly different from that for the centerfire .25 ACP Jetfire.

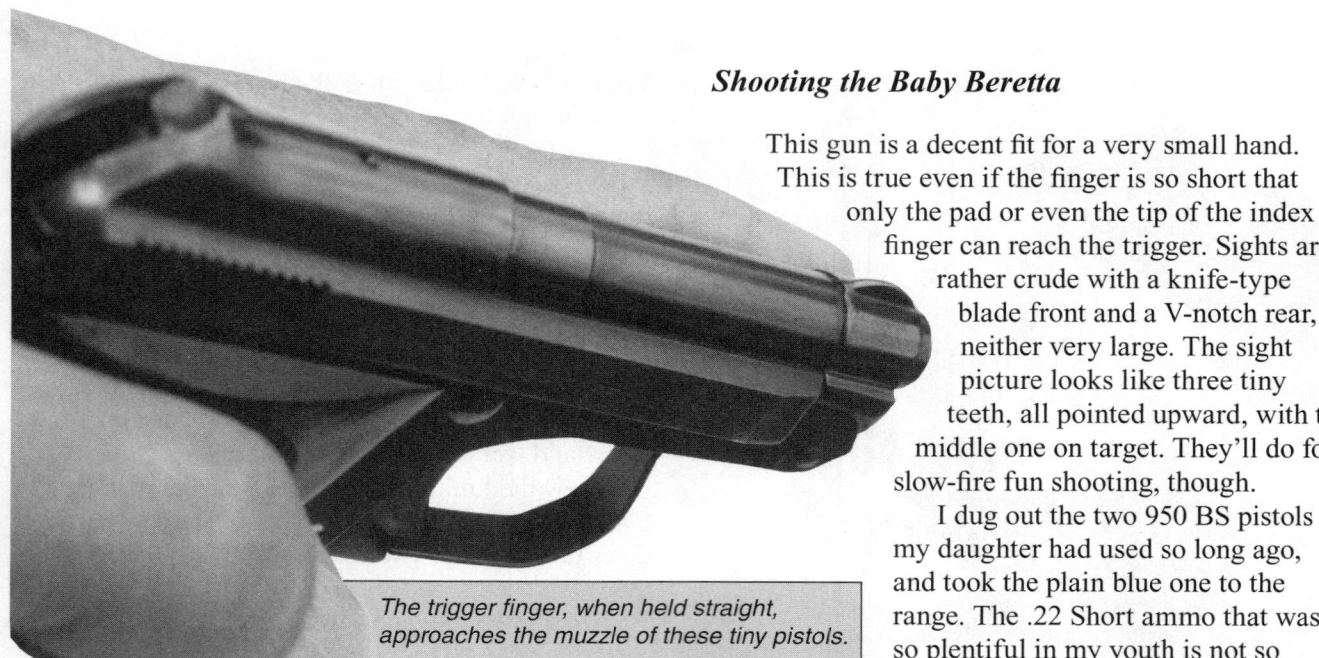

Shooting the Baby Beretta

This gun is a decent fit for a very small hand. This is true even if the finger is so short that only the pad or even the tip of the index finger can reach the trigger. Sights are rather crude with a knife-type blade front and a V-notch rear, neither very large. The sight picture looks like three tiny teeth, all pointed upward, with the middle one on target. They'll do for slow-fire fun shooting, though.

I dug out the two 950 BS pistols my daughter had used so long ago, and took the plain blue one to the range. The .22 Short ammo that was so plentiful in my youth is not so available today. I finally found the CCI brand at a well-stocked local gun shop. It came in three flavors: target, standard and hollow-point.

The phone hadn't stopped ringing at the office, and by the time I got to the range it was past the dark side of the end of the day. Even in the car headlights, I couldn't distinguish the aiming point crudely drawn in pencil on the white side of the IPSC targets, nor could I get a good visual fix on the miniscule blade that is the Minx's front sight.

Even so, the wee pistol easily delivered thorax-sized groups. Five hollow-points went into 6 inches even, five target loads into 5 inches even, and a like number of the standard copper-washed solid bullets delivered a group that measured 4 9/16 inches. (The distance was 25 yards.)

The trigger finger, when held straight, approaches the muzzle of these tiny pistols.

I recently accepted an assignment to teach in a foreign country where I could be licensed to carry a gun, but couldn't carry anything larger than .32 caliber. We were able to postpone the trip long enough for me to decide on a .32 Magnum or a .30 Luger auto pistol. I expect it will be the latter. If I were to find myself in a country that said I could carry a gun, but it had to be a .25 caliber or smaller, I would unhesitatingly carry a Beretta Jetfire .25. Or two. Or three.

But I wouldn't carry a .22 Short. It's tough enough to get a sharply rimmed round to feed in a small semiautomatic pistol without making it a Short rimfire round. As it is, Beretta had to build a little ramp into each magazine to make this pistol work in .22 Short. Not for nothing did John Browning design the .25 ACP cartridge expressly to feed in small auto pistols.

Here is the the John Lawson Custom "Sugar and Spice Special." Note the porting of .22 Short barrel.

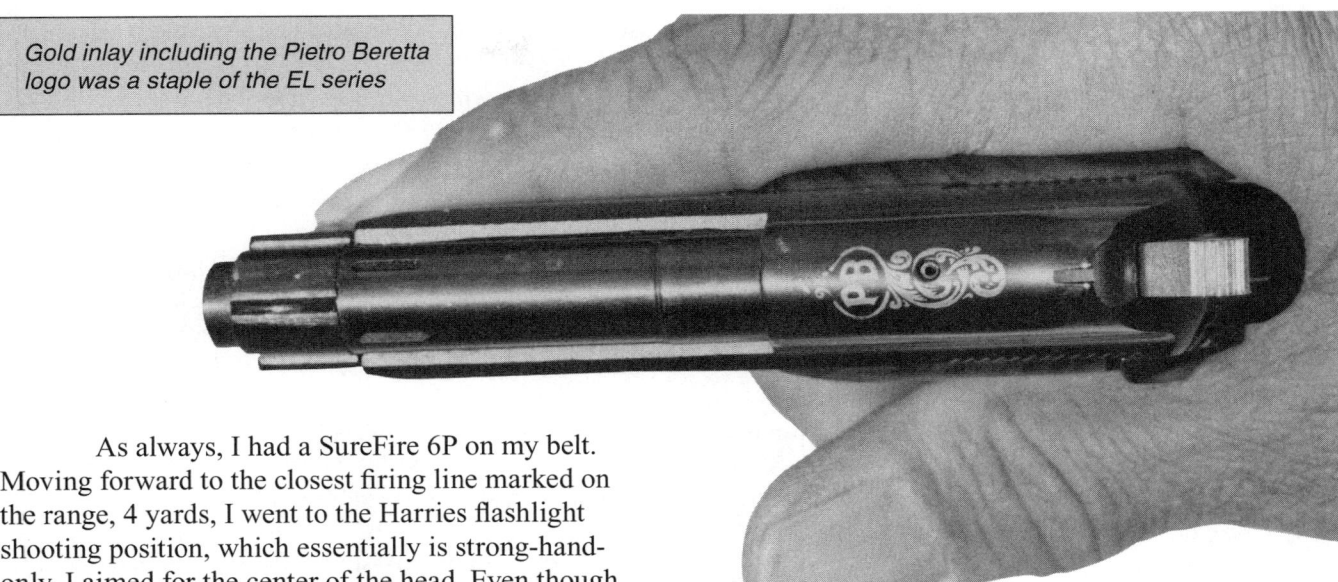

Gold inlay including the Pietro Beretta logo was a staple of the EL series

As always, I had a SureFire 6P on my belt. Moving forward to the closest firing line marked on the range, 4 yards, I went to the Harries flashlight shooting position, which essentially is strong-hand-only. I aimed for the center of the head. Even though the front sight was still awfully indistinct, the pistol delivered surprising accuracy. The five HPs punched a group measuring just 9/16 of an inch. The target loads were again tighter, with all five in 3/8 of an inch. And once more the standard load was most accurate of all, with five shots in 1/2 of an inch and four of them in a cluster measuring 5/16 of an inch.

We moved to the indoor range, which is only 50 feet long at this facility, to give the gun a fair chance. I laid out some rapid-fire bull's-eye targets. Alas, I discovered that it wasn't the light. Aging male eyesight had struck again. I couldn't get a focus on a front sight that small and that close without taking off my prescription shooting glasses.

Under these conditions, the hollow-point bullets delivered a 4 3/4-inch group, the best three in 3/4 of in inch. The target loads plunked five shots into 5 3/16 inches. The standard ammo delivered a 5 1/4-inch group, with the best three in 2 1/8 inches.

Given the "old guy's eyes" problem, I don't think the above was a fair test of the gun's accuracy. I'm sure it can shoot better than that. However, that will do for barnyard rats at close range.

It will also do in terms of accepted accuracy standard for small-caliber pistols. These are not 25-yard guns, though this one kept everything well inside the 8-inch circle of an IDPA target's center zone at that distance, even under terrible eyesight conditions and worse light conditions.

Some perspective is in order, though. Officer survival authority Terry Campbell has called the little .22 and .25 automatics "nose guns," on the theory that you can only survive with them if you stick them up your attacker's nose before you pull the trigger. At 12 feet from the target, even with poor light and vision circumstances, this gun gave groups tight enough that you could not only put the bullet up the nose, you could pretty much select which nostril.

The accuracy is quite sufficient for tin cans, plastic soda bottles and the like. I personally see this as a close-range plinking gun for beginners. It'll do fine there.

I can't help but notice that muzzle flash was mild with the low-powered .22 Short, and this was especially true of the target load. The latter gave just enough flash signature to silhouette the sight picture in the dark, and give the shooter feedback on where the sights were when the shot broke.

I did not experience any malfunctions with any of the CCI .22 Short cartridges in the 950 BS. In the past, I had noted that the Minx in .22 Short didn't even come close to the reliability of the Jetfire, the same gun in .25 ACP. I can't recall ever seeing a Jetfire jam in any way. When my older daughter was a little girl we figured out that the Minx was jamming once every 29 shots. However, we were using a brand other than CCI. From now on, the CCI ammo will be my load of choice in the Beretta .22 Short pistol.

For Defense?

I was the first guy to say it, and I'll say it again: "Friends don't let friends carry mouse guns." If "defense" means defending the chicken coop from rats at close range, the .22 Short Beretta will do the job. Some squirrel hunters I know have told me the

.22 Short is just right for those most edible of rodents, if they can be killed at short range. But a squirrel is to an aggressive human assailant as a man is to a Tyrannosaurus Rex. You wouldn't take a .38 Special as your primary armament if you went to Jurassic Park to hunt the elusive T-Rex.

You shouldn't take a close-range squirrel pistol as your primary weapon if you think there's a chance you'll be attacked by a 200-pound speed freak armed with a stolen .45 automatic. It's just Logic 101.

Velocity, energy and most other measurements of power drop off radically when fired from the 2 3/8-inch Beretta barrel. Tests by Phil Engeldrum and others show that in short-barrelled pocket pistols, the .25 Auto clearly outperforms the .22 LR. If that's the case, where do you think that leaves the .22 Short?

Still Deadly

Make no mistake, the .22 Short is still lethal. Smith & Wesson introduced the cartridge just before the Civil War, and it's been killing people ever since. Just for the heck of it, I took the Beretta to my basement along with an old, hardcover Reader's Digest Condensed Book, and shot it with each of the rounds I had tested at the range.

The hollow point went in 1 3/16 inches, expanding to 1/2 an inch at its widest point and shedding some lead. The standard copper-washed solid round nose projectile went in 1 1/2 inches, expanding to 3/8 by 1/2 an inch. Even the slow-moving lead round-nosed target bullet pierced to 1 3/8 inches, though there was more deformation than expansion.

How does this equate to performance in flesh? You can't really correlate it, scientifically. I can tell you that a .45 ball round will go through a good 6 inches of the same type of material, and will pierce some 26 inches of simulated solid muscle tissue (Fackler formula ballistic gelatin). That's about a 4.3:1 factor, which would extrapolate to the .22 Short solid bullet going in roughly 6 1/2 inches, and the hollow-point a good five inches. That's less than half of what the FBI accepts as adequate penetration for defensive handgun ammo, but it's more than enough to cause death. The .22 Short is not a toy. When used improperly it can be deadly. When used for self-defense, however, it would take surgical bullet placement through an open part of the skull (such as the nasal cavity) into the brain stem to guarantee an immediate cessation of violent action.

Final Notes

Even with its tiny sights, the Beretta 950 BS in .22 Short is an excellent "starter gun" for close-range plinking and firearms safety training. It would be better if they had made more of them with the 4-inch barrel. That's a gun I've rarely seen and never could find to purchase. Even the 950 BS in .22 Short is no longer offered in the U.S., though they seem to be plentiful at gun shows (doubtless traded in by people who bought them for self-defense and smartened up).

The Beretta 950 BS is, quite simply, a neat little pistol. It occupies a special niche in the handgun world.

Beretta has not offered the Jetfire since the end of 2002, and they stopped making the Minx even before that. Says de Plano, "The market made the decision. Sales of the Jetfire and Minx had become miniscule because the people who used to buy them were buying the Bobcat instead." Certainly the double-action feature and the optional .22 LR chambering of the slightly larger Model 21 made these guns highly desirable. Today the Bobcat is available in blue or Inox, and either .25 ACP or .22 Long Rifle.

Beretta's .22 Caliber Fun Guns

Beretta has built a lot of .22 rimfire pistols over the years, including many fine ones. Those produced today include ultra-compact pocket pistols designed for last-ditch defense. They can certainly be applied to informal target shooting – plinking – but aren't geared for something like a pistol match, and don't have the precise accuracy you'd want for small game hunting. For that, you need to branch to three other points in the Beretta line.

In the current Beretta catalog, I see three options that make particularly good sense for the recreational shooter. The choice will depend on what the shooter's needs are. Will it be preparation for defense with a bigger Beretta? Small game hunting? Match shooting? Or just general plinking? As always, we need to tailor the tool to the task. Let's examine each of Beretta's .22 caliber "fun guns" in their own right.

Upper: The Beretta Neos in short-barrel …
Lower: … and long-barrel configuration.

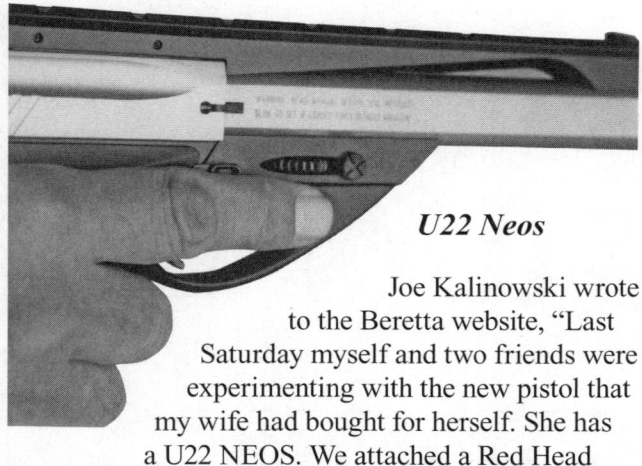

> Ayoob does not like the front trigger guard shape of the Neos. It goes too far forward leaving the fingertip on an incline that wants to slide back to the trigger, getting in the way of the "finger out of the trigger guard" safety principle.

U22 Neos

Joe Kalinowski wrote to the Beretta website, "Last Saturday myself and two friends were experimenting with the new pistol that my wife had bought for herself. She has a U22 NEOS. We attached a Red Head red dot sight to it. Using standard .22 LR ammo, we were hitting a 5-inch target consistently at 100 yards. We found it to be just a great pistol for target shooting. Both of my friends went out to purchase one after we were done shooting!"

The Neos is a futuristic pistol that would look at home in a Buck Rogers or Flash Gordon comic. The frame is polymer. The grip sweeps backward at a rakish angle that puts the shooter in mind of the German Luger or a 1950s era High Standard Supermatic .22 target pistol. Rising high above the frame, the flat-sided barrel and sleekly sculpted slide flow upward into a full-length rib with a ventilated space that makes you think of an ancient Roman viaduct. To that look of Rome, Beretta adds a touch of Greece.

"The pistol gets its name from the Greek word meaning 'new.' And the Neos is one neat gun, thanks to its ultramodern styling," says friend and fellow gun writer Wiley Clapp in the *Guns & Ammo* on-line magazine, www.gunsandammomag.com. At 25 yards, firing with a two-hand hold from a sandbag rest, Wiley was pleased with the results. "Early on it was obvious that this was a decent gun," he wrote. "The creep in the trigger system was annoying and made me wonder what a good pistolsmith might be able to do. But even with the annoyance – you don't get a match trigger in a plinker – the accuracy was there. Shooting six premium .22 Long Rifle loads produced an overall group average of 1.40 inches. That is smaller than the X-ring of the Standard American Pistol target (1.695 inches). And the best single group, fired with Eley Tenex, measured .97 of an inch. I think that is far better than we have any right to expect."

Handgun hunter and all around *pistolero* Paco Kelly got good accuracy with his Neos, too. Using Remington/Eley target rifle ammo, with a 4-power Simmons handgun scope mounted on Neos' handy rail, he was able to get a 1.6-inch group. With PMC's cost-effective new Scoremaster .22 LR match load, he got an outstanding 1.1-inch group. And these were *10*-shot groups, not the usual five-shot sequences. Impressive!

Helping them achieve these excellent accuracy results was the full-length mounting rail that constitutes the topmost portion of the pistol.

> The wheel above the trigger releases the barrel, a'la the old High Standard Duramatic. The slide stop is ergonomically placed, but check out the location of the thumb safety, near the grip tang.

Continuing the viaduct allusion, the edges look like the hand-rails on a bridge. The flat surface is great for pointing rather than precisely aiming. It's like looking down an aircraft carrier's deck in one sense, and for a clay bird shooter, it's more like looking down the wide ventilated rib of a Browning BROADway shotgun.

The sights themselves are an integral part of this design theme. The rear sight takes up the entire width of the sighting plane and proved to be reliably click-adjustable. The front sight rises boldly to give a clearly visible outline to the marksman's eye. Explains Clapp, "Out front there is a superb front sight. It is really just a block of blued steel, but this one was cleverly designed. It's tapered from the rear edge forward. This means the shooter who wants a crisp sight picture focuses on the front sight where he is looking at three edges (top and both sides) and not three surfaces. It is a small contour change, but it pays big dividends. Also, the top rib on the Neos is set up as a full-length Weaver base that allows for the mounting of various projected dot or scope sights."

The Neos is a combined effort of Beretta engineers and the house of Guigiaro, the Italian designers. As noted elsewhere in this book, I thought the Guigiaro-designed Beretta 9000 was a spectacular failure, a triumph of eye candy over ergonomics and

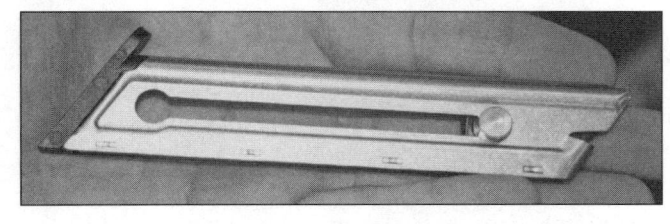

The front profile of U22 Neos gives good view of the protected muzzle.

The open-side Neos magazine has clean lines and an easy window through which to count rounds.

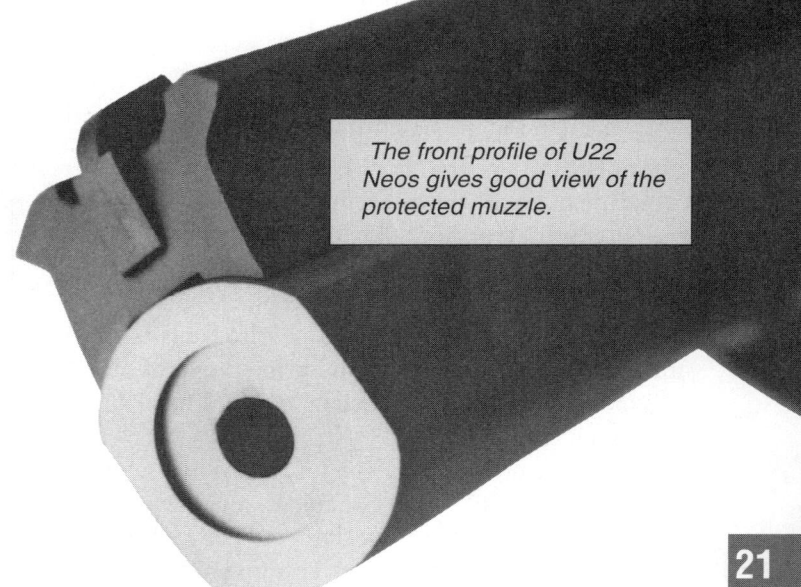

good mechanical function. But not all Guigiaro-styled Berettas are clueless. Witness the excellent ergonomics and function of the Extrema shotgun. In the case of the Neos, the engineers didn't let the designers go nuts. They merely let them fancy up a very solid, functional .22 pistol.

I recently had a chat with one of the Beretta engineers who did the internal design work on the Neos project. He has since moved on to accept a similar position elsewhere in the industry. He told me, "Mas, it took us four years to get the Neos perfect with the whole range of American .22 ammo as well as the European ammo it was originally tested with. But we got it right ... "

And that's the key. Most .22 Long Rifle is not an interchangeable commodity, as it might look to the uninitiated. There are lots of subtle differences between ammo types and manufacturers. But those four years were well spent. Everyone I know who owns a Neos or has shot one is without complaint as to the gun's reliability.

"J" Stuckey runs a busy gun shop, Southern Sportsman in Live Oak, Florida. He says, "The Beretta Neos is by far my best selling .22 handgun. I order them half a dozen at a time, and they sell right out. And, you know, I've never had one of them come back."

To find a Neos that

From this angle, we can see the fluted slide and ambidextrous safety of U22 Neos.

"came back," I had to "surf the net." This particular customer didn't post to beef Beretta, but to compliment them. He had found something wrong with his Neos, and Beretta had instantly made it right. He now had a Neos that worked perfectly.

Priced similarly to the Bobcat pocket pistol, itself an extraordinary good value, the Neos is an amazingly good buy. It's in the price range of other polymer-frame plinkers, such as the Walther P22 and the Ruger 22/45.

I have friends who use the U22 Neos as entry-level bulls-eye target pistols in local league competition. They do OK with them. They tell me the guns never miss a lick, unlike some of the finicky target autos the heavy hitters use, which jam more frequently. When I was at Camp Perry this year, I saw flyers from one entrepreneurial individual who is apparently doing trigger jobs on Neos pistols and attempting to turn them into full-fledged bull's-eye guns. I wish him the best.

I didn't see any Neos pistols on the firing line at Camp Perry. One reason is that the heavy hitters there want handguns that can shoot 1.1-inch to 1.6-inch groups at *50* yards, their standard slow fire distance. Never mind the 25-yard line they use for timed and rapid fire, and gun writers use for bench rest testing most handguns. A primary reason you won't see an out-of-the-box Neos in the hand of a High Master bull's-eye shooter in competition is the trigger pull. It is in the 4-pound plus range. While this is not a bad thing by itself, it is a chore to manipulate when the gun itself weighs only 2 pounds with the 4.2-inch barrel, and 36 ounces with the 6-inch barrel.

Clapp found the Neos' trigger "OK except for a small amount of creep." Trigger creep, for those new to the term, means a trigger movement that starts and stops, giving the sensation of parts grating against each other. It's an uneven pull that impairs good shooting in a lot of ways. A smooth but heavy trigger pull is far more manageable than a light trigger pull that has creep in it.

I've also found the Neos to have a creepy trigger in every one of the several specimens I've tried. Some are worse than others. Some are downright spongy. This is not conducive to doing your best shooting. On the other hand, having some felt movement before the pistol discharges can be a safety feature that lets you know under stress that the gun is about to go off. As there is "good" cholesterol and "bad" cholesterol and there is "good" creep and "bad" creep. For a gun that will be used for training new shooters, palpable movement in the trigger before discharge may actually be a good thing, in that it might prevent some premature discharges.

Where do you draw the line on that trigger pull? When the neophyte shooter becomes sufficiently experienced to want to shoot bull's-eye, an unforgiving game where only one hand may grasp and stabilize the pistol. It is there that a crisp, easy trigger pull goes past "want" and becomes "need" if

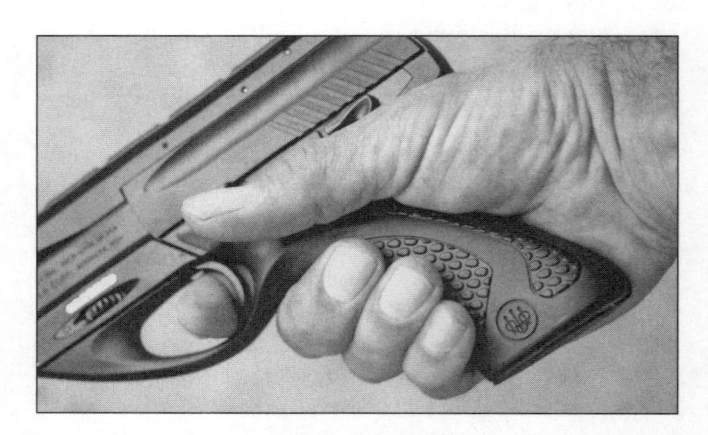

Above: Most shooters like the way the U22 feels despite the steep grip angle. The trigger finger of average size adult male can reach to the distal joint, which assures that short fingers can reach it with fingertip contact.

Left: From this perspective we can see the Neos' radical grip angle. Thumb safety is on-safe. Note that it extends downward slightly from frame, where it can contact the flesh of shooter's hand. Ayoob doesn't like this element of the design.

it's important to you to shoot the best possible score.

A shooter named Beth found that out. In the "BULLSEYESHOOTERS" SECTION of Yahoo.com's Sports Groups, she wrote, "Hi all, I have only been shooting bull's-eye for about a year and a half but I felt I should reply about the Neos ... before I started BE (bull's-eye shooting), after only a very basic pistol class, I knew I wanted to give BE a try. So w/ a .22 league getting ready to start here at our local range, I went out and bought a Neo (sic) – because it was kind of 'cute.' Well it was a mistake. It was very frustrating and discouraging for me as a new shooter ... I could hardly keep my shots on the paper let alone score ... I was then taken under the wings of some experienced shooters – one, after trying my gun, told me 'This is the worst trigger I have ever shot!!' I soon tried a few of their guns, shot much better, and bought myself an IZH. In my last .22 league I finished as high lady and reached the Expert level and am not too far from my DE (Distinguished Expert rating). I have since bought an accurized Ruger 22/45 w/ a Volquartsen trigger from a fellow shooter ... I plan on using that to teach my daughter ... it is much better than the Neo (sic) ever was and I only paid a small amount more for it ... so I would say to new shooters considering the Neos – unless of course they have changed the triggers – try a Russian or a Ruger."

Thus, we see that some like the Neos as an entry-level gun for match shooting, and some do not. Remember, however, that Beretta designed the gun as a plinker. Most casual shooters these days fire with a two-hand hold.

With a strong man holding it two-handed in a firm grip with a bench for support, the trigger on the Neos will not be an impediment to tight groups, as evidenced by those turned in by Paco Kelly and Wiley Clapp. However, when the gun is held one-handed at arm's length with no artificial support and aimed at a bull's-eye target 50 yards distant, it's going to be a different story. The Neos simply isn't made for that kind of shooting.

There are things I like about the Neos and things I don't. As noted above, I think the sighting system is excellent. So is the fit in the hand. So is the trigger reach dimension. The all-metal magazines are extremely easy to load, manipulate and clean, thanks to their open-sided design. The takedown is very efficient, using a wheel at the front of the frame to secure the barrel in place and harkening back to the old High Standard Duramatic in that respect.

Some features are less likeable. The magazine release is a push-button in an unusual place: directly in front of the trigger guard and above it on the right

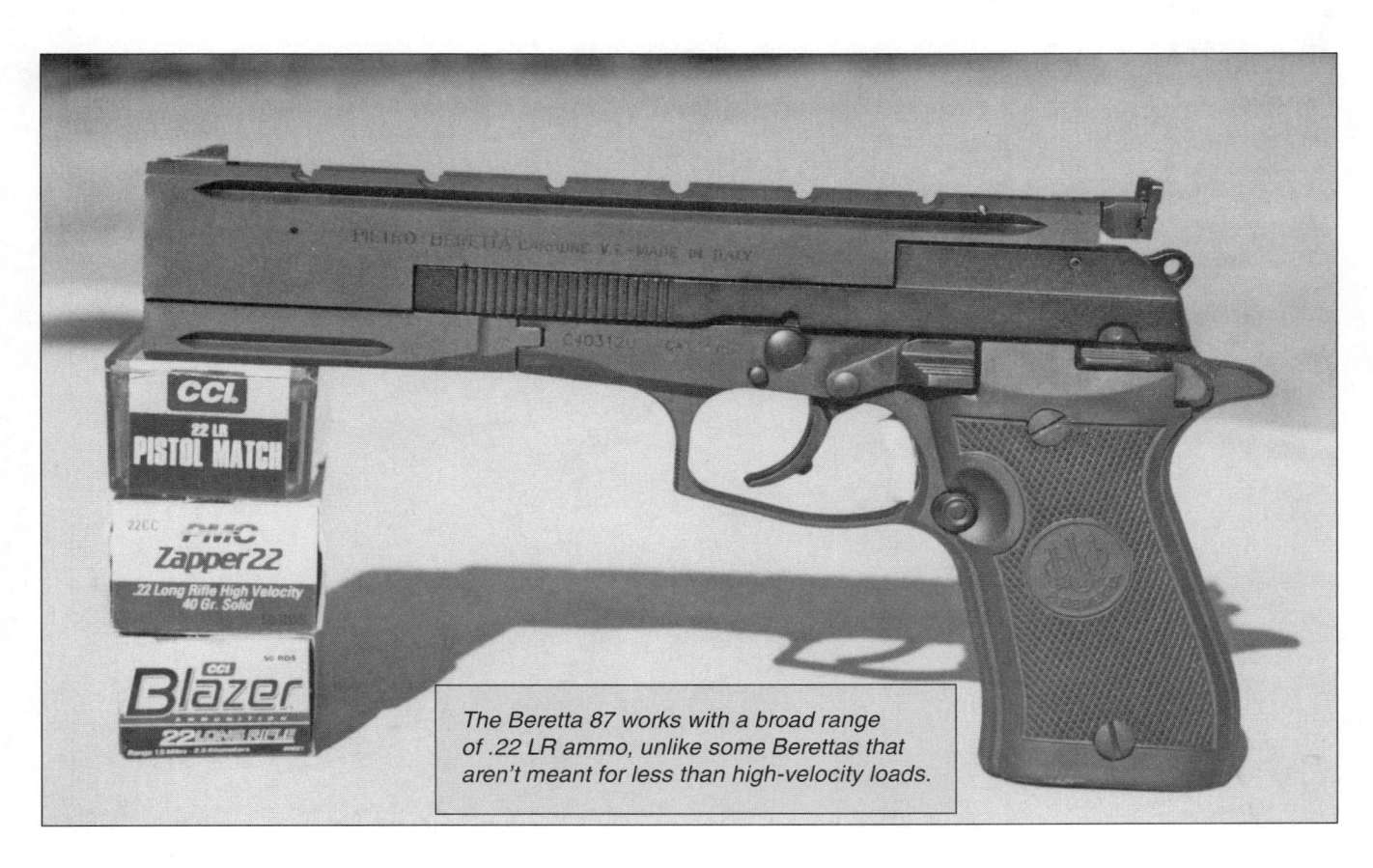

The Beretta 87 works with a broad range of .22 LR ammo, unlike some Berettas that aren't meant for less than high-velocity loads.

side of the frame. With my average size male hands, and being right-handed, I found it easy and quick to hit the mag release with my trigger finger. This is a good thing, as far as it goes, because it gets the trigger finger out of the trigger guard at a time when it shouldn't be in there. However, I don't think left-handed shooters will find it nearly as convenient as we righties do. The drop of the magazine was clean and efficient.

The manual safety is ambidextrous, a pleasant surprise and one too rarely seen on .22 caliber pistols. Unfortunately, the design of the safety catch is not ergonomic at all. When on safe, two sharp little pointy "ears" project downward toward the web of the hand. The camper who has picked up the gun when something in the woods went bump in the night may be tempted to off-safe the gun prematurely to relieve this sharp-edged discomfort. A cocked, off-safe pistol is now in hand. Not a great thing. Moreover, the angle at which the safety moves to put it in fire position is quite awkward.

The trigger guard is very large and roomy, which is a good thing for a gloved hand. All recreational shooting is not done in balmy weather. However, the shape of the inside front of the guard disturbs me a little. It's deeply niched out. This, apparently, is to allow the finger to slide quickly into the guard. This it does … all too quickly. One thing that will be hammered into you in any competent pistol-handling program is, "Keep your finger out of the trigger guard." Most of us prefer to keep that finger up on the frame. Unfortunately, some like to rest their trigger finger at the front edge of the guard. As the hand tightens in a stress situation, this tends to hold the finger taut, and if muscles are convulsed by a startle response or postural disturbance, the finger tends to snap back onto the surface of the trigger, often with enough force to inadvertently fire the pistol. The shape of the trigger guard on the Neos will, unfortunately, be conducive to that, I think. I'm not sure a redesign is necessary, but anyone using one of these pistols needs to be reminded that *unless one is in the act of intentionally firing, one's trigger finger should be up on the **frame** of this or any pistol, and not poised on the forward edge of the trigger guard!*

Above: The slide stop lever, safety lever, and magazine release lever are all ergonomically placed on the Beretta 87. The extended magazine holds 10 shots.

Right: Now, here, on the back of one of the author's 81-series Beretta .380s, is a functional trigger stop! He thinks Beretta should put one of these on the Model 87.

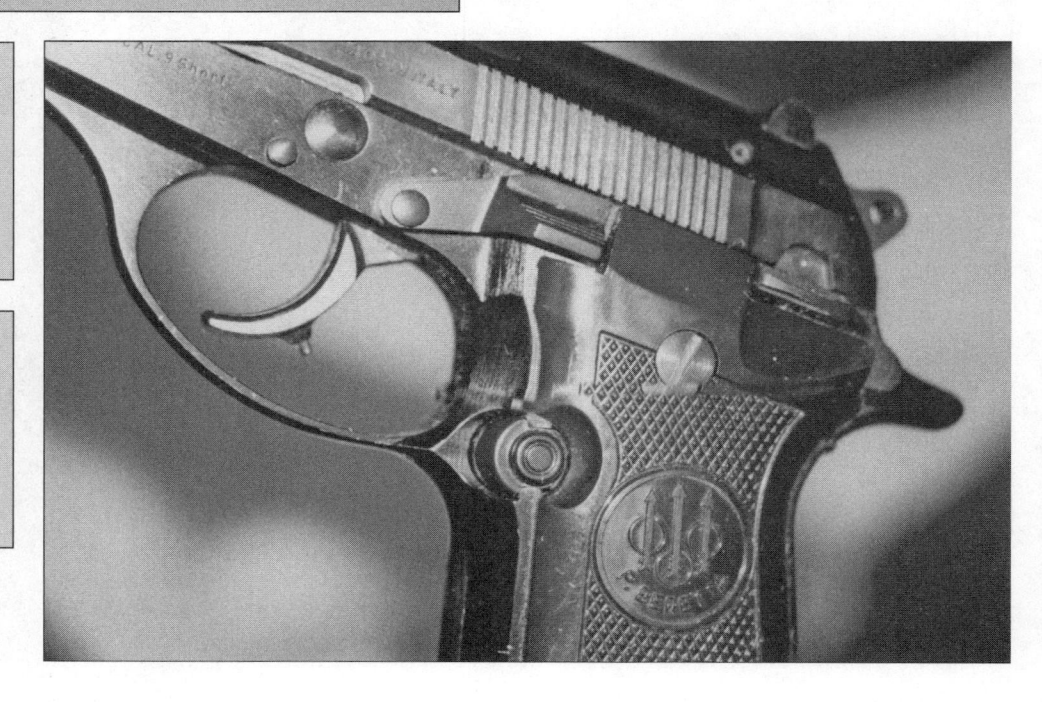

All things considered, though, the Neos is a cool little gun. I like it better than any of the other Guigiaro-designed Beretta handguns. It's built for fun, and in a safe, responsible recreational shooting environment, it will consistently deliver that fun. Its price, reliability and inherent accuracy, make it a splendid value, and that low price makes it a very affordable portal through which to enter the world of high-quality Beretta firearms.

The Model 87 Series

Beretta introduced the Cheetah Model 87 in 1988. It was a companion gun to the Model 84 and Model 85 series .380 caliber pistols and was functionally identical except for being chambered for the .22 Long Rifle cartridge. The same year, the firm offered the Model 89 Gold Standard, an aptly named target pistol that was built on the same frame but in single-action-only mode, with a skeletonized slide running under a high sight-ribbed barrel. The Gold Standard came with an exquisite target-grade trigger pull.

Along about 2000, the Model 89 Gold Standard seemed to disappear from the line, replaced by the Model 87 Target. Where the Gold Standard had resembled a cross between a Cheetah .380 and a Hammerli match pistol, the Model 87 appeared to be a

This impromptu "trigger stop" made a world of difference in the shootability of the Model 87.

Cheetah frame with the trigger squared a little in front. It also had a barrel/slide assembly that was in essence the one from the Gold Standard, but trimmed down a bit from the top and with a Weaver-style scope rail that also acted as a low-profile sight rail. The Model 87 Target pistol has its own 10-shot .22 LR magazine and will not accept the seven-round magazine of the .22 caliber Model 87 Cheetah.

At a solid 41 ounces, this gun still is not as heavy as most of the dedicated .22 caliber target pistols

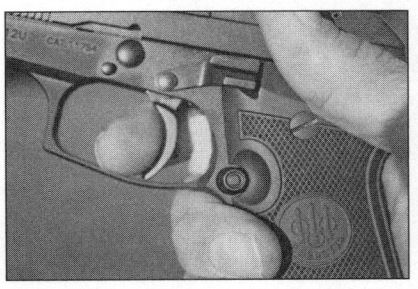

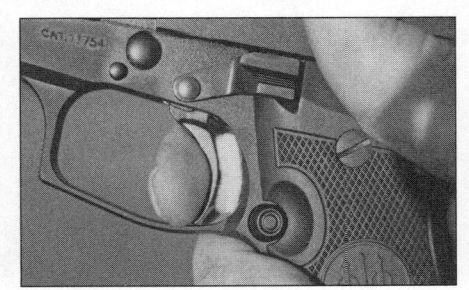

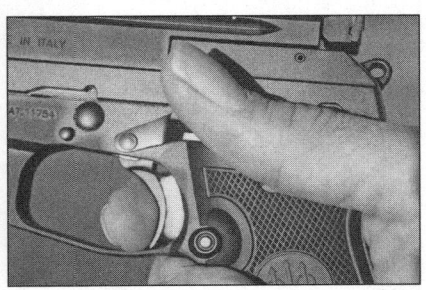

Top left: The backlash problem is diagnosed and solved. Out of the box trigger resistance begins at this point ...
Top center: ... and sear releases at about this point, at which time ...
Top right: ... the trigger lashes this far back to the frame, which can move the gun just as it's firing, ruining accuracy. The solution ...
Bottom left: ... is a trigger stop, here quickly rigged with a bit of floor protector. Pull starts here with the trigger at rest ...
Bottom center: ... and breaks at the same point ...
Bottom right: ... but now immediately comes to a soft, cushioned stop. Backlash cured!

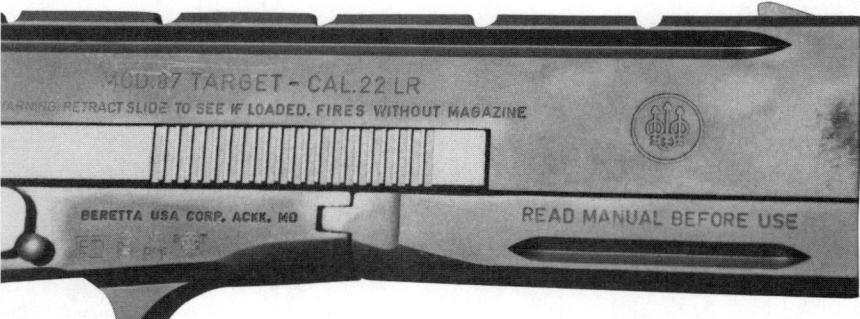

The muzzle weight has grooves to allow additional weights to be added. Matte finish is evenly applied to this businesslike pistol.

that find their way to the national championships at Camp Perry. It can be described as "target pistol lite." However, its compact grip frame fits exquisitely in smaller hands. Remember, it has evolved upward from a frame size that many categorize as a "pocket pistol." Trigger reach is excellent for shorter fingers.

Taking a sight picture, it's as if you were looking down a long pier going out toward the water; a pier with a handrail on each side. This slim pistol's balance is excellent, and there are attachment points provided to hang weights from the front if the shooter wants a more muzzle-heavy feel. Overall, this blue steel pistol, despite its matte finish, just reeks of quality. The skeletonized slide runs smoothly under a rugged sight rib that sits above the action like a bridge, keeping the sights solidly oriented to the barrel. In this, it reminds the shooter of two of the most proven American match target .22 pistols, the High Standard Victor and the Smith & Wesson Model 41. Its frame composition has been described as "zirconium-aluminum alloy." The slide has extensions running on either side toward the muzzle, with finger grooves. This is one pistol that you pretty much have to operate by reaching up underneath the front, with thumb on one side and fingertips on the other, and push back to activate the gun. The good news is that these grooves are a safe distance back from the muzzle, making this a much safer handling protocol than doing the same with, say, a Beretta 92 or a 1911 pistol with trendy forward slide grooves.

The trigger pull is smooth, with an easy roll, reminding the shooter of the old Model 34 .380 or Beretta's middle period pocket pistol in .22 LR, the Model 70. However, it had horrendous backlash, perhaps the worst I've ever encountered on a .22 caliber single-action auto. When the sear released, the trigger and finger took a long plunge straight back until they stopped against the frame. This unfortunate circumstance, called backlash or overtravel, is ruinous to accuracy.

The Model 89 Gold Standard, as I recall, had an adjustable trigger that was hugely better. It is sad that this attribute did not survive in the Model 87 Target incarnation.

My friend and fellow gun writer David Fortier recently wrote up the Model 87 Target in the *2005 Shooting Times Handgun Buyers' Guide*. He tested a dozen different match-grade .22 loads at 50 yards. This is twice the distance at which most handguns are accuracy tested, and is the yardage at which precision slow fire takes place in classic American bull's-eye matches. All 12 loads grouped well under 2 inches at 50 yards. Two grouped under an inch: Eley 40-grain Tenex delivered 0.87 inches, and Wolf 40-grain Match Gold did 0.67 inches. David wrote that he was firing off sandbags with a Burris 2x to 7x variable telescopic sight attached to the Weaver rails.

That, my friends, is match-winning accuracy. It's built in at the plant in Italy. The trick is getting that accuracy out of the pistol.

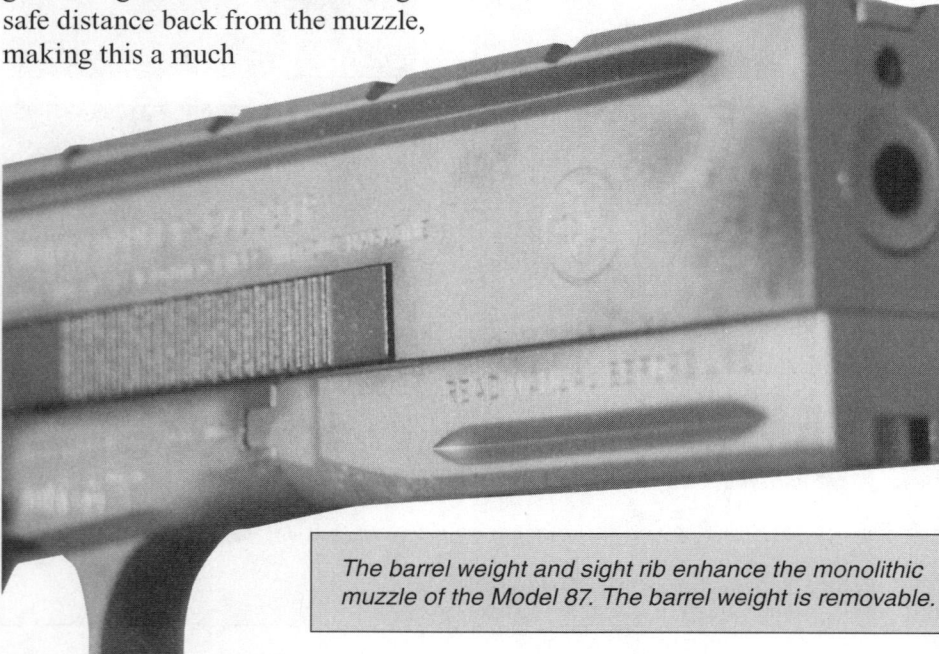

The barrel weight and sight rib enhance the monolithic muzzle of the Model 87. The barrel weight is removable.

David explained that he shot his at a seminar that Beretta held for the writers at the company he works for, Primedia. He described his test pistol's trigger pull as follows: "The trigger was a bit heavier, 4.5 pounds, than I like. Don't get me wrong. It was crisp with zero creep, no overtravel, and only took 3/16 inch of forward travel to reset." [1]

I re-read that. "Huh? *No* over-travel? How come David and his buddies at Primedia rate? Where do *I* get an 87 like that?"

Apparently, the test gun provided had been specially tuned at the factory. Much more overtravel, resulting in backlash, is present in every out-of-the-box Model 87 Target I've run across.

Now, by the time I read David's article, I had been shooting a test sample Model 87 Target provided by Beretta for this book. It was certainly a sweet-shooting little gun, but I wasn't getting nearly the five-shot groups David was. I was using the iron sights, not a 7X scope, and that could have been part of it. I've seen David Fortier shoot, and I can tell you he's a superb marksman, and *that* could have been a part of it. But after fighting with the trigger group after group, while the "best three shot" clusters were indicating tremendous accuracy potential, the fact that his pistol had no overtravel and mine had enough overtravel to qualify for frequent flyer miles probably also had something to do with the less than stellar performance.

Earlier, a friend and fellow firearms instructor in Michigan, Jeff Brooks, had bought a Model 87 Target for his young son. He was not any happier with the backlash than I was, or with the heavy (for a bull's-eye pistol) trigger pull weight that left Fortier dissatisfied. Jeff told me of his specimen, "Trigger overtravel is absolutely horrible and very excessive." He asked me to recommend a pistolsmith.

I told him to try Ernest Langdon, who specializes in Berettas, and that if Langdon didn't handle that model, to try Teddy Jacobson at Actions by T in Sugarland, Texas. It turned out that Langdon preferred to do major work only on Model 92 and 96 pistols, and light action hones on Cougars, and didn't work on 80-Series Berettas at all. Jacobson, on the other hand, took on the job. Jeff reported after he got the gun back from the masterful Texas pistolsmith, "We love the 87 Target. Teddy Jacobson did an outstanding job on trigger pull weight, smoothness, and travel." He sent me some pictures of young Jonathan and some of his targets, and it's clear, both shooter and pistol are doing fine.

The test gun I had belonged to Beretta, not to me. I'm used to heavy triggers, generally specifying around 4.5 pounds single-action in my pistols,

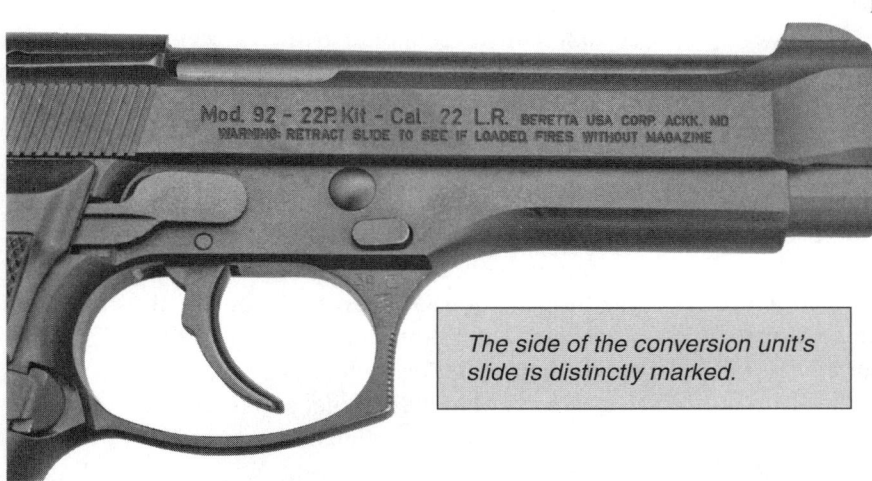

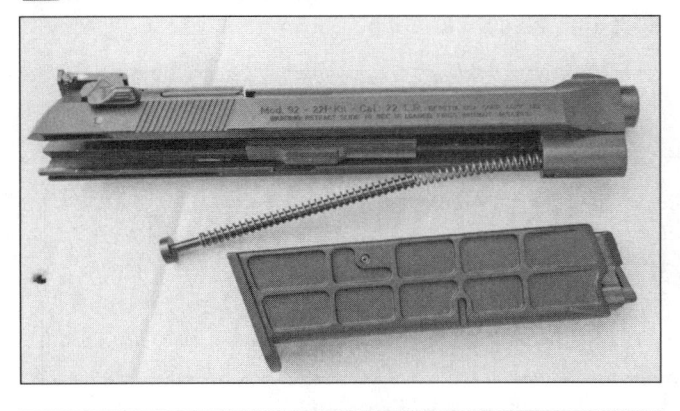

The side of the conversion unit's slide is distinctly marked.

This is Beretta's own .22 conversion unit for full-length Model 92 and 96 traditional double-action pistols. It includes a magazine.

The conversion unit, in place, duplicates all functions of the M9 barrel/slide assembly it has just replaced.

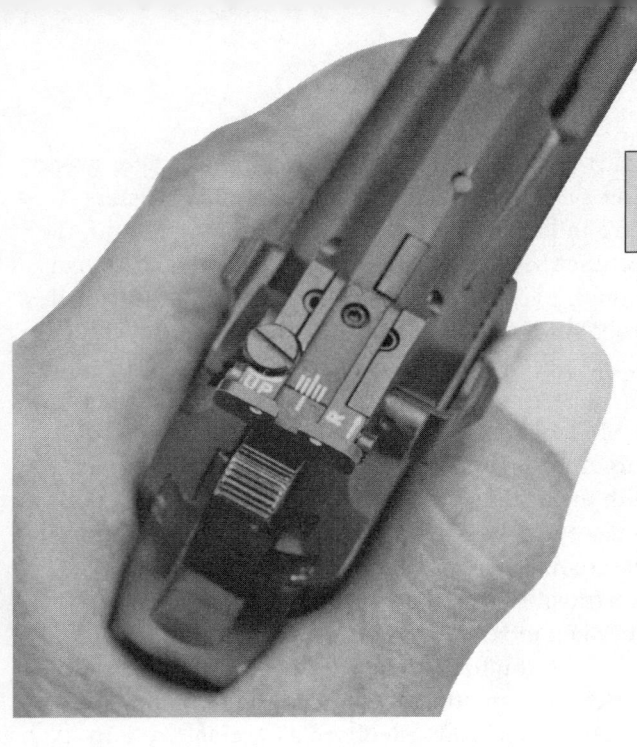

The rear sight of the Beretta .22 conversion unit appears to be the Italian LPA. It works extremely well.

so that didn't bother me. My test Model 87 Target's trigger was also quite smooth out of the box. It was the backlash I wanted to fix, and I wasn't about to drill a hole through the frame of a pistol that belonged to Beretta, to install a set screw to act as a trigger stop. I joked with my buddy Jon Strayer, "I oughta take a piece of pencil eraser and duct tape it to the inside back of the trigger guard."

Jon said, "I can do better. Be right back." A short time later he returned with the test gun. He had taken a small piece of floor protector – the heavy fiber pads that adhere to the bottoms of things like table legs to keep them from scarring the floors they stand on – and applied it to the inside rear of the trigger guard.

What a difference! The makeshift trigger stop worked. All of a sudden, the sights did not move off target when the hammer fell. Groups shrank immediately. My first five shots with CCI Pistol Match with the trigger stop installed, off an MTM pistol rest at 25 yards, landed in a group measuring just 0.95 inches. The best three shots, probably the best indicator of the gun's mechanical accuracy potential without putting it in a machine rest, were all touching and center-to-center measured 0.35 inches. And this was still with iron sights.

I've had better luck in terms of reliability than Fortier, who wrote, "Reliability during testing was very good but not flawless. Occasionally (perhaps eight times total during testing) the pistol failed to eject. Habitually, though, it would fail to chamber a round from slide lock. Simply hitting the slide release would cause the bullet nose to stop on the feedramp. Pulling the slide to the rear and releasing it, though, and I was good to go. No other problems of any kind were experienced." [2]

Now, I oughta be jealous of David because he got to test a primo Model 87 Target with no backlash, and I got stuck with one that seemed to backlash from Terni to Brescia. I should grind my teeth because my 0.35 inches group was only the best three shots, and his 0.35 inches group was for all five. However, I'm about 20 years older than David and can forgive him his sharper eyes and steadier hand. Moreover, that old thing about nature compensating seemed to be in play here … because my test Model 87 Target did not malfunction once. My friends and I all liked the way this little pistol was set up, and a bunch of us have put a bunch of ammo through it. Not enough bricks to build a house, but enough bricks of .22 ammo to know that Beretta Model 87 Target serial number C403120 is an extraordinarily reliable little pistol.

There is no reason this otherwise excellent little sporting .22 should not be coming out of the factory

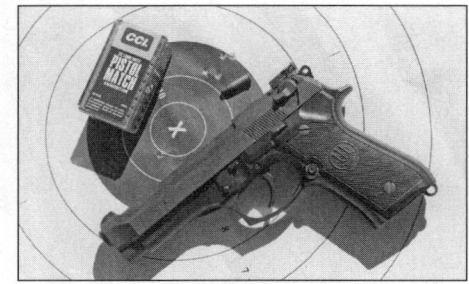

Left: The conversion unit gave this good five-shot group at 25 yards with inexpensive Blazer ammo.
Center: The first shot went out of the group, but the next four CCI Pistol Match rounds landed in a pleasingly tight cluster at 25 yards.
Right: These Federal .22 LR rounds exhibited good grouping potential, but fell victim to the unit's "4+1 syndrome."

with a better trigger. There was even a very tiny contact point where the toe of the trigger touched the bottom edge of the trigger guard. Not enough to palpably drag, but enough to have left a tiny drag line on the finish inside the guard. Maybe my trigger finger is just getting numb. That minor drag point didn't get in the way of shooting, but it shouldn't have been there.

The gun comes with a vestigial little stop on the back of the trigger that does absolutely nothing. I *know* that Beretta can do these triggers better. I know it because I own a Beretta .380 of this series with an excellent trigger stop attached at the factory. You see the same neat little trigger stop on the picture of the Beretta 85 that appears in the owner's manual. It belongs, properly adjusted, on this neat little single-action .22 pistol.

In summary, the Model 87 is an endearing little gun. I like its feel. I like its balance, and I love its splendid inherent accuracy in a slim and compact package. It is a little more than twice the price of a U22 Neos, but in my eyes (and in my hands) it seems like more than twice the gun. I don't think it's overpriced. I would like to see Beretta bring back the Model 89 Gold Match, but in the meantime, this will do.

I intend to buy this sample pistol from Beretta. And as soon as I do, I'm going to install a proper trigger stop in it.

Beretta 92/96 Conversion Unit

There are multiple .22 LR conversion units out there for the full-size Beretta service pistol. Some of them are quite good. But, from what I've seen, the very best is made by a little known source, and is a very well kept secret. That maker of the best .22 conversion unit for the Beretta is ... Beretta.

For the military man or woman whose MOS may include the need for a pistol ... for the cop who carries a Model 92 or a Model 96 on duty ... or for the armed citizen who has chosen one of those models, the Beretta .22 is a hugely practical adjunct to the system.

Surprising accuracy and full functionality make it a perfect practice companion!

The Beretta 92 series pistol is a modern classic. Bill Wilson has called it the most reliable out-of-the-box double-action auto on the market, and he has frequently made a point of shooting one in the competition he started, IDPA, the International Defensive Pistol Association. IDPA's national championship has been won more than once with a Beretta 92, with the double-action 9mm outshooting supposedly more "shootable" single-action autos like the ones Wilson himself is famous for building and customizing. The Beretta is the preferred DA auto of former World Champion Ray Chapman.

More to the point, it is the national military pistol of numerous countries both inside and outside of NATO, including the United States of America, which adopted it as the M9 in the mid-1980s. It remains extremely popular among civilians, too. Even with 10-round magazines that are altogether too stingy for its ample size, the Beretta 92 continues to sell to private citizens on the strength of its accuracy, reliability, and smoothness of action. In the Chicago area, where there is no concealed carry option and, suburbanites buy handguns for sport and home protection only, a veteran gun dealer with a huge stock told me recently that the Beretta 92 is his single best-selling handgun model.

And then, there are the cops. The Beretta 92 9mm remains standard issue at this writing for both LAPD and Los Angeles County Sheriff's Department, two of the nation's largest law enforcement agencies, though both give their members a short list of other optional guns they can buy on their own. These days, even more departments purchase the Beretta 96, the 92's twin that is chambered for the .40 S&W cartridge. The state troopers

The Beretta conversion seamlessly duplicates the functions of the standard 92 and 96 series pistols.

of Rhode Island, Indiana, and Florida are among those who adopted the Beretta 96.

When a gun is that popular, a market develops for conversion kits that will allow training with inexpensive .22 Long Rifle rimfire ammunition. It happened long ago with the 1911. It happened with such exotic auto pistols as the SIG P-210, and HK's M4 and P7 .380 pistols. It's happening right now with the GLOCK and Beretta, courtesy of Jonathan Arthur Ciener.

And Beretta is finally on board with a .22 conversion unit of their own.

While it appears on their website, Beretta does not actively advertise their neat little .22 conversion unit. This is a shame. It may be true that if you invent a better mousetrap, the world will beat a path to your door, but first the world needs to know that you have a better mousetrap.

I first learned of this unit from a National Guard pistol team that I've had some small input in training. They asked me what I thought of it compared to Jonathan Arthur Ciener's unit. I told them I was familiar with the Ciener conversion kit and thought very highly of it. My only criticism was that it was a "slick-side." To keep manufacturing costs down and make the unit affordable, Ciener did not fit it with a safety/decock lever. This required lowering the hammer by hand, as on the very first Beretta 92 and its early Taurus clone way back when.

The unit leader replied that they also had tested the Ciener unit and liked it, but really wanted something with a decocker/safety device as on their issue weapons. They weren't just looking at something for cheap bulls-eye target practice, he explained. They wanted a unit that would help them fulfill their training commitment to military police, security personnel, and others for whom the M9 pistol would be a primary duty and combat tool. Since the Army and National Guard mandate on-safe carry of the holstered 9mm service pistol, this had to include a system that would allow the troops to drill on releasing the safety and on decocking the pistol during a lull in the firing action.

The unit leader told me that the Beretta conversion apparently had this feature, and asked what I could find out about it. I immediately ordered one, tested it, and got it to one of his people for testing.

Gun Details

We picked up the Beretta conversion unit at the Manchester Indoor Firing Line in Manchester, New Hampshire. We were eager to, in a common figure of speech, "see what it was made of."

The barrel is steel, and the slide is aluminum. Aluminum slide plus aluminum frame makes for a very light pistol indeed. The action is simple blowback. The ten-round magazine (one only provided with the unit) is polymer. The finish appears to be Beretta's familiar Bruniton.

A neat little adjustable sight is provided, always a big help when you're shooting for precision. My boss got to it first and sighted it in for himself, which puts it a little low-right for my eyes. Clicks seemed to be positive and replicable. Sight picture was excellent with a little white dot inset for iffy light conditions.

The slide locks back on the empty magazine, and can be manually locked back via the slide lock lever. Some conversion units don't have these features.

The slide runs smoothly and effortlessly. The safety/decock lever is that

Clearly marked "22 L.R." on the barrel, the conversion unit features a very functional ramp and an efficient magazine that delivers the cartridges on a good feed angle.

of the F-series pistol, but it also works with the G-series, the designation for a spring-loaded lever, which functions as a one-stroke decocker, but not as a manual safety. However, the Beretta website does not list it as being compatible with the D-series, the double-action-only (self-decocking) variation, which makes mechanical sense.

According to Beretta, the unit is compatible with any Model 92 from the S- and SB-series on up. These are the ones with the slide-mounted safety-decock levers. The very first 92, with frame-mounted manual safety and no dedicated decocking mechanism, is not compatible with this conversion unit. Neither is the Billenium, Beretta's limited run single-action steel-frame target auto with the frame-mounted manual safety. Nor are the short frame compacts, the 92FC and the 92M. However, the unit is compatible with the Centurion (short barrel/slide assembly on full-size frame) and the Brigadier (full-size frame with reinforced heavy slide).

What is true of the 92 is true of the 96. The conversion unit will work on all .40 caliber Beretta 96 pistols of the F- and G-series, according to Beretta, including the Brigadier and the Centurion but not the compacts. Nor, of course, will it work on the more recent designs, the 8000 series or the polymer-frame 9000 series, which are different pistols entirely.

Endurance

Beretta recently made a series of special Model 92 pistols to commemorate Operation Enduring Freedom. The epoch of the Beretta 92 itself could be called Operation Enduring Reliability. Despite rumors spread by Internet commandoes to the contrary, the military armorers I've talked to have been virtually unanimous in their opinion that the Model 92/M9 is an extremely reliable pistol. Its endurance, in terms of breakage, seems no worse than that of the other mainstream high-capacity 9mm service pistols. It has merely gotten a lot more negative publicity for its miniscule number of failures. This is due in at least some part to competitors who were jealous that their gun didn't win the huge U.S. government contract.

The .22 conversion unit lives up to this reputation. Before it went to the military pistol team, I lent it to my chief of police, who is a big Beretta fan. He put it on his own commercial M92 frame, and proceeded to hammer about 1,000 rounds of Remington .22LR through it. "Love the accuracy," he reported

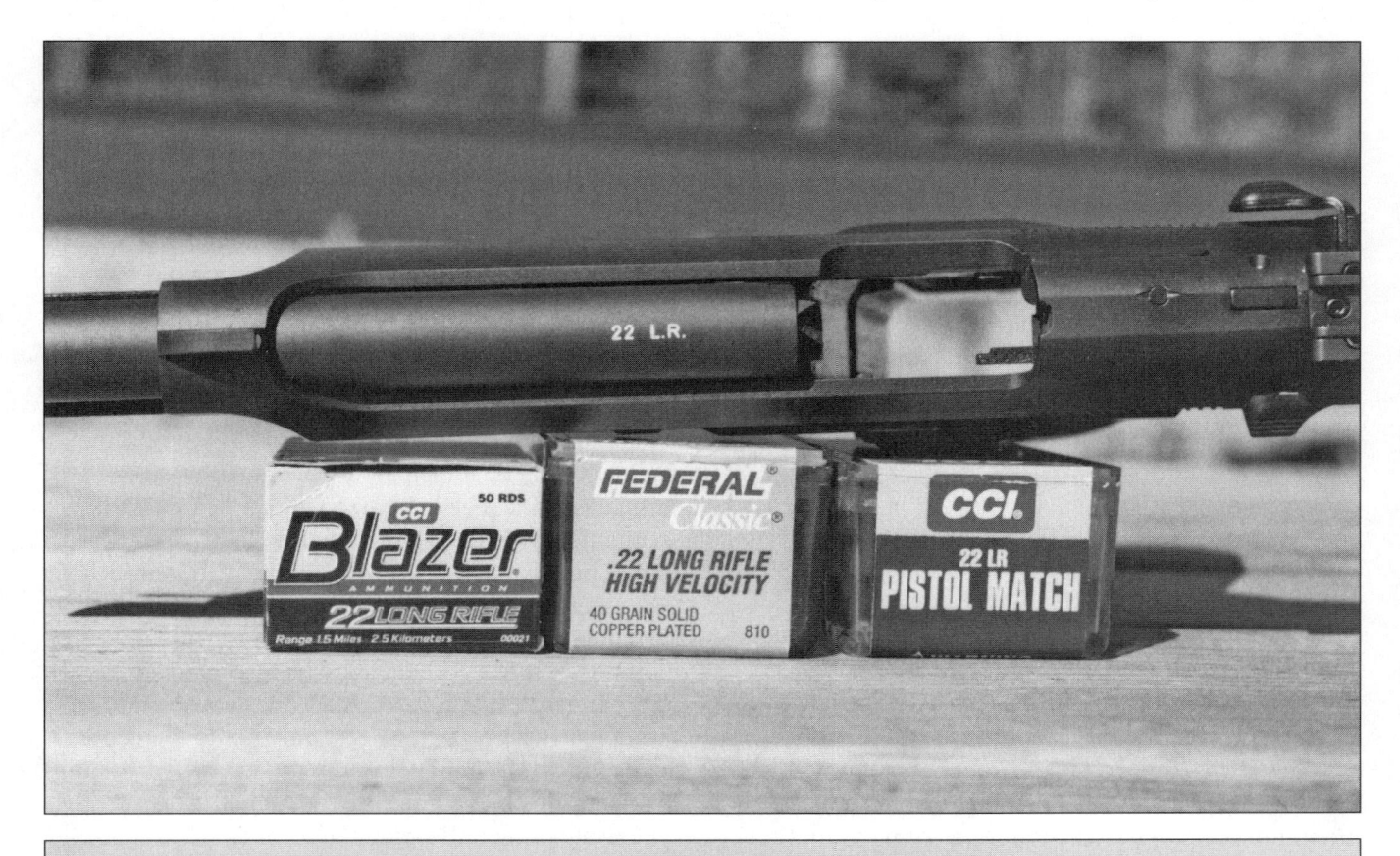

The .22 conversion unit is less picky about ammo than many other .22s, including some other Beretta options in the caliber.

enthusiastically, "and it didn't jam once." I then ran a few hundred rounds of assorted ammo through it myself.

Bear in mind that at this time, approaching 1,500 rounds, the conversion unit had not yet been cleaned. Carbon and lead buildup were visibly present, but the pistol kept chugging along. I say "chugging" advisedly. At least half of the ammo my boss put through it was standard-velocity, lead-bullet target stuff. This ammo has a very mild recoil impulse that will not operate a number of .22LR pistols and even some .22 auto-loading rifles. About half of what I put through it was less than high-velocity too, mostly the inexpensive Blazer.

As crudded up as it was, the converted pistol would very occasionally go "chug, chug." By that I mean the slide would come back, it would start forward, seem to stall, then finish its forward movement and go into battery. This happened only with the low-velocity ammo. With plated-bullet high-velocity ammo, the standby of plinkers, cycling was crisp and perfect with every shot.

One malfunction finally occurred when I handed it to a friend to try. He held it very casually, wrist and elbow both bent, and obviously with a very light grasp. A few rounds of Blazer into the magazine, the slide went only part of the way back and remained back. "I limp-wristed it," he said immediately. I told him to go ahead and clear it. He jacked the slide back smartly, the pistol went back into battery; and he continued without further problem.

Twice, again with light loads, the slide came back just enough to clear the spent casing but not far enough to pick up a fresh round. In both cases, oddly enough, the pistol decocked itself when the slide came forward, though the safety/decock lever was still firmly up in the "fire" position. Each time, the slide was racked again, and firing continued normally.

With any .22 auto pistol, it's a good idea to clean the gun every 500 rounds or so. By the time these few problems occurred, the gun was approaching three times longer than normal between cleanings. With conversion units I've found it's better to clean them every 50 to 100 rounds. It's hard for me to blame the gun.

Now it was time to put it through its accuracy paces. Remember, the pistol still had not been cleaned after almost 1,500 rounds. We were trying to find out how many rounds it would take to make it stop running without being cleaned and lubed.

How Accurate

Accuracy testing was done with ammo at three different price levels, sort of like the old Sears, Roebuck thing of "good, better, best." The shooting was done outdoors with two hands braced on the bench at 25 yards. Each five-shot group was measured overall, and also for the best three shots. I discovered several years ago that if five shots were fired from the bench and all felt perfect, measuring the best three factored out unnoticed human error and came remarkably close to what the same gun/ammo combo would do for five shots out of a machine rest.

For a low-priced generic round I chose the CCI Blazer with a lead bullet at what felt like standard velocity. The five-shot group measured 3.25 inches. The first shot had gone wide. The next four went into a cluster measuring 1.63 inches. The best three shots were in 0.75 of an inch. Federal's standard line Classic round-nose, plated, high-velocity load put five shots into 3.88 inches. Not counting the first shot, the group would have measured 0.94 of an inch, and the best three were in 0.88 of an inch. CCI's elite Pistol Match, with lead bullet at standard velocity was the priciest load tested. The five-shot group measured a disappointing 3.75 inches, but that was once again due to the first hand-chambered shot. The subsequent four shots went into a diamond pattern that measured an inch on the nose, with the best three clustering into a group of 0.75 of an inch.

The Blazer, which I bought over the counter for $9.95 per brick, had actually given the best accuracy, beating even the Pistol Match by a very slight margin. The cheapest load coming out on top for precision isn't something that happens every day, particularly in .22LR.

The first shot always going somewhere other than where the subsequent shots went was disappointing, but hardly a surprise. This is called "4+1 syndrome" and is widely documented. It occurs with semiautomatic pistols (and to a lesser degree with semiautomatic rifles) when the first hand-chambered round puts the parts in a very slightly different firing alignment, or "battery," than what they go into during firing when the mechanism cycles automatically and auto-loads each subsequent cartridge. Interestingly, the standard Beretta 92 in 9mm does not seem to be particularly prone to this, certainly not to the degree I saw in the test sample of Beretta's .22 conversion unit.

Does this make it useless? Not at all. Whether you're shooting bull's-eye, IDPA, or IPSC, you go to the firing line cold each time and then load for the string of fire. Thus, competition with a gun that suffers from 4+1 syndrome can be a problem. Remember, though, that Beretta does not market this accessory as a match gun, they market it as a practice gun. Since practice is less formal, it should be no problem to load the gun with one round extra (.22 ammo is cheap, after all) and fire the first shot into the backstop, then simply keep the magazine topped off. By running the range "hot," every subsequent practice shot can be fired with a round automatically cycled into the firing chamber by the gun's mechanism, allowing the shooter to take advantage of what is obviously an otherwise "match-grade" level of inherent accuracy in this unit.

For bull's-eye practice, I would load each magazine with six and would have two targets up. I would take my time and put one slow-fire practice shot into the first target prior to each string, then set the timer and fire the next five in whatever Slow-, Timed-, or Rapid-Fire sequence I had chosen. The conversion unit tested was reasonably consistent, putting the first hand chambered shot high, and usually left, of point-of-aim in roughly the same spot.

I loaded six Blazers and gave that a try. Sure enough, the first bullet flew to 12 o'clock, landing about 3 inches away from where the rest of the group followed. But those next five automatically cycled shots landed in a group that measured 1.44 inches, with the best three in 1 inch even.

Verdict

I like the Beretta 92 conversion unit. I like it a lot. It is more reliable and less maintenance-intensive than any other .22 caliber handgun conversion unit I've ever worked with. The fact that it duplicates the manual safety and decocker function of the service-caliber F-series guns is, to my way of thinking, a big plus. Even if you chose to carry your Beretta off-safe, if your gun is the F-series you need drawing, firing, and malfunction-clearing techniques, which verify that it's off-safe. Working with a slick-slide practice gun that can't accidentally be put on safe, it's easy to get sloppy about those important subtleties of technique. This conversion unit's design will keep us sharp with those things.

I'm not sure how much of that errant first shot problem will clear up with scrupulous cleaning. We couldn't find out because the gun was earmarked to go to a military firearms training unit after we were done with it, and the one thing being studied was how many rounds it could handle before it choked on the dirt.

The accuracy for all but that hand-chambered first shot was a pleasant surprise. We took this gun out to the NRA Hunter Pistol range, where we tried it on steel silhouettes cut for small-bore shooting. They happened to be set up only at 40 meters (chickens) and 50 meters (pigs). However, they proved to be easy work for the Beretta conversion unit, even from the standing position. Given that NRA Hunter Silhouette uses half-size animals in comparison to the International Handgun Metallic Silhouette Association, this was good accuracy indeed. The "chickens" are about as big as pigeons, and I've owned housecats bigger than the "pigs."

Final Notes

How good is the conversion unit? I bought the test sample. What's more, I'm gonna have to buy another. My chief has dibs on the first one. Is Beretta gonna make a million bucks on this neat little setup? Well, there are over seven figures worth of guns out there to which they can be fitted. If every gunowner purchases a unit for it, and if Beretta makes a profit of a dollar per unit …

For more information contact: Beretta, 17601 Beretta Dr., Dept CH, Accokeek, MD 20607; 301-283-2191; www.berettausa.com

Endnotes

(1)"Beretta's Model 87 Target Is A Rimfire Masterpiece," by David M. Fortier, *2005 Shooting Times Handgun Buyers' Guide,* Peoria, IL: Primedia, Page 48.

(2)Ibid., P. 49.

The Beretta Tomcat .32

Colt named many of their revolvers after dangerous snakes: The Cobra, the Python, the Diamondback, the Viper, the Anaconda. Few arms companies have named their guns for dangerous cats, though a copy of the Winchester 1892 carbine that was long popular south of the border, usually in caliber .44-40, was given the name "El Tigre." Beretta, however, has an affinity for feline nomenclature.

I am not sure why, after calling their little .22 LR pocket pistol the Bobcat, they would choose to name the distinctly more powerful .32 ACP the Tomcat. Not that I don't think the name is appropriate. You see, the .32 caliber is a pussycat in every respect, but, comparatively, naming a .32 after *felis domesticus* and the .22 after a wildcat seems a bit over-reaching insofar as the latter. It's a little like naming your goldfish "Moby Dick."

Beretta's Tomcat has earned itself a lot of friends. Some owe it their lives. A fellow identified only as GB wrote the following first-person account of such an instance in the "It Happened to Me" section of *Combat Handguns* magazine: [1]

"That day had started like any other for the last 15 years. I've had a jewelry store and pawn shop in West Palm Beach, Florida, but this day would change my life forever. I set up the showcases for the day. It's a beautiful South Florida day, hot and humid. (Two young males dressed in black) were hanging around looking at rings and things. The first guy was in the shop in the morning and was looking to sell his 14-karat gold chain. I thought he was going to make a trade for a ring or some cash. The pair just kept looking at more and more stuff. After about 35 minutes I asked, 'Do you have any cash?' The first guy just showed me a pocket with nothing in it. He still had the 14-karat gold chain to work with, so I went on waiting on them.

"Not one person came in all of the time they were

Even the short-barreled Centurion 9mm dwarfs the Tomcat .32, below.

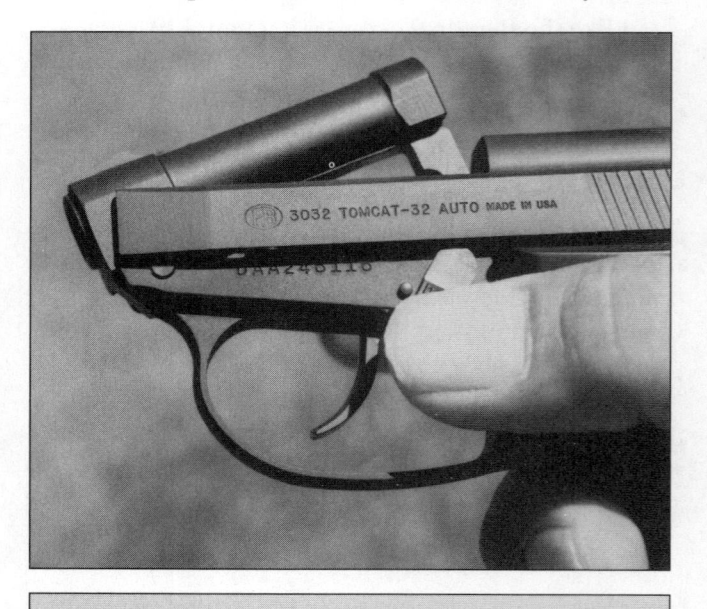

Key features of the Tomcat are tip-up loading, seen as the thumb pushes the release lever forward, and a barrel held rigidly in place so the pistol won't jam if a muzzle-contact shot is attempted.

in the store. The first guy said he was going to buy his girl a ring and I went to show him diamond rings. I pulled a tray of diamond rings out of the showcase and when I raised my head up, the other guy was pointing a gun right between my eyes. It was about two inches from my head. I looked down the gun barrel, a .25 caliber. In a split second I swung my hand and hit the gun. At that point I ducked behind the counter and crawled on my hands toward the back room, hoping the pair would just run off. The next thing I knew I had one of them on my back and he's calling for his friend to help him get me down. I told his accomplice that he'd better run. I managed to pull my Tomcat from my side pocket. I got it in my hand and hit him with it so hard that I broke the trigger guard, and he went down. He was still calling for the other guy. With no time to waste I had to even up the odds.

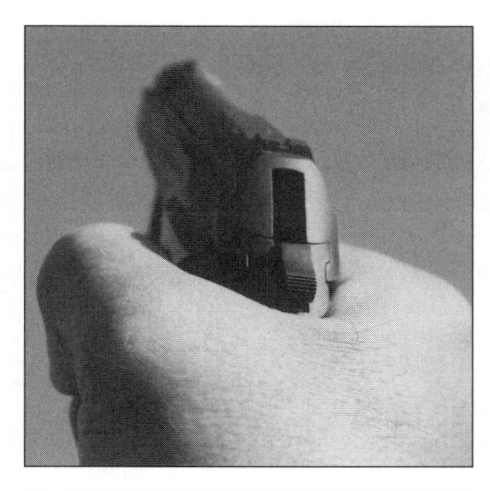

"Now he was getting back up from the floor so I flipped off the safety on my gun and put it to the side of his head. I kept second-guessing myself. He was getting up and calling out for help from his accomplice in crime. I didn't know if the accomplice was going to come in the back room so I put the gun to the side of his head and pulled the trigger. Bang the gun went off and he went down to the floor half over a chair. I heard the doorbell ring as the accomplice ran out. I locked up and called 911. He was still where he fell, dead.

Sitting low in the hand, the Tomcat has low bore axis and minimal muzzle rise. The slide abrading the hand is much less a problem than with many other pistols in its class.

"Two days before the holdup I'd just picked up the Tomcat from the gun store across the street. For some time before that I hadn't been carrying a gun. My 9mm was just too big."

There are those who like the Tomcat as a police backup gun, too. My friend and colleague Mike Boyle is one of the nation's top police gun experts, and an outstanding trainer whom I've seen teach in such venues as the American Society of Law Enforcement Trainers, and the International Association of Law Enforcement Firearms Instructors. In a roundup article discussing pocket pistols for backup in a police-oriented publication he and I both contribute to regularly, *Guns & Weapons for Law Enforcement*, Mike had the following to say about the Tomcat in the February, 2005 issue.

"Carried in a Tomahawk holster from Pocket Concealment Systems, the Tomcat doesn't cramp my style at all. Magazine capacity is seven rounds. I have considerably more trigger time with the Tomcat than the other pistols tested and to date my experience is most favorable. The manual of arms for the DA/SA Tomcat is a bit more involved than the DAOs, but the single-action trigger makes hitting small targets or distant targets easier. On several

The Model 3032 Tomcat is a fast-moving pistol in the gun shops.

While very compact, the Tomcat has a grip frame that allows two fingers to wrap solidly around it. Some pistols in its class allow only one and perhaps part of a second.

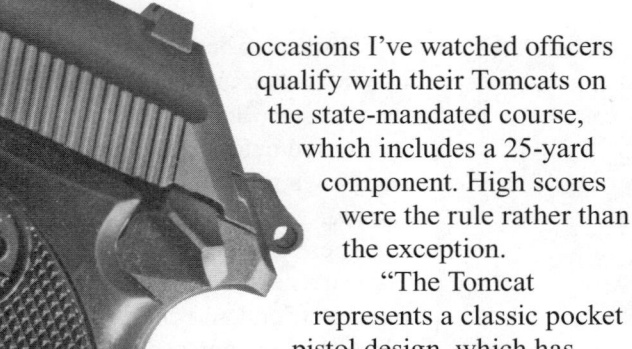

occasions I've watched officers qualify with their Tomcats on the state-mandated course, which includes a 25-yard component. High scores were the rule rather than the exception.

"The Tomcat represents a classic pocket pistol design, which has clearly benefited by the power boost to the .32ACP. As a last-ditch backup, it offers a great deal of potential." [2]

Nothing has really changed since, except for the intro of a couple of still smaller .32s by other makers, such as the Kel-Tec P32.

GB showed in his incident subsequent the efficacy of the muzzle-contact shot. The tip-up barrel design of the Tomcat not only eases loading and unloading for many people, but also holds the gun's parts rigidly in battery allowing the pistol to fire when it is in hard contact with the target. Many, many auto pistols will have their parts "pushed out of battery" by such contact, and will be rendered incapable of firing.

GB's statement that he had bought the Tomcat because a 9mm was just too big to carry, really says it all. While slightly larger than some of the other new-generation subcompact .32s such as the defining Seecamp, the almost impossibly light little KelTec P32, and the North American Arms Guardian, the Tomcat .32 is spectacularly easier to shoot by comparison. Not in a class with the Beretta .380, by any means, but certainly better in that respect than the other true pocket pistols in .32 caliber.

Personally, when danger threatens I'd like to have the cry of angry 9mm leopard speaking for my side, or the snarl of a .45 caliber lion, or the roar of a .357 caliber Siberian tiger. But, you know, the meow of the Tomcat is still a better sound than the whimper of a victim …

The Meow Of The Tomcat

Beretta is a company that believes, like Burger King, that you, the customer, should be able to "have it your way." A recent Beretta ad in a foreign gun magazine showed a range of Model 92 options from the old frame-mounted safety style that hasn't been imported into the U.S. for many years, to the familiar 92FS, the shorter Centurion, and the heavy-duty Brigadier. And of course there's the double-action-only 92D that's popular among U.S. police.

Similarly, Beretta USA offers a wide power range to the good guy or gal who draws a weapon in the face of imminent, unlawful use of deadly force. You can respond with the roar of the Cougar (9mm Parabellum, .40 S&W, .357 SIG, or .45 ACP caliber). You can reply with the growl of the Cheetah (.380 ACP).

And now, you can answer with the meow of the Tomcat, the smallest .32 auto that Beretta has offered.

This is not your grandfather's Beretta .32, which would have been the single-action 1935 model, a solid and chunky gun that was optimistically named the Puma when Beretta sold it here commercially years ago. Nor is it the .32 version of the Model 84, the high-capacity DA first-shot pistol of recent years. Both of those autos were much better in their natural caliber, the .380 ACP. Their recoil was negligible, and they were hell for accurate. Unfortunately they were also big for the power they put out.

The Tomcat, whose name is a quintessential tribute to truth in advertising, is not particularly accurate and, in the feline menagerie of the Beretta catalog, is pathetically feeble. Comparing the Tomcat .32 with a Cougar .40 is rather like putting your own little housecat up against a mountain lion. Consider the following ballistics, courtesy of Winchester:

Top: The Tomcat can be carried three ways with a round in the chamber, though all contravene the owner's manual. Here is its optional cocked and locked mode …

Center: … here the hammer is down, and safety engaged …

Bottom: … and here the pistol is off safe, ready to fire in double-action mode.

Caliber	Bullet Weight	Muzzle Velocity	Muzzle Energy
.40 S&W Silvertip	155 grains	1205 ft. per sec.	500 foot-pounds
9mm Luger Silvertip	115 grains	1225 ft. per sec.	383 foot-pounds
.38 Special +P Lead HP	158 grains	890 ft. per sec.	278 foot-pounds
.38 Special Silvertip	110 grains	945 ft. per sec.	218 foot-pounds
.380 Auto Silvertip	85 grains	1000 ft. per sec.	189 foot-pounds
.32 Auto Silvertip	60 grains	970 ft. per sec.	125 foot-pounds
.25 Auto Expanding Point	45 grains	815 ft. per sec.	66 foot-pounds

Mouse Gun Factor

Yeah, I know, I'm the guy who says "Friends don't let friends carry mouse guns." Why then am I writing this article?

Mouseguns are a fact of life. There are X number of good people who will carry a tiny gun or no gun at all, either as backup or as first line of defense, and a basic law of life is that "something is better than nothing." Jeff Cooper once said he'd rather have a hatchet than a .25 auto for self-defense. At belly-to-belly distance, me too, though I'd likely trade the hatchet for my Richard Sokol custom Arkansas Toothpick. However, Jeff was always big and strong, and I am comparatively little and weak. At a range of 20 feet, if the bad guy has a firearm, I'd rather have the mouse gun than the hatchet since I know he can empty his weapon into me in the second and a half it'll take me to reach him with a blade.

Thus, we take it as a given that this article won't be a diatribe against mouse guns, but rather an inquiry into how well the Beretta Tomcat fulfills the mouse gun role.

The Pistol

Built to be sold to the people who are tired of waiting in line for the Seecamp LWS-32, a hard-to-find pistol in the Czech double-action-only pattern that has no sights and is the size of a small .25, the Beretta Tomcat partially succeeds. It's available now at your local gun shop, and at a remarkably affordable price, not the scalper's ticket so many charge for a Seecamp. It's the size of a .25, all right, but the size of Beretta's own double-action first shot, 11-ounce Model 21 Bobcat .25 auto, which is 4.9 inches long with its 2.4-inch barrel. Somewhat more ruggedly constructed, the Tomcat weighs 13.1 ounces with chamber empty and magazine removed, and 16.6 ounces on my calibrated electronic scale when fully loaded with seven rounds of 71-grain ball in the magazine and an eighth round, the Gold Dot 60-grain hollow-point, in the launch tube.

The Tomcat is a cooler looking gun. Its trigger guard looks like it was part of the design instead of a piece of sheet metal folded over and stapled. Where the little Beretta DA .22/.25 has a thin blade front and V-notch rear sight, the .32 version has a small but much more visible square post/square notch rear sight picture.

It has a tip-up barrel, perhaps a tiny bit stiffer in the lever to operate than that of the other pocket .22 and .25 Berettas, but easier to manipulate than the 180-degree lever on the Model 86 .380. Good news. Weak or handicapped people can load the chamber easily without having to actuate a spring-loaded slide. Bad news: there's no extractor, the design trusts blowback force to clear the spent casing out of the chamber, and if there *is* an extraction failure, you can't just work the slide to clear it. Doing that will merely bring up another round against the jammed spent casing, the dreaded and erroneously-named "double-feed jam."

More good news, however is that during tests, the gun *never* failed to extract, and a poll of half a dozen

A frontal view of the Beretta 3032 Tomcat. The barrel cannot move back if the muzzle is pressed into the target, an important consideration at the distances at which small pocket pistols are likely to be used, and an advantage it shares with smaller frame Berettas.

A push forward on this lever with the thumb pops the barrel up for cartridge insertion or removal, saving you from working the slide. This can be a godsend for those with limited strength in hands and upper body. Note also that chamber can be loaded or emptied

other owners showed the same collective experience.

The Tomcat is bigger, significantly bigger, than the Seecamp .32. However, it's smaller than any *other* .32 automatic on the market. (Yeah, I know, at least two companies are supposed to be offering Seecamp clones. Call me if you see one in a gunshop. I haven't.)

Comparing the new Beretta .32 to my preferred off-duty backup gun, the S&W 442 Centennial Airweight .38 Special, the Beretta is a little smaller in height and distinctly smaller in overall length. Remove the barrel from your J-frame revolver, and what's left of your gun will be the length of a fully assembled Tomcat. Weight, however, is less dramatically favorable to the .32. Empty, the Tomcat weighs 13.1 ounces and the S&W Airweight hammerless, 15.2 ounces. Fully loaded there's even less difference. With five 158-grain +P lead hollow-points in the chambers, my favorite pocket .38 weighs 17.9 ounces. With seven Federal ball rounds in the magazine and a 60-grain Gold Dot hollow-point in the chamber, the Beretta .32 weighs 16.6 ounces. One and three-tenths ounces ain't a helluva lot of difference.

Eight rounds for the .32 versus five rounds for the .38 is a significant difference, until you factor in the potency per shot. The total deliverable muzzle energy of .38 Special +P, times five, dramatically exceeds that of a .32 ACP times eight, even when you allow for the 2-inch barrel of the .38 and the 2.4-inch barrel of the Tomcat.

Does a Beretta Tomcat .32 beat a Beretta Bobcat .25? Oh, my, yes! A .32 auto is by any standard about twice as powerful as a .25 auto. This must, of course, be kept in perspective. A .380 auto is half again more potent than a .32, while a .38 Special can deliver more than four times the raw power of a .25 and more than twice that of the best .32 auto round. So often, there is time for only one shot …

Field Testing the Tomcat

I bit the itty-bitty bullet, as it were, and carried the test Beretta Tomcat, as a backup gun for almost the whole month of April 1997. Just under two weeks of that were in the Pacific Northwest, a week was in the South, and the remainder was in Northern New England. I was legal to carry loaded and concealed in all three jurisdictions.

I'm not gonna give you a lot of crap about getting in touch with my feminine side, or being secure enough in my masculinity to carry a .32 for backup. I will tell you

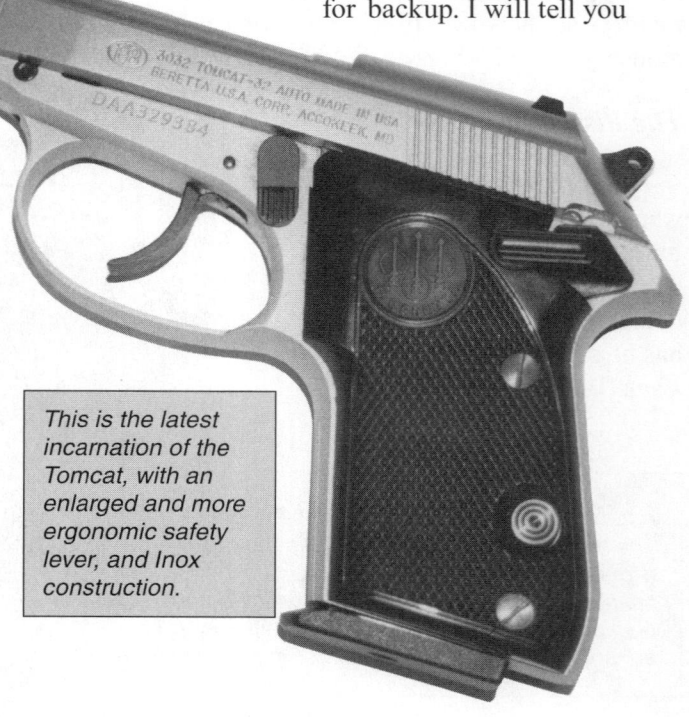

This is the latest incarnation of the Tomcat, with an enlarged and more ergonomic safety lever, and Inox construction.

that for all but a week of that time, the .32 was a third gun, since I had an Airweight .38 on my left ankle and a Glock .45 on my right hip. But during the week where the .32 was my only backup I didn't start going through withdrawal symptoms or anything.

For all this time I used one holster: Jerry Ahern's excellent pocket scabbard. While some pocket holsters, like the Kramer, require an upward draw to strip off the holster and clear the sidearm, the Ahern design needs you to rock the gun back with its muzzle pointed tactically toward the threat. Now it clears both pocket and holster, the holster perhaps hanging out of the pocket lining as the separation takes place. I found it unerringly effective.

However, I discovered that while the Beretta .32 was almost as fast out of the Ahern pocket holster as a snub .38 out of one of my usual pocket holsters when I was wearing loose trousers (i.e., BDUs), this changed in tight jeans. With the jeans it wasn't nearly as fast. This isn't a fault of Ahern's holster design or anything unique to the Beretta Tomcat; rather, it's a fact of life with tight-to-the-body carry of any semiautomatic pistol. An autoloader's grip profile is flat on the sides and tight clothing or holsters hug it close to your body requiring your fingers to sort of claw in to get a drawing grasp. The rounded profile of a small revolver's grip frame allows a much easier draw in these types of carry. The rounded edges of the revolver's stocks sort of guide your hand quickly into position.

Accuracy? The first thing I saw with this little gun was that it shot way low. At 7 yards, while it would put a decent group together, that group would be some two or three inches below point of aim. The trigger pull didn't help. While it improved with lubrication, the double-action pull never got better than mediocre and the single-action pull had "bad creep" with about four stopping points through an almost interminably long stroke that seemed to reach all the way back to the rear of the frame before the gun went off.

The action and trigger were very rough when we started. Wear and lubrication took off the "very" but couldn't eradicate all of the "rough." This little gun is not the glass-smooth Beretta 92/96, whose exquisitely polished moving parts and contact surfaces are the envy of the rest of the handgun industry.

Reliability? We ran just under 300 rounds through this gun. There were only two malfunctions, steep-angled 12 o'clock misfeeds that could not be cleared without stripping the mag from the pistol. Both occurred, surprisingly, with full-metal-jacket ball ammo, Winchester's USA brand which is normally utterly reliable. Yet the gun was flawless with Federal ball, and with 20-some rounds of Speer Gold Dot and 50 of Winchester Silvertip, both 60-grain hollow-points. Go figure.

The two jams were cleared by ripping the magazine out of the gun, thumbing the topmost round either out of the mag or back in place, and then "reload, cycle, shoot." As previously noted, there were no extraction failures. (Interestingly, we got into a bad batch of contaminated old .22 ammo when shooting a Beretta 21 next to the Model 3032 Tomcat. These rounds failed to cycle. We had to pop the barrel up and pry the spent rimfire casings out with a pocketknife. Determining what we *would* do if a Tomcat failed to extract a .32 hull if the round was too feeble to cycle the gun, we found that a #2 pencil would go down the barrel to punch the casing out. Colleague Marty Hayes, no fan of small-caliber pistols, commented dryly, "If you have to carry a #2 pencil anyway, cut out the middleman. Leave the .32 at home and just carry a sharp pencil. If you're attacked

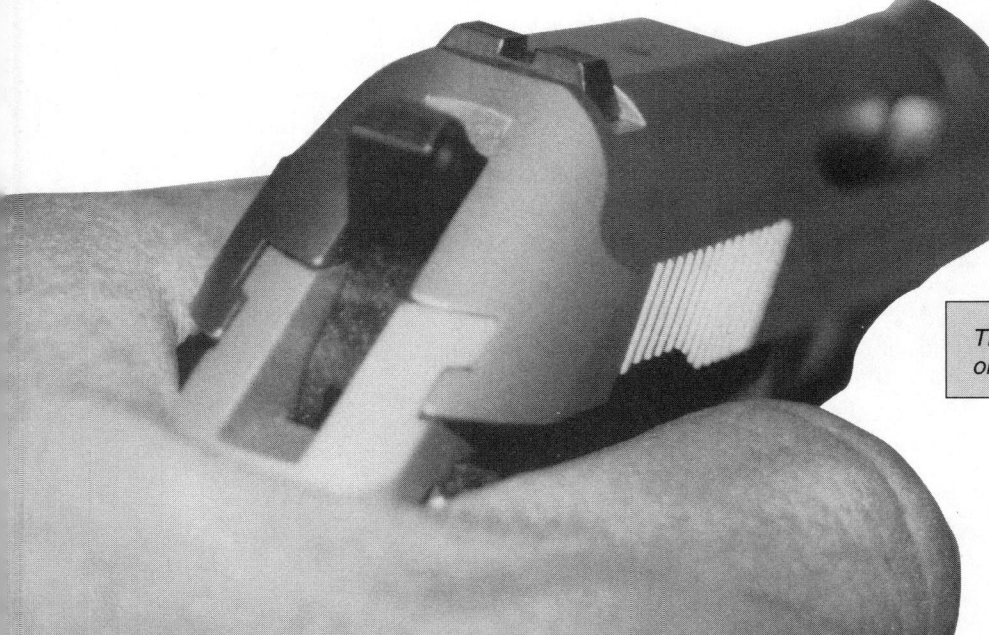

The rear sight on Tomcat is better than those on most guns its size ...

by a violent criminal, stab him with the pencil until he dies. You'll probably have about the same wound profile anyway.")

But I won't make any mouse gun jibes here. I *won't* ...

The tradition is to test pocket pistols at no farther than 7 yards, the theory being that this is the greatest distance at which you'll have employ one. I'm sorry, but I can't buy that. I'll go with Affirmative Action hiring so long as it's *enlightened* Affirmative Action hiring.

What that means is, Affirmative Action hiring does no one any good if it's construed as lowering the standards to let in people who otherwise wouldn't qualify for the job. *Enlightened* Affirmative Action hiring is, you let people of every size, color, gender, and belief system compete and the ones who can do the job better are the ones you put to work. The history of it is, if you hire people who can't do the job because it seems politically correct or convenient, the job doesn't get done and people who needed the job done right end up suffering. But if you throw out height and weight and color and similar requirements and hire people who can do the job well however they do it, you end up getting the job done.

When cops were whining in the 1970s and 1980s about having to be backed up by women and small-statured men, they shut up after the new hires showed they could do the job.

With this in mind, I test even pocket guns the way I test service pistols, including 25-yard shootability tests. If the bad guy doesn't cooperate with your game plan of being in close when the fight starts (and, let's face it, he didn't cooperate with your game plan when he started the fight in the first place), you need equipment that will allow you to engage successfully at parking lot distance. My Tomcat .32 shot so low that with a 12 o'clock hold on a piece of 8½- by 11-inch typing paper, Federal 71-grain ball put five rounds in 5¼ inches, the best three in 2¾; Winchester ball put the five in 7⅛ inches, the best three in 3¾. Some people find that acceptable. I find it beyond the edge of acceptability, having perhaps been spoiled by the exquisite accuracy of Beretta's .380, 9mm, and .40 pistols.

Yet all is relative. Its group is enough to shoot a 300 out of 300 on the police qualification course's generous B-27 target, assuming you have your Kentucky windage right. While I've qualified with the sightless Seecamp on that course, I wouldn't bet my life on shooting a 300 with one.

Feedback From Others

One career cop I know bought two Tomcats and carries one in each front pocket. He likes the portability, hates the trigger pull, and doesn't find the gun hurts his hand. Neither of his Tomcats shoot where they look.

A male civilian I know liked the grouping capability but didn't like it being someplace other than where he was aiming, and found the sharp edge of the safety catch painful. A female civilian noted similar concerns and found the slide and the barrel tip-up lever difficult to operate. Both of them found the gun hurt their hands.

Another woman found the gun too weak in output, too inaccurate, and painful to shoot due to sharp edges. A large male cop found its slide bit his hand when he shot it and went back to a .38 snub for his second gun. A large male civilian fell in love with it, finding it easier to shoot every shot in the same place than his Seecamp .32, even though his Beretta didn't shoot spot on.

Personally, I found hand bite – a common thing with pocket autos and male hands – to be minor. Like the other users, I was disconcerted that the gun was not sighted in at the factory. The other Tomcat users, like me, carried the gun off safe because its sharp-edged safety worked too stiffly to rely on in a crisis.

... as is the front sight.

The Owner's Manual

Many have lauded the Seecamp owner's manual for its refreshing approach to user instructions, such as, carry it loaded with a round in the chamber ready to fire. It is, after all, something you bought to protect your life in an emergency. Duh! Kudos to Seecamp.

I was disheartened when I compared that to the Tomcat owner's manual. "IN THE FIELD, the pistol should be carried unloaded (empty chamber, magazine removed, the hammer fully-lowered and the safety 'ON') in a holster, with the magazine in a pouch or pocket. It takes only a second to insert a loaded magazine and to retract and release the slide for chamber loading and cocking." (Page 6.) "WARNING!! If the pistol is carried chamber loaded (NOT RECOMMENDED) with the hammer full-lowered, ENGAGE the SAFETY: DO NOT try to override the Safety by asserting (sic) excessive trigger pull force. Also, the mechanism may be damaged by forceful manual hammer cocking." (Page 11.) "The Model 3032 has an INERTIA type firing pin which, when used with the hammer down, external safety engaged and with the double-action trigger pull, assures the greatest degree of safety if it is necessary to carry the pistol chamber loaded (NOT RECOMMENDED)." (Page 3.) "Extreme care must be taken to avoid hitting or dropping a loaded firearm. Even if on SAFE, accidental discharge may occur – some ammunition have (sic) very sensitive primers." (Page 4.)

Does this just mean that Beretta has more lawyers than Seecamp? It can't mean they have better lawyers than Seecamp, which was represented by current NRA director Howard Fezell in the lawsuit that beat the Maryland Gun Board's attempt to ban that pistol in that state. I have to go on the assumption that the gun's maker knows the pistol better than the gun's user, and if they worry about me carrying it chamber loaded, I worry about it when I carry it. For most of a month I had a Gold Dot in the chamber, the barrel closed on an already lowered hammer, and seven rounds of easy-feeding Federal ball in the magazine because I hadn't put the requisite 200 rounds of any one hollow-point through the mechanism and don't trust any handgun until I have. And ... I thought about the safety factor and the owner's manual every day I carried this gun.

Beretta Tomcat vs. Seecamp LWS-32

Let's get right down to it. How does Beretta's entry in the Seecamp market compare to the gun that defined that market?

The Beretta points much better. The Seecamp points low, a tough thing for a gun that has no sights. Most anyone will hit better with the sighted Beretta, even though the Tomcats all seem to shoot low. The Seecamp is a lot more portable: slightly shorter than the Tomcat, much smaller in height (you can get one finger on its grip, but two on the Beretta's), and a significant 3 ounces lighter, while holding only one less round of ammo. The LWS-32's double-action-only trigger is smoother and more controllable than the Tomcat's. The Seecamp is on a restricted diet by its manufacturer: Winchester Silvertip and Glaser Safety Slugs only, while the Beretta has no such limitation.

Seecamp endorses carrying their .32 with a round in the chamber. Beretta does not.

Perhaps most important for many, the Beretta .32's suggested retail price is much lower than that of the Seecamp.

Bottom Line

The Beretta 3032 Tomcat came to me with only one magazine. This is the way most pocket pistols are sold. The industry has come to believe that any blithe spirit who trusts his life to a sub-caliber firearm probably isn't into carrying spare ammo. This tells you something about the market profile you're matching yourself to when you consider buying one.

I'd rather you carried a .32 auto than a .25, or no gun at all. But this is not the accurate, point of aim/point of impact, glass smooth, and sufficiently potent Beretta that the U.S. military adopted for soldiers, and that INS adopted for U.S. Customs and Border Patrol. It's a damn good pocket pistol, more affordable and more available and more accurate than the Seecamp .32 whose market it was designed to invade, but that's all that it is.

If that's good enough, buy one. If not, buy a bigger caliber Beretta ... and if you ever need a defensive handgun for its intended purpose, you'll thank me and Beretta after it's all over.

Endnotes

1. "A Timely Tomcat," by GB, Combat Handguns magazine, New York City, November 2004 issue, P.6.
2. ".32 ACP Triple Play" by Mike Boyle, Guns & Weapons for Law Enforcement magazine, New York City, February 2005 issue, Pp. 32 and 84.

The Beretta .380s

When I was young, if you wanted to purchase a high-quality .380 automatic pistol, you basically had three choices: Beretta, Browning, and Walther. The classic Colt Pocket Model had been gone since World War II, though since it was a John Browning design many of its features lived on in the Belgian pistol that bore his name. The sleek, but complicated, Remington Model 51 was likewise long since discontinued.

The First Wave

My first centerfire handgun was a Beretta Model 1934 that had come back from the European theater as a souvenir of WWII. This .380 had been standard issue in the Italian military. The Model 1935 was functionally identical, but chambered for .32 ACP. The .380 ACP (**A**utomatic **C**olt **P**istol) was the American term for a cartridge known as the 9mm Kurz (9mm "short"), 9mm Corto, 9mm Browning Short, or simply 9X17mm.

Over its many years of service – and its many more as a popular concealed carry handgun all over the world – the 1934 series earned a reputation as perhaps the most rugged and heavy-duty .380 made. It was certainly the most shootable. Its solid weight helped to absorb recoil and unlike some contemporaries such as the Walther PP and PPK, its slide did not bite the hand upon firing. When sold commercially in the United States, imported by Galef, the .32 was known as the Puma and the .380 as the Cougar. These guns were manufactured until 1959.

There are a lot of these rugged old pistols still out there, and a lot of shooters who still appreciate them.

The Second Wave

By the time John F. Kennedy replaced Dwight Eisenhower in the White House, the 70 series Berettas had begun to replace the 1934 style. Known as the Model 100 in the U.S. market, this new pistol was sleeker than the 1934, though similar in many ways including the open slide

An early Beretta 86 shows its relative size in an adult male hand. The pistol is ambidextrously "cocked and locked," making it easier for weaker hands to operate.

A current production Model 84 is shown on safe with the hammer down in the double-action mode …

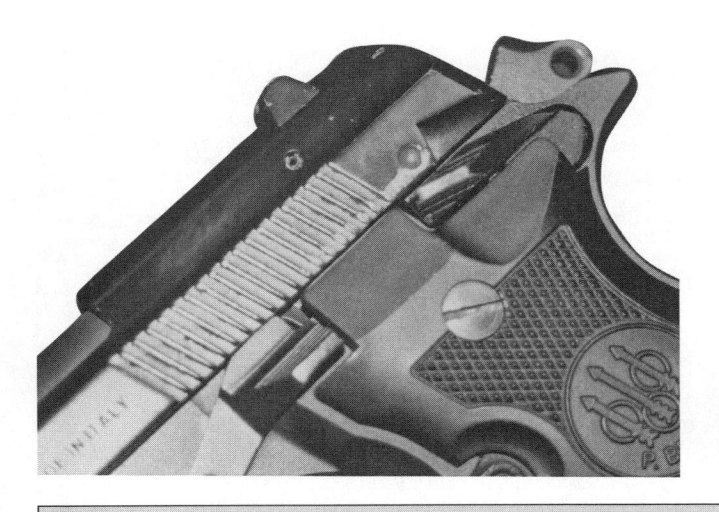

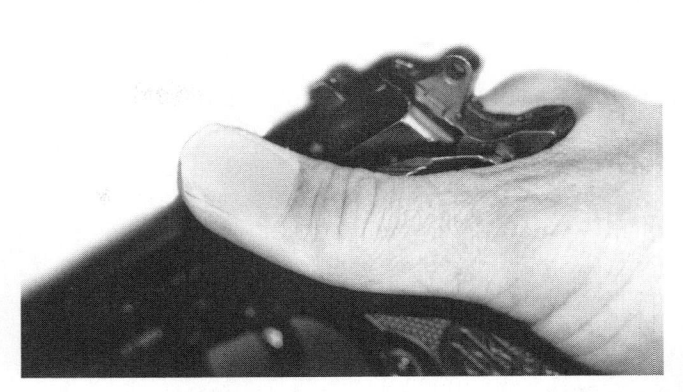

Left: ... off safe, cocked and ready to fire ...
Right: ... and being decocked, which on later models is accomplished by thumbing the frame-mounted lever up past the on-safe position.

and the single-action design. It also retained the good shooting characteristics. However, there were some distinct differences.

One strange safety catch was exchanged for another. The awkward lever above the trigger guard on the left of the 1934's frame had to be rotated forward, down and then up, 180 degrees, to get it into the "fire" position. The Series 70 had a cross-bolt safety forward of the grip tang. In theory, the median joint of the right thumb would press it inward to "fire," and it would have to be pressed back out from the other side for "safe." In practice, most people found it not only different, but just plain difficult. The same had proven true earlier, when Beretta had put it on their 1951 model 9mm Parabellum service pistol. Once the safety was disengaged, though, the 70 series demonstrated superb shooting characteristics. Its more steeply angled grip felt better in many hands (including mine) and made it point more naturally for many shooters (including me.)

The 1934/35 pistols had come with conventional "European-style" butt heel magazine releases. The 70 models had a push-button release low at the rear of the left grip panel. This was seen as a more ergonomic way for thumb and fingers of the left hand to remove the magazine from the butt, and this feature was found on Beretta 9mm Parabellum pistols throughout the third quarter of the Twentieth Century, and remains on the small-frame Beretta pocket pistols.

The more or less conventional slide stop lever on the left side of the frame was a welcome addition on the 70 series pistols. Most had the "little finger extension" on the magazine that was commonly, but not exclusively, seen on its predecessor guns. Particularly nice were the .22 Long Rifle versions. Their good trigger pull, good accuracy, flat silhouette and reasonably compact size made them a favorite of discriminating plinkers and outdoorsmen. With aluminum alloy frames, they weighed just over 16 ounces. Variants in .22 LR included the standard Model 70S and the Model 71, which lasted until 1985. The Model 72 came with a barrel almost 6 inches long, as well as a standard length (3½-inch) barrel. The Model 73 had both front and rear fixed sights attached to the barrel, on the theory (long since proven by High Standard and Smith & Wesson in the U.S.) that a front sight on a fixed barrel and a rear sight on a moving slide would not always be in a constant relationship with one

Here is the ambidextrous, 14-shot Beretta Model 84 Cheetah .380.

another. The Model 74 had adjustable sights, also with the rear sight mounted on the barrel. This pistol also featured an adjustable trigger pull. Larry Wilson quotes factory literature of the period: "The trigger pull is adjustable by means of a conic screw acting on the sear (remove right grip panel, adjustment screw for trigger located near disconnector)." [1]

You may have read that the Mossad, the Israeli intelligence/counter-intelligence agency, was long quite partial to the Beretta .22 pistol. This is the gun. Its flatness made it carry very comfortably and discreetly when concealed, and its excellent pointing qualities lent themselves to the Israeli doctrine of point-shooting with pistols. Since Israeli handgun doctrine also required that the pistol be carried off-safe with the chamber empty, and a round jacked into the spout when it was drawn for serious purposes, the odd cross-bolt safety proved no problem at all.

All these Berettas, indeed all Beretta semiautomatics, had been single-action pistols. Their first double-action in this caliber was the Model 90, introduced in late 1968 and produced through early 1982. Writes Wilson, "The medium-frame Model 90 was the first Beretta automatic pistol with a double-action trigger system, barrel of stainless steel, enclosed slide with ejection port on the right side, and the magazine release located by the rear of the trigger guard. The frame was of aluminum alloy; the hammer was exposed; the slide remained opened after the last shot was fired. Although the pistol did not prove a success, the future of the double-action system was assured." [2] Only some 22,000 were

Right: While the author prefers the more powerful Berettas at his hip and in a tactical thigh holster, he admits the shootability of the Model 86 .380 he is holding. Note the group in the target ...

Left: ... which was fired as fast as he could pull the trigger.

Bill Goldstein, an authority on self-defense for senior citizens, strongly recommends the Model 86 for its easy-handling features.

Barbara, a senior citizen with arthritis, is a deadly shot with her Beretta 86, finding it the easiest pistol to operate efficiently.

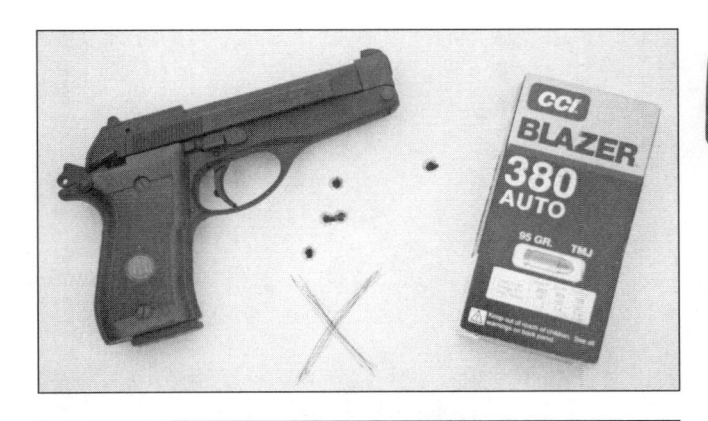

This Beretta Model 86 gave decent accuracy at 25 yards with cheap Blazer ammo, which it fed perfectly.

Beretta's modern .380s offer good trigger reach.

produced.

The Third Wave

In the early 1980s, the 70 series and the pioneering Model 90 both gave way to what became known as the 81 series, though it has also been called the 80 series. With some refinements these are the .380 Berettas that are with us today, along with their .32 and .22 caliber companion guns, in the current Beretta catalog.

This generation saw the return of the open-top slide, the departure from which had not been a hit for Beretta with the Model 90. A frame-mounted manual safety, similar in shooter operation to that of the first-generation Model 92 9mm, was installed. The 81 series also had a magazine release button in what combat shooters considered the appropriate location, behind the trigger guard on the frame.

These guns also had magazine disconnector safeties, not a usual Beretta feature. This means that if the magazine has been removed from the gun and it has been left with a round in the chamber, if someone picks up the gun and pulls the trigger, the chambered cartridge will not discharge. Wilson lists this feature as "available on request; magazine safety on trigger mechanism when magazine extracted."[3] However, I have never seen a Beretta .380 of this generation that *didn't* have the magazine disconnector feature.

The first of the 81 series was the actual Model 81, with a double-stack magazine in caliber .32 ACP (7.65 mm.) It was quickly joined by a twin in .380, the Model 84. Both remain in production. The Model 81, curiously, held 12 rounds in its magazine, while a magazine of the same dimension managed to contain 13 fatter cartridges for the Model 84. The .380 proved quite popular and remains so to this day. The Model 81 is seldom seen in this country. It was realized early on that a 13-shot .32, generating 125 foot pounds of energy per shot with 60-grain Silvertip jacketed hollow-points and 129 foot-pounds per shot with 71-grain full-metal-jacket ammo, would not sell well to Americans when for the same price they could get the identical gun as a 14-shot .380 generating 189 foot-pounds with 85-grain Silvertip JHP and 211 foot-pounds with 95-grain FMJ. It was a "do the math" thing. The relevant decision-makers on both sides of the water knew Yanks would take the .380 hands down over the .32 and chose not to bother bringing the latter to U.S. shores. They made the right decision.

The Indiana State Police bought a Beretta 84 .380 for each of their troopers, as an off-duty and optional backup gun. The pistol was issued simultaneously with the Beretta 92G 9mm that was adopted to replace the agency's traditional .357 Magnum service revolvers. When ISP later "powered up" to the .40 S&W service pistol, they chose the Beretta 96G, but kept the Beretta .380s for the backup/off-duty function.

A fascinating variation of the

Unlike many .380s, the Beretta Cheetah has sights that are easy to see.

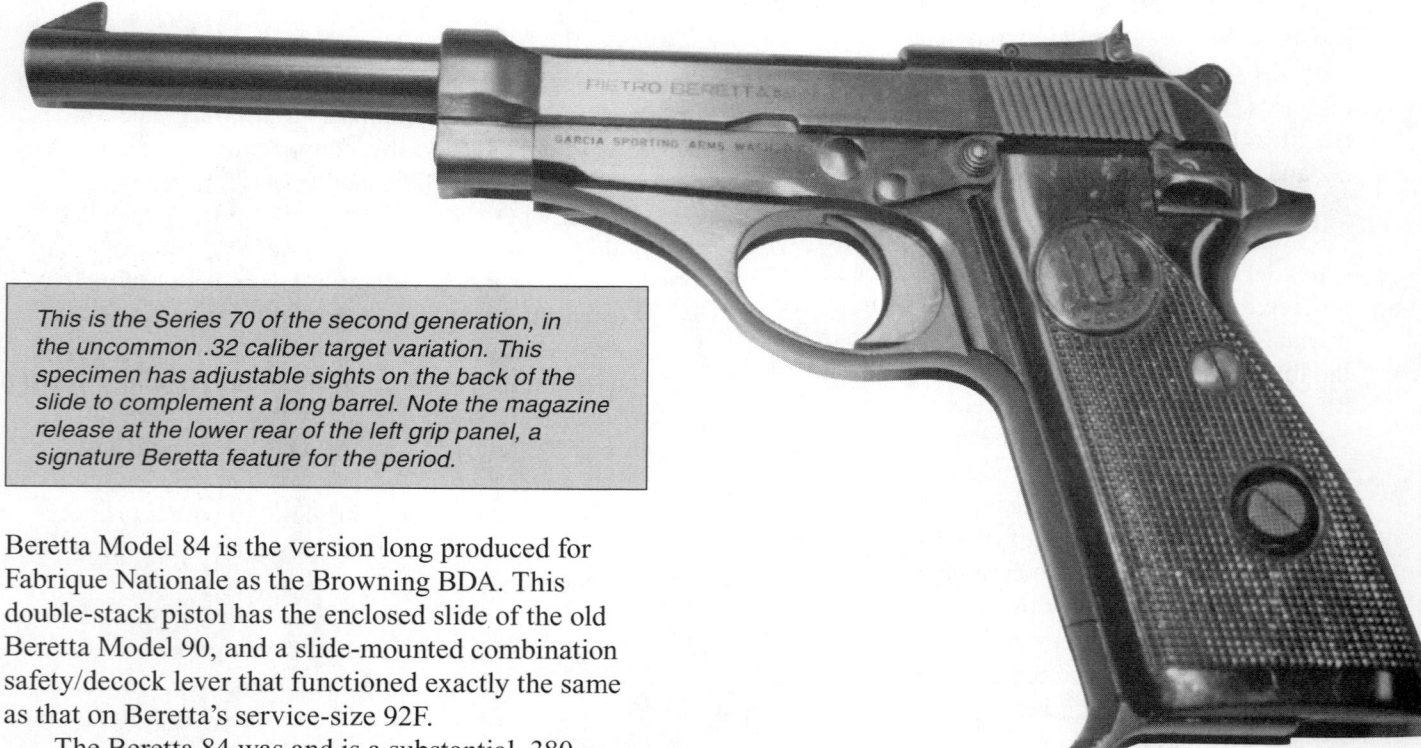

Left: This is the 1935 Model .32 with the hammer at rest and off safe. Of the Beretta intermediate-frame pistols this is part of the first classic generation. …

Right: … and here it is cocked and on safe. The 180-degree safety catch proved awkward. This pistol appears to have been chrome plated after market.

This is the Series 70 of the second generation, in the uncommon .32 caliber target variation. This specimen has adjustable sights on the back of the slide to complement a long barrel. Note the magazine release at the lower rear of the left grip panel, a signature Beretta feature for the period.

Beretta Model 84 is the version long produced for Fabrique Nationale as the Browning BDA. This double-stack pistol has the enclosed slide of the old Beretta Model 90, and a slide-mounted combination safety/decock lever that functioned exactly the same as that on Beretta's service-size 92F.

The Beretta 84 was and is a substantial .380. There are a lot of .380s that are smaller. Hell, there are 9mm and even .40 S&W pistols that are smaller. With this in mind, Beretta introduced the Model 85 a few years later with a slim single-stack magazine that held eight .380 cartridges, allowing a proportionally slimmer grip frame.

The 85's slender grip frame and magazine size were retained for the Model 86, which is my personal favorite Beretta .380. The dust cover (the forward part of the frame) was extended to allow for a tip-up barrel a' la the 950 series. While the lever that pops the barrel up is located on the left side of a 950's frame and requires only a short arc of movement, the one on the .380 is on the right side and demands a full 180 degrees before the mechanism tilts the barrel upward.

Though the Model 86 looks bulkier than the 85, it is not really so in any given dimension, and its added weight is but a single ounce. A Beretta 86 tips the

Right: ... the 1934/35 style fit solidly in the hand, and established a reputation as a .380 unbeatable for reliability and accuracy.

Below left: For much of the 20th century this was the defining shape of Beretta pistols. The author's first centerfire handgun, a Model 1934 .380 ...

Below right: ... had a patina from WWII combat use, and the manual safety was removed ...

Author's favorite .380 is the Model 86. It is the most powerful tip-up barrel design. This is a feature that enables use by those with crippled or weakened hands.

scales at 23 ounces unloaded, an 85, at 22 ounces.

I'm partial to the Beretta 86 for the same reason a lot of firearms instructors are: it serves as a special-purpose "orthopedic gun" for a certain type of student. This is the individual who, for reasons of illness, injury, age, or whatever does not have the strength to operate the slide of a semiautomatic pistol.

Circa 1992, the Models 84, 85, and 86 became the Beretta Cheetah series along with the Model 87, which was the same gun in .22 Long Rifle. The design was updated to make the frame-mounted safety lever function as a decocking lever as well.

This, for the most part, is a good feature. Lowering a double-action pistol's hammer by hand is asking for an accident. There is huge potential for slippage.

If you're going to carry a double-action Beretta .380 *in* double-action mode, the Cheetah series (or the Browning BDA) makes enormous sense. If you are accustomed to carrying a 1911 or other type pistol with a frame-mounted safety that is pressed down for "fire" and up for "safe," you will have commonality with the Cheetah in its double-action mode, and that makes awfully good sense, too.

At the same time, one thing I liked about the earlier design of the Model 86 was that its manual safety design made possible cocked and locked, single-action carry. It was my experience that a person whose limited upper body strength made it hard for them to operate an auto pistol's slide, often also had fingers so weak or so limited in reach that the long, heavy first shot pull of a double-action trigger would be difficult for them, too. I've encouraged a number of people in this situation to go with the older style Beretta 86, and as long as they could live with the .380 ACP power level, they were happy with it. Those same people, almost always, found themselves carrying the gun cocked and locked because it was much faster and much easier for them to get off the first shot. Sometimes, that was the only way they *could* get off the first shot.

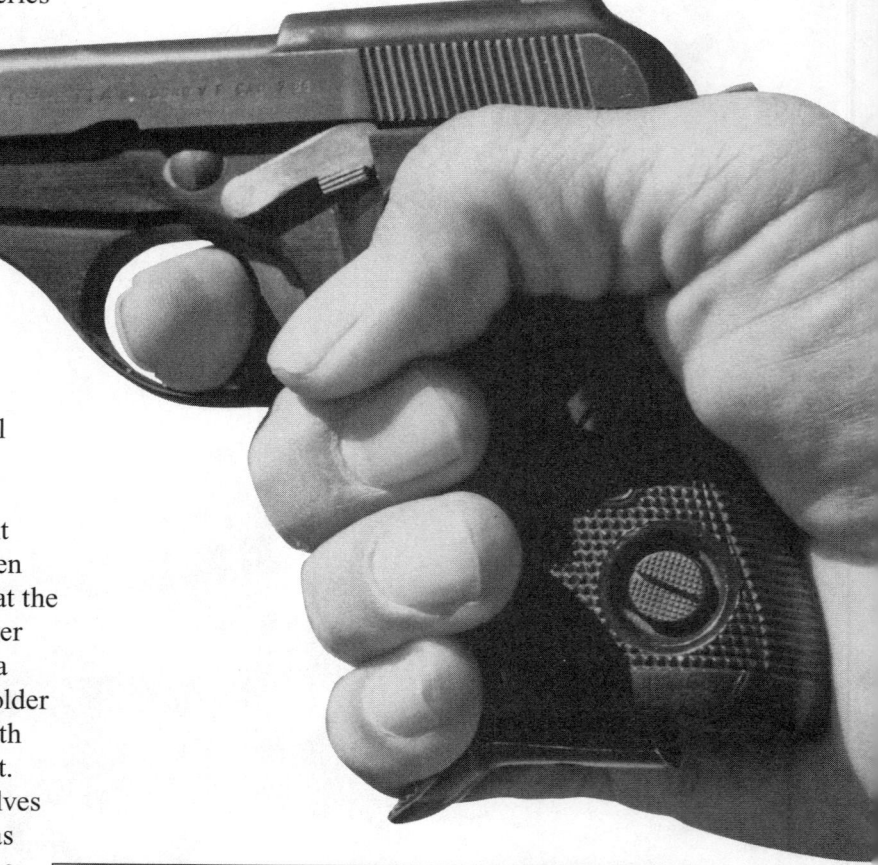

The author thinks the best casual sporting .22 Beretta ever made was the Model 70. This one has adjustable sights, factory thumb-rest stock.

Few pistols point as well as a series 70 Beretta, or feel as good in the hand.

The Beretta Model 70 .22 became famous as an issue weapon for Mossad, the Israeli secret service.

Cocked and locked, the second-generation Model 70 is seen with its ergonomic thumb safety, which replaced the previous cross-bolt design.

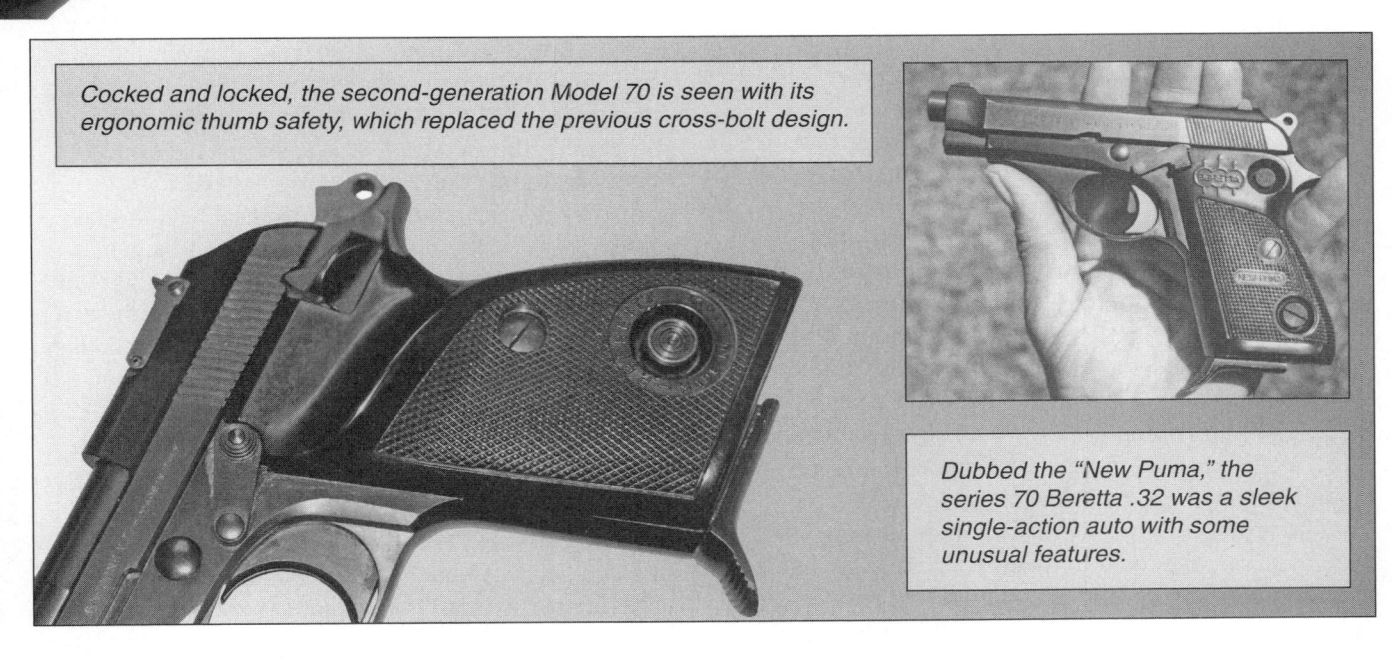

Dubbed the "New Puma," the series 70 Beretta .32 was a sleek single-action auto with some unusual features.

Unlike first-generation guns, the second-generation intermediate frame Berettas had this efficient, ergonomic slide lock design.

Shooting the Beretta .380s

Not until a year or so into production of the third-generation guns (81 series) did Beretta .380s start coming with internal firing pin safeties. This rendered them drop-safe. Prior state-of-the-art was such that if a semiautomatic pistol with a round in the chamber and no internal firing pin lock should be struck sharply on the muzzle or hammer end, the firing pin could be driven forward enough by inertia to fire the weapon. Thus, if you have any pistol without an internal firing pin lock, it is an excellent idea to carry it with an empty chamber and jack a round into the firing chamber Israeli-style when the gun is drawn in an emergency or any other situation where it may be appropriate to fire. The current Beretta .380s with internal firing pin lock are, however, safe to carry with a round in the chamber, the way U.S. police and most of us "in the business" carry our semiautomatic pistols.

I personally thought those sweet, second-generation 70 series models had the best feel of all, but the current generation is awfully close in that positive attribute. This is subjective, of course, but the reader can easily test a given handgun for this factor without firing a shot. Triple check that the gun is unloaded. Pick a spot that could safely absorb a bullet. Lower the gun, close your eyes, and keeping the eyelids shut, bring the pistol up and point it by feel at that pre-selected spot. Freeze everything, and open your eyes. If the gun is aimed where you wanted it to be, that gun "points well for you." It's a subjective thing. It's about *you* and the gun, not about me or anyone else and the given pistol.

The top of a Series 81 pistol's slide is somewhat rounded. This makes it more comfortable for inside-the-waistband carry, and is esthetically pleasing. However, it also means there's less flat area at the rear of the slide with which the shooter's support hand can engage the grasping grooves. This can make jacking the slide awkward. It's another reason why I'm partial to the Model 86 with its tip-up barrel. There are some other .380s, notably the SIG P230 and P232, whose slides are easier to operate than those of a Beretta 84 or 85.

The modern Beretta .380s normally come with ambidextrous safety levers. This is always a good thing. You might be right-handed, as I am, but either of us might have to lend our gun to another good guy or gal who will be using it southpaw. At any time, either of us could suffer an injury to our dominant hand or arm that requires us to carry on the weak side for a while. That's a lousy time to have to call the gunsmith and see how long it will take to install an ambi safety on our carry gun.

If what you want is a smaller, lower-powered version of a modern military or police style Beretta, consider looking for the Browning BDA variation. Remember, its safety/decock lever is operated exactly the same way as the similarly slide-mounted lever on an F-series Beretta.

Like the second-generation Beretta .380s, the current third-generation has a .22 caliber understudy gun available that works exactly the same way. It is the Model 87. This is a handy thing for practice and training.

Recoil of the Beretta .380 is markedly soft. Virtually everyone who shoots one comments on that. When editor Harry Kane and I were putting together the 2005 edition of the annual *Complete Book of Handguns,* we included an article on very small hideout guns. These ranged from the little Guardian .32 auto, to Beretta's .32 Tomcat, to the J-frame S&W Airweight .38 Special revolver, the sweet little Kahr PM9 micro-size 9mm Parabellum and the Beretta 86 .380. There was no question that of all these guns, the Beretta .380 was by far the easiest to shoot and to hit center with at high speed.

Muzzle jump is minimal with the Cheetah-class .380s. The low bore axis is one reason and a grip frame that allows a full purchase and a strong grasp is another. I and the other fans of powerful guns can make all the "mouse gun" jokes we want, but the fact is, there are some people who are just intimidated by more powerful pistols but are confident in their ability to shoot fast and straight under stress with a gun like a Beretta .380. Let's say that you and I have to go into one of those dangerous situations that I've come to call The Dark Place. We can choose one of three people to back us up. One has a 12-gauge shotgun, but is totally intimidated by its savage recoil. One has a .45 automatic, and cringes and jerks the trigger with every shot. And one has a Beretta .380, and shoots it fast and straight even when the pressure's on.

The one with the shotgun will probably miss, if the courage is mustered to fire it at all. The one with the .45 will likely jerk low, and maybe achieve a thigh shot if we're lucky. But the cool hand with the .380 is most likely to hit dead center in an emergency. The one with the .380 gets my vote. How about you?

The trigger pull is quite good in both double- and single-action. As with their modern service pistols, the current Beretta .380s have generously sized sights that are easy to see, particularly for those of us with aging eyes.

But let's look at the biggest advantage of the Beretta .380s as currently produced …

The damn things work!

My experience with the elegant and stylish Walther pistols is that some of them feed hollow point ammo and some of them don't. If you have a good one, the splendid little Walther-influenced SIG .380, will work as well as a Beretta. If you don't have a good one, it'll show up in the first few hundred rounds, and you'll have to send it back to the factory to make things right. The SIG .380s will also slice your hand with the slide as it comes back, and most of the Walther pistols will do the same; they don't bite as much since S&W started importing them a couple of years ago and made Walther extend the grip tang, but they still bite some. I've seen Colt .380s that worked with JHP, and Colt .380s that didn't. Contemporary .380s from Colt are scaled down versions of the Government Model .45, and if you have average size adult male hands and shoot with a strong grasp in which your thumb is curled down, there's a good chance that you'll accidentally depress the magazine release and dump the magazine on your foot.

None of these problems occur with the current Berettas. They feed JHPs. They don't bite your hand. They're accurate as hell, right up there with the Walther and the SIG, tied for braggin' rights as "best of breed" among the .380 pistols past and present in terms of precision shooting potential.

While putting this chapter together, I took a Model 86 out to the backyard range with the only two types of .380 ammo I had in the house, both inexpensive "generic ball" loads. Remington-UMC easily kept all five shots in the head of an IPSC target at 25 yards, with a group measuring 3.05 inches. The best three of those bullet holes were in a cluster spanning only 1.4 inches center-to-center. CCI Speer's aluminum-cased Blazer delivered a five-shot group of 3.20 inches, with the best four in 1.65 inches and the best three in 0.80 of an inch. Bearing in mind the proven rule of thumb that the best three of five shots handheld from a bench rest will come awfully close to what the same gun/cartridge combination will do for all five shots from a machine rest, that's damned impressive pistol performance.

Downsides? Really, only a couple. If you have the earlier double-actions with the hand-lowered hammers, you're almost better off to carry them cocked and locked. Also, to get the great reliability and accuracy and easy shooting of the Beretta .380s, you have to accept that, as Wilson accurately categorizes them, they're medium-frame guns. If you want a small-frame pistol, small enough for a pocket or ankle holster, and you want it to be a Beretta, you're probably going to have to go down to the Tomcat .32.

But if you're looking for a .380 that will be carried in or on a belt, worn in a shoulder holster, packed in a purse, or stored in a lock box or glove box, the Cheetah size Beretta will be awfully tough to beat.

Endnotes

(1)Wilson, R.L., "The World of Beretta: An International Legend," New York City: Random House, 2000, P. 204.

(2)Ibid., P. 202.

(3)Ibid., P. 205.

Model 92:
The Flagship of the Beretta Fleet

Brace yourself for the longest chapter in this book. There's a reason for that. The book is about modern Beretta pistols, and we're going to talk about the gun that wrote the most complex and significant chapter in the history of those handguns. The Model 92 is the defining Beretta pistol of modern times. Adopted by all branches of the United States military in 1984, one of the three or four most popular law enforcement pistols in the nation and one of the most distinctively recognizable handguns in the world, the Beretta 92 has become a modern classic, like it or not.

I say "like it or not" advisedly, because with the arguable exception of the Glock, no other pistol has been the subject of such controversy in modern times, if ever.

The great are envied. The great are resented. Therefore, the great are attacked. It is human nature. When you get elected president, some people will want to tear you down. When you win the richest single contract anyone in your industry can remember, the same thing will happen. As soon as it became apparent that the Beretta Model 92 was a great pistol, and that its maker was going to be richly rewarded for it, the envy, resentment, and attacks reached epic proportions.

The defining shape of the Beretta pistol today: the 9mm Model 92FS.

It became the standard military service pistol of the United States, replacing an iconic piece of ordnance that was one of the most beloved guns in history, the 1911A1 .45 automatic. The American police, half a million strong, were switching from revolvers to semiautomatic pistols and the Beretta 92 was the sales leader in that market. The American public had historically based many firearms purchases on what their nation's police and military were carrying. Accordingly, by 1997, Beretta would sell *2 million* of these pistols.

With no lever on the slide, the 92D has room for more grasping grooves than F or G models.

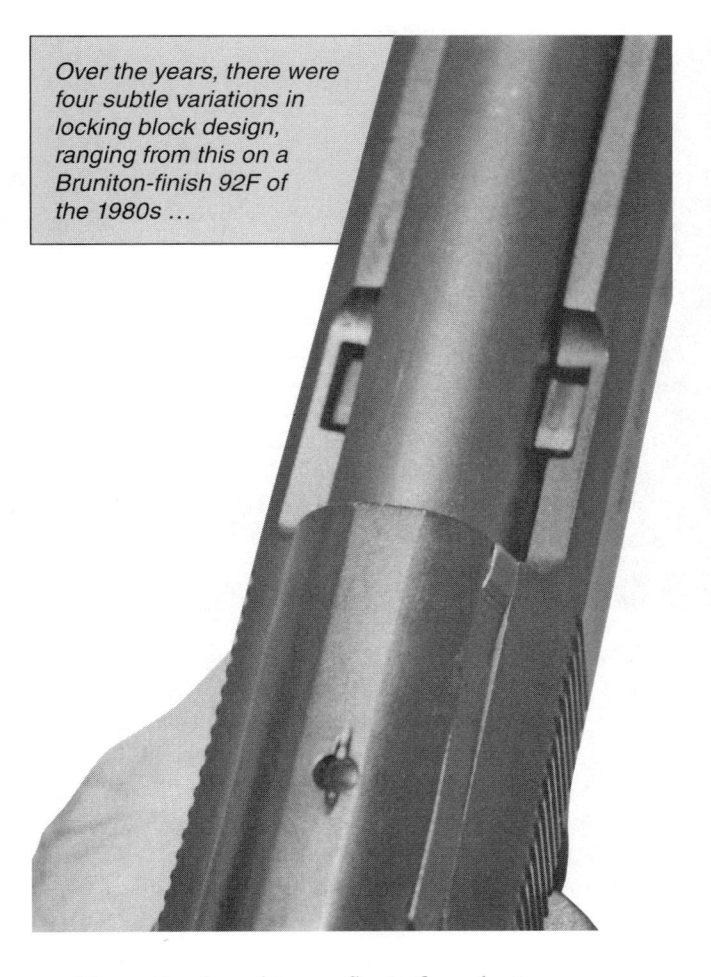

Over the years, there were four subtle variations in locking block design, ranging from this on a Bruniton-finish 92F of the 1980s …

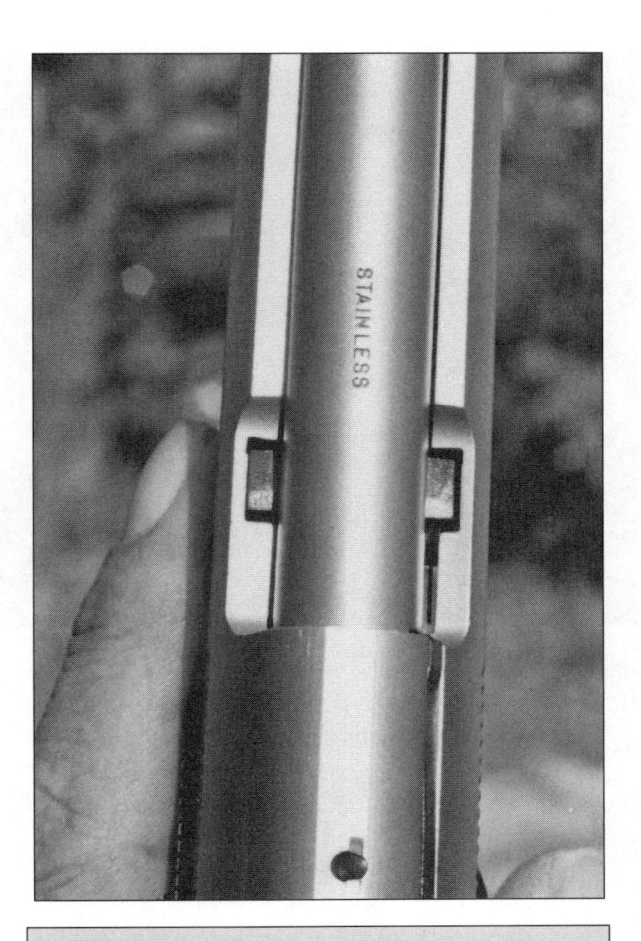

… to this on a stainless 92FS produced in 2004.

No matter how huge a fleet of products a manufacturing company floats, it will have at least one flagship, one product that is hugely successful. For Smith & Wesson it was the K-frame revolver, introduced in 1899 and now with a history and popularity that touches three centuries. For Colt, the first flagship was the Model P single-action revolver, designed in 1873 and still in production. Now it is the Model 1911 semiautomatic pistol. For Winchester, it was the lever-action Model 94 and the bolt-action Model 70 rifles.

For Beretta the flagship is the Model 92 pistol. To understand why it is as good as it is and as widely used as it is, we have to go back to its roots.

The Derivation

The key design elements that distinguish the Beretta Model 92 from other auto-loading pistols are its open-slide design, its distinctive locking mechanism, and its double-action lockwork. None are unique. The uniqueness came from the nature of their combination by Beretta, and from the collective design genius of Carlo Beretta, Giuseppe Mazzetti, and Vittorio Valle.

Says Beretta historian Larry Wilson, "The family tree of the Model 92 is one of the more complex within the domain of automatic pistols, with its roots in the relatively simple design of Tullio Marengoni's Model 1915. Contrasting the two shows the sophisticated level of Beretta's research and development team, as well as the advanced state of its manufacturing facility." [1]

On June 29, 1915, the first patent was issued on the handgun that would be known as the Beretta Model 1915. A blowback pistol chambered for the 9mm Glisenti, then Italy's military pistol cartridge, it had a "hammerless" look with an enclosed firing mechanism, enclosed barrel, and extremely simplified design and construction. It was followed by a series of 7.65mm and 9mm Glisenti pistols (models 1917, 1922, 1923, etc.) with partially exposed slides, leaving the barrel less and less enclosed by the slide mass. The true "open-slide look" would come with the Model of 1934, the blowback 7.65mm and 9mm Corto that would be the definitive Beretta pistol of the early 20th century, and which would remain so until the coming of the Model 92. By then, the Beretta pistol design

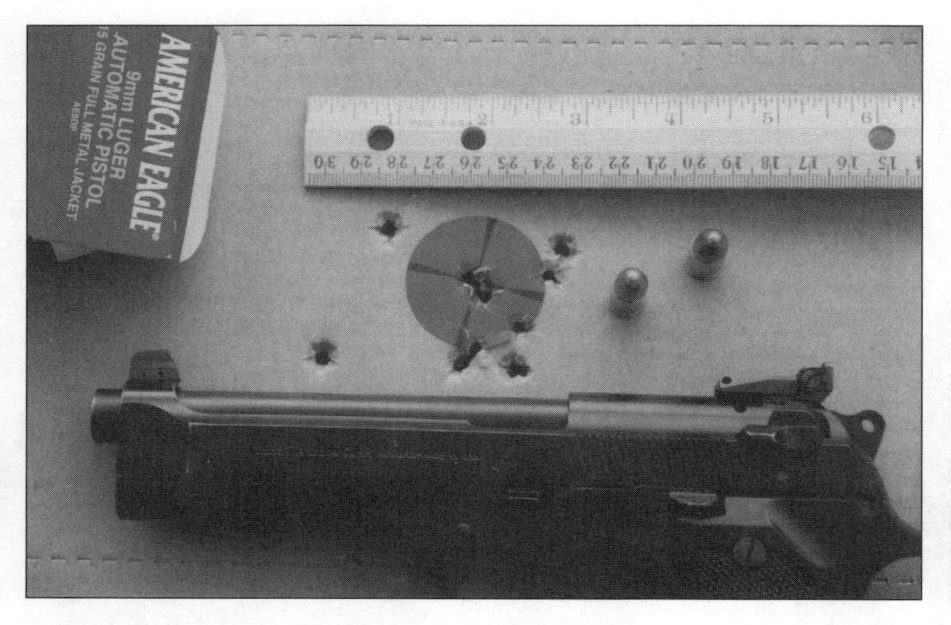

The Beretta 92 is accurate. This 92F is box stock save for LPA sights just attached by Bill Pfeil. Five shots from 25 yards and five from 50, hand-held from right-hand barricade position, resulted in this 10-shot group of less than 3 inches with inexpensive Federal American Eagle ball.

had evolved into a burr-style outside hammer format, though the pistol was still single-action.

In the shape of the barrel and slide, and to some degree the overall shape of the gun, the Model 34 presaged the Model 92. But other major design elements were drawn from elsewhere.

The locking block design of the Walther P-38 pistol in 9mm Luger, adopted in 1938 by German armed forces as their primary service pistol, would also find its way into the Model 92. Gun expert Charles M. Heard explained, "The P-38 fires 9mm Parabellum rounds handled by a short recoil system with the barrel being disengaged by cams which are movable inclined planes."[2]

The Walther P-38 also featured a mechanism in which the initial pull of the trigger, "double-action," first raised and then dropped the exposed hammer to fire the chambered cartridge. As the gun cycled, the slide cocked the hammer, and subsequent shots would be fired with the easy single-action trigger pull. The hammer would be lowered by an internal decocking mechanism, activated by pushing down a lever on the left side of the slide, which when in the down position also functioned as a manual safety catch. This in turn derived from an earlier Walther, the PP/PPK series of pocket-size pistols in .22 LR, 7.65mm, and .380. These pistols had debuted in 1928. While Czech pistols had been built around the double-action feature earlier than that, they had been double-action only, even after the first shot. Walther was the first to produce a double-action mechanism that functioned only on the first shot, cocking itself to single-action for follow-up rounds. Smith & Wesson would

Heavy dust accumulation from too much holster carry with too little cleaning will not impair the function of this Beretta 92.

adopt it before it was adopted by Beretta, but this Walther concept would find its way to the Model 92 as surely as the P-38 lock-up design.

Thus, we see that the key design elements that would distinguish the Model 92 were in place on various handguns well before World War II. However, they were not yet ready to be lashed together into that particular pistol. One more bridge had yet to be built: Beretta's first 9mm Parabellum service pistol.

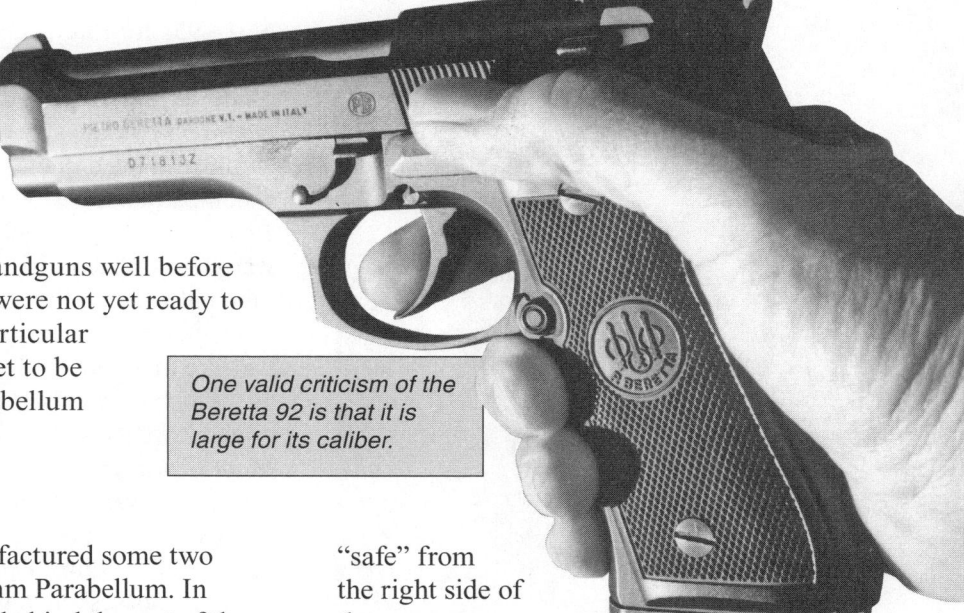

One valid criticism of the Beretta 92 is that it is large for its caliber.

The Beretta Precedent

By 1950, Beretta had manufactured some two million pistols, but not yet a 9mm Parabellum. In this, the company was decades behind the rest of the European small arms industry. It was time to catch up.

The catch up gun was the sturdy Model of 1951. Over the following decades it would go through various refinements and permutations, and be given various names. Model 1951. Model 51. Model 951. Brigadier. Model 104. In all cases, it was essentially the same rugged pistol. Its single-stack magazine held eight 9mm Luger rounds. The hammer was the common burr or rowel type, but more oval than circular, and in this it differed from earlier Berettas and most other European autoloaders.

The magazine release was a button recessed into the lower rear corner of the left grip panel. The safety was a cross-bolt, which was pressed to the right for "fire" from the left side of the pistol, and to the left for "safe" from the right side of the weapon.

Produced primarily in 9mm but also in .30 Luger, the gun featured the open slide concept of Marengoni. With no upper slide to snag a spent casing during its ejection arc if something went wrong, it was remarkably jam-free. The common "stovepipe" malfunction, in which a spent casing is caught in the ejection port and sticks up like an exhaust pipe, was virtually unknown with this gun. Similarly, the open top above the barrel eliminated a major area where sand and dirt could accumulate and create friction against the barrel that could jam the weapon.

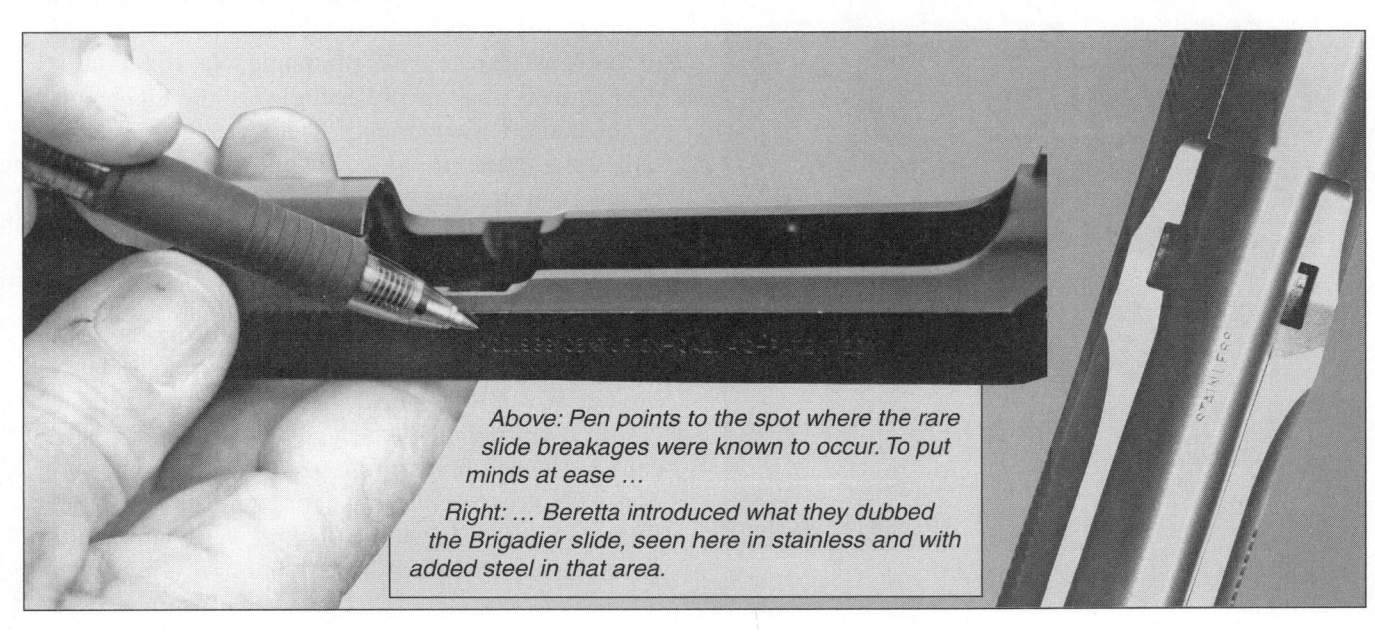

This feature was almost immediately recognized and appreciated by the fledgling nation of Israel, and by the Arab states surrounding it. The Maadi

Above: Pen points to the spot where the rare slide breakages were known to occur. To put minds at ease ...

Right: ... Beretta introduced what they dubbed the Brigadier slide, seen here in stainless and with added steel in that area.

F-series/M9 pistols are carried on safe by many private citizens and police officers, and by the U.S. Army and U.S. Marine Corps as standard doctrine.

F-series/M9s are carried off safe by many cops, civilians, and the USAF.

Company was licensed by Beretta to build copies of the 951 for Engineering Industries of Cairo. This Egyptian-made pistol was known as the Helwan.

Beretta was prescient as to the role pistols would play in the short-term future of military conflict. Wilson quotes the brochures that originally accompanied the Model 951 pistols in the early 1950s. "The experience of the recent (Korean) war proved that an individual defense weapon of high ballistic qualities is still required, the more so against the dangers of enemy raids and partisan warfare met with (by) the supply and contact service, and which demands a ready reaction based upon efficient weapons of outstanding offensive power. Modern warfare, in fact, created the phenomena of (guerrilla) warfare which takes place at the flanks of the operational army units, and the use of pistols and light machine guns, despite the development of new weapons possessing a very high destructive power, cannot yet be considered as obsolete even in modern theatres of war." [3]

As this book is written, that lesson is being proven in Iraq and Afghanistan. While not universally issued to all personnel, the Beretta M9 pistol is dramatically present, strapped to the bodies of a greater percentage of American combat troops than in any conflict in collective modern memory.

The Model 951 did not set the pistol world on fire. It lacked what a marketing specialist might call "the hook," a distinguishing feature to set it apart from the competition. There was not something it could do that the others couldn't. It didn't have the double-column, high-capacity magazine that had been seen as a desirable feature since the Browning High Power of 1935. It didn't have the double-action of the Walther P-38. It didn't have the raw, crushing power of the American Colt .45 automatic. Nor did it have the exquisite target pistol accuracy of the SIGs built at Neuhausen, Switzerland. There was, however, a target-model Beretta 51 that would be made for the Egyptian army called the Berhama, which would later be put into Beretta's regular line as the 952 Special.

Experts of the time, military and civilian, saw the gun as functional but boring and undistinguished. One of the leading handgun experts during the 951's heyday was Henry M. Stebbins, who wrote, "The Model 1951 or 951 Brigadier is a business Beretta: 9mm Luger caliber, 4½inch barrel (not bad for this caliber), locked-breech action, exposed hammer. There is a cross-bolt safety at the top rear of the frame, a poor location; but the gun has a hammer, too, which most servicemen in any country, right now, probably would say is a good thing on a pistol. Eight- or ten-shot mags are available, and a butt spur for the shooter's little finger. After the last shot the slide stays open as we should expect with a military handgun. Perhaps the Brigadier has the ambition to become just that: a military sidearm officially adopted by one, two, or how many countries? A lot of them once used the Luger, but now it costs too much to make Lugers, at least as standard items." [4]

Tepid words, but at the time the Beretta 9mm was not seen as a hot gun. Stebbins had a point about the safety catch design, at least as seen by those of us accustomed to more conventional placement of that component. Not all agreed, however. One who took a warmer view of that feature in particular, and of the 1951 Beretta in general, was a later expert, Timothy J. Mullin, author of *Training the Gunfighter* and *The 100 Greatest Combat Pistols*. In the latter book, Mullin said of the Model 951, "… this is actually quite a good weapon. The design is similar to that of the Beretta M92 and has shown itself to be quite reliable. Of course, the M1951 Beretta uses a single-column magazine, which features a single-action trigger style, but that configuration has some advantages. It has a straight-line feed, thus increasing its feeding reliability. The single-column magazine avoids grip bulk, and the single-action trigger makes it easy to shoot.

"The magazine release is located on the butt, and that is always slow. It also requires two hands to use and has a tendency to get pushed off by car seats. The front sight is narrow and low, and the rear sight is small and shallow, thus indexing is slow. Painted white, they would show up much better. The sights and the gritty trigger on the Egyptian example tested combined to yield a 3 1/6 -inch group on the formal range.

"The safety on the M1951 is a cross-bolt variety. This is unlike that found on most other combat handguns, and when you first see it, you will probably view it as awkward and slow. But you will be mistaken. The safety is one of the pistol's best features. It reminds me of the safety found on the Star Z-63 SMG, and I found that on both the Star and the M1951 you could flip the safety off and on rapidly without shifting your hand at all. In fact, it was faster to operate than a Colt Government Model. All you need to do is take up your normal firing position, with your right thumb (assuming a right-hand grip) resting with the knuckle on the button. Merely extending the thumb slightly will bump the safety off. To reengage, merely straighten the trigger finger out, flex the finger straight out, hitting the button with the inside of your knuckle, and it will flip on. In actual practice, I found it fast and easy. For left-handers, the procedure is reversed, but it is equally simple. You have no need for an ambidextrous safety, extended safety, or

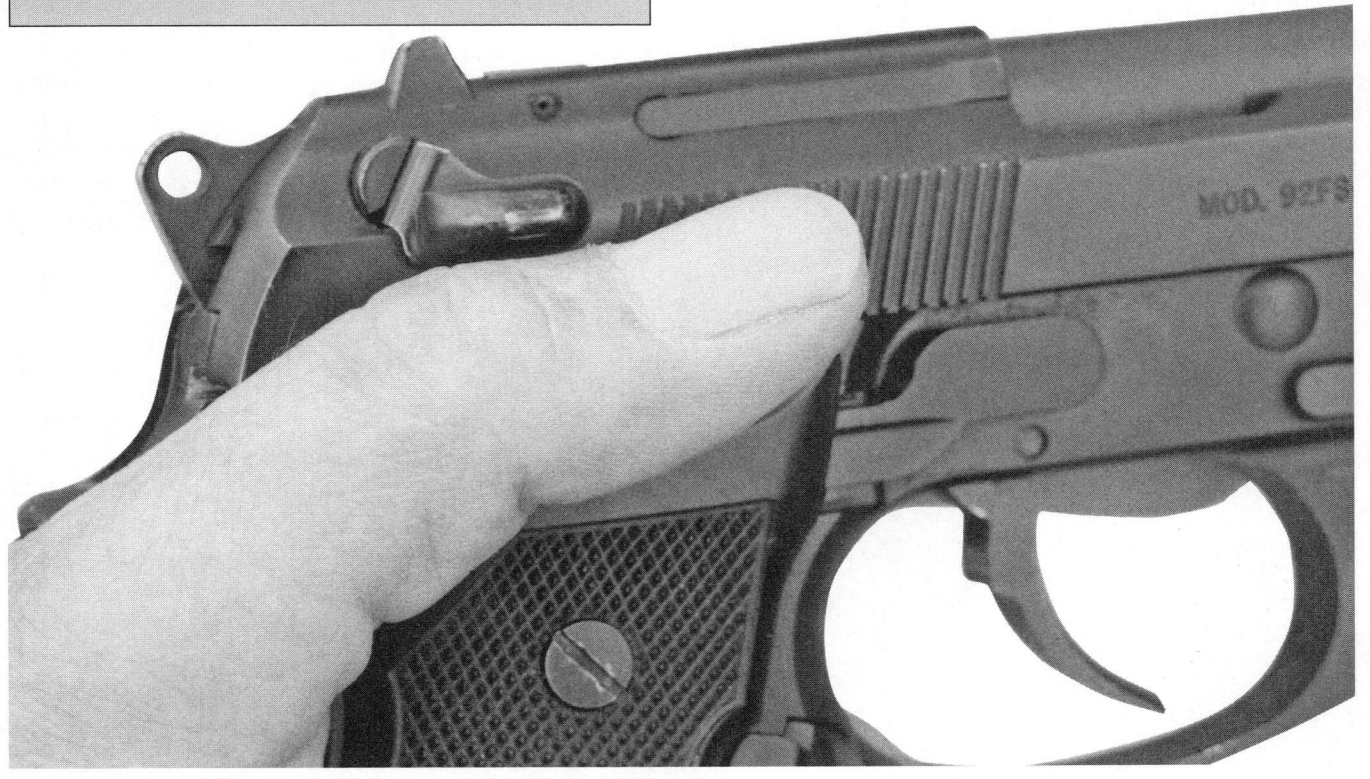

> Long before the U.S. adopted the Beretta 92, it had been fitted with an ambidextrous safety/decocking lever as standard. It is a very southpaw-friendly pistol.

external safety, and since the pistol grips are flush with the safety, you avoid the problems associated with flipping the safety off while in the holster. I really like this safety system." [5] (Note that when Mullen refers to the "knuckle" of the thumb, he is describing the median joint, not the proximal joint.)

The Model 1951 proved that Beretta could build a rugged, reliable 9mm Parabellum service pistol. The foundation had been laid for the Model 92.

Genesis Of The Model 92

In 1970, perceiving the double-action 9mm to be the pistol of the future, the Beretta company began work on such a gun. It would be Beretta's first double-action 9mm, and its first pistol with a double-stack, high-capacity magazine. Giusseppe Mazzetti and Vittorio Valle, reporting directly to Carlo Beretta, led the design team, which reportedly at one point had some 15 designers working on the double-action mechanism alone. Much of that development would ultimately transfer to the forthcoming Series 81 pistols, medium-framed autos in calibers .22, .32, and .380.

The first prototypes, reports Larry Wilson, were complete by 1975. This original incarnation of the Beretta Model 92 had the open slide and "oval" burr hammer, and unique magazine release, of the 1951. The shooter operated a frame-mounted safety, pivoting on a pin, the same as a 1911 or a Browning. The trigger guard was rounded.

Its first major contest to become a national military firearm took place in Brazil. Beretta won handily with the Model 92, building the Brazilian military Berettas at a factory it would later turn over to Forjas Taurus. But a much bigger contract was in the wind: after talking about adopting a 9mm pistol since the end of World War II, it appeared that the US Government was finally going to go ahead and do it. Reports Wilson, " … in 1978 the House Appropriations Committee of the U.S. Congress issued a directive recommending to the Department of Defense that the time had come for a new service handgun." He quoted Jeff Reh of Beretta, who would be deeply involved in the process, "The idea to purchase a new military sidearm was initiated by the House Appropriations Committee, where Chairman Joseph Addabbo's staff conducted a study which verified that an unnecessary proliferation of different types of weapons and ammunition existed in the military stockpile. Addabbo's staff recommended a reduction of the number of weapons in the inventory to ease maintenance burdens and eventually the recommendation was made that a new service sidearm be considered to replaced the venerable Colt Model 1911 .45 pistol." [6]

On the prize table was a contract for probably half a million guns. It was the most lucrative single prospect that anyone still living could remember ever having been placed in front of the handgun industry. It triggered one of the bitterest battles that the industry had ever experienced. In the end, some of the guns fell by the wayside, and some evolved of necessity into better pistols than they had been. The Beretta Model 92 was among the latter.

Stainless ("Inox") construction was a natural evolution for the 92FS, here demonstrated by gun dealer and small arms expert Jim McLoud.

The Fight To Succeed The 1911

The story of the military testing is long and complicated. The most detailed and informative accounts appear in Wilson's book, and in the *United States Marine Corps Diary 1990* in a segment by Matthew T. Robinson, the associate editor of the *Marine Corps Gazette*. That account was called "The Long Road to Change: Procurement of the Beretta 9mm M9 Service Pistol," and Larry Wilson dubbed it "the most succinct and straightforward piece" explaining the complex testing procedure and its various "back-stories." The following is a necessarily brief synopsis.

The testing began in the late 1970s, under the Joint Services Small Arms Program (JSSAP), an entity mandated by Congress. It was determined that the United States Air Force would be the service branch that would lead the testing, which kicked off at the USAF's Eglin Air Base in Valparaiso, Florida.

There were many entries. Colt fielded their double-action SSP, which did not do terribly well and which never made it into full-scale production. Smith & Wesson entered their Model 459 high-capacity, lightweight 9mm with a double-stack magazine. Ironically, this was a second-generation version of the S&W Model 39, a 26.5-ounce update of the Model 39 of 1954, which had been developed by S&W in the late 1940s the first time the government had indicated that it might be interested in adopting a new 9mm duty pistol. Heckler and Koch fielded two models, their P9 – preceding the Glock as the first polymer-framed pistol– and their VP70, a semi-auto pistol version of their machine pistol. Fabrique Nationale sent three different 9mm pistols to the contest, and Star of Spain sent one. Beretta, fresh from winning the Brazilian Army competition, sent in the Model 92.

The evolution of the Model 92 took place quickly, and of necessity as it faced the most modern high-tech handguns the free world had to offer. Gene Gangarosa, Jr. is a handgun authority who has written an eminently readable book on Beretta pistols, and several great articles. He encapsulated the 92's development as follows.

"In 1976 Beretta introduced their 9mm Model 92 pistol. It made a big hit worldwide with its 15-round magazine and double-action trigger. In its first version the Model 92 featured a sear-blocking manual safety lever located on the frame's left side in the manner of a Colt Government Model. Later that year, to appeal to military and police forces, Beretta introduced its Model 92S, a Model 92 with a hammer-decocking manual safety lever on the left side of the

Slide markings help track the Model 92's evolution in America. Beretta's U.S. corporate base was in New York when this 92F was imported from Italy ...

... while Beretta U.S.A, had been established in Maryland by the time the sun shone on this 92F ...

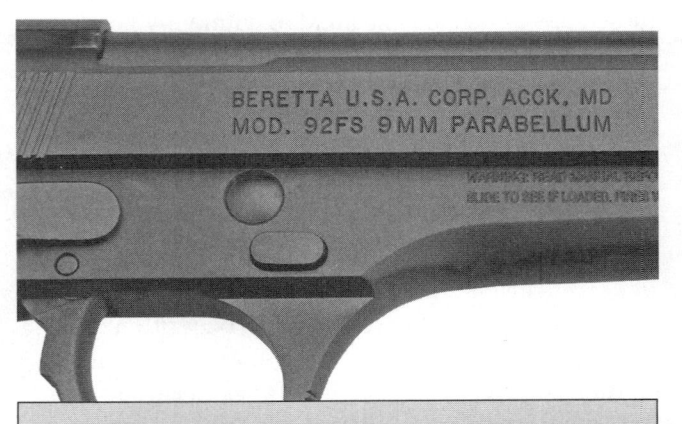

... and this contemporary 92FS was proudly "made in U.S.A."

slide. An upgraded variant of the Model 92S, the Model 92S-1, appeared in 1978 in response to U.S. armed forces interest in issuing a 9mm service pistol. This added an ambidextrous safety lever, enlarged sights and grooved grip straps to the Model 92S, and placed the magazine release behind the trigger guard. Beretta placed the Model 92S-1 changes into full production in late 1980 when the company introduced the Model 92SB. In addition to all the improvements of the prototypical S-1 variant, the SB version also incorporated fully checkered grips, safety levers reshaped to the current configuration, an overtravel shelf on the trigger and a firing-pin lock. Further changes made to the Model 92SB, in response to continued U.S. armed forces testing, led to the Model 92SB-F, evaluated by the U.S. Army in 1984 and adopted in January 1985 as the M9. Beretta also released this variant for commercial sale and police issue as the Model 92F. Changes included a black enamel 'Bruniton' finish, squared combat-style trigger guard, chrome-lined bore, slight flaring of the frame's bottom front portion, fourth-finger rest on the magazine bottom, relieving the grips' upper rear corners to allow easier access to the safety lever, and enlarging the grips screws' screwdriver slots. In 1990, following several slide separation incidents in the U.S. armed forces' training and experimentation, Beretta incorporated a 'slide retention device.' This quick fix consists of an enlarged hammer axis pin, which, if the slide's rear end separates during recoil, engages in a groove machined inside the slide's lower left rear portion to keep the slide on the frame. With the slide retention device fitted, Beretta designated the pistol Model 92FS, advancing the gun to its current configuration." [7]

The 92FS with slide catch device was designated the M10 pistol by the military. However, in all these years, not a single military person who works with these guns has called one an M10 within my hearing. Without exception, with slide catch or without it, FS or F style, the soldiers, sailors, Marines, and airmen who carry them call these guns "M9s". If a tree falls in the forest and no one is there to hear, did it really make a sound? If a name is changed and no one uses the new name, was the thing in question really re-named?

The entire, every-viewpoint-represented story of the giant cluster-coitus that was the test for the new 9mm U.S. military pistol has yet to be written. Very thorough accounts exist thus far, however, in the writings of Matthews and Wilson, cited earlier, and in Gangarosa's work. Suffice to say that after a long string of tests, lawsuits, and exchanged allegations, the Beretta Model 92 won virtually all of the tests. In the very last, it finished neck and neck with SIG-Sauer, and very slightly underbid the manufacturers of the SIG P226. Because it had been understood that the military would adopt the winner of the test, and because there were then so *many* tests over several years, various historical accounts differ as to the year that the Beretta Model 92 was actually adopted as U.S. Service Pistol, M9.

However, the weight of the evidence indicates that the pivotal approval and official adoption came in 1985. There would be many subsequent tests, all of which verified the selection of the Beretta as having been "the right thing to do." Suffice to say that Beretta considers 1985 to have been the official year of the U.S. adoption.

Lawsuits and trash-talking newspaper stories came into play. There were those who vilified the Beretta. In 1997, one of my editors at Publishers Development Corporation, now Firearms Marketing Group, asked me to research an article on the matter. The research was already pretty much done. I had followed the Beretta testing from the beginning. A good friend of mine, Jack Robbins, was one of the key men involved in the JSSAP project at Eglin. He had told me that the reason the Beretta had won was that it had simply outperformed everything else, and that Beretta had shown a different attitude than most of its competitors. The majority had figured they made the best gun and it would stand on its own. Beretta, more than any other player in the race, had sent its top people back and forth between the U.S.A. and Italy to ask the testers and the military in detail what they wanted and demanded, and had custom-tailored what became the 92F – and ultimately, the M9 – to those wants and needs.

When the slide separations started happening, I was on it like white on rice. I had for many years done the "Industry Insider" column for *American Handgunner*, and was proud that I had earned a reputation of telling it like it was. I had exposed a number of bad firearms, and a lot of manufacturers didn't like me for it. I had been banned at various times from Charter Arms, Glock, Smith & Wesson, and Sterling Arms for writing things about their products that the executives didn't appreciate. One company had pulled over a million dollars worth of advertising out of the PDC magazines, with a senior exec telling the publisher that they would buy again as soon as I was fired. To his enormous credit, founding publisher George Von Rosen told them to stuff it. Later, when that particular executive was fired, his gun company determined that I was no longer the problem. By then, the company had addressed every one of the shortcomings that I had mentioned in the long article series on their guns that had so enraged their former decision-maker.

In short, I was ready to find the fire that was generating the smoke, and expose Beretta for its shoddy workmanship. I had taught at the U.S. Army Marksmanship Training Unit at Fort Benning, and still had honest and trustworthy sources there and in the other services, and in the many major police departments that had adopted the Beretta 92.

I contacted those sources. They told me that the allegations against Beretta had been hugely overblown. The term they most frequently used was "bullshit." The guns, they said, were working great. Offered total protection from any comeback in the form of anonymity, they had no reason to lie for Beretta.

My job was to find out the truth, and tell it to the readers. I did. What I found out, and what I told those readers, is as follows.

The Beretta Continues

Few modern pistols have been so vilified as the Beretta 92 ... and fewer still so thoroughly redeemed by excellence in wide-ranging field performance.

Known as the M9 in U.S. military parlance, the Beretta 92 is now the primary standard handgun of all the United States' armed forces and has been the official service pistol for more than a decade. Other nations have been similarly impressed, ranging from the region Jeff Cooper calls "the sandbox" where it was in use by both sides during Arab-Israeli conflicts, to South Africa where it is produced locally under license as the Z-88.

Similarly, the free world's police establishment has been responsive to the 92 series. The French national gendarmes carry the 92G, and the South African police issue the Z-88. But nowhere have police taken to the Beretta with more street-proven enthusiasm than the United States. Crisscrossing the nation, major departments carry it: Maine State Police to Los Angeles County Sheriffs, Washington State Patrol to Florida Highway Patrol, and countless major agencies in between. From New Orleans (92F) to St. Louis (92D) to San Francisco (96G), the Beretta is as well represented among city cops as among their state and county cousins. Of the four types of handguns authorized to LAPD personnel, the 92F is the overwhelming favorite and the one issued to new recruits at the academy.

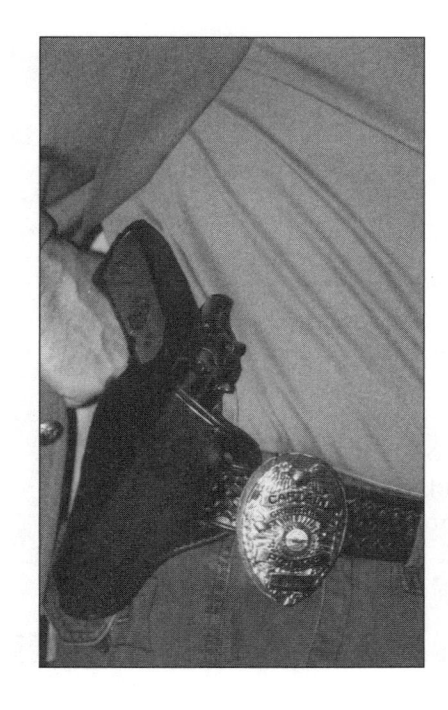

Nor have the Feds ignored the Beretta. When I taught at the DEA Academy I noticed a

The Beretta 92 has been – and still is – widely carried by American law enforcement officers.

Seen from below the pistol, this is the subtle yet difficult movement a criminal would have to perform, while an officer held his Beretta still for him, to disassemble the gun in the cop's hand. The concept of such a disarm is simply an urban legend.

disproportionate number of 92Fs on the hips of agents training for the high-risk Operation Snowcap in South America, despite the fact that most Drug Enforcement Agents preferred something smaller on the list of approved 9mm pistols for daily plainclothes carry. The U.S. Postal Service inspectors are said to have adopted the Beretta.

FBI made headlines in the firearms press with their adoption of the S&W 10mm, subsequent large-scale purchases of the SIG 9mm, and orders for a few hundred Para Ordnance and Springfield Armory .45 autos and a small contract for .40 caliber Glocks. Yet almost lost in the shadows was the vast purchase of thousands upon thousands of Beretta 96D Brigadiers as standard sidearms for the Immigration and Naturalization Service, a volume acquisition that dwarfs all the auto pistols the FBI has purchased, combined.

The Beretta is also extremely popular among armed citizens as a home and store defense weapon, its frame size being somewhat large for concealed carry. American civilians have historically followed their military's choice of small arms, and have historically been satisfied. The Beretta pistol seems to be no exception.

Praised by Faint Damns ...

Those who've raised their voices to condemn the 92 series Beretta fall into three categories: competitors beaten out on testing, .45 fans, and those who detest double-action autos in general. All three fit another category: sore losers.

The military's adoption of the Beretta over certain other brands brought threats of lawsuits and Congressional hearings and put the rumor mill into three-shift overtime. Yet subsequent endurance tests validated the Beretta's durability, reliability, and longevity.

No, the Beretta didn't and doesn't come in .45 ACP. Nor did any other gun the U.S. military was going to adopt in keeping with NATO ammo inventory specs. Had the contract been won by the SIG P-226, the S&W 659, the Ruger P-85, or the HK P7M13, *that* gun would have been the target of the "poodle shooter" and "pea-shooter" brickbats thrown at the Beretta by the .45 traditionalists.

Yes, the Beretta is double-action for its first shot, and for all its shots in the "D" models. But so would any other gun adopted by the military or police services that happened to adopt the Beretta. Current institutional thinking on small arms tends toward double-action, with cocked and locked single-actions like the 1911 seen as the province of elite, highly-trained, dedicated personnel. This is no fault of the Beretta.

The three primary fire control systems. Top, the F, with safety/decock lever on slide; Center, the G, with lever performing only the decocking function; and D, double-action-only with no lever necessary on its slick slide.

Those who don't care for the gun point smugly to its sales figures having dropped since the coming of the Clinton high-capacity magazine ban. *Duh.* Parallel sales decreases have been noted in every other large-frame autoloader whose main design feature, high cartridge capacity, has been similarly reduced.

... and Praised with Real Praise

Officials of LAPD, LASD, Border Patrol (INS) and other major police agencies that have adopted the Beretta tell me they're thrilled with it. Extremely high reliability, a superb frequency-of-repair ratio, outstanding accuracy, and excellent hit potential both on the qualification range and in street shootings have been the hallmarks of the gun in actual field service.

Now that the initial overreaction to a few separated slides has settled down, every single military authority I talk to (currently serving military, not gun writers who've never been involved in monitoring the Beretta in action) tell me the guns require much less service than the worn 1911s they replaced, and that most of their troops like them better. Those that don't seem to be the ones who miss .45 ballistics, and that was a fait accompli determined by the Pentagon long before the Beretta's adoption.

In the private sector, it would be hard to find a more knowledgeable authority on semiautomatic pistol reliability than national champion, master gunsmith, and handgun manufacturer Bill Wilson. Ask Bill what's the most reliable semiauto pistol you can buy out of the box today, and he'll tell you what he told me: "Beretta 92." His opinion is shared by such master trainers of advanced pistolcraft as Ray Chapman and Ken Hackathorn. Significantly, both Wilson and Hackathorn told me they had chosen to shoot Beretta 92s at the inaugural IDPA (International Defensive Pistol Association) national championship ... and both placed high with them against the highest-tech modern service pistols available.

Setting the Record Straight

The grist from the rumor mill is not biodegradable. It seems to pollute the firearms environment forever. Let's clear up some persistent rumors about these guns.

Rumor: The slide will break off and smack you in the face. **Inside story:** A handful of slides did indeed separate. Most were traceable to a lot of NATO ammo that approached 50,000 psi chamber pressure: proof loads of nearly .30/06 rifle intensity. Some of the SEALs' breakages came with silencers attached, which had levered the barrel forward and overstressed the locking blocks and broken the slides. Berettas simply aren't designed for suppressors. The number of separated slides represent something like one ten-thousandth of one percent of production.

Rumor: The Beretta can be made to fire by manipulating the trigger bar on the outside of the frame. **Inside story:** I haven't seen anyone who could demonstrate this, and neither has anyone I've spoken

"Rack grade" M9s ready to issue at a National Guard armory.

with at Beretta. Have you actually *seen* it? Me, neither. Do we hear an alligator in the sewer?

Rumor: Street gangs are training to disarm cops and citizens by using the Beretta's fast takedown system to rip the gun apart in the good guy's hand. **Inside story:** No case of this happening either deliberately or accidentally "in real life" has ever been documented to the best of my knowledge. It can be done in demonstration, but it takes about twice as long as it would take to rip any whole gun out of a user's hand and would require the good guy to stand there and let it happen. This seems to be another urban legend like the alligators in the sewers, apparently promulgated by some Southern California gun buff cops who wanted their department to adopt a single-action .45 auto instead of a double-action 9mm. One such cop who put out a police teletype to the effect that this was happening was reportedly reprimanded for issuing a false statement.

Rumor: Berettas jammed epidemically in the sandy environment of the Gulf War. **Inside story:** By all accounts from military armorers and instructors, the Berettas stood up as well as any small arms to the Gulf environments, and better than most. Think about it: This is the pistol that the Israelis, the acknowledged masters of modern desert warfare, use extensively themselves.

Three generations of Beretta 92 magazines. If made by Beretta or MecGar, they tend to always be functional.

Beretta Attributes

There is simply no other combat auto that comes from the factory with as smooth running a slide as the Beretta 92 style. It's the envy of the industry in this regard. Its open-top design all but eliminates stovepipe malfunctions unless underpowered ammo is used, or bad technique that binds the slide with the shooter's thumb.

Its double-action trigger pull is, if not the best, right up there among the top two or three. Its single-action pull is also quite manageable. In the double-action-only models, with one less sear as a friction point, the DA pull is smoother and easier still. In the standard model, the spring-loaded safety catch is the easiest and quickest of its kind in the industry to operate.

Soldiers who disliked the Beretta's accuracy were comparing it to the customized target guns produced in the gunsmith shops of the Marksmanship Training Units. With BarSto or Jarvis barrels, the Beretta will equal even those match-grade target pistols. In

State and regional IDPA champion David Maglio carries this on-safe 92FS at work, and had need to fire it in line of duty, resulting in a dead stop with 100 percent hits.

service mode, it easily outshoots not only the 1911 but virtually all of the contemporary 9mms. Only the SIG can equal or barely exceed it in accuracy on a level playing field. Vince O'Neill, the famous police trainer from Oklahoma, notes that local cops who shoot on pistol teams with duty weapons tend to choose the Beretta for its superior accuracy.

One valid complaint leveled at the big service gun is its long trigger reach for small hands. Beretta has answered this on two fronts. One was the introduction of the new generation Cougar series with reshaped frame that brings the web of the hand deeper under the slide and gives the finger better access to the trigger, but another more to the point was the development of a retrofit short-reach trigger for the 92/96 models. First offered only to police armorers, it should be available for civilian retrofit by the time you read this.

Have It Your Way

Beretta currently offers these pistols in several formats. Some are strictly target models and not within the purview of this publication. They've been made in 7.65 mm Luger and Heaven knows what other calibers for special markets internationally, and Jonathan Arthur Ciener makes a .22 conversion unit. Just looking at combat/defense variants in calibers commonly imported into the U.S., we have the following.

The 92 series guns were designed for 15-plus-1 round capacity in full-size guns, and are chambered for 9mm Luger (9mm Parabellum, 9X19). The 96 series guns are chambered for the .40 S&W cartridge and were designed for 11-plus-1 cartridge capacity. Both are now limited to 10-round magazines for current importation, though grandfathered magazines from pre-ban production are legal, and in 9mm, still exist in relative abundance. They sell for about $40 each in my region. (Editors Note: With the sunset of the Clinton Gun Ban, the high-capacity magazines are once again available.)

The "F" suffix is the current designation for the standard double-action first shot model. Its slide-mounted safety/decock lever is extremely easy to operate thanks to the spring-assist feature earlier noted. This is the gun of the U.S. military, of LAPD and LASD, and by far the most popular version in use by law-abiding private citizens in the United States and the rest of the world.

The 92FC, no longer in production, is the compact 14-shot version of the 9mm. It always fit my hand better than any other gun in the Beretta catalog. My daughter, Cat, used mine, tuned by Jim Horan, to win High Woman honors at the 1996 National Tactical Invitational. This was the first semiauto pistol adopted by Maine State Police and the Rochester (NY) Police, both agencies being famous for good R&D before they adopted equipment. They reasoned that the same gun would work well for uniform wear and plainclothes/off-duty carry.

The 92M, recently reissued, is the slim-gripped single-stack 9mm. I wouldn't be surprised to see a 96M before long, given the re-assessed priorities of the civilian market in the U.S. after the high-capacity magazine ban.

The "D" suffix means that the gun is double-action for every shot, a "slick-slide" with no safety catch or decocking lever, and with a bobbed hammer. INS, NYPD's Emergency Services Unit, and the state police forces of Ohio and Pennsylvania, among others, all chose this option. Fewer than 1,000 "DS" models were produced, all in 9mm, double-action-only with the slide lever now a dedicated safety catch.

The "G" suffix comes from "gendarme," since it was the French police who first ordered this variant with the slide lever modified to function only as a decocker, and not as a safety. It has received good acceptance stateside by departments who like that doctrine. Indiana State Police adopted the 92G in 9mm, and San Francisco PD, the 96G in .40 S&W caliber. Due to the added internal spring that forces the lever off safe, it is a little stiffer to decock than the standard model, though one less thumb motion is required in its manual of arms.

The Brigadier, a resurrected name from Beretta's mid-20th century progenitor of the Model 92, now designates a heavy-duty reinforced slide. The INS Beretta .40s are all Brigadiers. I'm not sure they were needed, but the slight extra weight does give the gun a good feel, and whether it was perception or reality, fears of cracking slides were now credibly answered.

The Centurion is essentially the shortened compact barrel/slide assembly on a full-size frame. You can get it in 9mm or .40, and in "F" or "D" configuration. It has exceptionally good balance.

Personal Comments

The reader always has a right to know the writer's personal bias or prejudice. I've been shooting service Berettas fairly extensively since the 1980s, and have carried them concealed and on police duty, and used them frequently as "teaching guns." The Beretta 9mm in either "F" or "D" configuration is the one auto pistol I'm most likely to issue a student who doesn't have his own autoloader. I've found them easy and safe to handle, and forgiving of the lack of maintenance that can occur in an intensive shooting class environment.

I've been enormously impressed with the reliability of the countless Berettas I've seen go through my school. The feed problems that showed up in the first year of the .40 caliber Model 96 production were quickly resolved. My daughter and I took only Berettas to the advanced pistol class at Thunder Ranch and didn't bring back a whole lot of the 4,000 rounds of Black Hills 9mm that we sent ahead. The only malfunctions we had occurred when we created them deliberately during required clearance drills. One round torn up in that fashion found its way into my 92 and stopped; a tap-rack instantly rectified an error that was mine, not the pistol's.

I can put any firearm I want next to my bed to protect my family and myself. The gun I do put there is a Beretta 92F stainless worked over by Bill Jarvis with one of his 6-inch match barrels, Mag-Na-Ported at the outer end, and with a SureFire flashlight mounted to the frame. With a pre-ban 20-round extended magazine (I swap between the excellent MecGar and Beretta's own, developed originally for their 93R machine pistol) I have 21 rounds of 115 grain +P+ 9mm that hits with .357 Magnum ballistics from the 6-inch barrel but kicks like a .380 thanks to the porting and the weight of the flashlight, and which can deliver 1-inch groups at 25 yards. It simply doesn't jam. It worked great for me in the darkened combat simulators of Thunder Ranch, drawn from a Safariland thigh holster.

The Future Beretta

Beretta's new Cougar 8000 series is a good gun, and will hit its stride with the new subcompact model. I'm not sure it needed a rotary breech, though its easy-reach frame makes sense for small-handed police users. For the citizen, Cougar full capacity magazines won't be available and grandfathered 92/96 mags will be. I'm partial to the 92 for its light recoil, utter reliability, and significant ammo reservoir. I like the feel of the compact – which should be re-introduced as an 11-shot 96FC in my opinion, since the 92FC magazine perfectly accommodates 10 of the .40 S&W rounds – and if anybody's worried about the supply of older mags drying up, the standard 96 series will do nicely. Going down to a 10-shot magazine from the 15 the 9mm Beretta was designed for hurts, even though Bill Clinton doesn't really feel our pain, but going down from an 11-shot .40 mag to a 10-rounder is a lot easier. A 10 percent bite doesn't hurt as much as a 33 $\frac{1}{3}$ percent bite.

Beretta should take a page from Ford in their advertising: "Ask the man who owns one." The proof,

The 92 is eminently shootable at high speed. Author has just fired 60 shots, 54 center "5s," and four slightly peripheral "4s," at quadruple speed with stages like draw and fire six shots in two seconds, strong-hand-only. Pistol is Langdon-tuned Beretta 92G.

really, is in the second-hand gun supply. In my neck of the woods, you simply don't see used Beretta .40s. People who have them like them too much to trade them in. You do see some Beretta 9mms on the used gun shelves, but they're mostly trade-ins from police departments who swapped up to Beretta .40s.

That, in the end, is the story. The people who own Berettas like them so much they keep them. The people who bad-mouth Berettas generally usually turn out to never have owned one ... and they don't know what they've missed.

What Now?

There has been a lot of water under the bridge since that article was published. None of it has flowed against the Beretta 92. During the Afghanistan and Iraq conflicts, current as this is written, there were recurrent complaints about the failure of the Beretta to put the bad guys down. The problem, obviously, was the long-standing impotence of 9mm ball ammunition, and not the fault of the Berettas that launched the bullets. Other complaints came in that the Berettas were jamming, but every single one of the many military sources I've contacted, who were given full anonymity if they requested it and had no reason to lie, said that the guns were working fine with Beretta magazines in the hostile overseas environments. The problem, they said, lay in aftermarket Checkmate brand magazines bought by the government on bid.

Meanwhile, stateside, the Beretta has been like a Timex watch: it "took a lickin' and kept on tickin'." Consider the following, which appeared originally in a publication of the Los Angeles County deputy sheriffs' union, and has since been reprinted in the Beretta armorer's manual. The title is "Keys for Survival," and the author is Carrol Hogue. He explains why the Los Angeles County Sheriff's Department bought the Beretta 92F as a standard sidearm for LASD's several thousand deputies, and why their counterpart city police force, LAPD, adopted the same gun as standard shortly thereafter.

"Let's start with the known facts. First, the Federal Government subjected a wide variety of weaponry to the most grueling comprehensive testing process imaginable in a five-year-long search for a gun to replace the venerable Colt .45; they selected the same model Beretta we are now receiving – the Model 92-F ..."

... Sam Marino is a 17-year LASD veteran who developed three of the first P.O.S.T. (Police Officer Standards and Training) approved semi-automatic training courses in the state. He has conducted extensive semi-automatic pistol combat training for units of our Detective Division and other law enforcement agencies including federal agencies throughout the state. Sam has taught officer survival since 1971. Much of his time goes into exhaustive research to improve and update his officer survival knowledge. In short, both of these gentlemen (the other is LAPD's famed shooting champion and gunfight veteran, John Pride) know their subject and speak with unquestionable integrity. What follows are their opinions...

"... The Beretta's overall design and workmanship provides superior durability, ease of disassembly and cleaning, swift and easy reloading, and a grip configuration which enables the greatest majority of hand sizes to easily reach the weapon's control mechanisms. It also provides all shooters superior weapon control, enabling them to maximize their marksmanship skills. In addition, Sam, with 30 years of experience as a gunsmith and precision machinist, fully concurs with comparative tests showing the Beretta to have superior quality control, workmanship and engineering to its competitors ...

"In the most recent training course conducted by Sam and John, 10,400 rounds of 9mm ammunition were fired by the 20 students. There were five malfunctions. One was a 'stove-pipe' empty case that failed to fully eject. This was caused by the shooter's failing to lock his left wrist while practicing shooting with his nondominant shooting hand. He merely swept the 'stove-pipe with the other hand and immediately continued to shoot. Two rounds failed to cycle the pistol's action on another student's gun. He cleared the temporary malfunction and fired the rounds. The problem was later diagnosed by Sam as a mere failure to clean the weapon. The student had fired over 750 rounds without cleaning it. A simple use of a bore brush and three drops of oil solved his shooting problem. The final malfunctions occurred when two empty cases failed to be extracted from the chamber of a Smith & Wesson pistol. The student's gun revealed a dirty and clogged extractor that admittedly had not been cleaned in the past two years of the pistol's usage. A toothbrush and pipe cleaner was used to solve that 'high-tech' problem and again, the gun continued to provide flawless service. None of these malfunctions were the fault of the pistol or its ammunition. Rather, it was a failure of the individual person to perform the most basic of required periodic maintenance and lubrication on a timely and necessary basis. I would challenge the reader to objectively compare the above training malfunction rate with similar conditions with similarly maintained revolvers." [8]

Beretta Accuracy

The Beretta Model 92 is an extremely accurate pistol as it comes out of the box. How accurate? When a firm run by my then-spouse decided to become a distributor for an excellent brand of ammo called Pro-Load, I took some 115 grain +P Tactical JHP to the range. I had with me an old DAO Model 92 traded in by the Indianapolis Police Department when it went to .40 caliber pistols. Hand held from the bench, double-action every witnessed shot, the Model 92 put five of these 1,300 foot-second combat loads into an inch and a quarter. The gun and the group appeared in a flyer put out by her company, Armor of New Hampshire.

A while back, when Cameron Hopkins was the editor of American Handgunner, he challenged me to defend my hypothesis that a good shot could fire five rounds from the bench rest and, if there were no called flyers, measure the best three hits and get a close approximation of what all five would do from the Ransom machine rest. Charlie Petty and I each took two of my guns, two of his, and three known accurate loads and lots of ammo for each. I did five hand-held five-shot groups with each, measuring all five and then the best three. Charlie did the same with five-shot groups from his Ransom Rest. One of the four guns, representing a stock police-type service pistol, was my Beretta 92D. It was right out of the box. All shooting was at 25 measured yards. Each round was one famous for being among the most accurate of 9mm Parabellum ammo.

With Federal 115-grain JHP, factory product code 9BP, we got a 2.70 inches average hand-held and 2.55 inches from the machine, with the best three shots averaging 1.40 inches and twice delivering one-inch groups. The best hand-held group was 1.45 inches, and the best machine rest group was 1.94 inches.

Winchester's famously accurate OSM (Olin Super Match) 147-grain subsonic JHP averaged 2.91 inches hand-held and 1.90 inches machine rest, each for five-shot groups. Best individual five-round groups were 1.55 inches by hand, and 1.39 inches by machine, with an average of 1.09 inches for the best-three clusters hand-held, including two groups that went under an inch.

We went back to Federal for their Gold Medal Match in 124-grain full metal jacket configuration. Hand-held, five-shot groups averaged 2.85 inches with 1.10 inches the average best-three clusters, and the machine averaged 1.88 inches for five-shot groups.

What do we see here? First, this Beretta was consistent. So was the ammo. Second, consider that the other three guns so closely correlated "best-three shots hand-held" with "all five from the machine rest" that in some cases, these measurements were closer than the best and worst groups from the machine rest with the same gun/cartridge combo. With the Beretta, for some reason, the hand-held five-shot groups were closer to the five-shot Ransom groups than the best three measurements. That should not have happened.

I thought at first that it might have something to do with the heavy DAO pull being managed less well by the machine than the cocked guns normally fired from a Ransom Rest. I later learned better. Visiting Marine Corps and U.S. Army pistolsmiths at Camp Perry, I learned that both had been disappointed in the groups they got from machine rests with rack-grade, standard-issue M9 Berettas, and worked hard to get their custom masterpieces down to 1-inch groups at 25 yards from the same machine rests.

Beretta expert Ernest Langdon, who has won multiple National Championships shooting the Beretta 92 against all manner of custom match guns, has the best explanation. "If you use a Ransom Rest to test the Beretta 92, you won't get the results you'll get when you aim the gun," he says flatly. "Repeatability of the rest is part of the issue, but the gun sights off the slide, not the frame. I've seen several guys on the Marine Corps pistol team who shoot a better group by hand. Some of that comes down to slide-to-frame fit. The Weapons Training Battalion, RTU Shop, takes slop out of the slide/frame fit, and those guns perform much better in machine rests for that reason."

BING! The light bulb goes on. When held in the human hand, the gun is aimed by the human eye. The inherent practical accuracy of the Beretta comes from its good barrel-to-slide fit, which can be achieved without compromise of reliability thanks to the open-slide design. However, the slide-to-frame fit has some slop in it, which is where that effortless glass-smooth feel of racking the slide partly comes from. It's there to guarantee function in mud and sand. But that slop between the barrel/slide assembly and the frame can result in the barrel and slide coming back into battery "aimed" at a different spot on the target than the one that preceded it when it is fired in the machine rest.

Today's Beretta 92 pistols are probably the most accurate they've ever been. Says Langdon, who in the past has worked for Beretta and now makes his living customizing those pistols and SIG-Sauers, "The millions of dollars worth of new machinery at the Accokeek, Maryland plant has improved the fit of the pistols without compromising their reliability. They feel tighter now. There's better slide-to-barrel fit, and better frame-to-slide fit. They're the best they've ever been. One Vertec I had came in sub-1 inch at 25 yards, out of the box, from a machine rest."

Reliability

Experts everywhere attest to the awesome reliability of the Beretta 92. Wiley Clapp and the late, great Dean Grennell published the *Gun Digest Book of 9mm Handguns* in 1986. They wrote of the Beretta 92, "The pistol is most reliable. Of all the guns listed in this book, this particular Beretta was fired the most … The performance has been most notably free of malfunctions – it is a reliable handgun."[9]

British gun experts Richard Law and Peter Brookesmith wrote, "The Beretta we tested notched up mileage quite quickly and passed the 50,000 round mark after about 18 months' service. We test-fired the pistol quite often, and allowed it to be used a great deal at our club, so it was used a lot without paying for the ammunition! The working parts showed no signs of uneven wear, and we paid particular attention to the slide, as cracked slides and even slide separations have been mentioned in American military experience. The latest models for target shooters have the slide beefed up a little in front of and around the wedge lock cut-outs in response to the problems with some production firearms, but that 'improvement' was clearly not necessary in our test gun, which is still banging on cheerfully without any sign of wear in that department."[10]

Design Updates

Over the years, there were updates to the Beretta 92 design. The FS slide catch system has already been discussed. An outside company, Phrobis, produced an enclosed slide to fit a Beretta 92, but that was seen by many users as about as unclear on the concept as a steel frame for a Glock, and never caught on.

Beretta resurrected the Brigadier name for Model 92 and Model 96 pistols whose slides were built up slightly in the area of the locking blocks. They have worked well, but so have Berettas with the standard model slides. Military armorers who built target Berettas for our armed services pistol teams tell me they like the Brigadier slides simply because there is more steel to work with in the area of the locking blocks when they are tightening the slide-to-frame fit of the pistols for maximum precision accuracy. The Border Patrol thought enough of the Brigadier configuration to specify it for the 96D pistols that they adopted as the first standard INS auto pistol in the early 1990s. They have stood up well by all currently available accounts.

The controversial locking blocks have been modified three times for a total of four subtly different designs. Explains Beretta expert Ernest Langdon, "The first locking block design had square shoulders. The second version had radiused corners on the ears of the block. The third version was nearly identical, but not radiused as radically, on the theory that the first fix took away too much material. Finally, the current version was re-engineered significantly. It will work with the original barrel design, but the way it contacts the barrel and the way the stress is placed on the locking block are reduced by changing stress points. This was done by raising the rib on the back and changing the geometry of the locking block plunger. The new block requires a new plunger. The new design moves the stress from the locking block wings closer in to the main body of the locking block, so the pressure of the round firing doesn't have the same effect on locking block wings as it did in the past."

Continues Langdon, "I still, proactively, replace my locking blocks at 20,000 rounds. I have not seen one of the newest style break yet. One fellow broke a third-generation block at 63,000 rounds, and that was one of only a couple of the third-generation that I've seen break. I can't remember seeing a generation four break, unless someone had done something stupid with it. One guy's broke at 2,000 rounds, and when he sent me the gun I found the back side of the locking block had been ground off and polished." This, of course, had artificially weakened the locking block.

Bear in mind, however, that many gun companies will privately tell you that their semiautomatic pistols are designed for a 10,000-round service life. Beretta puts no limit on theirs, nor have they warned against +P, +P+, and NATO high-pressure 9mm ammo. The guns are designed, they say, to handle that. So how many rounds can you look at?

No one shoots Beretta 9mms more intensively than Ernest Langdon. "I've put about half a million rounds through 9mm Berettas since 1985, when I was still in the Marine Corps," he says. "I just haven't broken that many parts. I usually have 40,000 or 50,000 rounds through one of my guns before I retire it, but I usually only retire them because I've thought of something new I want to try that I need a new gun to start with."

Major Variations

Changes in the locking blocks were the sort of normal product evolution that one would expect in something that has been used widely and heavily for decades. Ditto the heavier Brigadier-style slide.

Some changes, on the other hand, were ludicrous. Beretta offered a "fix" for the perceived danger of a bad guy grabbing the Model 92 and disassembling it in the officer's hands. Yeah, I know, people "saw it happen" in one of the "Lethal Weapon" movies. Well, we saw a giant robot kill cops wholesale in a "Terminator" movie, but it's safe to say that neither bad guys disassembling pistols in people's hands nor killer robots have ever been a real concern.

Talk about "ingenious solutions to non-existent problems." The short-lived order to military armorers to change Beretta slides every 3,000 rounds was rarely observed, and quickly passed away, but people talk of it as if it was still in effect.

On the other hand, there were significant branchings in the Model 92 line that created newer and sometimes better guns. The more powerful .40 caliber Model 96. The shorter, handier Compacts and Centurions. The ergonomic, updated-in-every-way Vertec. The factory "performance enhanced" Elite series.

Each of these was a meaningful change important to the epoch of the modern Beretta pistol. Each wrote its own chapter in Beretta's history, and each is worthy therefore of a chapter in this book.

Endnotes

(1) Wilson, R.L., "The World of Beretta: An International Legend," New York City: Random House, 2000, P. 234.

(2) Heard, Charles M., "Complete Guidebook of Handguns," Los Angeles: Trend Books, 1960, P. 59.

(3) Wilson, op.cit., P. 225.

(4) Stebbins, Henry M., "Pistols: A Modern Encyclopedia," Castle Books, 1961, P. 138.

(5) Mullin, Timothy J., "The 100 Greatest Combat Pistols," Boulder, CO: Paladin Press, 1994, Pages 233-234.

(6) Wilson, op. cit., P. 227.

(7) "Beretta 92FS INOX 9mm" by Gene Gangarosa, Gun Buyer's Annual 2005, New York City: Harris Publications, 2005, Pages 58-59.

(8) Hogue, Carrol, "Keys for Survival," undated, from "92F Series Armorers Handbook," published by Beretta USA.

(9) Grennell, Dean A., and Clapp, Wiley, "The Gun Digest Book of 9mm Handguns," Northbrook, IL: DBI Books, 1986, P. 217.

(10) Law, Richard, and Brookesmith, Peter, "The Fighting Handgun," London: Arms and Armour Press, 1996, P. 133.

The Beretta 92/96 Combat Compacts

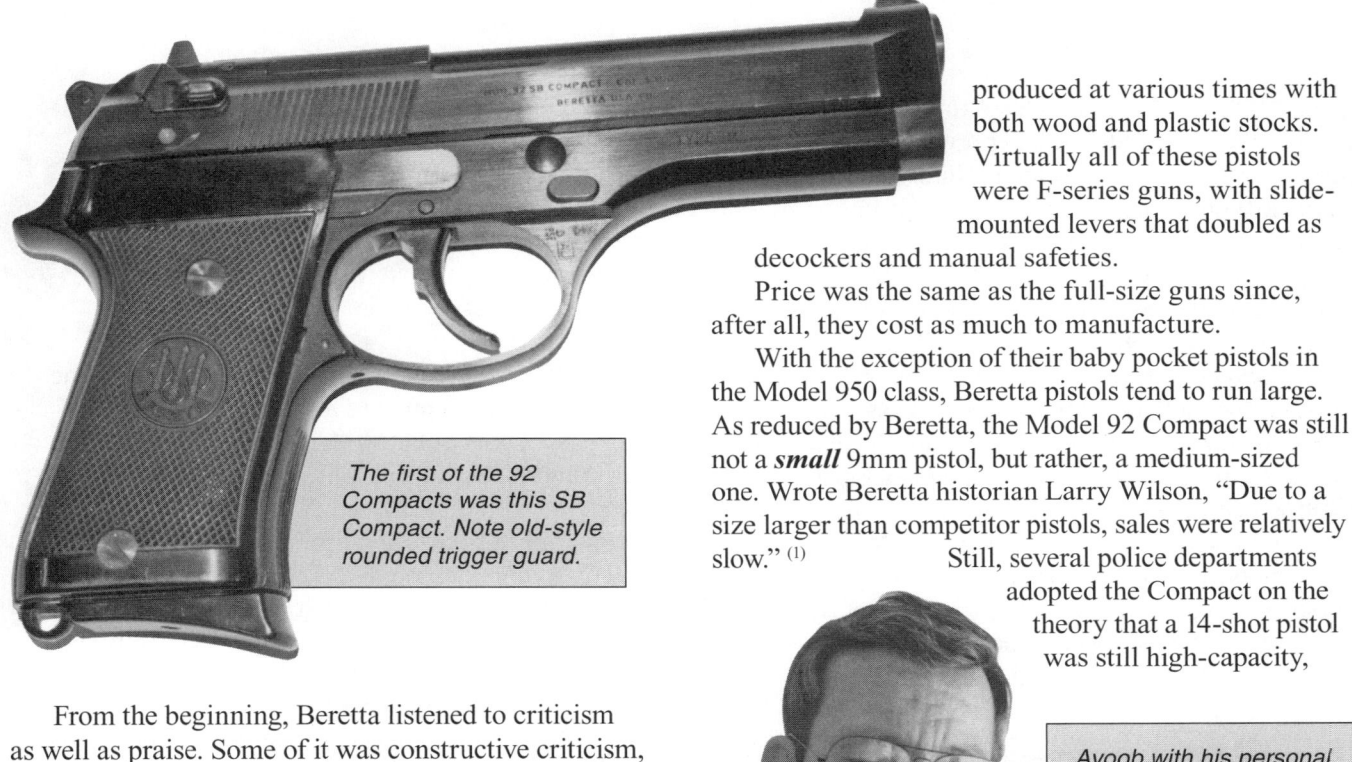

The first of the 92 Compacts was this SB Compact. Note old-style rounded trigger guard.

produced at various times with both wood and plastic stocks. Virtually all of these pistols were F-series guns, with slide-mounted levers that doubled as decockers and manual safeties.

Price was the same as the full-size guns since, after all, they cost as much to manufacture.

With the exception of their baby pocket pistols in the Model 950 class, Beretta pistols tend to run large. As reduced by Beretta, the Model 92 Compact was still not a *small* 9mm pistol, but rather, a medium-sized one. Wrote Beretta historian Larry Wilson, "Due to a size larger than competitor pistols, sales were relatively slow." [1] Still, several police departments adopted the Compact on the theory that a 14-shot pistol was still high-capacity,

Ayoob with his personal favorite Beretta, the 9mm 92F Compact (92FC).

From the beginning, Beretta listened to criticism as well as praise. Some of it was constructive criticism, even if much of the rest wasn't. One honest complaint with the Model 92 was that it was a big pistol. The company set about making a smaller version.

The High-Capacity Compact 9mms

In 1980, Beretta introduced the Model 92 SB Compact 9mm, which was shortened at the butt, reducing magazine capacity to 13 rounds. This was the first of the high-capacity compacts. The barrel was shortened from the standard 4.9 inches to 4.3 inches. The 92 SB Compact remained in production until the late 1980s, when it was replaced by the 92 FC Compact. This updated pistol had all the upgrades that had evolved in the 92F.

The 92FC Compact was also eventually discontinued. It had been

and this one was of a size that could allow a single weapon to serve as a uniform duty pistol, a gun for plainclothes detectives, and as an off-duty weapon for all armed personnel. The Maine State Police and the Rochester, New York PD were among the departments that standardized on the 92FC across the board.

The Model 92FC was shortened proportionally more at butt than at nose.

By 1987, the United States Army had adopted the combat shooting system I had previously developed, StressFire™, and incorporated it into their combat pistolcraft doctrine. If you get a copy of the Army's combat pistol manual FM23-35 and compare it to a copy of my 1983 books *StressFire*, you'll see that many of the illustrations have been traced as line drawings from photos in the *StressFire* book, then embellished by dressing the figure with modern uniform, helmet, and M9 pistol. I was asked by the Army to come to Fort Benning and teach a cadre of StressFire instructors for the Marksmanship Training Unit, which is headquartered there.

I knew that they would issue me an M9 for teaching purposes, but I wanted a pistol I had personally sighted in, and one that would stay with me when I left the post. While I had shot and otherwise tested many Beretta 92s, I did not personally own one at the time. I dropped down to Riley's Sport Shop in Hooksett, NH, one of the largest gun shops in New England, to look over the current crop.

They had a broad range of Berettas, but the one that really hooked me was a second-hand 92FC Compact. The regular Model 92 felt a little large in my hand, but this one was just right. With the magazine with its extended floorplate in place, the bottom of the frontstrap of the grip frame came exactly to the bottom edge of my little finger. Measuring the guns, the reach to the trigger from the center of the frame's backstrap was exactly the same as with the full-size gun, but for reasons I can't explain, the shortening of the butt had somehow changed the ergonomics. It felt as if I could get more finger on the trigger of the Compact than on the full-size pistol, and it seemed that my thumb came just a little bit more naturally to the safety catch.

With its short butt, it concealed well inside the waistband in one of the LFI Concealment Rigs I had designed for Ted Blocker. Here was a true teaching gun, compact enough to wear 24/7, accurate and powerful enough to get the job done, and with the same utter reliability that characterized the larger pistol from which it had been cloned. If it had been a puppy, it would have wagged its tail, licked my hand, and silently begged me to take it home. "How much is that doggie in the window?"

I bought the pistol and took it home that day. It became my favorite

A Model 92 Compact with the finger extension on the magazine's buttplate is "just right" for an average size adult male hand. The price was a reduction of magazine capacity to 13 rounds of 9mm.

The author's pet 92FC wore Farrar grips and a Millett fixed rear sight.

Beretta. It fit my hand like no other gun in the Beretta catalog. I took it with me to Fort Benning, and wore it later when I taught another cadre of Army StressFire instructors out of Fort Lewis. To steal a line from Humphrey Bogart, it was "the start of a beautiful friendship."

It is our nature to embellish our weapons to suit personal tastes. This one was fine-tuned for me by Jim Horan, who unfortunately is no longer in that business. It is discussed in greater depth in the chapter on custom Berettas.

In 1996, while preparing for the National Tactical Invitational, my daughter Cat discovered that she shot faster and straighter with a Beretta than with any other combat handgun, including the custom Colt .45s and 9mm Brownings she had been shooting up to then. The Compact in particular fit her hand. When the NTI was over, she was High Woman at the national event, and had won a national championship at the age of 19. I commemorated the accomplishment by giving her my cherished Horan Custom 92FC Compact.

I often thought about getting another, but by then, I had acquired several more 92 Berettas, and couldn't really justify purchasing one more. While the little one *felt* better in my hands than the full-size, I shot them equally well. Among those Berettas was a pair of Centurions, one each in 9mm and .40 S&W, which I had won along the way. Beretta had introduced the Centurion around 1993. It was simply the standard Beretta frame with a Compact barrel/slide assembly on top. It was analogous to the Colt Commander vis-à-vis the Colt Government Model. The difference between the two Berettas is less than that between the two Colts. Standard spec for a Government Model was always full-size all-steel frame and 5-inch barrel, bringing unloaded weight to 39 ounces. The Commander's frame was full-size, but made of lightweight aluminum, and its barrel was shortened to 4.25 inches with a proportionally shortened slide, bringing total unloaded weight down to 26.5 ounces, a quantum improvement. By contrast, the full-size Beretta already had a lightweight aluminum alloy frame, and bringing its barrel down from 4.9 inches to 4.3 inches was a proportionally less radical shortening. A standard Beretta 92FS weighs 34.4 ounces; the Centurion weighs 33.2 ounces. It's not nearly as much difference, which is probably why the Centurion is not so popular among Beretta fans as the Lightweight Commander is among Colt enthusiasts.

Still, the Centurion was well liked, particularly by plainclothes officers who had acclimated to the Beretta during their earlier years in uniform. When Cat and I shot Thunder Ranch with Berettas, we found ourselves naturally bonding with one other shooter in that particular Advanced Pistol class who was also shooting a Beretta 9mm. He was an

The 9mm loads of +P and +P+ strength were no problem for the 92FC.

LAPD detective. He said that a surprising number of his fellow investigators had bought the Centurions. The gist of his explanation was that most of them carried outside-the-belt scabbards, and that the shorter barrels and proportionally shorter holsters let them wear shorter outer garments for concealment. They had been deeply trained in the Beretta 92F system by the department, loved it and trusted it, and simply wanted something shorter. That it seemed to balance better in the hand for many of them was simply icing on the cake. Bear in mind, these men and women had each been given the free 24/7 use of a standard Beretta 92F by the city that employed them and they had paid cash out of their own pockets to purchase their own Centurions. That's a classic example of "voting with your wallet."

Suffice to say that while the Model 92 Compact is not in the catalog at this time, the Centurion most certainly is and has remained there since its introduction. The Centurion pistol simply seems to strike a responsive chord with those who carry a gun for a living.

Though it seemed counter-intuitive, the grip only having been shortened at the butt of the 92FC seemed to give Ayoob's hand an easier reach to the safety catch and trigger.

The .40 Caliber Compacts

Beretta brought out the Model 92 in .40 S&W as the Model 96 in the early 1990s, and quickly offered it in the shorter format. The Centurion is quite popular in .40 S&W. Still, I always wanted a true compact version of the .40 Beretta, with shortened butt as well, a clone of the 92 FC in the more powerful chambering. When the onerous Clinton Crime Bill became law in 1994, banning further production and sale to the public of magazines holding more than 10 cartridges, it seemed an opportune time for Beretta to look at such a gun. I found that *exactly* 10 .40 S&W cartridges would fit in the Beretta Compact double-stack magazine that had been designed to hold 13 of the 9mm Luger rounds.

I strongly suggested this to the company in 1995 when I wrote, "The infamous Crime Bill may affect Beretta's civilian sales. A 9mm the size of a Beretta 92 loses a selling point when the capacity is cut from 16 rounds to 10 or 11.

"Some time ago, Beretta unfortunately discontinued the neat little 14-shot 92 FC and its sister gun with flat grip and slimline single-stack magazine, the 92M. I would not be surprised to see the latter come back. I think it would also be a smart move for them to offer both in .40 S&W chambering. A 10- or 11-shot 96FC the size of my little compact and spitting the powerful .40s would be an excellent defensive handgun." [2]

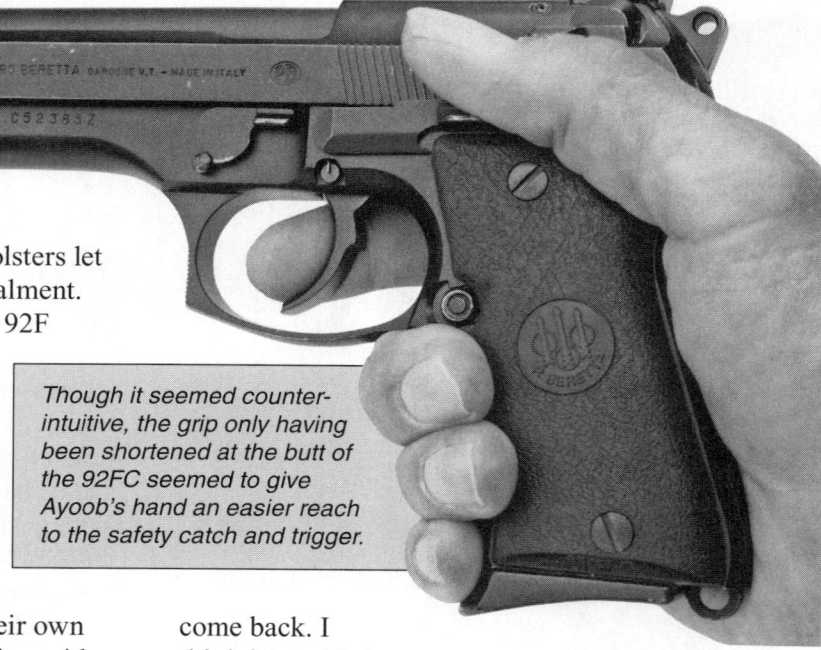

Not only were folks listening, it turned out they'd gotten there ahead of me. Unbeknownst to yours truly, a very few such guns had been produced three years before. In the fine print of Larry Wilson's excellent history of Beretta, one finds the following gem: "**Model 96 Compact**: matched in size to the Model 92F Compact; introduced 1992; nine-shot version of the Model 92FC." [3]

While that gem could be found in the pages of Larry's superb book, this gem of a gun could not be found in gun shops. Most shooters, including this writer, never saw one. Gun collecting authority Ned Schwing, in the 2004 Standard Catalog of Firearms, reports a type M single-stack magazine Beretta 96 Compact, in both stainless steel (Inox) and blue, introduced in 2000. I recall that introduction. It came and went, with very few of the guns imported into the United States. I *still* haven't gotten my hands on one, and I'm better connected with Beretta than most shooters.

It's a shame, because – particularly in the time of the 10-round magazine limit – a nine- to 11-shot Beretta Compact in .40 would have been a primo self-defense pistol.

The Mini-Cougars

In 1997, the existing Beretta 8000 Series Cougar line expanded to include the new Mini-Cougar. It has been produced in 9mm, .40 S&W, and .45 ACP. The approach taken to this gun was the opposite of that taken with the Centurion in the classic line service pistols. Instead of keeping a full-length grip frame and shortening the barrel, Beretta kept the Cougar's already short barrel/slide assembly, and shortened the grip frame. Notes Ned Schwing in the 2004 Standard Catalog of Firearms, "This (the regular Cougar series) is a compact-size pistol using a short-recoil rotating barrel … Overall length is 7 inches, barrel length is 3.6 inches, overall height 5.5 inches, and unloaded weight is 33.5 ounces … the (Mini-Cougar) pistol is fitted with a 3.6-inch barrel (3.7 inches on .45 ACP). Empty weight is … between 27 oz. and 30 oz. depending on caliber." [4]

The result was a radical looking pistol that appeared, in proportion, to have "a long nose and a short handle." This sold well enough that Beretta followed with more of the same, bringing out their Model 8000F Cougar L in 2000. The butt was shortened fully four-tenths of an inch more.

The result is a pistol that conceals *extremely* well with absolutely minimum bulge or "print" at the back of the concealing garment when worn on or behind the hip. However, with proportionally less of the shooter's hand on the gun, there is not a lot to hang on to. This creates a sensation of increased recoil and muzzle jump that does not occur in the Model 92 Compact or Centurion lines. Also, with less hand mass on the grip frame to stabilize the pistol against rearward slide pull, it seems more difficult to "jack" the slide. This can be eased by bringing the hammer back before retracting the slide, thus alleviating mainspring pressure against the slide and allowing less force to operate the cartridge feeding and ejecting mechanism by hand.

The Type M Single-Stack Compact

Because there was no significant difference in grip girth or trigger reach between the Model 92 in 16-shot double-stack full-size and 14-shot double-stack compact, Beretta continued to hear the demands for a "smaller" 9mm pistol. This was answered with the Type M, which came with a single-stack magazine that held eight pounds. Production began with the SB series in 1981, but according to Wilson, these guns were not imported into the United States until 1989. By this time they incorporated the improvements of the 92-SB Compact Second Series which included grip panels scalloped out for better thumb reach to the safety/decock lever, a trigger with an over-travel stop protrusion, and the SB's series of internal refinements, which in turn evolved into the FS series. Wilson lists a subsequent 92FCM model that had the "Bruniton matte black finish, chrome-plating to barrel, squared front trigger guard, (and) slide retention feature." [5]

The Model 92 Type M allowed better hand reach to the trigger, and seemed to orient in the smaller to average size hand better than its double-stack brothers. It worked just as well with hot loads as did the double-stack version. It had its fans, to be sure, but the marketplace still saw the Beretta 9mm as a *high-capacity* pistol, and one with a single-stack magazine apparently seemed, well, incongruous to a lot of buyers.

The single-stack Type M gun reached its zenith with the Custom Carry II variation, a part of Beretta's aptly named Elite series, it proved to be a splendid little pistol.

Some think Beretta pistols are big for the power they put out. That has historically been true of their .380s and to some degree their 9mm service pistol, though not all other models. It was in answer to this criticism that, some years ago, Beretta introduced the Model M variation of their full-size 9mm. Barrel and slide were the same as the popular 92 FC Compact, just over 4 inches of tube, and the grip-frame was slimmed down and now housed a single-stack eight-round magazine. It did not sell particularly well and was soon gone from the Beretta catalogue.

The firm reintroduced it as the Concealed Carry, a limited-production special run of 2,000 pistols. That *did* fly, perhaps due to enhanced interest in compact fighting handguns generated by the recent and welcome spate of "shall-issue" carry laws. Beretta has continued the concept with the Concealed Carry II.

Overview

Take the original Model M. Give it a stainless slide, and finish the lightweight aluminum frame to sort of match, giving the gun a subtle but pleasing two-tone hue. Have Wayne Novak design one of his famous streamlined sights for it, compact on the outside but with a wide, deep notch where it counts. Install a blue/black safety-decock lever and slide stop for contrast. Apply tasteful, classy-looking lettering confirming that it is a special-run pistol. Complete with black plastic grips to continue the stark visual contrast. *Voila.* You have the Concealed Carry II.

This pistol is a conventional DA/SA design. That is, the first shot is double-action with a long, fairly heavy stroke, and the gun self-cocks itself after that, so subsequent shots require only the short, easy single-action pull. The slide-mounted lever is pressed down to decock, then pushed back up if you wish to return to "firing" status. The lever if left down functions as a safety, leaving the pistol "on safe."

Although a very few Model 96 Compacts were produced in .40 S&W, most of the compacts were in the 92 series and chambered for 9mm Parabellum, like this one.

Unlike most other Berettas of this type, the safety-decock lever is not ambidextrous and is designed for right-handed use only.

I recently spent a couple of weeks carrying and testing this gun. Match season was pretty much over so I didn't get to compete in a combat shoot with it, but I was able to use it as a teaching gun for an LFI-I class. Due to travel demands I was able to carry it in places ranging from frigid Northern New England in winter to balmy and sometimes humid Florida. It rode well under winter mackinaw and untucked summer shirt alike.

Compactness

If pure size is a your big concern, you might choose a Kahr K9 with one less round, or a Smith & Wesson 3913 or SIG P-239 with the same eight-plus-one cartridge capacity. Slightly thicker in the slide than the little S&W 9mm, the Beretta's barrel/slide assembly is somewhat longer, and therefore, overall length is greater.

The short, thin "handle area" of the Concealed Carry II is what reduces its "bulge factor," particularly in an inside-the-waistband holster. I once spent several weeks in Florida with a 3913 inside my belt in an LFI Concealment Rig, and never once needed a covering garment. For the whole time, an untucked tee or polo shirt sufficed to hide the pistol and its slim spare magazine in the companion pouch on the opposite side of the belt. There's no doubt in my mind that in the same type of rig, the Concealed Carry II would have hidden just as well.

I used one of those LFI Concealment Rigs, made by Ted Blocker and designed for the 92FC, for hideout needs with the Concealed Carry II. The rest of the time I had the gun in one of Safariland's fast, comfortable "universal fit" paddle holsters when the gun was hidden by coat, jacket, or vest. Discretion and comfort levels were high throughout.

No doubt about it, the Concealed Carry lives up to its name.

The Centurion, with its Compact-length barrel/slide but full size grip frame, was the most popular. This one is an F-type Model 92 in 9mm.

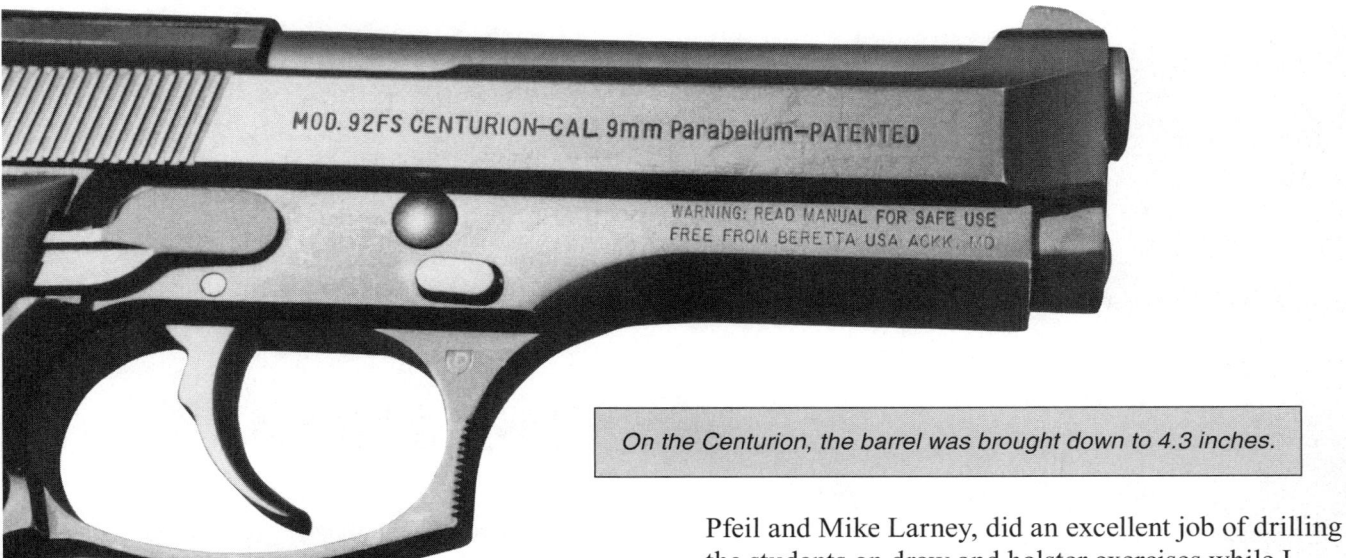

On the Centurion, the barrel was brought down to 4.3 inches.

Reliability

The Beretta 92 series has earned an enviable reputation for reliability. From the U.S. military to such private sector gun experts as Ken Hackathorn and Bill Wilson, the 9mm Beretta 92 has been acclaimed the single most reliable service pistol of its kind. Everything I've seen in the police sector, the military sector, and the private training sector tells me that they may well be correct.

Hundreds and hundreds of rounds were fired during two weeks with no takedown and no cleaning. I shot it, friends shot it, students shot it. Ammo ranged from 115-grain to 147-grain, from ball to wide-mouth hollow-points, from subsonic velocity to screaming high-pressure +P+.

There was not a single malfunction of any kind. Zero. Nada. Perfect performance in this regard. Plain and simple, 100 percent reliability.

I wasn't surprised. It said "Beretta 92" right on the slide, didn't it?

Accuracy

Weather at home was inhospitable for accuracy testing when this gun came in, with howling winds that brought the chill factor to sub-zero. I tried Federal 9BP and Winchester subsonic hollow-points, perhaps the two most consistently accurate rounds in the kingdom of the 9mm Parabellum, and got no better than 3-inch to 4-inch groups. I quit trying … there.

In a few days I was in sunny Florida, teaching a class for Herman Gunter in Live Oak, near Jacksonville. Herman and his able colleagues, Bill Pfeil and Mike Larney, did an excellent job of drilling the students on draw and holster exercises while I adjourned to an adjacent range to test the Concealed Carry II for accuracy a second time. There were no benches in place at this particular range, so I shot from the rollover prone position Ray Chapman had taught me many years ago. Distance was 25 yards, and the targets were the heads of IPSC targets that had been laid out for the students. They would, at least on the first day, be shooting at the body anyway. Each five-shot group was measured overall, center to center, farthest hit to farthest. Then, the best three shots in each group were measured. The first lets you know what you can do with the gun at that distance under practical circumstances if you can stay cool, while the second measurement generally comes close to what the gun could do from a machine rest with five shots. That is, the second measurement helps to exclude the human error factor.

Results were as follows:

Cartridge	Bullet Weight	5 Shot Group	Best 3 Shots
Federal Classic FMJ	123-grain	2.15"	1.30"
CCI Blazer Lead Free FMJ	124-grain	2.95"	1.10"
Federal Classic JHP ("9BP")	115-grain	3.15"	1.10"
Pro-Load Tactical JHP +P	124-grain	3.35"	2.00"
Winchester OSM subsonic JHP	147-grain	3.55"	1.35"
American Eagle FMJ	124-grain	3.65"	1.75"
Winchester Ranger Talon +P+ JHP	127-grain	4.20"	1.15"
Winchester +P+ JHP ("ISP Load")	115-grain	4.25"	1.50"
Remington JHP	115-grain	4.75"	1.85"

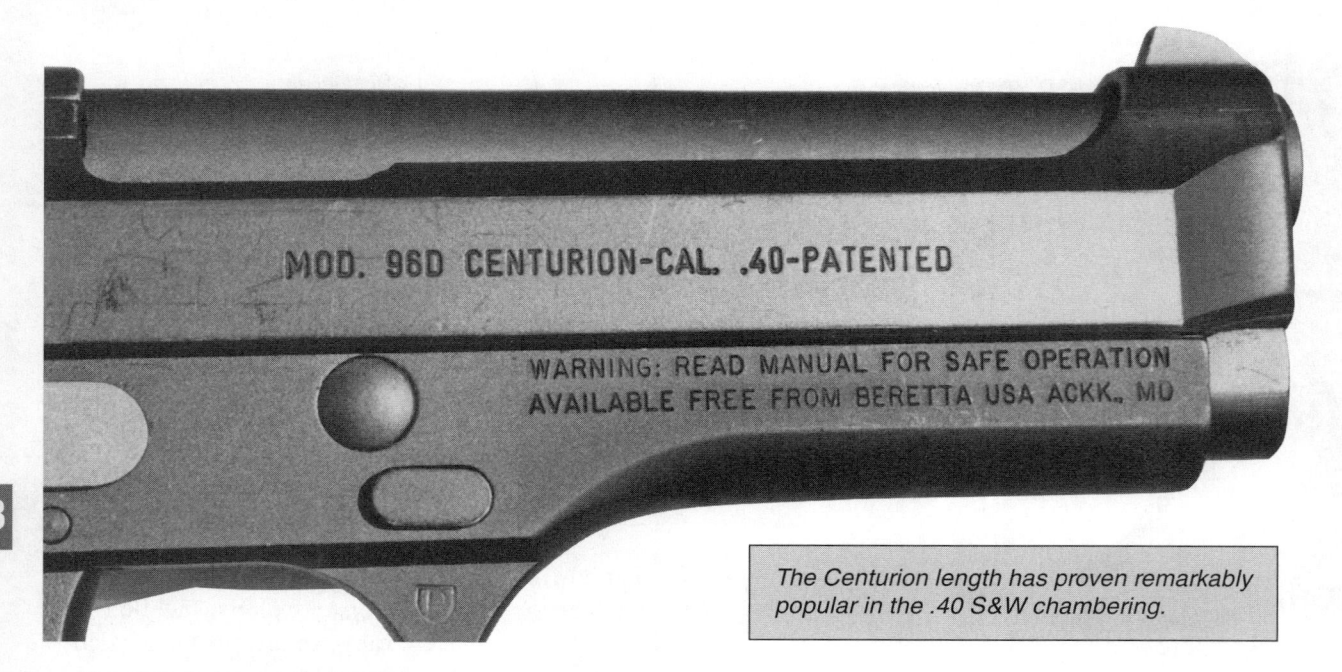

The Centurion length has proven remarkably popular in the .40 S&W chambering.

Cartridge	Bullet Weight	5 Shot Group	Best 3 Shots
Triton Hi-Vel +P JHP	115-grain	6.85″	2.40″

The overall groups only tell part of the story. The stainless front sight is milled out of the frame and appears silvery white to the eye. The rear sight is plain black. For my eyes, this is a terrible combination. Yes, you have the big, blocky sight picture we've all come to expect (and some of us have come to love) on a Beretta pistol. However, my own eyes just couldn't line up that great sight picture except in silhouette. Most of my other Berettas are blue, and don't cause me a problem in sighting. The stainless one I keep by the bed has Trijicon night sights that line up beautifully for me. This one didn't.

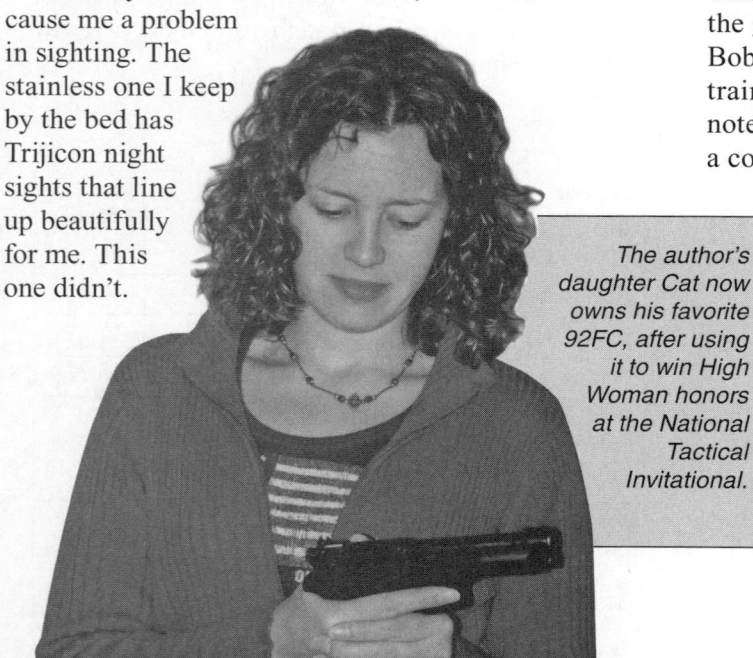

The author's daughter Cat now owns his favorite 92FC, after using it to win High Woman honors at the National Tactical Invitational.

What I'm saying is, I don't think the 5-shot groups above give a fair assessment of the pistol's inherent accuracy, because of the way the shooter's eye saw the sights. Look instead to the 3-shot groups, which I think give a much truer prediction of this pistol's inherent accuracy. *Note that 90 percent of the "best 3" measurements were 2 inches or less at 25 yards.* This is more in keeping with what I've learned to expect from Beretta 92s with good ammo over the years, whether full size or compact like this one.

On the last day of the class, I used this gun to shoot the "pace-setter" before the students qualified. This goes back to a factor in adult learning that the great officer survival instructor and super-cop Bob Lindsey brought to the attention of the police training community, called "modeling." Lindsey noted that if you expect your student to perform a complex skill like drawing and firing a gun to maximum standards, you should show him or her exactly what they should be doing just before you demand their performance. It gives them a mental image, and helps set a "mental clock," for what the instructor is looking for.

The test in this case was a 60-shot close combat course, from 4 yards (one-hand-only with each hand) to 15 yards on the tough IPSC silhouette. Shooting the American Eagle up close and that deliciously accurate top-line Federal hardball at the longer ranges, the Concealed Carry II gave me a clean 300 out of 300 points on the IPSC target, putting the 60 bullet holes in a group measuring about five and three-eighths inches.

Shooting under pressure (in a match, or before the eyes of paying students who are wondering if he who teaches can also do) is a very good test of a pistol's ergonomics. Except for the sight visibility (and the fact that this gun shot slightly left, which had to be adjusted for at the 10- and 15-yard lines), I couldn't have asked for better performance.

The trigger was heavy at a little over 12 pounds double-action and 5 to 6 pounds single, but it was smooth. Such triggers are very defensible in court against the frequent false accusations of accidental discharge that ruthless, politically-motivated prosecutors and unscrupulous, money-motivated plaintiffs' lawyers like to lodge against both cops and armed citizens in the wake of deliberate, justified shootings. In short, the trigger in both double- and single-action is just what you want on the Concealed Carry II: controllable, yet "lawyer-resistant."

Bad News

In the mid-$700 suggested retail range, this pistol is a bit pricey, but not out of line with most of its competition in that regard. I found a couple of sharp edges on this gun that aren't usually present on 92 or 96 series Berettas, either standard size or compact.

Two were at the back edge of the grip tang. I've considered the Beretta 92FC, their first short-barrel 9mm compact with shortened butt and 14-round staggered magazine, to be my favorite of its kind since I bought one in the late 1980s. I took it with me to Fort Benning back then, to teach the first cadre of the US Army's StressFire instructors after the Army adopted my method of combat pistol shooting. In 1996, my oldest daughter Cat, then 19, used the same Beretta Compact with hot Black Hills 115 grain +P hollow-points to win High Woman at the National Tactical Invitational. It became her gun thereafter, and I just used full size 92s when I needed a 9mm Beretta. None of them ever dug into the web of my hand at the grip tang. This test pistol did.

The other sharp edge wasn't so much painful as protuberant. Rather than the usual ambidextrous safety-decock lever seen on most 9mm Berettas, the Concealed Carry II has only a right-hander's lever, mounted on the left rear of the slide. On the right where the other "paddle" should be is merely a stud. I found that carrying "Mexican style," just shoved into the waistband, this protruding stud would snag if the gun was carried down deep. I've never experienced this with any other Beretta. While Mexican carry is something all of us in the business recommend against, we also recognize that most users will do it at one time or another out of expedience.

This is the least of my concerns with this particular component of the Beretta. In the class I taught with the Concealed Carry II, three of the 19 people present were left-handed. They were effectively "out of the loop" as far as the design of this particular model. That's unacceptable. Any of the rest of us might have had to use it left-handed, too. This pistol should have an ambidextrous safety like previous models, full size and compact.

While they're at it, Beretta also needs to reconsider the color contrast of this black part with the silver slide. Many who carry a Beretta 92 (myself included) carry it on safe. The pistol is certainly not going to go off if dropped or struck while the lever is in the "fire" position. The reason I carry mine on safe is as a weapon retention safety net in case a perpetrator gets it out of my holster and momentarily gains control. The contrasty color draws the eye right to the safety, and any bozo who looks at it will quickly figure out that one of two levers needs to be manipulated to "turn the gun on."

Please, Beretta, make this gun for us with the stainless, ambidextrous safety you'd put on a regular 92FS stainless service pistol!

Good News

There's far more good news than bad with this slick little 9mm. Recoil is very mild, allowing you to take advantage of the smooth trigger pull for good, fast shot placement. While the sights weren't the ideal color combo for my eyes, that doesn't mean they won't be right for yours. The reduced size of the grip-frame does indeed aid concealment, while the extension on the magazine gives the loaded gun an excellent "feel" in the hand.

That 100 percent Beretta reliability is there, always a comforting thing in a handgun whose purpose is to protect your life and the lives of your loved ones. Rumors to the contrary, these guns hold up quite well to hot loads and are warranted from the factory to handle +P and +P+ ammo. After all, their big brothers stand up to even hotter NATO ammo. (Yeah, I know, the old story about the tiny fraction of 1 percent of more than a million Beretta 92s fracturing their slides with military ammo. Some of those were with a particularly hot run of NATO ball that was almost "proof load level" in pressure, and some were with silenced guns whose heavy "cans" cantilevered the barrel so far forward it stressed out the locking blocks and caused slide fractures. Neither of these anomalies is likely to impact an armed citizen or plainclothes police officer buying a Concealed Carry II.)

The gun's ability to handle hot loads is important. Most any hollow-point .45 slug will get you through the night, and the same is true of the .40 caliber, but these small 9mm bullets are awfully "cartridge specific" in their stopping power. To put it bluntly, some work and some don't as far as stopping lethally violent human activity. In the old days, when there weren't "some 9mm rounds that work," the caliber earned a reputation as an impotent man-stopper. The rounds that Evan Marshall and Ed Sanow found in studies of gunfights to be in the 90 percent range for likelihood of stopping the fight quickly tended to be 115-grainers in the 1,300 feet per second range.

During the test period, when this was my main carry gun, I kept it loaded with the famed Illinois State Police load; Winchester's 115-grain +P+ at 1,300 fps. From frigid Chicago in winter to sultry Cairo in summer, the Illinois troopers found it to open up and work from their 4-inch S&W service pistols for almost 20 years, no matter how much heavy clothing the opponent might be wearing. In all their many gunfights, the Illinois troopers never did have a "stopping power nightmare" of a bad guy soaking up six or 13 solid hits before going down. They and brother officers they had studied *had* experienced that in the past with other, lesser 9mm rounds, which is why Winchester and Federal developed the 115-grain +P+ especially for their needs. I hope their new Glocks with 180-grain .40 caliber subsonic hollow-points work out as well for them.

These Winchester +P+ rounds have never been available officially to civilians, but identical if not superior ballistics, produced with superb quality control, are available from such smaller makers as Triton (Hi-Vel line) and Pro-Load (Tactical line). Such rounds make a 9mm pistol a viable defensive handgun in those terrible moments when you may only have time for one shot to save your life. The Beretta will handle them.

Recoil isn't bad at all thanks to the good ergonomics of the Concealed Carry II.

Bottom Line

The Beretta Concealed Carry II is a good little gun, a *very* good little gun. I've mentioned a few things I thought might make it better, but that's one shooter's habituation talking. For you, it might just be the ideal piece for the job it is named after. If you're in the market for a 9mm personal protection pistol, you owe it to yourself to check out the Beretta Concealed Carry II before you finalize your decision.

Endnotes

(1) Wilson, R. L., "The World of Beretta: An International Legend," New York City: Random House, 2000, P.245.

(2) Ayoob, Massad, "1995 Complete Book of Handguns," New York City: Harris Publications, 1995, P. 42.

(3) Wilson, op.cit., P. 245.

(4) Schwing, Ned, 2004 "Standard Catalog of Firearms," Iola, WI: Krause Publications, 2003, P. 140.

(5) Wilson, op.cit.

The Beretta Vertec

The continuing evolution of the Beretta 92 series did not stop with the modifications done at the behest of the U.S. government. Other things were going on. New developments had emerged that could be adapted to the pistol, and Beretta's people had their fingers on these changing pulses.

There were those of us who would have preferred a dovetailed front sight. Hitherto, the front post had been machined out of the slide. The integral sight was certainly strong, but for precise adjustments of point of aim/point of impact, it always helps to be able to install a higher or lower front sight. For some, this writer included, the previous slide construction had meant a stainless steel front sight on a stainless steel pistol, and for us that could cause glare in bright sunlight that got in the way of a good sight picture. The dovetailed sight would allow something with more contrast and answer that need, too.

It had come into vogue by the year 2000 to make pistols with integral Picatinny rails in the lower front of the frame, the dust guard, to allow the quick installation (and equally quick removal) of white light, laser sight, or combined flashlight/laser modules. Some departments were issuing the lights to officers with belt pouches, to be snapped on the guns when performing a building search or a manhunt in the dark. A growing number of departments were even authorizing special holsters that would hold the pistol with the light already mounted. This setup had become virtually standard for SWAT teams and K9 handlers.

Finally, Beretta had long since faced the fact that the size of their 92 series guns left the trigger reach just too long for people with very short fingers. A couple of different fixes had been tried on the 92 series, and Beretta had brought out the Cougar line with a shorter trigger reach. It was decided that a dramatic reshaping of the Model 92's grip frame would be worth a shot. However, part of the design parameter was to keep interchangeability with old-style Model 92 and Model 96 magazines.

The result was the introduction of the Beretta Vertec in 2002. The new pistol embodied all those features: the radically reshaped grip, the dovetailed front sight, and the integral frame rail. The Vertec was designed to complement the standard-frame pistol, not to replace it.

Viva! Vertec

The classic Beretta Model 92 9mm, known as the M9 to our military and as the Model 96 when chambered for the .40 Smith & Wesson round, is an endearing pistol. People like master gunsmith Bill Wilson and master instructor Ken Hackathorn have proclaimed it the most reliable of service pistols. It is match-winning accurate, as Ernest Langdon proved winning overall top score at the IDPA National Championships multiple times with his 92G. The biggest complaint by shooters was that it "had a big handle" that made it hard for them to reach the trigger properly if they didn't have long fingers.

Beretta has listened. In the past, they have tried to reach out to those smaller-handed shooters in at least three ways. First was the little-known experiment done for the Los Angeles County Sheriff's Department, which issues the Model 92. The back of the grip-frame at the web of the hand area was relieved to allow better trigger reach. This option never caught on.

Next, they picked up on a concept from SIGARMS and engineered a new trigger that would sit farther back, somewhat reducing trigger reach. This was much more successful and has been widely applied by Beretta-trained police armorers, but some thought it didn't go far enough.

Third came the Cougar series. These guns were drafted on a new sheet of paper and use a rotary breech. The grip shape was geared for small hands, "niched out" where the web makes contact, and the result was a much more reachable trigger. However, the Cougars never quite caught on like the classic 92/96 series.

Demand remained for a big Beretta service pistol with a smaller grip-frame. The demand was answered this year with the Vertec. Topside, it's the Beretta 92 or 96 that you know and love. The frame has been redesigned in two ways. First, a much slimmer, straighter grip with thinner panels combines with the short-reach trigger (standard on all Vertecs) to get past the hand fit problem. Second, a bigger dust cover (forward end of frame) is shaped to accommodate attachable flashlights.

The Vertec In Hand

Design credit on the Vertec concept goes to Len Lucas, Todd Green, Gabriele DePlano, and Drew Ursin. Lucas, who first suggested the dual texture, designed the grip panels. As the photos on the next page show, this is a mix of "checkering feel" and "stippling feel." What the pictures can't show is that it feels good in the hand. No bite, and no slip.

The combination of the short-reach trigger, the redesigned grip frame, and the thinner grip panels results in a trigger reach that is 3/16 of an inch shorter than that of a standard M9, says Green, the firm's director of law enforcement activities.

I have those "average size adult male hands" gun designers always talk about. I've always been partial to the Beretta, but could never hold it properly with the barrel in line with the long bones of the forearm and still get the distal joint of my index finger onto the trigger. That distal joint placement gives maximum leverage for a double-action trigger pull. With the Vertec, it was as if Lucas and company had built the new frame to fit my hand. The distal joint of the finger was perfectly centered on the trigger.

The test gun was the 92F, my own preference on Beretta's list of fire-control systems. The F-series is the traditional style. It is double-action for the first shot and self-cocking to single-action for each follow-up round. The ambidextrous levers at the rear of the slide serve as both decocking levers and a manual safety.

Beretta also offers their G-series. Still double-action for the first shot only, a 92G's slide lever is spring-loaded and functions as a decocker only. The gun cannot be put "on safe."

Finally, there is the D-series. A gun like the 96D is double-action-only, with a spurless hammer and a "slick slide" since the gun is self-decocking. These have proven particularly popular with police.

Indeed, Todd Green tells me that current policy is that with the exception of the competition-oriented Elite series guns, which are decocker only, the D- and G-format are limited to police. This is ironic, since cops who carry their guns hanging out where everyone can grab at them are the ones who need the weapon retention feature of an on-safe gun more than anyone else. From the Los Angeles County Sheriff's Department to the North Carolina Highway Patrol, there are countless police officers who have survived gun grabs because the Beretta F-series pistol was "on-safe" when a suspect gained control of it, pointed it at them, and pulled the trigger. It is for this reason that I personally prefer the F-series for my own use.

The Beretta has always had one of the most easily manipulated safety/decockers of its kind. While the one on the test gun was a little stiffer than the ones I'm used to, which tend to be either well-worn or customized, it worked just fine. The web of the hand being a little forward seems to give the thumb more leverage to activate this lever.

A Wisconsin police equipment shop owner demonstrates the Vertec, in hand, compared to standard 92FS on showcase.

The trigger was also a little stiffer than usual for a Beretta, but perhaps it just wasn't broken in enough yet. Single-action felt like about 7 pounds, double-action, maybe 11. The finish was the handsome, evenly applied Bruniton that we've come to expect from this brand. The barrel was different, though: blackened stainless. Explains Todd Green, "Bruniton is so lubricious that with stainless, you can't get it to stick. They finally came up with a special stainless steel in Italy, and a primer they can put on it that allows the Bruniton to be applied. The result is an even more durable and corrosion-resistant barrel."

The barrel, by the way, is 4.7 inches instead of the usual 4.9. In addition to making the gun a little shorter, it makes for a better-looking pistol. Some thought that the muzzle protruding from the slide on the familiar M9 looked a little, well, ungainly. Notes Green, "The only reason for the extended barrel in the first place was to have room to cut threading so you could add a sound suppressor."

Shooting The Vertec

The Beretta 92 is an accurate, mild-kicking pistol, and that continues in the Vertec variation. My gun had the traditional big Beretta sights, so beloved by geezers like me because our aging eyes can still see them.

Eight loads were tested, representing six manufacturers. These included the "big four" and also two of our finest OEMs (Original Equipment Manufacturers), Black Hills and Pro-Load. Six different bullet weights were used.

Surprisingly, this gun just wouldn't shoot tight with 115-grain ball ammo. Two brands noted for quality and accuracy averaged around 5-inch groups at 25 yards. However, five hollow-points and a frangible round designed for steel targets and indoor ranges all shot under 3 inches at that distance, and half of the loads we tested did better than 2½ inches. Each group was measured center-to-center, twice, to the nearest 0.05 of an inch. The first measurement was the whole five shots. The second was the best three, which, if all the shots seem to have broken cleanly, will give you a good prediction of what the gun could do with all five from a machine rest. And we did not have such a rest available for this testing of the Vertec.

The distinctive new Vertec grip frame is, to Ayoob's way of thinking, a marked improvement over the older style.

The reshaped grip frame of Vertec allows greater trigger reach, allowing the finger to be placed on the trigger at the distal joint for maximum leverage, especially critical in fast double-action shooting.

Manufacturer	Load	5 Shot Group	Best 3 Shots
Black Hills	115-grain FMJ reman.	5.15″	4.30″
Federal	123-grain FMJ	4.95″	2.45″
Pro-Load	124-grain FMJ +P Qualifier	2.30″	1.30″
Remington	115-grain JHP	2.10″	1.35″
Speer	100-grain RHT frangible Cleanfire	1.85″	1.15″
Winchester	115-grain Silvertip JHP	2.80″	1.15″
Winchester	127-grain +P+ Ranger LE JHP	2.15″	1.25″
Winchester	147-grain OSM JHP subsonic	2.75″	1.00″

There were a few surprises in shooting the Vertec. The Winchester OSM (Olin Super Match) is one of our most accurate 9mm loads. It did the tightest "best-three" group with an inch even, and four shots were in 1.45 inches. I was delighted with the Speer RHT (Reduced Hazard Training) ammo. We don't expect great accuracy from frangible projectiles, nor yet from lead-free primers like CCI/Speer's Cleanfire. They tend to be less consistent than conventional primers with lead styphnate, and less consistent primers generally result in altered ignition patterns that in turn cause vertical stringing at the target. This is my second test of a 9mm pistol in which the Speer RHT has won the accuracy sweepstakes. This is proof that CCI/Speer is doing a difficult job right. With frangible and lead-free rounds more and more becoming a requirement on certain indoor ranges, it's good to know that this round is available.

I am frankly stumped by the Vertec's problem with the 115-grain ball rounds. I've won accuracy-intensive PPC matches with Black Hills reloads, and the ammo used here was from a batch that was already proven. Even more puzzling was what happened with the Federal ball. Not only did we get a lousy group (and this, from an old and cherished batch that I know to be particularly accurate, the kind we target shooting competitors save for special occasions), but three of the five virgin rounds split their casings. Beretta is also at a loss to explain it, since countless thousands of cops use Federal ammo in Berettas daily and Beretta uses a lot of it in testing and demonstrations.

In any case, split casings notwithstanding, the gun spat out every empty and cycled a fresh cartridge every time. The gun is on its way back to Beretta at this time for examination and if they can figure out what happened with those three split casings.

Note that split casings often result in extraction failures. That did not happen here. True to its heritage, the 92F Vertec performed 100 percent malfunction-free through several hundred rounds.

I shot a qualification with it, just to get the feel of the new gun. It's very quick on target. For some, the straighter grip angle may make it "point better" or "point worse." I was looking for that, and honestly couldn't find a problem with it, though I didn't find an advantage in that regard, either. I'm habituated to the conventional Beretta and it points well for me. With the flatter backstrap, conventional wisdom would have the Vertec pointing slightly low, but that was not the case. Closing my eyes and bringing the Vertec to target, I raised my eyelids to find the sights spot on where I wanted them. Even for those of us who

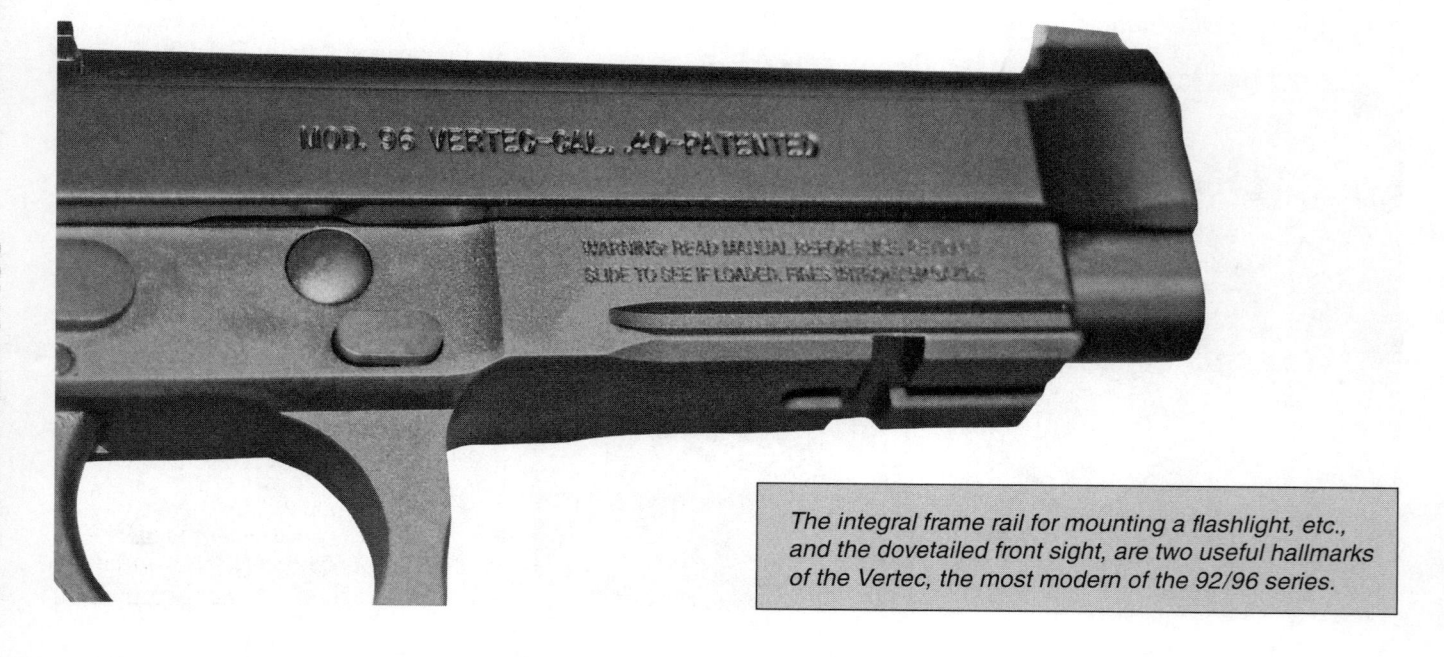

The integral frame rail for mounting a flashlight, etc., and the dovetailed front sight, are two useful hallmarks of the Vertec, the most modern of the 92/96 series.

have doubts about most "point-shooting" systems and prefer the visual verification of at least a coarse sight picture, a gun that points well gets those sights on target a little faster. For me, this gun delivered.

The 60-shot qualification course involved weak-hand-only, strong-hand-only, two-hand standing, kneeling and other cover postures as the distance went back. I wound up shooting a perfect score on the target, an IDPA silhouette. The 60 shots were in a group measuring just under 5½ inches. One shot had gone high right, or the group would have been an inch or more tighter, about what I average with the standard Beretta. The starboard shot came from overcompensating; the fixed sights on this particular gun went left for me and a little high.

With the Vertec, this is not a problem. The gentle kiss of a Beretta sight-changing tool will true up the rear sight for you to get the windage perfect. New with the Vertec is a dovetailed front sight. If elevation isn't right for you, your eyes, and your preferred or mandated load, a front sight of different height is easily installed to bring you to perfect zero.

Reloads were quick and clean. Green notes that these guns have beveled magazine wells. This is gilding the lily on a gun designed for a high-capacity magazine, which is tapered toward the top and goes into a magazine, well, like greased lightning anyway.

Good news: Despite its radically changed grip-frame, *the Vertec takes high-capacity 92/96 magazines!* Now, if you're a private citizen who favors the .40 S&W, this is no big whoop. The Beretta 96 in .40 S&W only took an 11-round magazine and wasn't out that long before the Clinton hi-capacity magazine ban. Good news: Now that the Clinton Gun Ban is history, you can once again fully load all the Beretta pistols.

The test 92F Vertec shot perfectly with a multitude of my pre-ban 15- and 20-round magazines. The Beretta 9mm has been so popular for so long that there are probably over a million pre-ban high-cap magazines floating around for it. And new ones are now being built every day.

Finally, let's look at the flashlight attachment thing. This makes huge sense on a home defense pistol. More and more police departments are looking at putting something like an Insights M3 light on every officer's belt in a pouch, to give him or her the same building search capability with a light-mounted pistol that any SWAT cop would be likely to have. In some jurisdictions, cops who think bad guys are inside a structure can call the SWAT team. For most of us, on smaller and farther flung departments, it's the regular street cop or road deputy or trooper who has to search the building for the burglar when the alarm has gone off. This is a useful addition to the Beretta line. Mark Maynard and I played with it with an M3. We found it lined up well and it went on easily. While it came off a little hard, that may have been because both pistol and light were fairly new.

Future Of The Vertec

Todd Green tells me that a Federal agency he can't name has already purchased a large quantity of Vertec pistols. There have been a number of lawsuits against police agencies by female personnel who were fired for failing to qualify with handguns that were simply too large in the grip for their short fingers to reach. It has been my experience that the department that fights this can expect to lose the lawsuit, pay a judgment of about $100,000, and rack up close to that in legal fees. It is just a *hell* of a lot easier to purchase for each such officer a Vertec to replace the standard Beretta. If the department prefers a decocker only or

This veteran shooter found his scores improving when he switched to the 9mm Vertec.

a DAO pistol, both are available to law enforcement from Beretta in the Vertec style.

Price isn't that much more. The standard model Beretta 92FS carries a suggested retail of $676 with the black Bruniton finish, or $734 in stainless, which Beretta calls "Inox." The Vertec version sells for $712 in Bruniton and $762 in Inox.

For those who always liked the Beretta but just didn't find it to fit their hand, the Vertec may finally mate you and the gun you desired. For those with small hands who *have* to use the standard size Beretta, the Vertec may prove to be nothing less than a godsend.

Vertec Update

The Vertec has been quite successful since its introduction in 2002. Cops in particular love it. Police departments that had been issuing 9mm or .40 Berettas appreciated a gun that would better fit a smaller officer's hand, and help stave off hugely costly and morale-draining lawsuits. Armed citizens appreciated the better fit and the better front sight arrangement, and also realized that a pistol with a flashlight attached could make enormous good sense as a home defense gun.

Interestingly, it has not eclipsed the standard models as much as some thought it would. Part of the explanation for this may be the war in Iraq and Afghanistan. Many gun dealers tell me that their sales of Berettas have been up since those hostilities commenced; they continue at the time of this writing. While American military personnel are not allowed to take personal handguns overseas under current regulations, I'm told, a number of our men and women in uniform have decided that practice with a Beretta 92 and a semiautomatic AR-15, privately owned, would be excellent insurance before being shipped over or, in the case of reserve personnel, called up. Since take-home guns for practice aren't in U.S. military protocol, these brave Americans have to buy their own. Often, concerned parents buy the guns for them. Since the standard frame is the one they've been trained with,

Doug Berg finds the Vertec lets him get "more hand around the gun," resulting in better recoil control. Note the spent casing in mid-air directly above the muzzle, yet the is muzzle already back on target.

have qualified on, and will be issued, that's the logical choice. Some buy commemoratives, killing two birds with one stone as it were. Most buy 9mms, but some purchase the .40, on the theory that it's *their* gun and will defend *their* home afterward, and they've heard gripes from returning comrades of the ineffectuality of 9mm military ball ammo in combat.

Still, the Vertec has been a success. I never heard back from Beretta on the problems I experienced with the split casings. Later shooting with the same batch of ammo confirmed that it wasn't the cartridges. I suspect that I simply got a very rare bad barrel in mine, which would also explain why the groups I got with the Vertec were less than I might have expected from one of my own standard-style Beretta 92s. The many Vertecs I've seen go through my school since have worked just fine.

There is no better endorsement of the Vertec than the fact that Ernest Langdon, the world's top Beretta shooter in practical handgun competition, has gone that route. He shoots a black 9mm Vertec 92G these days, after a year and a half shooting SIG .45s in competition. He loves the feel of the pistol, and feels it's a far better choice as an issue gun since it fits so many hands. He also appreciates the dovetailed sights and the beveled mag well, and of course, the quick-attaching and -detaching flashlight option.

After discussing this with Ernest, I'm more convinced than ever that the Vertec I was sent for test had an anomalous bad barrel. Langdon insists that Beretta has never produced a better pistol with better tolerances than the Vertec. He tells me that in a recent test of a customer's stock gun, the factory barrel gave him five-shot groups of less than an inch at 25 yards.

The Vertec is a natural progression of the 92/96 series, and for many shooters – particularly those with need of an attached flashlight, or those with small hands – may be the key that finally opens the door to their appreciation of these superb handguns.

The Beretta 96

This is the 96G Centurion, decocker only. It has earned an enviable reputation with Florida Department of Law Enforcement.

In 1990, Beretta U.S.A. had reason to worry. They had once achieved market dominance in the police "wonder-nine" field with their Model 92 9mm, but SIG-Sauer's P226 was neck and neck with them and perhaps gaining in the race, and their margin of lead had been a slim one in any case. Glock's new "plastic pistol" had risen up out of nowhere like Godzilla coming up out of Tokyo harbor, and if trends continued it would soon be the dominant police 9mm in the USA.

Then, in January of 1990, Smith & Wesson and Winchester announced the new .40 Smith & Wesson cartridge at the SHOT Show in Las Vegas. It soon became clear that the perfect compromise had been reached between those who wanted a 16-shot 9mm and those who preferred an eight-shot .45 ACP. There was now a 12-shot .40 S&W. Smith & Wesson, with ample research time to de-bug the new gun and tune it to the new round before introducing it, was ahead of the rest of the field. Their entry, the Model 4006, was a traditional double-action pistol in all stainless steel construction, beefed up for the high pressure curve and extreme slide velocity produced by the new cartridge that bore their name. Police orders were almost immediate, and soon skyrocketed. Beretta realized they would have to follow suit.

Different companies took different approaches. SIG waited the longest to come out with a .40, carefully beefing up their guns before they did so and crafting their rugged P229 pistol for this hot cartridge and its new sibling, the .357 SIG round. Glock had made the mistake of jumping in too soon with a 9mm rechambered for .40, and the early prototype of the Glock 22 failed durability tests at California Highway Patrol, which adopted the Smith & Wesson 4006 instead.

By 1991, Beretta had adapted the Model 92 to fire the new cartridge. They could equal S&W's capacity, 11 rounds in the magazine and another in the firing chamber, but not the 16-round capacity of the Glock 22. (Considerably strengthened after the embarrassing CHP failure, complete with a new reinforcing pin in the frame, the Glock 22 would

Here is a Maryland State Police issue Model 96D and duty leather. The department seems extremely happy with the pistol.

go on to become the best selling of all .40 caliber service pistols in the police sector). Beretta named its new .40 caliber the Model 96.

Many departments that wanted to "power up" and liked the idea of the compromise .40 S&W cartridge, had also had splendid success with the Beretta 9mm. Some others had not yet adopted a 9mm, but liked the Beretta features and reputation as well as the potential of the .40, and chose the Model 96 for those reasons.

The performance of the guns in service was not, in the beginning, as stellar as that of the predecessor Model 92, at least not in every case. The results might best be described as spotty, with some having excellent experiences and some being less pleased.

One satisfied customer was police chief Joseph Faughnan, a former Connecticut State Police trooper, who adopted the Beretta 96 for his new department. Larry Wilson quotes him at length in his book on Beretta, and the following excerpts are particularly noteworthy. He was with the CSP when it became only the second State Police department in the United States to adopt a semiautomatic pistol, actually standardizing on the 92F before the U.S. military did. The troopers were prejudiced against these strange new automatics. Said Faughnan,

"It fell upon the State Police Academy to be entrusted with overcoming this age-old prejudice, to impart confidence in the troopers of the dependability of the Beretta. Over the course of 1982 to 1983, all of the Troopers were given extensive classroom and range hands-on training in the nomenclature, operation, and safety of the 92F. Troopers found this new 9mm to be more accurate and far quicker to reload than the issued revolver. Over 900 members were certified to carry the new sidearm with no untoward incident during training.

Upper: The Model 96 Beretta is a very controllable .40. Here, the Model 96F is leveled at the target for its last shot ...
Lower: ... and here it is in full recoil.

This is a full size 96D, with Farrar grips and Trijicon night sights. Note the squared floorplate of the magazine, a signature of most – but interestingly, not all – Beretta 96 magazines.

"As a result of the State Police conversion to high-capacity semiautomatic pistols, most other police departments in Connecticut followed suit. With the crime rate accelerating, and the number of gun-related incidents increasing, this change not only made good tactical sense, but also became necessary to allow police officers to be equipped with similar modern weapons that many criminals now carried.

"In July of 1991, I was appointed police chief of Clinton, and learned that its 24 officers still carried revolvers. Based upon

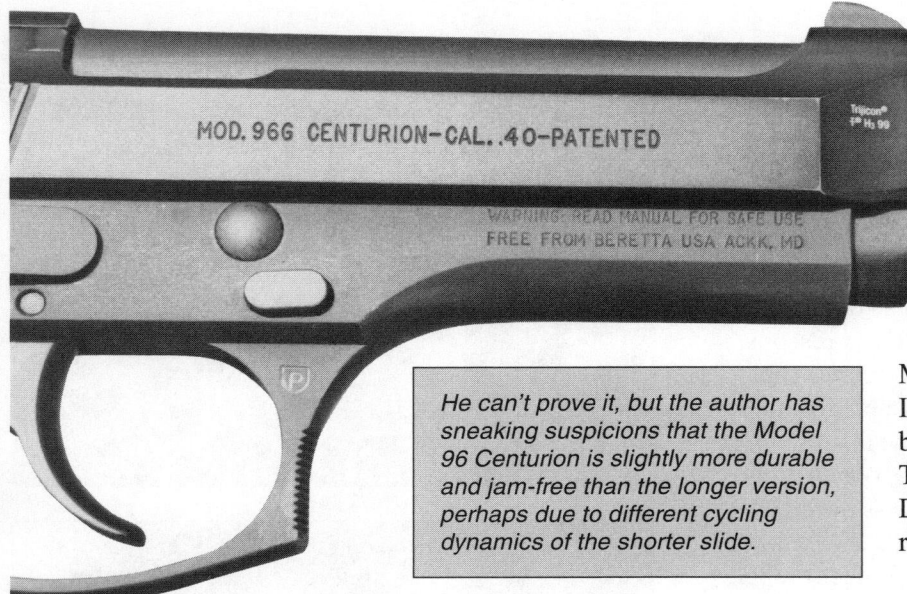

He can't prove it, but the author has sneaking suspicions that the Model 96 Centurion is slightly more durable and jam-free than the longer version, perhaps due to different cycling dynamics of the shorter slide.

the positive experiences with the 92F, I instructed the department's range officer, Corporal Albert Hawkes, to obtain a test weapon in .40 caliber S&W from Beretta for trial. Beretta had just then begun manufacture of the Model 96, double-action, in that caliber, which was very similar to the 92F (our test gun was the 13th made). One significant difference between these two models was the magazine capacity: 15 for the 92F and 10 for the 96. It was felt that the smaller magazine capacity would be compensated for by the .40 caliber, which we considered better suited for law enforcement needs.

"Tests of the new pistol proved that this new model was as dependable and reliable as its older cousin, so the decision was made to equip the entire department. A training program that was basically copied from the State Police was instituted in Clinton, with similar positive results.

"The minimal repairs that have been necessary in subsequent years of service have shown the reliability of the 96. Its relatively simple design and strong construction has led officers to have complete confidence in this weapon. My experiences with both the 92F and the 96 have been totally positive, and it is no surprise to me ... that law enforcement and the military worldwide continue to adopt Berettas."[1]

While the early guns sent to the chief for testing may have had 10-round magazines, the standard for the Model 96 became an 11-rounder, bringing the gun up to a total capacity of 12 .40 caliber rounds. This equaled the capacity of the gun that had the head start, Smith & Wesson's Model 4006. In 1994, the Crime Bill became law, banning magazines holding more than 10 rounds, so all but the cops were back to the 10-rounders. As the chief had noted, however, 10-round magazines could be viewed as a fair trade for .40 caliber performance.

After heavy testing, the City of San Francisco Police Department chose the 96G as its first standard-issue semiautomatic service pistol. In similar fashion, the state police of Connecticut, Maryland, Pennsylvania, and Rhode Island also adopted Model 96 pistols, but double-action-only, D series. The Providence, Rhode Island Police Department adopted the 96D also, and reported splendid performance.

An extraordinarily exhaustive test led the Immigration and Naturalization Service, which encompasses the gunfight-heavy Border Patrol, to adopt the Beretta 96D pistol. Concerned about the high intensity of their chosen round, a .40 S&W cartridge with 155-grain bullet at 1,200 feet per second velocity, they became the first institutional purchaser to opt for the Brigadier design, which encompassed a slightly heavier slide that was reinforced in the area of the locking blocks.

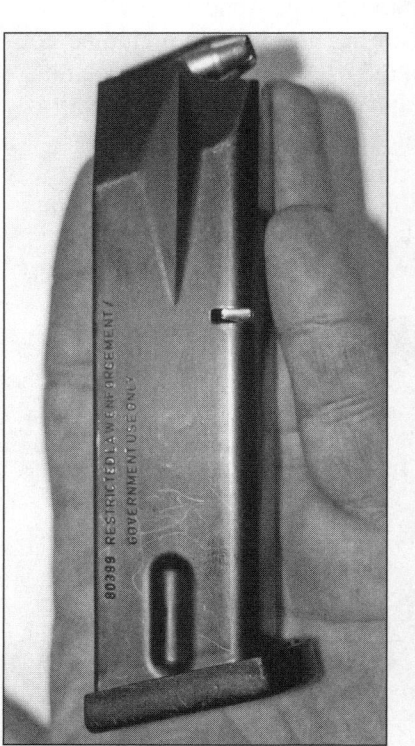

Some other departments simply swapped their 9mm Berettas for .40 Berettas. After intensive testing that showed it met their demanding accuracy and reliability standards, the Model 96G was adopted by the Indiana State Police to replace their superbly-functioning but less powerful Model 92G pistols.

For a decade, only police could buy 11-round Model 96 magazines, which were so marked. Note the characteristic square floorplate of the Model 96 magazine.

Trouble in Paradise

Ray Chapman was famous for saying, "Pistols work best with the cartridge for which they were originally chambered." He cited as examples the fact that the Colt Government Model pistols in .38 Super and 9mm were never quite as reliable without custom gunsmithing as they were in the caliber for which John Browning originally designed that gun, .45 ACP.

Over the years, that proved true in many other handguns, even revolvers. Six-gun historians have said that the slightly bottle-necked case of the .44-40 Winchester would sometimes back out of the chamber of the Colt Single Action Army, a.k.a. "Peacemaker," locking up the gun. They cite this as the reason the Colt .44 was never as popular on the frontier as the Colt .45, which was originally constructed around the .45 cartridge. In the latter half of the 20th Century, Smith & Wesson discovered that their K-frame revolver, originally built around the low-pressure black powder .38 cartridge, would overheat, lock up, and jam when fired extensively with .357 Magnum ammunition. This was particularly true in the stainless steel version. In late 2004, Smith & Wesson announced that, fully 50 years after the introduction of their K-frame .357 Combat Magnum, this gun would henceforth be produced on the larger L-frame. It was a tacit and late admission that a gun designed to be a .38 could lose some of its splendid performance and much of its long service life when chambered for the much more powerful .357 Magnum cartridge.

Something similar happens when a 9mm size gun is chambered for the .40 S&W. While the .40's design parameter was to fit in a 9mm envelope, it brought to the table an extremely high slide velocity and early pressure curve that beat up guns. This happens across the spectrum of manufacturers. Browning had to put a .45-size slide on its 9mm Hi-Power when it rechambered that gun for .40 S&W. S&W, of course, beefed up their 5906 pistol for the more powerful new round. SIG literally re-engineered the line before introducing .40 caliber pistols. Even the famously durable Glock had to go back to the drawing board after its first attempt at turning their 9mm into a .40, and it is no secret even so that today's Glock .40 caliber pistols show more wear with the same number of rounds than their otherwise identical 9mm pistols.

Another analogy would be taking a standard configuration 1911 .45 pistol and running it constantly with +P .45 ammo. One of the premier makers of 1911s is ParaOrdnance of Canada. Thanos Polyzos of ParaOrdnance once told me, "Suppose you have an automobile built to run 100,000 miles of normal driving, and then you run it all the time at 100 miles an hour. That's more stress than it was engineered for, and it will reduce its life. You'll be lucky to get 50,000 miles out of it. Similarly, a pistol engineered to last for 100,000 rounds of standard-pressure .45 ACP will be lucky if it reaches 50,000 before falling apart, if every shot is at +P pressure."

There are laws of physics and laws of metallurgy at work here that cannot be denied. A more powerful pistol in the same format as a less powerful one will wear out sooner and break parts sooner, because of the much greater buffeting those parts take from the recoil force every time a shot goes off.

All this is why the Beretta 96 has not developed the same reputation for extreme longevity as the Beretta 92.

The Vancouver, BC police adopted the Beretta 96D as soon as their government made all police departments switch from revolvers to autoloaders as an occupational safety issue. The department feels that the guns have stood up well enough, considering the power of the ammunition put through them constantly in training, and they continue to issue the 96D. However, at least one of their constables went through three pistols due to breakage. Admittedly, he was a

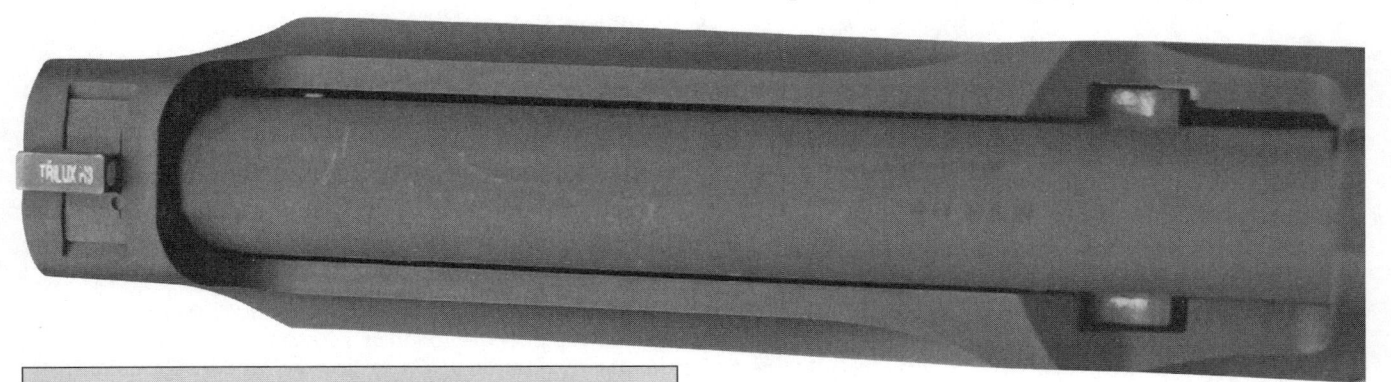

Note uneven wear on the locking blocks of this Model 96.

firearms instructor and member of the pistol team, and shooting the guns heavily.

Another department with mixed results was Tacoma, Washington. Tacoma had adopted the Glock early on, prior to the voluntary product upgrade circa 1990. There had been an accidental discharge issue, and the department decided to dump the Glocks and adopt the .40 caliber Beretta, based largely on the excellent experiences the Washington State Patrol had enjoyed with the Beretta 92.

I was teaching frequently in the Northwest then, and I saw Tacoma officers having jam after jam with their very early production Beretta 96s. The 135-grain bullet, the lightest practical load available in terms of bullet weight, seemed to cause feeding problems in a number of Model 96 specimens. (A spokesman for a large ammo company later told me that his firm developed a special 165-grain load expressly to feed in Model 96 pistols).

Tacoma did another series of pistol tests. The result was a new policy that gave officers broad options in their choice of duty handgun, including something that seemed radical to many, the cocked and locked 1911 .45. Tacoma approved one brand, the Kimber. This was sufficiently newsworthy to make most of the gun magazines. It left the shooting public with the impression that the department had adopted the Kimber as standard. In fact, the Beretta .40 remained on the approved list, and the Glock was also listed as an authorized weapon, along with the Kimber .45.

Tweaking and Shaking Down

Beretta shook down the design here and tweaked it here and there. Soon, the malfunctions seemed to disappear in newly manufactured guns. Meanwhile, the Model 96 benefited from the same design updates as the Model 92. These included the locking block improvements; the Brigadier slide option that seems to have worked out so well for the Border Patrol; the short slide/barrel configuration known as the Centurion; and stainless or INOX construction. Elites and Vertecs were manufactured in .40 S&W as well as 9mm Parabellum.

However, the damage had been done. By now, the Glock pistol was far and away the most popular .40 caliber on the market. Departments and police unions saw no reason to argue for a 12-shot .40 when Glock offered them a *16-shot* .40. Before long, Glock held a huge lead in the .40 caliber service pistol market, with SIG a distant second. The Beretta 96 was reduced to dueling with Smith & Wesson for third place.

During the irritating decade of the Clinton ban on magazines holding more than ten rounds, law-abiding private citizens who owned Beretta 92 pistols discovered a good use for 10-round Beretta 96 mags. It turned out that the "Clinton legal" 96 magazine, designed for 10 .40 caliber cartridges, would function passably in a Model 92 while holding thirteen 9mm cartridges.

Personally, I rather liked the Model 96. It is accurate and controllable. Although I own several Beretta 92s in 9mm, I have but one Beretta 96 in .40, and I won it. That said, though, I've carried it and trusted my life to it. It has fired thousands upon thousands of rounds and malfunctioned but once, an easily corrected failure to go into battery. I've lent it out often to students, at 500 rounds a crack, and the one time it ever jammed was a failure to fully chamber on a freezing day when I was wearing a heavy coat that forced me to bend my elbows more than usual. I expect I simply limp-wristed the gun.

The wedge-shaped magazine floorplate is characteristic of the 9mm Model 92, but this gun is the author's 96D Centurion in .40 caliber. The magazine is simply one of the uncommon Beretta USA magazines for the 96 produced with 92-style floorplate.

This pistol is a Centurion, with the 4.3-inch barrel and proportional slide. Interestingly enough, most of the Beretta .40 complaints I've heard have involved the full-size guns. I wonder if the shorter, lighter slide might not be rocketing back and forth with a little less force than the full length one on the 4.9-inch barrel gun.

In Florida, two analogous agencies switched from the Beretta 92F to the Beretta 96G. The Highway Patrol, a uniformed force, bought full-size pistols. The Department of Law Enforcement, a force of plainclothes investigators, bought the shorter Centurion models for better concealment.

The uniformed troopers' instructors tell me they've seen a very slight increase in malfunctions with the full-size .40s over the virtually jam-proof 9mms they had before, something they attribute to limp-wristing. Says one instructor, "Every time I see a .40 Beretta jam, I take the recruit's gun and run a magazine and it works fine. Then I make sure the recruit is locking his or her wrist, and it works fine for them, too. The Beretta 9mm is very tolerant of a shooter with an unlocked wrist. The Beretta .40 just isn't quite so tolerant."

The plainclothes DLE investigators, on the other hand, tell me they found the same splendid level of reliability with their .40 Centurions as they did with their previous 92F 9mm pistols. This would tend to confirm the theory that the shorter slide version of the Beretta is a little more forgiving in terms of reliability when chambered for .40 S&W.

The Ohio State Patrol adopted the Model 96D early on, and since switched to the SIG-Sauer P226 DAO in the same .40 Smith & Wesson caliber. Two malfunctions during field actions were cited as the reason. One trooper's pistol reportedly jammed while he was shooting a dog. The other involved Trooper Angela Watson, who killed the man who shot her with a .44 Magnum. As she returned fire, she found her pistol inoperable, proceeded with the jam-clearing technique she had been taught, reloaded and kept shooting. She told me she is not certain whether, as the Beretta people surmise, she might have simply failed to return her double action trigger all the way forward.

Today, the general consensus is that the Beretta 96 has been tweaked up to the same level of reliability as the Beretta 92, but it will never have the longevity of the 9mm Beretta because the powerful .40 round simply gives it too much of a beating. This is not unique to the Beretta. No matter what the brand, if you have two analogous pistols of the same type and weight, one in 9mm and one in .40 S&W, the .40 will wear out sooner simply because it is "being used harder" by its faster-cycling cartridge.

As all this was happening, Beretta worked hard to field other pistols in the caliber that was now the most popular in American law enforcement, the .40 S&W. In the next couple of chapters, we'll look at how all the Beretta .40s stand vis-à-vis one another.

Endnotes

(1) Wilson, R.L., "The World of Beretta: An International Legend," New York City: Random House, 2000,
Pages 251-253.

Beretta Cougar 8000 and 8048

Top: A Mini-Cougar with extension magazine duplicates the feel of a standard model, but with a sort of finger groove at the bottom.

Center: Standard size Beretta Cougar.

Below: Mini-Cougar with short concealment magazine. All are F models with ambidextrous safety/decock levers.

In 1997, continuing to respond to the common perception of their standard line 9mm and .40 S&W pistols being too large, Beretta introduced the 8000 series. In years past, back when J. Galef & Son was importing the commercial version of the 1934 Beretta .380 to the United States, they had called that gun the Cougar. The name was resurrected for the 8000 series. In 9mm, the standard-size Cougar was dubbed the Model 8000, and when chambered for the .40 Smith & Wesson cartridge, it was called the Model 8040.

Beretta historian Larry Wilson says of the Cougar, "Beretta built the new handgun in hammer and spurless hammer models, with an enclosed slide, the ejection port on the right side. Production of this pistol has been in the Gardone factory …"[1]

Wilson continues, "Trying to scale down the Model 92 series was not going to work, unless the typical Walther-Beretta barrel locking system was abandoned in order to shorten the overall length of the barrel. Beretta's philosophy was that in order to ensure maximum accuracy, the barrel has to remain in the axis of the target, thus excluding the use of a tilting barrel (the John M. Browning approach). A rotating barrel was the chosen alternative, consistent with Beretta's belief that whenever the barrel remains in the axis it is more accurate. Another advantage was that the energy, when firing, is dissipated all along the rotating barrel creating less stress and a longer life of the pistol. The only perceived drawback of the new system was that, whatever solution was chosen, Beretta would have to issue a pistol without the typical 'open slide design' that happens to be the company's signature."[2]

Beretta finally had a pistol that fired police/military service power ammo, in the size range of their user-friendly .380s. In addition to their claims for accuracy, they had also taken into consideration complaints that the big 92 and 96 frames, with their

Reduced recoil of the rotary breech system is a demonstrable fact in the Beretta Cougar. Here, Doug Berg cracks off a shot. The spent casing is spinning out of the ejection port, but the gun is already back in battery for the next shot, and already back on target.

The Mini-Cougar is the most versatile style in the Cougar line. It has the same length on top as a standard model, and with the "filler" magazine, shown here, can have the same capacity and feel as the bigger gun when the owner chooses.

long trigger reach, were too long for those with short fingers to reach well enough for top performance shooting. The Cougar's grip frame was reshaped so drastically that existing 92 and 96 magazines would not interchange without modification. The rear grip frame had a hollow shaped for the web of the hand that brought the web deeper into the gun, bringing the trigger finger closer to the trigger and thus improving the trigger reach dimension.

In addition, Beretta determined that the rotary breech mechanism softened recoil. This was cited in the 1997 Beretta catalog: "Inherent accuracy is built in. The Cougar's short recoil, straight in-line feed system delivers exceptional reliability and accuracy. When the Cougar is in battery, the positive lock-up of barrel to slide assures perfect alignment of barrel and sights. Upon firing, the barrel travels and rotates with axial movement. By channeling part of the recoil energy into barrel rotation, and by partially absorbing the barrel and slide recoil shock through the central block before it is transferred to the frame, the Cougar achieves unusually low felt recoil. The result is superior accuracy and quicker recovery for second shots ... One of the most ergonomically advanced pistols in its class. All edges are rounded or beveled and carefully finished ... virtually snag-proof and exceptionally easy to draw and conceal. The ... contoured frame and grips make this Cougar exceptionally easy to control during firing. By taking hand anatomy and instinctive hold into account, the cougar accommodates smaller hands and also protects larger hands from being pinched by the slide." [3]

The Cougar was successful in its improvement of trigger reach. Many liked it better in that respect than its older siblings.

Cougar 8000 9mm

The Cougar 8000s that I've shot have had mild recoil, but it's hard to tell how much of that comes from the rotating barrel. The gun still weighs 32 ounces, and a solidly built 9mm that size shouldn't kick much anyway. I've found over the years that you don't really notice much difference in 9mm kick when a recoil-reducing device is installed. I didn't feel that much difference in the SIG P226 9mm, for example, with or without the mercury-filled Harrt's Recoil Reducer installed, but there was a palpable improvement when one of these units was installed in the .45 caliber P220.

The Cougars, with their different design, lack that glassy and classy feel when you rack the actions. The ejection port is smaller than on many enclosed-slide semiautomatic pistols, but still ample to eject a live cartridge when unloading. Though the factory promised that all sharp edges had been removed, I found the ambidextrous decocking levers pointy in the front. This was a definite annoyance when manually operating the slide "levers up," with the safety in firing position. On the 8000F, where those levers also function as a safety catch, simply moving the levers down into the "safe" position when operating the slide solved the problem. This kept the pointy tips of the levers down and away from the shooter's fingers and thumb.

I observed some malfunctions in early 9mm Cougars and began not to trust them, but the factory apparently got on top of that problem and tweaked the design, because in the last few years several 9mm Cougars have gone through courses I've taught, and didn't seem prone to stoppages.

Beretta quickly offered a "Mini-Cougar" which essentially was the same gun on top, with the butt shortened radically and magazine capacity proportionally reduced. In 1994, Congress had passed the Crime Bill, which for the following decade would make it illegal for private citizens in America to purchase pistol magazines that held more than 10 rounds. It offended Americans to have to buy a pistol with a 10-round magazine that should have held 15, which was the original design capacity of the Model 8000, identical to that of the Model 92. As a result, sales lagged. This was not because the 8000 was a bad gun, it was because of the psychological reaction to the way such guns had to be sold. The same was true of the Model 92's sales to the American public during the same 10-year period. Other manufacturers, including Smith & Wesson and SIGARMS, had like experiences with plunging commercial sales of their high-capacity 9mm service pistols.

This being the case, the Mini-Cougar seemed more desirable, and sold reasonably well in comparison to the service-size version of the Model 8000. Americans didn't mind going down to a lower cartridge capacity if they got value in return for it, and the value that the Mini-Cougar returned was distinctly improved concealability with its shorter butt.

The Cougar 9mm was accurate, though certainly no more so than the Model 92. The Cougar was touted as having passed 30,000-round torture tests, and winning NATO approval. In the 1990s, it passed the rugged battery of tests mandated by the NYPD, and was approved as an optional off-duty pistol for New York's Finest.

Cougar 8040 .40

In the United States, the .40 S&W cartridge had already eclipsed the 9mm in popularity among domestic police at the time of the Cougar's introduction. Thus, it was not surprising that police departments were more interested in the Model 8040 than in the smaller caliber Model 8000.

About 2000, I trained a police firearms instructor whose department had adopted the 8040D, in double-action-only "slick-slide" format. He was the top shot in his class, drawing swiftly from his department issue Safariland SS-III retention holster and hitting unerringly with the Gold Dot 180-grain ammo that, like his 8040D pistol, was department standard. He told me, "We've been really happy with these guns. No malfunctions, no breakage. The officers with smaller hands don't seem to have any problem with it. They're compact enough that several of us carry them off duty. Our issue gun for plainclothes detectives is the same 8040D that patrol division has, not the Mini-Cougar, and they conceal well enough under suit coats and windbreakers."

As a twelve-shot .40, the 8040 appealed to cops more than the 16-shot 9mm Model 8000. One department that powered up from the 9mm to the Model 8040, choosing the double-action-only "D" series, was the Utah Highway Patrol. The UHP explained the change in the following message on their website:

"Since 1986-87 the Department of Public Safety has utilized the Heckler & Koch (H&K) P7 (M8-M13) 9mm auto loading pistol as the issued duty handgun. Even though the H&K is an excellent weapon, it became apparent by 1996 that the P7 was no longer a viable weapon of choice for DPS. The price of a new

H&K with night sights and two magazines, increased from $425 in 1986 to over $1,100 in 1996. After a decade of use, many of the weapons needed routine maintenance; however, replacement parts were expensive and difficult to obtain.

"In the spring of 1995, the Utah Highway Patrol Training Section began an evaluation and testing program to look at other available weapons. Sergeant Jim Maguire coordinated this weapons evaluation and recommendation program. Thirteen weapons were obtained from various major manufacturers for testing and evaluation. Only auto-loading, 9mm and .40 caliber pistols were considered. Both double action only (DAO) and double/single action (DAS) versions were evaluated.

"On March 7, 1995, an evaluation shoot was held at the Salt Lake Airport Authority Range. Seventeen evaluators graded the weapons by completing an evaluation sheet immediately after firing each weapon. The evaluators consisted of members of the administration, training staff, firearms instructors, and department armorers. Each weapon was evaluated in 23 specific areas. Following tabulation of all evaluations, the top five weapons were identified for further testing and evaluation.

"During the following year, the UHP Training Section continued to evaluate and make recommendations regarding these weapons. In February 1996, DPS requested input from all sworn officers regarding the selection of the top weapon choice, the Beretta-8040D (DAO) in .40 caliber. This relatively new weapon, known as a Cougar, utilizes a rotating, locking barrel system. While a majority of the sworn officers supported this selection, a few disagreed. During the following month, those officers that disagreed with the choice were given an opportunity to test and evaluate the Beretta Cougar.

"The results of all testing and evaluation were presented to Commissioner Doug Bodrero on March 11, 1996. Following this meeting, the decision was made to move forward with the selection of the Beretta Cougar as the new issued sidearm of the Department of Public Safety. This extensive evaluation and selection process, involving all levels of the department, is indicative of the longstanding tradition of DPS to make responsible decisions and to provide the highest quality equipment to its troopers and agents."

There were also private citizens who felt that the .40 Cougar served their needs better than anything else. On a thread on www.packing.org, "andya" said, "I carry a Beretta Cougar 8040 and it's great. I have never had a problem with it, although it is a little larger than some. It is a little shorter than the 92, however, so is a little easier to conceal. I also own the 96 Brigadier Elite. I have also never had any trouble with that gun, and have shot well over 3,000 rounds … and it looks brand new."

Doug Berg speed-reloads his standard-size Beretta Cougar. The pistol is handled exactly as one would handle the larger, older model Beretta in the same 9mm or .40 caliber.

The rotary breech mechanism's tendency to soften recoil becomes more apparent as the shooter moves up from the 9mm Parabellum to the .40 Smith & Wesson round. Recoil is subjective: some find the Cougar to kick *dramatically* less than other .40 pistols of similar size and weight, and some perceive the difference to be less significant. But no credible observer with lots of experience shooting the various .40s finds the 8040's recoil objectionable.

This is also true of the Mini-Cougar version of the 8040 with shorter grip frame, which brings cartridge capacity down from the 11-plus-one it was originally designed for to a still-acceptable eight in the magazine plus one in the chamber. The gun proved appealing to John E. Jasen, who sent the following account to an Internet chat room: "The local public pistol range finally had some of the Beretta Cougar series to rent out, and so my SO (significant other) and I just had to spend a Sunday afternoon playing with them.

"First thing, both she and I are caliber-bigots, dismissing the 9mm as 'not enough fun.' The second thing is, they only had the Mini-Cougar in .40 S&W. Oh, well, close enough. We rented it, slapped in the magazine with the pinky rest, and prepared to party.

"Fit and finish is what we've come to expect on a Beretta – everything fit nicely, there was no looseness or too much 'rattle' to the piece, and there were no visible machine or tooling marks.

"Ergonomically, the piece is excellent – it fits deeply in both my SO's and my firing hand, is not too heavy, and the trigger is easily reachable. My only gripe is the location of the safety. Useability – the gun is *S*T*I*F*F* — the safety, the slide, the magazine release all scream 'factory fresh.' So much so, that my SO experienced a few problems racking the slide. Fireability – excellent. Something about the firearm, be it the size, shape, rotating lock-up, or magic, eats recoil. Compared to my standby, the Beretta 96, the Mini-Cougar 8040 had less felt recoil, and was just as easily controlled. My SO, who is fighting wrist problems, noticed this immediately, as she switched back and forth."

Using a student's 9mm Cougar 8000 the author fired this group offhand from 25 yards with inexpensive Sellier & Bellot full-metal-jacket training ammo. The sights needed to be adjusted slightly, but the pistol otherwise performed just fine.

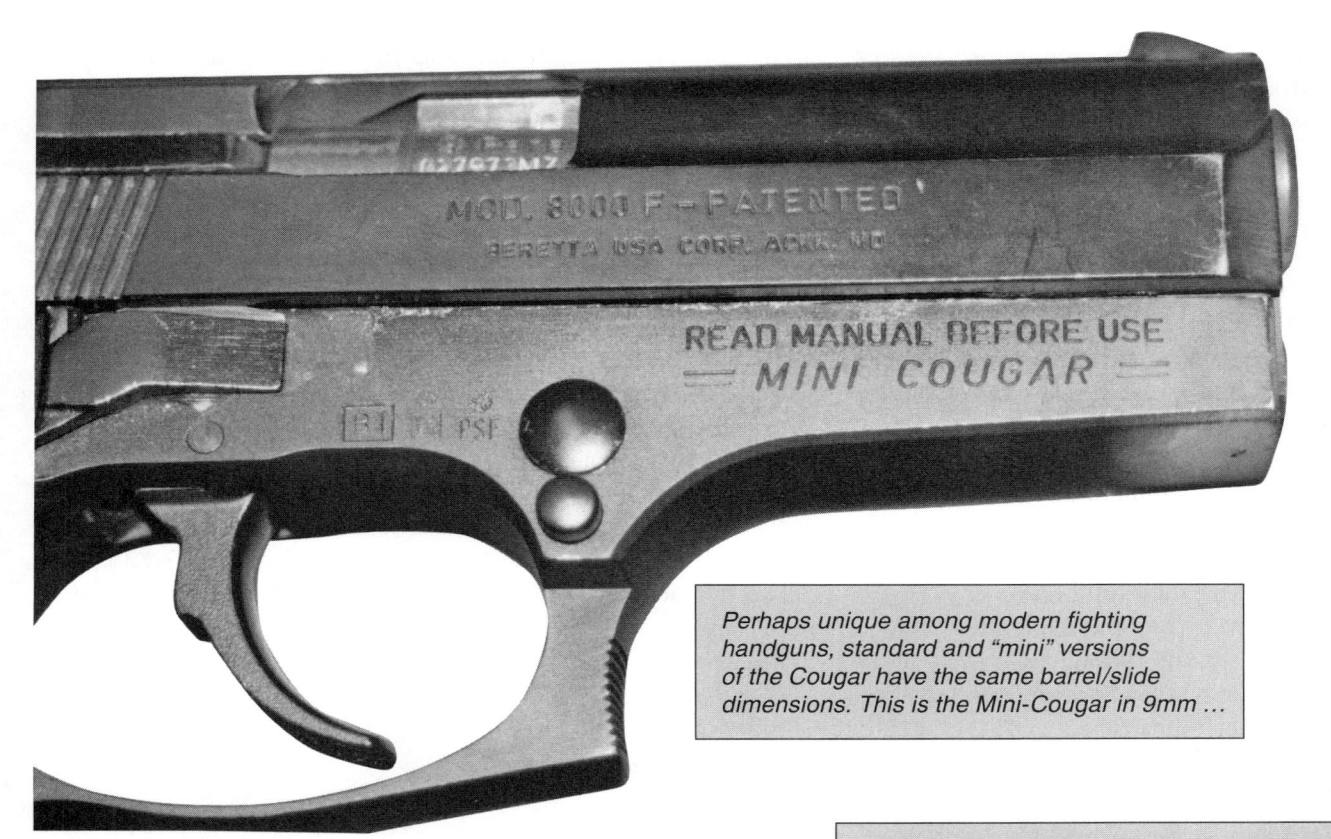

Perhaps unique among modern fighting handguns, standard and "mini" versions of the Cougar have the same barrel/slide dimensions. This is the Mini-Cougar in 9mm ...

... and this is the full-size Cougar in .40 S&W.

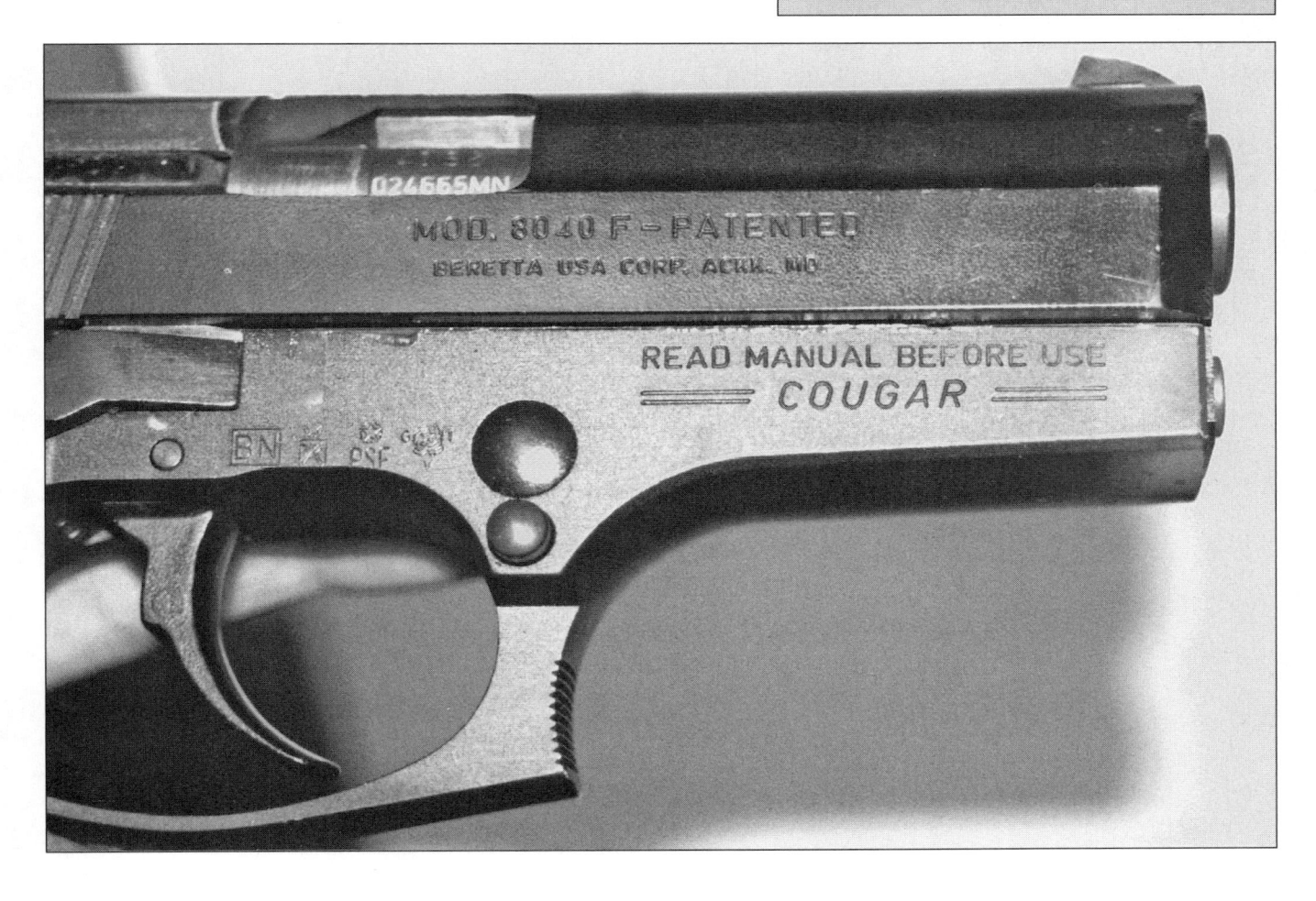

Personally, I haven't found the safety catch more troublesome on the Cougar than on the 92 or 96. Working the slide on the F or G series is made easier by cocking the hammer first, to alleviate the mainspring tension that, via the hammer, is helping to hold the slide forward. Mr. Jasen finished by saying, "I kinda like it, and would feel comfortable recommending something from the Cougar line-up to my friends. However, it did not especially excite me, especially since it has to contend with the opinions of a jealous Beretta 96. My SO will probably test it out a few more times, and is considering the purchase of one, as the reduction in felt recoil is a blessing on her wrists."

Jasen summed up the whole Cougar aura when he said, "it did not especially excite me." The gun has a "generic" look to it. It does not have the cachet of the 92 and the 96. It is a tool, not an icon. To a lot of shooters, the Beretta 92 is to handguns what a Lamborghini or an Alfa Romeo is to sports cars. The Beretta Cougar is seen as, well, kind of a Fiat. Good, functional, but nothing to make your blood sing, nothing to "amaze your friends and confound your enemies."

It has turned out to be a pretty good tool, too, and it was about to become a potentially better one. Mr. Jasen and his lady were not the only "caliber-bigots" out there. Many shooters and police departments still weren't convinced that the 9mm had enough oomph.

The .40 S&W in its original 180-grain subsonic load essentially duplicated the ballistics of the Old West's .38/40 round, which was never seen as equal in power to the legendary .45 Colt. And the .45 shooters of the world wanted *.45s*, dammit, and cops who had learned to trust the devastating power of the 125-grain Magnum hollow-point in their .357 service revolvers felt a bit cheated being issued the equivalent of a .38/40 when their department switched from wheelgun to autoloader.

Beretta, of course, knew this. It was time at last to come out with some powerful semiautomatic combat pistols. The company decided that if their most recent design could handle the .40 Smith & Wesson so well, it could handle a .357 SIG, and if they beefed it up by a couple of ounces, it could handle the larger .45 ACP cartridge.

The Cougar was about to become the first "big blaster" in the history of Beretta pistols.

Endnotes

(1) Wilson, R. L., "The World of Beretta: An International Legend," New York City: Random House, 2000, P. 207.

(2) Ibid.

(3) Beretta Catalog #470, 1997.

Beretta's Big Blasters:
The .357 and .45

One constant complaint that has been levied against the classic Beretta models is that they lack the power of the .45 ACP. That complaint began as soon as the M9, in the NATO 9mm chambering, replaced the 1911. Even in .40 S&W, there are those who feel that the power is just not enough. When that cartridge first came out, .45 fans derided it as the ".40 Short and Weak." Jeff Cooper, the "high priest" of the .45 and, many feel, the man directly responsible for the development of the powerful 10mm Auto cartridge, scoffs at the .40 as merely a "10mm Short."

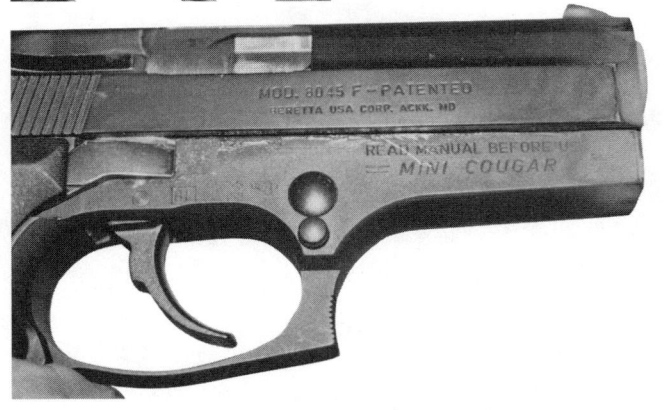

The full-power Cougar is available with handsome wooden stocks like these, with a Cougar logo.

The fact is, the .40 S&W was developed as a compromise between the 9mm and the .45, and there are those who simply do not compromise. They have faith in powerful cartridges like the .45 ACP and the .357 Magnum, and as much as they might appreciate Beretta quality and workmanship, they will go to other brands to get that power.

Seeing this, the Beretta decision-makers did what any businessman would do. They set about making more powerful pistols to capture this market. The results, both in the Cougar line, were the Beretta 8357 chambered for the .357 SIG, and the Beretta 8045 in caliber .45 ACP.

The Beretta .357 Auto

Not many people realize that Beretta, whose name is a byword for semiautomatic pistols, has also produced revolvers. In the late 20th Century, the firm developed a double-action .357 Magnum with integral recoil control ports in the barrel. It resembled a cross between a German Korth, a French Manhurin, and an American Ruger. Those who handled it said it was superb. I wouldn't know; I never got my hands on one.

Top: Like the smaller caliber Cougars, the .45 version is available in standard size, as shown, which will have the same barrel/slide length…
Above: …as the .45 Mini-Cougar, though the latter will have a much shorter grip frame.

These guns were never commercially imported into the United States.

Beretta does, after a fashion, manufacture a .357 Magnum revolver today. A few years ago, the company took over Uberti, one of Italy's leaders in that country's cottage industry of producing duplicates of American Frontier-style sixguns. If the Stampedes I've tested are any indication, Beretta has done a lot to improve Uberti's quality control. A fellow gun writer was at a seminar where some of the first of these guns were offered up for testing, and they failed miserably. The modern-style transfer bar on one specimen, he told me, fell out of the gun while they were shooting it. He told me that Beretta U.S.A.'s Cathy Williams, a professional's professional, left the range with tight lips and some angry words for the folks back in Italy.

They apparently listened to the dressing down she must have delivered. My own Stampede .357 Magnum is a thing of beauty. As noted in the chapter in this book on the Stampede, it shot remarkably well with the devastating 125-grain .357 Magnum load, with which it exhibited very mild recoil, and with an old batch of remanufactured .38 Special 148-grain wadcutter ammo, it delivered five shots into a 1-inch group at 25 yards.

However, Beretta is in the business of making defensive guns for an international market that includes law enforcement and the police service, and we all know that single-action revolvers like the Stampede had been rendered obsolete for both of those jobs by the dawn of the 20th century. No, those who wanted a more powerful Beretta handgun wanted a more powerful Beretta *automatic*.

One answer, of course, lay in the .357 SIG cartridge. Developed jointly between SIGARMS and Federal Cartridge in about 1993, it was intended to duplicate the ballistics of the round that outperformed all others as a manstopper in gunfights during the epoch of the police revolver, the .357 Magnum 125-grain semi-jacketed hollow-point.

Basically, the .357 SIG is a bottlenecked casing with a lower body so similar to that of the .40 S&W cartridge, that two otherwise identical pistols can be converted between the two calibers by simply changing the barrels.

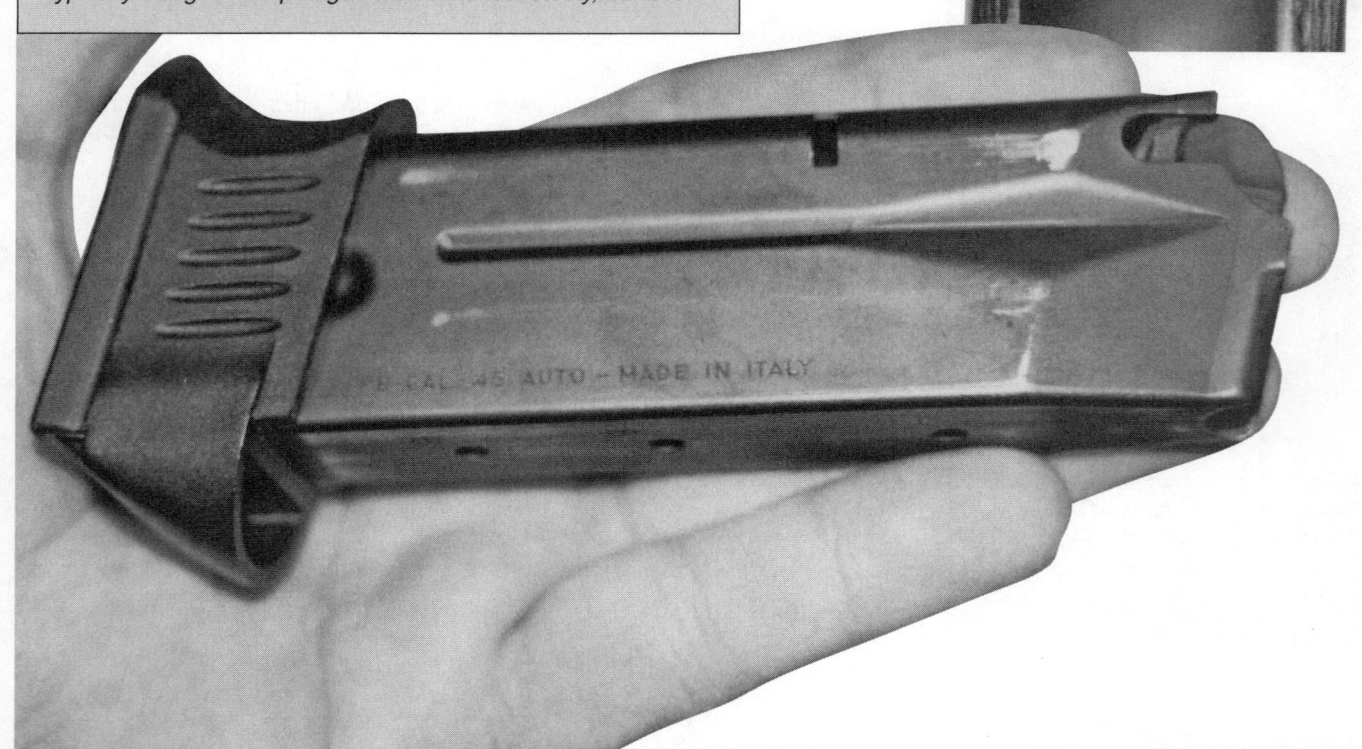

Below: As with the .40 and 9mm Cougar, if you get the 8045 .45 ACP in the "Mini" format, you can bring it up to standard size dimensions and cartridge capacity with this extension magazine available from Beretta.

Right: Cougar .45 and .357 SIG have the same big, generous sights as other modern Beretta service pistols. Note the "typically Cougar" sharp edges on the manual safety, however.

The same breechface, extractor, ejector, ejection port, slide, and recoil spring will work for either. The bullet is a 125-grain fully jacketed 9mm hollow-point, and solid-nose full-metal-jacket practice rounds are available.

The .357 Magnum was advertised as spitting its 125-grain bullet at 1,450 feet per second from the 4-inch barrel of a service revolver. Some production runs performed as advertised. Some came in a little lower, in the high 1,300 to low 1,400 feet per second range out of a standard service revolver. Velocity drops off quickly with this revolver round as the gun's barrel is progressively shortened. Going to a 3-inch barrel or a 2½-inch barrel could cost more than 100 feet per second of bullet speed. I chronographed the 125-grain Magnum out of a Colt Magnum Carry snub-nose revolver with a true 2-inch barrel, and the machine recorded only 1,220 feet per second on the average.

By contrast, the .357 SIG out of a 4-inch autoloader's barrel will generally come somewhere between 1,325 and 1,350 feet per second. Some lots of 125-grain .357 SIG ammo would go over 1,400 fps. Thus, the new auto cartridge was equaling or exceeding the performance of the old revolver cartridge in shorter barrel detective guns, and sometimes duplicating and in rare tests even exceeding the performance of 4-inch .357 Magnum service revolvers.

Since a great many bad guys had been shot with the 125-grain Magnum, and no police department had ever noticed a reduced effectiveness when they were shot with a detective's 2.5-inch or 3-inch revolver instead of a uniformed patrolman's 4-inch gun, this meant that the .357 SIG was indeed delivering the ballistics of the .357 Magnum, at least in the testing environment and on paper. However, part of the Magnum load's success had come about due to the early and violent disruption of its bullet in flesh. That bullet had been *semi*-jacketed, with a substantial amount of exposed, soft lead up front to aid the expansion process. We were not certain that the same performance would happen with a fully jacketed hollow-point, a design necessary for semiautomatic pistols because exposed soft lead could deform when it hit the feet ramp and jam the autoloader.

The answers were not long in coming. The Delaware State Police, fed up with the poor performance in the field of their 147-grain subsonic 9mm ammo, became the first large police department

> *A minor downside is that the 8045's magazine is relatively fat for the eight rounds of .45 ACP it holds. Three .45 Auto magazines, from left: Wilson-Rogers mag for 1911, Beretta 8045 mag, and SIG P220 mag.*

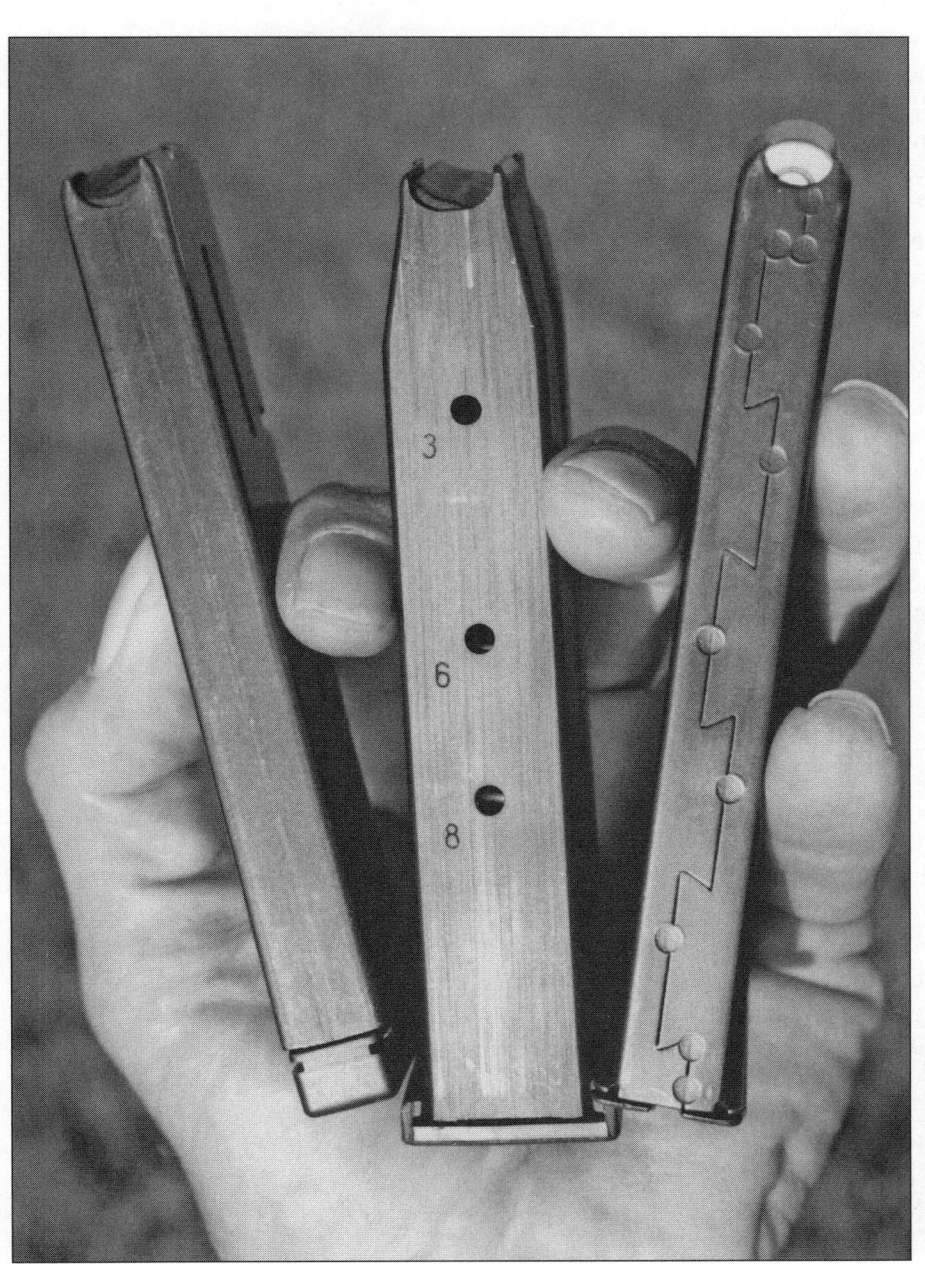

The large-frame Cougar fits well in the hand, and gives good trigger reach.

to adopt the .357 SIG. They reported complete satisfaction. Almost immediately, they were followed by two larger state police agencies, those of Virginia and Texas.

In those states, particularly Texas, greater population equaled more crime, and more crime equaled more gunfights involving lawmen. Virginia, like Delaware, had gone with the .357 SIG to replace the 147-grain subsonic 9mm, which they had found to perform poorly on humans and vicious dogs alike, each often requiring altogether too many shots to get the job done. After the .357 SIGs had been in the field for a while, Virginia troopers told me they were delighted with the performance of the 125-grain Gold Dot. The one-shot stop on charging pit bulls had now become the rule rather than the exception. Perhaps most impressive, they told me, was the number of violent men who had gone down when hit with a single .357 SIG Gold Dot in a non-vital part of their anatomy.

Texas had even more shootings than Virginia. Their DPS (Department of Public Safety) had been issuing .45 autos with ammo that ranged from 185-grain hollow-points at 1,000 feet per second to 230-grain high-tech JHP at velocity approaching 900 fps. They had been satisfied with the .45 ACP's performance, but old hands on the force said they missed what some described as the "lightning bolt" drops that had been documented with felons shot with the 125-grain Magnum rounds the department had carried during their revolver days. With the .357 SIG in the field – this department also using the 125-grain Gold Dot – bad guys again began "dropping as if hit by lightning bolts." The Texas DPS continues to be extremely pleased with the performance of this caliber and ammunition.

Quietly observing all this was the North Carolina Highway Patrol. NCHP is not by any means the largest state police agency in the United States, but it is one of the most advanced in terms of research. In 1983, concurrent with the Connecticut State Police, NCHP had become one of the first major departments in the nation to adopt a high-capacity 9mm auto, the Beretta 92F. From the beginning, they carried these guns "on safe," rigorously teaching recruits and in-service troopers to disengage the safety reflexively as they brought it on target. They never had an officer fail to do so and get hurt when he needed to respond with gunfire, but they documented many lives saved when someone got the gun away from the trooper and tried to murder him or others with it.

They had good luck with their 115-grain JHP 9mm ammo, and found it to be an adequate manstopper. However, their monitoring of the collective police experience elsewhere in the country showed them that not every department could say the same thing. "We didn't want to wait for a horror story," one rangemaster there told me. "We went to the .40 proactively."

Having been delighted with the performance of the 92F, the NCHP adopted its twin in .40 caliber, the Model 96F Beretta. Pistols fit the same holsters, and magazines fit the same pouches. The slight increase in recoil did not bother the troopers. They continued to make on-safe carry a requirement, and the on-safe Berettas continued to save lives. NCHP range officials told me they were delighted with the performance of the 96F pistols. When their troopers needed to shoot violent criminals and vicious animals, the .40 S&W round got the job done expeditiously.

But, the North Carolina Highway Patrol still had its feelers out. A few incidents occurred around the country where bad guys were shot with .40 S&W and did not go down. Once again, seeing a potential trend developing that might one day endanger one of their troopers' lives, the NCHP experts reached out to other state police agencies that had adopted the .357 SIG and gathered field experience with it. They liked what they learned.

NCHP had been extremely happy for nearly 20 years with the service they had gotten from the Beretta factory in maintaining their many guns, and they and the individual troopers had been enormously satisfied by the quality and reliability of their Beretta pistols the entire time. They wanted the new cartridge, but they wanted to stay with Beretta.

Et voila: in a most timely manner, the Beretta Cougar Model 8357 presented itself. Offering the same magazine capacity as a .40 Cougar, the F-series offered the same life-saving manual safety that had kept so many troopers from being killed with their own guns when criminals had gained control of their Beretta 92F and 96F pistols.

The North Carolina Highway Patrol became the first police department in the nation to adopt the Beretta Cougar 8357F pistol. They carry it to this day. They report that they are extremely satisfied with their choice. The guns are still carried on-safe by department mandate, and this policy has still worked out to have 100 percent positive results. At various times, I understand, they have issued 125-grain Gold Dot and 125-grain Winchester Ranger as duty ammunition, and had good luck with both. A few months ago, I asked a North Carolina state trooper what kind of ammo he was carrying, and in answer he presented from his ammo pouch a magazine of 125-grain Gold Dot.

I've shot this pistol, and been very pleased with it. The bottleneck case design makes the .357 SIG cartridge feed very smoothly, its taper guiding the round into the firing chamber. The gun I shot exhibited 100 percent reliability as I recall, which is pretty much what the NCHP experienced in transitioning their entire armed force to the 8357F. It was also very accurate. The .357 SIG has been an inherently accurate cartridge since its inception, and the 8357 in that caliber may well be the most consistently accurate of all Beretta Cougars. I consistently got five-shot 25-yard groups in the 2-inch range.

The .357 SIG is a success story. Early problems with the cartridge involving case neck separation seem to have been pretty well worked out. If you want a double-action police-type service pistol in this caliber, there are several choices. However, if you want one with the added "handgun retention insurance" of a manual safety, there is only one: the Beretta Cougar 8357.

It is simply an excellent pistol.

That said, though, there are still many for whom the long-established history of the .45 caliber as a fighting handgun makes it the defensive sidearm of choice, the only one they're really psychologically comfortable and secure with.

The Beretta .45 Automatic

On the military side, there is no military force in the world that uses the .357 SIG, but the .45 ACP was documented as the most effective military ball handgun cartridge of the 20th century, and nothing has changed about that in the 21st. Even with jacketed hollow-point ammunition, cold weather brings out heavy clothing that can plug the bullet's hollow cavity

While the large-frame Cougar may have a relatively fat magazine, its taper toward the top and the gun's proportionally wide magazine well make reloading a snap.

and cause it to fail to expand. When duty may include arctic conditions and thickly clad opposing personnel, the .45 comes into its own. The decades have proven that even if it doesn't expand, its big bullet still tends to neutralize opponents with solid hits.

Which brings us to the long-awaited Beretta .45 automatic, the Cougar 8045. The one I have now is an excellent pistol. It has jammed but once, a feed stoppage with a low-powered target round. This particular gun is an F-series, and I carry it on-safe, finding it very quick to disengage the safety when I draw the pistol. As with the F-series Beretta 92, the safety lever is spring-loaded, and the easiest of its kind to manipulate under stress or other adverse conditions.

I wrote the following article for a gun magazine when the 8045 came out. Note that the test gun was a "D" series, double-action-only, with "slick slide." I mentioned that while it had sharp edges, none were in a place to bite the hands. That is not true of the 8045F model that sits beside my keyboard as I write this. As with other Cougar models, its ambidextrous safety/decock lever comes to a point at the front. This can dig painfully into the operating hand when the slide is jacked while the levers are straight forward, in the "fire" position. This problem is solved by simply lowering the lever to the "on safe" position, "pointing the points" downward and out of the way of most hands during manual slide operation.

Beretta's .45 In Action

I like Beretta pistols. I like .45s. A lot of people who liked .45s didn't like Berettas because they only came in smaller calibers.

That's over now.

Long promised – hell, it was hinted at when Beretta first introduced the Cougar series in calibers 9X19 and .40 S&W – the Beretta .45 is now a reality. Not just for gun writers and regular visitors of the SHOT Show, but for people who buy guns in gun shops. It carries eight fat sluggers in its staggered magazine and a ninth in its rotary breech. Its shape is streamlined and its lightweight aluminum alloy frame gives it portability that makes it weight-efficient for the .45 ACP power it puts out. It's worth the weight and it's worth the wait.

In The Hand

This biggest of Beretta Cougars, the Model 8045, feels good in the hand. The company engineers spent a lot of time on the ergonomics. The back of the frame is kind of "hogged out" to bring the web of the hand more forward and thus allow more of the index finger to reach the trigger. They listened to all the short-fingered folks who complained about the long trigger reach on the classic 92/96 series Beretta service pistols.

I would describe it as semi-compact. The barrel

Firing at the second target in from the left, Ayoob lets go a .45 ball round from 8045F. The spent casing is visible airborne at 1 o'clock to the gun muzzle, but the Beretta is already back on target. The rotary breech mechanism really does soften recoil.

is 3⅝ inches long from the face of the rotary breech to the muzzle, and the squarish slide is proportional. The grip frame is full length, however. This gives a good hold but requires a little more attention to concealment.

The slide is radiused in part on the front and swept back at the rear, which on the spurless hammer double-action-only version may cause problems interfacing with some safety straps. The angle is steep enough, and the back surface of the hammer/slide area smooth enough, that the gun could slip out from under all but the most perfectly sized strap.

There are some sharp edges. I found them at the front of the muzzle, and on the edges of the slide along its length, where I would expect the finish to quickly wear with a lot of drawing and holstering. However, in manipulating the gun, and shooting it, and putting it through considerable administrative- and combat-type handling, I found there were no sharp surfaces anyplace that bothered my hands.

I found the magazines easy to load by hand all the way to full capacity. Release was smooth, positive, and easy. The magazines went into the gun swiftly, thanks to the tapered feed lips of the double-stack design. Funneling the mag well would be a redundancy. The magazines were just a little bit snug in leather pouches made for Beretta 92 mags, and wouldn't fit at all in the Kydex ones.

I have those "average size adult male hands" you read about in gun magazines. I found I could get a good grip on this gun and a good purchase on the trigger, but I would have liked to get a little bit more finger on the trigger. However, I make contact with the trigger using the distal joint. If you prefer to shoot with the pad of the finger on the trigger and have the same size hand, the 8045 should be perfect for you.

NCHP carries these guns on safe and reports multiple lives saved in the field during struggles for the troopers' guns.

The slide release is easy to reach. Perhaps too easy. As with earlier Beretta service guns, it extends well back to the point where if you shoot with a high thumb position like Jeff Cooper or a straight thumb grasp like most IPSC shooters, your dominant thumb will ride the slide stop and prevent it from locking the slide open when the pistol runs dry.

Like other Beretta duty guns, it is available in three configurations. The "F" series has the conventional slide-mounted safety/decock lever, and goes into single-action mode after the first double-action shot. As with the 92/96 pistols, this lever is lightly spring-loaded and is among the easiest of its kind to flick "off safe."

The "G" series is also double-action for the first shot and self-cocking for follow-up rounds, but the decocker lever is spring-loaded and dedicated to that purpose. It

The most powerful Cougars handle quickly. Caught by the camera in mid-draw from a Bianchi Accumold duty rig, Ayoob's big-frame type F Cougar is already off safe.

All the Cougars inherited ambi safety/decock lever, and niched-out grip panel to facilitate reaching it, from the 92F.

cannot be put "on safe." Of course, all these guns have integral firing pin blocks and are totally safe against accidental discharge from dropping or other impact, according to the factory.

Finally, the "D" series is double-action for every shot, and comes in "slick-slide" configuration with no slide-mounted levers at all. This is increasingly popular with police departments who buy into the KISS principle and like the simplicity of "insert magazine, jack slide, and then shoot like a double-action revolver." The inability for the gun to be cocked to a "hair trigger" single-action mode (and the inability of a shark with a bar association card to allege that it had happened even when it didn't) makes DAO appeal greatly to police chiefs and the legal advisors of law enforcement agencies.

Which to choose? I'm personally partial to the "F" style Berettas carried on safe, because I've seen so many cases where a criminal got an on-safe auto from a good guy, tried to shoot him, and couldn't do so before the good guy, or his back-up, rectified the situation. However, if I was going to carry off safe for immediate draw-and-fire capability but still wanted double-action-only on the first shot, I would unhesitatingly recommend the "G" series. The reason is that the safety can't accidentally be engaged rendering the gun inoperable for the moment in the hand of a good guy or gal who isn't familiar with popping off the safety catch. I have also seen more than one person who shot the DAO (double-action-only) model *better* because of the uniformity of pull from first to second shot, and because of the "surprise break" inherent in the rolling pull of a long double-action trigger.

You pays your money and you takes your choice. Beretta, like Burger King, lets you "have it your way." My test sample was a DAO Model 8045 D.

On The Bench ...

I tested for accuracy with half a dozen popular .45 ACP loads from a bench-rested, hand-held position at 25 yards. A peculiarity of the gun immediately became apparent: it shot fine with some loads and all over the place with a couple of others.

Winchester's quick-expanding, low penetration 185-grain Silvertip is extremely accurate in most .45s. Not this one. The same was true of Pro-Load's match-grade 230-grain ball round. Both boxes of ammo were from lots that had previously proven extremely accurate in other guns. The Silvertip ran 6 inches for a five-shot group, the Pro-Load, almost 5 inches with even the best three shots a full 3 ½ inches apart. The gun liked the four other rounds better. Go figure.

Manufacturer	Load Type	5 Shot Group	Best 3 Shots
CCI Blazer	200-grain JHP	4 1/16"	1 9/16"
Black Hills	230-grain Gold Dot	2 1/2"	1 7/8"
Federal Classic	185-grain JHP	3 1/2"	1 13/16"
Federal	230-grain Hydra-Shok	2 1/2"	1 3/16"

Using the barricade for support enhances accuracy, but also enhances recoil. As light as the 8357 and 8045 kick for their calibers, it's no problem with them.

It should be remembered that this was hand-held shooting with the gun braced on a bench, not a sandbag. It replicates shooting over the hood of an automobile at the same 25-yard distance. Experience has taught me that the best three shots will generally equal a five-shot group from a Ransom machine rest if there are no called flyers. The three-shot group gives me an idea of the pistol's inherent mechanical accuracy, and the five-shot group gives me a predictor of what I can do in the field from that position if I keep my cool.

Bear in mind also that all these shots were fired double-action-only. I find that with a top-quality double-action revolver, I do the same or better double-action as I do single-action. With a double-action auto, however, the linkage is rarely as smooth as on the best sixguns and I'll generally shoot a bit tighter in single-action mode. This gun almost certainly has more inherent mechanical accuracy than I could wring out of it.

The double action pull on this pistol runs around 9 or 10 pounds in pull weight. There is a very slight "stack," or increase in resistance toward the end of the pull. I find the older 92/96 DAO Berettas to be a little smoother, lighter, and more uniform in trigger pull.

With the loads it liked, the big-bore Beretta was giving me the same good accuracy I have come to expect from the brand in the smaller calibers. One other idiosyncrasy was noted. Usually, bullets of the same weight and velocity by different makers will shoot to the same point of aim/point of impact. With this gun, it wasn't so. Consider the two most accurate loads: 230-grain Hydra-Shok shot a little high and needed a six o'clock hold for center hits, but 230-grain Black Hills with the Gold Dot bullet shot dead center with the center hold. Go figure.

But, in any case, you test "pure" accuracy off the bench, and you test "practical accuracy" on your legs in combat simulation.

... And On The Qualification Range

I shot the 8045D on two qualification courses on a near-freezing (mid-30s Fahrenheit) day at the outdoor range. The first run was a state-approved course for off-duty and backup guns comprising 60 rounds fired strong-hand-only, weak-hand-only, and two-handed from exposed shooting positions, while kneeling and in other positions replicating cover. Distances ranged from 4 to 15 yards.

I used a potpourri of ammunition. The score was 300 out of 300 on the tough IPSC Brussels target. The farthest hits were with the rounds the gun liked least, the accurate-in-most-everything-else Silvertip and Pro-Load. Still, all 60 bullet holes were within 5 inches center-to-center.

I noticed that the recoil was very controllable. I had just come off two weeks of training during which I'd fired over 1,000 rounds through a Beretta 92F and had become accustomed to mild 9mm kick, but this .45 gave me no sense of a harder-kicking gun. There was no discomfort and it snapped right back on target. There may be something to the claim that the rotary breech mechanism reduces recoil.

Next up was the NRA's Police Service Automatic course, comprising 48 rounds at distances from 3 yards to 25. Again, I used a mix of ammo. The target was the B-27. In qualification mode ("8" ring and in counts for five out of five possible points, "7" ring is four points, and a shot anywhere in the black, from earlobe to cuff link, is three points) this may be the most forgiving of all police targets. However, if you go with it in competition mode ("10" ring measuring 4 by 6 inches, and anything outside the "7" ring considered a miss) it becomes singularly unforgiving. I kept track of the hits stage by stage.

3 yards: Draw and fire six shots, strong-hand-only, eight seconds. The DAO Beretta put all six Pro-Load ball rounds well inside the tie-breaking center X ring within the "10" ring. The B-27's "X" measures 2 by 3 inches, and this group was half of that. Nine feet is easier than 75 feet.

7 yards: Draw, fire six, reload from slide-lock, fire six more, two-hand standing, 20 seconds. One mag of Silvertip and one of Blazer went home nicely, 11 Xs and one "10" ring. The single shot outside the X-ring

The Cougar is equipped with an ambidextrous safety that is well placed and easy to operate.

was me; not the gun or the ammo.

15 yards: Same drill as at 7. I got frisky on the trigger and pulled a shot into the "9" ring. Everything else was in the "10" and "X" zone. Both mags were Federal 185-grain hollow-points.

25 yards: Draw and fire six shots kneeling, six standing left-hand barricade (left hand firing the gun), and six standing right-hand barricade (right hand firing gun) in 90 seconds. After my first four shots from kneeling, I glanced downrange to assess the group and was horrified to see all four Black Hills rounds clustered in the "9" ring. I had been thinking "Hydra-Shok" and holding the wrong elevation. I corrected and held center for the left-hand barricade, forgetting that this magazine was Hydra-Shok that shot higher out of this gun. Whine. Whimper. By the time I was done, the 25-yard stage had cost me eight points.

In qualification mode, of course, it was an easy "240 out of 240" for 100 percent. In competition scoring, however, it was a 471 out of 480 possible with only some 30 of the 48 shots in the tie-breaking center X ring, a 98 percent delivery.

I thought the gun did great. This is because: 1) Its pilot was an aging writer with weakening eyes, not a national champion. 2) The score that won that event this year at the national championships was only eight points higher. 3) The score was fired with different loads that shot to different points of aim, and 4) It was the shooter's first time through the course with it.

This gun had shown me that with four of the six loads I had tried in it, it had the inherent accuracy to shoot a perfect 480 out of 480 in more competent hands than mine.

In short, I was pleased with its ergonomics under pressure *and* its inherent accuracy potential. Bottom line: the Beretta Model 8045 *shoots,* even in its "toughest to shoot well" incarnation as the double-action-only Model 8045 D.

Reliability

In terms of reliability, the new .45 Beretta has big shoes to fill, those of its famous older brother, the 9mm Beretta 92. The performance of that gun in military torture tests has been extraordinary,

Right: Cougar shootability, big-bore style. Ayoob has just completed a 60-round 4- to 15-yard close combat qualification with 8045 and full-power ammo. Score is 300 out of 300 with all 60 holes in approximately a 5-inch group.

Above: This group is 12 shots in 20 seconds including draw and reload, from 7 yards with a Cougar .45.

exceeding that of the legendary 1911 pistol in terms of reliability. We hear the same from police departments using that gun.

I put several hundred rounds of ammo through the test .45, including the CCI "flying ashtray" 200-grain hollow-points. There were no malfunctions of any kind. This included one magazine that was new out of the box without the oil wiped off it, which was dropped in the dirt and immediately clotted with fine grains of sand. The 8045 chewed up the dirt and spat it out, along with the bullets it sent downrange.

A Few Words About The Sights

Beretta service pistols come with big, blocky sights. My aging eyeballs and I love them. Before 1986, I used to practice now and then shooting with uncorrected vision. Then came the tragic sacrifice of FBI Special Agent Ben Grogan in the notorious Miami gun battle. A superb marksman and officer survival practitioner, Grogan was severely myopic and lost his eyeglasses in an automobile collision that preceded the shootout. He fired his 9mm S&W blindly and failed to hit. He was heard to say, "Where is everybody," before his killer crept up on him and shot him down. I tried to learn from his sacrifice, and ever since, I've shot one match a year and one qualification a year with plain shooting glasses and no correction for my own myopic dominant eye.

Not until 1998 did I shoot a clean 300 on the tough IPSC target that way. The pistol was a Beretta 92D, and I owe the score in large part to those humongous Beretta sights.

The same were on the 8045 D they sent me. I had requested night sights. There was also a matter of a deadline, and I asked them to rush the gun.

I shouldn't have done that.

Being a slow learner in his second half century on this planet, I have finally learned certain basic truths. Right up there with "Don't eat the yellow snow" should be the caveat, "Don't rush the people who are putting your gun together for you."

Taking the gun out of the box, I noted it had a Trijicon module only on the front. Hey, that was cool.

Some officer survival instructors, like Jim Horan, *recommend* that you have just the one insert up front. It's cheaper, so you can afford to get it on your gun sooner, and besides it's a little faster in close than lining up the three dots, though I find that with any serious distance, I personally want a glowing rear sight to index it with.

The rear sight was also marked "Trijicon," but looking down the top of the slide I could see only two blind little sockets facing me. It took me a while to realize what had happened.

The rear sight had been installed backwards. Two perfectly functional night sight modules were now looking away from me and facing my target.

When I stopped laughing, it occurred to me that even though the opponent would see the rear night sights and the defender wouldn't, it would be survivable on this end. I pictured a crackhead who forced someone to shoot him with such a gun and surviving, testifying from his wheelchair: "It was weird, Dude! I thought I was in control, and then I saw these little green snake eyes lookin' at me out of the dark, and then there was this orange flash…"

That sort of error is highly unusual for Beretta. I really think it's my fault for rushing the order.

That said, the sights as installed shot true. It's tough to tell you how pleasing that was. In the past year I've almost lost count of the high-priced guns with fixed sights that didn't shoot where they looked because the factory hadn't bothered to sight them in. With every load it shot, this pistol centered its group for windage and once I knew whether the particular load went high or low, I was able to put the sights either center or six o'clock and deliver the shot "spot on." I should have wept for gratitude.

Bottom Line

If my Beretta .45 automatic is any indication, yours will be utterly reliable, easy to shoot fast and reload fast, and will shoot pretty much where it looks. It will be accurate with loads it likes, and you'll have fun finding out which those are.

The .45 Beretta really *was* worth the wait.

The Beretta 9000

By the dawn of the 21st century, the Glock pistol had become overwhelmingly the most popular police handgun in the United States. Its polymer-frame construction made it cheap to manufacture, light to carry, yet strong enough for constant training fire. It had excellent pointing characteristics and ergonomics. Some 70 percent of new police purchases of handguns were said to be Glocks.

Now perhaps third place in the police sales race, and far behind the leader, Beretta knew that it needed to come up with a new police handgun. In a classic example of "If you can't beat 'em, join 'em," the oldest of the world's gun makers at last departed from its tried and true formula of blue steel and walnut and introduced its first polymer-frame handgun in 2001. It was dubbed the Model 9000.

The Beretta 9000: sleek and racy to look at, its problems don't show up until you go to shoot it.

Do The Math!

Beretta offers three models that chamber the .40 round. However, that understates the real breadth of what's offered, which doesn't become apparent until we realize that barrel length and firing system options widen the Beretta .40 field considerably.

First came the Model 96, essentially the famous and well-proven Beretta 92, but in caliber .40 S&W. Next came the 8000 series, which the company dubbed the Cougar. In 2000, Beretta introduced a third platform, the modernistic Model 9000 with a polymer frame. I've had the opportunity to shoot all three.

But, as noted, the choices don't end there. The 9000 at this time comes only in one size: compact. The standard 8040 Cougar is best described as "compact/service size," and is also available in a much smaller version, the "Mini-Cougar." The 96 is available in full size (4.9-inch barrel) and as the shorter Centurion with a 4.3-inch tube. Counting the different sizes, that's five separate .40 models in the Beretta line. But, there's more: the full-size 96 is also available in Brigadier format with a beefier slide. The 96 can also be had in stainless. That's seven.

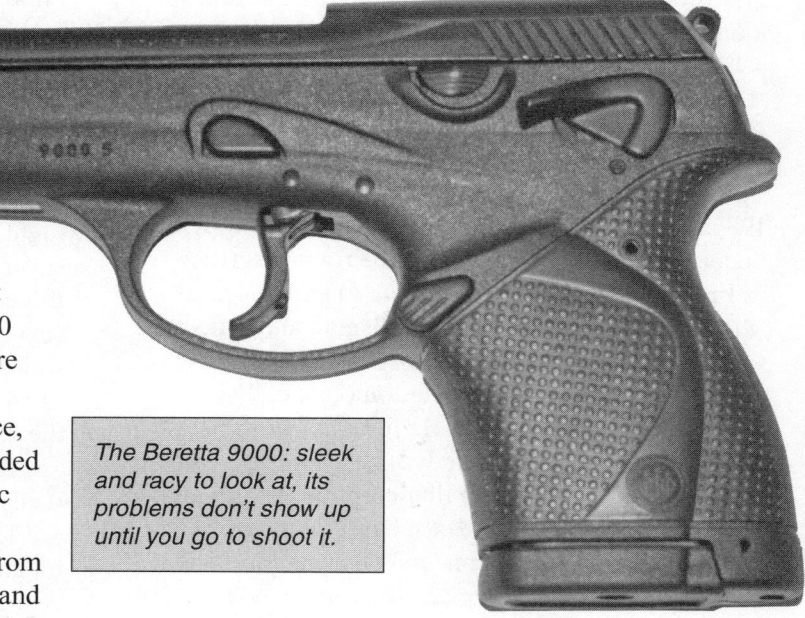

Times Three

However, each of these models is available in a choice of three fire control systems. The conventional double-action first shot style, self-cocking thereafter, with a combination safety/decocking lever is the "F" style. This is what the Army uses in their Beretta M9 9mm. The same system but with a spring-loaded slide lever that decocks only and is always in the "fire" position is the "G" style. The double-action-only — called the "slick-slide" by Beretta insiders because it needs no levers of any kind on the slide — is known as the "D" style.

We now have a *smorgasbord* of 21 .40 caliber Berettas from which to select.

Let's look at the fire control systems first. The "F" is the oldest and most proven of Beretta's systems. On-safe carry gives you a weapon retention fallback. If the bad guy gets your gun, he has to find the safety catch before he can shoot you. Being lightly spring-loaded, it's among the quickest to release. If you have

Trigger reach on the 9000 in double-action is all but impossibly long. Here, the index finger of an average adult male hand can barely reach to the whorl of the fingerprint. Note also the very narrow slide manipulation area offered by the design. DA trigger pull was heavy and creepy.

long enough a thumb, a downward swipe like wiping off a 1911's safety will activate it.

If you don't like the idea of the pistol being locked on safe, the "G" model is your best bet. This is because the safety can't accidentally get engaged when you're not expecting it to, which could slow down an emergency reaction draw and shot. The gun will still be self-cocking with the easy trigger pull for every shot after the first until you hit the decocking lever. Because of the heavier decock lever spring in the "G" model, this action will require a little more thumb effort than with the "F."

In addition to the sleek, uncluttered look from which it derives its nickname, the slick-slide "D" style appeals to police chiefs because of the long, fairly heavy double-action pull for every shot. Actually, because of its slightly different mechanism, this DA trigger stroke is a little lighter than the first DA pull on the "F" and "G" variants.

The theory is that DAO will eliminate accidental discharges traceable to those who forget to decock their guns under stress, and holster them or run around with them while the hammer is cocked

… Newest

When I was a kid, the futurists said that by the dawn of the 21st century, we'd be riding cars on cushions of air, we might have mass transit space travel, and handguns would look like the Beretta 9000. So far, all we've got to show for it is the Beretta 9000.

Rendered with a polymer frame, the pistol weighs only 26.8 ounces with its 3.4-inch barrel, and measures only 6.6 inches overall. A softer polymer comprises most of the gripping surface of the frame. The safety/decocker ("F") and decocker ("G") are mounted on the frame instead of the slide. This design has returned to Beretta's signature open slide.

What this sleek little pistol has going for it is those wonderfully big sights, and the Beretta name, and …well … based on the one sample I've shot, that's about it.

The trigger is unbelievably far from the backstrap, worse for small hands than the biggest Model 92 or 96 that ever left a Beretta plant. When grasping the pistol properly (barrel in line with the long bones of the forearm) I can just get the whorl of my fingerprint onto the trigger. This means that a petite female with proportional hands will barely be able to **touch** the trigger, much less exert enough leverage to make a fast, controlled shot, unless she curls her hand so far around the gun that recoil control will be severely impaired.

The one I tested was double-action-only. No "G" models were available, and the "F" had been recalled. It seems that a batch of the investment-cast safety/decock levers had made it through inspection with detents that weren't deep enough. When the pistol was brushed, bumped, or just set down, the lever would slip from "safe" to "fire." Of course, the gun was still "drop safe" in the sense that it wouldn't fire from impact, and contrary to rumor the levers weren't falling off of the guns, but Beretta did the right thing and issued a recall.

Gabriele de Plano tells me that the factory spec for double-action pull weight on a 9000 is eight to 12 pounds. Mine is on the high side of that at best, and probably over the top. With the poor leverage afforded by the ridiculously long trigger reach, it feels like about an 18-pound pull. And it's a *lo-o-ong* pull, about seven-eighths of an inch.

Manipulation of the pistol proved extremely awkward. Perhaps in the name of racy looks, the slide is so narrow top to bottom at the grasping point that there's only about three-eighths of an inch of serrated steel to hang onto. This made racking the slide extremely difficult, no matter what the size, shape, or strength of the users' hands.

The slide's polish wasn't what I'm used to seeing from Beretta, inside or outside. The roughness was visible. The front sight sat up out of its dovetail notch with lots of light between it and the slide. That sight is shaped like a shark's fin, but on a shark the fin is attached all the way from front to back. Seen in silhouette, this front sight looked more like a sailboat sail on a mast. Beretta has gone to great and laudable lengths to cultivate pride of ownership among its customers. The newest .40 simply doesn't make the cut on subtleties of workmanship. I've never had to say that about a Beretta before.

Accuracy was not at all up to what I expect from a Beretta. Despite the heavy trigger, the sights were dead on target each time the shot broke (I just brought the trigger back more slowly). Five out of six loads I tested with ran from 5 inches to more than 7 inches for five-shot groups at 25 yards. The best I could do was one 2.9-inch group with Winchester's 180-grain police-only load, the Ranger Talon.

Was it just me? I went back the next day and tried again, and had some friends of known high skill shoot with me. Same dismal results. This time I had brought along my 96D Centurion. It gave me a 2.1-inch group. I tried each over a combat course, using tactical instead of speed reloads with the 10-round mags since only two came with the 9000, and some 15-shot stages required two mandatory reloads.

At ranges of 4 to 15 yards, all under time, the 9000 was tough to shoot well. "Trigger finger fatigue" took its toll. At 15 yards I honked two shots high left, costing me three points and leaving me with a 247 out of 250 possible points on the IPSC target, or 98.8 percent. I then shot the same course with the 96D and the same American Eagle 180-grain subsonic .40 ammo, and got a perfect 250. I checked the record later and the last such course I'd shot with a Cougar had also delivered a 100 percent score.

This doesn't mean the 9000 was only 1.2 percent below the Cougar and the 96D. The group with the 4.3-inch Beretta 96 measured 3⅜ inches center to center, with 40 of the 50 bullets going through one ragged hole. The record showed that the Cougar had delivered about a 5-inch group. By contrast, the shot spread with the 9000 was *8¹/₁₆* inches, and the 47 out of 50 shots that were in the center "A" zone were more of a pattern than a group. They measured 7⅛ inches.

By that standard, the old Beretta .40 "shot more than twice as good" as the new one.

Finally, and most unforgivably, my test 9000 jammed. Every stoppage was a 12 o'clock misfeed. It was the last thing I expected with a tilting-barrel design so radical that it's patented. I was getting about one jam to every 60 or so shots, and they did not clear easily. I had to rip the magazine out of the gun, allowing the choked round to fall, then reload and continue. By contrast, in the several years I've owned my 96D, carried it, and lent it out to students, I can recall but one stoppage. It was a failure to go into battery (i.e., a failure to completely close the slide) on a 180-grain Winchester hollow-point. I began to do a tap-rack, but as soon as I slapped the butt the round chambered fully, so I just kept shooting.

My sample Beretta 9000 11-shot .40 is almost exactly the same height, length, and thickness of my

To press the operating lever upward sufficiently to decock a cocked 9000, one must reach completely out of a firing hold, as demonstrated here.

Glock 30 11-shot .45. The Glock is a tenth of an inch longer, actually lighter, and much more accurate and reliable, and easier to operate, to boot. A reason to buy a Beretta 9000 has not yet become clear to me.

What went wrong with the newest Beretta? Gabriele de Plano thinks I got a lemon, and assures me I got a lemon. I hope he's right, but if he's wrong, the problem could be that our oldest firearms manufacturer went into the 21st century too fast and via the wrong avenue.

Drive two hours west from Beretta's headquarters in Brescia, and you come to Torino, the home of Giorgietto Giugiaro Design. Beretta has made much of this gun having been shaped by Giugiaro. Unfortunately, while this design firm has created neat helicopter interior and trim, and designed helmets and eyewear and automobiles, their only experience with firearms prior to the 9000 was Beretta's AL-391 shotgun. The 9000 is their first pistol. It shows.

Italy has a long and magnificent history of both art and design. A paradigm exists. Consider the Sistine Chapel. Its ceilings and west wall are adorned with the frescoes of Michelangelo, considered by some the greatest painter who ever lived, and this may be his masterpiece. However, Michelangelo was commissioned to paint them in 1508 by Pope Julius II. We cannot help but notice that no Pontiff was stupid enough to commission an artist to **build the whole chapel!** The master architect Giovanni dei Dolci under the supervision of Pope Sixtus IV, for whom it is named, designed the historic edifice, which was completed in 1481.

The lesson was there. Beretta began manufacturing firearms 480 years ago, when this was fresh in their nation's memory: *let an engineer do the design, and then let the artists fancy it up!* Alas, this lesson appears to have been missed in the latest Beretta .40.

Has the 9000 merely been plagued with misfortune? Is my sample, serial # SN000365, just a lemon? I hope so.

The Line Continues

I'll reserve judgment on the 9000, but I also won't buy one until the design matures and improves significantly. I could be very comfortable with the Cougar .40. I *am* very comfortable with my .40 Centurion.

I'm not so comfortable with the 9000.

What About Now?

Well, it's been a few years since I fired the Model 9000. That gun was, in fact, the 365th Model 9000 off the production line. A lot of water has gone under the bridge, and I've seen a lot of Model 9000s on the firing line. I can no longer reserve judgment.

When I wrote the **Gun Digest Book of SIG-Sauer: A Complete Look at SIG-Sauer Pistols** a bit ago, I left SIGARMS' Mauser M2 out. I explained in that book, "The Mauser M2, which has been marketed by SIG, is left out entirely. Despite its excellent accuracy potential, its poor human engineering, second-rate workmanship, lack of reliability, and minimal projected service life don't make it fit to appear in the pages of a book concerning SIGARMS. I don't have any say what goes into the SIGARMS catalog, but I do have a say on what goes into this book, which is why we'll focus on the proven and enduring excellence of the true SIG-Sauer pistols."[1]

This time around, I have to take a different approach. It's easy enough to leave a Mauser brand pistol out of a book about SIGs. I can't leave a Beretta brand pistol out of a book about Berettas. So, in a nutshell:

> *Cocked and locked override would have been a useful feature if the rest of the gun had lived up to potential, in Ayoob's opinion.*

The single-action trigger pull on the F model isn't bad, but certainly isn't great. Based on what I've seen on the firing line, the guns still jam, and are still awkward to clear and to operate because the core design has not left enough slide for the human hand to effectively grasp when operating the action under stress. Accuracy remains mediocre.

On the F and G models, decocking is performed by pushing the Model 9000's safety/decock lever upwards. This requires so much force that even a strong man usually has to reposition his hand on the gun to gain enough leverage to do so, which takes the pistol out of firing grasp. This is simply tactically unacceptable.

At this writing, the very end of the year 2004, 9000G and 9000D models are no longer being manufactured. Beretta has apparently given up on selling this gun to cops; I know of no law enforcement agency that has adopted it, which speaks well of my brothers and sisters in that profession.

Despite rumors that the 9000 has been totally discontinued, I am told that the company's official line is that the 9000F is still available. "It is not being discontinued, it is being de-emphasized," said one Beretta executive diplomatically. Remaining stocks of Model 9000 pistols are being dumped to distributors at fire-sale prices, and distributors are trying to unload them at major discounts to dealers, who in due course are offering them at very low prices. I've seen dealers offering them in the $250 range. Now, $250 for a real Beretta does indeed seem like a bargain, but you have to ask yourself this: if the hallmark of the Beretta name is a well-engineered pistol that is utterly reliable and easy to shoot well, *is* the Model 9000 a "real Beretta"? For the same price you can purchase a .22 Neos or a .25 Bobcat that will operate reliably and will let you shoot it well.

Every family has its black sheep. I sympathize. (In my family, I probably *am* the black sheep). HK had the VP70Z, SIG had the Mauser M2, Colt had the egregious Model 2000, Smith & Wesson had its disposable Sigma .380, and so on.

When the Model 9000 had been out a year or two, and my first slam of it was already in print, I had a chat with a Beretta executive and asked him what he thought of the gun. He asked, "Off the record?" Well, that means I can't print what is said. I counter-offered, "How about not for attribution?" That means it gets said, but his name isn't on it and he will have immunity for his honesty. He agreed.

He took a deep breath and said, "Beretta makes the finest pistol in the world." He then paused and added, "Unfortunately, we also make the Model 9000."

Enough said. The Beretta 9000 is a piece of crap. I predict that it will soon be completely and officially discontinued, and none too soon. It was a blot on the honorable and distinguished Beretta coat of arms.

At one of its Italian facilities, Beretta maintains a splendid firearms museum, which includes samples of virtually all the fine firearms produced under that honored name for nearly five centuries. As I have had to include the Model 9000 here, the museum curator will have to include at least one specimen of the Model 9000 there.

I hope they display it in a separate case, draped with black crepe.

The Model 9000 pistol will leave a legacy, however, to all in the handgun industry. Remember the Sistine Chapel analogy. Let the experienced engineers design the gun, and only thereafter allow the "designers" near it, and then only to trim and decorate the surfaces.

Endnotes

(1) Ayoob, Massad, "The Gun Digest Book of SIG-Sauer: A complete Look at SIG-Sauer Pistols," Iola, WI: Krause Publications, P.14.

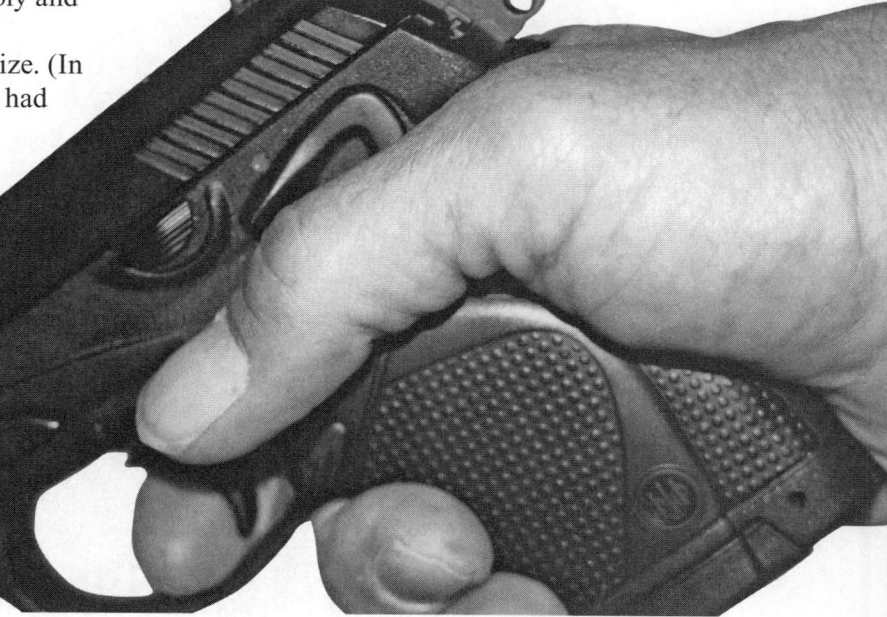

Even in single-action mode, 9000's trigger reach is longer than it should have been if the design parameter was to include a broad range of hand sizes.

Beretta Oddities

Beretta is a prolific manufacturer, and there are more variations in its product line than can be treated in depth in a book of this length. There have been numerous commemorative models. They are very nicely rendered. However, mechanically, they are not appreciably different from the mainstream Berettas. With a word limit, there is room for steak but no space for sizzle.

Some Beretta variants have proven so popular and useful that they have earned their own chapters. The Elites are an example. The compact versions of the Models 92 and 96 are also important.

But there have been others of note, and they deserve to be included in this book.

The Beretta Billennium

This silvery commemorative of the second millennium was distinct not just in appearance, but in engineering. It was a dedicated single-action pistol, all steel, surfaced for beauty but engineered for performance. It came with extra front and rear sights, all dovetail-fitted, to allow them to be adjusted to the individual's eyes and chosen load while retaining the traditional ruggedness of fixed combat sights. The silver finish, Beretta's Gabriele de Plano told me when the gun was introduced, was a nickel alloy. Said Gabriele, "The proprietary alloys that make it more wear resistant were developed jointly by Beretta and one of our outside vendors. We've used it in the past on some of our over/under shotguns. You'll see it on the Silver Pigeon II. I would call it more of a pewter finish." It contrasted strikingly with the dark carbon fiber grips, which sort of made their own fashion statement. The traditional grasping grooves at the rear of the slide were replaced with a snake-scale motif, first seen on some of the Smith & Wesson Performance Center top-dollar guns, and later on another upscale pistol, Ed Brown's Kobra Carry 1911 .45 auto.

The beautiful Billennium presented a distinctive silhouette, here in its natural cocked n' locked mode. At 43 ounces unloaded, it didn't need a compensator to deliver minimal recoil in 9mm.

The Billennium came with a frame-mounted ambidextrous safety of generous shape that worked exactly like that of the first Model 92, which is to say, exactly like that of the popular 1911 pistol. It was not accurized per se, and inherent accuracy was the same as that of a stock Model 92 service gun. However, being made entirely of steel, the Billennium kicked even less.

There was good news and bad news here. The good news was that the recoil was now even lighter; I shot one extensively, and it is not an exaggeration to say that its recoil with 9mm Parabellum ammunition felt as if I was shooting a Beretta with a .22 conversion unit. The bad news: the Billennium

Carbon fiber stocks. Snake-scale slide-grasping grooves. A single action trigger, albeit set farther forward than the author would have liked. All things considered, the Billennium was a striking Beretta.

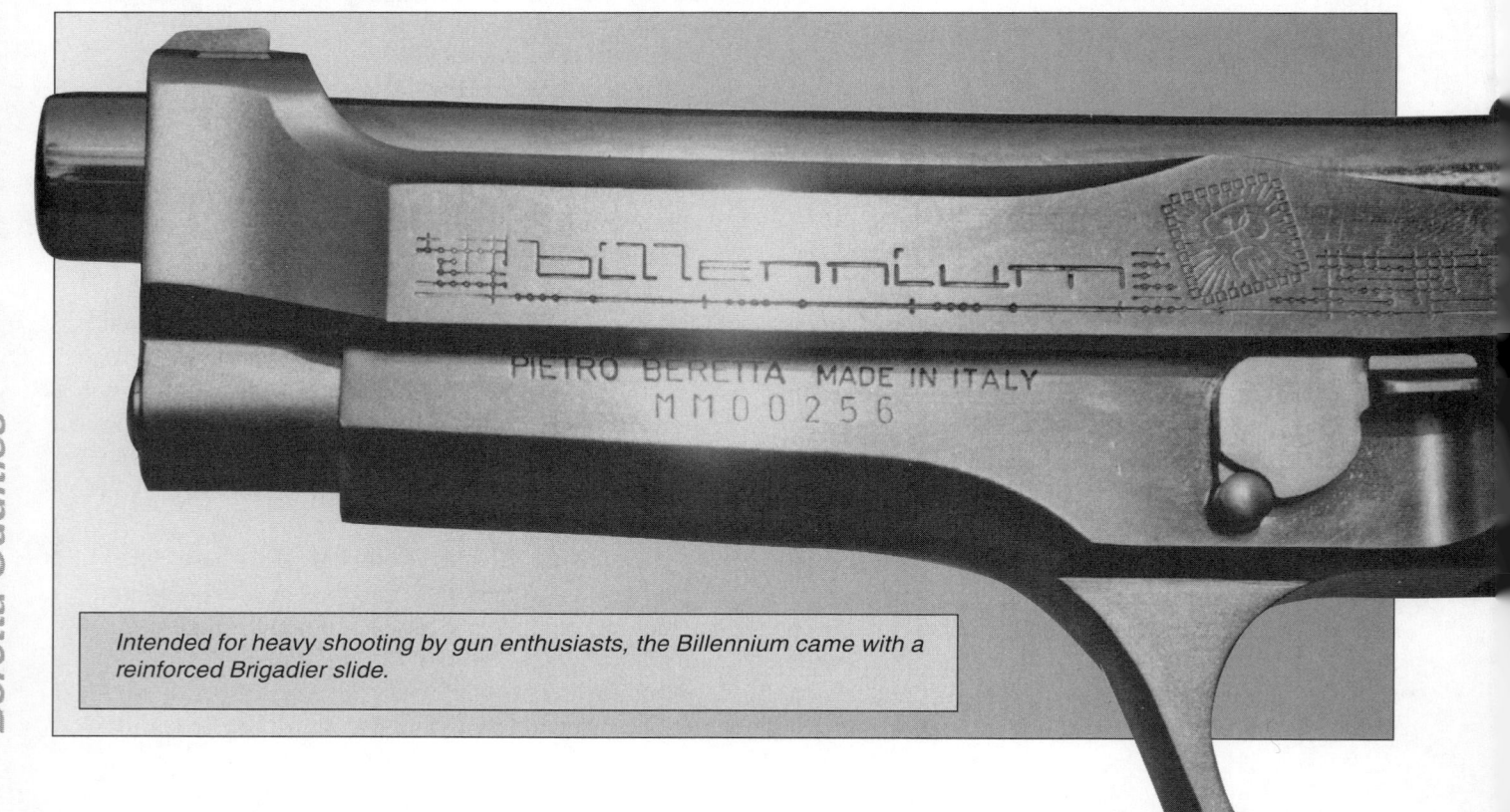

Intended for heavy shooting by gun enthusiasts, the Billennium came with a reinforced Brigadier slide.

was one hefty piece of gear. At 43 ounces empty, it weighed about the same as a fully loaded all stainless steel Smith & Wesson Model 5906 service pistol, which also holds 16 rounds of 9mm. And the Smith 5906 was always considered a heavy service pistol.

Todd Green, a helluva shot and a very sharp guy, was working for Beretta when the Billennium came out, and doing a fine job of winning IDPA trophies with his Langdon-tuned 92G. I asked him if he was going to switch to the sweet-shooting Billennium for International Defensive Pistol Association competition. He told me sadly, "The Billennium is not legal for IDPA competition. It's about two or three ounces over the weight limit for an Enhanced Service Pistol."

The Billennium is one of those guns that is not designed for a particular kind of shooting competition, and is probably too heavy for comfortable all-day carry, but is just a joy to shoot and a paean sung to the gunmaker's art. It's the kind of gun that's worth owning as an *objet d'art*.

Built to celebrate the Year 2000, the Billennium was limited to a production run of 2,000 guns. Its suggested retail price was $1,357, just over twice the price of two plain-vanilla Model 92 pistols at the time.

Cocked and locked, the Billennium shows off its "adjustable fixed sights," handsome grips and trim, and one of the padded-bottom competition-style magazines that came with it.

The Strange Tale of the Frankenstein Beretta

Dr. Frankenstein, in Mary Shelley's classic novel, built a monstrous caricature of a man from the body parts of other people and brought it to life. The monster was so grotesque that he was repulsive to normal people, but under all his bad karma, he was actually a pretty decent sort.

There was once a Beretta 92 like that.

Back in the day when the "wonder-nine" pistol was ascendant, some officers of the Indianapolis Police Department felt that they were losing the firepower race and told the chief they needed high-capacity auto pistols like those that so many other law enforcement agencies were issuing. The Indiana State Police itself had cashiered their Smith & Wesson .357 Magnum service revolvers for the Beretta 92G, after an exhaustive test that even included machine rest testing and 50-yard accuracy measurements. The Beretta had won on the strength of its reliability and accuracy, and the ISP theorized that since their people weren't used to releasing safeties after their long time with revolvers, the decock-only variation was the way to go.

The head of the firearms unit for Indianapolis PD at the time tapped into ISP's exhaustive research and recommended that the chief adopt the same Model 92G. This was done, and the guns were issued, along with the 147-grain 9mm subsonic ammo that had become trendy since the FBI's approval of the round in the late 1980s.

All went well for a while. Then the day came when a criminal struggled with an IPD officer and managed to get his Beretta out of the holster and turn it on him. The 92G is like a SIG-Sauer or a Glock or a revolver: a point-and-shoot gun following the Keep It Simple, Stupid principle. The bad guy hosed a good part of the 16 rounds now at his command in the direction of the officer.

The officer ran, ducked, bobbed and weaved, and made his way to cover without being seriously hurt. The suspect turned and ran to his vehicle to get away. As he jumped behind the wheel, the would-be cop-killer tried to shove the stolen Beretta into the front of his waistband.

Well, no one had taught *him* to decock after firing, nor had they taught him to keep his finger off the trigger if he did not intend to shoot. The hammer was back and the trigger was in the easy, short-pull single-action mode with his finger still on it as he shoved it into the front of his pants. The finger caught on the belt or the waistband and, along with the trigger, stopped. The gun, however, kept moving as the suspect pushed on it.

BANG! The pistol discharged, and delivered justice. Without going into details, it would be correct to say that there was indeed a "de-cocking" involved, but it just didn't involve the Beretta's hammer or the lever on its slide.

Now, if I had been that officer's instructor, I would have gone to a convent and made a donation and asked the good sisters to light a candle and thank the Lord above for the miracle of deliverance that had saved my officer from death when a man tried to murder him with a barrage of bullets from his own pistol. I then would have called Beretta U.S.A. in Accokeek, Maryland, and said, "Um, upon review, it seems like that 'F' model of yours with the proprietary manual safety might be a good idea after all. What would it take to turn our 92Gs into 92Fs?"

The guy in charge in Indianapolis took a different tack. Apparently the training officer assumed that if an untrained idiot cop-killer can emasculate himself by not decocking the gun, leaving his finger on the trigger, and thrusting it down the front of his pants, some officer under his command might have been stupid enough to do the same thing.

So, instead, he called Beretta and had them convert all the 92Gs to double-action-only.

This was done. Each was converted to D configuration, but of course, each had begun its existence as a 92G and still had that model number stamped on its slide. It now had something else on its slide: an ambidextrous, spring-loaded safety/decock lever that on this model had never been a safety, and now wasn't a decocking lever either. After all, one definition of a double-action only pistol is "self-decocking." There was no longer anything *to* decock. The lever was now absolutely vestigial. It would flip down and snap back up on its spring load, but it did absolutely nothing. It was sort of like the snaffle bit a horse plays with, with its tongue.

I thought of it as the uncatalogued Beretta GD. A G to start, a D to finish.

Forgive a brief digression. When I was young, my mother, who thought it unladylike to use bad language or take God's name in vain, would use the abbreviation "GD" when my dad would have said, "God damn!" I am sure that the wanna-be cop-killer who emasculated himself must at some point have blamed that "GD Beretta." As I was putting this book together, each chapter needed a filecode in the computer, and I used "GDBeretta" for *Gun Digest Book of Modern Beretta Pistols*. I confess that as deadline loomed closer and things came up that made the book's completion more hectic, I uttered the phrase "that GD Beretta book is due" more than once.

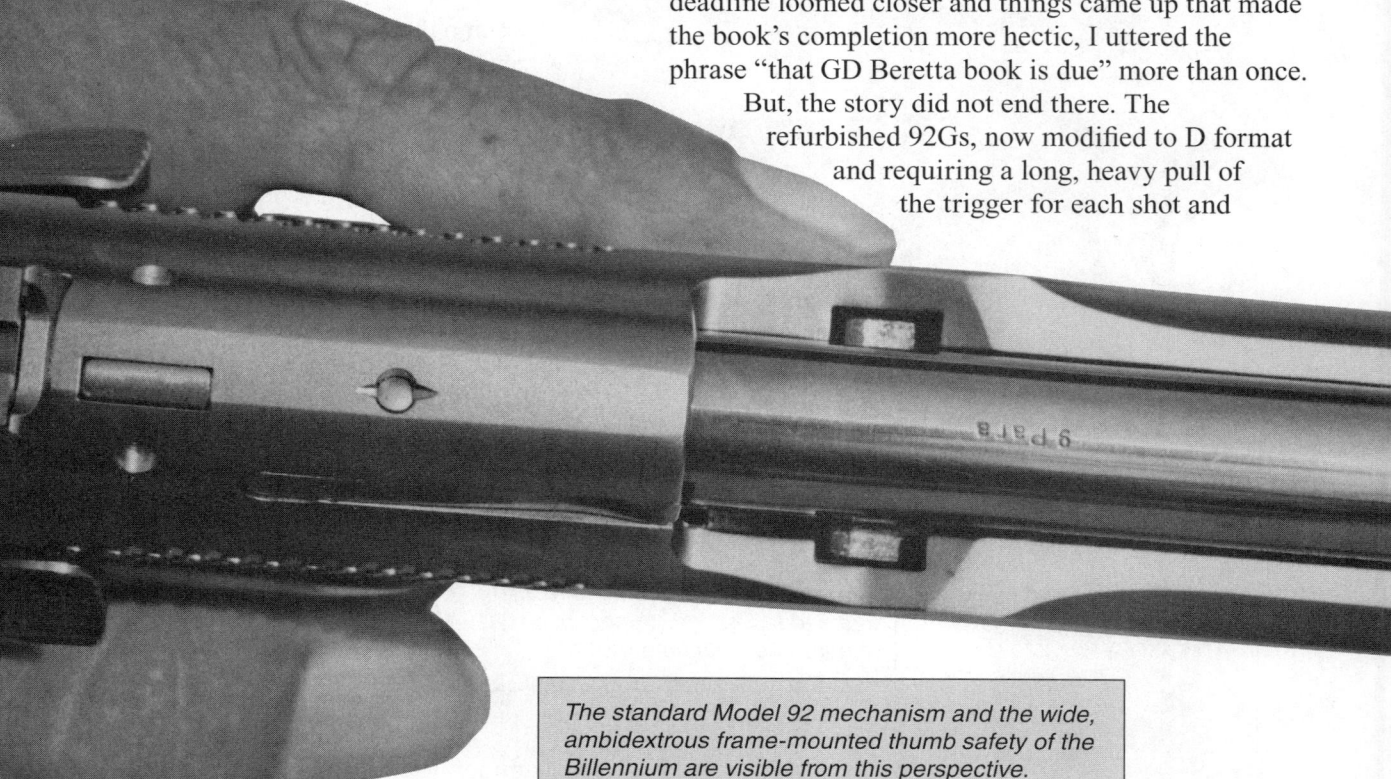

But, the story did not end there. The refurbished 92Gs, now modified to D format and requiring a long, heavy pull of the trigger for each shot and

The standard Model 92 mechanism and the wide, ambidextrous frame-mounted thumb safety of the Billennium are visible from this perspective.

ZEISS CONQUEST VS. .50 PEACEKEEPER
www.gunsmagazine.com
MAGAZINE
ZEISS IN ICE
WIN A CUSTOM NAA GUARDIAN
WIN OVER $10,000 IN PRIZES!
DISPLAY UNTIL APRIL 28, 2003
MAY 2003 $3.95
$5.95 IN CANADA

Above and previous page: Ayoob's article on the Billennium was the cover story for the May 2002 issue of Guns magazine, with photography by the incomparable Ichiro Nagata.

therefore an equally long trigger return between shots, went back on the street. I am told that there was no refresher training to allow the troops to get used to the completely new trigger mechanism. After all, they had the same guns, didn't they?

Later, the day came when an officer got involved in a shooting with one. The incident was caught on video, I'm told, and the camera captured more trigger pulls than shots fired on the officer's part. Accustomed to the short, easy pull for every shot after the first, he had apparently reverted to training. Accordingly, he failed a few times to return the trigger sufficiently to fire again, although he finally got the job done and came out the winner of the gunfight.

Now, throughout all this time, the department and its officers had discovered that going from .357 Magnum 125-grain hollow-points to 9mm subsonics is a change that comes with a price. IPD, back in the 1970s when Dick Riley was the guy in charge of guns and related training there, had become the first metropolis to adopt the then-new 125-grain Magnum load. In more than 200 shootings, it had dropped the bad guys like lightning bolts, sometimes with hits to arms and legs. The 147-grain 9mm at under a 1,000 feet per second had nowhere near that level of "stopping power," and that had become apparent in the field.

Admitting that there had been a retraining failure and a less than perfect choice in duty ammunition would not do. The department decided that it was the 9mm cartridge, not the 147-grain subsonic load, that was inadequate, and moreover that the answer to the trigger thing was to simply adopt a gun that had a shorter trigger pull for every shot. The department adopted the Glock 22 in caliber .40 S&W.

Now, that Glock 22 happens to be an excellent pistol, and I am not surprised that it has worked out well and IPD carries it to this day. However, it does strike me as a classic case of making a good choice for bad reasons.

When the new guns were acquired, the old ones were traded in, and were sold off by a distributor in Kentucky. I bought one. I wanted it for my collection as a monument to the sort of bureaucratic idiocy that can sometimes bedevil large organizations.

I would show it to friends, and – particularly those

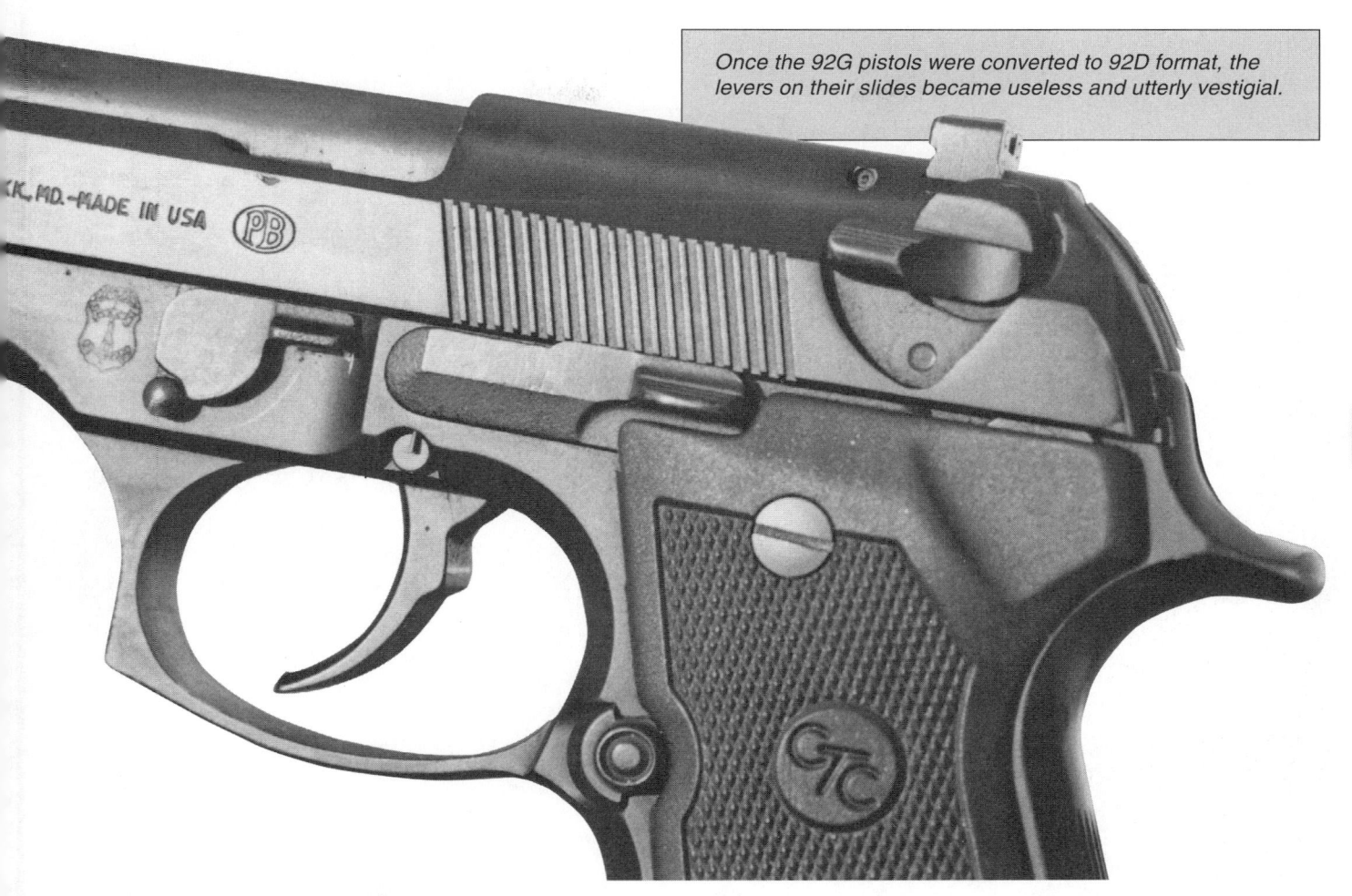

Once the 92G pistols were converted to 92D format, the levers on their slides became useless and utterly vestigial.

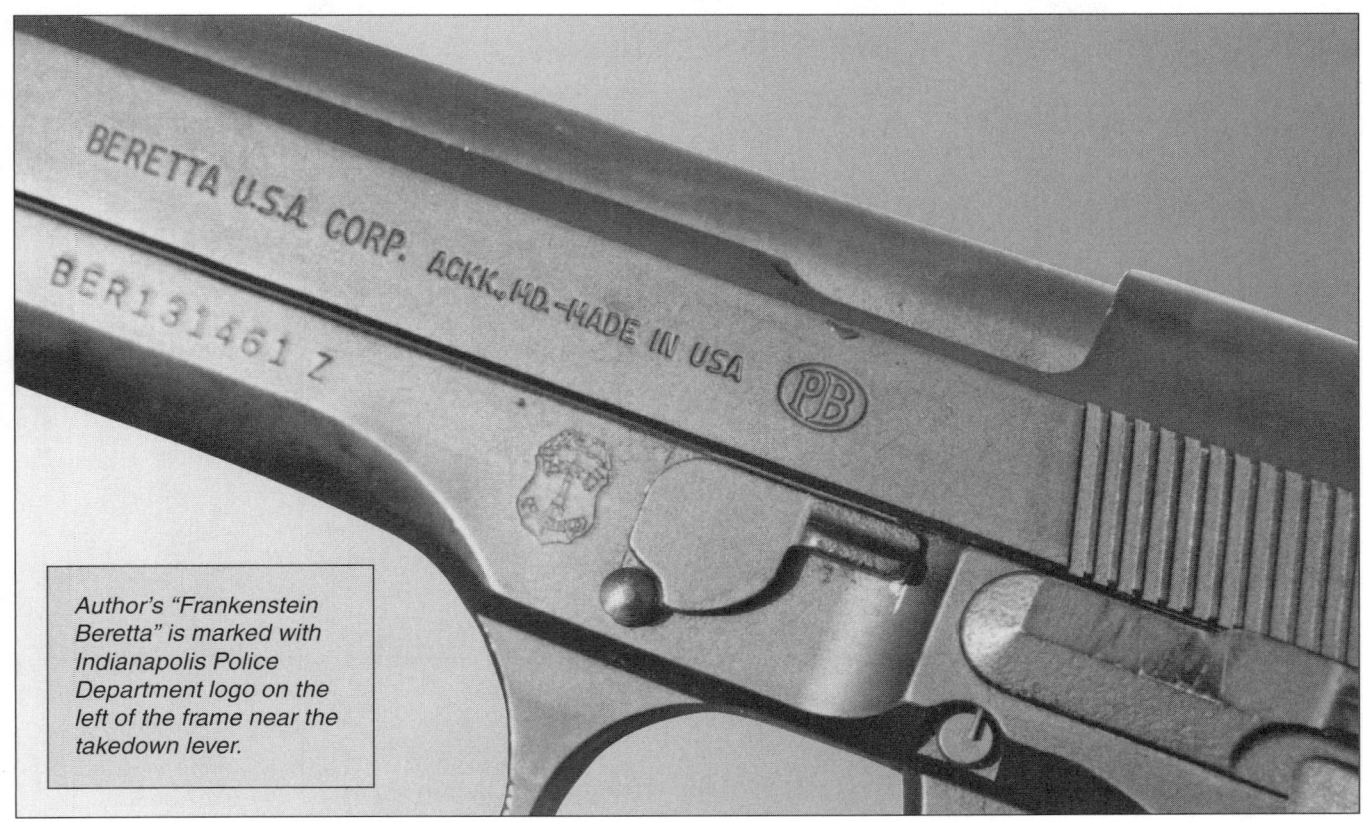

Author's "Frankenstein Beretta" is marked with Indianapolis Police Department logo on the left of the frame near the takedown lever.

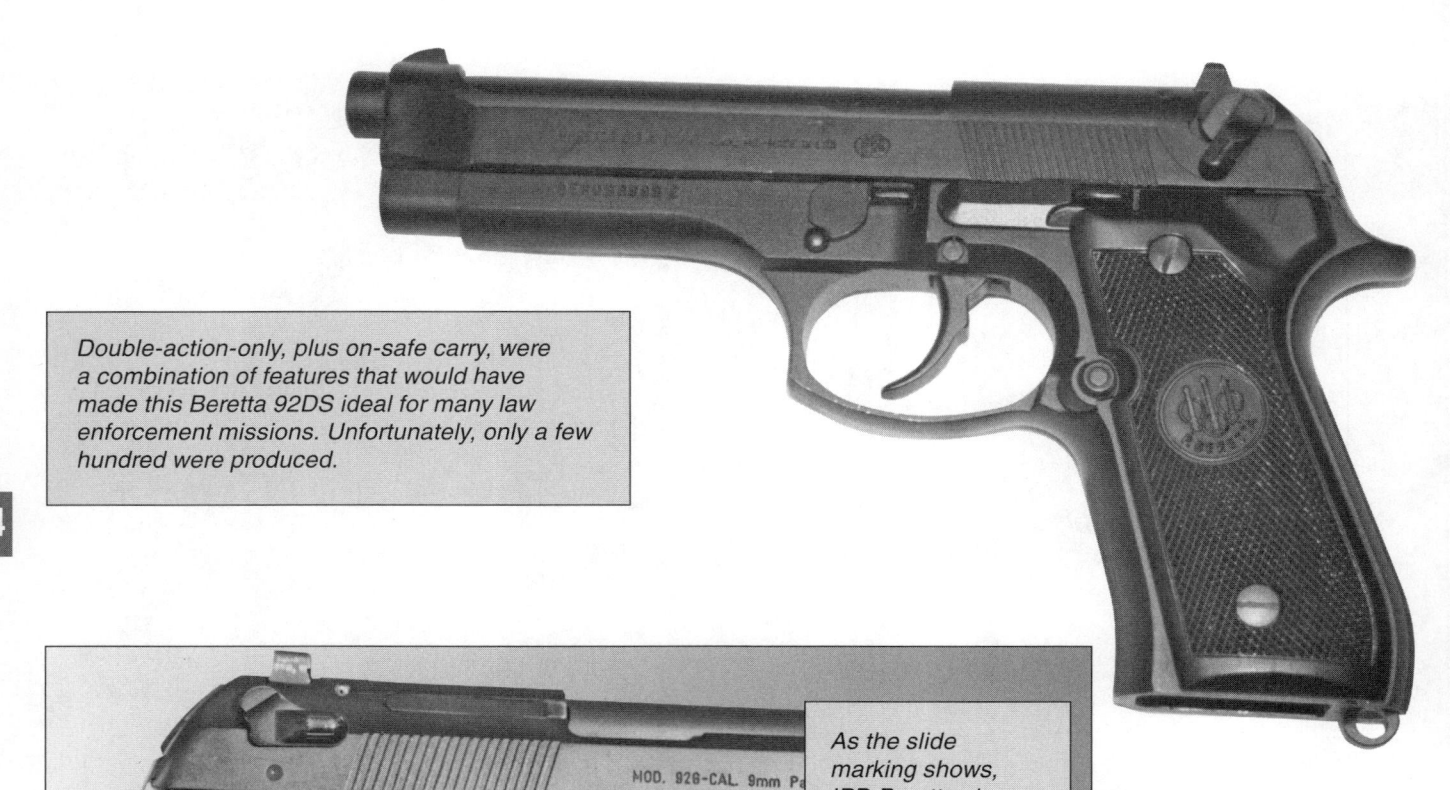

Double-action-only, plus on-safe carry, were a combination of features that would have made this Beretta 92DS ideal for many law enforcement missions. Unfortunately, only a few hundred were produced.

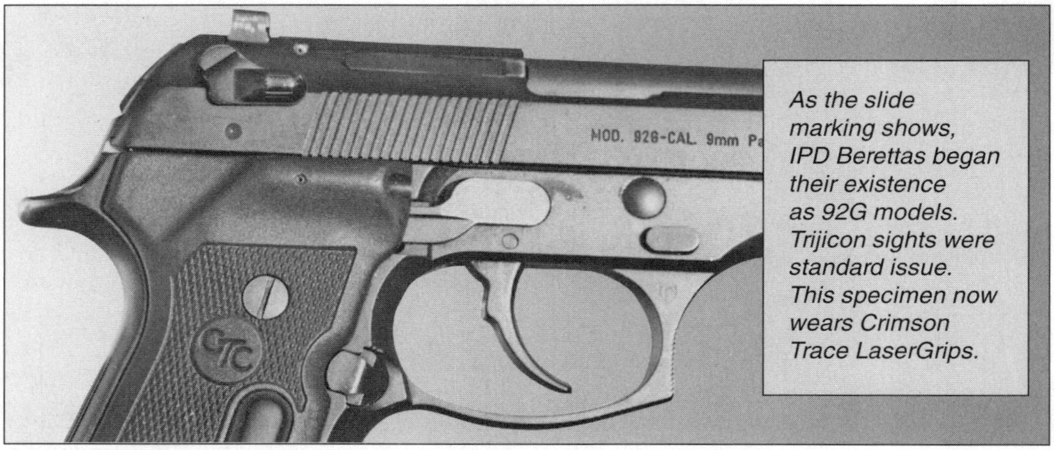

As the slide marking shows, IPD Berettas began their existence as 92G models. Trijicon sights were standard issue. This specimen now wears Crimson Trace LaserGrips.

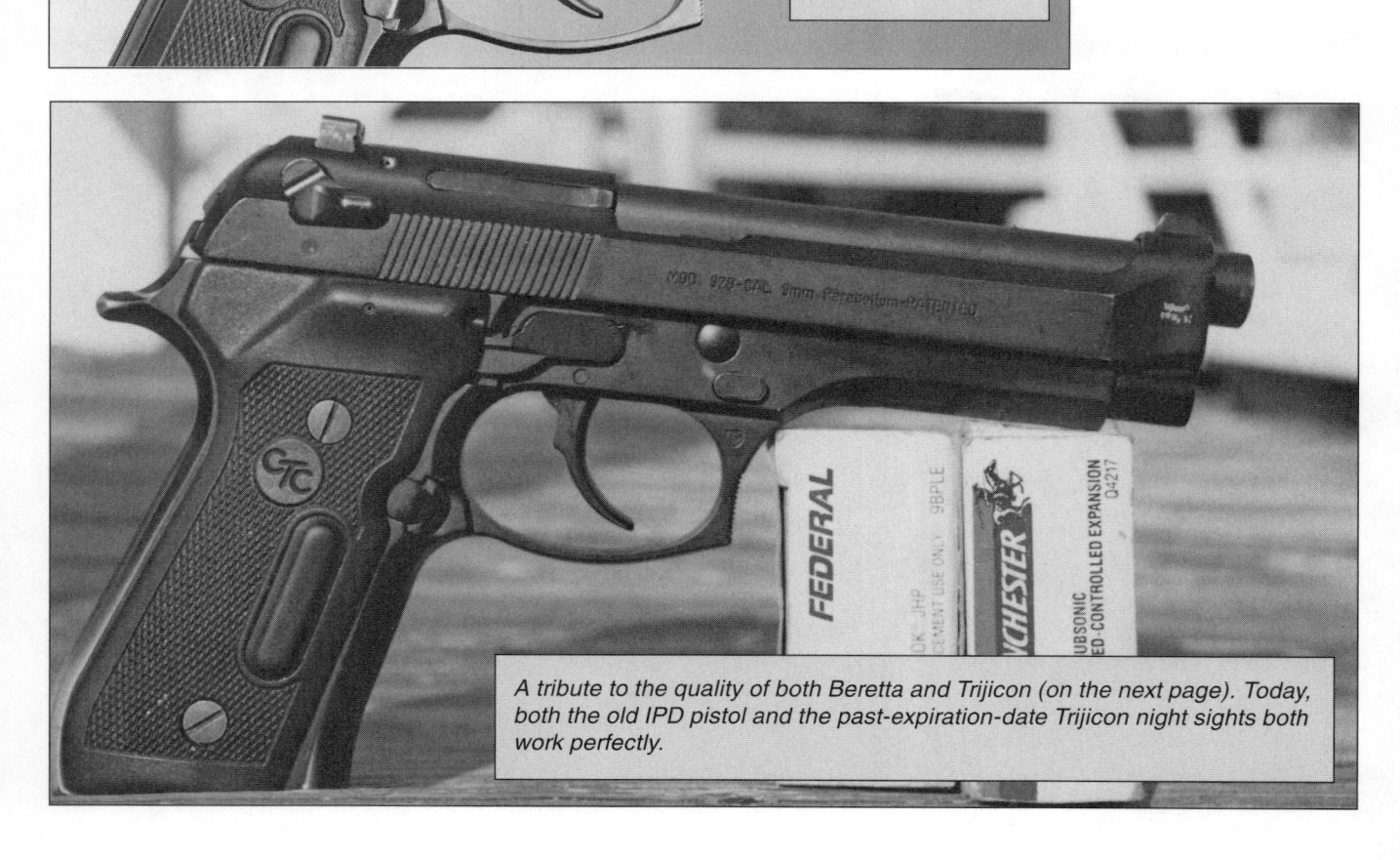

A tribute to the quality of both Beretta and Trijicon (on the next page). Today, both the old IPD pistol and the past-expiration-date Trijicon night sights both work perfectly.

who knew and understood the Beretta – they would shake their head at the Frankenstein gun that was made up partly of the creature known as a 92G and partly of a creature known as a 92D. The gun, let's face it, was a freak.

The hell of it was, like the monster in Mary Shelley's novel, it wasn't bad per se. My particular gun, serial number BER131461Z, is a helluva nice pistol. When it came to me, its DAO pull was smooth as butter. Part of that is Beretta using an easier spring for the D series than for the F or the G, and part of it is that there is one less sear for the mechanism to have to trip, but part of it too is that this gun was just worn smooth by constant shooting or at least, dry firing. Its anodized frame was worn down to the white in several places, a clear sign that it had been carried much in an exposed holster exposed to the elements, and to bumping and scuffing.

I was going to just stick it in the safe with the rest of the "strange gun" collection, but there's no point in having a shootin' iron that you don't *shoot,* so I took it to the range. I was pleasantly surprised to discover that its Trijicon night sights were absolutely spot on for my eyes, point of aim/point of impact perfectly coinciding at 25 yards. It was also accurate: This was the pistol I used to fire the 1.25-inch 25 yard group with hot Pro-Load +P Tactical 115-grain ammo that appeared in the Police Bookshelf catalog.

It was immediately promoted from the "freak gun collection" to the working battery. I often issued it to students who hadn't brought their own pistols: it was accurate, it was safe, and its long, smooth pull taught them to stroke a trigger without jerking it. I found it was particularly suited to PPC-type shooting. I don't remember it ever jamming.

I find myself carrying it now and again. Its Trijicon night sights are way past warranty and should have gone dark a long time ago, but they still glow brightly. I took it to Thunder Ranch one time as a spare. Sue me: it's not the style of Beretta I usually prefer, but I *like* it, and the little freak is a unique bit of handgun history.

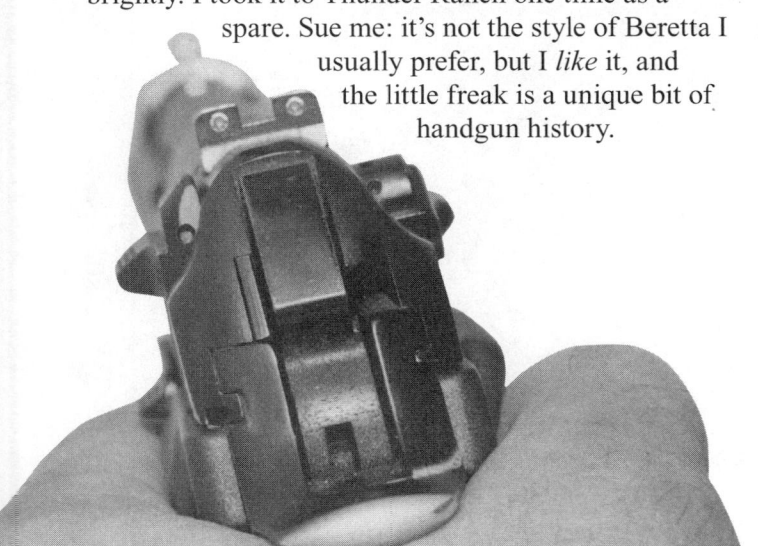

The Beretta 92DS

Around 1994, Beretta introduced a variation of the 92 called the DS. The D still stood for double-action-only. The S stood for Safety: while the usual D model was a "slick-slide," this one had the ambidextrous lever of the F model, and it functioned as a manual safety.

The 92DS was the yin to the 92G pistol's yang, as it were. On the G, that lever was a decocker only; on the DS, self-decocking as it was, that lever was a safety catch only.

All the civil liability advantages of the double-action-only design were there, *plus* the feature that had saved the lives of so many cops who carried Beretta 92F pistols on safe and had to deal with a gun grab. I for one thought it was a smart idea.

The marketplace did not. Civilians didn't want DAO, they wanted traditional double-action where they only had that hard, heavy pull for the first shot. Beretta, like Smith & Wesson and SIG and HK, found their sales of DAO pistols to the shooting public to be minimal. The cops, meanwhile, were in full sail with the KISS principle of "Keep It Simple, Stupid" and still thought releasing a manual safety might be too complicated. They wanted the D series, and they wanted it in the slick-slide format, thank you very much.

Brian Felter was at Beretta at the time, and he told me only a few hundred 92DS pistols were manufactured before the variant was discontinued for lack of buyer interest. In Ned Schwing's excellent *Standard Catalog of Firearms* it is reported that a 96DS in .40 was also offered, though I've never seen one.

It's a shame, because the double-action-only feature combined with a manual safety is the ideal rig for a lot of users. Maybe it was just before its time. Taurus reports that their recently introduced 24/7 pistol, DAO with a frame-mounted manual safety, is selling just fine.

The 92DS is already a collector's item. I'm keeping mine. If you'd like one, it's easy enough; the gun just won't say "DS" on it. Send your Beretta F-series pistol to armorer Rick Devoid at Tarnhelm Supply, 431 High St., Boscawen, NH 03303, www.tarnhelm.com, (603)796-2551. Ask him to install D-series parts and convert it to double-action-only. You'll get back a DAO Beretta with a functioning, dedicated safety. While you're at it, you might want to talk to him about an action slick, night sights, or similar needs. He's good at that stuff.

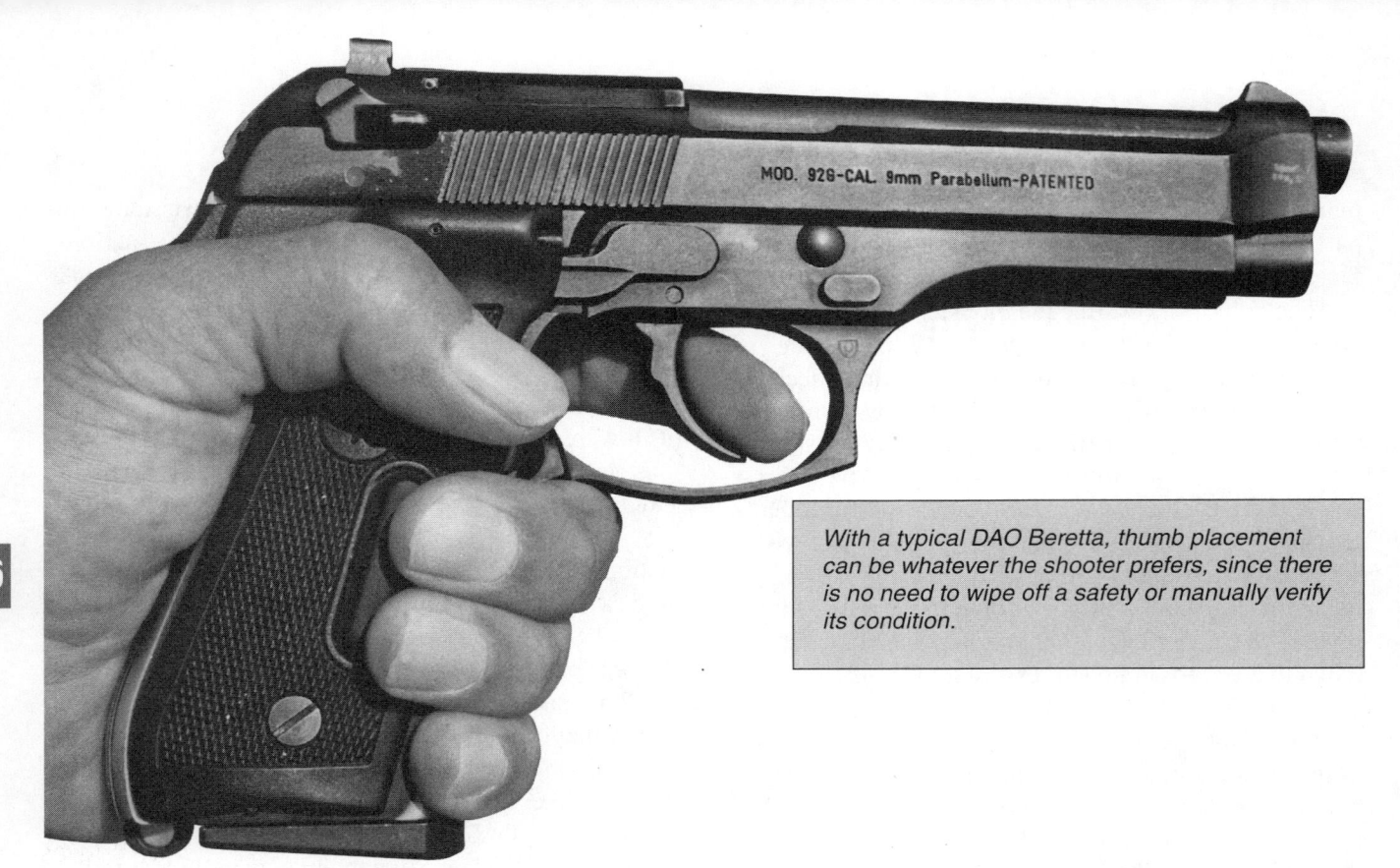

With a typical DAO Beretta, thumb placement can be whatever the shooter prefers, since there is no need to wipe off a safety or manually verify its condition.

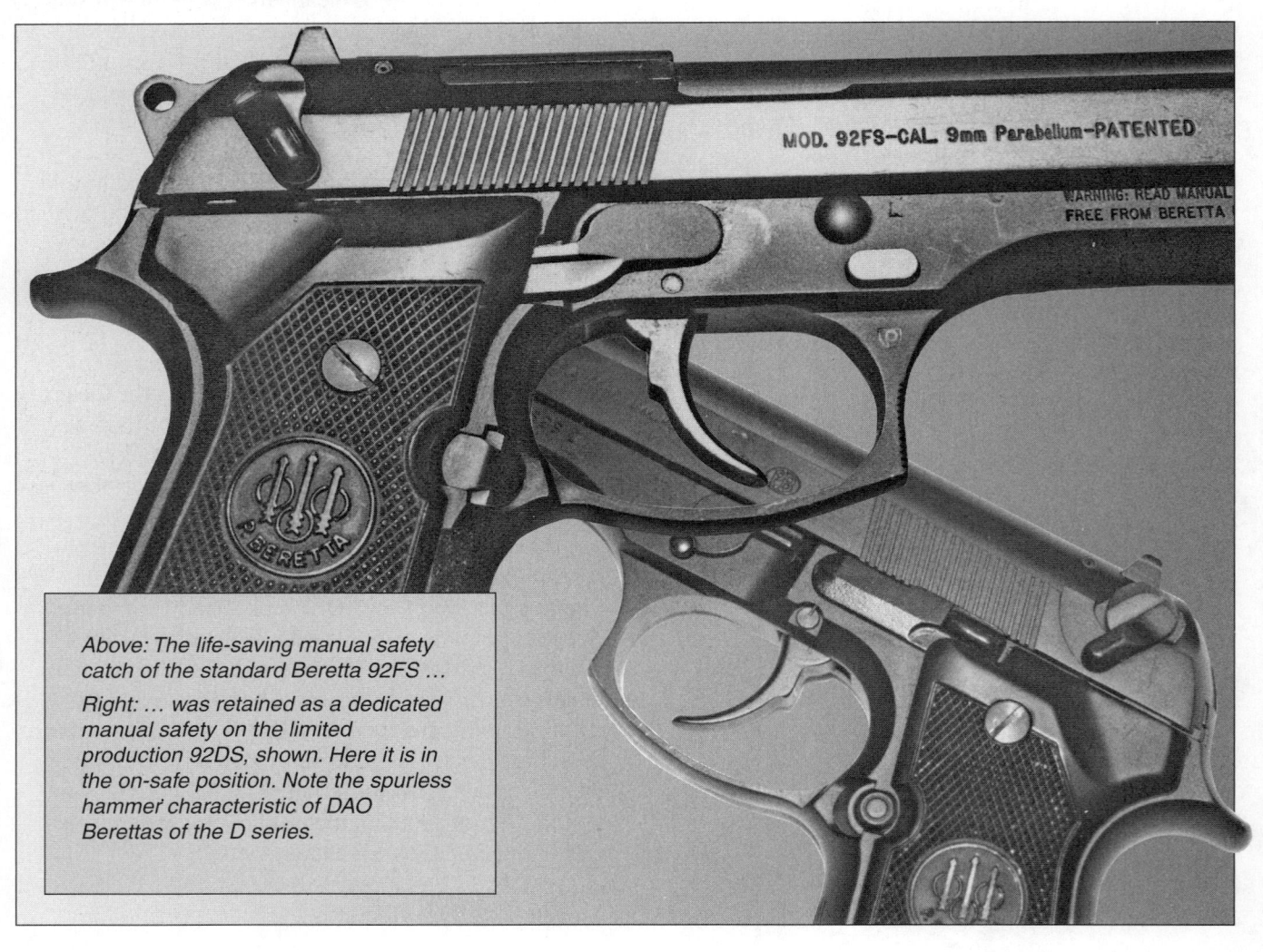

Above: The life-saving manual safety catch of the standard Beretta 92FS …

Right: … was retained as a dedicated manual safety on the limited production 92DS, shown. Here it is in the on-safe position. Note the spurless hammer characteristic of DAO Berettas of the D series.

Today's Beretta Revolver

In a dealer's showcase in December 2004, the three Beretta Stampedes on the left are priced slightly lower than the silvery, "ivory"-handled Ruger Vaquero at right.

Beretta *revolvers?* No, it's not a misprint. Beretta is a byword for semiautomatic pistols and has been for almost 90 years, but the fact is, they've sent a whole lot of revolvers out into the world.

In the 19th century, from the pinfire era on, Beretta had a bunch of revolvers in their catalogue. For the most part, they were produced at other factories and sold under Beretta auspices, which is the paradigm to which the company returned in the early 21st century.

In the 20th century, Beretta sold a line of wheelguns under its own name that they called Tenex revolvers, which bore a remarkable resemblance to the Taurus. Later, they came out with a high-tech revolver of their own, a double-action .357 Magnum replete with integral recoil compensation, though it was never marketed in the United States.

In recent years, Beretta's continuing acquisition of other gun manufacturers made them the owners

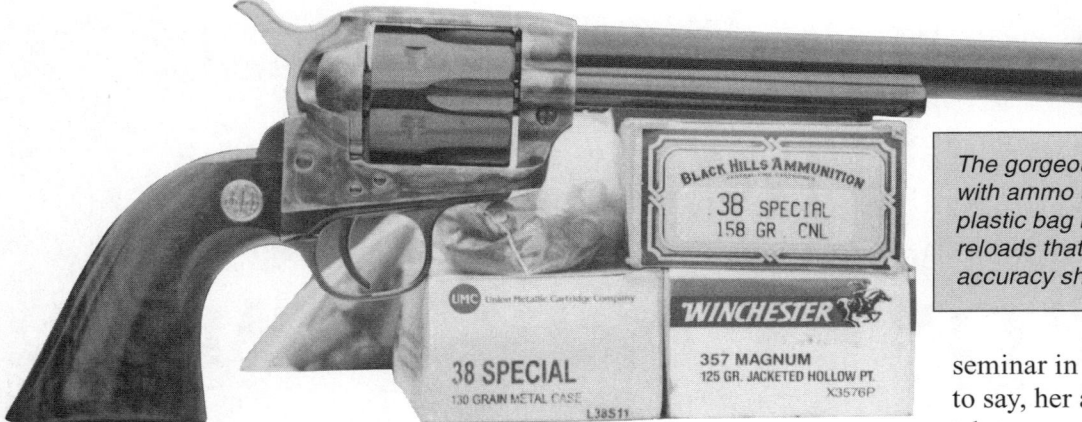

The gorgeous deluxe-grade .357 with ammo used in the test. The plastic bag holds the .38 wadcutter reloads that were the star of the accuracy show.

of Uberti. That firm is a manufacturer of, among other things, replicas of the Colt "Peacemaker" style single-action revolver. People knowledgeable about such guns have had mixed reviews of Uberti quality over the years. When Beretta decided to put their own name on one line of Uberti cowboy-style six-guns all that quickly changed.

One of my gun writer buddies was at an early introduction of the Beretta Stampede by Uberti. He told me that the guns' performance was less than stellar. At one point, the transfer bar mechanism fell out of one of the guns, he said.

Present was Cathy Williams, Beretta's public relations liaison, and one of the very best in the industry. She is not someone to be trifled with, and I would not have wanted to be the one who made the defective guns that brought her back from that seminar in a cold fury. Suffice to say, her advice was apparently taken.

The Uberti guns coming through now under the Beretta Stampede moniker are absolutely gorgeous. Not just in looks, but in performance.

Uberti of Italy has been making clones of 19th Century American cowboy guns for years and years, and getting better at it all the time. In the meantime, Beretta – the oldest gunmaker in the world, let alone Italy – has been making strategic alliances with other firearms manufacturers. They've done so with Uberti,

Below: Ayoob fired from this rickety improvised "bench" at 25 yards, but the Stampede deluxe …

Opposite page top: … delighted him with this group of five remanufactured .38 Special wadcutters …

Opposite page bottom: … measuring exactly an inch center-to-center. Great accuracy!

129

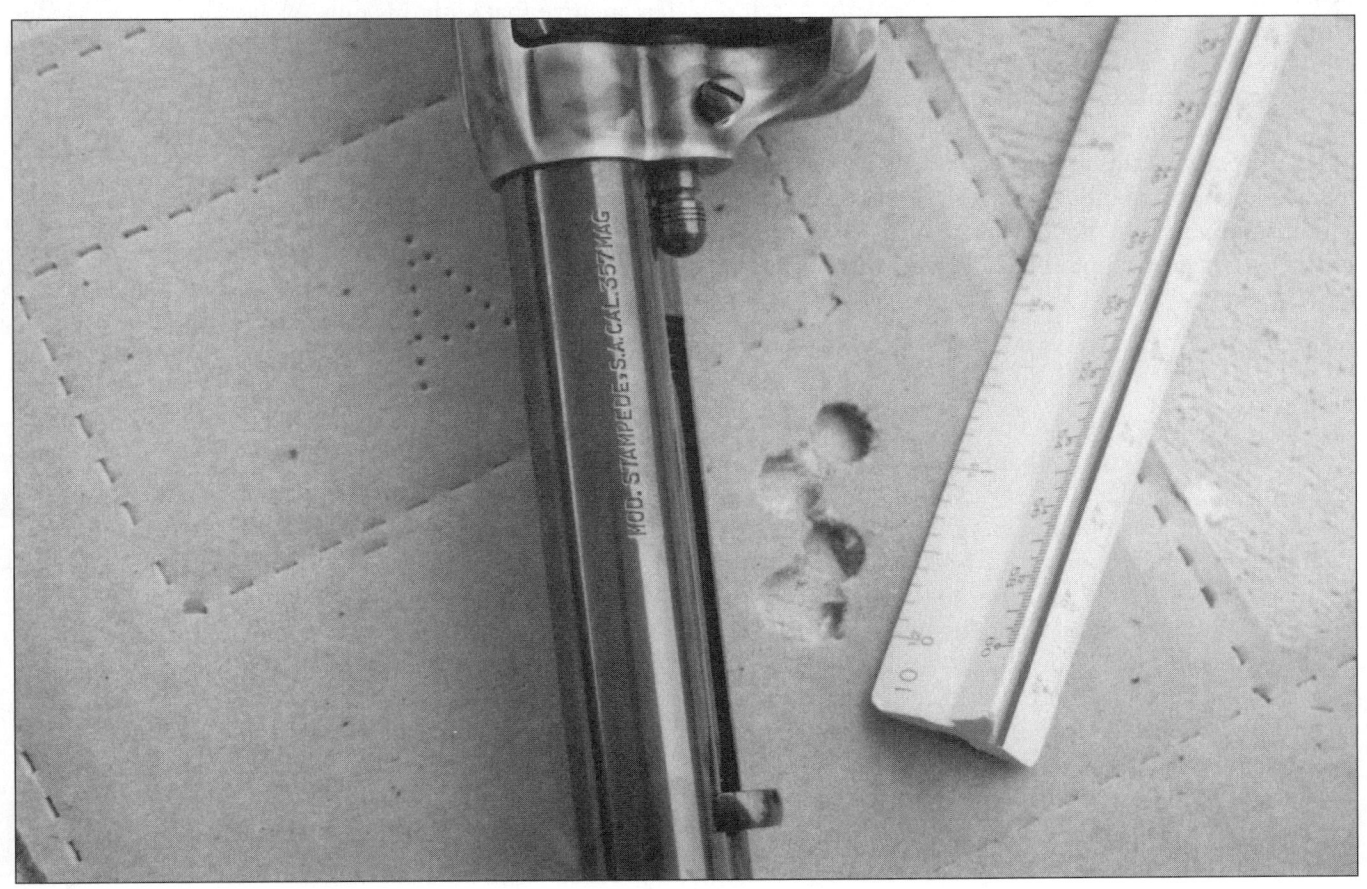

The Gun Digest Book of Beretta Pistols

which was purchased by the Beretta holding company in 2000. If the resulting Beretta Stampede revolver is any indication, then as Humphrey Bogart said, "This could be the start of a beautiful friendship."

Though they hit the gun magazines quite some time ago, the Stampede only recently finished the long trail to retail sales. The company offers three popular calibers in the three most popular barrel length. The chamberings are .45 Colt, .44-40 Winchester, and .357 Magnum. The barrel options are the cavalry style 7½-inch, the artillery style 5½-inch, and the "civilian style" 4 ⅝-inch. The styling is reasonably authentic to the original Colt Model P of 1873, the Single Action Army, better known as the Peacemaker.

My first Colt single-action, acquired when I was in junior high school, was a Frontier Six-Shooter, the Model P in .44-40. I never did bond with that cartridge, though, and don't keep much .44-40 ammo on hand. Accordingly, I ordered the test samples in the other two calibers. .45 Colt was, of course, by far the most popular of the dozens of cartridges for which the Model P has been chambered since 1873. Though I don't care for it in double-action revolvers or lever-action rifles because its disproportionately narrow rim causes occasional extraction failures, this fine old cartridge is in its element in a gate-loading Peacemaker. Colt had chambered the Single Action Army for the .357 Magnum cartridge shortly after Smith & Wesson developed it in 1935, and today it makes sense because, firing the .38 Special cartridge, it gives great accuracy with light recoil. Mild, lead-bullet .38 Special ammo has become the choice of many champions in today's hot sport of cowboy action shooting. Why not just make it in .38 Special? Because the .357 Magnum chambering is famously more versatile.

About The Design

In the heyday of the Peacemaker, people knew enough to keep an empty chamber under its hammer. By the last half of the 20th century, that common sense gene had died out of a lot of bloodlines, leaving a generation of bozos who put live cartridges under the firing pins of traditional single-action revolvers. They paid a terrible price when the guns were struck or dropped and, predictably, discharged. Thus was born a whole new spate of redesigned single-actions that resembled the Model P on the outside, but were redesigned internally to prevent the firing pin from coming forward unless the trigger was pulled.

The Stampede is of this latter breed. If Bat Masterson came back to life and thumbed a Stampede's hammer back, he would be horrified to see that it had no firing pin. It would take him a moment to realize that the firing pin now floats, spring-loaded, in the frame, and a transfer bar is present to bring the impetus of the hammer fall to the firing pin and thence to the primer when the trigger is pulled. The system works fine, and we experienced no ignition problems.

The action is sufficiently altered, however, that the four clicks of the original Colt single-action hammer is absent. This, to the true traditionalist, is an unforgivable deviation from authenticity. That said, though, the hammer comes back easily enough and smoothly enough that the ergonomics are essentially the same. Alas, however, the shooter will feel only three clicks by the time the hammer reaches full cock. The old-timers said that those four clicks spelled C-O-L-T. Well, on this revolver, I guess the three clicks will have to spell N-E-W.

Beretta proudly advertises that the updated lockwork makes the gun perfectly safe to carry with the hammer down on a live round. Having a torpedo in each of the six launch tubes does, of course, increase firepower by 20 percent, but it still gives me the creeps to do it, and any serious shooter of my generation will tell you the same. Cognitively, we recognize that with this gun, or the Ruger New Model series or Colt's own Cowboy, it is now mechanically safe to have a live cartridge under the hammer

However, we are uncomfortable doing so. It feels as if we are violating a taboo, and it takes the pleasure out of carrying a single-action. Besides, we know if we get into that habit with our Stampedes and our Ruger Vaqueros and our Colt Cowboys, we will eventually slip and do it with our old original Colts, and set the stage for tragedy. So, we just leave the chamber under the hammer empty as in the old days, and we advise others to do the same. And, cowboy action shooting rules require that only five rounds be loaded.

Other Beretta Stampede features include a wide trigger that, as with most handguns, is symmetrical to both sides of the trigger guard. This will throw off some of us geezers accustomed to the trigger of the original Colt, which is narrow and slightly off from center, and thus in a subtly different place for the left hand than it is for the right.

Some modernized single-actions, notably the current production Rugers, have cylinders that aren't as free in back-and-forth movement during the loading and unloading process. That is, it is very easy to roll the chamber past the loading gate, at

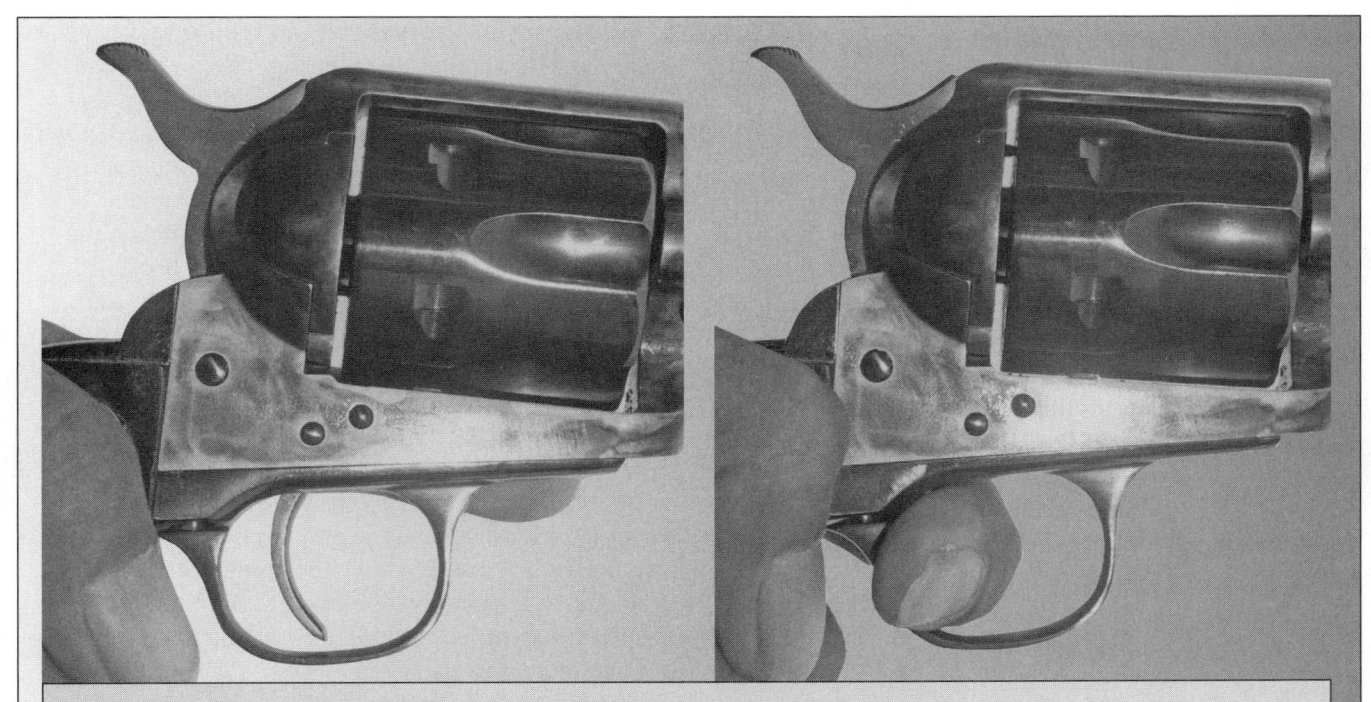

Left: Look at back of cylinder in line with the hammer. At rest, the Uberti/Beretta's firing pin does not protrude, allowing safe carry with a round under the hammer ...

Right: ... because the firing pin will not come through until the trigger has been pulled.

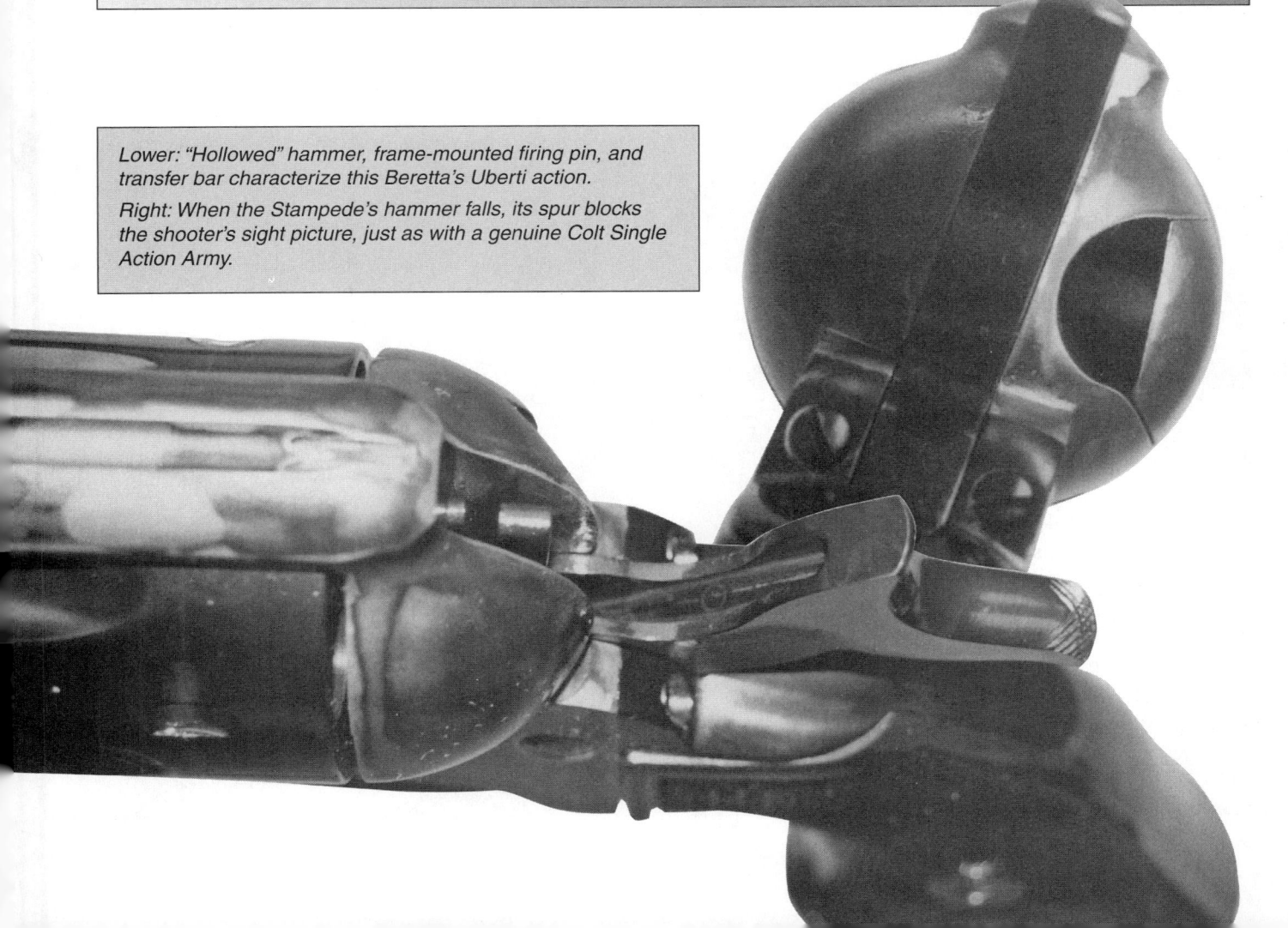

Lower: "Hollowed" hammer, frame-mounted firing pin, and transfer bar characterize this Beretta's Uberti action.

Right: When the Stampede's hammer falls, its spur blocks the shooter's sight picture, just as with a genuine Colt Single Action Army.

With the hammer cocked, we can see the small, square notch of the rear sight milled into the top of the frame.

With more cylinder rotation play in loading and unloading, the Stampede makes those operations easier.

which time you discover you can't roll it back, and you must do another complete, clockwise rotation of the cylinder to get a second chance to align that chamber. On the Ruger, a gunsmith can cure that with no compromise of safety with access to the requisite parts. On the Uberti Beretta, it's not a problem. If the chamber you wanted rolls its edge just past the loading gate, why, you can simply roll it back.

Another variation from the original Colt: the genuine article was filled up with a "load one, skip one, load the next four" sequence to put the empty chamber naturally under the hammer. With the Stampede, the mechanism is just different enough that as you put in the fifth live round, you can close the loading gate and roll the cylinder back counterclockwise, and the empty chamber will naturally lock itself under the hammer. As with the Colt, the hammer must be brought back to half cock to free up cylinder rotation for loading and unloading. When punching spent casings out, the shooter will be happy to find a generous ejector button hanging discreetly under the ejector rod housing.

Both the standard grade and the deluxe grade come with a *faux* case hardening on the frame. The multi-colored look is nice, and a lot of people like it. The Beretta website (www.BerettaUSA.com) describes this as "Beretta Color-Case finish – our durable and particularly attractive interpretation of the traditional color-case look." If you don't care for two-tone six-guns and want the whole thing finished the same, you'll have to go with the optional nickel finish.

Plain blue, fancy blue, or nickel. .45 Colt, .44-40, or .357. 4⅝-inch, 5½-inch, or 7½-inch. Podnuh, yuh kin outfit yer whole posse with Beretta Stampedes an' not have any two of 'em jes' 'zackly alike.

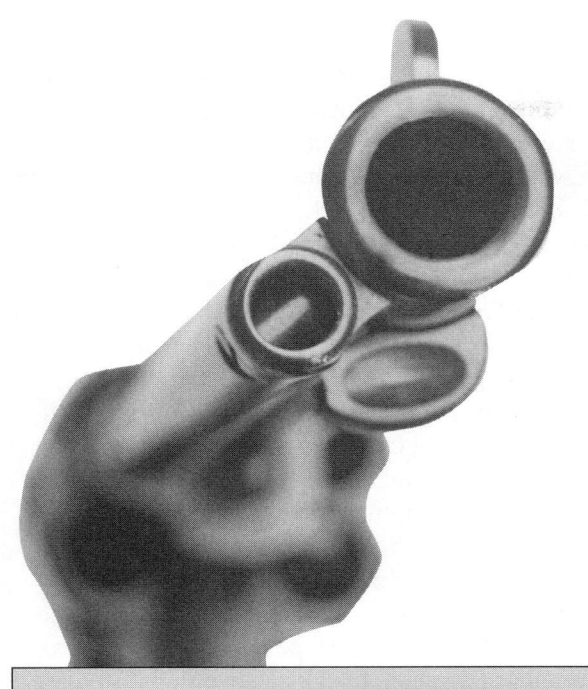

The imposing muzzle profile of the 4¾-inch .45 Stampede. Note the generously sized ejector button.

This is the stock style of the standard grade Beretta Stampede.

How's *that* fer celebratin' that thar individualism of the Old West?

The test guns we ordered were a 4⅝-inch .45 in Standard grade, and a Deluxe in .357 with a 7½-inch barrel.

The Standard .45

Weighing a portable 36.8 ounces and measuring 9½ inches overall, the 4⅝-inch Standard revolver came out of the box looking fine. Its plastic two-piece stocks were checkered, duplicating the feel of the original gutta percha, or 19th century "hard rubber," that Colt put on so many Model Ps. Where the Colt pony ran rampant, of course, this gun has the Beretta shield, and instead of an eagle on the bottom of the grip, we see an American bison. The grip panels' fit to the frame was very slightly imperfect, with the panels extruding just a bit past the frame at the bottom rear edge.

The finish, on the other hand, was beautiful. A friend of mine has written that fine bluing should look like a pool of black oil that appears wet even when the surface is bone dry. That, my friends, is the look the Uberti/Beretta Stampede has achieved with its standard-grade finish. The polish is excellent, and the color is a deep blue-black. It earned compliments from each of the many gun-wise testers who handled and admired it.

Mechanical timing was excellent. With the hammer at rest, there was no play in the cylinder at all. Nor was there any palpable play with the hammer at full cock. And, when the hammer fell and pushed the business end of the firing pin out through the breechface, there was *still* no play to be felt. Examination of spent casings showed perfectly centered firing pin hits on each. Alignment of every chamber with the bore was perfect. There was no "side-spit" from its barrel-to-cylinder gap.

The trigger broke cleanly in the 3-pound pull weight range. While the cylinder occasionally felt as if it was dragging during the loading and unloading process, nothing snagged. In firing, the hammer came back with the same easy movement every time.

This gun shot a bit to the left with each of the three loads I had available for it. We used all "cowboy" ammunition, factory flat-point lead bullets at mild velocity. Black Hills .45 Schofield, the shorter S&W cartridge issued by the U.S. Cavalry

The fire blued front sight of the deluxe was easier to see and, the author believes, resulted in improved accuracy.

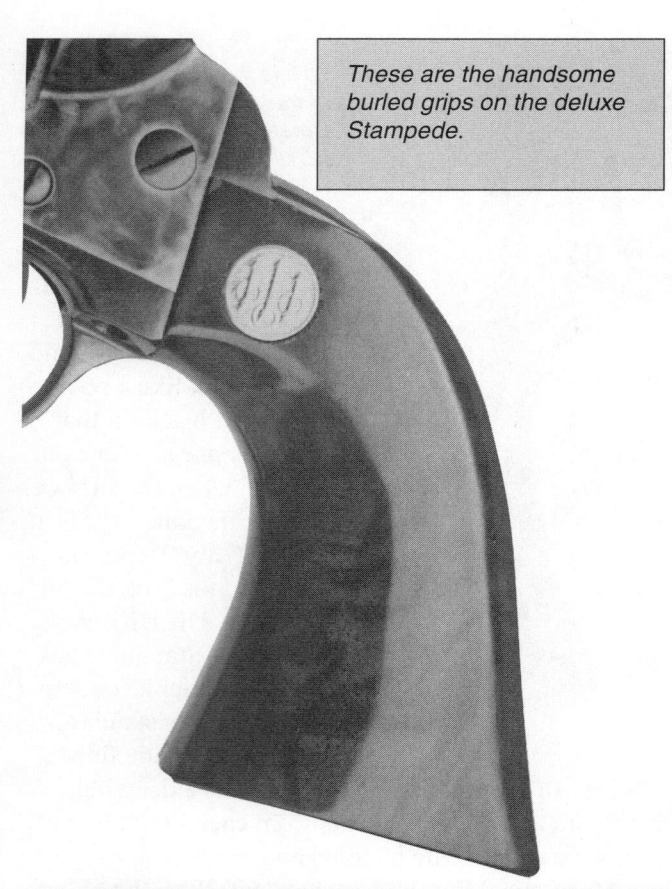

These are the handsome burled grips on the deluxe Stampede.

because it worked in the .45 Colt guns as well, spat a 230-grain bullet. At 25 yards from a makeshift rest, it put five rounds into 3.7 inches. The best three of which were in a 1.2-inch cluster. These shorter, slower rounds hit about 4 inches below point of aim.

Master brand 250-grain .45 Colt virgin ammo gave me a group of 4.8 inches, the best three in 3.35 inches. MagTech's cowboy load, also a 250-grain flat point .45 Colt, was the clear winner with a 2.8-inch five-shot group, the best three of which were in a triangle measuring only 1.15 inches. Both .45 Colt loads were pretty much "on" for elevation.

I think the gun and ammo are both more accurate than that. That fine polish on the front sight, which is rounded, reflected light off the top and made it difficult to get elevation exactly perfect. There is a long history of guns with that kind of front sight doing that. I think if the surface facing the shooter was dulled or flattened, the groups would be smaller. As tightly and finely as this revolver is fitted, there is no reason for it not to shoot with much more accuracy than I was able to coax out of it.

Recoil with all the cowboy loads was mild, strikingly so with the stubby Schofield round.

Cocking was smooth and virtually effortless with both test revolvers. This is the deluxe.

Left: These are gate-loading and unloading revolvers, of course, and the Stampede design makes these procedures easy.

Below: Deluxe (above) and standard grade Stampedes come out of the box ready for cowboy action matches.

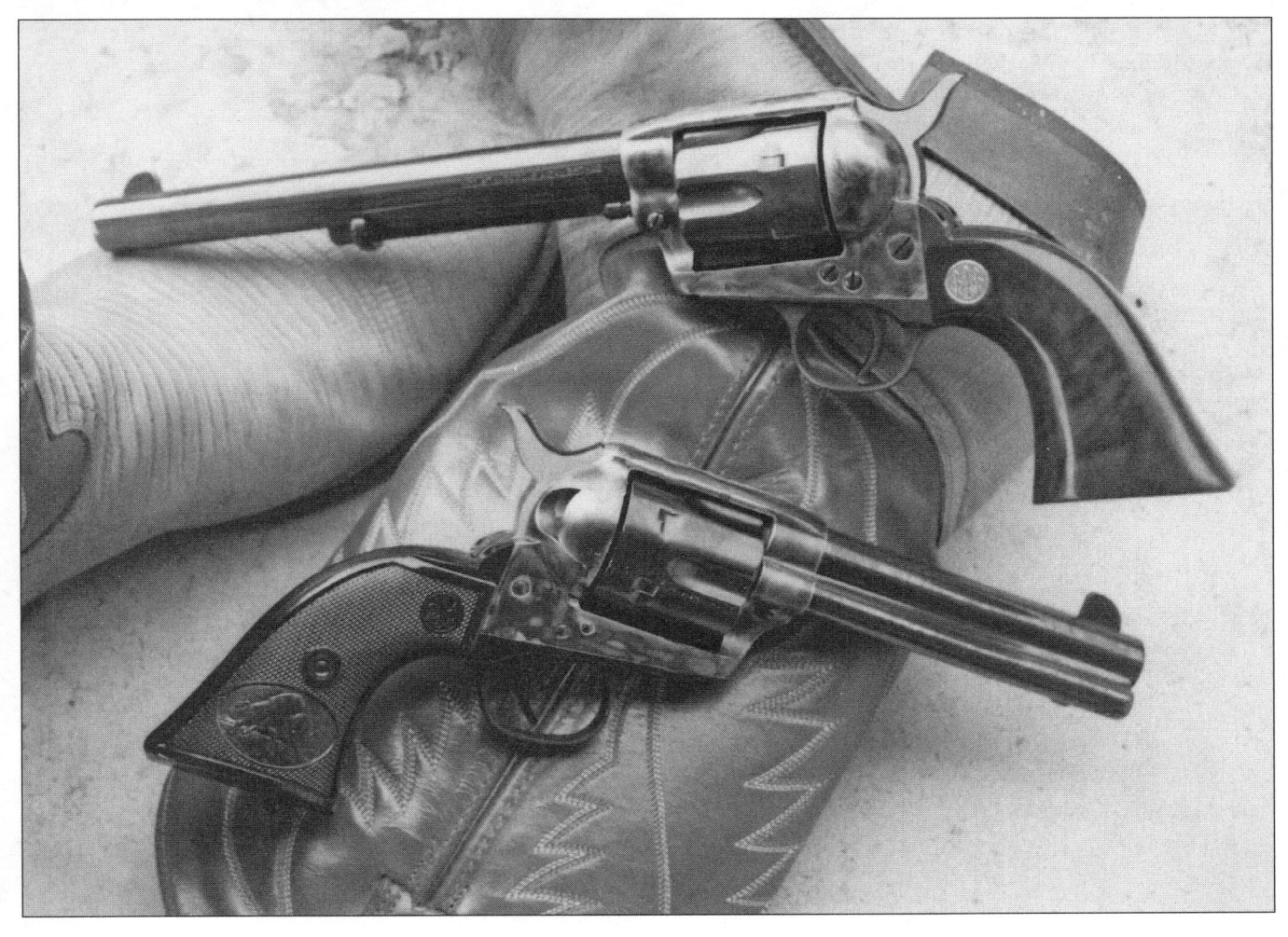

Above: With cowboy match ammo, the .45 Colt is an easy-shooting caliber. Ayoob is about to let off a shot …
Below: … and minimal muzzle rise is apparent.

Deluxe .357

The standard-grade Stampede impresses. The deluxe-grade Stampede *stuns*.

Beretta calls this gun's finish "charcoal blue," but it's something that has become perhaps more widely known as "fire blue." It's an electric blue, a not-quite cobalt blue if you will, and when it's applied to a gun whose underlying steel is as nicely polished as this one's, well, it just reaches out and grabs you by the eyeballs. Cylinder, barrel, cylinder pin, trigger, screws, grip frame and trigger guard, and the top of the hammer are all fire blued. The contrast with the "color-case look" is nothing less than striking.

The stock is one-piece hardwood, nicely polished, with a very subtle burl. Again, though, there is a fitting problem: air space between the left side of the stock and the frame, and the same overlap in the same place as was noted with the standard-grade gun and its black plastic grips. It has a bright gold-color Beretta medallion. Some shooters find this incongruous (hell, Colt didn't even start putting them on single actions until the 1950s, to the best of my knowledge). If we don't like it, we can do what we did with our second- and third-generation Colts and simply get new grips.

This gun was chambered for .38 Special/.357 Magnum rounds, and with its 7½-inch barrel was 13 inches in overall length, but weighed less than 2 ounces more than the short-barreled .45. Balance was distinctly different, though. Where the 4⅝-inch .45 Stampede had a "neutral" balance, the 7½-inch .357 had a pleasantly muzzle-heavy feel that seemed to help it stay on target when shooting without a rest.

The deluxe was fitted differently from the Standard. The barrel/cylinder gap was much tighter, only a couple of thousandths compared to the 5 or 6 thousandths of the .45. Many consider this too tight for reliable function, but we had no problems with it. The cylinder turned smoothly and effortlessly during all administrative handling. With the hammer at rest, there was very slight cylinder play; ditto when it was cocked; and ditto again with the trigger back and the hammer fallen. The hammer came back with the same

The deluxe gun shot a bit to the right with all loads tested; elevation of point of impact varied with ammo's velocity.

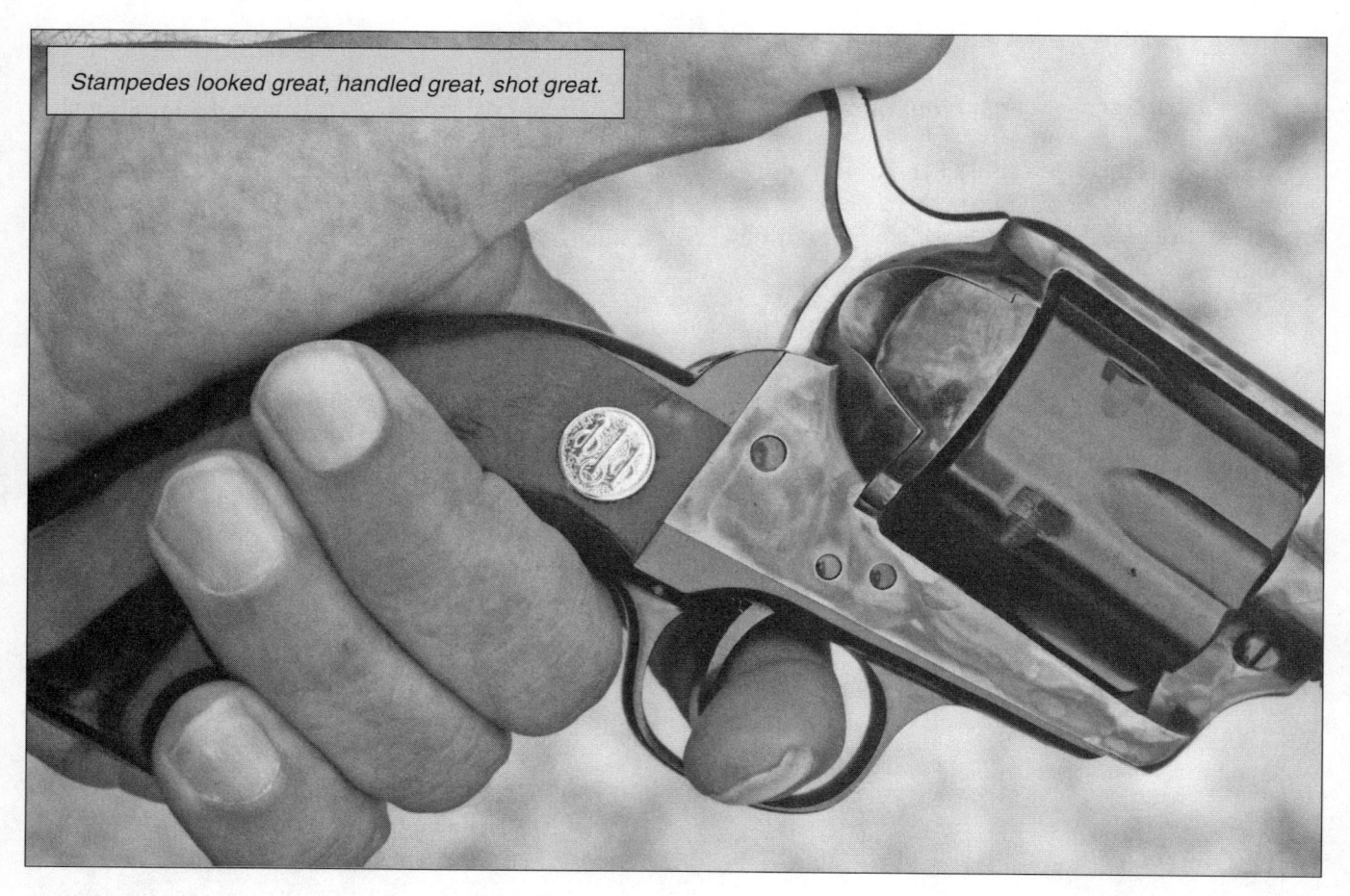

Stampedes looked great, handled great, shot great.

sweet ease as the .45's, and its trigger pull was a few ounces lighter and even crisper.

Groups were much tighter with the deluxe version. Having only one cowboy load in the caliber on hand, I threw in some loads that would take advantage of the .357 chambering's legendary versatility: .38 wadcutters, .38 "plinker" ammo, and the famously potent 125-grain Magnum hollow-points.

Winchester 125-grain SJHP .357 Magnum, rated for over 1,400 foot seconds from a mere 4-inch barrel, must have been screaming when it left the muzzle of the 7½-inch barrel Stampede. On the shooter's end, though, there was only a gentle bump and a very slight rollback of the plow-handle-shaped grip frame in the hand. Very fast bullets tend to hit lower than standard velocity, and sure enough, the Winchester 125-grain Magnums clustered about 3 inches low from point of aim and, like everything else we shot in this gun, just a tad right. The five-shot group measured 2.3 inches, with four of those shots in an inch and a quarter and the best three in 1.05 inches.

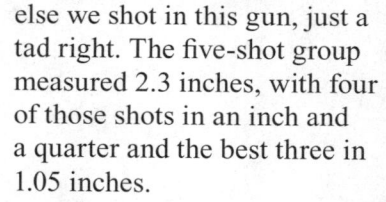

Remington UMC "generic" 130-grain full-metal-jacket .38

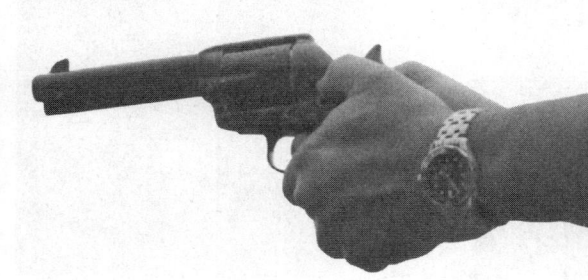

Soft shootin'. Steve Denney lines up the standard-grade Stampede ...

Special ammo is cheap and popular for informal recreational shooting. It delivered a 2.65-inch group for five shots, 1.7 inches for the best three. Recoil was mild, of course, and the center of the group was about an inch and a half below point of aim.

Black Hills .38 Special Cowboy ammo is what I'd take to a SASS match with this gun, and that's apparently the sort of load it's sighted for. At modest velocity, the 150-grain lead flat-point bullets were spot on for elevation, though a little right like everything else in this particular specimen, and the group measured 2.2 inches for all five shots. Four of those rounds were in a little nest 1.1 inches in diameter, and the best three were in a triangle that measured but three quarters of one inch. Now you know why Black Hills is the brand I take to cowboy matches. Recoil, as you might imagine, was inconsequential.

But the best group by far came from the load that, before SASS, was the light practice round of choice in a .357 Magnum. I had on hand some remanufactured (commercially reloaded) 148-grain .38 Special mid-range wadcutter from Warwick Precision in Sanbornton, NH. The five-shot group from the makeshift bench measured 1 inch, on the nose, center-to-center. That, my brothers and sisters of the single-action posse, is not the kind of accuracy you see every day at 25 yards from a fixed-sight, out-of-the box "cowboy revolver." The best three shots in the group, which I always measure in hopes of factoring out human error, were in a single clover-shaped hole measuring only 0.35 of an inch center-to-center. A tribute to the excellence of Warwick Precision ammo, with which I won a lot of matches with high-tech, custom double-action revolvers when I shot PPC a lot, this group was no less a tribute to superb engineering and execution by Uberti for Beretta. The wadcutters, by the way, clustered just above point of aim.

Why did the .357 group so much better than the .45? The greater sight radius afforded by its longer barrel was, I think, the least of it. It had a tighter barrel-to-cylinder gap, but that's not so great a component of revolver accuracy as solid lockup, and the .45 was even tighter than the .357 in that regard.

No, I think the big difference was the fire-blued front sight. Lighter in color, it stood out in marked contrast against the target inside the small, square notch of the rear sight. It didn't give the glare effect of sunlight on top of its rounded surface as did the blue-black sight of the same configuration on the .45. It's one of those human factors. No matter how much inherent, mechanical accuracy the firearm possesses, the ability of its user to translate that into consistent aim and surprise trigger break will be critical to the final performance.

The guns shot to different elevations with loads of different velocities. This is why there are adjustable sights. However, most single-action competitors don't think adjustable sights are "the cowboy way" and some competitions require fixed sights. So, as has been done since the dawn of fixed-sight revolvers, you settle on one load and have your gunsmith zero your piece in for that. Ditto the .45 shooting left and the .38/.357 shooting right. So it was before, and so it shall be.

High Value

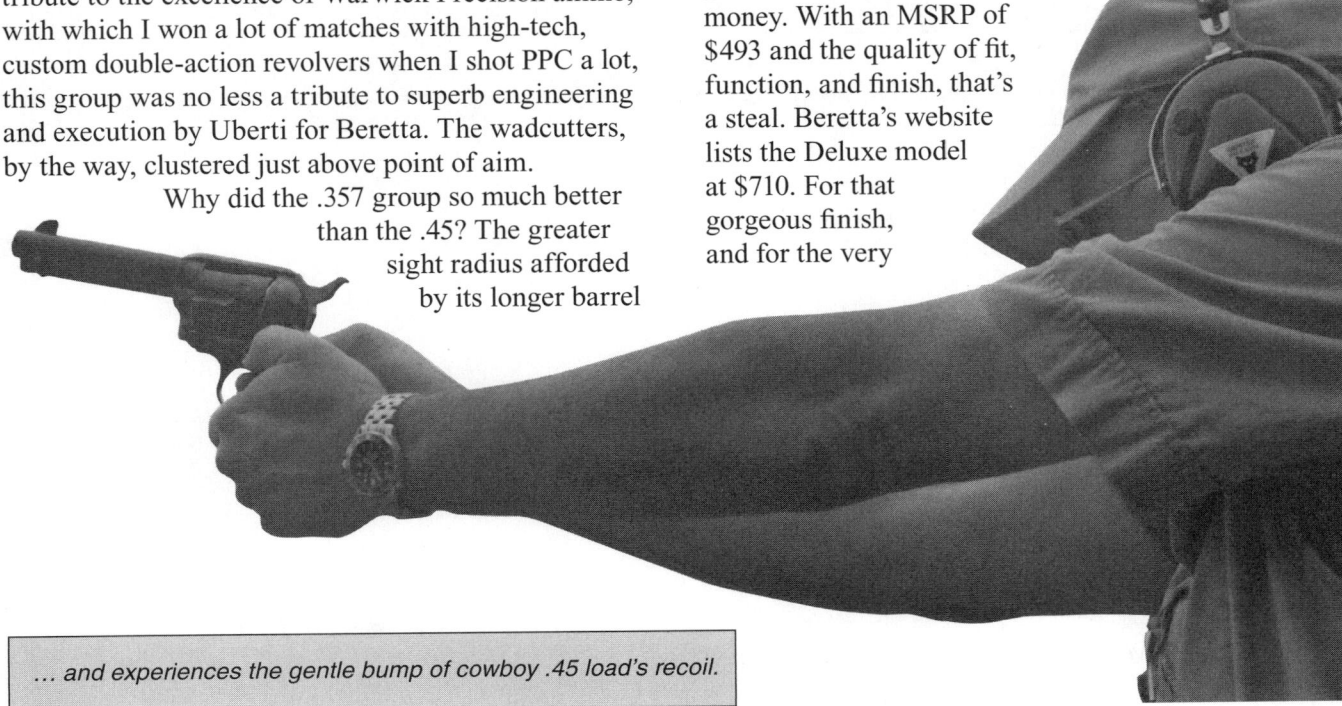

I, like all who shot them, was very pleased with the two Stampede revolvers. The Standard grade is a beautiful little gun, and absolutely worth the money. With an MSRP of $493 and the quality of fit, function, and finish, that's a steal. Beretta's website lists the Deluxe model at $710. For that gorgeous finish, and for the very

... and experiences the gentle bump of cowboy .45 load's recoil.

practical reason that I can see the "charcoal blue" front sight better and therefore can hit with it better, that's a damn good price, too.

These guns give top value for the money. They are aptly named. Once cowboy action shooters find out how good these Beretta Stampedes are, and how little they cost for their quality and performance, there's gonna be a stampede to the gun shops to buy them.

But a chapter about Beretta *revolvers* seems rather anomalous to a book about Beretta *pistols*. So, let's return to the topic of those high speed, low drag, way cool Beretta semiautomatics, and how to get the most out of them…

The .45 caliber standard model was exquisitely tight, and shot very well with these three factory cowboy competition loads.

Beretta Accessories

Fobus synthetic holster and magazine pouches are popular in IDPA matches and for concealed carry. These were mail-ordered from Brownell's.

You wouldn't buy an Alfa Romeo and put cheap two-ply retread tires on it. Don't accessorize your Beretta on the cheap, either.

The fact is, there isn't much that one of these guns really *needs* as it comes out of the box. Let's say you've bought a stock Beretta Vertec. The Bruniton finish on the chrome-molybdenum gun will age nicely, rubbing off a bit on the frame if you give it a lot of wear, which imbues a pleasant "salty" look to the gun, sort of like a scarred and dented police baton. It's a patina that says, "Been there, done that." If you've chosen the Inox version, as Beretta calls its stainless guns, it's sufficiently rust-resistant that an additional aftermarket finish probably won't be necessary.

As noted elsewhere, the sights will be excellent as they come out of the box. Between the dovetailed front sight of the Vertec and the generously sized dovetail rear sight on all the 92s, it will be no trick

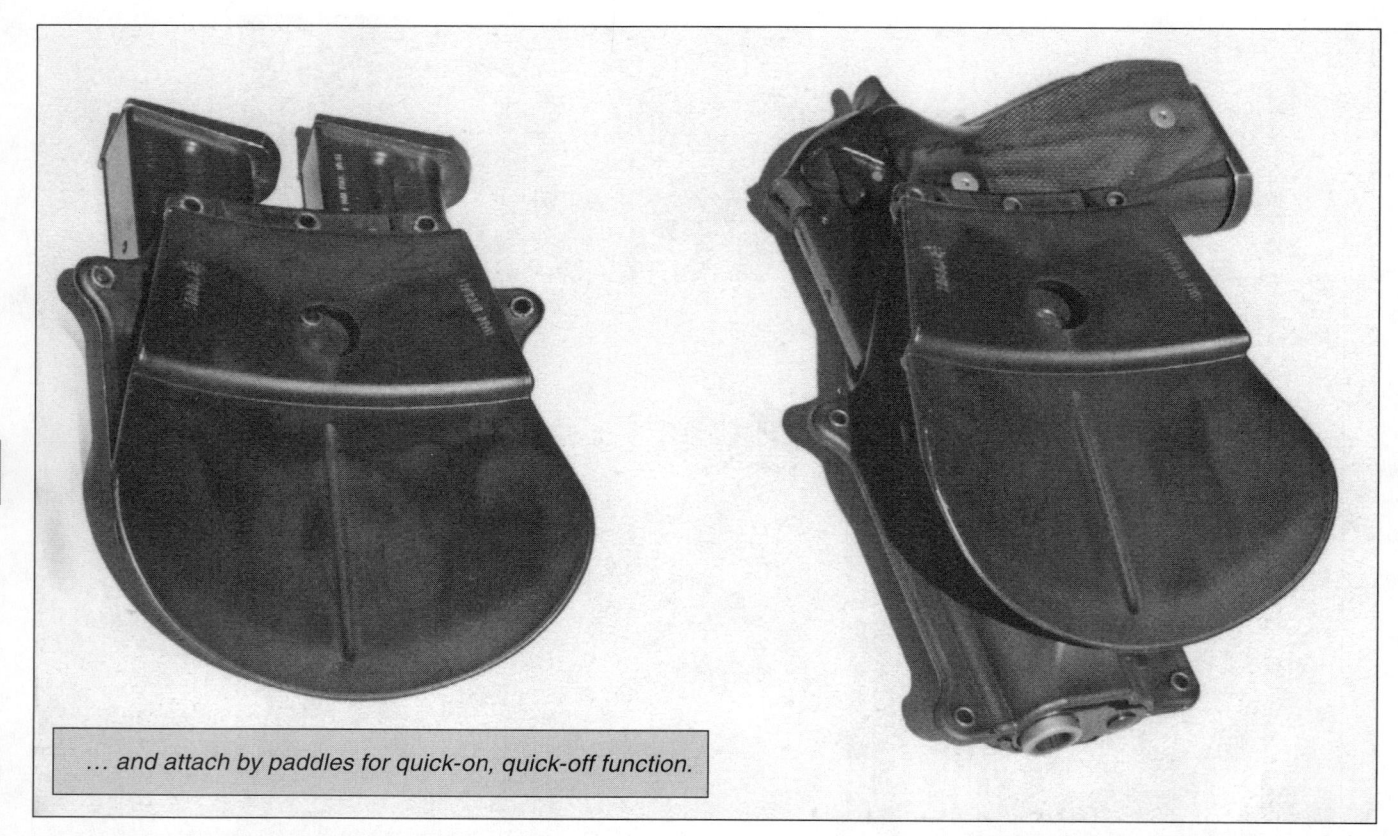

... and attach by paddles for quick-on, quick-off function.

Left: A Don Hume holster offers quick on/off with snapping belt loops.

Below: Conventional thumb break scabbard holds Cougar 9mm with one level of security; add one more if it's an F series on safe.

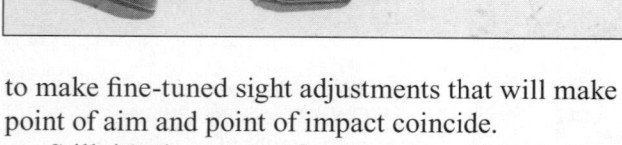

to make fine-tuned sight adjustments that will make point of aim and point of impact coincide.

Still, it's the nature of men to customize their weapons. Elsewhere in this book, we'll talk about hard-core customizing of the Beretta. Often, all it takes to make the Beretta just a little more perfect for your needs is this or that bolt-on accessory.

Even if your new carry Beretta is fine for you as it comes out of the box, you still need something to carry it in. Since the serious fighting Berettas are good-sized pistols, holster selection becomes particularly important. That makes "gun-wear accessories" a good place to start.

Kydex speed scabbard for 92F Vertec; very fast, but Level 0 security. It would be equivalent of Level I if the pistol was on safe.

Above: This handy business portfolio by Andrews Leather looks harmless …
Opposite page top: … but carries a loaded 92F and spare magazine of 15 rounds …
Opposite page bottom: … cleverly concealed inside.

Holsters, Etc.

Concealment Holsters. For your smaller Berettas, the pocket is the logical place to carry. If the gun is just in there loose, it can shift around and not be perfectly placed for a draw when the time comes that you need it. A pocket holster does a lot of good things for you. A good one will break up the outline of the gun in your pocket, maintaining discretion. It will keep the gun upright and ready for your reaching hand. It will keep pocket lint and dirt from getting into the mechanism.

Uncle Mike's makes a decent nylon pocket holster. Greg Kramer makes the Cadillac of leather pocket rigs, with a stiff square backer to disguise the pistol's shape. Jerry Ahern makes a nifty little pocket rig for the tiny autos. Perhaps the most efficient are the Kydex ones, with flared shape designed to catch on the edge of the pocket lining to guarantee that holster and gun come apart as they should during an emergency draw. Ky-Tac and Mach-2 are my favorite brands in that genre.

Coming up from the Tomcat .32 and the little .22s and .25s, we get to the .380s. Beretta's 80 Series guns are big for .380s. That's what makes them so fast and accurate and easy to shoot, but it also makes them harder to conceal. Be thinking in terms of belt rigs and shoulder rigs.

The shoulder rig is handy for the person who only puts the piece on when he or she goes out. It is particularly useful for women, since it solves a wardrobe problem. Dress gun belts are no longer needed. Women are able to reach to their armpit easier than men. Bianchi, Cobra Gunskin, Galco, Safariland, and Ted Blocker all make suitable shoulder rigs with horizontal or semi-upside down carry that work beautifully with Beretta .380s.

The belt is a more sensible location for most men. Inside the waistband carry is the most discreet, though even with these compact pistols they'll be tight. You bought the pants for you, after all, and now they're occupied by you and a holstered Beretta, and perhaps a spare magazine. You want to get the pants about two inches larger in the waist than you normally

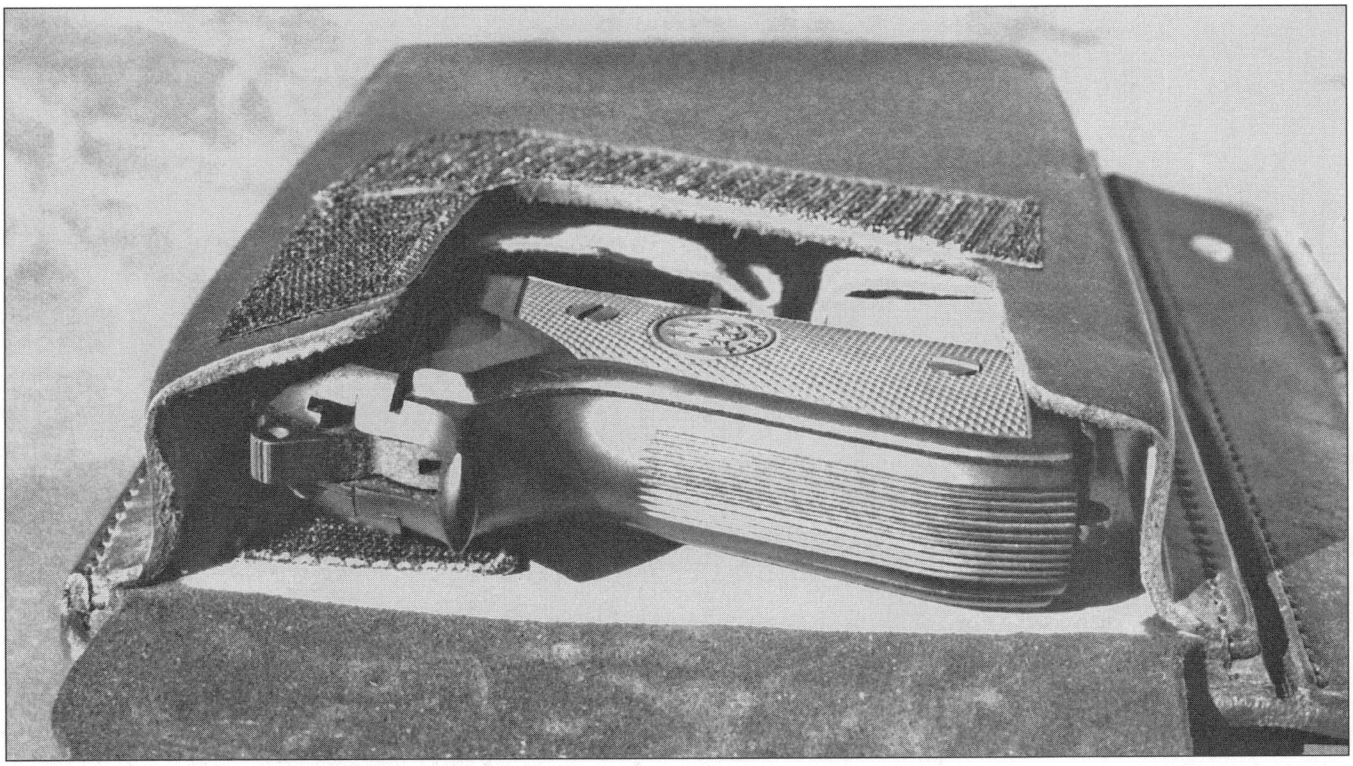

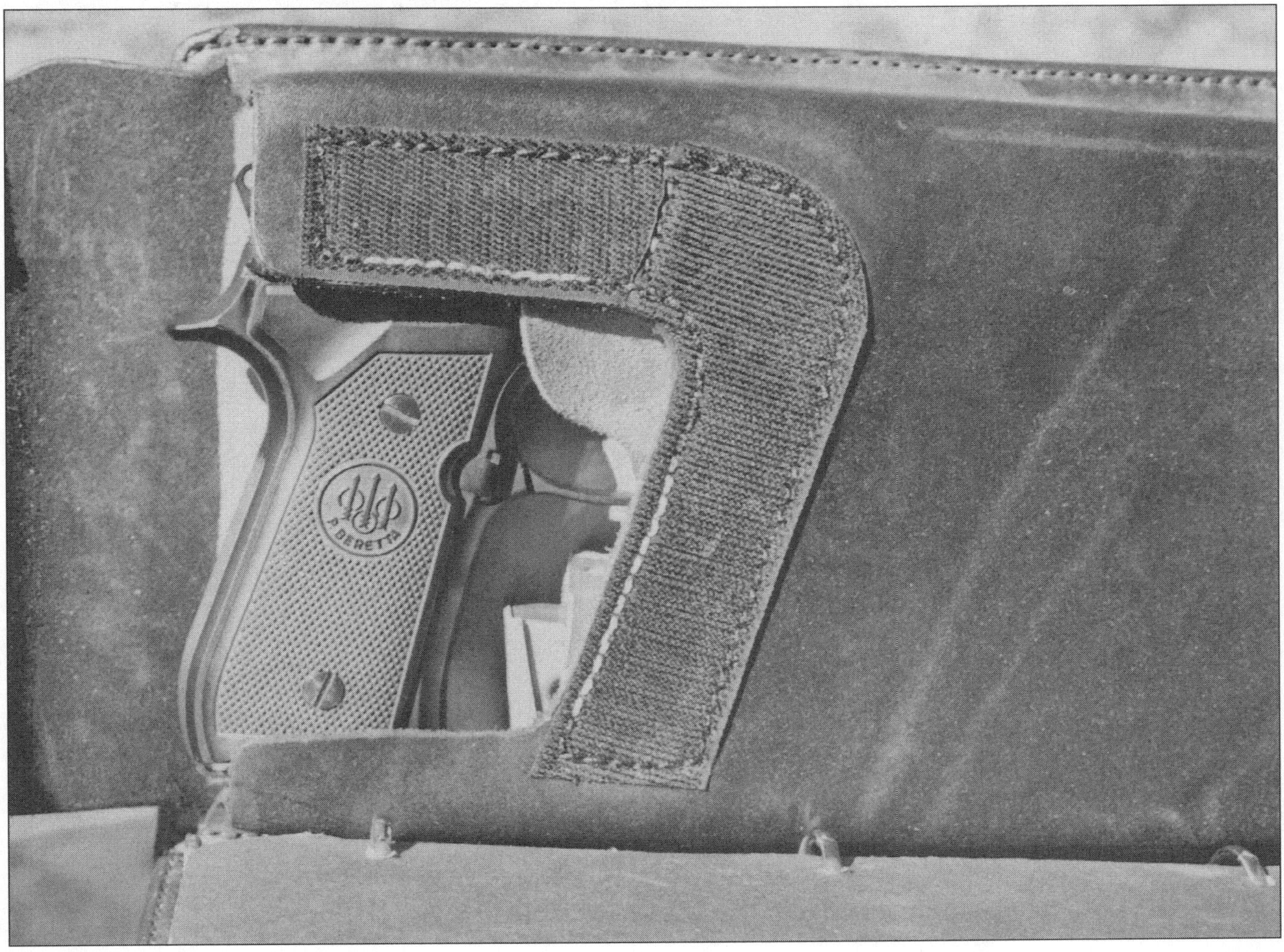
P. BERETTA

Galco thumb-break keeps this lawman's Beretta 96 discreetly concealed when he's in plainclothes.

If you carry on safe, you want a holster design like this one by Dillon that gives the thumb early access to the safety lever.

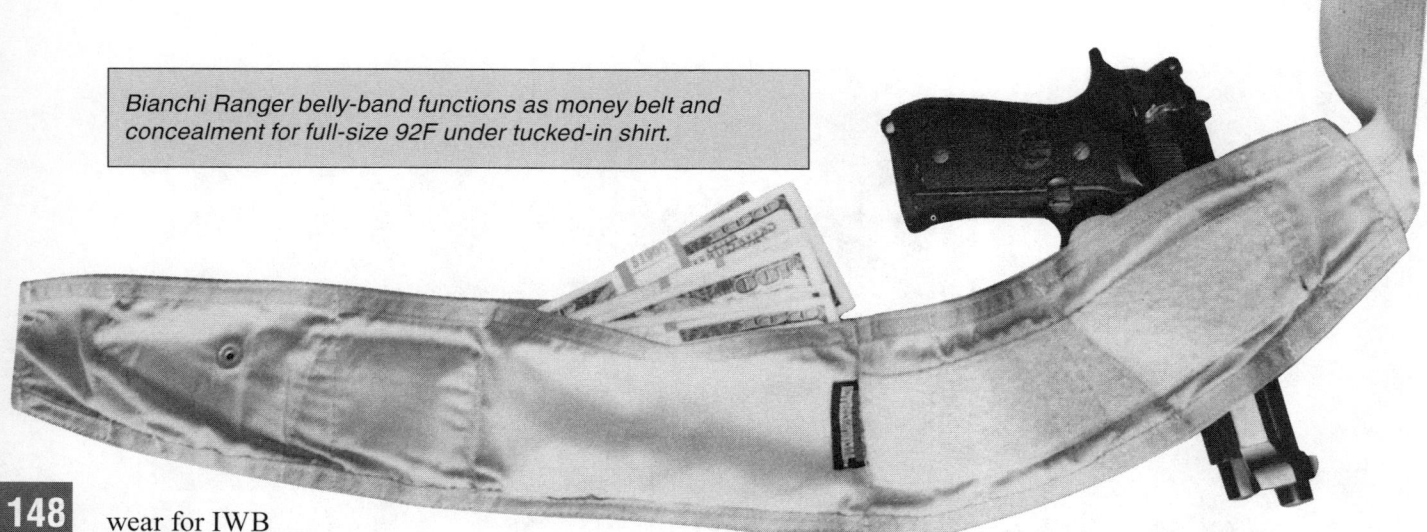

Bianchi Ranger belly-band functions as money belt and concealment for full-size 92F under tucked-in shirt.

wear for IWB (inside the waistband) carry to really work for you.

That goes double if you're carrying a serious-size fighting Beretta: Model 92 or 96, or Cougar. Make sure you get a good, strong dress gun belt designed to fit the loops of your holster. This will help distribute the weight, and help hold the package of gun and holster snugly and discreetly to your body.

A good belt scabbard may be easier and more comfortable, though the reality is it will bulge more and therefore require a looser, longer concealing garment for discreet concealed carry. The holster makers listed above all have several good options. Ditto Blackhawk, Blade-Tech, Dillon, Elmer MacEvoy's Leather Arsenal, Milt Sparks, Mitch Rosen, Orca, Strong Holsters, Uncle Mike's, and more. Fobus also makes a synthetic line of holsters for Berettas.

In the IWB area, the two I'm most partial to are, not surprisingly, the ones I designed. The LFI Concealment Rig by Ted Blocker is made of good quality grain-out leather, and rides inside the belt secured by a Velcro tab that mates to the lining of a dedicated, matching gun belt, as does the similarly designed spare magazine carrier. This arrangement allows the shooter almost unlimited adjustment as to the angle at which the gun is raked, and significant adjustment as to how high or low the pistol sits. It's also very quick to put on or take off. It stays in place securely, held by a combination of belt tension and Velcro shear factor.

The other is the ARG, which I designed years ago for Mitch Rosen. Made of high-quality leather with superb workmanship, this IWB holster has a leather strap located at the rear to lever the gun forward. It's particularly suitable for concealing a gun with a large grip frame such as the Beretta 92 or 96, since the placement of the belt loop levers the butt forward and keeps it from tilting back and "printing" under the coat. Asked by Rosen to name it, I called it the Rear Guard, since the loop was designed to guard against bulge at the rear of the jacket. Mitch, who likes to name holsters after their designers – a good thing – dubbed it the Ayoob Rear Guard. This was fine until I realized the initials would spell ARG, which when uttered in one syllable sounds like "Arrgghh!" I was just glad I hadn't called it *S*uper *H*olster *I*nside *T*rousers. After 9/11, Mitch re-named the holster the American Rear Guard.

Another option that seems inviting with a large auto pistol is off-body carry. Some of the above firms, including Bianchi and Galco, make purses with built-in holsters, and some other firms such as Guardian Leather specialize in them. Guardian Leather also makes a superb leather briefcase with built-in holster that accepts a ballistic panel that will defeat 00 Buckshot and Magnum handgun rounds. Various makers have produced everything from cell phone and DVD player carriers that will hide a Bobcat or Tomcat, to big Daytimer-type rigs that actually do that job, but also have a hiding place that can conceal a big Model 92. If you like to just stick your gun in the glove compartment, an on-safe F-series Beretta minimizes the chance of anything hitting the trigger and firing the gun if you get into an auto accident.

One point specific to the Beretta F-series, or any pistol with a slide-mounted safety that might be carried on-safe: make sure you can reach it. Many holsters are designed with a leather flare that comes up between the body and the pistol, especially the inside-the-waistband styles. This design has two purposes. One is to protect the gun from your salty sweat. The other is to protect your skin from possible sharp edges on the gun. However, with a slide-mounted safety to manipulate during an emergency draw, you want to be able to get the thumb to that

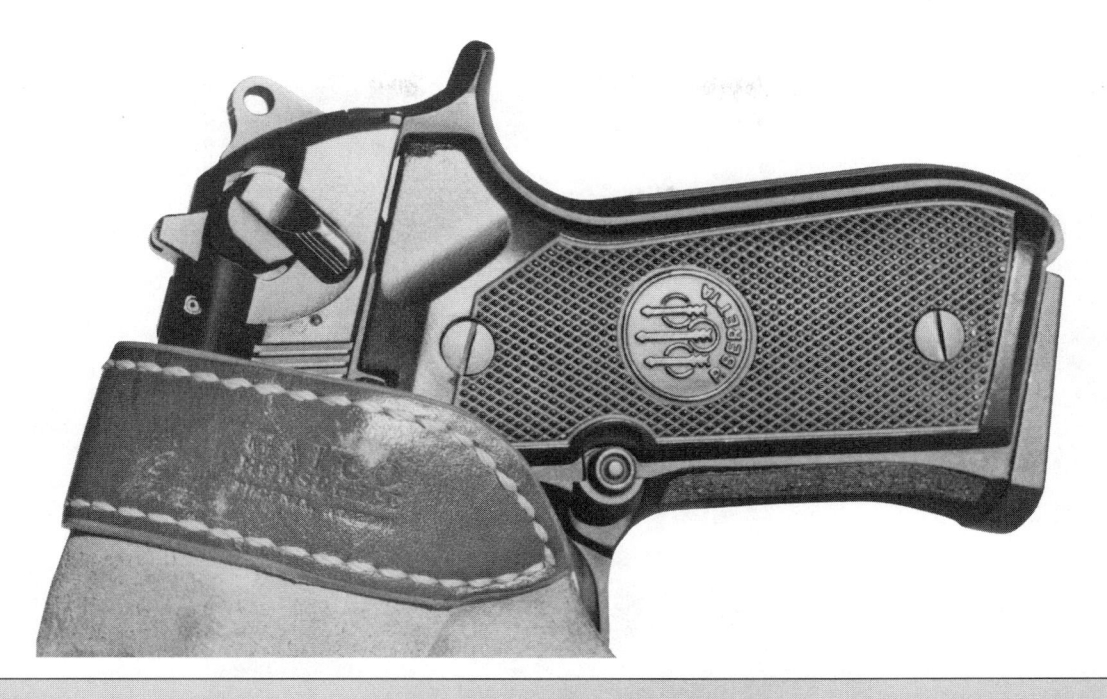

Below left: Galco's "NSA" inside-the-waistband holster strongly resembles the Ayoob Rear Guard by Mitchell Rosen …

Below right: … sharing a reinforced mouth for smooth, one-handed holstering by feel, but deviating in that it is rough-out instead of grain-out …

Above … and sharing also a cut that exposes the slide lever if the Beretta is carried on safe.

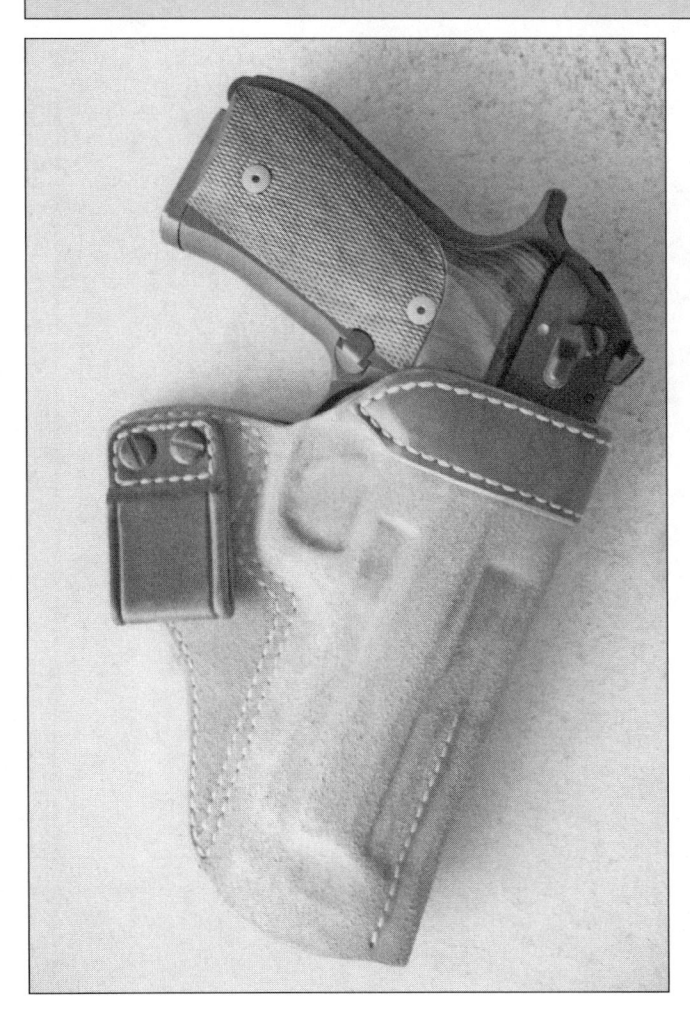

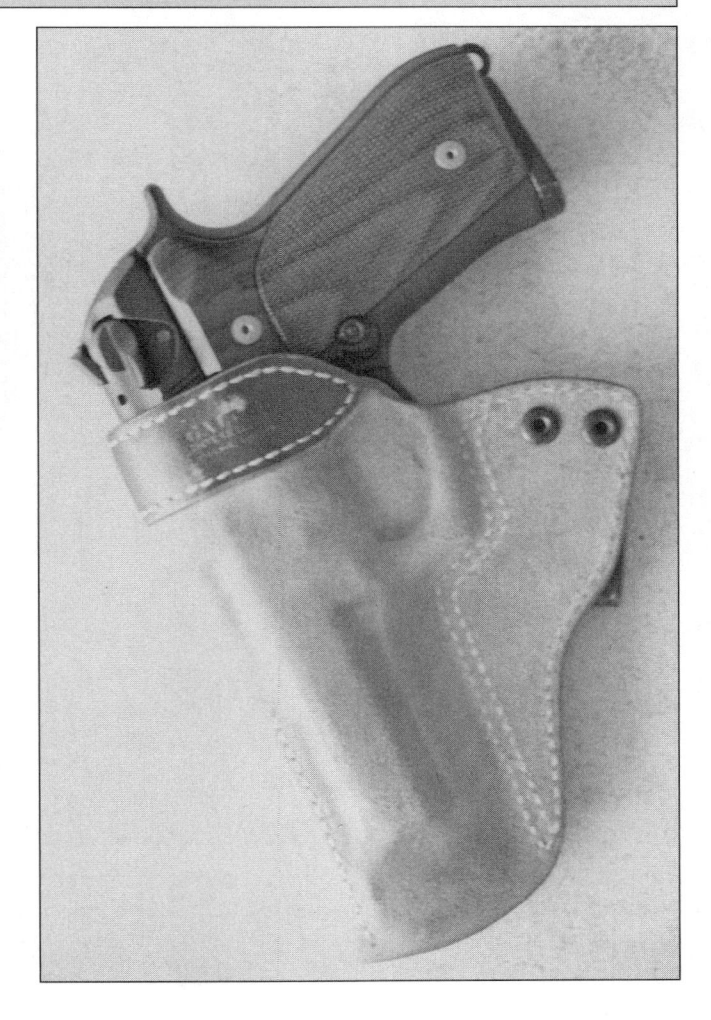

If you must keep the loaded gun in a glove compartment, the author feels that a double-action Beretta – especially an on safe F series like this one – represents the safest possible handgun type to use.

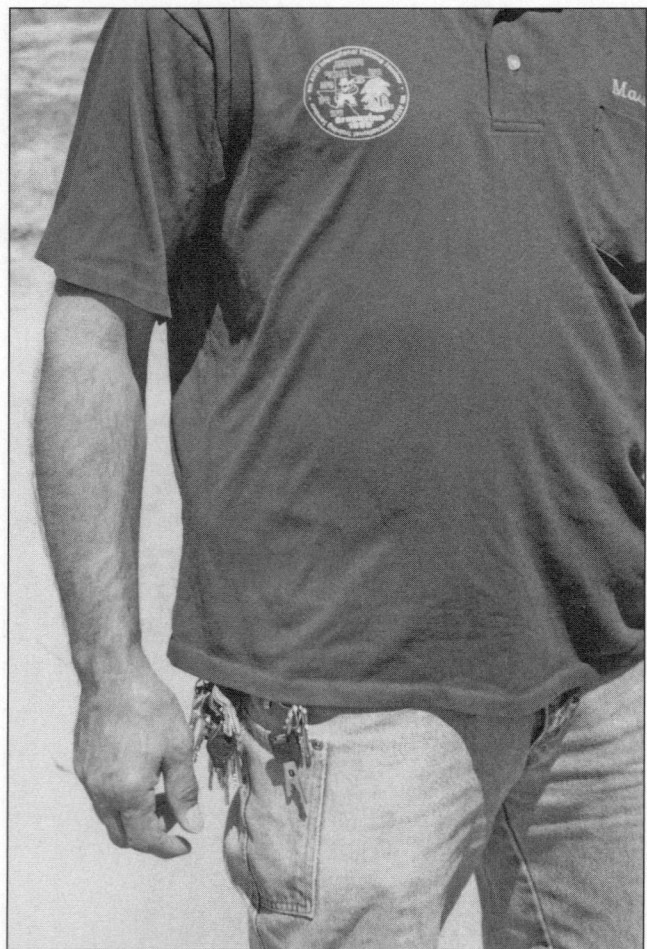

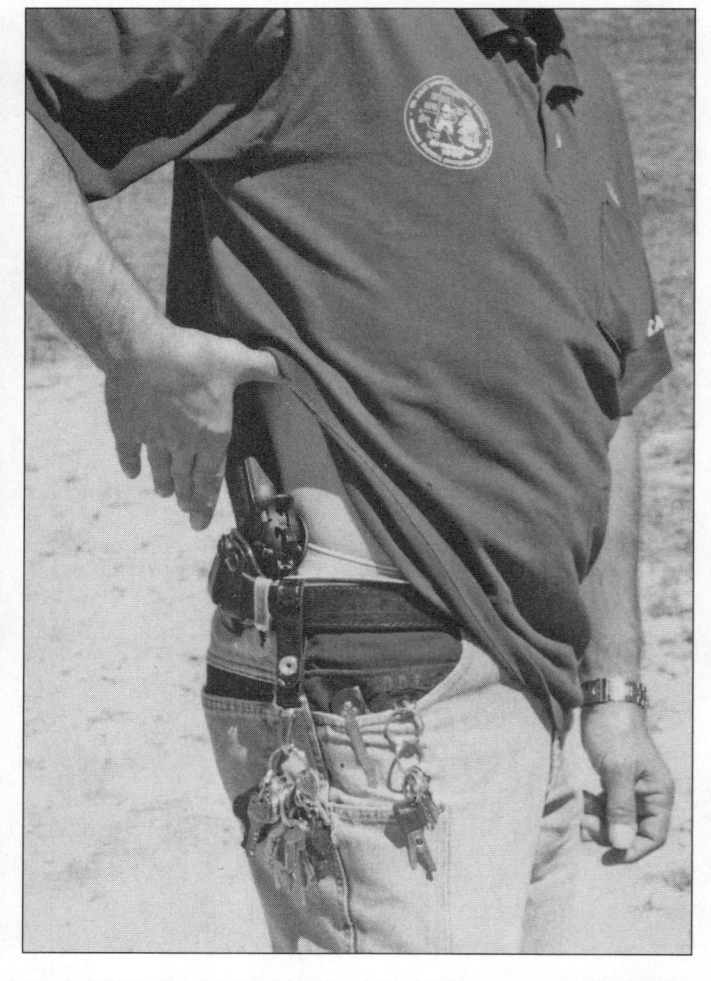

Above left: With an inside-the-waistband holster, even a full-size Beretta …
Above right: … can be reasonably well concealed under an untucked polo shirt that is one size large.

Above left: The sliding tab on Ted Blocker DA-2 holster's front belt slot allows adjustment of forward cant, straight up draw, or crossdraw. The same holster is available with thumb-break as DA-1.

Above right: Orca's inside-the-waistband holster is practical and concealable with this 92FS.

Left: Dillon's open-top scabbard is very fast, very concealable, and very affordable, but like all open-top holsters is "Level 0" for security against gun snatches. The pistol is a Langdon Custom 92G.

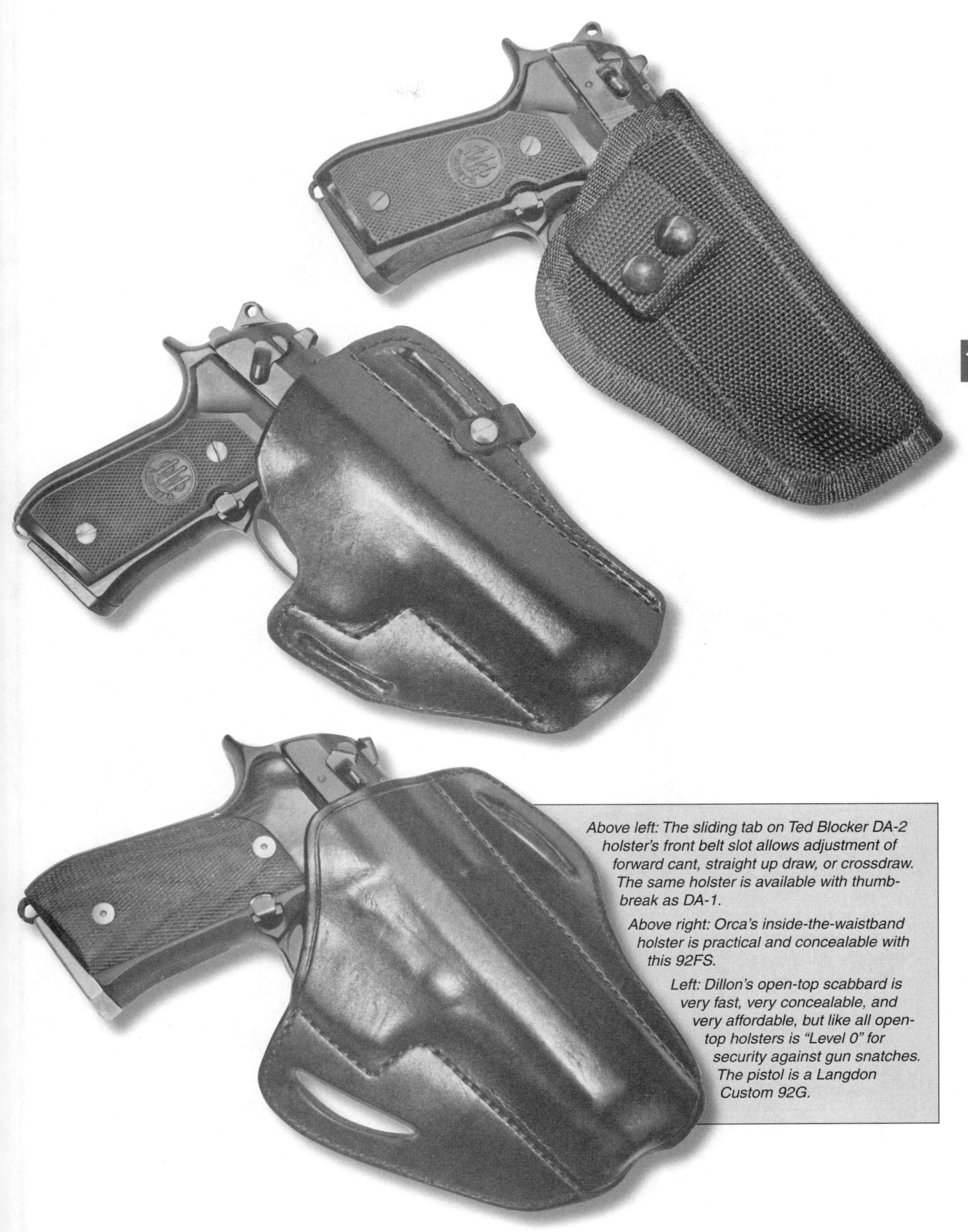

Above left: Milt Sparks Executive Companion is an excellent inside-the-waistband holster …

Above right: … whose design includes a leather shield to protect you the from gun and the gun from you …

Below: … but because leather blocks the safety, it is better suited for a Beretta not carried on safe.

lever as soon as the draw begins. That means that the leather should be cut away in that area.

Uniform duty holsters.

A police officer's Beretta, and that of a uniformed security professional, is hanging out for the world to see … and to reach for. Speed of access is important, but so is security. This has led to a continuing evolution of snatch-resistant holsters that still offer swift access to the authorized wearer who is properly trained and practiced.

Safariland is the best-selling maker of police security holsters. Several years ago, the firm came up with a rating system for such rigs that has come into wide use. Each is deemed to have a certain "level" of security. For each movement required to draw the gun and have it in hand ready to shoot, a level of security is added.

An open top quick-draw holster would be "Level 0." It offers no security against a gun-grab. It will yield its deadly cargo to an offender's reaching hand as quickly as to the legitimate owner's.

"Level I" security is typified by the common thumb-break holster. One movement, the release of the safety strap, is all that is required to free the gun for a draw-and-shoot movement.

"Level II" security is reached when two movements are required before the draw can get under way. Most break-front holsters are Level Two, with a thumb-break and then a movement in a certain direction that releases the holster from an internal securing niche and allows the draw to begin. Strong's Piece-Keeper holster is Level II, since the shooter has to rock the thumb-lock back and then perform the conventional thumb-break movement before the pistol is released. The Safariland Model 295, quite popular in law enforcement, is Level II. So is the same maker's SLS. The name stands for Self-Locking System. A push downward on the release paddle unlocks the design, allowing the same thumb to move from the same position in a forward rocking motion to clear the holster for draw. The SLS gets its name from its automatic locking feature, which kicks in when the officer simply pushes back on the safety strap upon reholstering. This makes it much faster and easier for an officer to secure the service weapon while handcuffing a suspect. This has become hugely popular, particularly in its optional thigh-carry style for tactical operators who wear heavy armor.

The two holsters most commonly used by the US military in combat today are actually Level II rigs. The M-12 Bianchi, a universal left or right hand rig,

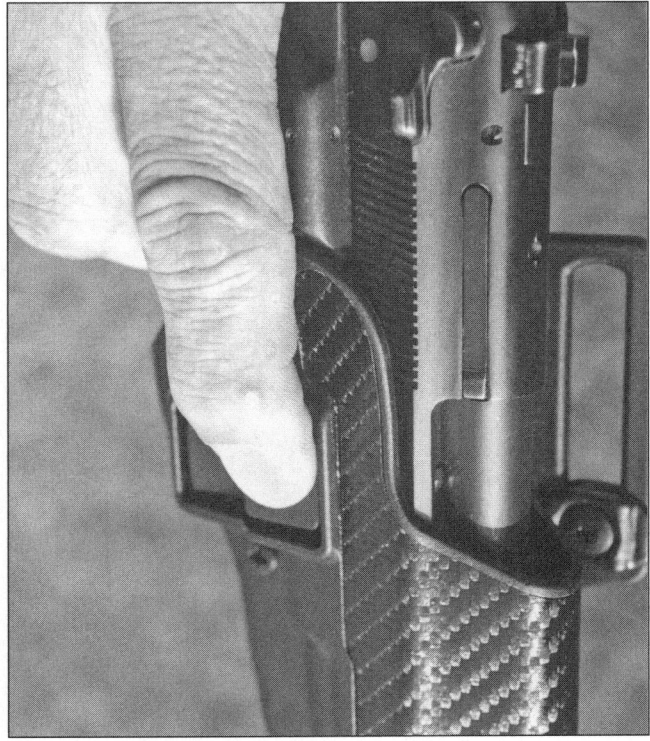

Right: Consider the new SERPA holster from Blackhawk, made of carbon fiber and with clever recessed trigger lock …

Below: … that keeps the gun in the holster until the owner, executing a proper draw, depresses the release paddle with the trigger finger.

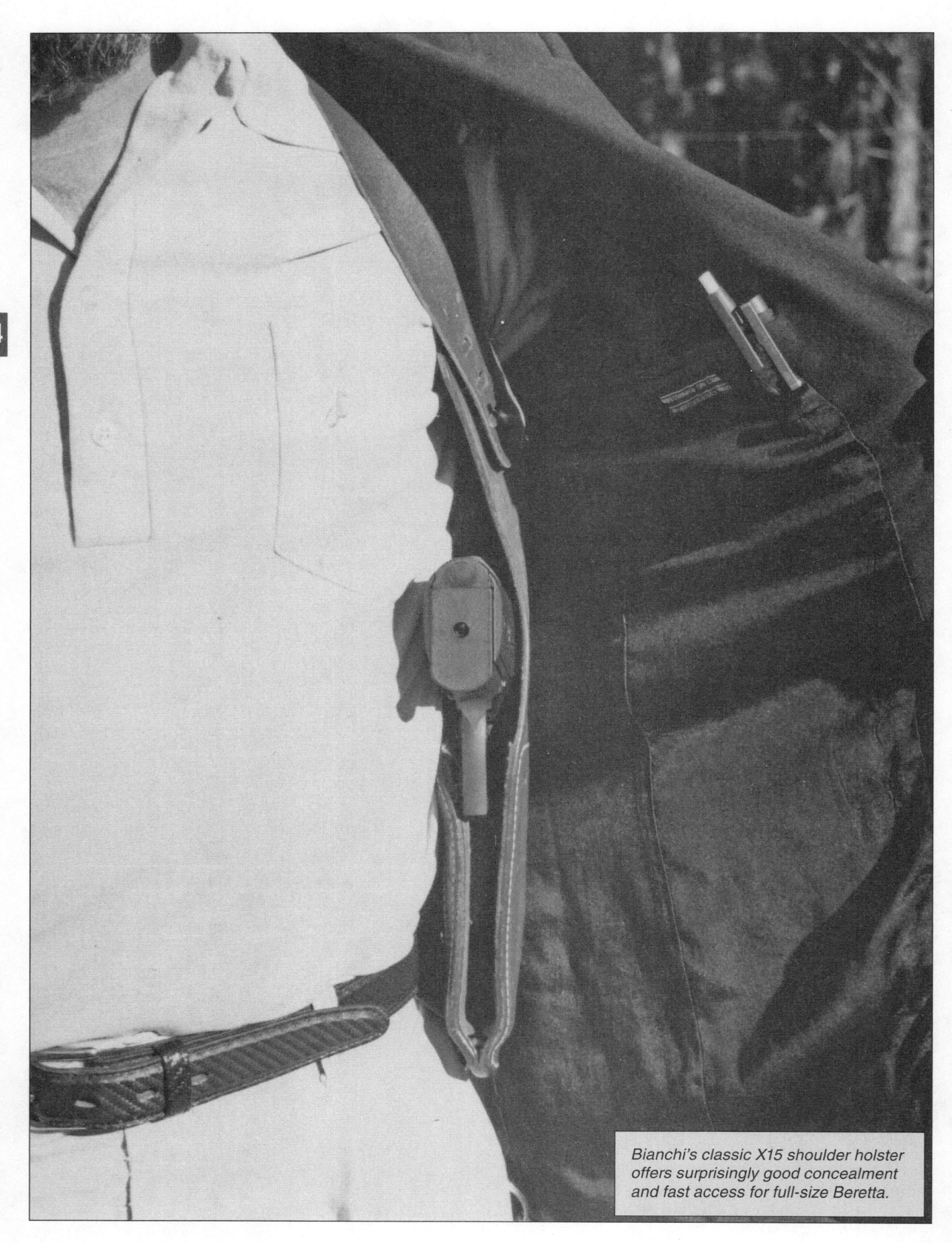

Bianchi's classic X15 shoulder holster offers surprisingly good concealment and fast access for full-size Beretta.

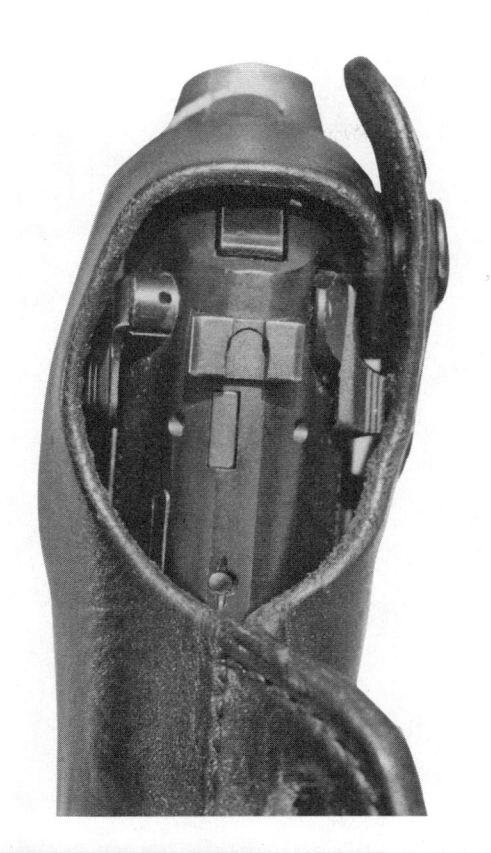

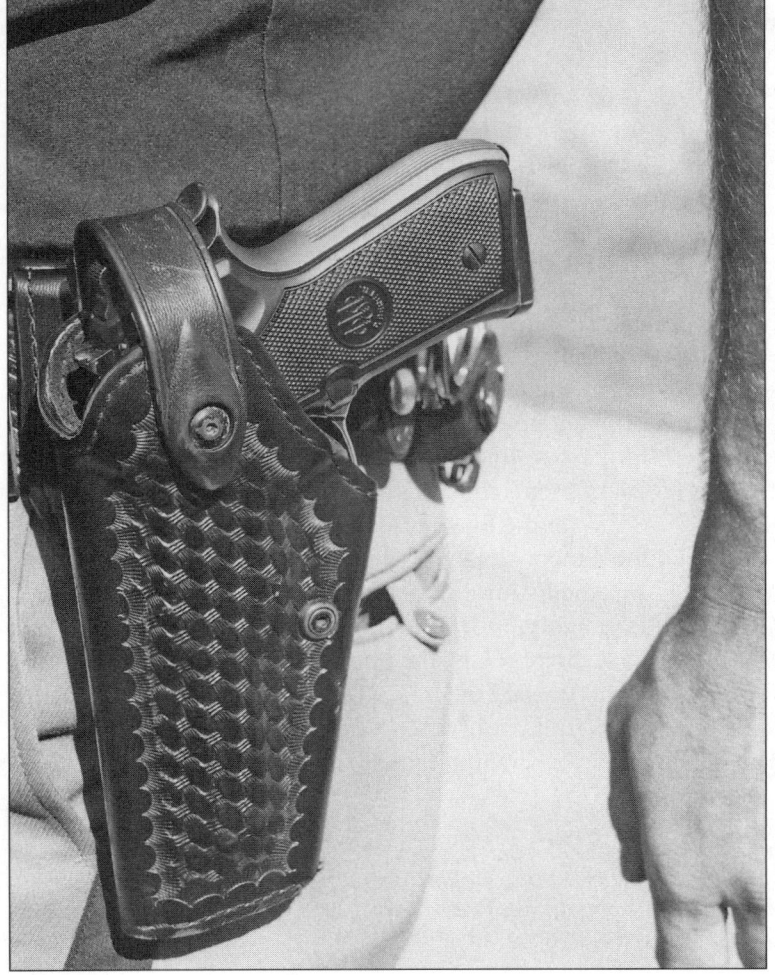

Left: Safariland SLS duty holster, Level II security, holds a department-issue 92F.

Above left: Simple thumb-break offers Level I security.

Above right: Simple duty thumb-break: effectively Level I security if off safe, Level II if pistol is on safe.

is the standard issue all-purpose military holster. The shooter has to pull down on an inconspicuous D-ring to unlock the flap. The second of the two movements that comprise the Level II status is the lifting of the flap. Designed by Richard Nichols and John Bianchi, this holster has served our military well for a score of years. At this writing, the Safariland SLS thigh holster is in very wide use by our troops in the Middle East, since it secures the Beretta M9 well and keeps it out of the way of the Interceptor body armor but still readily accessible.

"Level III" came into being more than a quarter of a century ago, the brainchild of the brilliant and prolific Bill Rogers. The designer of the SLS and many other modern rigs, he created the most popular Level III holster, Safariland's SS-III, also known as the Model 070. Two straps, one broken by the thumb and the other released by the middle finger during the draw, can be released simultaneously in a practiced movement by the officer. The gun is then rocked back to release it from an internal niche, the third element of the Level III design, and the gun can now be drawn in the conventional manner. Countless police lives have been saved when Berettas and other guns were kept in their holsters, because the SS-III design refused to yield them up to even the most determined gun-grabber. This writer's police department issues the SS-III. It has worked extraordinarily well for us.

"Level IV" was achieved when Rogers combined the SLS feature with the SS-III. Some consider the result, the Raptor holster, to be Level III, but with a middle finger hit (1), thumb release (2), and the forward roll of the SLS feature (3), *plus* the necessary rock to clear the internal niche (4), that adds up to four movements in my book and qualifies for Level IV status. Rogers later designed an optional add-on, an additional discreet lock that could be retrofitted to the Raptor, which brings it up to Level IV or the hitherto unimagined "Level V," depending on whose count seems most logical to you.

With the F-type Beretta carried on-safe, another movement has to be accomplished by the person who snatched your gun before he can shoot you with it. Personally, I feel that this qualifies as one more level of security. Thus, the open-top scabbard that was Level 0 when the 92F was carried lever-up becomes in effect Level I when the same gun is carried with the lever down in the on-safe position, and so on.

Rugged, lightweight, synthetic duty holsters by Uncle Mike's are available in Levels I, II, and III.

The rotating thumb lock on the safety strap release paddle brings this Strong Piece-Keeper holster up to Level II security. It is available in plainclothes and uniform duty rig versions.

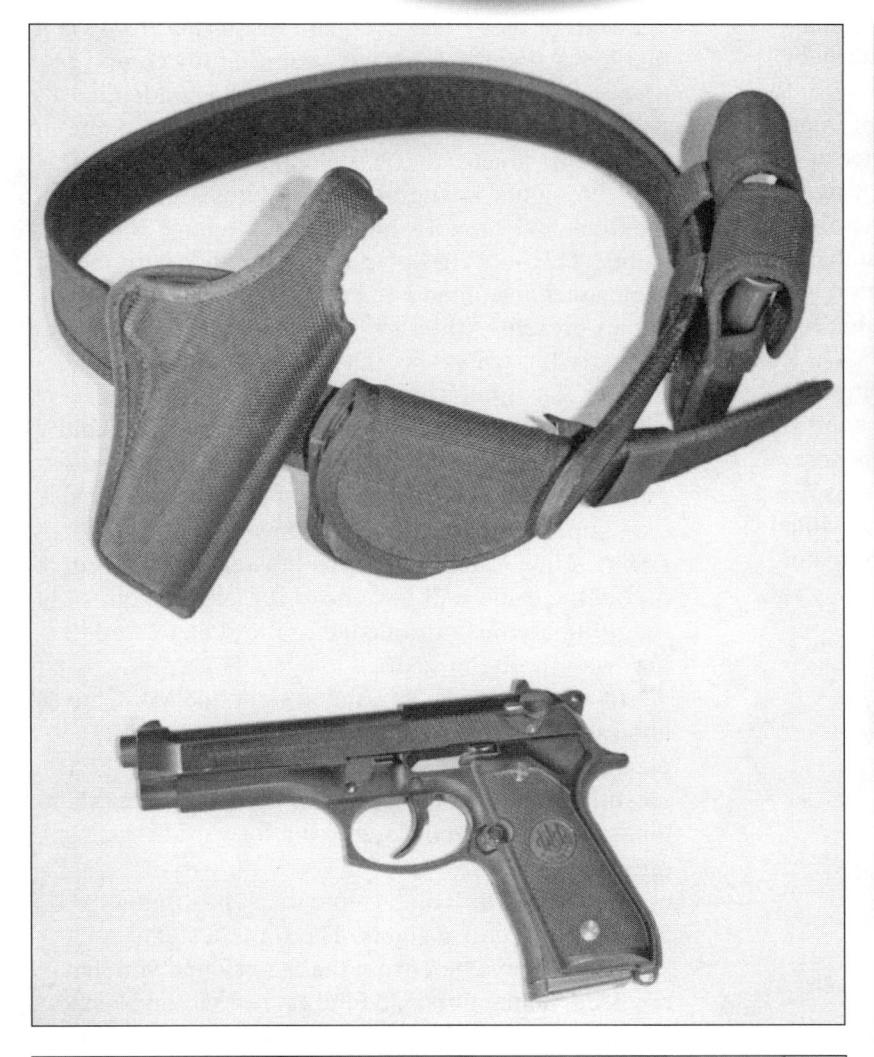

This left-hand belt scabbard by Greg Kramer, made of horse-hide, is an excellent piece of work. Here it carries a Beretta 96G Centurion.

A minimalist, lightweight duty rig, the Bianchi Accumold.

Safariland SS-III, the author's favorite duty holster, holds a state trooper's Beretta 96G. It defined the Level III security holster.

Useful accessories on the author's "Bedside Beretta," a Jarvis Custom 92FS Inox, include a dedicated SureFire white light unit, Trijicon night sights, Beretta 20-round extended magazine developed originally for the Beretta 93R machine pistol.

Sights

Precision marksmen want the best, most finely adjustable sights to tailor the point of aim/point of impact to their eyes, their load, and the known distance at which they're shooting. For the U.S. military shooting teams that use the Beretta in competition that generally means the biggest and most precisely adjustable of such sights, the BoMar. Another useful option, one I've had good luck with, is the LPA adjustable sight from Italy. I have one on an otherwise stock Model 92. It was fitted perfectly by Bill Pfeil and installed so professionally that the gun was dead on at 50 yards without having to touch the sight adjustment screws. The LPA appears to be the sight that Beretta is using on their excellent .22 conversion unit for the Model 92 and 96 pistols.

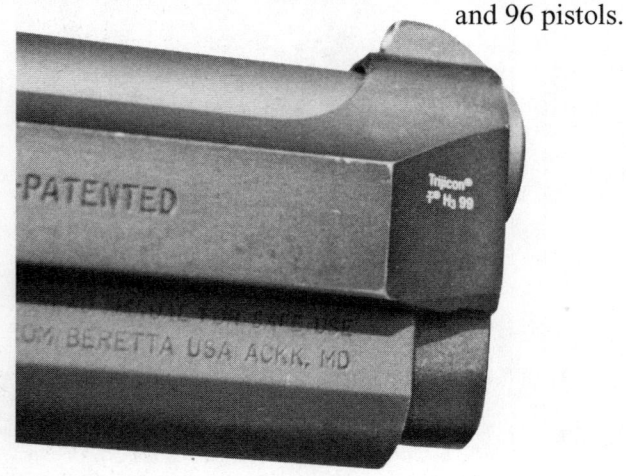

Ayoob says you can't beat Trijicon for night sights.

Both of these, however, can result in a front sight that looks like a submarine's conning tower, and a proportionally high rear sight. All of a sudden, a whole lot of holsters won't fit anymore. I have one Don Hume holster that will barely take the 92 with the LPA sights, snagging and slowing slightly on the draw, but even it won't accept the huge BoMar sights. The only rig I own that will work with the grotesquely changed and enlarged gun profile these babies present is the Law Concealment Holster, formerly known as the Shadow Concealment Holster. The gun is slow to get back in, and not particularly fast to draw, but nothing will snag and the rig works ambidextrously and will fit many other guns, both oddly and conventionally shaped. (Resist the temptation to carry one of these high-sighted Berettas in a Yaqui Slide type holster. It will seem to fit, but the stage will have been set for the front sight snagging on the bottom edge of the skeleton holster part way through the draw.)

In a lower-profile adjustable sight, the MMC gives good service, though of course it won't give you the precision of an LPA, let alone a BoMar. Novak's has recently brought out a version of their sleek rear sight that's adjustable, and I'm looking forward to testing one.

Where Novak's comes into its own is in low-profile fixed combat sights. The Beretta sights are so good as they come from the factory that you may not need them, but it's good to know that the Novaks are there because they can be a stark improvement to some of your other guns. If you don't mind a slightly higher profile, the sleek Aristocrat rear sight that Jim

Left: Big, high-visibility sights are a plus, both front …
Below: … and rear.

Below: The Bianchi Cobra holster adjusts like this to exactly fit the flashlight-mounted pistol …
Right: … and finishes as this businesslike package.

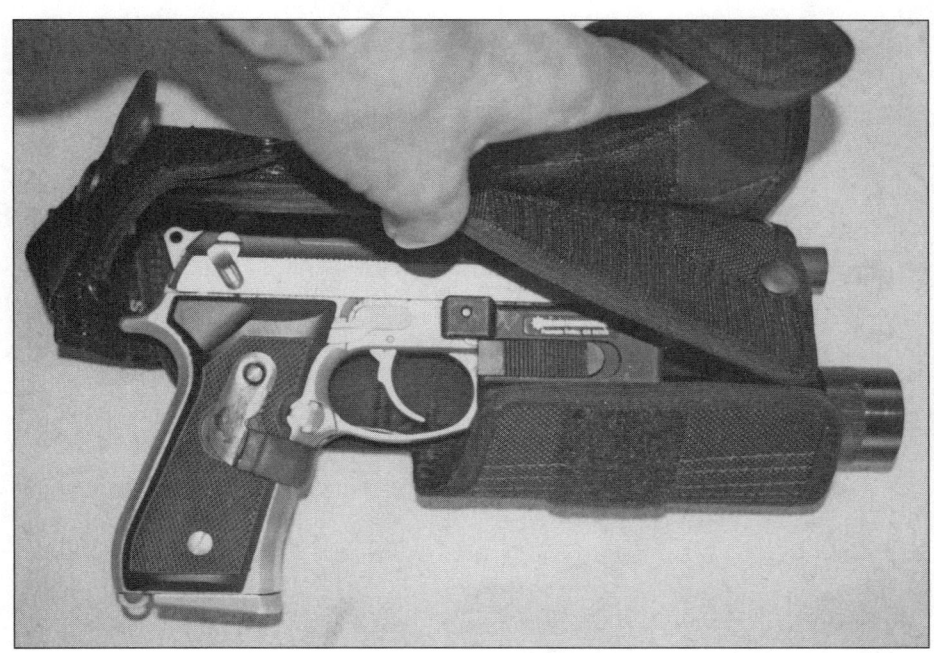

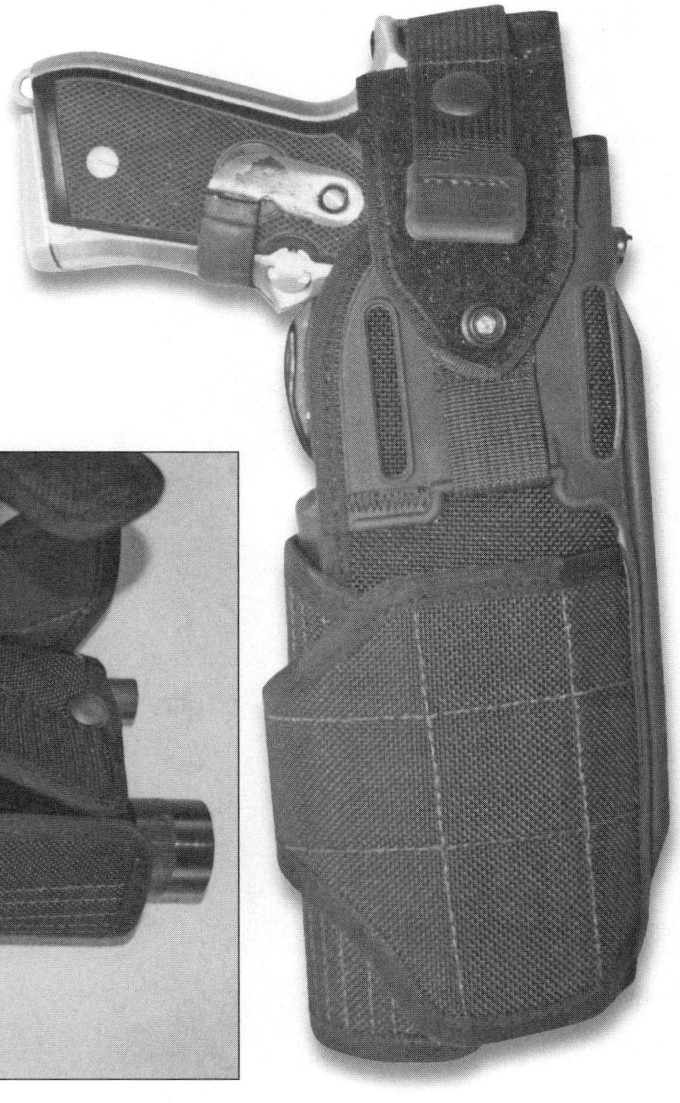

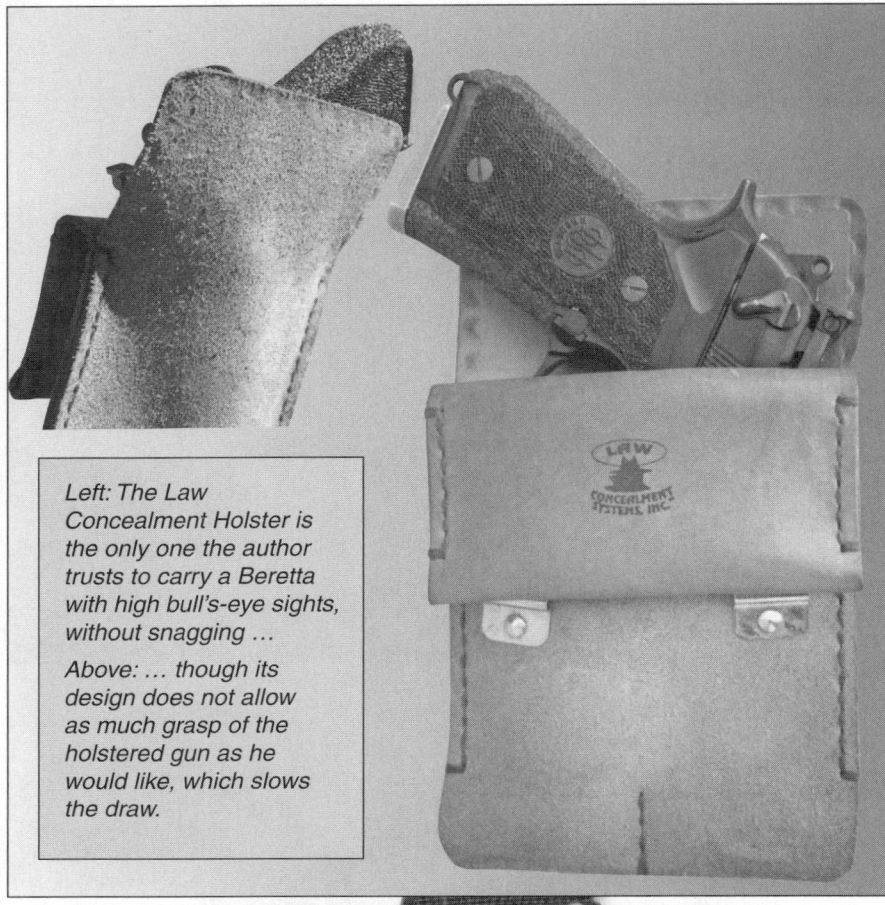

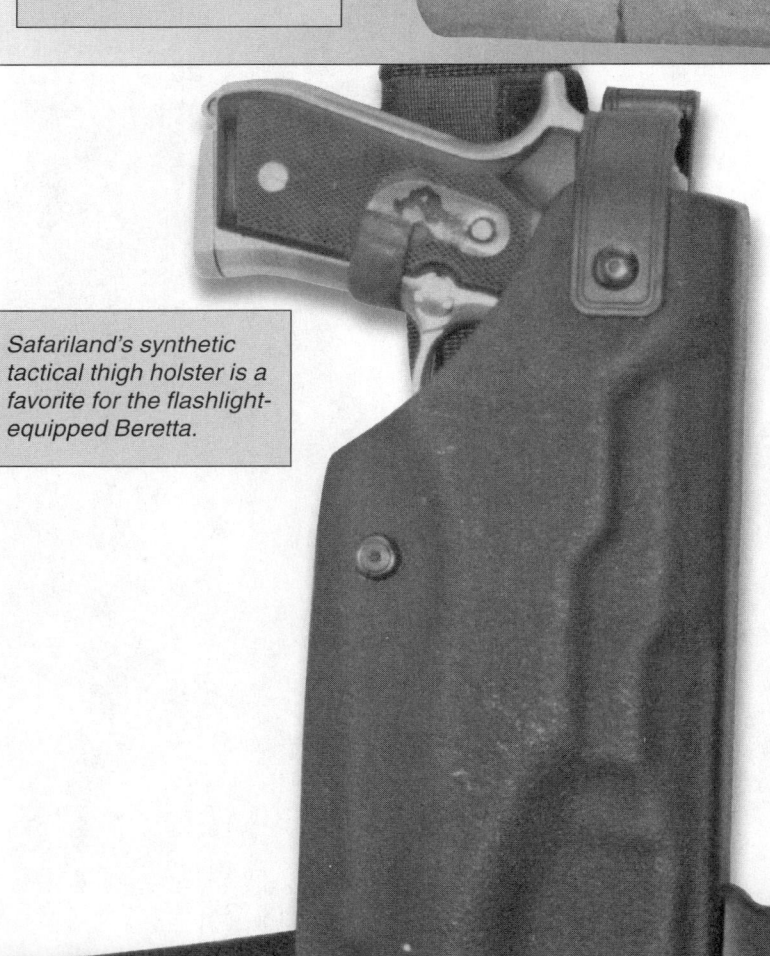

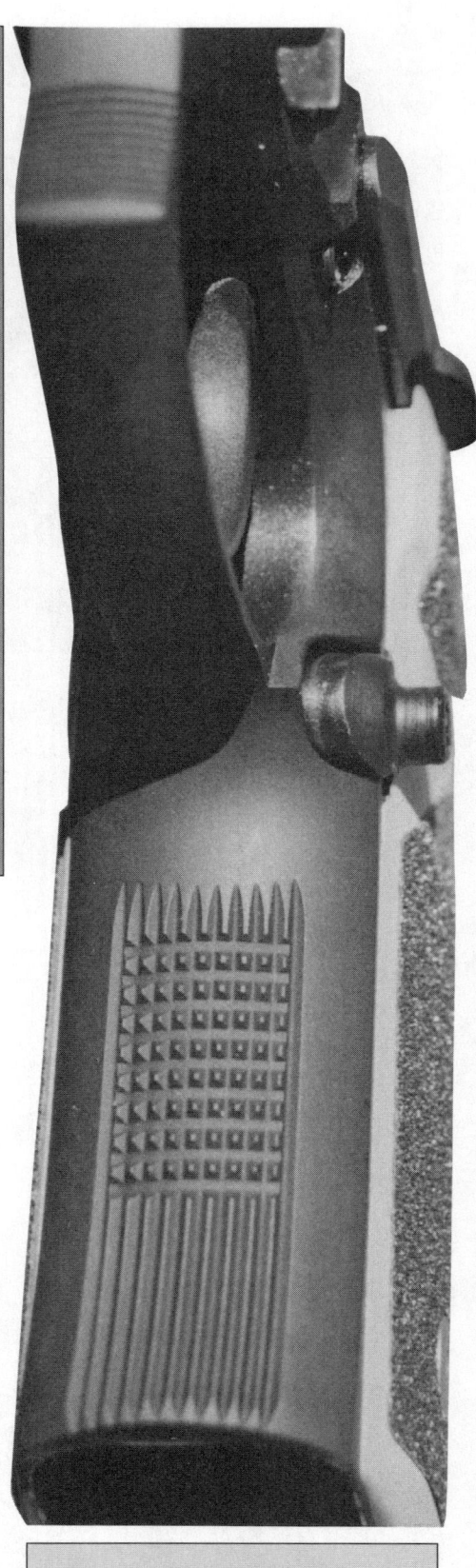

Left: The Law Concealment Holster is the only one the author trusts to carry a Beretta with high bull's-eye sights, without snagging …

Above: … though its design does not allow as much grasp of the holstered gun as he would like, which slows the draw.

Safariland's synthetic tactical thigh holster is a favorite for the flashlight-equipped Beretta.

The extended magazine release designed for the Elite series competition pistols can be transferred to standard models.

Horan put on my pet 92F Compact gives a wonderful sight picture.

Night sights make huge sense on a combat gun. You can order them from Beretta, or send the gun back to Beretta for installation. (Call first for shipping details.) If you're going aftermarket, you can't beat Trijicon night sights. I like the fact that their metal-encapsulated design provides a silver ring that enhances the three-dot sight picture during daylight. The IWI brand (Innovative Weaponry Inc.) is also good, and the Meprolight night sights have improved greatly in past years.

XS sights, which began as the Ashley Express created by my friend Ashley Emerson, are ideal for close-range employment. They're very fast on target. Once you start getting out to seven yards or so, though, it becomes difficult to hold a tight group because you have a coarser than usual sight picture. Combined with tritium in the Big Dot format, you have a globe hanging out front over a shallow "v"; in the "v" is a vertical line. For a precision shot, put that line under the globe until it looks like a lollipop. I've seen people who do a lot better with them than I do. They're particularly nice on the little pocket guns. Beretta offers them on their little Tomcat .32, which when so fitted is listed appropriately in the Beretta catalog as the Alley Cat.

Stocks

Call them stocks, call them grips, call them whatever – just don't call them "handles," or you'll upset the purists. The grasp on the handgun is the interface between man and machine, and quite apart from dressing up the pistol, these can perfect the interface and help you to shoot just a little bit better.

Personally, I find that the factory-provided stocks on most Berettas work just fine. However, hands differ extraordinarily in size and span and adaptability to different grasps. Thus, it is important to know that custom stocks are available if you need them.

For good looks, I've seen nothing better than the handsome Cocobolo stocks by Hogue that Ernest Langdon put on my Beretta 92G when he customized it. Checkered 20 lines to the inch, they give a superb hold. The price is remarkably reasonable.

For pure non-slipperiness, you want synthetics. Most choose one or another variation of what are colloquially called "rubber" grips. For the truly huge hand, nothing may feel as good as Pachmayrs. However, the 92/96 Beretta is already a "big-handled" pistol. I can only say that in my average size hand, the Pachmayrs are just too much girth.

If you like traction plus finger grooves, go with the Hogue. However, be advised that these are designed for thick male fingers. Most women, for example, find the finger grooves to be spaced too widely apart, forcing them to spread their fingers slightly and thus weaken their grasp.

A good compromise are the Farrar grips, the only such that Beretta used to authorize, though we've seen some cobblestone Hogues with Beretta logos coming on some guns in Beretta factory boxes. Slim and flat, but still giving an extremely secure hold, the Farrars are my personal choice. But what we're talking about here is feel, and feel is always a subjective element.

For the truly hard core, there is what can only be described as the "skateboard tape over aluminum" grip offered by "David McGonical, English Gunsmith" at Cape Custom Guns in Blaine, Washington. Career street lawman Nick Bolton turned me on to these when I saw him kicking butt at a FASTactics match at Firearms Academy of Seattle with a pair of these on his department-issue Beretta 96D. I ordered a pair, and set them aside until the day I was coaching a tough young Sabra through my LFI-I class. This woman was of average size with average length fingers, and the Beretta being so popular where she came from (Tel Aviv), she had ordered the best available, a Model 92 Inox Elite II. Unfortunately, she had Hogue finger groove

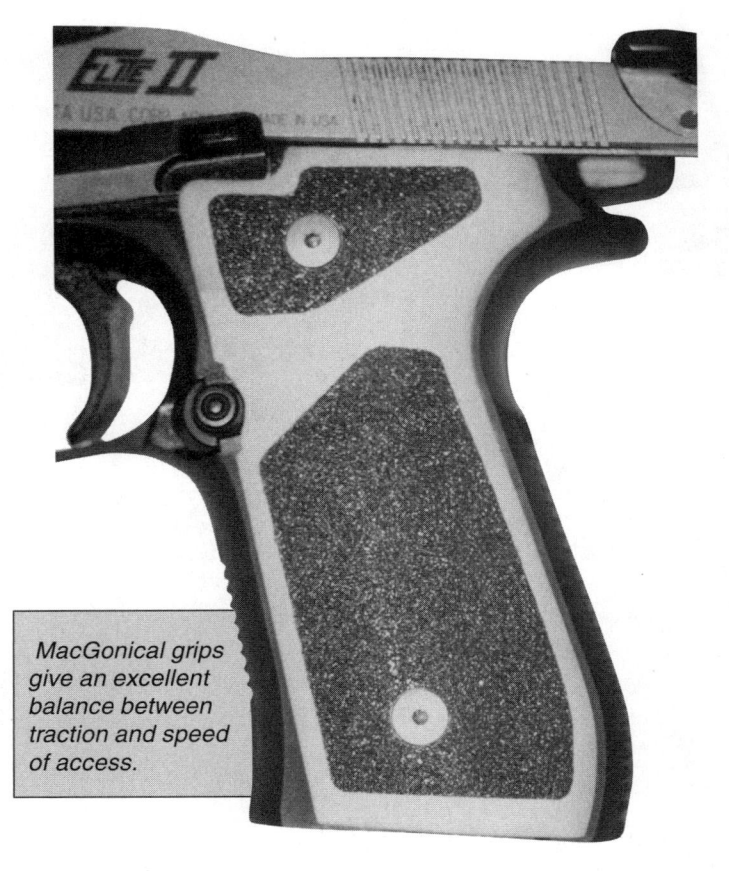

MacGonical grips give an excellent balance between traction and speed of access.

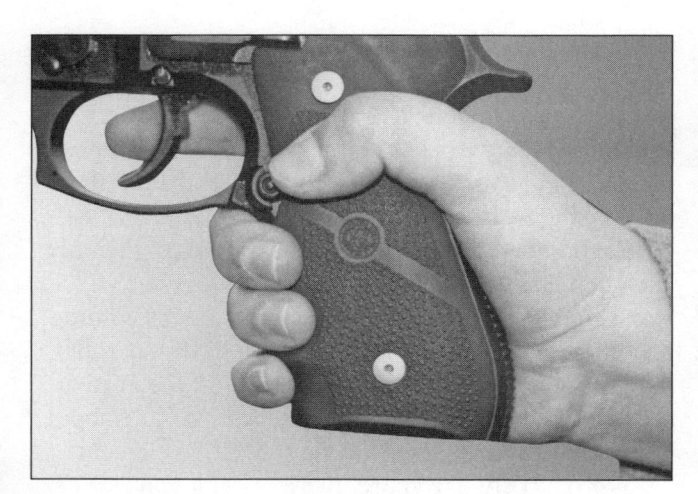

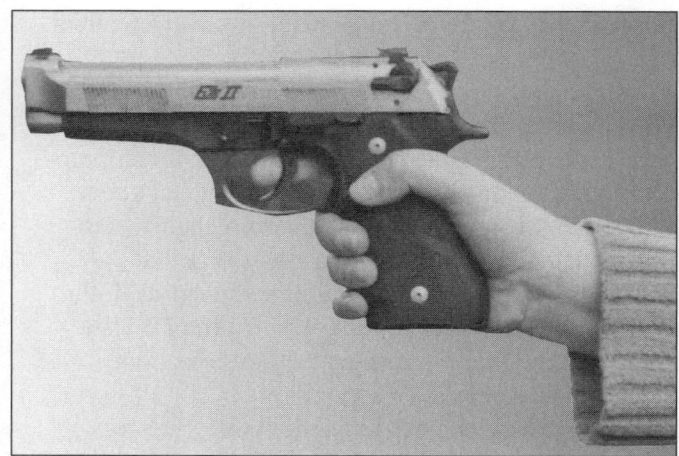

Above left: Handgun stocks are the interface between operator and machine. Young Rotem here was having trouble getting the proper grasp on her 9mm Elite II …

Above right: … with Hogue grips with finger grooves that fit large male fingers better than they fit hers …

Left: … so LFI staff put MacGonical stocks on her Beretta …

Below: … which dramatically enhanced her control and performance.

grips on it that were designed for a much larger hand than hers, and she wasn't doing her best with the gun. I swapped her into the McGonical grips, and the improvement was phenomenal. Now she, too, was kicking butt. I tried her pistol at 15 yards, and offhand, put 15 shots into a 2-inch group. I think I'm going to be spending more time with brother McGonical's Beretta stocks.

Jerry Barnhart offers his Burner grips for the Beretta. Basically, they're "skateboard tape on the grips, out of the box, and it stays there." I've tried these on one of Langdon's Model 92 pistols, and once the hand is in place they work great. However, the traction to the hand is so strong that if you don't get the right grip in the first place, it'll take you a small moment to adjust it. There's enough smooth aluminum surrounding the sandpaper-like panels on the McGonical interpretation that David's design may be a little faster, while Jerry's is more secure. Bull's-eye shooters who prefer the Beretta 92 need to know about Barnhart Burner grips; they seem to be ideal for that purpose.

Even rougher is the custom stippling job that military armorers do on Berettas. It can be duplicated by gunsmiths who choose to take the job. These will definitely slow down your draw, and if you tuck the pistol into your waistband under your shirt against your bare skin, this treatment of the grip panels will chew up your flesh and leave you red and sore. How do I know this, you ask? Trust me, I know this …

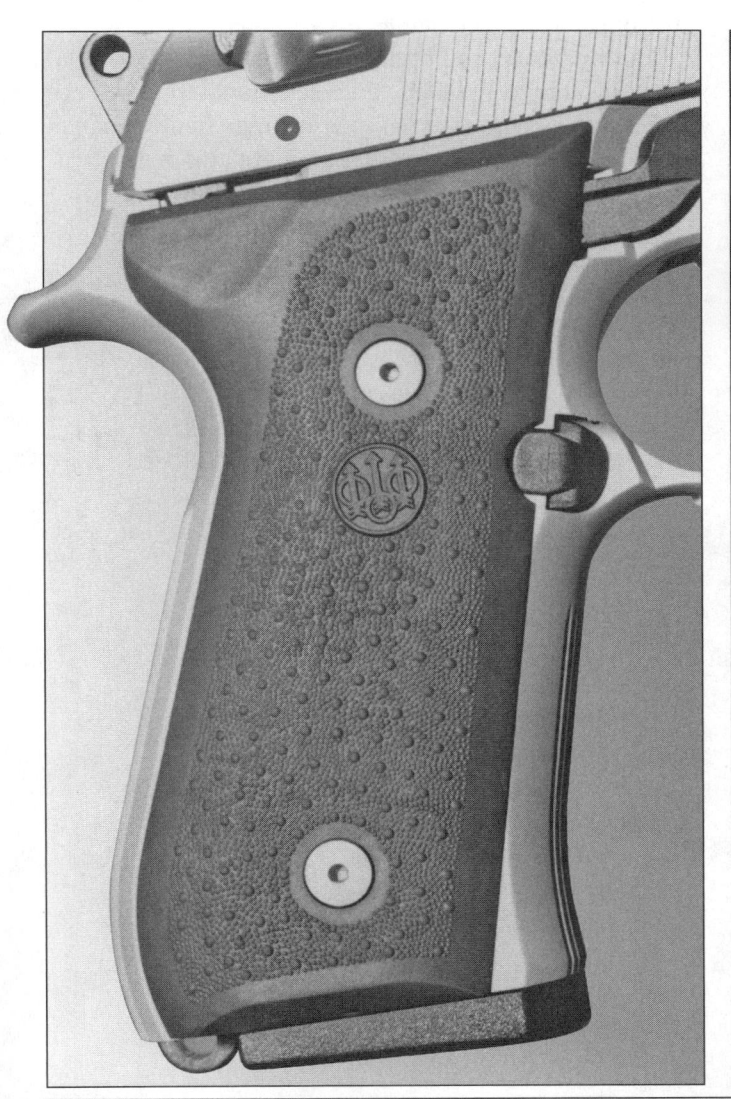

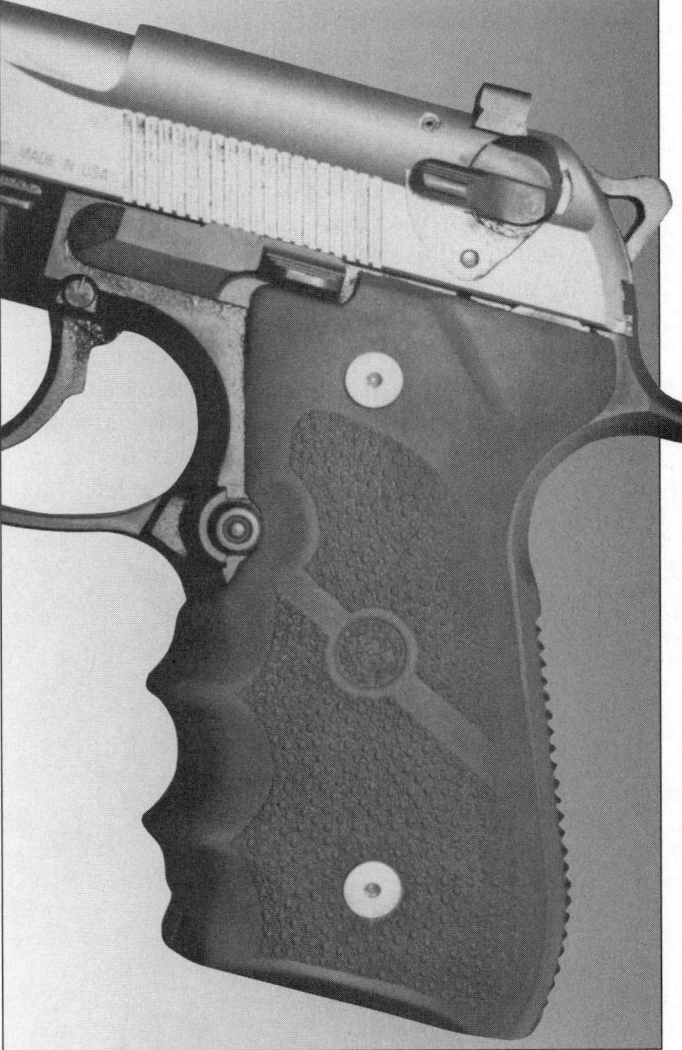

Left: Hogue makes excellent stocks for Berettas. This soft cobblestone style fits medium sized hands well …
Right: … and, in the author's experience, this finger-grooved version fits best in large male hands.

Laser Sights

Laser sights are coming into their own. The big, clunky ones that hung off the gun are still available, but long obsolete and won't be recommended in these pages. Low-profile laser sights that are integral to the gun and will work with a conventional holster are the ticket. The only hang-on laser modules worth looking at are those that provide their function as an adjunct to white light, and we'll talk about those later.

Basically, your choices are two: LaserMax, and the Crimson Trace LaserGrips. Numerous police departments have approved each, and each is easy to install yourself. The LaserMax takes the form of a tube that replaces the recoil spring guide, running parallel beneath the barrel. A crossbolt push-button switch located at the point of the slide stop pin activates the unit. This means that it has to be either turned on when you draw, or left on in the holster, the latter not being a very smart protocol. However, it also won't go on by accident and give your position away unexpectedly. When activated, it projects a pulsing red dot on the target. It is not adjustable, but the bullet will usually hit quite close to the dot, typically just above it.

The LaserGrips simply replace the right panel of the Beretta 92 or 96. A vertical bar on the grip is depressed by the firing grasp. It is activated by the pressure of the palm of the hand near the finger joints when held in the right hand, and by the tips of the middle and ring fingers when grasped in the left hand. It projects a bright, steady, solid red dot. This dot runs below the barrel and to the right of it, of course, so if you sight it

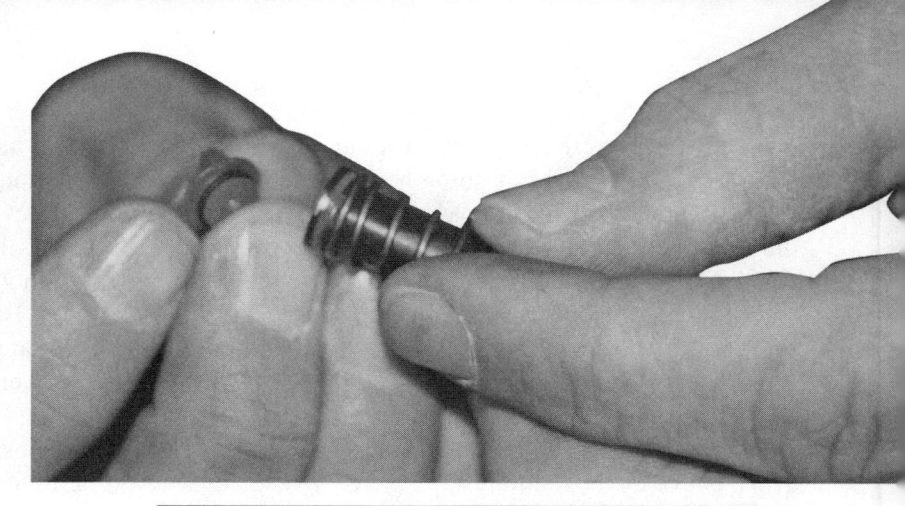

The recently redesigned LaserMax unit takes a small but powerful battery.

dead on at a certain point it will really be set *only* for that certain point. I prefer to sight mine in parallel to the bore, so I know that at any reasonable distance I'll hit a tiny bit left and high of the dot. The LaserGrip is adjustable for windage and elevation with discreet little screws built into the grip; a tiny Allen wrench is provided. A downside is that the light automatically goes on when you grip your Beretta firmly, which may or may not be something you want to happen. Knowing that this might be a concern, Crimson Trace has a switch on the bottom of the panel of most LaserGrips, including those for the Beretta 92/96, that allows you

With LaserMax, the kit includes a replacement takedown lever, which houses the laser sight's cross-bolt push-button activator.

Below left: A warning label must accompany laser units of a certain power.

Left: Originally developed as a demonstration tool for sales, the LaserGrip Ring's Beretta dummy gun from Crimson Trace is also an excellent teaching tool.

Below right: Crimson Trace LaserGrips have proven popular on Beretta 92 and 96 series pistols. A grasp-activated pressure panel seen running vertically down the right front of the grip panel controls the laser. The power switch is at the bottom edge of the grip panel directly beneath the lower grip screw.

to turn off the laser function beforehand.

Which to choose? It's your call, based on the features that best appeal to you. I find myself using the Crimson Trace more often because the solid dot works a little better for my eyes. But some other shooters have found just as certainly that the pulsing dot of the LaserMax suits them better.

While I personally think the intimidation effect of the red dot on a suspect at gunpoint has been hugely overblown and oversold, there is no doubt that it has happened sometimes. Anything that could help you in a fight is something worth having. If you are down and hurt so bad you can't raise the gun to aim, the laser dot gives you an aiming indicator that can neutralize your opponent before he finishes you off or hurts you permanently. When working with a raid shield, a laser-sighted pistol lets you keep a more locked wrist, reducing the chances of stoppages, and lets you keep much more of your gun arm in behind your ballistic protection. The latter is also true when firing from behind hard cover.

For firearms instructors, the laser sight is an extremely useful tool. On a deactivated gun (just strip the barrel/slide assembly off your Beretta) you can demonstrate the effects of smooth pull versus trigger jerk, and the concept of the wobble zone, without firing a shot. A student who is jerking the trigger can quickly learn to hold the gun steady on target by keeping the laser dot motionless while pulling the trigger.

Attachable Light Units

White light – the current high-speed, low-drag, way cool tactical term for a powerful flashlight – can be an enormous asset when attached to the firearm. I was hugely grateful for the SureFire tactical light bolted onto my stainless 92FS when I took it through The Tower at Thunder Ranch, and that feeling goes to the power of 10 for any cop or armed citizen who's doing a for-real building search for someone who is armed and wants them to die. The light can find the foe, identify the target, and blind the threat.

Obviously, common sense must be used.

Dummy guns are extremely useful tactical training accessories. This 92FS is identically matched by the ComTac dummy.

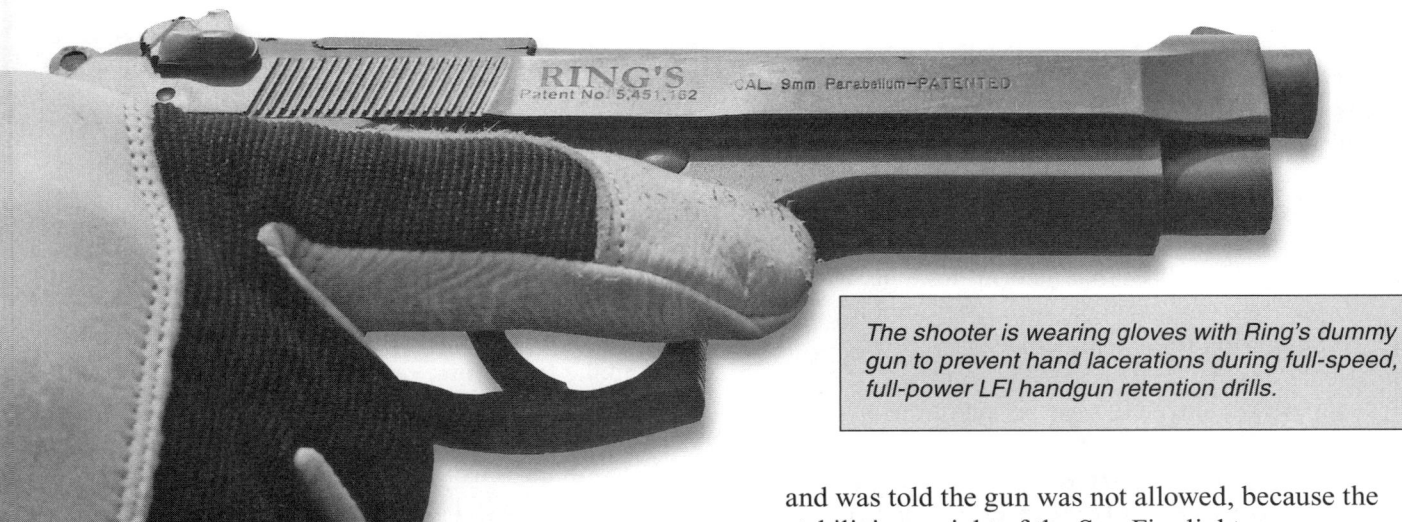

The shooter is wearing gloves with Ring's dummy gun to prevent hand lacerations during full-speed, full-power LFI handgun retention drills.

Remember that anything you point the light at, you're pointing a gun at. Now more than ever it will be imperative to keep the finger clear of the trigger guard, and now more than ever you will appreciate things like the smooth but safe double-action pull of a Beretta service pistol, and perhaps even the manual safety on the F models.

Beretta's Vertec comes from the factory with integral light rails that will take the InSights (Streamlight) M3 or M6, or SureFire's equivalent, the X200. Older model Beretta 92/96 pistols can simply be fitted with a dedicated SureFire tactical light. These are bigger and heavier, and less convenient. However, they offer a new magnitude of power, and their weight helps hold the gun down during fast firing of powerful ammo. How much control do they add? I tried to shoot my SureFire-equipped Beretta 9mm in a practical police course (PPC) match and was told the gun was not allowed, because the stabilizing weight of the SureFire light gave me an unfair advantage. As a general rule, anything that gives you an unfair advantage in a game is something you want to have on your side in a fight.

Safariland and Bianchi make tactical holsters for Berettas and other pistols equipped with the big SureFire tac-lights. The Bianchi Cobra offers a wide range of adjustment, but I've personally found the Safariland to work a bit quicker and smoother for me.

Several companies now offer holsters that will carry your pistol with the smaller SureFire or InSights light attached. I can't speak for all of them, but I can say that the Blade-Tech makes sense for concealed carry under a substantial covering garment, and the Safariland SLS will work fine for uniformed patrol.

If you're buying your first Beretta 9mm or .40, the flashlight rail alone makes it wise to purchase the Vertec model of the pistol. The easy on/off feature of the flashlight attachment is an enormous convenience.

You can also get a combined laser/white light unit, which will be only slightly larger but considerably more expensive. My choice would be the InSight M6 or the heavy-duty version, the M6X. Of the two functions, I personally think the white light is by far the most important. If cost is an object, as it is for most of us, it's better to buy a simple M3 and have it now than save up for an M6X you won't have until later.

Magazines

I personally see magazines as integral to the gun. Calling them accessories is like saying the tires on your car are "accessories." But some see it that way, so a few points bear repeating here.

There are only two brands worth owning: Beretta and MecGar. That's not just an opinion, it's an earnest warning. (Some don't even think that's two brands, since MecGar has produced so many of Beretta's factory magazines.) When you

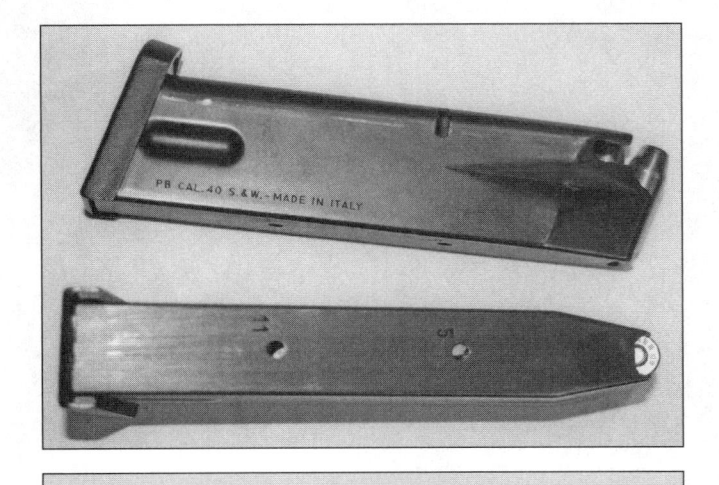

The author strongly advises shooters to use ONLY Beretta or MecGar brand magazines in Beretta pistols.

see feeding problems in a Beretta 92 or 96 pistol, it always seems to be either inappropriate ammo or bad aftermarket magazines. Remember that earlier analogy of the Alpha Romeo with two-ply retread tires. The system is only as strong as the weakest link, and the magazine is one of the most important links in the cycling chain that determines a pistol's reliability. We're not talking sporting equipment here, we're talking life-saving emergency rescue equipment.

By the way, the dark 10-year period of the magazine ban is over. As soon as you can, invest in a couple of 20-round magazines for your Beretta 92. They make huge sense for home defense or police emergency team use.

Now only a quaint reminder of a grim period in the civil liberties of American gun owners, 10-round "Clinton magazines" are still useful for training purposes.

Dummy Guns

A solid, non-shooting mockup of your pistol is a useful thing to have. We use them primarily for disarming training and weapon retention drills. Weapon retention being the art and science of defeating someone else's attempt to disarm you. However, they are useful for demonstrating techniques in front of a class, particularly things best seen from the front, since the audience isn't looking down the business end of "a gun" per se. They are useful for very basic students as well: if they "cross" someone with the muzzle, they aren't as set back and traumatized as if they had done it with a real gun, loaded or empty.

Finally, the dummy gun is great for custom-fitting a holster. With leather rigs, this process includes wet-molding, and you can practically hear your pistol rusting as it sits in the holster overnight, no matter how much you've greased it. Using the dummy gun for this takes the worry out. The brands I personally prefer are Odin Press (all metal) and Ring's (identical plastic copies). The latter are available with LaserGrips fitted, from Crimson Trace, as demonstration and teaching tools.

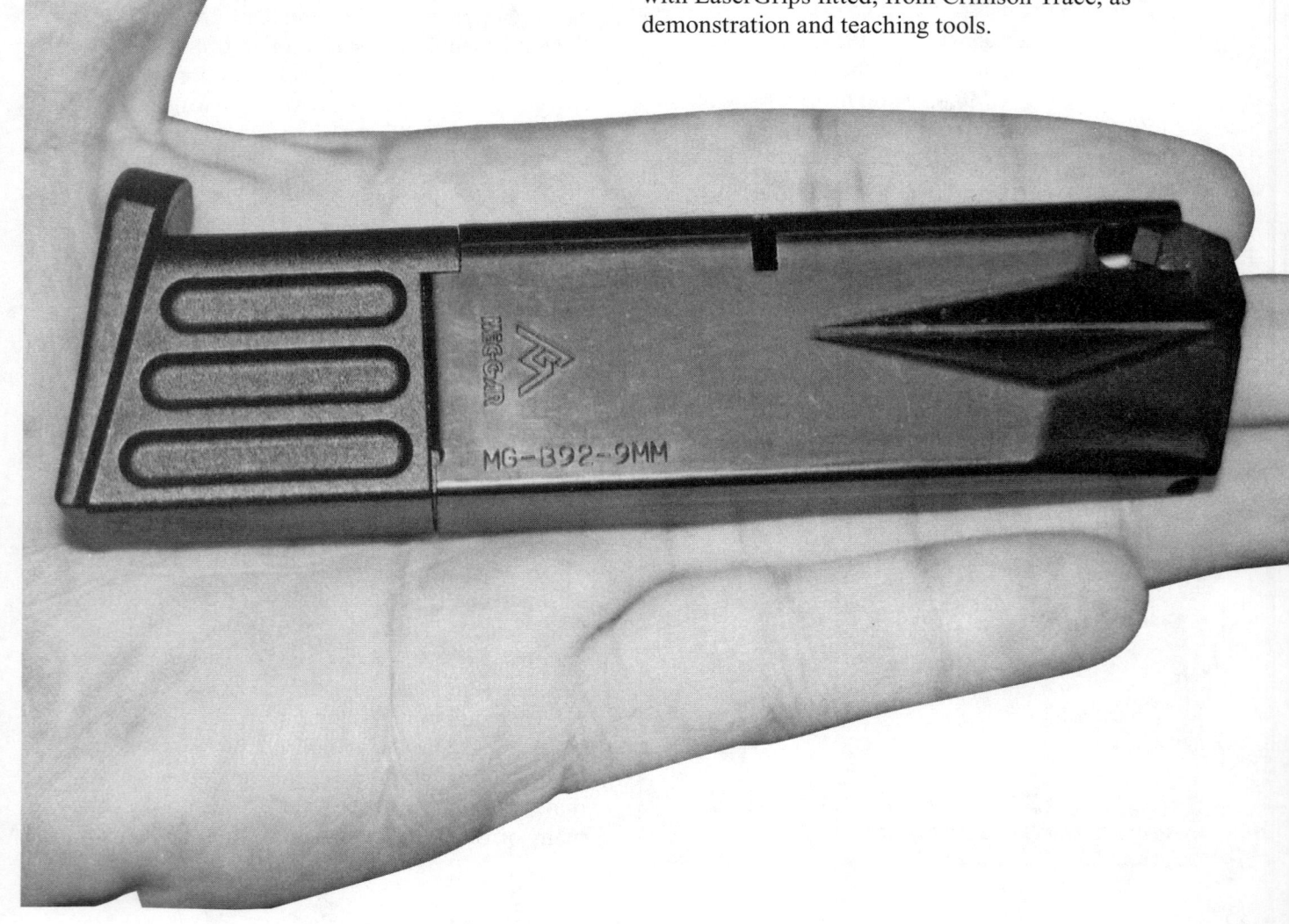

Above: Sold by a martial arts supply house for disarming training, this generic copy of a Beretta made in China is in the author's opinion too soft for the purpose.

Below: Ring's dummy Beretta is an exact likeness, useful for holster molding.

The Gun Digest Book of Beretta Pistols

The Beretta Elite Series

It has become customary among the manufacturers of fine firearms to incorporate deluxe lines which offer not just an increased grade of "fanciness," but a level of features and performance that might only be appreciated by the *connoisseur* of the product, who would naturally be willing to pay the extra price that such lavish attention entailed.

With the Smith & Wesson brand, it's the Performance Center line of guns. With Colt, it's the heady products of the Custom Shop.

With Beretta, it's the Elite series.

The Beretta service pistol is a modern classic. Standard-issue for uniformed U.S. military personnel as the M9, it is also one of our most popular service handguns in law enforcement. It is likewise well appreciated in the civilian sector. The Beretta 92 has won national titles in IDPA (stock service pistol class) and IPSC (production class) in the hands of champions like Ernie Langdon and Rob Haught.

A few years ago, Beretta decided to improve on a good thing with their Elite version. Enhancements included a nicer finish and many other features. The shooting public's reception was warm, and the concept is back. Now comes Beretta's Elite II.

Form And Function

The original Elite had a stainless barrel, duty style. On the Elite II, both barrel and slide are stainless, or "Inox" as Beretta puts it, the European terminology, keeping with the origin of the pistol's design. The frame and furnishings (sights, decocking lever) are a handsome blue-black, and the overall result is striking.

The muzzle is reshaped into a "target crown." I am not certain how much this enhances the already famous accuracy of the duty-grade gun. I've personally shot 1.5-inch groups at 25 yards with hot Pro-Load Tactical 9mm using the standard-grade Model 92 service pistol, and 1.25 inches with a Langdon Custom version. Using machine rests, Indiana State Police wrung superb accuracy out of the Model 96G service pistol with assorted .40 S&W ammunition and adopted that weapon. Does the subtle target crown improve things? Well, it can't hurt, and a certain kind of discriminating buyer gains confidence from knowing his sidearm has every possible feature that can positively enhance its performance.

Beretta makes its big combat autos in three formats. The most common is the "F" series, a traditional double-

Scott Hattrup shows his award-winning form with the Elite II.

At 20, this young lady already has a taste for fine firearms. Here, she cleans up weak-hand-only with her Beretta Elite II at an LFI-I course.

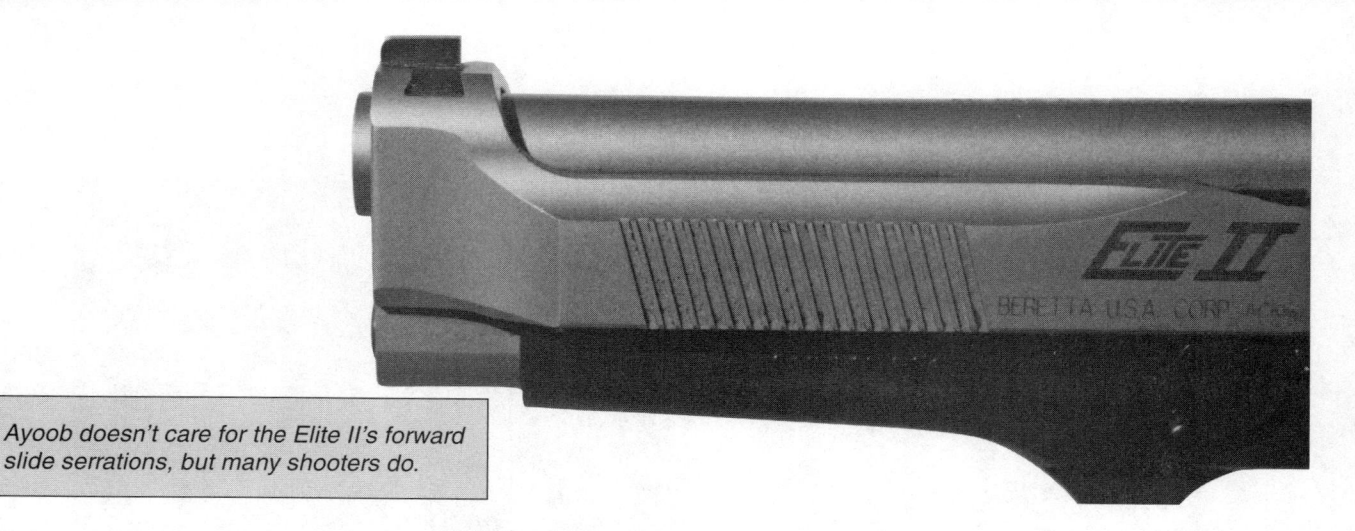

Ayoob doesn't care for the Elite II's forward slide serrations, but many shooters do.

action (TDA) pistol that is self-cocking after the first shot, and whose slide-mounted decocking lever also functions as a manual safety when left in the down position. Many police departments have gone with the "D" series, which is double-action-only (DAO). The Elite is produced in the third format as a "G" model. The fire control mechanism is TDA, but the ambidextrous lever on the slide functions strictly as a decocking lever and not as a manual "safety catch."

Also catching to your eyes is the skeletonized hammer. This first appeared on the original Elite. Some felt that it was a little too light to guarantee ignition with the hardest primers, and as a result, it has been beefed up with more mass for the Elite II. With revolver and autoloader alike, one of the trickiest balances to strike is that of ignition time versus ignition reliability. A lighter hammer falls faster, giving quicker ignition time and allowing less movement of the gun from the perfect alignment with the target when we pressed the trigger back and allowed the sear to release. Properly executed, the faster hammer strike can actually enhance ignition reliability. However, if the balance of mass, and speed is not perfect, light hits can result, causing misfires, particularly if there has been significant wear on the mainspring. This is totally unacceptable. Beretta was right to redesign the hammer after light hits were sporadically reported with the earlier design, and feedback from Elite II users in the field indicates that, this time, they have found the perfect balance.

Elite pistols go through a special muzzle-crowning process at the factory.

Returning to the barrel, what is more noticeable than the crown is the truncated length. At first glance, many handgunners mistake this gun for the Centurion model with a shorter barrel and slide. Actually, the slide is full-length, but the barrel has been cut back to 4.7 inches, which I personally find more visually pleasing than the long nubbin of barrel that protrudes from in front of the slide on the standard full-size Beretta 92 and 96 pistols. Can I honestly say it improves handling? Not so I can quantify it objectively. It just looks more proportional. Does the slight reduction in barrel length reduce ballistic performance? Not to a degree anyone or anything on the receiving end would notice.

There are forward grooves factory-cut into the slide of the Elite II, intended to make it easier to perform a chamber-check. Of course, Beretta's trademark extractor that palpably protrudes when there is a round in the chamber is in place too. No serious user trusts such a mechanical device to determine if a gun is loaded or not; a visual check is always preferable. Recognizing this, Beretta has designed the Elite II to facilitate both.

That slide, by the way, is the rugged Brigadier style. This is what the Border Patrol specified for their standard-issue Model 96D pistols. It is designed to handle a lifetime supply of hot loads.

What the serious shooter will most appreciate is the sights. The front is a sharp, clear Patridge post, inserted into a dovetail that runs on a 180-degree angle across the front of the slide. This allows reasonably easy removal and replacement. The rear is a genuine Novak, sleek in looks and efficient in function with the desirable huge rear notch that makes a fast sight picture easy to achieve. By loosening a set-screw, the rear sight can be drifted in its dovetail. The result is de

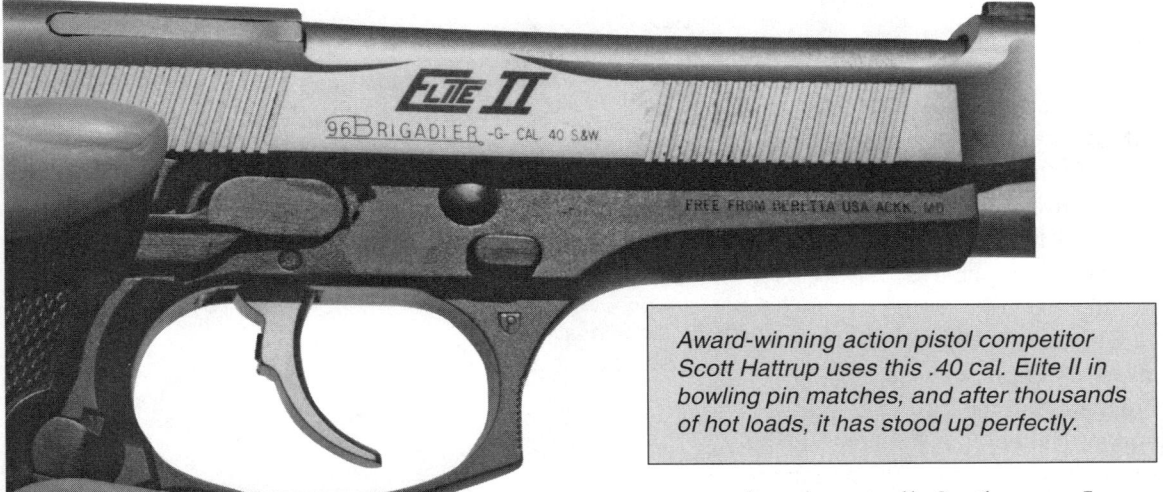

Award-winning action pistol competitor Scott Hattrup uses this .40 cal. Elite II in bowling pin matches, and after thousands of hot loads, it has stood up perfectly.

facto adjustability of sights if you don't mind some inconvenience in return for the ruggedness that we've always expected from fixed sights.

Gilding The Lily

Scott Hattrup of Kansas provided the test guns for this article. If the name sounds familiar, it speaks well of you because it means you're active in gun owners' rights causes. Scott is one of our most active and most articulate spokespersons for the right to self-defense and gun ownership. He practices what he preaches, actively shooting in IDPA, IPSC, and NRA Action Pistol at the Bianchi Cup. An advanced graduate of the Lethal Force Institute, he has also studied the high-performance manipulation of the Beretta pistol under no less an authority than Ernie Langdon. That champion shooter is not only a fine marksman, but a skilled instructor and a masterful gunsmith who confines himself to Beretta pistols.

Three Langdon-tuned Beretta Elites were examined for this piece. One was Scott's original 9mm Elite, now known to some Beretta enthusiasts as the Elite I. It had received Ernie's "Level II" work, best described as a superb "slick for the street" that includes his trademark "speed bump trigger" with the anti-backlash device and an Elite II hammer.

A part of the deal with the Elite II is that you get a particularly smooth trigger action in addition to the super-slick slide-to-frame function that has always been a Beretta hallmark. However, some enthusiasts are just never satisfied. On Scott's Beretta 96 .40 and Beretta 92 9mm Elite II pistols, Ernie performed his competition job. This is the meticulous honing that characterizes the Level II "street action" job, plus some judicious lightening of the springs to allow an easier trigger pull. On the guns I examined, Langdon had brought the double-action trigger pull weight down to about 7 pounds, and the single-action down to 4 pounds or a little less. Langdon's intensive knowledge of a Beretta's innards, coupled with the ingenious design of his "speed bump" retrofit trigger, also seems to allow the system to reset faster for subsequent shots. Simply put, pulling the trigger of a Langdon gun is pure pleasure, whether in single or double-action mode.

For information on Langdon's work, contact him at Langdon Tactical Technology, Inc., P.O. Box 10759, Dept CH, Burke, VA 22009. You can phone for info at 703-978-1262, or check out his website at www.langdontactical.com.

The Elite's special muzzle crown is shown in detail.

Elite II Shooting

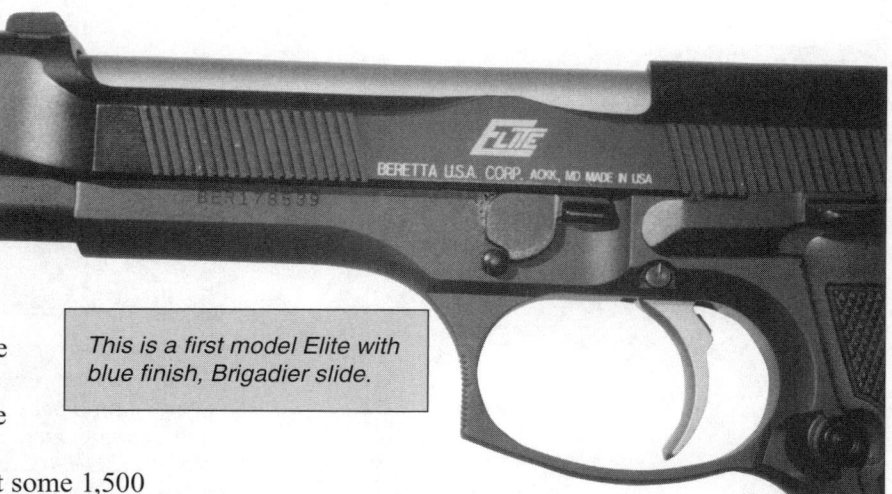

Reliability is the cornerstone of Beretta's reputation. Scott put several thousand rounds through his 9mm Elite II. Everything functioned 100%, including Winchester U.S.A. brand inexpensive "white box" ammo until he got to some loads with tough CCI primers. With these, he experienced about one misfire per 100 rounds. Since having the gun gone over by Langdon, Hattrup has put some 1,500 to 2,000 rounds through it, with no malfunctions or failures of any kind.

Scott's Elite II in .40 has some 2,000 rounds of assorted ammo through it so far. He reports no malfunctions of any kind.

Explains Hattrup, who lives in a state that does not yet have the concealed carry option, "I keep a straight-up Beretta 92 for home defense, and just bought a 92 Vertec for the flashlight rail feature. Berettas are known for their reliability, especially in 9mm, and reliability is my prime consideration in a self-defense firearm. The advantage of being able to use full-capacity 15-round military surplus magazines is a nice bonus."

Once he had selected the Beretta 92 for home defense, it seemed logical to shoot with the same system in competition to build his skill. Notes Scott,

This is a first model Elite with blue finish, Brigadier slide.

"I felt the competition would make me a faster and more accurate shooter, and I brought the Beretta concept with me to the competition field. I shoot primarily bowling pin matches at a local club, and USPSA (IPSC). USPSA's Production division seemed like a natural fit for the Beretta since I didn't have to buy a whole lot of new equipment to get into it."

He continues, "Reliability in the competitive environment is almost as important as in self-defense. After having paid to travel to an out-of-town match, having a gun break or choke can be a financial loss, not to mention killing both the match and the mood for you. My Berettas have never failed me in a match, large or small. From speaking with other Beretta shooters, I believe my experiences are quite common regarding reliability. Plenty of my fellow shooters (with other brands) have spent much more on their guns, only to have them fail or jam in the middle of a shooting string."

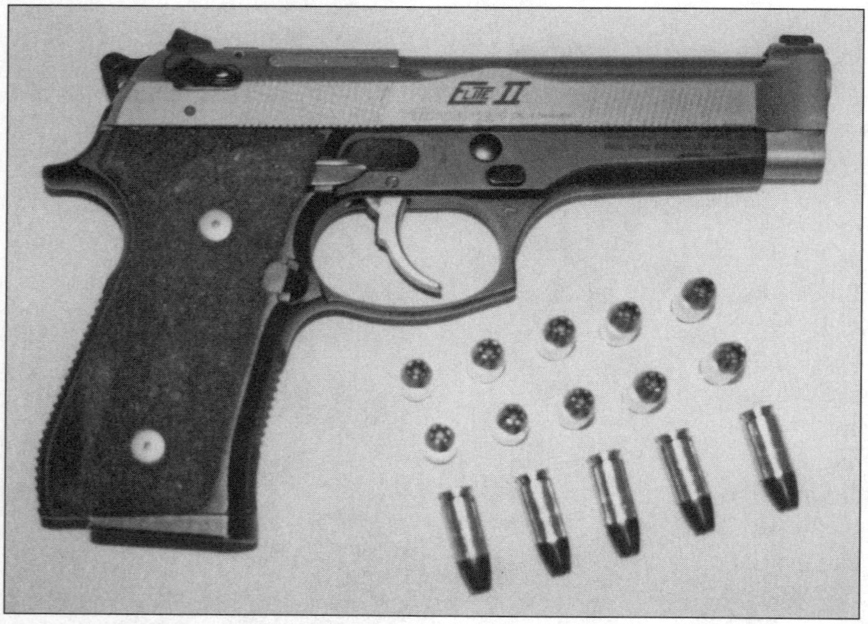

Shooting guns like these is always a pleasure. Even with the hot +P and +P+ loads Scott likes for home defense, a 115-grain JHP at 1,300-plus feet per second (fps), the 9mm Beretta with the Brigadier slide is a pussycat to control, its light aluminum frame notwithstanding. Recoil is gentler yet with his competition 9mm load, a 135-grain Zero FMJ bullet with a moderate charge of Hodgdon Tite-Group powder that brings it to a sedate velocity of about 1,000 fps. "This is all you need for IDPA or USPSA production-class shooting," explains Scott, who got the load data from Langdon.

In the Beretta .40, a pin-shooter will have no trouble clearing the table with Winchester Silvertip, a 155-grain

With 15 Winchester 127-grain +P+ rounds in each magazine and one more up the spout, the Beretta Elite II 9mm is a formidable defensive handgun.

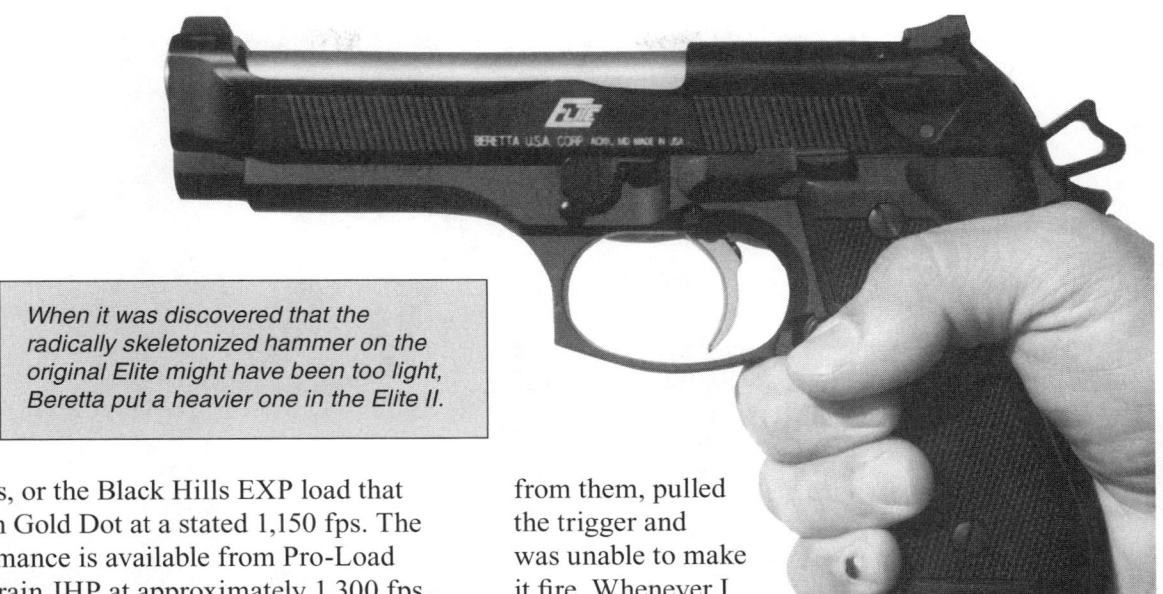

When it was discovered that the radically skeletonized hammer on the original Elite might have been too light, Beretta put a heavier one in the Elite II.

JHP at 1,200 fps, or the Black Hills EXP load that spits a 165-grain Gold Dot at a stated 1,150 fps. The .357-like performance is available from Pro-Load Tactical's 135-grain JHP at approximately 1,300 fps. All three are fine self-defense loads as well.

Wish List

The Beretta Elite II is an excellent pistol as it comes from the box. About all I could ask for would be for the firm to produce it in the standard 92F/96F configuration. From coast to coast, I've documented stories of cops who are alive because their F-series Beretta was on safe when the bad guy got it away from them, pulled the trigger and was unable to make it fire. Whenever I carry a Beretta pistol in the "G" style, ready to shoot, I have a sense that I'm lacking a tactical feature I could have if I had simply gone with the "F" model. Note that Hattrup uses a conventional 92F for his actual home-defense hardware, both the older model and his new Vertec with attachable white light.

I would also like to see Elite II treatment given to the 96 Compact. The double-stack Beretta Compact magazine, designed to hold 13 rounds of 9mm, was always "just right" for 10 rounds of .40 S&W.

For more information, contact: Beretta USA Corp., 17601 Beretta Dr., Dept CH, Accokeek, MD 20607; 301-283-2191; www.berettausa.com.

Top, and Elite II with Jerry Barnhart's Burner grips; below, first model Elite.

Right: Elites are distinguished by splendid trigger pulls, both double-action …

Below: … and single-action.

Hattrup demonstrates the match-winning stance he learned from Ernest Langdon.

Top to bottom: Original Beretta Elite 9mm (retrofitted with Elite II hammer); Elite II 9mm; Elite II .40.

Here is the Beretta Elite II in 9mm.

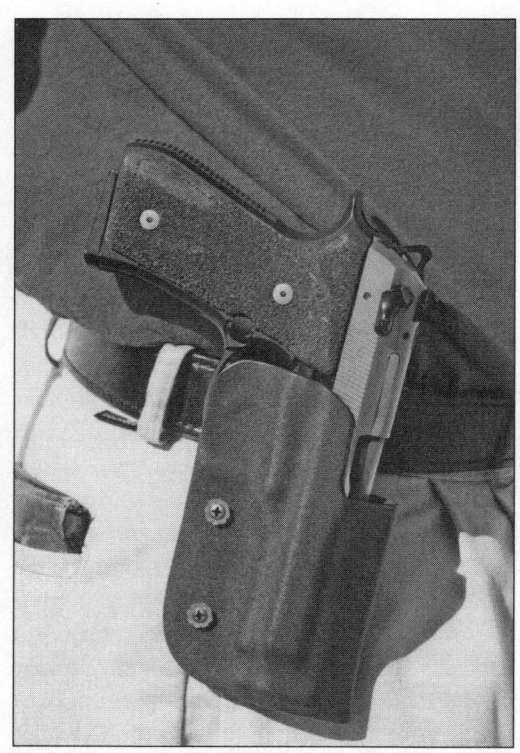

Hattrup's Elite II 9mm is match-ready with a Ky-Tac speed holster and Burner grips.

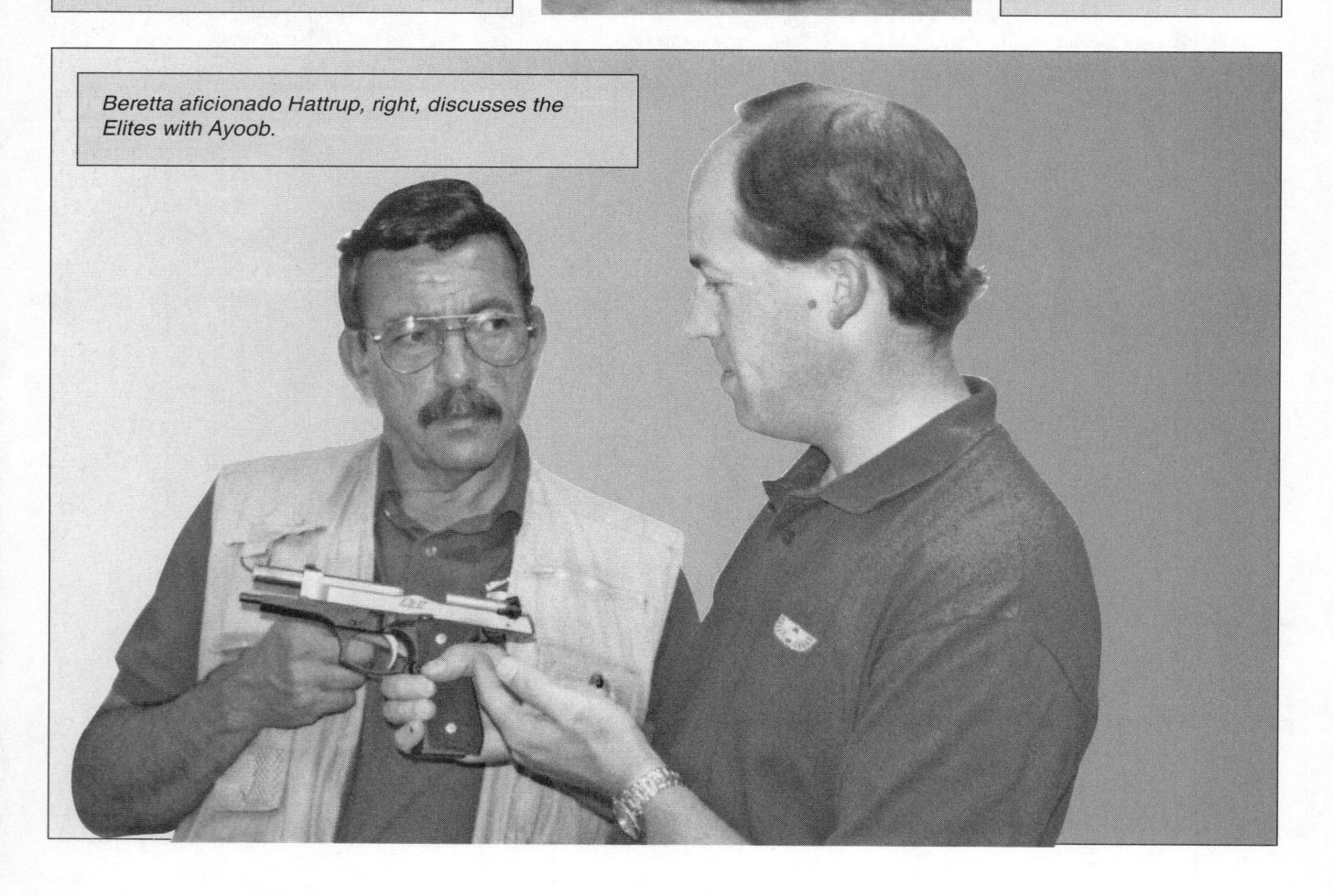

The Novak rear sight gives an excellent sight picture.

Beretta aficionado Hattrup, right, discusses the Elites with Ayoob.

Deeply cut grasping surfaces on the frame fore and aft allow excellent control. The magazine is competition style.

The skeletonized speed hammer, Novak sights and contrast-color G-type decocking lever are signature Elite features.

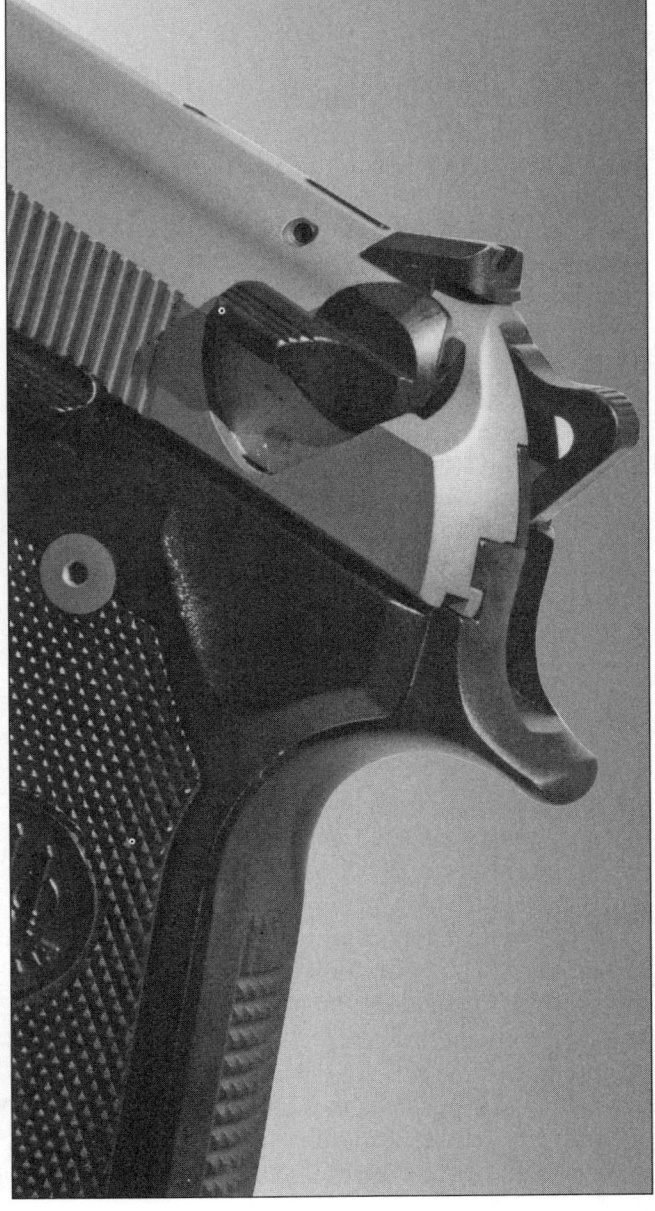

Maintaining Your Beretta

If you own a fine automobile, I expect that you take care of it. You fill it with quality gasoline, you put in good oil instead of cheap crap, and you inspect it regularly. You know that if you don't, it will wear out prematurely, break down on you, and perhaps even endanger your life and the lives of your loved ones.

It's the same with defensive firearms like the great majority of Beretta pistols. They are fine machines. They have a good "frequency of repair" ratio, and they are more tolerant than many other guns to a lack of maintenance. But to keep them in perfect working order all the time, and to make sure they last you want to maintain them well.

Keep them clean. Takedown procedures on all the Berettas tend to be fairly simple and straightforward, and the newer the model, the simpler they seem to be. With the tip-up barrel guns, pay *particular* attention to keeping the chambers shiny clean. These guns don't have extractors, which would get in the way of the tip-up barrel feature. The mechanism is counting on the recoil force of the spent casing to drive the slide rearward until the spent case is kicked out by the extractor. Binding the case into the chamber with accumulated crud could defeat that important dynamic, and jam your pistol.

The Beretta 92 manual makes an excellent point that more manufacturers of semi-automatic pistols should emphasize in the printed materials that come with their guns. It says, "Every time the pistol is fired or at least once a month, cleaning and lubricating is recommended." [1]

Review that carefully. Clean and lube it every time it's fired, *or* once a month. You wouldn't believe how many smart people who carry guns think they only have to clean their weapon after it has been fired. If

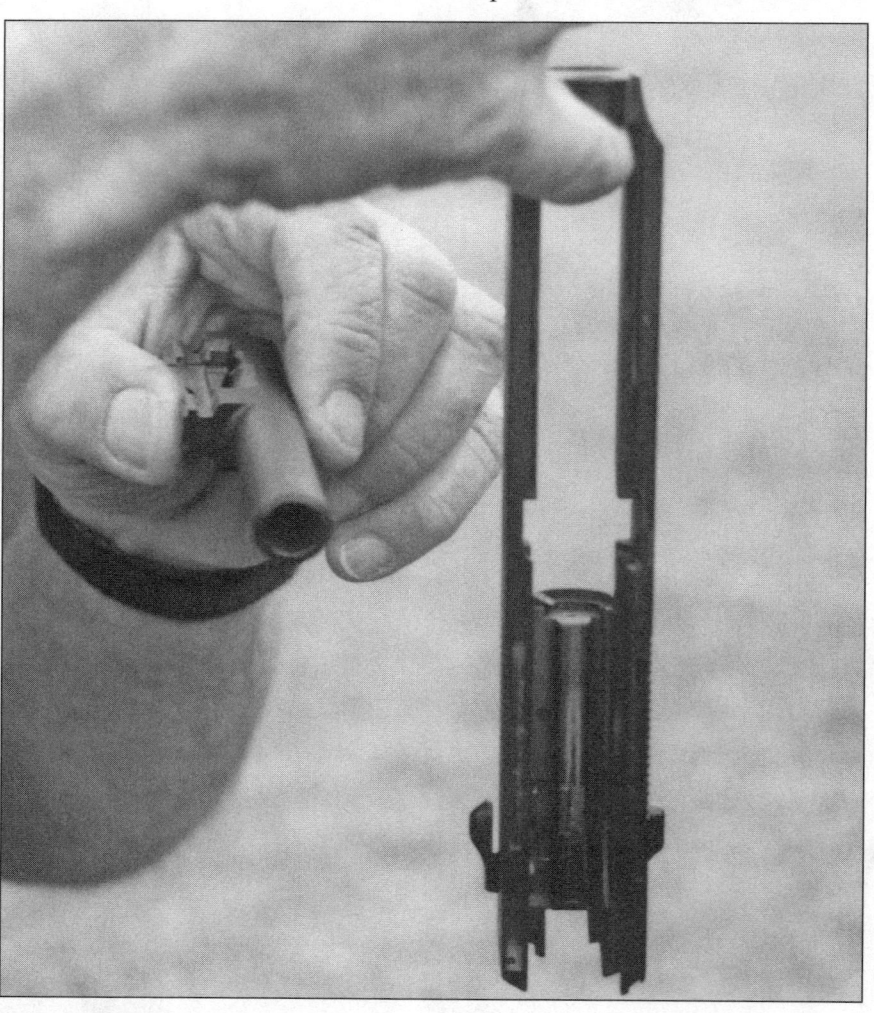

Holding the slide with the little finger like this, rap the side of it slightly. If it rings, you know there's no crack. Here, as an expedient, the pistol's barrel is used for the light tap, but a soft-nosed hammer is recommended.

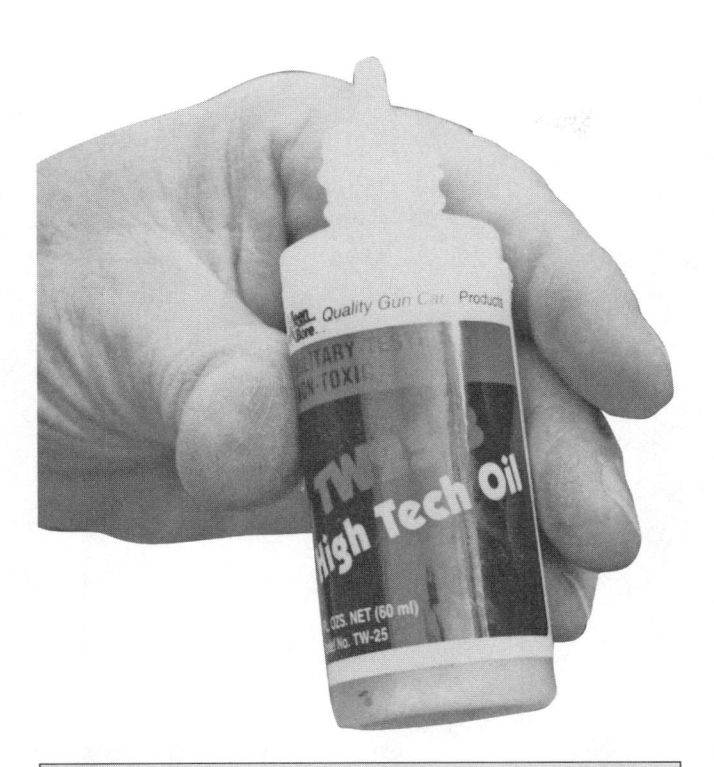

TW25 B High-Tech oil is the lube of choice for one experienced Beretta armorer.
It is an excellent lubricant, but not a cleanser.

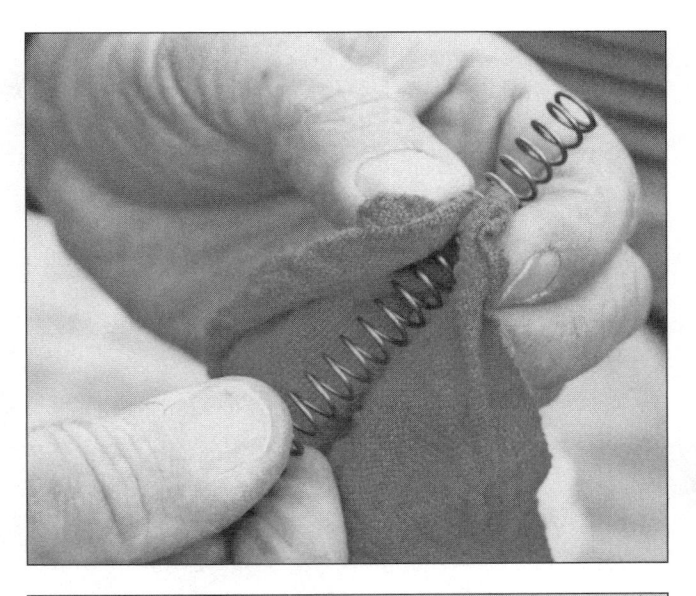

Cleaning the recoil spring. Get a bit of lightly oiled rag between the coils, and turning with thumb and forefinger …

The Beretta factory armorer's manual is a treasure trove of useful information.

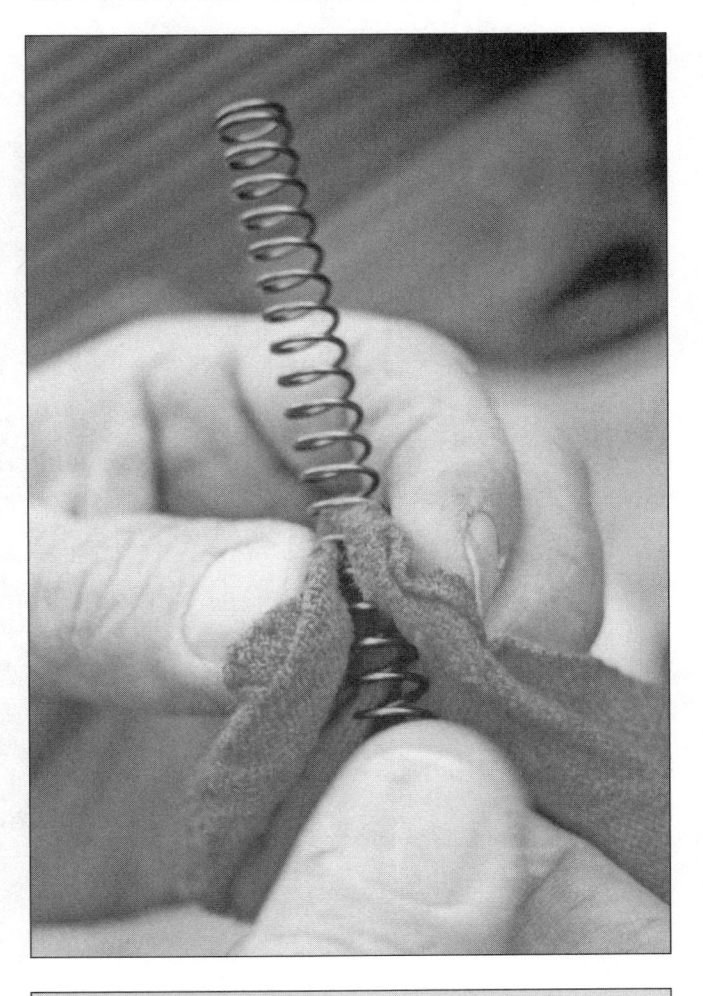

… roll the spring until the rag has gone all the way through.

Beretta armorer Bill Pfeil inspects a couple of police guns behind the firing line.

it is carried exposed to extremes of dust and dirt – a soldier or Marine in Afghanistan or Iraq would be in this situation – a *daily* cleaning, or at least a daily field-stripping and inspection, is warranted. If you carry a small Beretta in an ankle holster, an area where dirt and dust and grit very quickly accumulate on the pistol, daily or at least weekly cleaning should be the routine.

Why monthly cleaning on a carry gun that hasn't been fired *or* exposed to hostile environment? Because any auto-loading firearm requires lubrication for its long bearing surfaces to work against each other properly when the day comes that it *is* fired. People forget that most lubricant is liquid. Liquid evaporates. Liquid drains. The lube along your slide rails heads south when your pistol is carried muzzle down in its holster. Soon the pistol is dry. Dry pistols do not work as well as lubricated pistols.

In one episode of the old, cult-hit British TV show, "The Avengers," the male character, Steed, faces off with a thuggish European counterpart. The latter snarls that the next time they meet, he will face Steed with "a well-oiled Beretta." Steed, a clubby upper crust type who affects a bowler hat and walking stick, replies, "I prefer a Smith & Wesson, myself. Magnum."

Now, let's set aside for a moment the incongruity of the suave, urbane Steed, a man of Continental tastes, preferring an American revolver to a fine European automatic. What the bad guy had right was the "well-oiled Beretta" thing. A well-oiled Beretta is what you want on your side of the fight.

A few drops on the slide rails, top and sides will get you through the day at the range if you've let your gun sludge up and you don't want to experience a stoppage. But nature is telling you at a moment like that to take it apart as per the owner's manual, and give it a good cleaning. This chapter includes captioned photos in which a seasoned and certified Beretta armorer shows you the fine points of "the well-oiled Beretta."

> With tip-up barrels like this Tomcat .32, you want to make certain that chamber is completely clean to facilitate ejection.

If you are going to be in a high-sand environment, then a dry lube, something graphite-based perhaps, might make enormous sense for you. In arctic cold, be very sparing with the lubricant, or it will gel up on you and make the gun sluggish instead of slick. In non-hostile environments, I just use Firepower FP-10, or Break-Free CLP. I don't use WD-40, which seems to be more of a cleanser than a lubricant and tends to set up on the gun and get sticky after a long period of time.

If your gun is *really* sludged up, contact my buddy Bill Laughridge at Cylinder & Slide Shop in Fremont, Nebraska. He advertises in all the major gun magazines. He can ship you a bucket of Dunk-it. Soak the metal parts in there for a while, and the crud just floats away.

Another high-tech modern solution is the ultrasonic gun cleaning system. It's expensive and takes up some space, but for people who own many guns and shoot them a lot, it becomes a sensible investment. If the cost of the system seems intimidating, at the next meeting of your gun club make a motion that the group purchases a communal ultrasonic unit to be kept indoors at the range. NOTE: When your pistol comes out of the ultrasonic, it will be bone-dry, and will need complete re-lubrication.

It's amazing how many people clean their guns, but don't clean their magazines. The magazine is the key to the gun's feeding properly! The magazine, unlike the gun, gets dropped in the sand and mud all the time during training! When you clean the gun, clean its magazines! The magazine brushes available from sources like Brownell's are extremely handy for this, worth their weight in gold as it were.

Follow the manufacturer's instruction manual for disassembly. Don't go beyond that point into detail stripping unless you are a certified Beretta armorer or gunsmith. A full overhaul is best left to the skilled mechanic who does that particular machine for a living, or at least for part of his living. If you shoot a lot, any gun that you trust for defense of life should have such a detail-stripping overhaul once a year, minimum.

When you disassemble a Beretta, or any pistol, check for cracks, burrs, dings, and other defects in

> You want to diagnose problems carefully. What looked like a 92F locked on safe …

the parts. It's a good idea with any auto pistol to change out the recoil spring every 3,000 to 5,000 rounds. When you take your gun to be detail stripped by armorer or gunsmith, if it's had a few thousand rounds through it, ask that expert to replace the firing pin spring, too. These parts are cheap, and it's cheap insurance.

One trick Beretta armorers use to inspect for cracks in the slide is one you can easily use, too. Stick your finger through the hole for the barrel, in the front of the disassembled slide. Let the bare slide hang down from your finger, its rear sight toward the floor. Rap the side of the slide with a soft-nosed hammer or rubber mallet. If the sound produced has a ringing note to it, the slide is not cracked. If you hear more of a dull thud, it's an indication that a crack may have started. If you don't have the soft-nosed hammer, in a pinch you can just rap it with the gun's barrel. It will work the same way, and the light tap won't hurt a Beretta barrel.

> … actually just had the part jammed there by a sight that had drifted sideways, loosened by the careless application of a sight-drifting tool.

The Feeding

Don't use the el cheapo surplus ammo with corrosive primers that is still floating around; low prices don't necessarily make a bargain. Even if you think you've got it clean, there may be bad juju happening deep in the gun. Use quality ammo with non-corrosive primers.

I wouldn't use ammunition with steel cartridge casings in any Beretta. Unless you have a weapon designed for steel case ammo, like the Russian Makarov, it will tend to break extractors. I've also seen a lot of the steel case stuff come with "bulletproof primers" that caused repeated misfires.

Some advise against aluminum-cased Blazer ammunition. Personally, I haven't had any problems with it in Beretta pistols. A lot of my students show up with it, run hundreds and hundreds of rounds of aluminum Blazer through their Berettas in various calibers, and leave happy without a single malfunction. In fact, I've done more than one accuracy test of a pistol for a gun magazine where the Blazer shot the tightest group.

Keep a fresh box of your duty ammo handy. Change out the round in the chamber every month or so. Every time you unload and reload, the extractor takes another bite at the rim and the ejector takes another kick at it. Dinged up brass is one reason reloaded ammo tends to be less reliable than virgin

Beretta has owners' manuals for all currently produced guns. Get one from Beretta U.S.A. in Accokeek, MD if you don't have one for your pistol.

factory ammunition. Moreover, each time the cartridge is rammed into the chamber is another chance to weaken the watertight seal between case mouth and bullet, which down the road can at least theoretically compromise the integrity of the powder charge. With some ammo, repeated chamberings can push the bullet back into the cartridge casing. This shortens overall length, which can cause a feeding stoppage the next time that cartridge finds its way into a magazine. Worse, it increases the pressure inside the casing when it is finally fired, which can lead to catastrophic results.

The round that has been in and out of the chamber a few times should be taken out of active service. If the bullet has been pushed back into the casing, disassemble it with a bullet puller or dispose of it by soaking it for a few days in metal penetrating oil and then bury it, but for heaven's sake, *don't fire it*. If overall length looks OK but it's just scuffed up, set it in with your practice ammo to shoot up at the range.

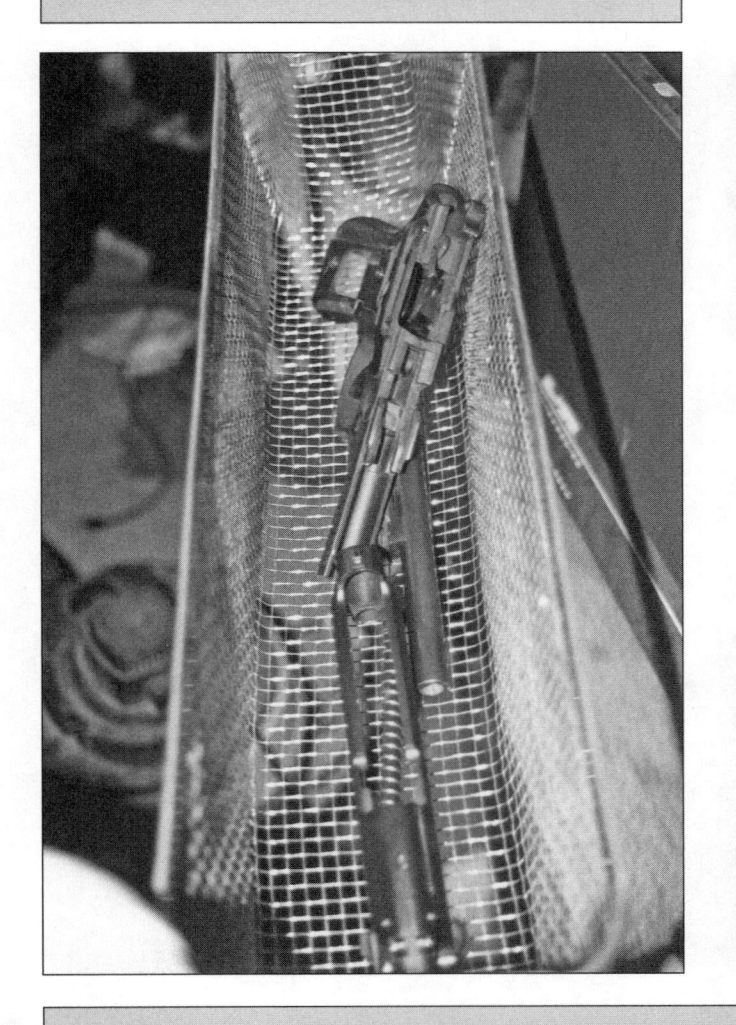

Left: Field stripped and with grip panels removed, the author's Beretta 92FS is ready for its bath ...
Right: ... in Marty Hayes' ultrasonic cleaning machine.

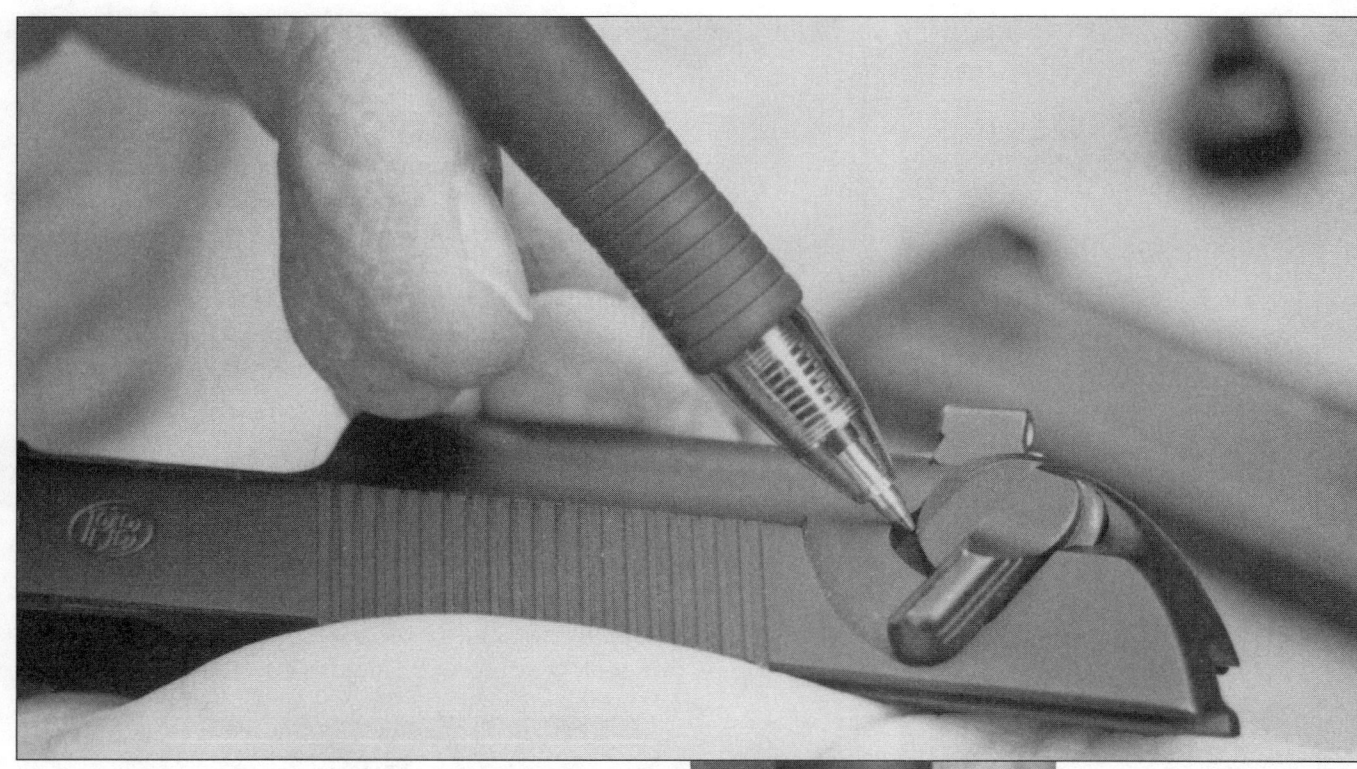

Above: How to achieve the proverbial well-oiled Beretta. A drop of oil goes on the safety/decock lever as shown, lubricating the plunger and plunger spring …

Right: … one drop in the rear of the firing pin channel …

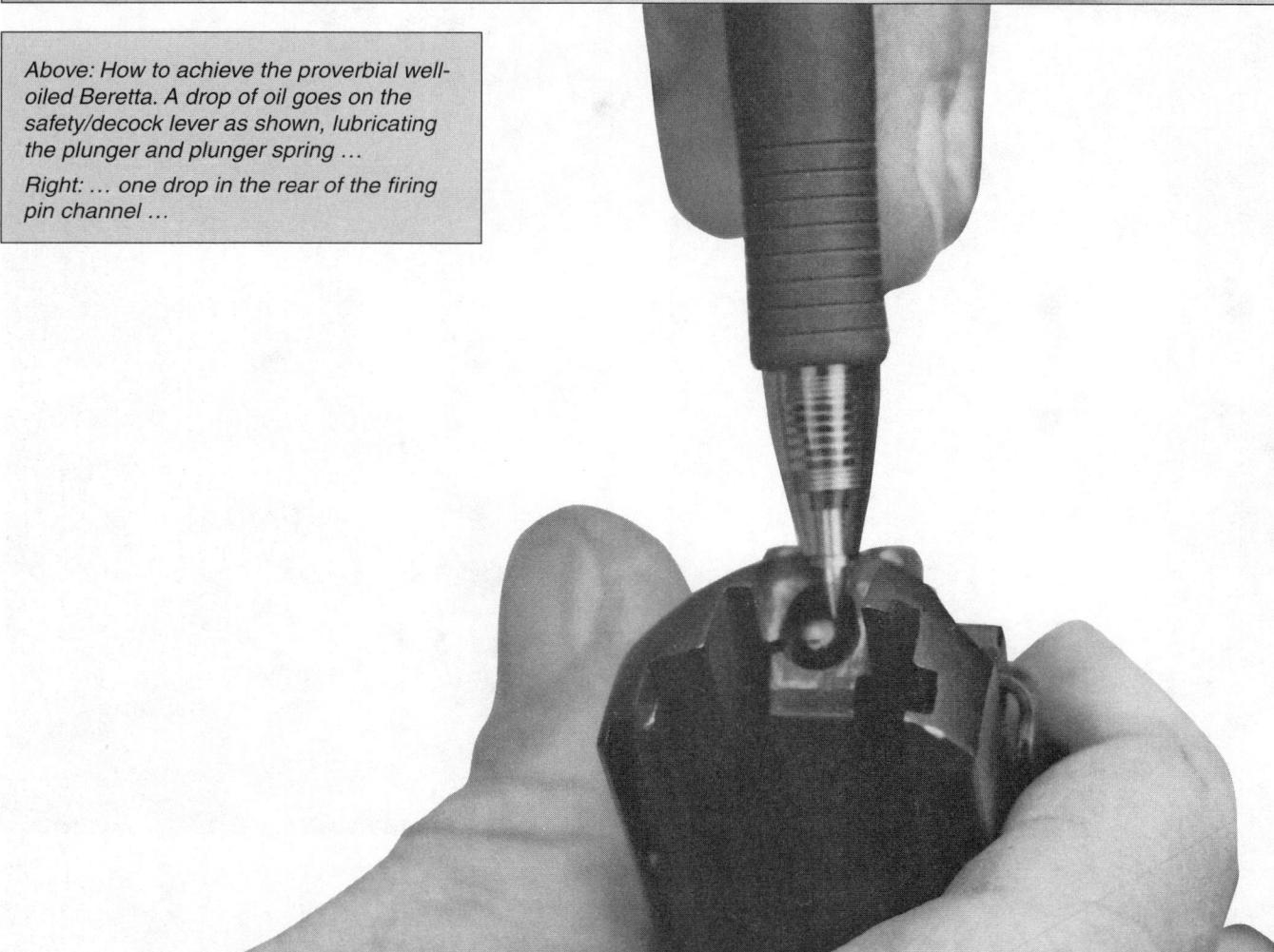

The ammunition in a defense gun should be factory fresh and in perfect condition in every respect.

When acquiring ammo for a Beretta 96, I'd recommend 155-, 165-, or 180-grain loads. I've just heard too many complaints about stoppages with lighter-bullet rounds. A substantial overall cartridge length seems to be critical to achieving perfect feeding in the .40 caliber open-slide Berettas. I've not heard that complaint with the Cougar 8040 series, however.

The 9mm Model 92, on the other hand, seems to be pretty much omnivorous. Don't worry about +P or even +P+ ammo. The factory warrants the modern 92 series for those rounds. Hell, it's rated for the 9mm NATO, which is higher pressure than either +P *or* +P+.

In 9mm Parabellum Berettas prior to the 92 series, you might be better off using standard-pressure American ammunition. Remember, too, that guns weren't throated for hollow-points back when the 1951 series came out. If you have one that malfunctions with modern, wide-mouth JHP, try some standard-pressure Remington 115-grain copper-jacketed hollow-point ammo.

Similarly, if you have a first- or second-generation .32 or .380 Beretta, the Remington standard JHP might be the load of choice for you. Not all of these old guns will feed modern JHP rounds, either. Third-generation (81 series) Berettas should have no problem with wide-mouth hollow-points.

As noted, reloads tend to jam more than factory ammo. If you're using reloads for an important match, disassemble your pistol the night before and drop each and every round into the firing chamber of the separated barrel, then turn the barrel upside down and drop the cartridge back into your palm. It should slip in smoothly and completely, and fall out smoothly and completely, of its own weight. If it doesn't, set it aside for a practice day, because you've just had a preview of a cycling failure waiting to happen.

This is mentioned elsewhere, but because many readers are like me and sometimes read a book by skipping around between the chapters, it bears repeating here. If we're talking about feeding a Beretta, part of that diet involves the primary feeding device, the magazine. More jams have been caused

... one drop behind the extractor...

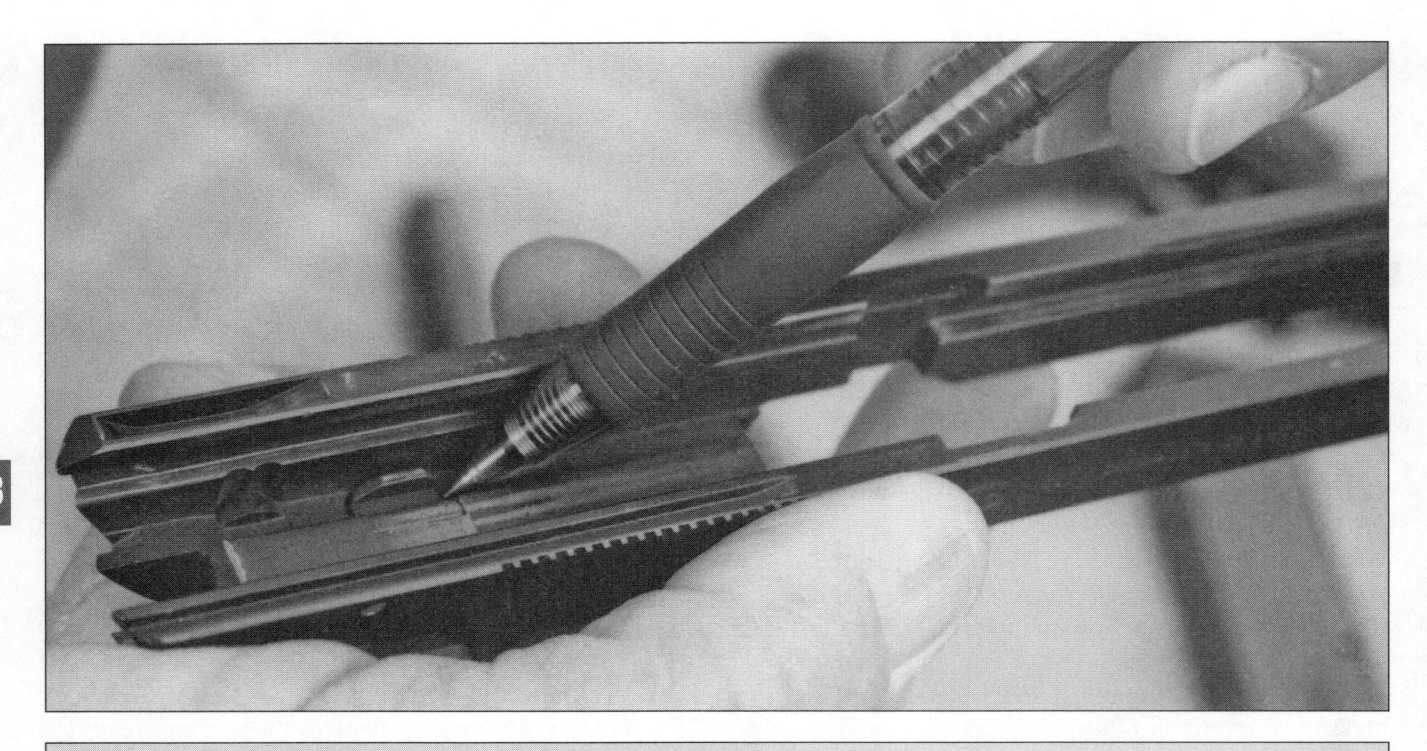

... one drop each in the front and back of firing pin catch ...

in Berettas by cheap, aftermarket magazines than by anything else. I use *only Beretta or MecGar brand magazines in my Beretta pistols,* and I most strongly urge you to do the same!

The defensive Beretta is there to take care of you. It's only fair that you take care of it in return. Inspect it routinely, clean it regularly and keep it properly lubricated. Use only Beretta or MecGar magazines, and only top-quality ammunition. In the end, you'll have a fine, fully operational pistol in perfect working order to pass on to your heirs after you peacefully die of old age.

Endnotes

(1)Beretta Series 92 Istruzioni per l'uso/ Instructions for operation/Mode d'emploi, P. 21

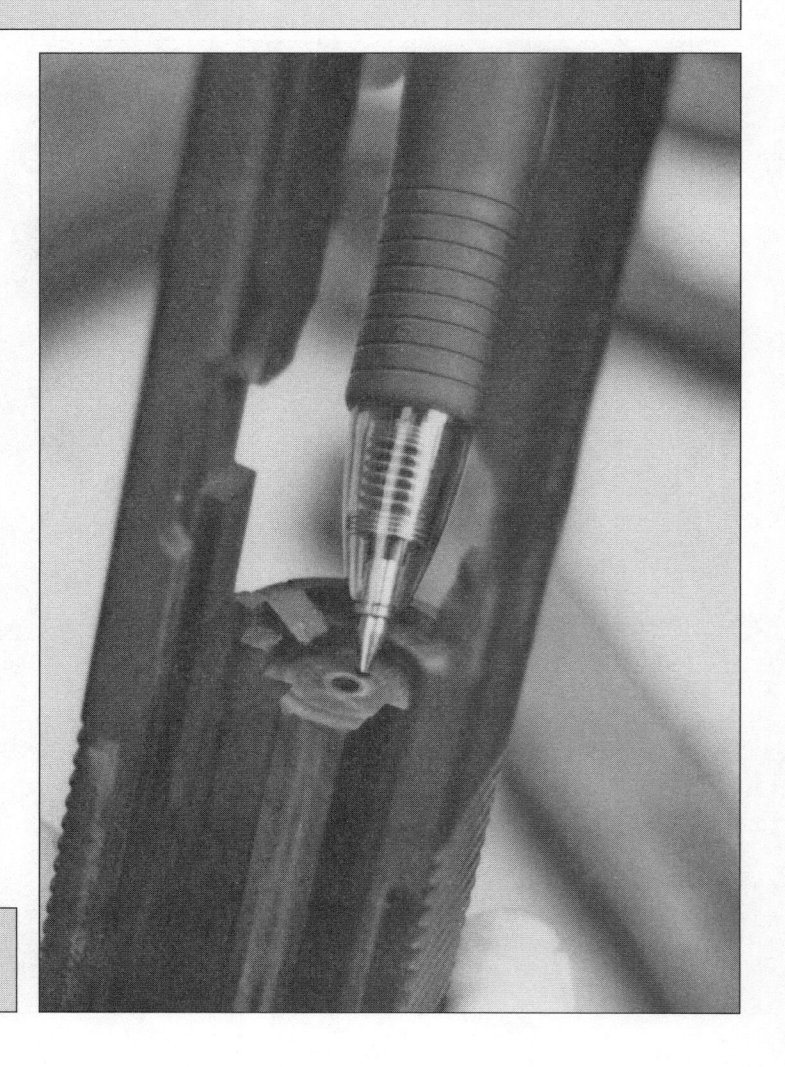

... one drop in the front of the firing pin channel ...

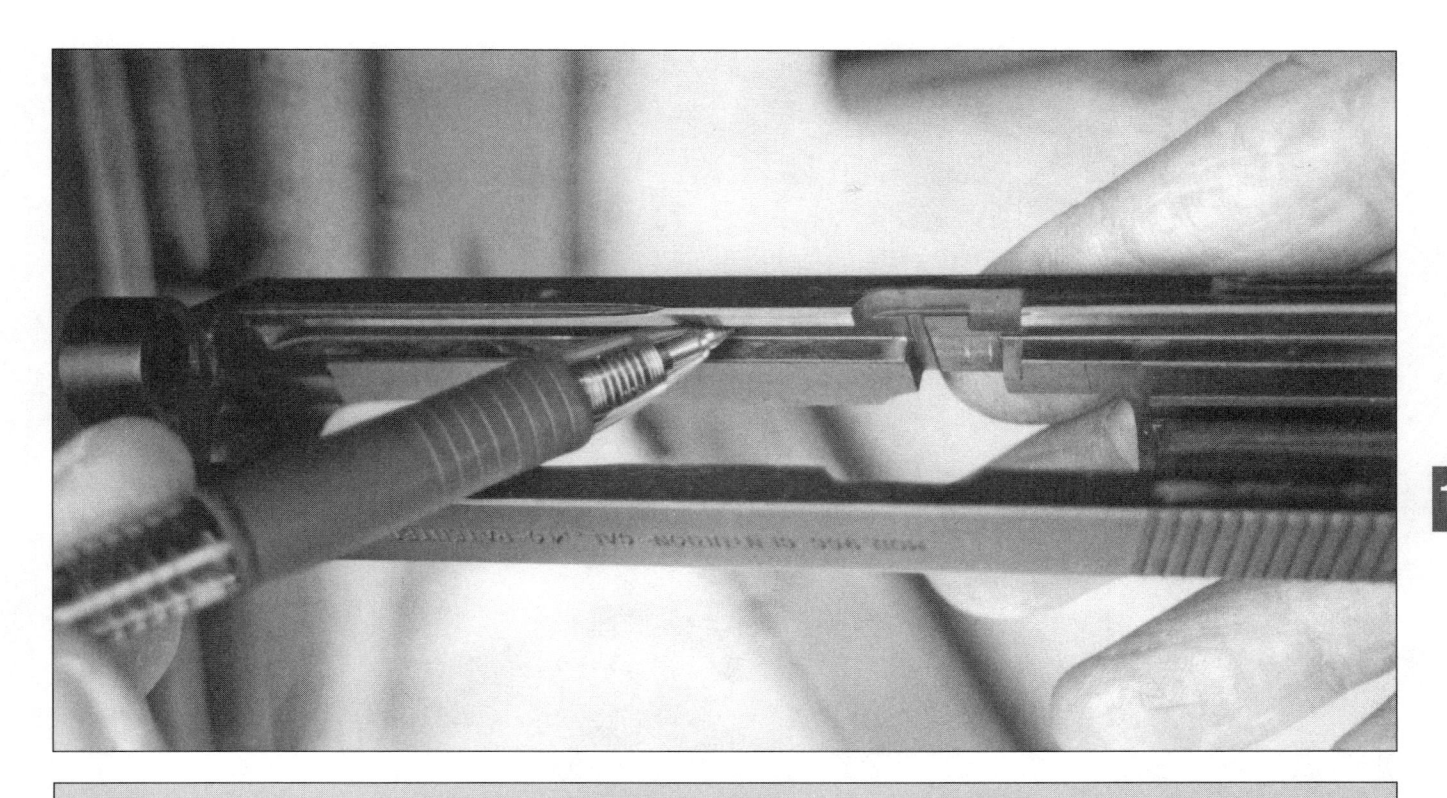

Above: … and a few drops in both left and right slide rails. Slide lube is completed, and it's time to go to the frame …

Below: … it won't hurt to put a drop on the trigger bar spring, a spot you have to be careful of while cleaning the magazine well …

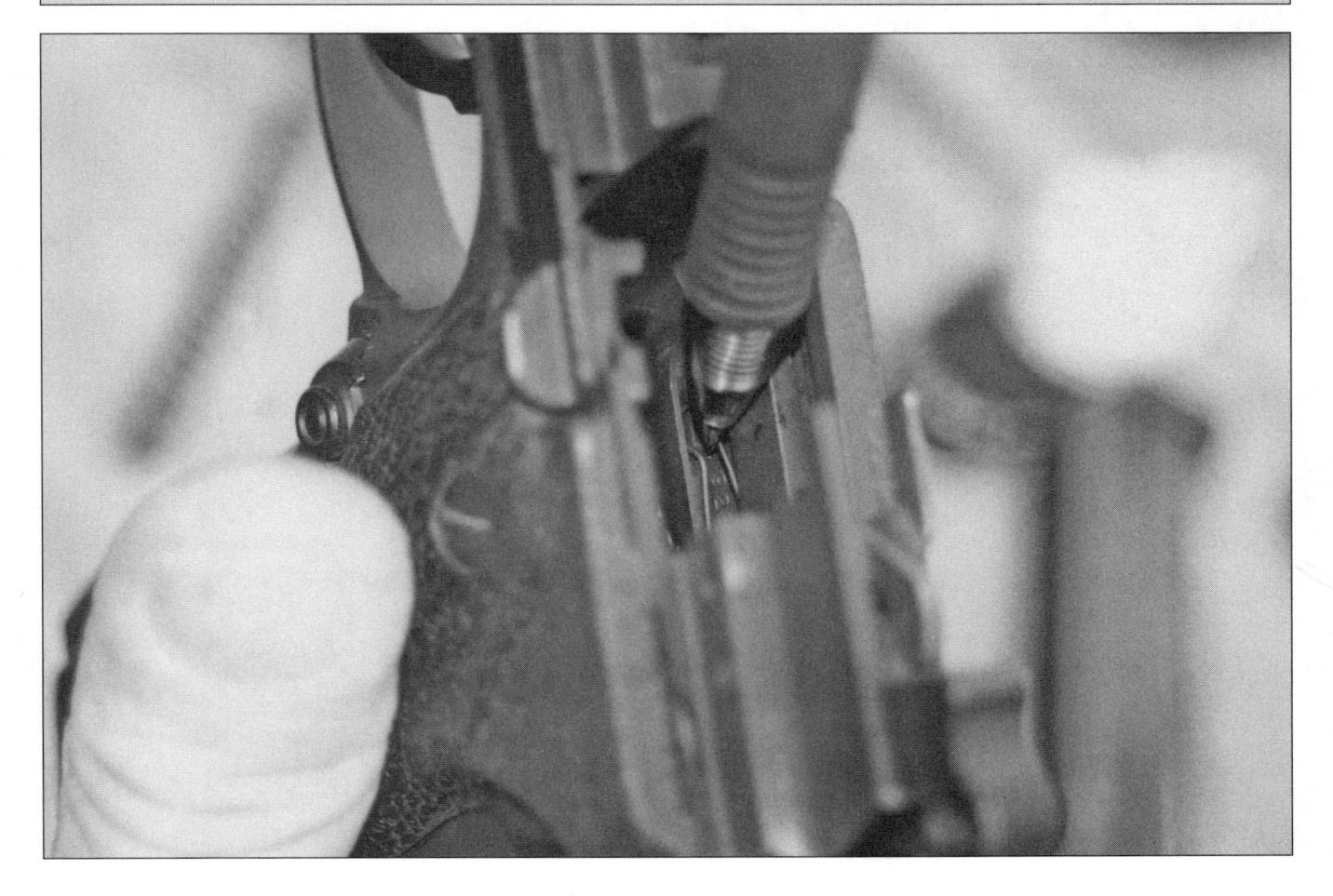

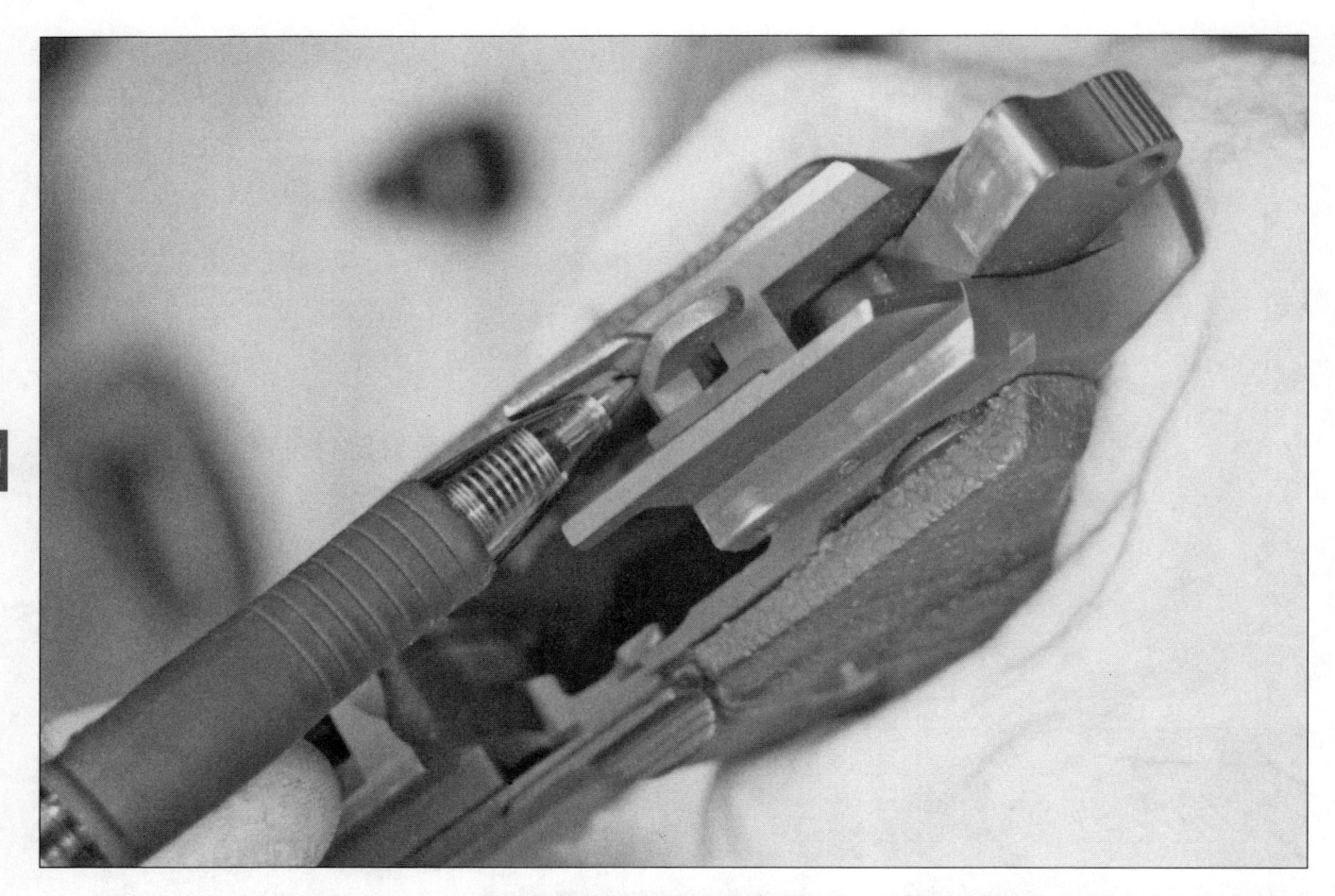

Above: ... put a drop of oil on each side of the firing pin block lever ...

Right: ... a drop on the hammer release lever ...

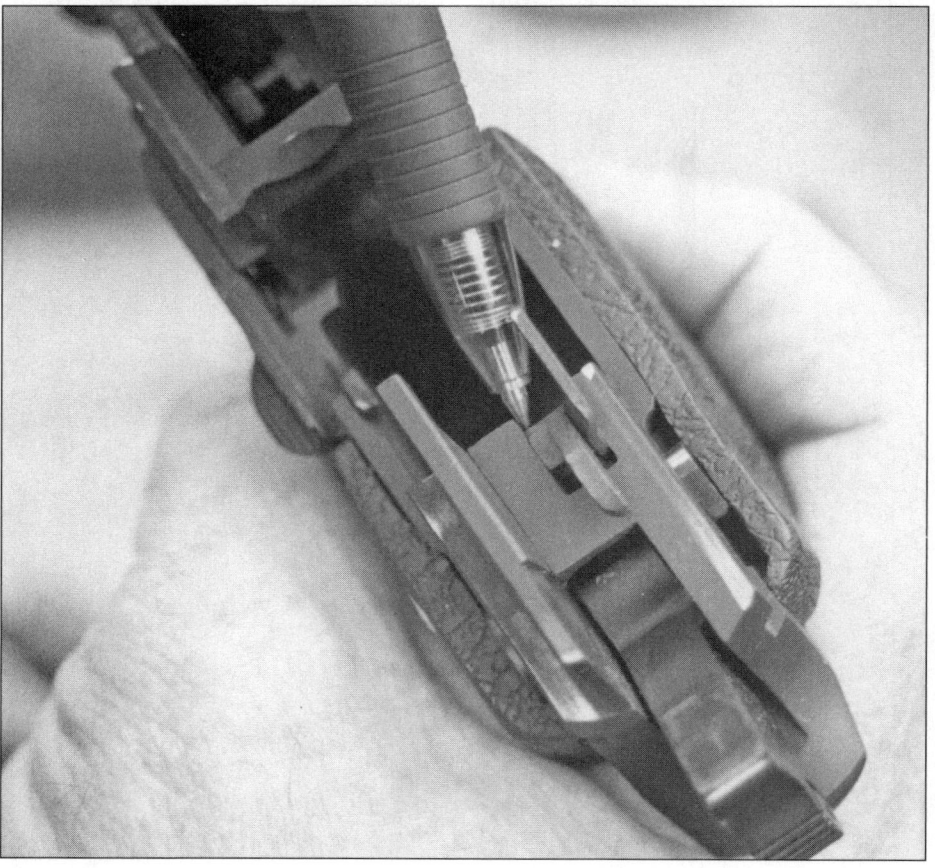

... a drop of oil between hammer and frame on both left and right side ...

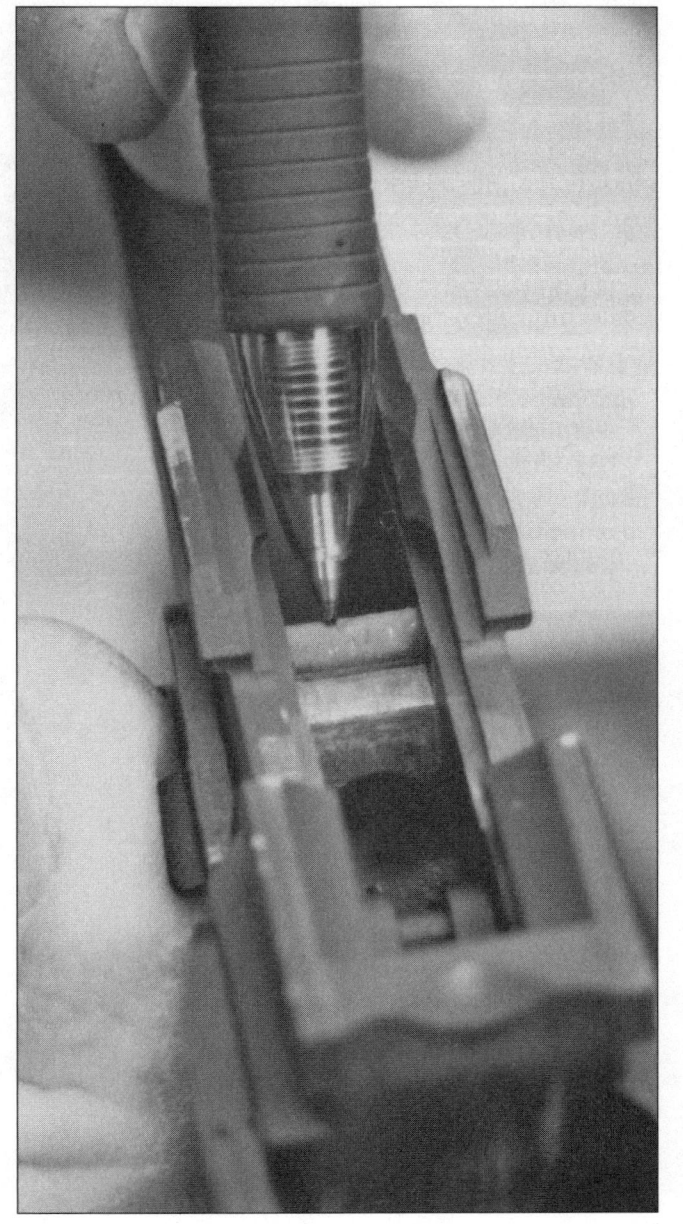

... a drop on the disassembly latch, a.k.a. takedown lever ...

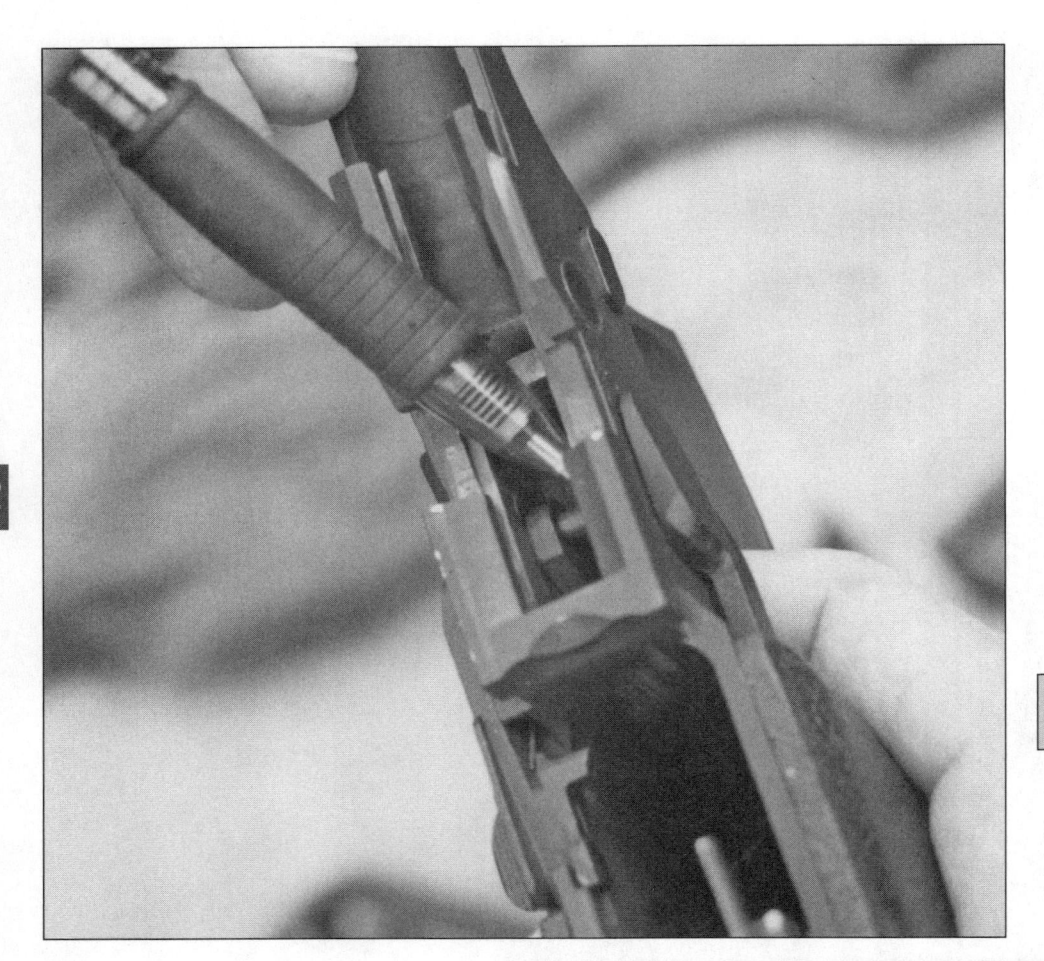

... a drop on the trigger pin ...

... a drop on the trigger pivot pin ...

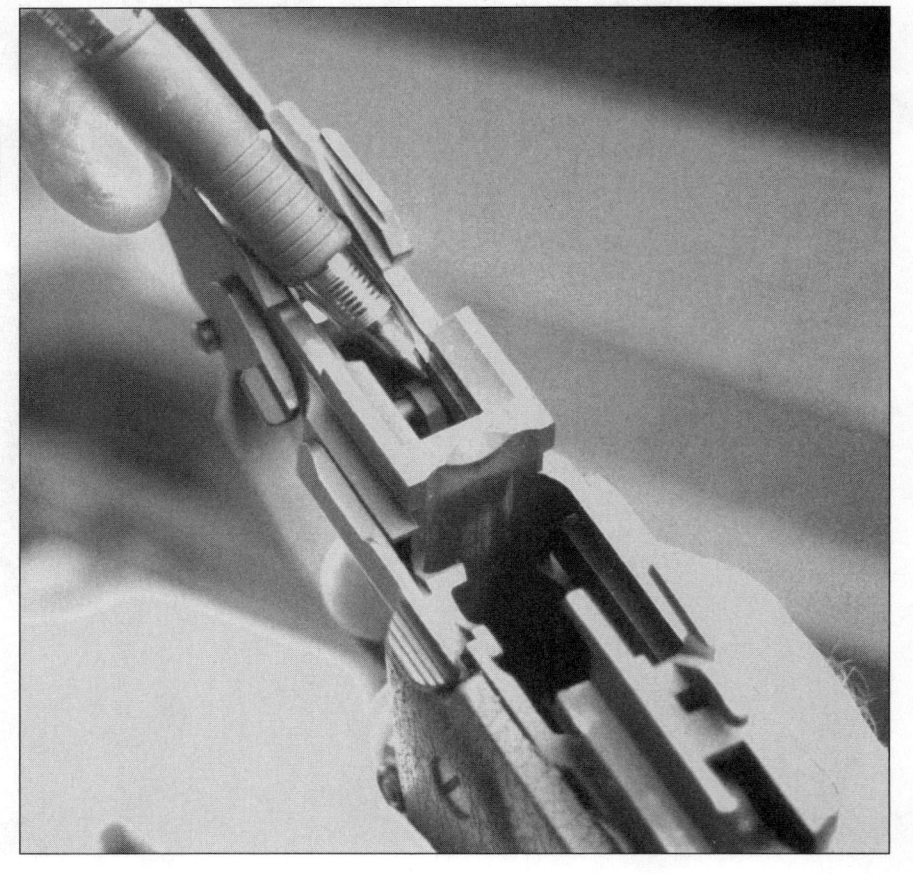

... a couple of drops behind the trigger bar ...

... and a drop or two on the sear, and the frame is lubed. Now to the barrel ...

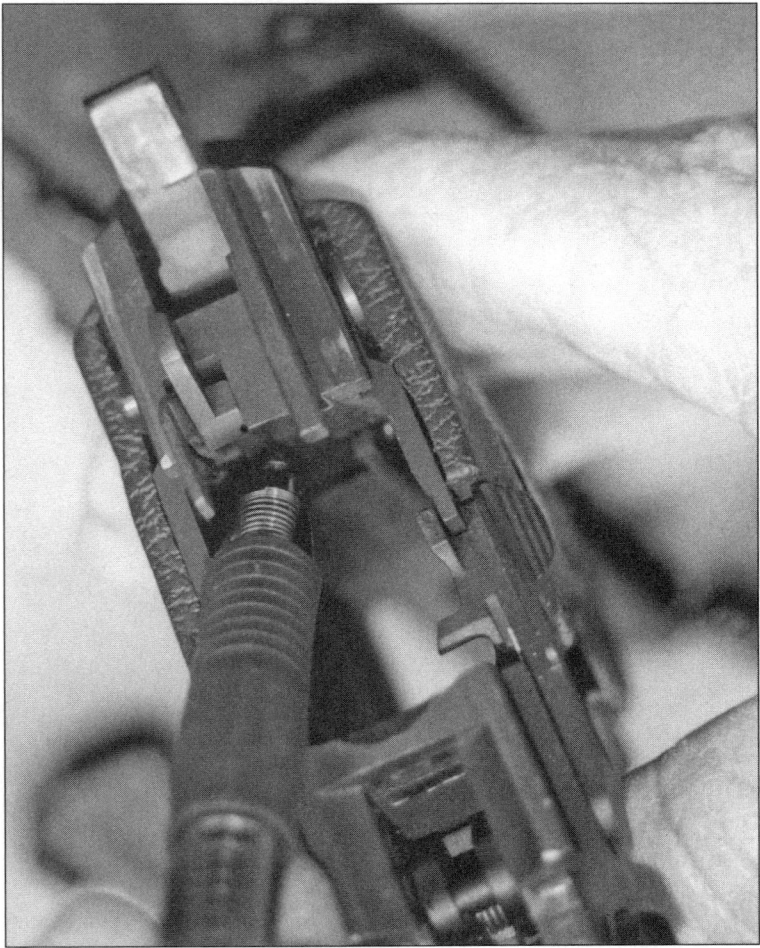

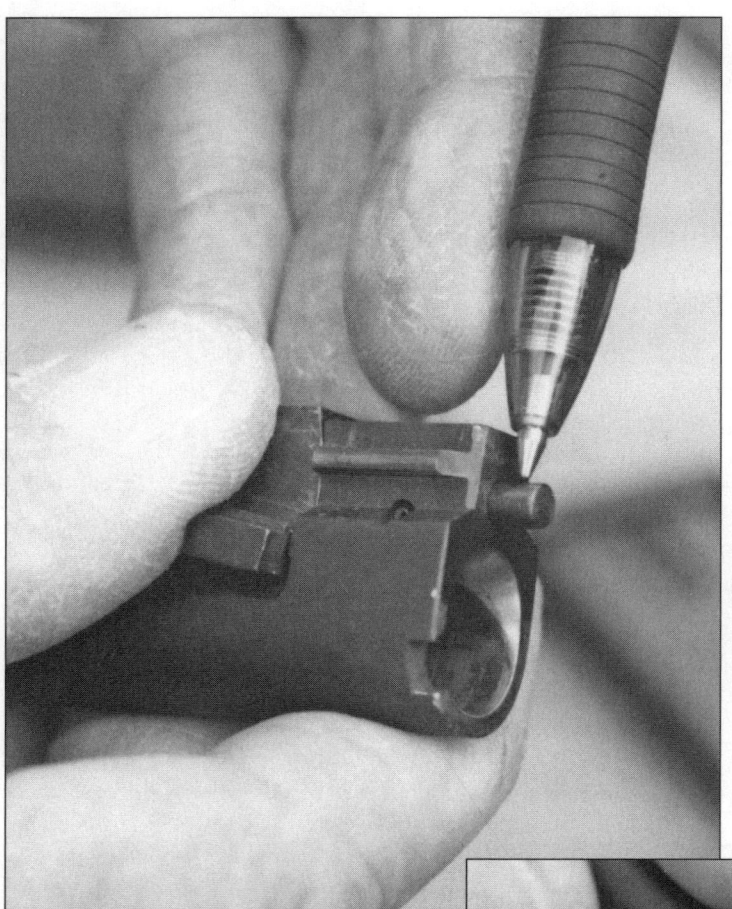

... where you want a drop of oil on the locking block plunger ...

... where you want to lube all bearing surfaces of the locking block area.

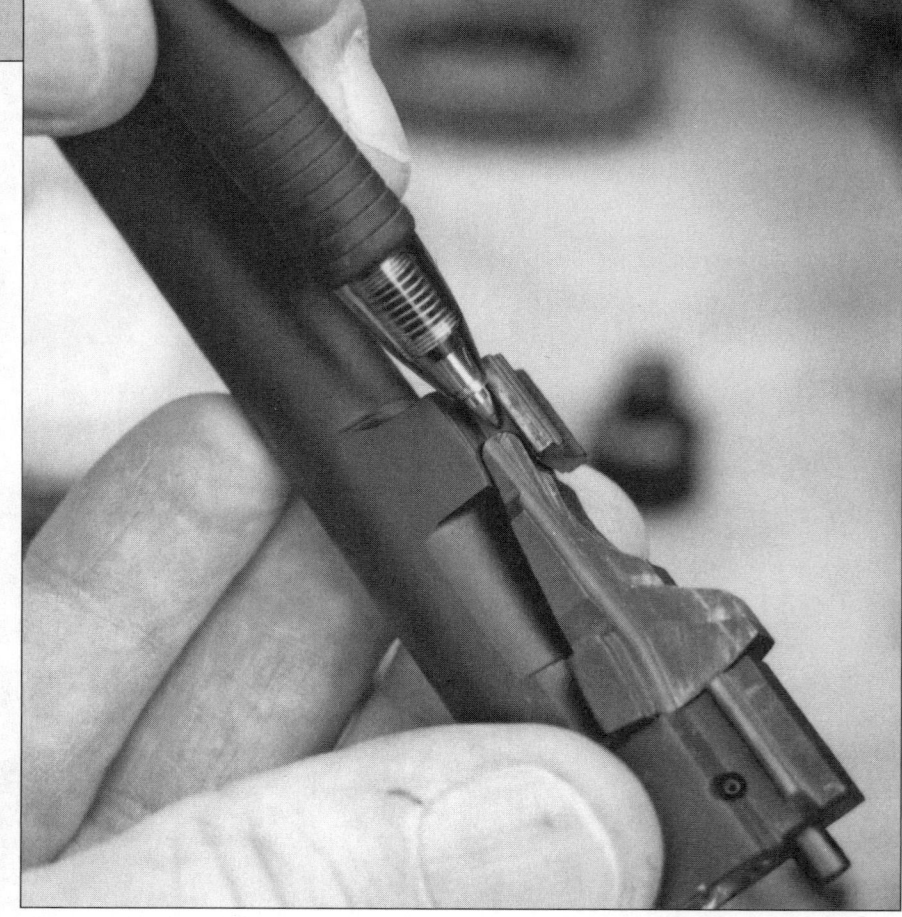

Careful Customizing
Can Make Your Beretta Better

Ayoob's Langdon-tuned Beretta 92G.

Maximum performance in the arena generally demands some degree of customizing of the equipment involved, so it can better fulfill its specific purpose. In handguns, this is true whether the arena is a pistol match or a dark alley in Los Angeles or a cave in Afghanistan.

The Beretta is a hard pistol to make better, but it can be done. Certain fine-tunings require such skilled labor that a manufacturer cannot perform them at the factory and still keep the price down to where most of those who need the gun can afford it. However, those who desire absolute maximum performance have historically found the money to pay for it, and learned to bring that money to a handful of extraordinarily skillful practitioners who specialize in the particular type of equipment in question.

I've had the privilege of seeing, shooting, and even owning Berettas customized by some of the finest craftsmen extant. Let's share the experience. We'll start with Ernest Langdon, widely considered the gold standard for combat pistolsmithing of the Beretta 92 and 96. I've used a Langdon custom pistol quite a bit over the years, and as it broke in more, it just got better and better. The last four IDPA matches I shot with it netted me two wins, and no finish lower than third place among some very skillful men and women with very fine guns. With a Langdon Beretta in your hands, you know that whatever else happens, you won't get hurt because your gun wasn't good enough.

Langdon Custom Beretta

The pretty gray Beretta 92 was empty, its slide locked back. I stripped its depleted magazine and went downrange to check the target, 25 yards away. Five Pro-Load Tactical rounds, each throwing a 115-grain Gold Dot hollow-point at some 1,300 feet per second (fps), had struck in a group that measured exactly an inch and a quarter center-to-center. The best three were in a clover-leaf that measured 0.30 of an inch center-to-center; less than one nine millimeter bullet's diameter.

I smiled. The target confirmed that sending this pistol to Ernest Langdon had been the right thing to do.

Langdon lightly bevels the magazine well, making reloading even easier.

The spurless hammer of a DAO Beretta gives the Langdon-treated TDA smoother lines and a more snag-free profile. Note the eye-pleasing contrast of the silvery barrel and trigger with the dark gray Teflon finish of the gun's main body.

Langdon & Beretta

The Beretta 92 is a mature design, splendidly manufactured. It has long been our nation's standard military sidearm, bearing the designation M9 in that service. It is reliable, accurate, and totally functional as a service pistol. Many felt that it couldn't be improved.

No matter how good any factory handgun is, it could be made better by craftsmanship, especially if that craftsmanship is guided by a deep knowledge of the pistol itself and how that pistol is used to maximum effect. Ernest Langdon was in a position to understand both.

I had been hearing about Ernie Langdon being the guy to beat in IDPA, and first saw him in action at the 1998 MidWinter National Championships. The guy was awesome. He won not only the Stock Service Pistol category, but the overall match, shooting what appeared to be a bone-stock Beretta 92. Today, Langdon is still the guy to beat in IDPA, and he continues to shoot the double-action 9mm. I've seen him take the overall from World Champ Rob Leatham and Bianchi Cup ruler Doug Koenig, who were shooting light-triggered 1911s at the time.

Langdon knows the real-world side as well as he knows the shooting match side. Eleven years in the Marine Corps took him from Panama to the Gulf, and saw him as the lead instructor in combat pistolcraft for four years in the High Risk Personnel Course at Quantico.

Since he is now a private citizen and multiple-time national champion, Langdon has naturally been inundated with offers to shoot this or that high-tech single-action auto as a factory team star. His response has always been, "Thanks, but no thanks." He remains convinced that the Beretta is unbeatable as a functional real-world defensive handgun, and he knows that with the right ammo, a 9mm is powerful enough to solve your problems. This is especially true of an accurate 9mm that holds 16 rounds and never jams.

Hogue cocobolo grips look great, feel great and help you shoot great.

A Bar-Sto barrel expertly fitted by Langdon allows the pistol to deliver precision accuracy.

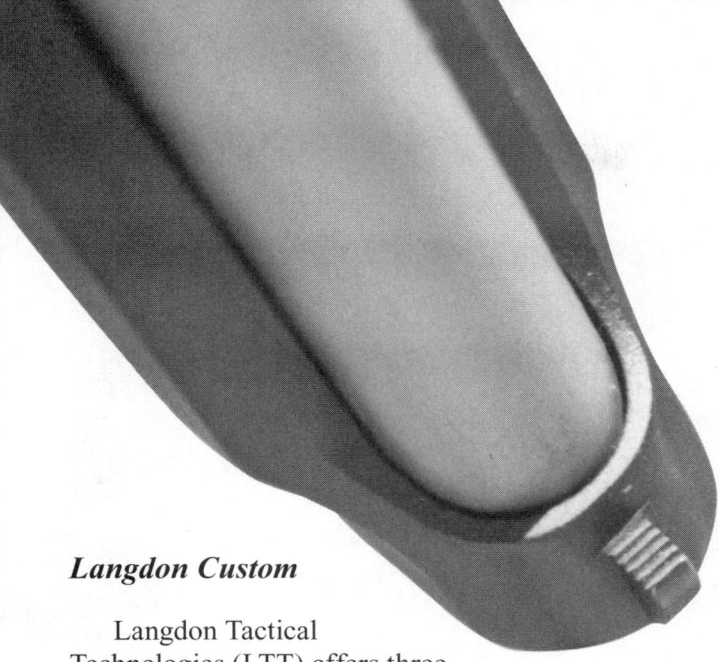

Langdon Custom

Langdon Tactical Technologies (LTT) offers three classes of action jobs. Ernest has found that the factory trigger pull goes 12 to 14 pounds in a 92/96 F or G model in double-action, and 5 to 6.5 pounds in single-action. LTT's Level I trigger job takes this down to a "smooth 8 pounds in DA and crisp 4 to 4.5 pounds in SA." A D-series (double-action-only) hammer spring is installed, and the action is honed. Cost is $85.

Level II is "the same basic action job … with the addition of the LTT Speed Bump Trigger (which) reduces the over-travel of the trigger pull. This gives the trigger pull a much better, crisper feel in both DA and SA as well as reducing the trigger reset, allowing for faster, more accurate follow-up shots." Pull weight is similar to Level I, with a smoother and shorter stroke, and also as with the Level I, this action work does not in any way compromise reliability. Cost is $125. As you'll see shortly, the difference in trigger control is well worth the extra $40 and this is what I'd recommend for a carry Beretta from Langdon.

The Level II competition trigger job goes a step farther. Langdon states clearly on his website, "Trigger pull after work is about 7 pounds in DA and 3 to 3.5 in SA. Note: This setup is not recommended for duty or carry pistols, and may not be compatible with some types of ammunition."

Right: The Novak rear sight gives excellent sight picture …

Above: … in tandem with front sight serrated by Langdon to break up reflection.

I asked him about the latter, and Langdon explained, "This is the lightest DA that I can get and still make it hit the primers hard enough. Some ammo will have problems with this setup. CCI primers will be a problem for sure. The best bet is to use something with Federal pistol primers, because they seem to work the best."

Langdon was requested to take this gun beyond the trigger job. A Bar-Sto barrel was installed for maximum accuracy. Plain black sights, as big and easy to see as he could make them, were requested. Since I never hand-cock a double-action auto, a spurless hammer was desirable. This would help forestall any false accusation of having cocked the gun and created a hair-trigger accidental discharge.

Finished Product

It was only a few weeks before the gun came back. I sent Langdon a 92G I'd had on hand for some time. This is the double-action first shot, single-action follow-up 9mm whose slide lever is spring-loaded and functions only as a decocker, not as a safety catch as on the 92F I personally prefer. It was going to be a match gun, and the targets don't try to kill you with your own gun at shooting events, so I didn't feel a need for a manual safety as a handgun retention "safety net." This pistol had been in use for some time as a loaner gun for students, and had never jammed to the best of my recollection with any factory ammunition.

The oversize magazine release button was never tripped accidentally and slightly enhanced reloading speed. The smooth surface of the trigger improved the rate of accurate rapid fire.

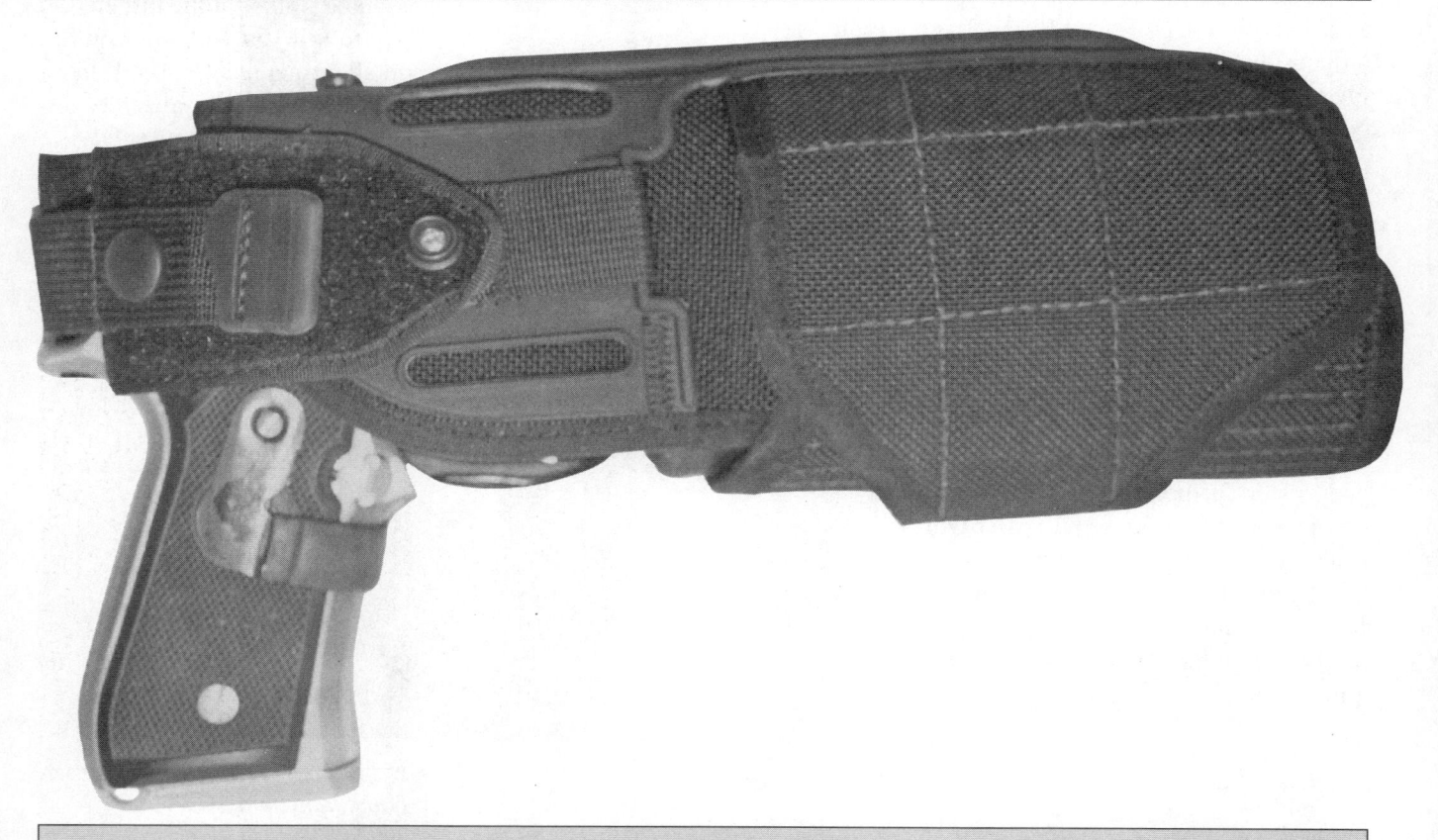

A Bianchi Cobra tactical holster can be mounted on a belt or thigh harness, and adjusts to hold large flashlight-mounted pistols.

When I took it out of the box after its return, I didn't recognize it. The black plastic grips had been replaced with exquisite Hogue cocobolo stocks, checkered 20 lines to the inch. Stainless Beretta hex-head screws held them in place.

The factory's workmanlike Bruniton finish had been replaced by a flat, dark gray matte surfacing. Langdon explains, "The frame was re-anodized and then Teflon-coated. Slide and decocking lever were flat blued and then Teflon coated. All of the finish work was done by John Setelin (Trapper) of T.T.I. International."

The Bar-Sto barrel had been cut down to 4.7 inches, a length Langdon favors for these guns. "It gives the pistol a much cleaner look," he feels. The stainless surface had been bead-blasted to match the silvery matte Speed Bump Trigger that now rode in the pistol.

There were no sharp contact points on the pistol. Ernest told me after he did the work, "Key points are the back of the slide near the frame rails. They can be very sharp on a Beretta. Also, the underside of (your) trigger guard has been rounded quite a bit. This is an area that most shooters have a problem with after they put a lot of rounds downrange. It tends to wear on the middle finger a great deal. All in all, I just knocked the edges off most of the outside of the pistol. I also took some off the decocking lever This lever can cause some shooters problems. Rob Haught has me do this to all his Berettas, as this lever really tears his thumb up. I have seen him bleeding after a long range session."

The man he's talking about is one of the best IDPA shooters around, and a street-wise cop. If there is ever a combat pistol championship for police chiefs, Rob Haught and Jeff Chudwin may be in a dead heat. Rob always shoots matches with a duty style Beretta, and his resorting to Langdon's services is a strong recommendation indeed.

The rear sight had been replaced by a Novak low-profile fixed unit, which Langdon had deepened and widened for maximum visibility. Where the

Langdon's proprietary Speed Bump trigger improves hit potential, especially in high-speed shooting.

Standing behind his product (and here, behind replicated cover) Langdon has used his own guns to win multiple national championships in various combat shooting disciplines.

Jarvis fitted his namesake barrel perfectly, resulting in outstanding accuracy with no compromise in reliability.

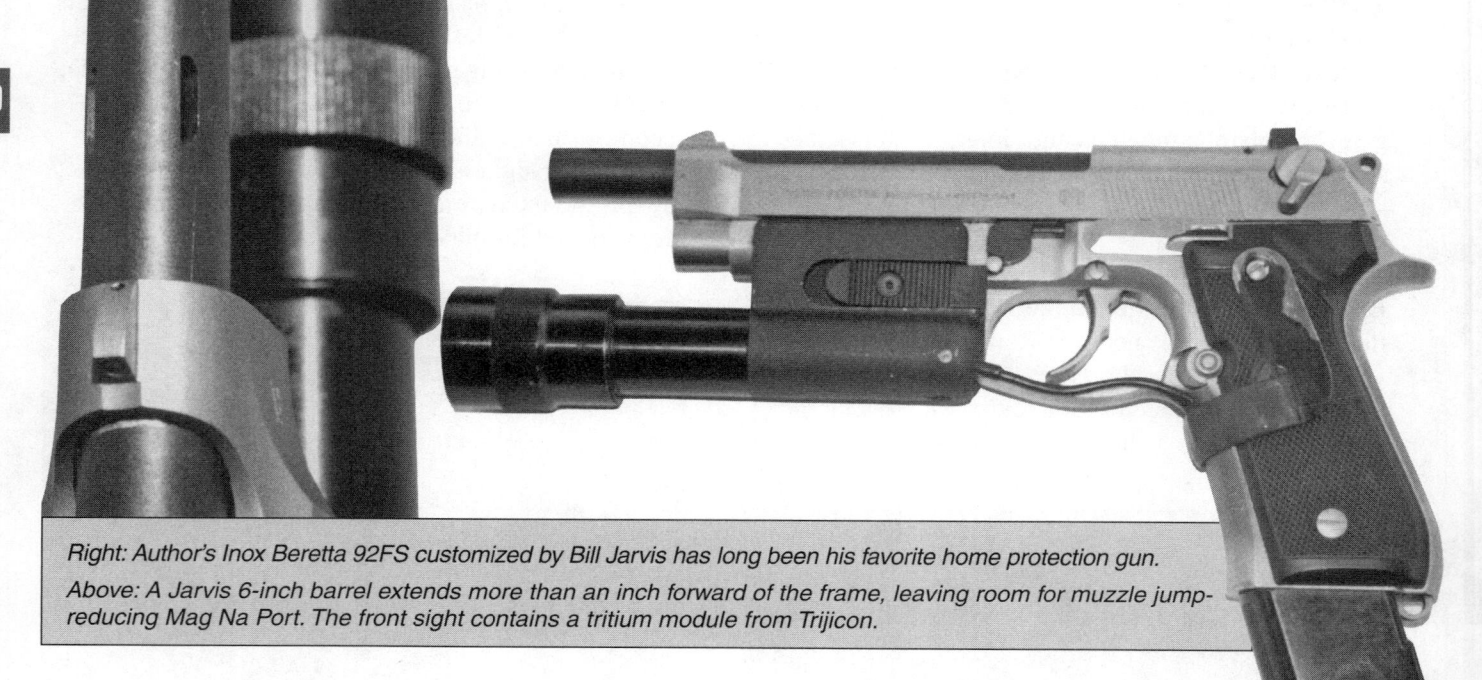

Right: Author's Inox Beretta 92FS customized by Bill Jarvis has long been his favorite home protection gun.

Above: A Jarvis 6-inch barrel extends more than an inch forward of the frame, leaving room for muzzle jump-reducing Mag Na Port. The front sight contains a tritium module from Trijicon.

A SureFire tactical light can be manually operated without the pressure switch, with the trigger finger of the gun hand as shown, or if in a two-hand hold, with the thumb of the support hand.

ordinary front dot sight had been now stood a sharply straight post serrated at 30 lines per inch (lpi). It would no longer "glare out" under bright overhead light. Explained the man who did the work, "I like 30 lpi because it is coarse and easy to see. I know some people like finer serrations for sights, but for picking up the sights fast, I think this is a better setup."

I had looked at this beautiful pistol long enough. It was time to take it to the range.

How It Shoots

When I stroked the Speed Bump Trigger, it didn't feel as if I was shooting a Beretta anymore. I didn't have tools to measure a double-action pull, but it was so light it felt as if the promise of 7 pounds DA had been fulfilled. My friend Brad Lewis measured the single-action pull at 3.5 pounds at the center of the trigger, and 3.25 pounds with weight applied to the toe (bottom tip) of the trigger, where there is more leverage. The trigger did indeed set more rapidly. As a Beretta shooter of many years, I can only say that the pull in both single- and double-action felt … shorter. The reset was also distinctly faster.

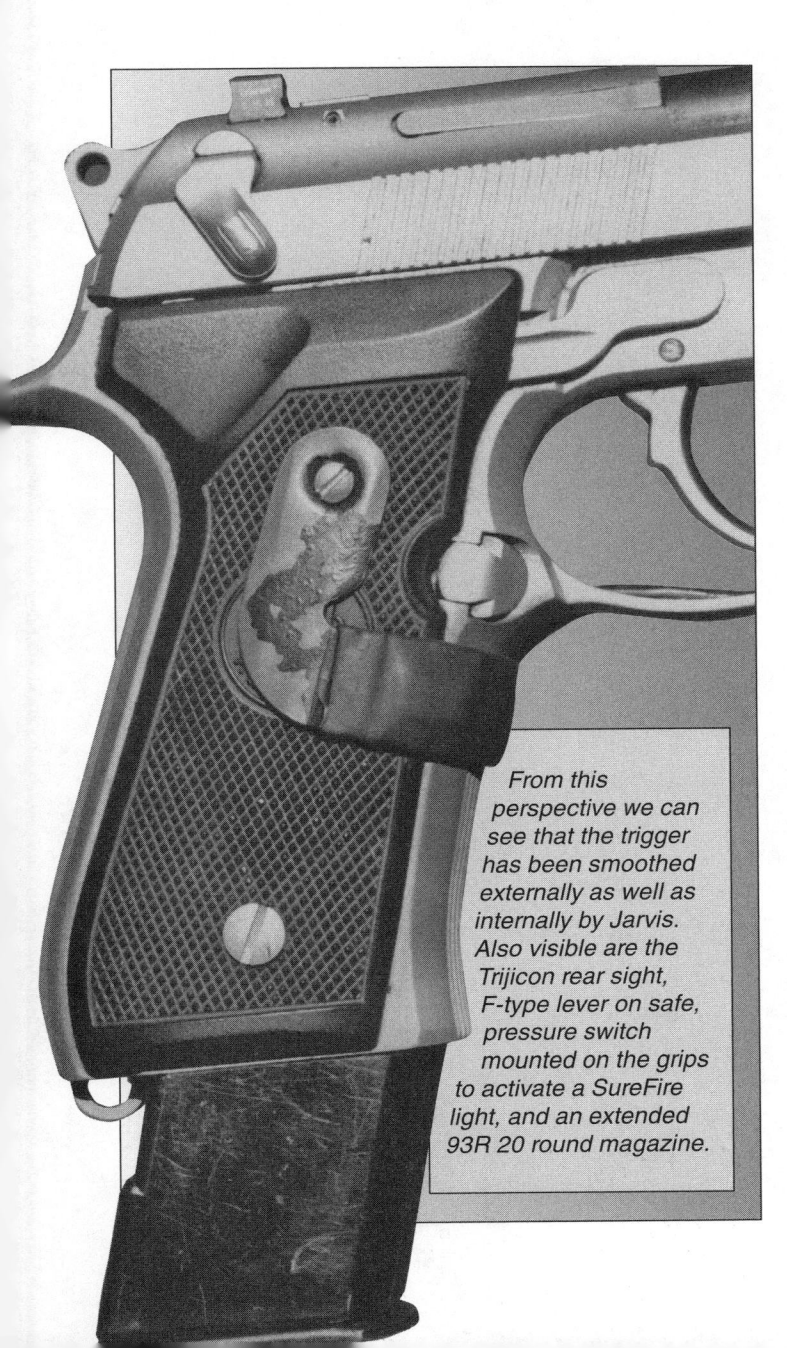

Langdon explains why his "trigger stop" approach takes the form of a full reshaping of the trigger instead of installation of a setscrew or any of the several other possible approaches. "I do not use a screw for several reasons. First, if it is adjustable, people will try to adjust it. No matter how good it is, they will mess with it to try and make it a little better. Then we end up with a pistol that will not go bang when you want it to. Second, it will not come out of adjustment (the way we do it). Finally, it does not tear up the frame as most of the triggers with screws do. When you're dealing with an aluminum frame and a steel set screw (the rubber bumpers and inserts never seem to last) the frame gives away and the setting is lost."

Was the gun accurate? You betcha. I tried nine different loads in this 9mm pistol, in five-shot groups hand-held off the bench at 25 yards. Each group was measured to the nearest 0.05 of an inch, center-to-center of the farthest bullet holes, and again for the best three shots. Experience has taught me that the latter measurement goes far toward factoring out human error and giving us a shorthand preview of the pistol's inherent accuracy, coming close to a five-shot group from a Ransom rest. The single most accurate round was that smashing Pro-Load Tactical +P, which drives the 115-grain Gold Dot at about 1,300 fps. This duplicates the famously decisive fight-stopping ballistics of the "Illinois State Police load" developed by Winchester, but with a more modern and effective projectile design.

Pro-Load led the field at 1.25 inches for all five shots, and that incredible 0.30 of an inch for the best three. Average was 2.70 inches for five-shot groups, and an extraordinary 1.055 inches for all of the "best three shots" groups.

This speaks well of Irv Stone's Bar-Sto barrels. It speaks equally well of Ernest Langdon's ability to install them. More than one famous master pistolsmith has told me that a Bar-Sto barrel is 90 percent of an accuracy job … and more than one person at Bar-Sto has told me that the key to their barrel's effectiveness is the craftsman's ability to install it correctly.

From this perspective we can see that the trigger has been smoothed externally as well as internally by Jarvis. Also visible are the Trijicon rear sight, F-type lever on safe, pressure switch mounted on the grips to activate a SureFire light, and an extended 93R 20 round magazine.

There were a few malfunctions with the test gun at first, and they bear discussion. Langdon had warned about CCI primers. The one misfire of the test, which involved more than 500 rounds of ammunition, occurred with a CCI Blazer 124-grain ball round. This was from the "Lead-Free" Blazer line, and it's well known that primers without lead styphnate are less reliable. NYPD has forbidden such "lead-free" ammo to be issued to the troops for field duty because of reliability concerns. The misfired round was extracted from the chamber and photographed. The hit was fairly deep into the primer. It didn't look like what a professional would call a "light hit." When the round was reinserted into the chamber of the Langdon Beretta, it discharged properly. There were no other misfires.

The Bar-Sto barrel in this pistol is a match barrel, and it's understood in the world of the gun that match barrels have extremely tight tolerances in every respect, including the chambers. It takes longer to break them in even when they have been properly fitted. Early in the testing, we saw failures of the gun to chamber rounds when loading from slide-lock. This does not usually occur in Berettas. The problem faded away as more rounds were fired and the gun was broken in.

The Jarvis Custom pistol puts 21 ferocious Winchester +P+ rounds, blinding white light, and a light recoil precision target pistol that can handle rescue shots in the hands of the SWAT cop, military trigger-puller, or home defender.

A greater concern was jams during strings of fire; all were 12 o'clock misfeeds. It appeared that the upper edge of the case mouth of the live round had stalled at the barrel hood or on the feed ramp. Every single time this happened, a "tap-rack" sequence was begun, and every single time, the "tap"—the slap of the support hand's palm to the gun butt—was enough to jar the problem loose and cause the round to chamber properly. Every single one of these problems also involved a subsonic cartridge firing a 147-grain bullet, sometimes ball and sometimes hollow-point.

Now, let's analyze this. At least one ammo company, Winchester, has warned that the light subsonic 147-grain loads the police community once demanded might not operate all auto pistols under less than ideal conditions. That said, I can't blame the ammo. Los Angeles County Sheriff's Department and St. Louis Police Department, among others, have used 147-grain subsonic in their many thousands of stock Berettas for many years with no jamming epidemic. I can't entirely blame the tight barrels: Bar-Sto barrels in 9mm autos using the superbly accurate Winchester Olin Super Match 147-grain or hand-

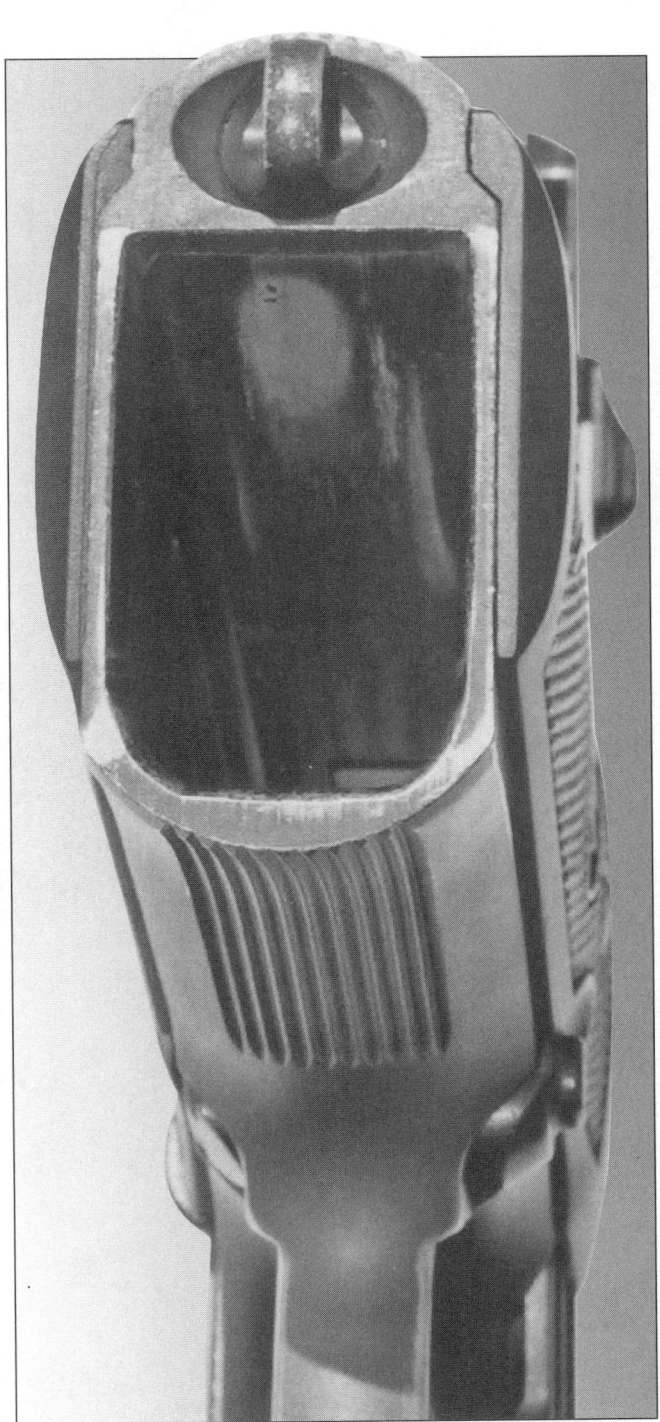

Beveling out a magazine well is a job that a home workman probably won't screw up so long as he is careful.

"Custom Lite." A bit of skateboard tape judiciously applied can improve grasp, won't damage gun, and can later be removed with no ill effects.

Above: Removal of the muzzle weight from Beretta Model 87 moved the balance point, made the gun less muzzle heavy and more "lively" feeling for some shooters …
Left: … with no loss of accuracy, as this 25-yard group shows.

The author's name was engraved on this Beretta magazine's floorplate by the pro shop at the Los Angeles County Sheriff's Academy.

The Beretta 9mm is taking over from the 1911 .45 as the dominant gun in NRA Distinguished pistol shooting.

loaded equivalents have won many Automatic events at NRA's national police shooting championships. What we have here is the combination of (a) a low impulse round, (b) a tight match barrel, and (c) a gun that had been shot fewer than 500 rounds through break-in.

I solved the problem the simple way. When the gun was broken in enough to be 100 percent with all the 115-grain and 124-grain rounds, I only used the 147-grain loads for play or practice, not for serious carry. By that point, the gun was running 100 percent with the lighter bullet, higher-velocity loads, and still delivering that splendid Bar-Sto accuracy.

Problem solved. The gun was reliable enough to carry, and I did that for a while, using an LFI Concealment Rig by Ted Blocker Leather inside the belt, and Safariland 560 Paddle and Greg Kramer scabbard designs outside the belt. The Beretta 92G is a big pistol, but thanks to its aluminum frame, not a particularly heavy one. The rounded edges from the bevel job made it all the more comfortable to wear 16 hours a day.

A final comment on lighter versus heavier bullets. In a stock Beretta, I find good accuracy with 147- and 115-grain ammo alike. Both were quite accurate in the custom Langdon pistol, but the 115s seemed more so. Langdon explained when I asked him, "The standard Beretta rifling is just under one turn in 10 inches. The Bar-Sto is one in 16. The slower twists like heavier bullets, and the faster twists like lighter ones."

The Final Measure

Testing a match service gun by Ernest Langdon should be the epitome of fun for a handgunner. But how do you test it where it hasn't already been proven better than you or I could prove it?

IDPA? Langdon won the IDPA Stock Service Pistol National Championship twice with one of these, and holds the current title. He has won three MidWinter National Championships in a row with the Langdon Beretta.

IPSC? That game's arm in this country is USPSA, the United States Practical Shooting Association, and Langdon won the national championship there in Production Class last year shooting a Beretta functionally identical to the one in this article.

S/Sgt. Joe Harless, U.S. Army, is one of the new breed of master pistol builders who have brought the Beretta 9mm to new heights of accuracy.

PPC, the police combat game? In what the NRA, who governs PPC, calls Police Service Automatic class at the national championships, the shooting runs from close range to 25 yards. The target is the B-27 silhouette. Its oval 10-ring measures about 4 by 6 inches, and the tie-breaking "center X" ring is just over 2 by 3 inches. The Langdon Beretta with the ammo it likes best, shoots inch and a quarter groups, and has the trigger pull to allow the shooter to deliver that inherent accuracy to the target. At 50 yards, it put five Winchester USA 147-grain ball round into 3.34 inches.

Fact is, the only match I could find to enter with this pistol before deadline was in a venue the Beretta pistol was never designed for, NRA Hunter Pistol. It's all done from standing (off-hand, two-hand) position, from 40 to 100 meters. It duplicates the steel critters of the International Metallic Handgun Silhouette Association, but with scaled-down targets. At 40 paces, the "chicken" is the size of a robin; at 50, the "pig" is no bigger than a house cat; at 75 meters, the "turkey" resembles a healthy chicken, and at 100, the "ram" is best described as a dachshund wearing a little helmet. In the Open Sight big-bore class, this is normally shot with something like a long-barrel Magnum target revolver or an iron-sighted Thompson/Center Contender single-shot precision pistol.

When it's the only game in town, you play.

A superb sight picture is gained with the BoMar rear and a custom 0.125-inch front sight.

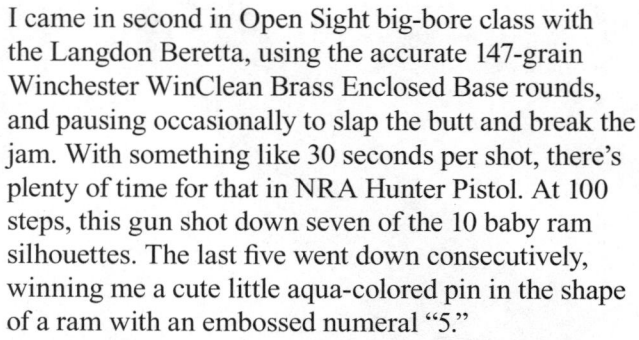

I came in second in Open Sight big-bore class with the Langdon Beretta, using the accurate 147-grain Winchester WinClean Brass Enclosed Base rounds, and pausing occasionally to slap the butt and break the jam. With something like 30 seconds per shot, there's plenty of time for that in NRA Hunter Pistol. At 100 steps, this gun shot down seven of the 10 baby ram silhouettes. The last five went down consecutively, winning me a cute little aqua-colored pin in the shape of a ram with an embossed numeral "5."

Does that replicate the purpose of the Beretta 9mm pistol? Frankly, no, but it shows you the deliverable accuracy that Ernest Langdon can build into that gun.

Bottom Line

I ordered a target pistol, and that's what I got: a precision machine that you have to break in before it works as reliably as its original heavy-duty version. It was the same with the 1911 pistol, wasn't it? Mine is broken in now, functioning with the loads I would use in it for anything serious anyway, and I am very happy with it.

For those who don't shoot competition, I would suggest staying with the Beretta barrel, which has more accuracy than any gunfight is likely to ever require, and focus on the splendid improvement that the Langdon conversion delivers to the trigger mechanism and the actual delivery of rapid defensive fire.

Leave out the match barrel, and go with the duty version of the Level II Competition package at the same price, and you'll have no reliability issues at all. You'll also save some money. Remember, the out-of-the-box Beretta will always do way better than 4 inches at 25 yards, and the center zone of an IDPA target is an 8-inch circle.

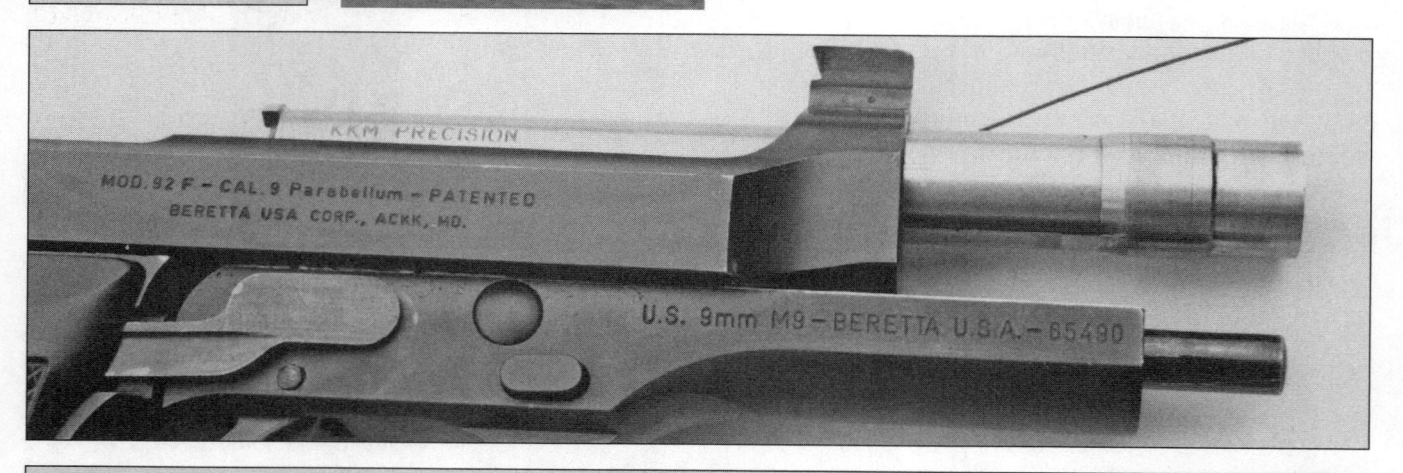

A KKM Precision barrel with a custom bushing is one approach to accurizing the M9.

Military-issue M9 Berettas jump on the firing line during the annual Small Arms Firing School at Camp Perry, Ohio.

The author shot this lightly customized Beretta in a Distinguished event at the NRA National Championships in 2004. The yellow tag on the trigger guard indicates it has passed inspection including trigger weight test.

Jarvis Custom 92FS

Some years ago, I decided to build a dedicated pistol just for home defense. My wife and daughters and I had things pretty well squared away in terms of strategy, tactics, and the whole "hardening the perimeter" thing. Excellent weapons were instantly available to authorized members of the family, and not readily available to an intruder who got in when we were not there. Still, I wanted something particularly suited to the task. We already had appropriate, high tech shotguns for the "artillery" function, but I wanted something more specialized for the "infantry" function if I had to move quickly and could take nothing but a pistol.

It would have to have ample rounds in-gun to handle multiple opponents if there was no time to access a second weapon or spare ammunition. If there wasn't time to grab a tactical flashlight, I wanted one right there on the gun. If I didn't want to give my position away to an enemy with that light but had already identified a deadly threat, I wanted night sights that would let me lock the missiles on target before the launch. If someone struggled with me for it, I wanted the gun to be at least somewhat proprietary to me and difficult for him to figure out how to use quickly if he momentarily gained control of it.

Made in-house, this trigger shoe would be dangerous for regular use, but is preferred by some military shooters for the Distinguished match. Grips have been "burned" and the front strap stippled.

The pistol I chose, with virtually all in the world to pick from and no thought that many years later I would be assigned to write a book about the brand, was the Beretta 92FS. This one happened to be stainless. It would hold 16 rounds of 9mm,

The Beretta M9 as modified by the U.S. Marine Corps for match shooting.

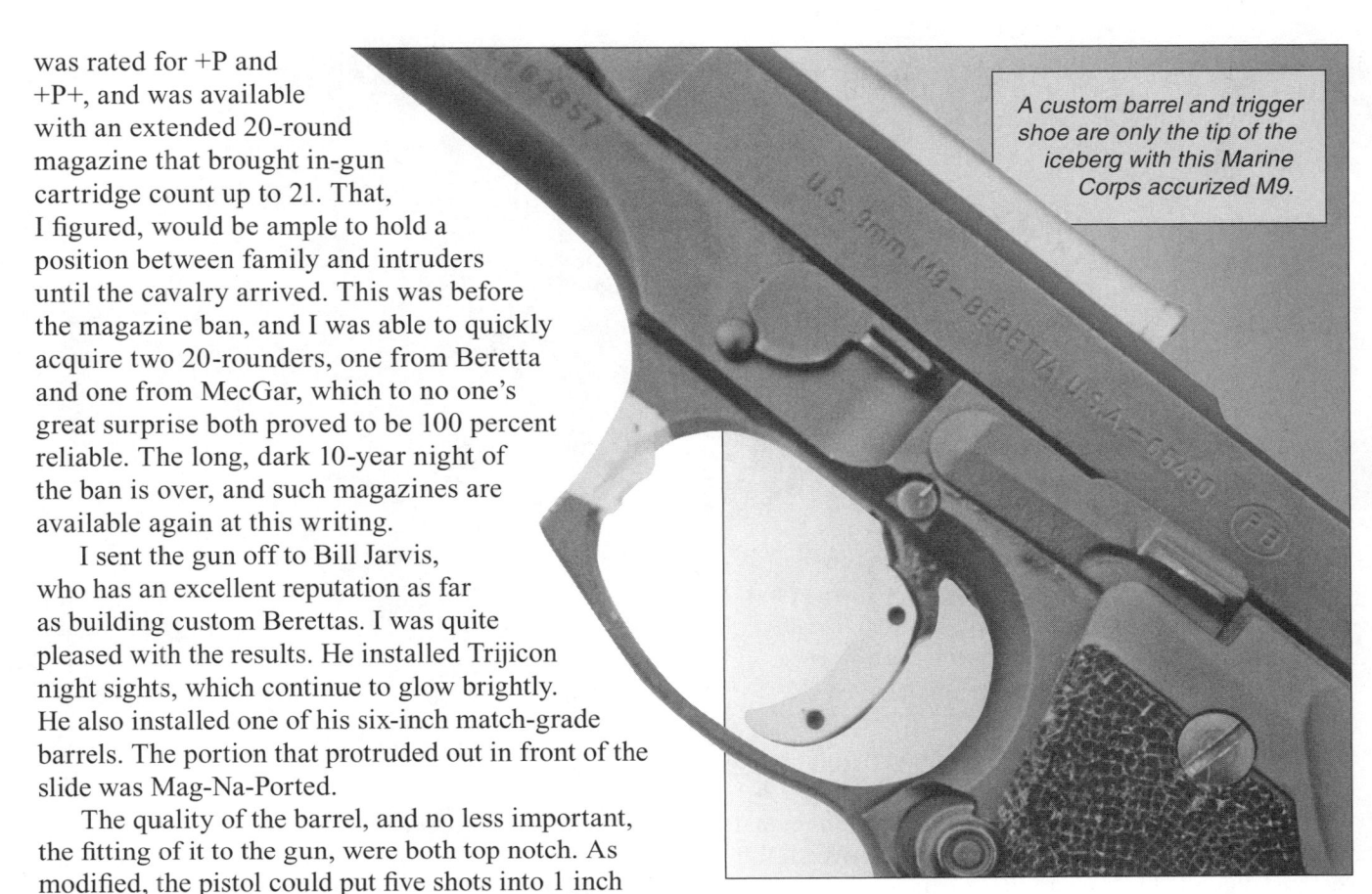

was rated for +P and +P+, and was available with an extended 20-round magazine that brought in-gun cartridge count up to 21. That, I figured, would be ample to hold a position between family and intruders until the cavalry arrived. This was before the magazine ban, and I was able to quickly acquire two 20-rounders, one from Beretta and one from MecGar, which to no one's great surprise both proved to be 100 percent reliable. The long, dark 10-year night of the ban is over, and such magazines are available again at this writing.

I sent the gun off to Bill Jarvis, who has an excellent reputation as far as building custom Berettas. I was quite pleased with the results. He installed Trijicon night sights, which continue to glow brightly. He also installed one of his six-inch match-grade barrels. The portion that protruded out in front of the slide was Mag-Na-Ported.

The quality of the barrel, and no less important, the fitting of it to the gun, were both top notch. As modified, the pistol could put five shots into 1 inch

A custom barrel and trigger shoe are only the tip of the iceberg with this Marine Corps accurized M9.

A USMC M9 modified for bull's-eye shooting, with service-issued Black Hills 9mm ball ammo.

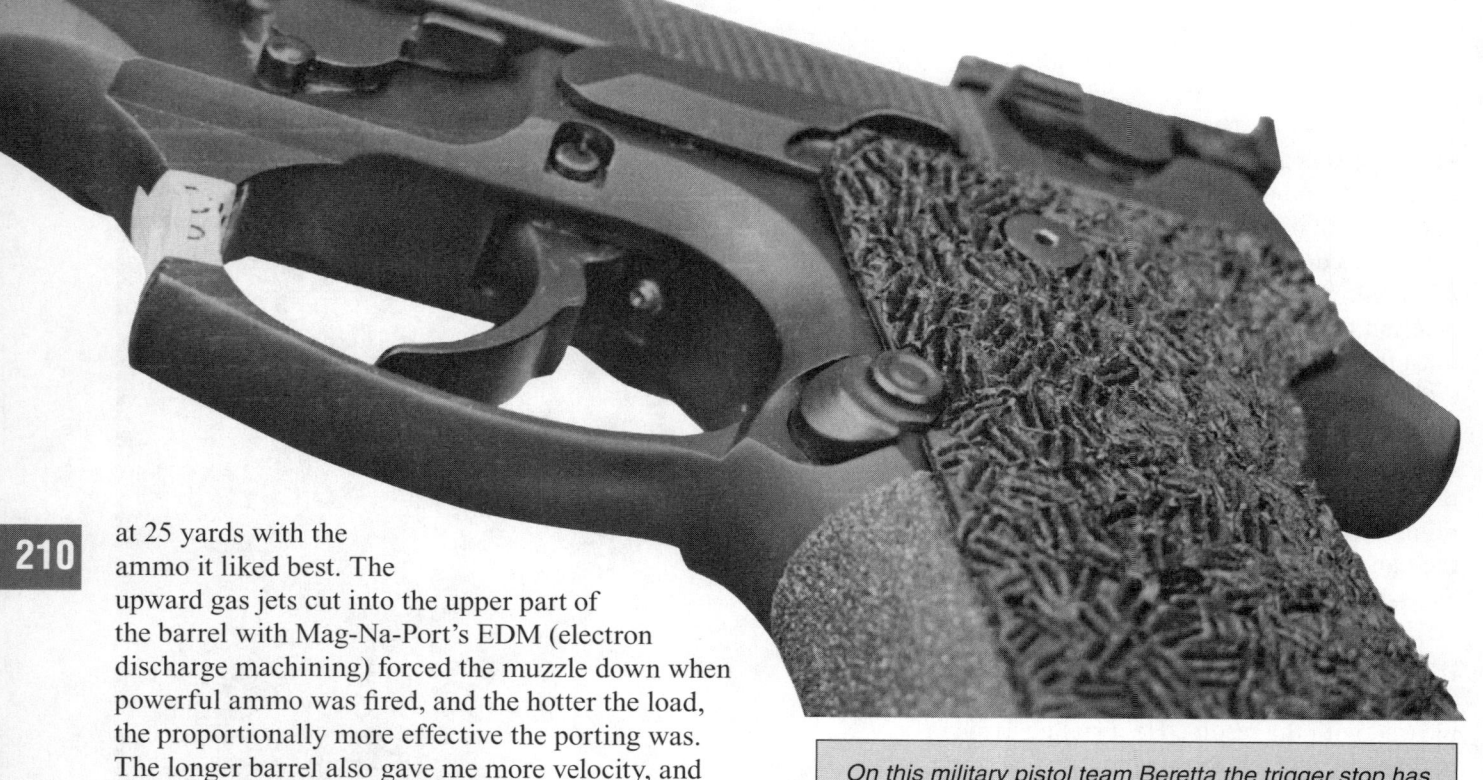

at 25 yards with the ammo it liked best. The upward gas jets cut into the upper part of the barrel with Mag-Na-Port's EDM (electron discharge machining) forced the muzzle down when powerful ammo was fired, and the hotter the load, the proportionally more effective the porting was. The longer barrel also gave me more velocity, and therefore, more energy per shot.

I started with 115-grain jacketed hollow-points rated for 1,350 feet per second out of a standard 4.9-inch Beretta barrel. Out of the 6-inch Jarvis tube, that ammo brought the chronograph readout to over 1,400 feet per second. That meant that each of these 9mm rounds out of the Jarvis pistol was hotter than the typical factory 110-grain .357 Magnum round, which sends that light bullet downrange at just under 1,300 foot seconds from a 4-inch service revolver's muzzle. These days, I use Winchester's Ranger-T 127-grain +P+ JHP. That stuff is rated for 1,250 foot seconds out of a standard service barrel and is probably over

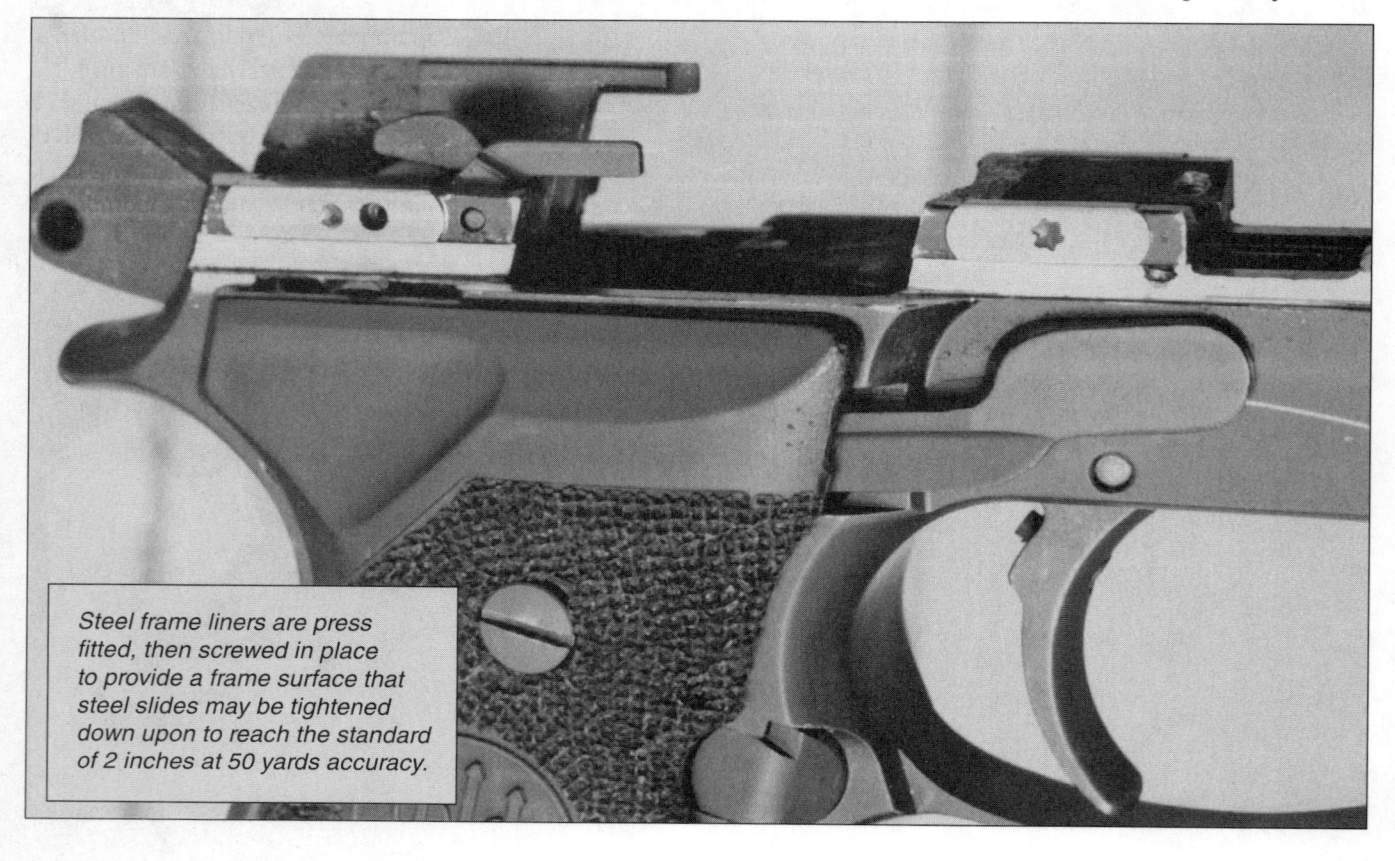

On this military pistol team Beretta the trigger stop has been inserted downward through hole drilled through the frame at the upper rear of the trigger guard.

Steel frame liners are press fitted, then screwed in place to provide a frame surface that steel slides may be tightened down upon to reach the standard of 2 inches at 50 yards accuracy.

1,300 foot seconds out of the longer Jarvis unit, which means that each shot is delivering impact in the .357 SIG's territory.

Bill also did a great action job. I told him I wanted the trigger pulls in both double- and single-action to be heavy enough to be court defensible, but smooth. This he delivered. The trigger doesn't pull so much as it rolls, feeding back a sense of polished metal moving against polished metal. It is a pleasure just to dry fire, and an absolute joy to shoot.

I affixed one of SureFire's dedicated tactical flashlights. The brightness of this unit is astounding when you first experience it. The lamp lights up everything in front of you, like turning on a high-intensity lamp – which, come to think of it, is exactly what you're doing when you activate it. The blinding light is almost enough for the shooter to hide behind.

The manual safety has always been left on. I'm habituated to popping it into the fire position when I come up with the gun, and if someone sneaks up and grabs it while I'm deep asleep, an on-safe pistol in such hands can buy me some time to rectify the situation.

I acquired tactical thigh holsters by Safariland and Bianchi to fit with the big flashlight. I t was handy for range work – you want to practice fairly frequently with your home defense pistol, since the history of armed citizens against the bad guys in this country shows that this is overwhelmingly the most likely situation where the law-abiding civilian may have to employ deadly force. It turned out that the leg holsters and the Jarvis pistol were awfully handy for things like building search simulation in training, and night shooting matches.

Between the weight of the flashlight and the MagnaPorting, the gun delivers "magnum force" .357 ballistic performance with only about a .380 level of recoil. That, my friends, is a heck of a deal.

All in all, I found Jarvis' work to be superb, priced right, and done quickly. I would recommend his custom work on the Beretta pistol without reservation.

Horan Custom

I've mentioned elsewhere in this book the excellent custom work done on my 92FC by Jim Horan. Sadly, he is no longer in the gunsmithing business. Having figured out just what a thankless task that is, now that he's retired from law enforcement he is working as a police equipment distributor. It's a loss to the Beretta shooting community, because he did a fine pistol.

The action smoothness was superb. The Aristocrat fixed rear sight he installed helped to promote accuracy at

In the delicate hand of Dr. Judy Tant, national women's champion bull's-eye shooter, this David Sams Custom Beretta is the most manageable of Distinguished guns.

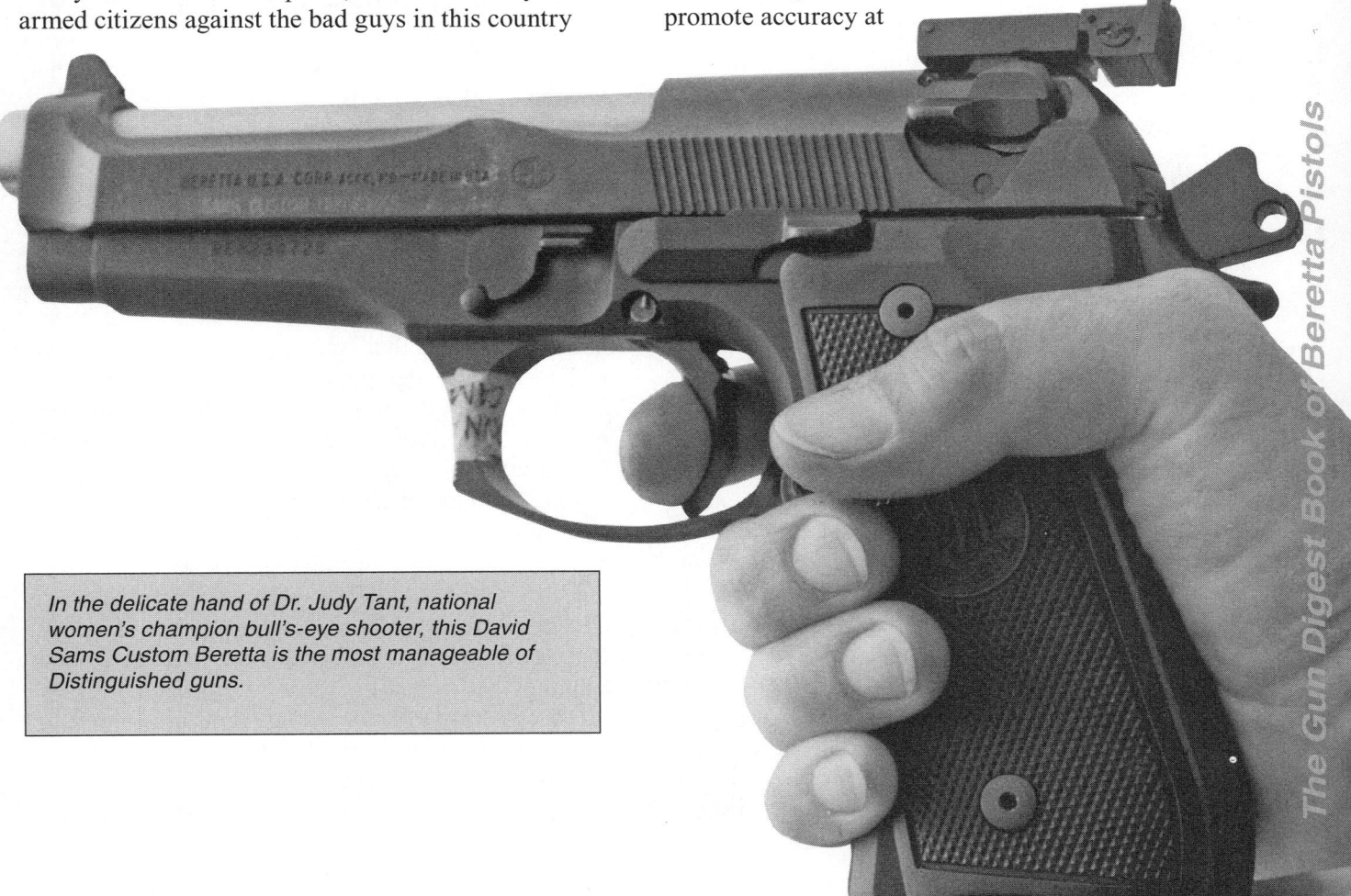

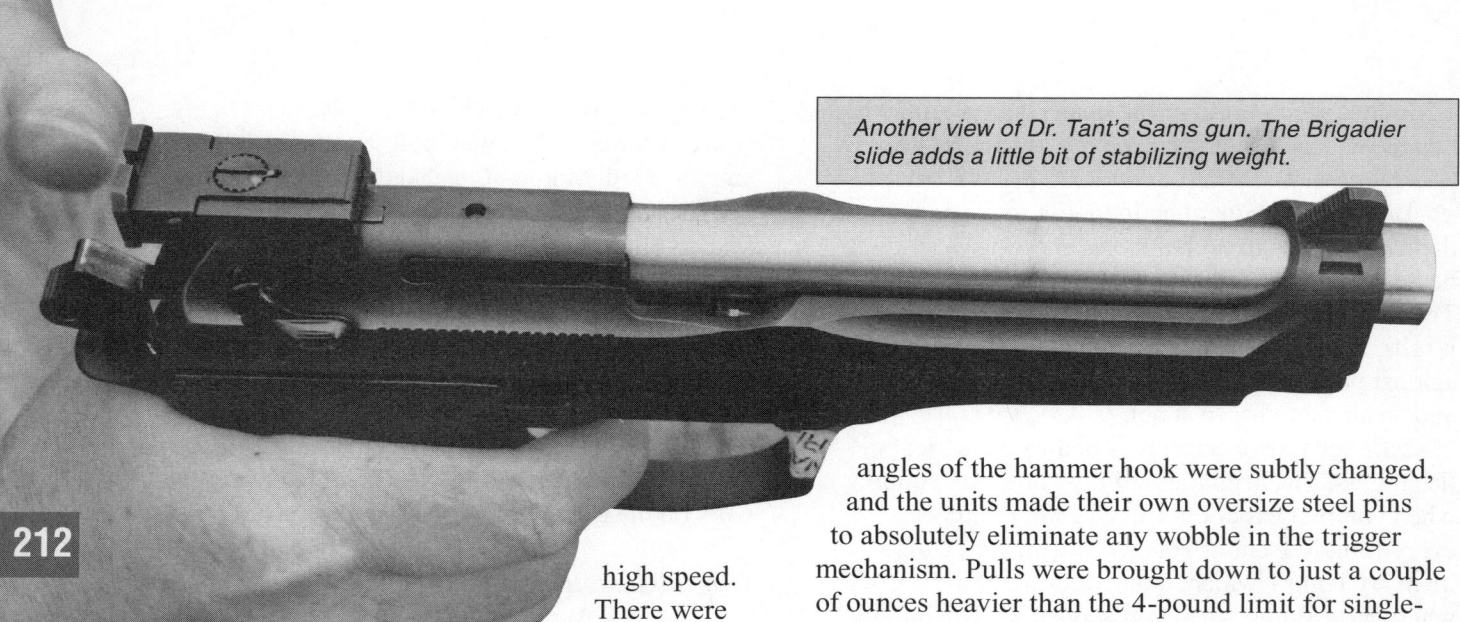

Another view of Dr. Tant's Sams gun. The Brigadier slide adds a little bit of stabilizing weight.

high speed. There were no sharp edges anywhere. And the pistol worked 100 percent. The gun now belongs to my daughter, and I'm happy that such a fine pistol protects my first-born.

Military Marksmanship Units

Led by the United States Marine Corps and the United States Army, our armed forces' marksmanship training units and pistol teams have learned a lot about the Beretta. Those two services are now using the Beretta M9 exclusively in "Distinguished" matches, events that require the U.S. military pistol to be used. This limits the military competitor to one of two guns: the Beretta M9 or the 1911 .45.

The conventional wisdom held that the .45 ACP cartridge was historically more accurate than the 9mm NATO round. Moreover, there was a long precedent for accurizing the 1911 to deliver very precise groups from the 50-yard line. However, this accurizing involved tightening the steel slide to the steel frame. This new Beretta thingamajig had an aluminum frame. How could a pistolsmith accurize *that?*

The answer was found in the good old-fashioned American ingenuity of our military armorers. First came steel inserts, hardened to 32 Rockwell, then cut to shape and press fit into the frame rails, and screwed in place for good measure. Now they could work steel to steel to tighten the slide to the frame.

The Beretta had a double-action trigger mechanism geared for fighting, not target shooting. The rules did not allow altering a double-action to single-action only, but Marine and Army pistolsmiths perfected the Beretta trigger job. Sears were stoned, angles of the hammer hook were subtly changed, and the units made their own oversize steel pins to absolutely eliminate any wobble in the trigger mechanism. Pulls were brought down to just a couple of ounces heavier than the 4-pound limit for single-action shooting specified in the rules. (The rules for bull's-eye shooting, that is. For the Army's action pistol team, the armorers have been able to safely bring trigger pull weights down as low as a pound and a half.) Trigger stops are fashioned, in the form of set screws brought through the frame at the rear of the trigger guard, or on the trigger itself.

High-visibility, precision adjustable sights were installed. These are almost exclusively the BoMar brand. A correspondingly high front sight, razor sharp and backslanted to prevent glare on its face, completes the sighting arrangement. The Army's Marksmanship Training Unit makes its own front sights, finding that a width of 0.125 of an inch works best.

The pistol's barrel is the heart of its accuracy. The military marksmanship units prefer the Bar-Sto and KKM brands. They have special fixtures for testing the accuracy of a rigidly held barrel that does not yet have a pistol wrapped around it, and only the most accurate are selected to go into the Berettas of pistol team members. From the special fixtures, these barrels will group their ammunition into less than an inch at 50 yards, the standard distance for slow-fire shooting. In the accurized pistols, when fired from machine rests, the accuracy is now on the order of 2 inches at 50 yards.

Choice of barrel depends on the ammunition the government has chosen to furnish the team members in a given year. Some 9mm ball rounds work better with one turn in 16 inches, while some stabilize better with a rifling twist that is twice as slow, one turn in 32 inches. Barrels are swapped out as necessary. Right now, about a third of the Army team is using 1:32 barrels.

Accustomed to flat-sided target pistols for the main parts of their shooting matches, the soldiers and Marines find a pistol like the Beretta, with a wide grip frame to accommodate a double stack cartridge

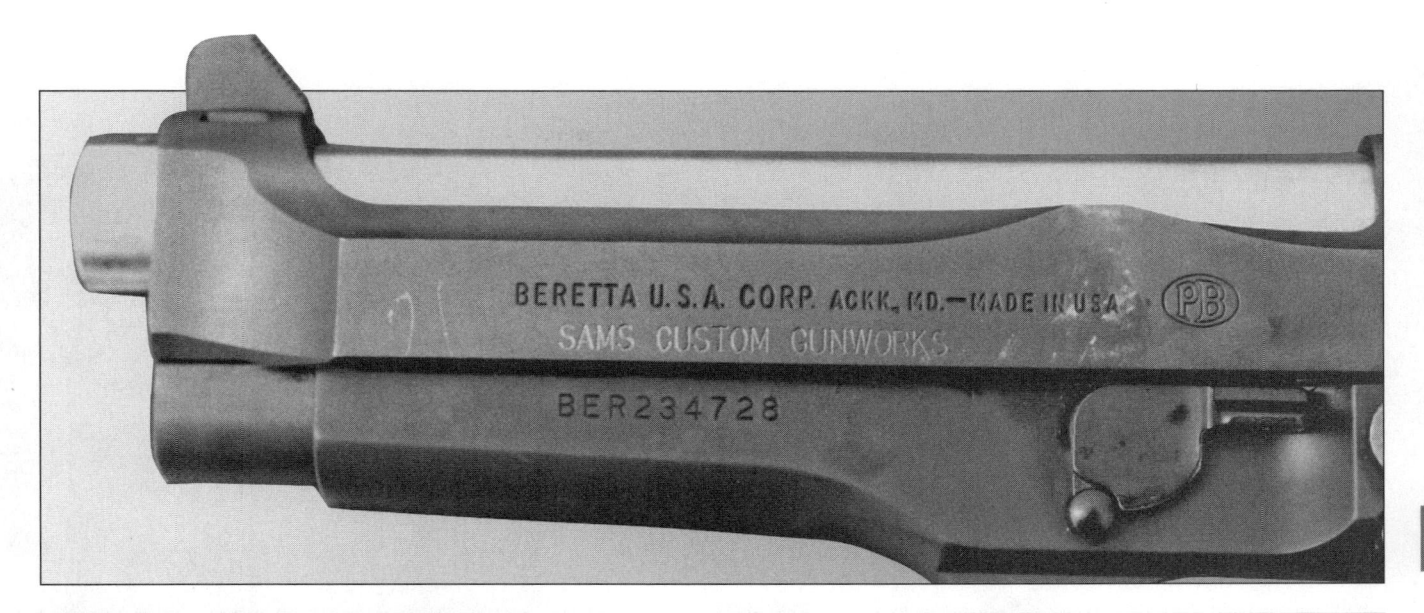

David Sams is to civilian custom bull's-eye Berettas as Ernest Langdon is to combat competition Berettas.

magazine, harder to "steer." They have found that a slippage-free grasping surface is particularly important when precision-shooting the Beretta one-handed. They "burn" the grips, in essence using heat to very roughly stipple the checkered plastic stocks that come on the service Berettas. The aluminum front and back straps of the grip frame are usually stippled to a similar consistency.

I've seen Berettas with Brigadier slides on several of the military pistols. The team gunsmiths find some of their shooters prefer the extra weight they offer, and they do not break the rules.

What the military teams have learned, the civilians who shoot with them at the bull's-eye matches at Camp Perry have learned, too. Ever since Steve Reiter won the Distinguished event back in the 1990s with a Beretta 9mm, stunning the purists, more and more of the civilians have followed the lead of the Army and the Marines, and switched to Berettas customized like theirs. Judy Tant, several times National Champion Woman and holding that title at this writing, told me she switched to her David Sams custom Beretta 92 for the Distinguished and Presidents' Hundred events because she appreciated the recoil being so much lighter than her .45 with the 230-grain hardball ammo the match rules require.

Fans of the great 1911 pistol may grind their teeth, but the fact is that the category of service pistol bull's-eye shooting, designed for the .45 and dominated by that gun for so many decades, is now virtually ruled by the Beretta 9mm. The skill, ingenuity, and craftsmanship of our military armorers – and the skill of our finest military handgun shooters – are the reasons why.

Custom "Lite"

There are minor improvements that we can perform on our own pistols without ruining them or resorting to professional pistolsmiths. If your need for more grip traction isn't fulfilled by new stocks, a judicious application of skateboard tape can do the trick.

If you don't have the tools for installing new higher-profile sights, Brownell's sells LPA sights that will slip over the standard factory fixed sights of a 92 or 96. Mine were installed by armorer Bill Pfeil, and shot spot on at 50 yards without needing further adjustment. Hand held, the gun delivered 3-inch groups at that distance with Federal American Eagle ball ammo.

Using a Dremel Moto-tool to very lightly bevel the edges of the magazine well can speed your reloads very slightly. The result may not look pretty, but if you're careful, you won't screw anything up and your performance might improve by just a tad. Engraving initials on the floorplate of the magazine or something like that shouldn't hurt anything either. It won't be as if a master engraver did it, but you'll be able to tell your Beretta mags from someone else's when they're lying in the dirt among many others on the range.

Sometimes – in a recreational gun, not a defense gun – you can go a little further with add-ons. The Beretta Model 87 target pistol tested for this book desperately needed something to stop its trigger backlash, and a bit of floor protector stuck in the back of the trigger guard with its own adhesive did the job. I wouldn't have done that with a defense gun – the material could come loose and block the trigger – but it was an acceptable risk in a pistol that would be used for target shooting only. On that gun, we even did the reverse and took something off. The front barrel weight on the Model 87, which turns out to weigh only an ounce on a postal scale, is out in the front where that single ounce feels like more. With it removed, the pistol *felt* lighter and better to some of the shooters testing it, particularly the two petite females on the test team. We found that removing it had no deleterious effect whatever. Five rounds of inexpensive Winchester high-speed .22 LR still grouped in just over an inch at 25 yards.

For any significant alterations, though, *seek out a professional who specializes in that particular gun.* It was such careful choice of the right "doctor" to perform the "surgery" that gave all the "operations" discussed above such successful outcomes.

Top of page: David Sams installed steel liners to accurize the frame and put a trigger stop through the trigger instead of frame on National Champ Tant's pistol.

Bottom of page: Sams takes advantage of front dovetail in the Brigadier slide to install a high front sight, and fits a special bushing to the custom barrel.

Selecting Ammunition
For Your Beretta

The purpose of the gun, it is said, is the bullet. The projectile does the job, and the launcher is merely an ancillary tool for accomplishing the primary objective. However, delivering that projectile to the exact intended spot has become so much of an art and science that we focus on the launcher and its manipulation, and find it easy to forget the importance of the projectile.

At Lethal Force Institute, I've long preached five criteria for defensive ammunition selection. **1. Reliability.** The gun is a safety rescue tool. Reliability is a completely non-negotiable baseline. If it doesn't work perfectly, it shouldn't go into a gun that could be used for self-defense. **2. Controllability.** A .50 caliber Action Express round will certainly hit with authority, but few people can control it in the accurate, rapid

Most ammo is accurate enough for most tasks. This Beretta 87, which will handle standard-velocity ammo, put five shots in just over an inch at 25 yards with inexpensive Winchester high-velocity plated round nose, a good choice in smaller Beretta .22 LRs and virtually guaranteed to cycle in them.

cadence needed with a self-defense pistol that may be deployed against multiple opponents. The gun should have a power level that the individual can control to the point where he or she can hit multiple targets the size of vital human organs swiftly and accurately. **3. Proven stopping power.** Instant cessation of a violent attack by a homicidal human or a vicious animal is, after all, the *raison d'etre* of the defensive handgun. Don't be the guinea pig for the newest ammo on the market. Carry something that has a good track record in actual gunfights. **4. Optimum Penetration.** The bullet needs to go "deep enough, but not too deep." Tailor the ammo selection to the predictable threat, just as a hunter tailors ammo selection to the intended quarry. You might want one round for an anticipated 200-yard shot at a small antelope, and another round entirely when hunting deer in thick, heavy brush. The round should be one that is likely to stay in the human body without exiting to endanger bystanders. Since most armed citizen self-defense actions generally involve opponents attacking them face-on without intermediate cover, a bullet that delivers 8 to 10 inches of penetration in muscle tissue-simulating ballistic gelatin, with a wide wound track, is ideal. For police, who often have to shoot running gunmen at inopportune angles from the side, and frequently have to fire through window glass and similar obstacles, a bullet that delivers 12 to 14 inches of penetration, even at the price of a narrower wound path, may be a better choice. **5. Reduced ricochet potential.** Round nose full metal jacket bullets are notorious for ricochet off hard surfaces, and ricochets can cause the deaths of innocent bystanders. The most knowledgeable experts who study actual gunfights recommend jacketed hollow-points for all center-fire semiautomatic pistols, and this is one reason why. Their "cookie cutter" nose shape tends to bite into surfaces and shatter or bury the bullet there instead of allowing it to glance off at high residual velocity.

The following recommendations fit those five criteria as well as possible. All are conventional rounds, for several reasons. First, exotic ammunition such as pre-fragmented or frangible rounds (Glaser Safety Slugs, Mag-Safe, etc.) are so expensive that they are rarely used in actual shootings, and develop little in the way of documented data. Ammunition selection is too important to be based on theories alone, particularly the theories of those who stand to profit by the sale of the ammo in question. Second, there have been shootings with Glaser where the bullet broke up too soon and did not get into the body to enough depth, or with enough force, to cause a disabling wound. Third, most such ammunition has a very light projectile going very fast, with a pressure curve different from what a given semiautomatic pistol's slide mass and spring compression weight were designed for. They may feed into the chamber, particularly when tested by hand, but they won't necessarily cycle the mechanism. Fourth, bringing us back to the cost factor, one should not consider a given pistol/cartridge combination trustworthy until at least 200 rounds of *that* ammo have been fired through *that* gun with *zero* malfunctions. In other words, to see if the most expensive exotic ammunition in .25 caliber will work in your particular Beretta Bobcat, it will cost you approximately twice the price of the pistol to purchase at retail enough ammunition to make that determination. This simply is not cost effective.

Let's go caliber by caliber. We'll pay particular attention to any incompatibility with the topic at hand, Beretta pistols. Fortunately, there are few such instances: today's Beretta pistols are pleasingly omnivorous weapons.

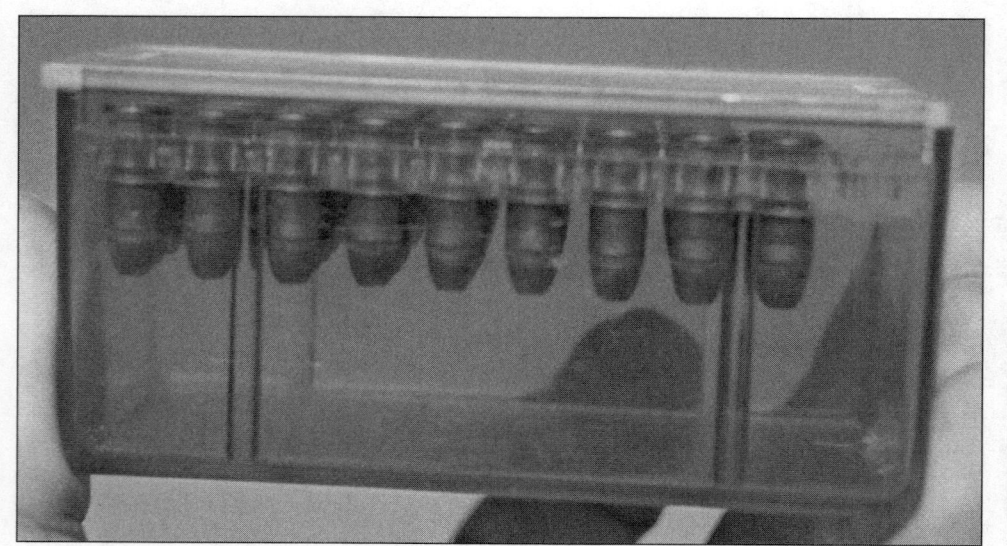

.22 Short

Not recommended. While people have been murdered with this feeble caliber, it is altogether too weak to count on for stopping

In the .22 Short Minx, Ayoob has found these CCI rounds to be the most reliable in terms of feeding and cycling, but considers the caliber pathetic for self-defense.

a violent aggressor. This writer has seen it bounce off the outer surface of automobile doors. There are numerous cases of it bouncing off human skulls. It is not guaranteed to go through an attacker's forehead on a straight-on shot. Moreover, the .22 Short round is notorious for jamming in small pistols, including even the Beretta Minx, probably the most popular semi-auto ever chambered for it. Use the Minx strictly for practice, and load it with copper-plated round nose, which is likely to feed better than anything else.

.22 Long Rifle

The tiny pistols like the Bobcat are notoriously difficult to make feed well with this long, thin, proportionally large-rimmed cartridge, and it's a miracle that the little Beretta 21 feeds as well as it does. Don't push it by going to hyper-velocity ammunition such as the CCI Stinger or Remington Yellow Jacket. Yes, they hit harder. However, in hollow point form they may break up too soon at that velocity and not get deep enough into a big man's vitals.

Nor do you want to err too much on the other side. On Beretta's website in late 2004 I found an entry by one fellow who cautioned, "If you are thinking of trying sub-sonic ammo in a Beretta Bobcat pistol, then hear me NOW!! DO NOT TRY IT, IT DOESN'T ALWAYS EJECT PROPERLY!!!"

Beretta responded, "Our small frame pistols, like the Bobcat, operate with a blowback principle. This, coupled with the reduced mass of the slide, requires the recoil spring to operate at a specific pressure from the ammunition in order to completely cycle. Use of subsonic ammo often does not provide enough pressure for complete cycling. The use of high-velocity ammunition will ensure correct function (please note that the use of hyper-velocity ammo is never recommended). Due to manufacturing tolerances on .22 LR ammo, .22 rimfire firearms of all makes will generally show a preference to a particular brand of ammo. This preference can only be determined through testing."

Since almost any .22 rimfire ammo can ricochet, I would tend in this one caliber range to go with round nose instead of HP to assure deep enough penetration. For some reason, the high-velocity Remington .22 Long Rifle with plated round nose bullets seems to produce particularly nasty wounds, tumbling through tissue with a buzzsaw effect, yet it feeds flawlessly and shoots accurately. It would be my first choice if I had to load any .22 caliber handgun to defend myself. That said, please be reminded that no competent expert will recommend a handgun this low in power for defense against lethal assault unless it is absolutely impossible to carry anything larger.

.25 ACP

In the smallest Berettas, the 950 size, the .25 caliber Jetfire is unquestionably a better pistol than its .22 Short twin, the Minx, in every respect except cost of ammo. It has it all over the even weaker .22 Short round. The Jetfire holds more rounds than the Minx, since "rimless" .25 center-fire cartridges can stack more efficiently than .22 Short cartridges with their relatively wide rims.

And, mainly, .25s work better. The great John Browning expressly designed this 6.35mm round in 1908 to work in tiny semiautomatic pistols. The 950 series single-action and Model 21 series double-action pistols in .25 ACP are famously reliable with the ammo Browning made for such guns, which was a 50-grain round-nose full-metal-jacket "ball" type.

There are several JHP rounds available for them. We've killed animals with two of them, performing necropsy (essentially, veterinary autopsy) to examine the wounds in detail and recover the bullets. These are the Winchester Expanding Point (45-grain bullet, 815 feet per second velocity, 66 foot-pounds energy at the muzzle) and the Speer Gold Dot (35-grain JHP bullet, 900 feet per second muzzle velocity, 62 foot-pounds muzzle energy). We found that the Winchester didn't expand in the "mushrooming" sense of the term, but did deform slightly and appeared to be less ricochet-prone than the traditional full-metal-jacket round-nose (50-grain FMJ, 760 feet per second, 65 foot-pounds). While this bullet may "mushroom" in gelatin, we found in flesh and bone that it would peel back on one side but not the other, or collapse into a fish-mouth shape. This still widened the frontal part of the bullet and gave it more of a cutting surface, and the shape of its nose at contact will definitely reduce the chance of an undesirable ricochet.

In the 21 series, a more modern design, the JHP seems more likely to feed than in a half century old design such as the 950. It is definitely worth the investment to see if it will work in your Beretta. My experience is that the JHP probably will feed 100 percent in the 21, and *may* feed 100 percent in the given specimen of the 950. If it doesn't, try the Winchester, whose more conservative nose design may be more amenable to feeding, and keep a few rounds of the Gold Dot handy to drop down the spout of the tip-down barrel. If any .25 does not feed reliably with such ammo, your only choice is to load it

The author's grandfather shot an armed robber with this Colt .32 auto, and won the fight, but Ayoob still doesn't care to rely on a caliber that small. For a .32 Beretta he recommends Silvertip or Gold Dot if it will feed reliably.

with full-metal-jacket. I have no particular preference as to brand.

As with the .22s, be reminded that there is a reason why experts recommend you not go to the .25 ACP for self-defense. The power just isn't there. I used to show my students a photo of an elderly man who committed suicide with a .25 auto. He lay down on his bed and shot himself in what he thought was his heart. Like many people, he had thought his heart lay somewhere under his left breast instead of in the center of his chest. Realizing after a while that the lung shot hurt but he was still quite alive, he got up and walked into the bathroom adjacent to the master bedroom, and judging by the bloodstain evidence apparently stood for some time in front of the bathroom mirror confirming that he had indeed shot himself in the chest. He returned to the bed and shot himself again, a bit to the right of the first wound, and lay the pistol down, which would be determined later from the distinctively shaped bloodstains on the bedclothes. Evidence indicates that he got up again and made a second trip to the bathroom to assess the damage. He returned and shot himself a third time, proving that "the third time is the charm." This wound proved fatal, but he still had time to lay the pistol down beside him and cross his arms peacefully over his chest as if an undertaker had laid him out before he gave up the ghost.

It should be noted that the blowback marks on his body indicated that all three shots were fired at muzzle contact, directing destructive muzzle blast into the chest cavity along with the bullets. I asked my students this question: "If this is the effect of three .25 caliber, muzzle-contact gunshot wounds on a frail, elderly man who wanted to die, what do you suppose their effect would have been on a big, strong, young criminal filled with adrenaline and drugs who wanted *you* to die?"

This is why I coined the phrase, "Friends don't let friends carry mouseguns."

.32 ACP

As recently as World War II, the OSS (Office of Strategic Services) issued the Colt .32 Pocket Model automatic to spies, and the United States Army issued them to general officers well into the 1950s. For decades after that, numerous European police forces felt .32 autos were adequate for law enforcement service. The South African Police Force issued .32s to detectives until almost the fourth quarter of the 20th century. Nazi officers used them, as well: the higher they went in rank, the smaller their pistols became. Adolph Hitler, according to the Russians, killed himself with one, a Walther PPK.

As a vestigial badge of office, the .32 is probably OK. It is probably adequate for committing suicide if, like Hitler, you put the gun in your mouth and fire with the muzzle only a couple of inches from the brain stem. However, you will notice that neither Yank nor Nazi ever issued a .32 to a soldier who was likely to face an armed enemy in combat. There was always sound reason for this.

As with the .25, the .32 tends to be the gun of the person who wants the psychological security that comes with carrying a gun, but either has not completed the reality check and committed to carrying something more substantial, or finds it so imperative that the gun be deeply hidden that he or she must carry something truly tiny. And, the fact is, when applied to a vital part of the body, the .32 can work.

Phil Engeldrum published a series of magazines back in the 1970s, the flagship of which was called *Pistolero*. It was a most iconoclastic publication. Phil was among the first in modern times to kill hogs with pistols and write about the effect of the pistols. He observed with alacrity that a .32 auto bullet that reached the brain would kill instantly, and a more powerful round that didn't…wouldn't. Phil was and is a physically brave man, a trait he passed on to his progeny. In late 2004, Phil's son – who had risked death as a New York City firefighter among the first responders to the Twin Towers horror – was killed in Iraq.

Phil believed that a .32 auto loaded with the hard-jacketed German Geco ball round would penetrate deeper than a .380 and be easier to shoot fast and straight, due to its light recoil. He was among the very few credentialed experts who preferred the .32 to the .380, in a time when most guns in each caliber were identical in size, make for make and model for model. Certainly, with proper placement it will do the job. Rex Applegate recorded a case of an OSS agent who was captured by a couple of Nazis behind their lines. Their quick pat-down did not reveal the Colt .32 auto the American operative had deeply concealed, and they over-confidently put him in the back of their staff car without restraints to bring him in for questioning. Knowing that execution at best and torture at worst almost certainly awaited him at the end of the drive the American drew the Colt and shot each of his Nazi captors once in the back of the head. Each was killed instantly, and the American escaped to tell his tale.

The trick is getting your attackers to turn their backs on you. Had he drawn his .32 against two Nazis aiming 9mm pistols at him, the outcome might have been different.

Still, something is better than nothing. In his study of thousands of actual shootings, Evan Marshall found the Winchester Silvertip .32 ACP cartridge to have an incredibly high percentage of one-shot stops, slightly over 60 percent. This is not only counter-intuitive; it boggles the mind. Evan doesn't pretend to be able to explain it. I think I may be able to: a close study of Evan's published anecdotes from this research shows that a significant number of these stops were men armed with something less than guns, who may well have "given up" out of sheer hopelessness when the first bullet in their body made them realize that the good guy or gal had a gun, and they didn't.

You want jacketed hollow-points (JHP) if your gun will feed them. There are Hydra-Shok and Gold Dot .32s out there, along with the Silvertip. All will reduce the ricochet problem that occurs with standard .32 ACP ball ammo, which carries a 71-grain round-nose full-metal-jacket projectile at 905 feet per second and produces 129 foot-pounds of energy. The Hydra weighs 65 grains, delivering 130 foot-pounds from a speed of 950 feet per second while the others weigh 60 grains and travel 960 to 970 fps, generating 123 to 125 foot-pounds. Fiocchi makes a 60-grain JHP at 1,200 feet per second, which hits with 205 foot-pounds of muzzle energy.

The ones we've tested in the slaughterhouse include the Silvertip, the Hydra-Shok, and the Gold Dot. All are more likely to expand than any .25, though they will still occasionally expand unevenly or in a fish-mouth shape. In an older model Beretta .32 – remember, the 1935 series and the Series 70 pre-dated jacketed hollow-point ammo in this caliber and were not necessarily designed to feed it – you may need to keep one of these JHPs in the chamber and load the magazine with FMJ. However, the Beretta Tomcat is a modern pistol expressly designed for hollow-points, and should handle all of the above. I would toss a coin and load one of the three in both chamber and magazine if I carried a Tomcat. It would be a coin toss as to which: I'd probably go with whichever shot best through my particular pistol.

.380 ACP

Lawyers speak of "bright line" doctrines, decisions or principles that clearly define boundaries. The .380 ACP round is a definite "bright line" in the pantheon of self-defense handgun cartridges. The trouble is, the bright line seems to go right through the center of it, with half of the people whose research qualifies them to an opinion accepting the .380 as the bare minimum, and the other half drawing the line just above that cartridge because they consider it marginal or sub-marginal.

This writer falls into the latter category. I stopped using .380s in slaughterhouse testing for a long time after six cases in a row where I shot a hog in the head in exactly the right spot with one, and it looked at me and squealed. In every case, a finishing shot from a 2-inch barrel .38 Special loaded with all-lead 158 grain +P hollow-points killed the critter instantly. Half the time, the .380 slug had stopped in the frontal wall of the skull and never reached the brain. The other half of the time, it had skidded off the front plate of the skull and along the side, usually winding up in soft tissue near the ear.

When the 102-grain Remington Golden Saber came along, promising greater penetration than other .380 JHP rounds, I took it to the slaughterhouse. It did not fully penetrate the hog's skull.

The .380 full-metal-jacket ammo carries a short 9mm diameter bullet weighing 95 grains and traveling 960 fps and churning up 190 foot-pounds of energy It is notoriously impotent as a manstopper and has been since its introduction in 1908. The cartridge's fans remind us that the late, great Charles "Skeeter" Skelton tested .380 ball next to 158-grain lead .38 Special round-nose ammo in the late 1950s and early 1960s and found they produced wound channels of identical width and depth. If .38 Special is adequate and "above the bright line," they ask, why doesn't .380 stand in the same position?

They miss the point. .38 Special round-nose lead 158-grain was *also* notoriously pathetic as a manstopper, so much so that every single police department in America eventually got away from it. The minimum accepted in the .38 Special these days is the high-performance hollow-point. The dimensions of the .38 Special case, and the sturdiness of the revolvers in the caliber, are such that it can be loaded with hotter rounds than can a .380 ACP cartridge casing.

This is probably why in their book *Street Stoppers: The Latest Handgun Stopping Power Street Results*, the aforementioned Evan Marshall and his colleague Ed Sanow wrote, "The .380 is another of those marginal calibers that individuals should carry with considerable caution. While the better loads offer significant advantages over the traditional full-metal-jacket rounds, they do not turn the .380 into a major caliber." [1]

That said; there have certainly been cases where .380 Berettas saved lives. However, be prepared to launch multiple projectiles to get the job done. Jeff Cooper once wrote of a case where he was brought in as an expert witness for the defense. The good guy under attack had saved his own life with his Beretta 84 .380, but he'd had to empty his 14-shot pistol into his attacker to do it. The prosecutor's office felt that this many shots was gratuitous and an obvious indication of malice, and brought a charge of murder. The defendant was acquitted after Colonel Cooper testified that the .380 was so feeble a manstopper that it was not at all surprising that it would take more than a dozen rounds to stop a violent human being's aggression.

It's true that .380 JHPs open up much more efficiently and more consistently than smaller calibers. This is probably because a hollow-point bullet expands from the inside of the cavity outward, as pressure builds up in that cavity from the flesh it is contacting. The larger the caliber, the more "meat" gets into the hollow cavity, and therefore, the more dynamically it will expand, all other factors being equal.

The Federal "Classic line" jacketed hollow-point .380 round, which spits a 90-grain bullet at 1,000 feet per second and 200 foot-pounds, has been at or near the very top of Marshall's list of the best .380 loads since the beginning of his research. The Federal Hydra-shok (same ballistics, but with a post in the center of the bullet's hollow cavity to force flesh outward and expand the projectile more efficiently with a venturi effect) and Winchester Silvertip (85-grain JHP, 1,000 fps, 189 foot-pounds) are right up there within a few percentage points. From what I've seen, I would have to agree with Evan as to the Federal 90-grain Classic being as good as anything, and I would consider it equivalent to the Hydra-shok or the Silvertip. None of the other .380 JHPs seem to have been involved in as many shootings as these, and however good they are, they remain unproven in the ultimate arena, at least not proven to the extent of these three rounds. For what it's worth, the PMC Starfire, whose 95-grain bullet goes 925 fps and generates 180 foot-pounds, seemed to disrupt slightly more tissue than anything else in its caliber in my slaughterhouse testing, but actual gunfights involving this cartridge are hard to find.

Modern (series 81) Berettas were expressly designed for hollow-points with virtually straight-line feed, and should work fine with any of the quality JHP rounds. Older models, particularly the 1934 series, were designed at a time when all that was available was military-specification ammo, and "mil-spec" meant round-nose full-metal-jacket. Thus, one specimen may feed JHP, and the next may not. If that is the case in your situation, load the gun with Remington standard line 88-grain JHP. Its bullet is made to similar dimentions as FMJ, and should feed in any gun that will feed ball. The Remington standard jacketed hollow-points don't seem to open up as dynamically as the Silvertips and the Hydra-shoks, but they're less ricochet prone than ball and for that reason alone a much better choice than FMJ.

9mm Parabellum

With us for more than a century now, the 9mm Luger has for the entire time proven itself to be impotent as a manstopper in combat when loaded with standard full-metal-jacket "ball" ammo. At this writing, the lesson is being relearned by American troops in Afghanistan and Iraq, with their excellent Beretta M9 pistols requiring hit after hit of NATO ball rounds to stop determined opponents unless those opponents are struck in the central nervous system.

This is a damn shame, and an unnecessary one. The United States Judge Advocate General's Office has long since determined that no convention or treaty to which the United States is bound requires ball ammo except in official, declared international warfare. What is going on at this writing is counter-terrorism, and American use of hollow-point ammunition is absolutely justified by all prevailing standards and law. Rumor has it that a number of U.S. fighting men have acquired their own JHP ammo, and that when they shoot the enemy with it, the other side's fighters go down with alacrity.

There are no surprises here. If we've known for more than a century that 9mm ball didn't have what it takes to stop armed men in a fight-or-flight state, we've known for more than a third of a century that *good* JHP 9mm *does*. It was in the 1960s that Lee Jurras created Super Vel, the first ammunition to use

The author often uses 127-grain Winchester Ranger SXT +P+ in his 9mm Berettas. They're warranted for it and stand up to its power. It's a police-only load; private citizens who can't get it can buy CCI Gold Dot 124-grain +P, the NYPD load, which virtually duplicates its ballistics.

lightweight jacketed hollow-points at higher than standard velocities. It made the .38 Special and the 9mm Parabellum true fighting handguns. The ammo got better over the years, reaching its zenith in the 1990s when more cops were carrying 9mm pistols than before or since.

Note that in the previous paragraphs I emphasized "*good* JHP 9mm." Some of it works, and some of it doesn't. "Expanding bullets" are not enough. A few decades ago, Cook County, Illinois sheriff's deputies got into a shootout with a heroin junkie who was high on smack and blazing away at them with a 1911 .45 automatic. They shot him no fewer than 33 times, and he was still on his feet trying to reload when two (yes, *two*) 12-gauge rifled slugs fired into his back put him down. The pistol bullets were 100-grain Winchester Power Point, a non-hollow-point "soft nose" design that seemed to work great in the Roma Plastilena clay and Duxseal popular among ballisticians at the time, but didn't expand worth a damn in human tissue. The bullets had just zipped through the junkie like ice pick wounds.

A few years later, a southern cop named Jim Martin came up against a homicidal/suicidal suspect who emptied a .357 Magnum at him and then tried to unlimber a .45 caliber Commando semiautomatic carbine. The suspect's first two shots, fired by surprise, hit Martin in the chest and back, but his Second Chance concealed body armor saved him from serious injury.

By now, the cop was behind cover and shooting back. He fired some 28 rounds from his high-capacity 9mm service automatic, pausing only briefly to reload. He hit the man 18 times or more, mostly solid torso hits. The ammo in his gun was PMC 115-grain jacketed hollow-point, which at that time was jacketed up and over the edge of the hollow cavity and did not expand. Again, it was a case of the officer's 9mm bullets acting like an ice pick. With his next to the last shot, Martin hit the suspect in the head; the man jerked his head back, but didn't go down, because hitting the head is not the same as hitting the brain. Martin steadied down, aimed more carefully, and put his last bullet through the offender's brain, killing him at last. PMC later upgraded their 9mm ammunition to much more efficient bullets, including Tom Burczynski's excellent StarFire design.

As time went on and more cops began carrying

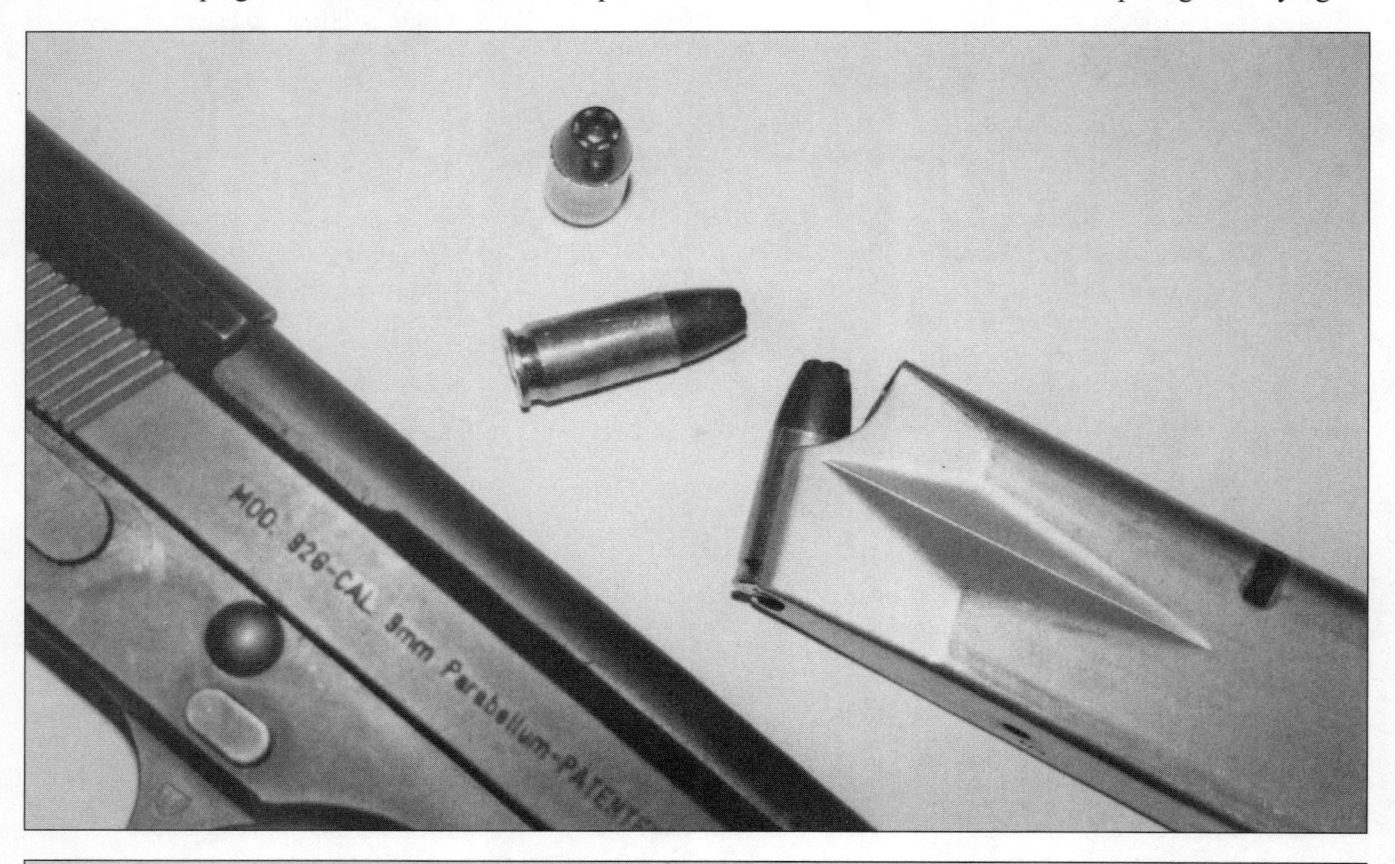

Winchester 127-grain +P+ in a Beretta 92G. Departments that issue this 9mm ammo are satisfied with it, and troops don't agitate for larger caliber guns because they know this ammo will do the job.

9mms, the manufacturers worked harder to come up with more effective ammo. One sidetrack occurred not long after Winchester developed their OSM round for the SEALs. Navy SEALs wanted a 9mm round so accurate that it would allow head shots on sentries at 50 yards with their MP5SD selective-fire weapons, fitted with integral sound suppressors. It was important that the bullet not break the sound barrier and alert other enemy troops to the sentry-killer's presence. Winchester, a subsidiary of Olin Corporation, named the cartridge the OSM for Olin Super Match. It was and is extraordinarily accurate. However, bullet expansion and tissue disruption where never its key design parameters.

On April 11, 1986, a gun battle occurred in Dade County, Florida that devastated the Federal Bureau of Investigation. Several of their agents took on two heavily armed robber/killers in a shootout that lasted over two minutes. When it was over, both perpetrators were dead, but one of them – Michael Platt, a Special Forces-trained ex-Army man – had used a stolen Ruger Mini-14 .223 rifle to kill Special Agents Jerry Dove and Ben Grogan, and to cripple for life special agents John Hanlon, Gordon McNeill, and Edmundo Mireles, and wound two other agents as well. By the time Agent Mireles had staggered up to their getaway car and killed them both with his pistol, the perpetrators had unwittingly changed the face of FBI firearms doctrine.

Platt, early in the gunfight, had been shot through the arm and into the chest with a 115-grain 9mm Winchester Silvertip bullet, fired from the Smith & Wesson pistol of FBI SWAT operative Dove. The bullet had cut an artery and inflicted a mortal wound, but it stopped short of the heart and left Platt up and running long enough to kill the man who shot him, murder another agent, and wreak more havoc. Two years later, the FBI convened a Wound Ballistics Workshop at their training headquarters at Quantico.

Among those present was Dr. Martin Fackler, formerly the head of wound treatment studies for the U.S. Army at the Letterman Institute at the Presidio in San Francisco. Fackler mentioned that while the 115-grain 9mm Silvertip would penetrate only about 8 inches of the muscle tissue-simulating ballistic gelatin formula he had developed, the new Winchester OSM round would pierce to a depth of about 14 inches. Had that round been fired into Platt's body on the exact same path as Dove's Silvertip, he pointed out, it would have gone into the heart and quite probably stopped Platt from killing two agents.

Though there were many, many other factors – elements of tactics and training – that were learned from the debacle, this was the element that the law enforcement world seemed to focus upon. The FBI adopted the subsonic 9mm, firing a 147-grain jacketed hollow-point at 990 feet per second and delivering 320 foot-pounds of energy.

This quickly became the "in" cartridge, and was soon the most popular 9mm round in law enforcement. There were high hopes for it, since it compared very favorably to the most effective .38 Special revolver round in police history, the "FBI load" which was comprised of a 158-grain lead semi-wadcutter hollow-point bullet of approximately the same diameter at 890 feet per second with 278 foot-pounds of energy.

Unfortunately, it quickly became apparent that even though in paper ballistics it slightly exceeded the most proven .38 Special manstopper, the 9mm subsonic was a *jacketed* hollow-point and the famously potent .38 Special load had been all-lead. The soft lead tended to upset even when fired through heavy clothing and from a 2-inch barrel. With its tough copper jacket, the 147-grain subsonic often failed to open up. There were many cases of over-penetration, and of bullets failing to expand … and of offenders who were not stopped as quickly as they should have been.

Meanwhile, the 1990 introduction of the .40 S&W cartridge had proven to be a seed sown in a fruitful field. It gave police departments not only a valid compromise between a single-stack magazine .45 and a double-stack magazine 9mm, but it gave them a face-saving way out of the corner they had painted themselves into by adopting a less than optimum 9mm cartridge.

Long before the 147-grain subsonic 9mm hit law enforcement, Federal and Winchester had provided the Illinois State Police – the first large American law enforcement agency to adopt a 9mm auto, in 1967 – with a +P+ 9mm JHP that weighed 115 grains and traveled 1,300 feet per second, generating a whopping 431 foot-pounds of energy. In numerous shootings, this round proved itself to be a very decisive manstopper.

Separate testing led to adoption of the 115-grain +P+ by the U.S. Secret Service, the Air Marshals, and in a pilot program for semiautomatic pistols, the U.S. Border Patrol. They among other agencies demonstrated it to be a decisive fight-stopper.

However, none of these agencies had the cachet of the FBI. The 147-grain round still ruled. Yet, department by department, failures of the 147 led to a branching into other concepts. Some admitted that they had made the wrong choice. Las Vegas Metro PD dumped the 147 subsonic after disappointing results and went back to their old 9mm duty load, the Winchester 115-grain Silvertip. Jacksonville (FL) dropped the 147-grain and adopted the 115-grain +P+, and ultimately switched to .40 caliber pistols.

Many more agencies simply adopted or at least approved larger-caliber weapons. The FBI itself went to the .40 as standard issue. So did New Orleans, St. Louis, Boston, and numerous other agencies. Fed up with the failure of the 147-grain subsonic 9mms in multiple shootings of vicious humans and vicious dogs alike, Virginia saw both their state troopers and the Richmond Police adopt the .357 SIG cartridge, whose performance in the field against both man and beast delighted both agencies. Chicago Police Department, Los Angeles County and Los Angeles City police authorized .45 caliber pistols and saw a massive transition to that caliber, even though the deputies and street cops had to buy the more powerful guns out of their own pockets.

Meanwhile, another 9mm load concept was developed and had borne fruit. This concept was exemplified by the Winchester 127-grain +P+ Ranger at 1,250 feet per second, and the CCI Speer Gold Dot 124-grain +P at the same velocity. Numerous police departments adopted each for their 9mm standard-issue service pistols, notably Orlando, Florida with the 127-grain Winchester +P+, and New York City PD with the Gold Dot 124-grain +P, had spectacular success with these rounds on the street. Indeed, they were so successful that street cops virtually stopped lobbying for more powerful guns. Word spread like wildfire among these agencies after each shooting: the ammo they had now made the 9mm *work* as a fight-stopper.

Where does that leave us in today's discussion, in a book about Beretta pistols? For police use, the 127-grain +P+ Winchester and the 124-grain +P Speer seem to be the way to go. They meet the FBI protocols for bullet penetration with and without intervening barricades, and most important, they have performed well on the street. They tend to deliver a wound measuring about 12 to 13 inches in depth, and effectively wide.

A strong second choice would be the 115-grain at about 1,300 feet per second. The Remington,

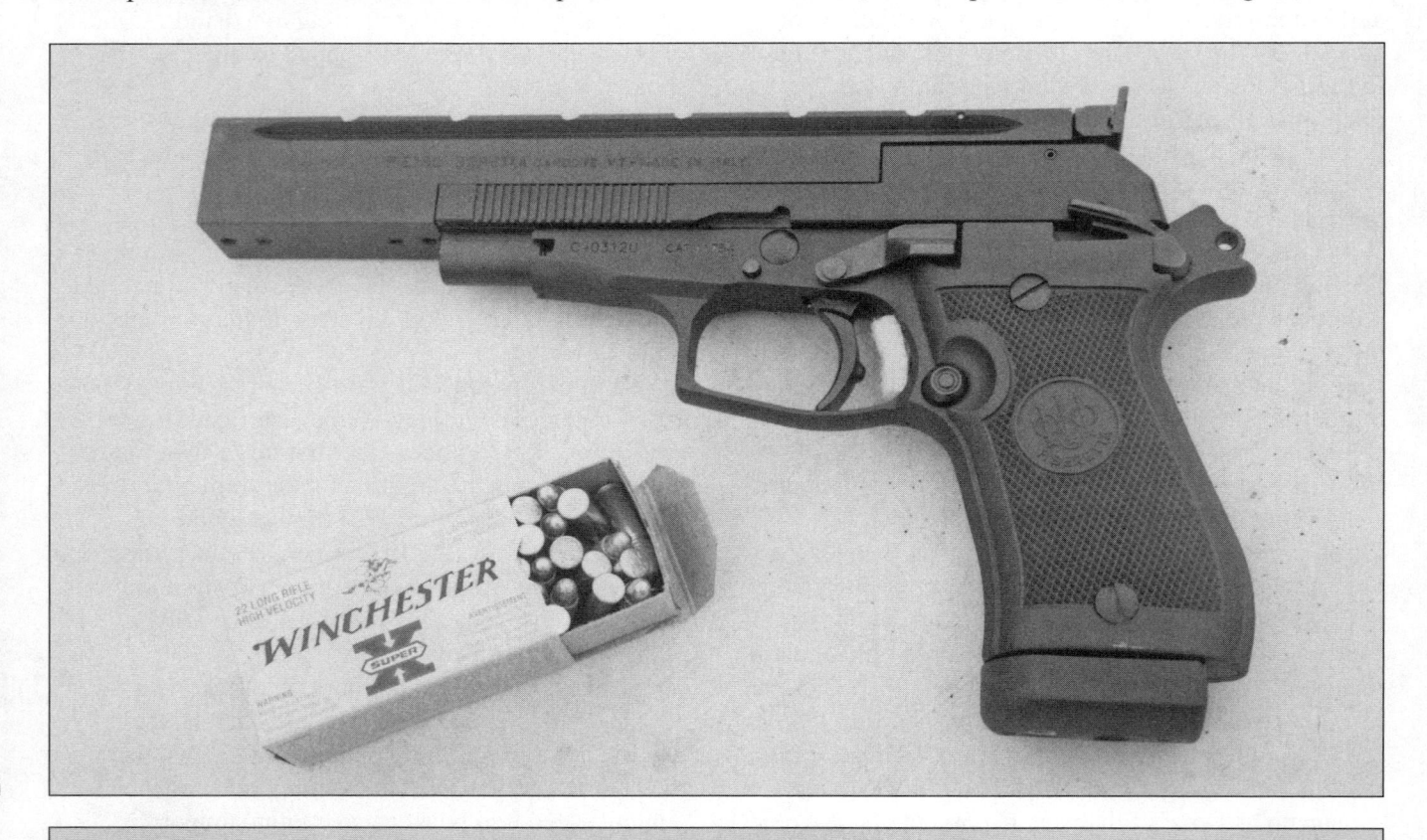

Most Beretta .22 LRs, including the 92/96 conversion unit, work best with plated high-speed ammo like this Winchester. This Model 87 shoots fine with the Winchester but will also handle standard-velocity, lead-bullet target ammo and shoot it even tighter.

Winchester, and Federal versions of this round are sold only to police departments, based on manufacturers' policy. However, civilians can purchase this excellent 115-grain ammo as CCI Gold Dot +P, Black Hills +P, Pro-Load Tactical +P, and Remington +P. Expect these loads to give about 10 inches of penetration, with a slightly wider wound channel than a 124-grain. While the Winchester 127-grain +P+ Ranger is not sold to the public per manufacturer policy, the CCI Gold Dot +P 124-grain, as issued to NYPD, is.

The +P and +P+ 9mm loads are a bit snappy in recoil, kicking about like a 180-grain standard-pressure .40 S&W round. This is not hard to control. However, for those who are particularly sensitive to recoil, I have to agree again with Evan Marshall and recommend Federal's 115-grain Classic JHP, which is product coded "9BP." In every shooting I've run across with that round, the bullet has mushroomed nicely and stopped at optimum depth in the opponent, quickly neutralizing him with few shots and often only one. Accuracy is also superlative, on a par with the famously accurate Olin Super Match.

It should be noted that all currently produced Beretta pistols in 9mm Parabellum are rated by the factory for +P and +P+ ammunition. This is not true of all their competition! The M9/Model 92 in particular was engineered for the NATO 9mm round, which is actually higher in pressure than a +P+ police load.

A final point before we leave the topic. Under the umbrella of "Beretta 9mm" are pistols manufactured more than half a century ago, before the advent of JHP bullets, some made without Beretta's approval or supervision. If your gun is an old Brigadier, an Egyptian Helwan, or a war souvenir Iraqi Tariq, it might not be wise to shoot it with high-pressure ammo *or* to expect it to cycle with wide-mouth hollow-point ammo. In either case, I would recommend the standard line, standard-pressure Remington JHP, 115-grain. As with their .380 (and .38 Super, and .45 ACP 185-grain) standard hollow-points, this round duplicates design cross-section of ball and should feed in any mil-spec gun that feeds hardball.

.40 S&W

Introduced in 1990 by Winchester and Smith & Wesson, the .40 S&W cartridge came at the right time for police firearms instructors and police chiefs who were beleaguered by their officers, who had split into two factions. One side wanted pistols more powerful than the 9mm, and were willing to accept the relatively low capacity of a single-stack magazine to get .45 caliber stopping power. The other side wanted lots of bullets, to put them at parity with what they perceived to be a firepower race with criminals who were trending toward higher capacity autoloaders. While some departments – Arizona Highway Patrol, for example, and the Georgia State Patrol – solved the quandary by giving troopers a choice between a single-stack .45 or a double-stack 9mm by the same maker, most chiefs wanted a single gun as standard issue.

The .40 made perfect sense. Whether in a Smith & Wesson 4006 or a Beretta Model 96, a cartridge capacity of 12 .40 S&W rounds exactly split the

The author's favorite .40 S&W load is this hot EXP from Black Hills, spitting a 165-grain Gold Dot at 1,140 to 1,150 feet per second. He finds it extraordinarily accurate in most .40 pistols, including his Beretta, and has won three state championships with it.

difference between an eight-shot .45 and a 16-shot 9mm. This seemed like Solomonic wisdom. It cut the Gordian knot. ".40" was close enough to ".45" to satisfy the big-bore advocates, and the double-stack magazine with twice the round-count of a six-shooter seemed a quantum enough a leap in round count for the firepower advocates. The .40 was a natural compromise.

The first generation of ammunition duplicated the old frontier .38/40 round, but with much more effective bullets that were designed to expand: 180-grain projectiles at 990 feet per second and hitting with 390 foot-pounds of energy. Though they often over-penetrated, they earned a surprisingly good reputation for stopping power, and remain the most popular cartridge in the caliber nationwide.

The second generation was lighter and faster, 155 grains at 1,200 fps for 1160 foot-pounds (Winchester Silvertip) and 165 grains at 1,150 fps with 484 foot-pounds (Speer Gold Dot, Black Hills EXP using the Gold Dot bullet, Winchester Ranger). These proved more dynamic. The Border Patrol went with 155-grain ammo in their Beretta 96Ds, primarily Remington standard-style JHPs, and reported awesomely effective street results. Departments like Nashville with the Winchester 165-grain bullets found their ammo much deadlier and faster-acting than the 180-grain .40s of the Tennessee State Police, who were so dissatisfied with the subsonic ammo that they changed calibers. This "medium range" of .40 caliber ballistics comes close to the 158-grain .357 Magnum round, but with a much more efficiently expanding bullet that satisfies FBI penetration protocols but does not seem to overpenetrate.

The third generation was the 135-grain at 1,250 to 1,300 feet per second. It is not particularly dynamic at the lower velocities at which it is sometimes offered, but at 1,250 to 1,300 feet per second it inflicts damage similar to that of the famously effective .357 Magnum 125-grain revolver round.

The 135-grain bullets give the .40 S&W cartridge a shorter overall length, and while that does not affect most guns, I've received a number of complaints about stoppages with 135-grain .40 rounds in the Beretta 96. I would urge something heavier. When Winchester was asked to develop a round specifically for the Beretta 96, the round they came out with was a full-speed 165-grain offering. I've seen no problem with current production .40s using a 180-grain load, but the 165-grain bullet at full speed seems to be the cartridge of choice for the Beretta 96, and seems to run fine in the Cougar 8000 series guns in that caliber as well.

Personally, I load my Beretta 96 Centurion with Black Hills 165-grain EXP. It is by far the most accurate load I've used in that gun – something that seems to be more the rule than the exception with that outstandingly accurate cartridge – and its awesome ballistics leave nothing to be desired.

.357 SIG

Developed in 1994, the .357 SIG cartridge can be described in oversimplified terms as a .40 S&W case necked down to 9mm, though of course it is a lot more complicated than that. Just necking down a .40 won't give you strong enough brass if you're handloading. This high-pressure round was designed to duplicate the power of a 125-grain .357 Magnum revolver cartridge, and it pretty much succeeds.

Though both lighter and heavier bullets are available, the 125-grain JHP at 1,350 feet per second, generating a devastating 510 foot-pounds of energy, is the overwhelming choice of both law enforcement and the private sector alike. All the shootings I know of are with the 125-grain load.

The Winchester Ranger load has been used by

In caliber .357 SIG, the original Federal (below) has set the reliability standard, while the very reliable Gold Dot (above) has the most awesome track record in stopping power. A Beretta 8357 should handle either just fine. Choose the 125-grain weight.

some agencies with spectacular success, but its performance does not exceed that of the Speer Gold Dot, which is overwhelmingly the most popular duty load in .357 SIG in American law enforcement. Therefore, we have the most shootings with it by far. There have been *no* horror stories of bad guys taking hit after hit before they stopped fighting. I'm aware of just one shooting, in Virginia, where the bad guy took hits in the double digits. He had just disarmed and wounded a cop, and multiple brother officers opened fire and riddled him so fast that he took ten to a dozen bullets before his corpse had time to fall.

The largest agency currently using the one Beretta in this caliber, the Cougar 8357, is the North Carolina Highway Patrol. They appreciate the on-safe option of the Beretta F-series pistol, which has already saved the lives of countless state troopers there. The NCHP is currently issuing the 125-grain Gold Dot, and reportedly is extremely satisfied with it. That's good enough for me …

.45 ACP

The good news with the .45 ACP is that its massive bullet size makes almost every load in the caliber an effective fight-ender. During a slightly shorter time frame than that in which 9mm hardball earned its reputation as being ineffectual, 230-grain .45 hardball became what almost every gun expert has called "a legendary manstopper."

As with the .357 SIG, Beretta makes but a single pistol line in this caliber, the Model 8045 Cougar series. As with the .357 SIG version, it works just fine. And, if you gave battle-experienced American troops a choice of Berettas, it's safe to say that many and perhaps most would go to the .45, just for the power. A number of American troops in the Iraq and Afghanistan theaters at this writing – including Marine Recon and the Army's Delta Force – are armed with 1911 .45s. For the most part, these guns are loaded with good ol' GI hardball, and that ammo – 230-grain bullets almost half an inch in diameter, traveling at about 850 feet per second with some 370 foot-pounds of energy – are reportedly putting the "bad guys" down decisively, just as this century-old round has done since the US military officially adopted it in 1911.

To put its reputation as a battle round in perspective, that round-nose full-metal-jacket bullet is acknowledged to be the least efficient bullet shape in common use. It is also extremely ricochet-prone and horrendously overpenetrative. A GI .45 ball round will pierce some 26 inches of Marty Fackler's muscle tissue-simulating ballistic gelatin. If you line three average size adult men up in a row, that means a through and through wound of the first guy, a through and through wound of the second, and a bullet that goes deep enough into the third to kill him before it lodges. That's fine for launching at enemy lines, but unacceptable for firing on an American street – or in a home, where the house defense gun's bullet can go through the offender and kill not just a random stranger, but a beloved member of your own family who is running in from behind him to help keep him from hurting you.

Fortunately, there are ample choices in JHP .45 Auto ammo, none of which seem to have any problem in feeding through the Beretta 8045. The only jam I've ever had with one of these pistols was a failure to cycle with a very light round that was loaded for competition, not serious use. And that only happened once out of 60 or so shots with that ammo.

If the US military was to adopt the Beretta .45 to replace the Beretta 9mm, it would already have in stock 185-grain +P JHP, produced to government-order spec by Olin/Winchester, which hits 1,140 feet per second velocity and delivers a whopping 534 foot-pounds of energy at the muzzle. This ammo was ordered for the special HK SOCOM guns acquired some time ago for the Special Operations Command, and it reportedly has delivered excellent performance in the field.

LAPD authorizes the Beretta 8045, and Chicago PD authorizes the same pistol so long as it is in double-action-only format. Chicago gives their officers a broad latitude as to just what weight and velocity of JHP .45 ACP they purchase to load in their optional large caliber service weapons, while LAPD issues ammo for its optional .45s. At this writing, the LAPD load is the Winchester 230-grain SXT. This is not a +P round, but it's on the high side of standard velocity at 880 feet per second and 396 foot-pounds of energy. It tends to open up very well. The last two shootings I'm aware of with this round from pistols with the same barrel length as the 8045 ended with instant one-shot fatal stops of men who were pointing rifles at the cops who shot them.

Bottom Line

Good guns want good ammo. Don't use corrosive military surplus. They don't call it "corrosive" for nothing. Personally, I don't use steel case ammo in any of my American or European handguns. That stuff, as currently produced, was designed by the Russians for Russian weapons, which in turn were designed with massive extractors expressly to deal with the way steel case ammo affects feeding. I've seen a lot of guns break their extractors on steel case pistol ammo.

Your gun is only as good as the ammo you feed it. Feed it the best, particularly when you load it up and make it ready to protect you, yours, and those you may have sworn an oath to serve. Bad ammo can ruin the best guns. The handful of slide breakages that hurt Beretta's reputation so badly came for the most part from horrendously overpressure cartridges that never should have left the ammo factory, and might have blown up lesser guns like hand grenades.

The gun and the ammo are symbiotic. Together, they comprise a life-saving emergency rescue tool. Don't scrimp. Use the best.

Your Beretta is worth it.

And, more to the point so are you and yours.

Endnotes

(1) Marshall, Evan and Sanow, Ed, "Street Stoppers: The Latest Handgun Stopping Power Street Results," Boulder, CO: Paladin Press, 1996, P. 151.

Beretta Field Performance: An Update

Some folks just never got over the fact that Beretta, instead of their favorite make and model and caliber of pistol, became the American armed forces' standard sidearm in the mid-1980s. They snipe at the M9 every chance they get.

This book is going to the publisher at the very beginning of 2005. At this time the Internet is rife with stories of horrible Beretta performance in Iraq and Afghanistan. "It jams!" "It doesn't put the bad guys down!"

The virtually universal consensus of *the U.S. military armorers who were over there* and *the American combat personnel who did the fighting* was that the Beretta pistols were fine and any problems involved Checkmate magazines bought on bid and pointy-nose full-metal-jacket ball ammunition that has been known for about a century to be a most unlikely manstopper.

You remember the book title, *When Bad Things Happen To Good People*? A history of the complaints against the Beretta Model 92 9mm pistol could honestly be titled, *When Bad Magazines and Bad Ammunition Happen To Good Guns.*

Elsewhere in this book I wrote about the accumulated complaints against the M9. There has been some water under the bridge. Let's update that and address the latest complaints about Beretta performance in the field.

The rumors rolling down the "information superhighway" tell us that M9 (Beretta 92) pistols are not working out well in Iraq and Afghanistan. We hear of jams in the sand, and enemy personnel shot multiple times with 9mm NATO ball rounds and still staying up and fighting.

Magazines have editors and other staff to review incoming information. They check facts. Alas, Internet chat rooms don't have that. This is why rumors need to be checked out before being accepted.

Berettas jamming in sand? Wait a minute. The Israelis are the masters of desert warfare, and they use Beretta pistols extensively. The Iraqis certainly knew their way around desert fighting, too, and their sidearm was the Tariq, a locally made copy of the Beretta 92. The Egyptians, with extensive experience in desert warfare, long carried the Beretta 92's predecessor, the old Brigadier, or clones of the same. The South Africans were no slouches in desert combat, either, since Namibia was for many years under their control as Southwest Africa, and they used the Z88, a copy of the 92 made under Beretta license in the Republic of South Africa.

The problem American forces had, it turns out, had nothing to do with the guns and everything to do with the magazines. Our government had purchased a large quantity of aftermarket magazines from the lowest bidder. "They're junk," one Army armorer told me after returning from a tour in Iraq. "To make them cheaper, they put something like a crackle finish on the outside, and to make them cheaper still, the same finish is on the inside. That gets in the way of a smooth travel of the follower and spring, and the springs on those magazines are weak, anyway. It's all you can ask of them to work in perfect conditions. When they get the least little bit of sand in them, they choke."

Army and Marine Corps armorers who work for their services' marksmanship training units are on top of the battlefield feedback from both fronts, Afghanistan and Iraq. They confirm that the pistols are fine. "Trust only two magazines: American Beretta mags, and Italian Beretta mags," they told me.

That basically gives you a choice of three, the third being MecGar magazines, since Italy's MecGar has made many of the "factory" magazines for Beretta.

Another problem cropped up with this. When soldiers and Marines wrote home and desperately asked friends and relatives to send them Beretta mags that worked, all that was available were 10-round "Clinton magazines." Even cops who attempted to purchase 15-round Beretta mags for department buddies who had been called up by the National Guard were stymied. "We can't sell you new 15-round magazines for them," they were told, "because they're for law enforcement only. You need a letter from a police supervisor on police letterhead saying that they'll be used in the performance of police duties. That doesn't cover military duties."

Until the sunset of the onerous and ill-begotten Crime Law in September 2004, all a well-meaning person on the home front could do for a soldier or Marine was send them a magazine of two-thirds capacity, or send Wolff aftermarket magazine springs for the Beretta M9. It was one more way in which the 10-year ban on full-capacity magazines had hurt the good guys without hurting the bad guys.

On another front, though, one complaint about the 9mm pistols was absolutely valid. This was the allegation that full metal jacket GI ammo in caliber 9mm was an impotent manstopper. Well, no kidding, Sherlock. This has been common knowledge since the advent of the 9mm Parabellum cartridge in 1902. Within little more than a decade, WWI became the classic proving ground of 9mm hardball versus American .45 hardball. The 230-grain full-metal-jacket slug from the large caliber Yank handguns became famous for one-shot stops in the fast and deadly close combat in the trenches, while returning vets spoke of the failure of the German Luger's 9mm round to drop doughboys and Tommies unless they were hit in the brain or the spine. This continued through another war. Not until the 1960s and the coming of high-speed hollow-point bullets did the 9mm get up off its knees as a fight-stopping cartridge.

There is some feedback to indicate that hollow-point 9mm ammo has been used in the current "War on Terror" with good success. Like the Internet rumors, it can't be substantiated, at least not without getting some good people in trouble for violating the letter of military regulations. That said, though, the Judge Advocate General's office long ago determined that the Geneva Convention and the Hague Accords, which can be seen as stipulating ball ammunition, apply only to declared international warfare. They do not apply to counter-terrorist fighting such as that which drove the American incursions into Afghanistan and then Iraq. Jacketed hollow-points should be technically legal, but require official military approval to keep the end users from getting into trouble. So far, that approval has not been forthcoming.

A number of .45s have found their way to the front in the current war, many in the hands of American combatants who simply brought their own. Certain special forces units are issued .45s: Delta Force gives each member a stipend with which to purchase his own customized 1911 in that caliber, and Marine Force Recon personnel are issued .45 caliber 1911s. As has been the case since WWI, .45 caliber is the most effective of hardball handgun ammo, putting down enemy fighters much more reliably than 9mm ball.

Let's look at two recently returned American combat soldiers. One has requested to remain nameless. He found the Beretta worked fine in Afghanistan, so long as it had good magazines and was kept reasonably clean. When he's not serving the National Guard, his job stateside is as a full-time police officer in a major metropolitan city. When his department allowed him to carry the gun of his choice, he wore a personally owned Beretta 92F. When he got into a gunfight with it, he unerringly drew from his SS-III security holster, smoothly popped off the safety, and killed his armed antagonist, who fell instantly to his Federal Hydra-Shok 9mm hollow-points. When the department adopted the GLOCK .40 for all officers, he went along with the program, but still carries his Beretta off duty. This man has trusted his life to the Beretta, here and abroad, and is still very comfortable in doing so.

The other man is Ray Millican, an Army Command Sergeant Major with a special forces assignment. Recently returned, he had the same observations on the American sidearms. Issued the M9, he trusts the gun but has little faith in full-metal-jacket 9mm ammo. He thinks so much of the Beretta that he bought one as a personal carry and home-defense pistol, but his experience with the 9mm soured him on the caliber and he chose a Beretta 96 chambered for the .40 S&W. I let him try my Beretta Cougar 8045, chambered for the .45 ACP cartridge. "Beautiful gun," he said after he shot it. "Very easy to control. Why couldn't the service adopt *this* Beretta instead of the 9mm? With military ammo, the .45 round gets the job done."

On The Home Front

The armed services aren't the only ones protecting America's shores with standard-issue Beretta pistols. The U.S. Border Patrol has for many years issued one standard sidearm: the Beretta 96D. As the "D" suffix indicates, this is a double-action-only pistol with "slick slide" and no safety/decocking lever. Lacking a single-action sear, the trigger pull is actually smoother and lighter by a small margin than the double-action first-shot trigger pull on the more traditional "F" series guns, such as the M9 pistol chosen by the military. The "96" model number connotes the Model 92 style pistol in caliber .40 Smith & Wesson. Where the 9mm Model 92 or M9 carries 15 rounds in the magazine and one more in the firing chamber, the .40 caliber Model 96 has 11 of the fatter cartridges in its mag, and another in the launch tube. Current-issue ammunition is the 155-grain Remington JHP, leaving the muzzle at some 1,200 feet per second. Border Patrol officials say that it has proven itself very effective as a manstopper in many gunfights involving their personnel. The Border Patrol Berettas have reinforced, heavy-duty slides.

Elsewhere among America's estimated 700,000 domestic law enforcement officers, the Beretta is probably the third most popular service pistol, second only to the GLOCK and the SIG. At this writing the Beretta 92 is still standard issue for America's third largest municipal police department, the LAPD, and for the country's single largest contingent of sheriff's deputies, the Los Angeles County Sheriff's Department.

Berettas come in three variations. Those with the "F" suffix are traditional double-action (TDA) designs, which are double-action only on the first shot. They then cock themselves to easy single-action pulls for subsequent shots, until the gun runs empty or is decocked with an ambidextrous lever on the slide. That lever is, on the F-series guns, a combination safety catch and decocking lever. This means the F-type Berettas can be carried on-safe. This practice has saved many cops in actual situations when someone got their pistol away from them and tried to shoot them or other officers, but were unable to do so because they could not figure out how to off-safe the weapon. LAPD and LASD are among the departments that use the F-series Beretta.

Next is the "G" series, which supposedly stands for "Gendarme" because the French police were the first to ask for the feature. A Beretta 92G or 96G is a TDA like the F-series pistol, but in the G-series, the slide-mounted lever is a dedicated decocker. Spring-loaded, it snaps back into the "fire" position as soon as the hammer has been mechanically lowered, and does not function as a manual safety. While a type F Beretta requires a double movement of the thumb, down and up, to decock it and then make it ready to immediately fire double-action, the type G requires only the initial downward movement. The spring that snaps it back up, however, also requires more pressure to operate than does the two-way lever of the F-series pistol. Major departments that have adopted the 96G (decocker-only .40 caliber) include Indiana State Police, Florida Highway Patrol, and the San Francisco Police Department.

Finally, there is the D-series. These are double-action-only (DAO) pistols, with spurless hammers that decock themselves after each shot. Some instructors believe that a single, consistent trigger pull every time makes these guns easier for officers to learn. Some chiefs believe that the DAO mechanism is less conducive to unintentional discharge and therefore more "liability resistant" than more traditional designs. The Beretta DAO has a full-length trigger stroke (unlike, say, the S&W DAO pistols, whose trigger throw is a little shorter than the first-shot pull on their TDA models), but it is very smooth and relatively light. One of the first Four-Gun Masters in IDPA competition, Mike Benedict, achieved that level in the Stock Service Pistol category using a Beretta 96D that had been traded in by the Ohio State Patrol.

The federal police who secure Veterans Administration facilities are armed with Beretta 92D 9mm pistols. The 96D in .40 is the standard service pistol of departments ranging from the Pennsylvania State Police and the Maryland State Police to, as noted, the U.S. Border Patrol. The 92D is extremely popular with the officers of the nation's second largest municipal police department, that of Chicago, which limits its personnel to double-action-only pistols but gives the officers a broad choice of brands.

Competition

Competition is conflict in sport, not battle. However, many forms of pistol competition are called "combat shooting" because they are intended to replicate as much as possible the stress and the marksmanship problems in real-world handgun fighting.

The Beretta has often been the victor in the "competition wars." Famed instructor Ken Hackathorn had a Beretta 92 with a 20-round magazine tucked in his belt to back up his .45 when he won the National Tactical Invitational. He has publicly stated that no factory-manufactured pistol is more reliable.

Rob Hought, a streetwise chief of police, has

won many IDPA (International Defensive Pistol Association) tournaments and other matches. He competes with a Beretta 92G.

For many years, to win the IDPA National Championships you had to beat Ernest Langdon and the Beretta 92G he customized for himself. He now makes his living modifying Beretta and SIG pistols for other potential champions.

The revolver once ruled police combat shooting, but as the auto pistol came to dominate in police uniform holsters, it was accepted in the competition environment too. The Beretta is well respected there. Vince O'Neil, several-time state champion PPC shooter of Oklahoma, is partial to the Beretta 92. He says he has not found any out of the box pistol that is both so accurate and so reliable.

Look next to the original American handgun sport, bull's-eye shooting. Two of the most important matches each year at the National Championships at Camp Perry are the President's Hundred and the Distinguished match. Each must be shot with a semiautomatic pistol of a type that is or has been standard-issue for the US military. This narrows the choices down to two: the Beretta M9 9mm, and the 1911A1 .45.

When the US military adopted the Beretta in the mid 1980s, traditionalists hung their heads, believing that this double-action 9mm autoloader with an aluminum frame could never come close to the accuracy potential of the steel-framed .45 auto originally designed by John Browning. Time has proven them wrong.

For the last few years, the Beretta has beaten the 1911 more often than not. Armorers learned to install Bar-Sto barrels or an equivalent, just as they had so long done with the 1911, to deliver maximum accuracy. BoMar sights were fitted atop the Beretta's slide, just as had been the tradition with the .45. Even as pistolsmiths had learned to install anti-backlash devices in 1911 triggers, armorers of the U.S. Army and Marine Corps marksmanship training units learned to go through the frame if necessary to install trigger stops in the Beretta. With the Colt .45 and its clones, they and their grandfathers had long since learned to do trigger jobs that brought the pull down from a mushy 8 or more pounds to a crisp 4-pound release. With the Beretta 92/M9, they learned to do the exact same thing, usually with an easier pull to start with.

The Bottom Line

Approaching its 20th year as the standard military service pistol of the United States, the Beretta 9mm demands only magazines as good – as *Beretta* – as the rest of the gun, to guarantee 100 percent functioning. For "manstopping," it demands manstopper ammo, and no other 9mm pistol would have done better or worse with the same ammunition in that respect. The Beretta is factory-warranted for +P and +P+ ammunition – the NATO-spec hardball issued with it is actually higher pressure than either – and for more than a quarter of a century, it has been proven on American streets that a hot JHP 9mm round is not wanting in the stopping power department.

The Beretta has received an unwarranted bad rap over the years. Some of it came from industry competitors jealous that Beretta, and not they, had won the lucrative military contract. Some came from a small handful of slide separations, which for the most part, were traced to horrendously overloaded ammunition and in some cases to use of improperly fitted sound suppressors.

On its own – the hard way, the old fashioned way – the Beretta 92 pistol has earned a reputation as an extraordinarily reliable, accurate, useful and functional combat pistol. And, in the end, no amount of unfounded rumor mongering is going to change that documented fact.

More update. The Border Patrol, by the time you read this, will be changing from Beretta pistols to SIG P229s in .40 caliber with DAK trigger groups. They and INS are under the umbrella of Homeland Security, which has approved only the SIG and Heckler & Koch brands for new handgun purchases. LAPD, a bastion of Berettas since that department first switched from revolvers to autoloaders for the rank and file in the late 1980s, now has a chief of police who is a well-known fan of the popular Glock pistol. Under his command, LAPD authorized several models of Glock pistols as privately owned duty or off-duty weapons, and it is said that he wants to make that brand the standard issue for the department. That may well have happened by the time you read this.

As the old cliché goes, "time marches on." Things change. It is worth noting that when Beretta loses a contract, they don't sue or scream or badmouth their competition, and that speaks well of them. The company has been with us for going on half a millennium. They're going to be with us a lot longer, because instead of sniveling about losing a battle, they move forward with research and prepare to fight the next war. It is an attitude that some of their competitors, and most of their detractors, would do well to emulate.

The Epiphany of the Beretta

Brand preference in handguns can be a funny thing. For generations, it was a family thing. A fellow might be a Colt man or a Smith & Wesson man because his father was a Colt or Smith & Wesson man. Today, though, the choice of firearms and the options of features have both become so wide that the smart shooter makes his choice based on experience and needs, not tradition.

Let's look at some folks who came to prefer the Beretta, and determine why they prefer it.

The Special Forces Vet

Ray Millican was introduced to the Beretta M9 in the service and took a liking to it immediately. "I love the way it shoots," he says. "Even when it's dirty, it'll work, so long as you have Beretta magazines. Every jam I saw or heard of in Afghanistan was with those cheap magazines the government bought on bid."

Ray liked the Beretta so much that, since the Army doesn't issue take-home guns, he bought one for himself as a carry and home-defense pistol. A big man, he has no problem concealing a full size Beretta, even in his native North Florida. "I bought a police trade-in, a 96G," he says. "The one thing I don't like about the 9mm Beretta is the stopping power of the cartridge. The Beretta 96 is a .40 caliber, and I like having a little more oomph."

Ray tried my Beretta 8045 Cougar in .45 ACP. "I *love* this gun," he said enthusiastically after strafing down a table of six Bianchi steel plates with six fast shots. "Why couldn't the military adopt *this* Beretta? With GI ball ammo, the .45 just makes so much more sense for combat than the 9mm!"

Now in reserve status and recently back from combat in Afghanistan, Ray has a stronger appreciation than ever of reliable fighting weapons that function in adverse

In "The Fighting Handgun," British gun experts Richard Law and Peter Brookesmith thought enough of the Beretta to use a stainless 92 on the cover to symbolize modern combat pistols.

conditions. "You can't beat the Beretta," he says, patting the Model 96 on his hip.

The Male Pistol Champion

I first met Vince O'Neill when he was a young street cop from Kansas who came to take an Advanced Officer Survival class from Ray Chapman and me at Ray's Chapman Academy of Practical Shooting in Columbia, Missouri. I watched him over his career as he became one of the pre-eminent officer survival instructors in the nation. Today, he teaches at a prestigious state law enforcement academy in the Midwest.

I've lost count of how many state championships Vince has won in police combat shooting. Many of them were with customized Smith & Wesson .38 caliber six-guns, back in the revolver days. Today, the overwhelming majority of cops carry autoloaders. "In our state," Vince told me, "most of the departments have the 'big boy' rule. They let their officers carry the sidearm of their choice, within reason." The same is true for instructors at the academy. Vince has his pick of guns. He was issued an excellent pistol, a .45 caliber Kimber. In the old days, on patrol, he shot up a storm with the SIG P226 9mm issued to him by his department in Kansas. Today, though, I see him carrying a Beretta more often than anything else.

I asked him once why he chose the Beretta. "For one thing, I've always liked fine guns," he replied, "and I just can't fault the workmanship on the Beretta. The trigger pull is easy to get along with, whether double- or single-action. It's probably the most accurate service pistol out there, and that's something I appreciate, too. There's a group of cops out here who shoot their duty guns in matches. I couldn't help but notice that a lot of the best shots carry the Beretta."

The last time I taught a class for Vince, his Beretta of choice was a 92G. He used it to clean the demanding Sky Marshal combat shooting qualification. It was the first time I've seen anyone shoot a perfect score on that extremely difficult course of fire. A few years before, he showed up at an advanced LFI class with a double-action-only 92D. The people who say DAO autos are impossible to shoot haven't seen a High Master like Vince O'Neill shoot the DAO Beretta. Vince was the top shot in his advanced class, beating a lot of heavy hitters who were shooting light-triggered, customized single-action autos.

A long career in law enforcement has left Vince convinced that shot placement counts for more than caliber, so long as the ammunition is efficient. He's comfortable with the 9mm Beretta, so long as it's loaded with light, fast, high-efficiency rounds. Well-connected in law enforcement, he has seen horror stories of stopping power failure with the 147-grain subsonic hollow-points he had to carry when his department in Kansas issued them, and he has seen how dynamically JHP rounds like the 127- or 124-grain at 1,250 foot-seconds, or the 115-grain at 1,300 to 1,350 fps, stop gunfights in the real world.

The Female Pistol Champion

My older daughter, Cat, started her pistol-shooting career at the age of 8 with a Beretta pistol. Specifically, a Beretta Minx in .22 Short. It fit her small hand, and she could reach all the controls. Ted Blocker, at the holster company that bears his name, made her the smallest ISI rig that ever left his shop. The tiny friction-tight speed scabbard, designed with input from the great champions Mickey Fowler and Mike Dalton at their school, International Shootists, Inc., worked perfectly with the tiny Beretta. A miniature double mag pouch accompanied the rig, which included the smallest gun belt to ever emerge from the shop: 18 inches, as I recall.

My buddy John Lawson was then the gunsmithing editor at *American Handgunner* magazine, where I was the law enforcement editor. He presented my 8-year-old with one of his inimitable "S n' S Specials." The "S n' S" stands for "Sugar n' Spice," and it's a gun he developed for little girl shooters, starting with one of his own nieces, as I recall. The gun was identical to Cat's, a Beretta Minx in .22 Short, but the fancy gold-inlaid EL model with high-polish blue finish. John had worked over the action to make it smoother, and – the cutest touch – had the little pistol Mag-Na-Ported.

Soon Cat was shooting Colt .45 autos, and set the little Berettas behind her like childhood playthings. At age 10, she carried a loaded Colt .38 on her hip when we went on safari together, and due to an anomaly of law in a certain African country, legally carried the same loaded gun concealed in major cities despite minor age. A year later, using a sophisticated High Standard .22 target pistol, she won her first pistol match against grown-up men. By the time she was 16, taking the Chapman Academy Advanced Pistol course on her own she had gravitated toward custom 1911 .45s and a Novak Custom Browning 9mm, identical to the ones used by the FBI's elite Hostage Rescue Team.

In 1996, Cat was 19 years old and ready for national competition. Preparing for the National Tactical Invitational, she was at the range with her

.45s and her Brownings when I told her, "Three of the 10 stages will be force-on-force. They use Simunitions ™, and every time I've been there so far, the issue guns have been SIG and Beretta 9mms. Tomorrow, let's bring out a SIG P226 and a Beretta 92, so you can refresh on their manual of arms.

This we did. I had been issued a SIG most often at previous NTIs, and we started with that. She shot it with aplomb, and had no problem activating its frame-mounted decocking lever. Then we switched to the Beretta, a full-size 92F.

About a box of ammo into things, I noticed something interesting. Not only was she adapting to the controls just fine, but she was shooting a little bit faster than with her custom single-action autos, and she was grouping just a little bit tighter.

I called her attention to it, but she had already noticed the difference. I asked, "What do you think it is?" She frowned, "I don't know. I can't say exactly. It just feels right in my hand." Now, as is detailed elsewhere in this book, the big Beretta 92 does not have a great history of winning the hearts of females, who tend to come with smaller hands than their brothers. However, Cat is the daughter of a tall, athletic woman and is tall herself, with very long fingers. Longer than mine, in fact. With this in mind, her statement that the gun just felt right no longer seemed counter-intuitive. "Let's run it a while longer," I said.

At the end of the session, she looked at me and said, "Are you thinking what I'm thinking?" I answered, "Hell, kid, if you shoot it better than the other guns, it oughta be your main gun for the match."

The next day we tried her out on some of my other Berettas. My own favorite, the 92FC Compact, fit her hand even better. She also shot remarkably well with my 92D. The long but smooth double-action stroke was no problem for her long, strong fingers.

My first-born showed up at the National Tactical Invitational with the 92FC in her Ted Blocker LFI Concealment Rig. For backup, she had the 92D.

To make a long story short, Cat kicked butt. She was up against a very strong field of the best female combat shooters in the country, including Gila May-Hayes, Vicki Farnam, and Lyn Bates. When the proverbial smoke had cleared, she was High Woman. She had won a national pistol championship at the age of 19. She had also beaten the overwhelming majority of the male contestants.

When she was 11, I had given her the Hi-Standard pistol she won her first match with. That turned out to be the start of an expensive tradition. I gave her my pet Beretta, the Horan custom compact, after she won the NTI with it. She had been licensed to carry concealed at the age of 18. She found that in cool to cold weather garb, she could conceal the Beretta Compact with its 13-round magazine under a jacket. In hot weather, she opted for a smaller Smith & Wesson Model 3913 in the same caliber. She carried both on-safe, loaded with 115-grain 9mm JHP at 1,350 feet per second, and found that they worked identically. She was fast and accurate with both, but a little faster and a little more accurate with the Beretta. It was about that time that she changed her email address to "BerettaGirl"...

Today, a teacher and grad student, Cat no longer has time for competitive shooting, but she still has her Beretta 9mm. She's married to an Army intelligence officer, who qualified Expert with every infantry weapon and was delighted to discover that his wife could beat him – and probably most anyone else on post – with the M9 service pistol.

The American Gun Expert

I've known Patrick Sweeney since the early years at the fabled Second Chance competition. Pat's a hell of a good shot, a hell of a good gunsmith, and a hell of a good writer. He's the author of several KP books, including *Gun Digest Book of the 1911, Gun Digest Book of the Glock,* and – most recently – Krause's third edition of *Modern Law Enforcement Weapons and Tactics.* He notes in the latter, in his chapter on the Beretta 92, "Its good points haven't kept its detractors from beating on it at every opportunity. Those good points are accuracy, reliability in function (except for some extreme conditions), ease of use and comfort. The M-92 is plenty accurate, as competitors in the USPSA Production Division have proven. Fit a match barrel to it, and it is fully capable of winning at Camp Perry, the national Bull's-eye championship. Given good ammo it will perk along for as long as you care to stand on the range and shoot it. And it will not bite you, jab you with sharp corners, or abrade parts of your hands." [1]

I don't think Patrick will mind if I quote him at length as to how he came to truly appreciate the Beretta service pistol. He had always, personally, had good luck with the gun, but like everyone else who reads the gun magazines and follows the Internet, had been inundated with stories of broken slides and locking blocks. Wrote Patrick, "One area that came in for continual improvement was the locking block. The latest version is the fourth design, and is now nearly indestructible. Ernest Langdon is a former Marine, IPSC competitor, and worked for Beretta for some time. He and I sat next to each other on the long bus ride from the airport to the range in South Africa for World Shoot XIII. I took advantage of the opportunity to find out a lot about the Beretta design, and found that my accurate and reliable pistol was not an anomaly. He can supply you with a brand new fourth generation locking block in case you're worried about yours not standing up to high shooting volumes. He can also improve the trigger pull and provide you with the small odds-and-ends parts that you should stock in your spare parts pouch of your maintenance bag. Keeping spare parts on hand is not an indictment of the Beretta. There are few pistols as rugged and reliable as the 1911, and I keep spares for my 1911s with me. There are few gunsmiths, competitors or writers with a greater appreciation and love of the 1911 than myself, and I own and have been known to carry, a Beretta M-92." [2]

In "Modern Law Enforcement Weapons and Tactics," gunsmith and ace competitive shooter Patrick Sweeney explains how he came to develop a new respect for the Beretta 92.

The British Gun Expert

Prior to the sad day in the mid-1990s when the Tony Blair government confiscated all modern handguns belonging to the British people, there were a number of staunch and highly competent handgunners among their number. Each year at the famous Bisley Camp not far from London was held Pistol Anno Domini, the world's largest handgun match. There were many highly competent handgun experts in the British Isles then, and among the very best was Richard Law.

His facility in Wales hosted a large gun club. One of his research projects was keeping track of "club guns," including their round count. It was in this environment that he developed his huge respect for Beretta pistols, first the 92 and later the Cougar series, which he found particularly ergonomic. In his excellent book "The Fighting Handgun," completed just before the ban, Richard had the following to say about the Beretta 92.

Picking up after his discussion of the American adoption of the Beretta as the M9 pistol, Law wrote, "The Beretta 92F was the ultimate winner of the U. S. Army trials, being adopted for service in 1985. The only serious competitors to this were the SIG Sauer P226, which was a rework of the P220 model specifically to compete in the trials, and Smith & Wesson's updated version of the Model 59.

"The Beretta we tested notched up mileage quite quickly and passed the 50,000-round mark after about 18 months' service. We test-fired the pistol quite often, and allowed it to be used a great deal at our club, so that it was used a lot without our paying for the ammunition!

"The working parts showed no signs of uneven wear, and we paid particular attention to the slide, as cracked slides and even slide separations have been mentioned in American military experience. The latest models for the target-shooters have the slide beefed up a little in front of and around the wedge lock cut-outs in response to problems with some production firearms, but that 'improvement' was clearly not necessary for our test gun, which is still banging on cheerfully without any sign of wear in that department.

"The Beretta does not have an ejector port because of the open-topped slide, so in recoil the whole of the top of the pistol opens and the empty case is released into fresh air with nothing for it to jam against. We never had a stovepipe jam or any other foul-up apart from the odd misfire, which could be blamed wholly on the ammunition. Jams are a nuisance at any time, and with inexperienced shooters they cause the additional risk of the muzzle straying if they try to rectify the fault on the firing line themselves.

"Not the least of the weapon's attractions was that the clear sight picture was easy to acquire, and the group printed where the sights pointed. There is probably nothing more irritating than fixed-sight pistols which shoot low left or otherwise off-centre. Aiming-off is an unsatisfactory way of getting a decent score, so any pistol which is not true should be adjusted if possible.

"One is entitled to expect a decent performance from a pistol which, out-of-the-box, is one of the most expensive of its type, but in this case at least one gets what one pays for a reliable tool which purrs on and on …"[3]

The Instructor

SSG James Mattimor recently emailed the following to the Beretta website. "I recently went through the NRA LEAD Tactical Handgun Instructor Development Course. I met great people, had fantastic training and an exceptional learning experience. I brought three Beretta 92s with me. We fired 1,500 rounds per man in five days. The only time my weapons stopped working was during the malfunction drills when we deliberately loaded dummy rounds. I was most pleased with myself when I was able to hit a steel silhouette target at 100 yards, standing, Weaver position. (Thank God for luck and a good optician.) I would not hesitate to train and send out my people armed with Berettas. All across the world good men are going into harm's way carrying your pistols. Thank you for keeping up the quality."

Mattimor later added, "While shooting at the NY Adjutant General's match in Camp Smith this year we had two competitors shooting the old Gov't Model .45. It was nothing but incessant jamming, magazine changes due to tap/rack procedures, etc. One of the 'gentlemen' was tossed out of the match because his jam clearing procedures looked dangerous to the range safety officer. At the end of the match I approached one of these 'gentlemen' and told him he was using a dinosaur. He was still sputtering nonsense about the .45 when I left in disgust. The U.S. military has been using Beretta for almost 20 years now and still the 'Dinosaur Lovers' carp, criticize and whine about their relics of the past. The .45 can't compete in a rapid-fire high-capacity world. I wish the gun writers and 'aficionados' would give it a rest."

The Security Professional

A man who identifies himself as Charles S. told Beretta, "I bought my 92F in 1992 from a local gun shop. This was my first Beretta firearm. I am a licensed security officer, and have been so from 1979. At the time I worked for the Federal Reserve Bank. I have used this handgun for home protection, work, and competition shooting. I've fired some 10,000 rounds without a malfunction. It's been one of the best handguns I have owned. Many police officers I work with say the same. I think so much of Beretta, I went out and got a 3032 Tomcat in 1998 as backup to my 92F. This handgun has worked without fail, and is one of the best small handguns I have owned. When a meth user tried to break into my home I had the Tomcat in my pocket. The fact that I had one of your handguns with me at the time stopped this crime and kept my family safe."

The Retired Cop

Ian Cunningham carries a Model 92FS, and told Beretta, "I carried a Beretta as a police officer and still carry one in my personal life today. I load lots of +P and wide JHPs. I've owned three Model 92s and have never had a problem. It is a robust, accurate, fast pistol. It is very easy to rhythm fire. For a long time I bounced between SIGs and Berettas but in the end the Beretta is where I'm gonna stay. Keep it up. Use Mec Gar or Beretta magazines and the damn things are bullet-proof reliable."

The Police Chief

The manufacturer learned from Chief Mike Lasniel, "I have been carrying Beretta Model 92s since I purchased an Italian-made 92SB in 1984 while I was in the Marines. I had zero faith in the crappy 1911s that we were issued at the time. I was a Primary Marksmanship Instructor, and shot on a Marine Corps Rifle and Pistol Team. The 1911s were incredibly unreliable, even though the armorers babied them. I was very happy when the Corps went to the Beretta, and got my 92F in 1987.

"When I went into law enforcement, I purchased a 92F, and carried it for many years while working as a city cop. I was the department high shooter with it for many years, and had also shot competitively while in the Corps, and on the SWAT team. It saw many tours of duty, since I was assigned to both narcotics and SWAT at the time. We would shoot at the sniper ranges, and after we were done with the rifles, we would grab some pistol ammo, and work on knockdown targets at 100 and 200 yards with our pistols. People were amazed at the accuracy of the Beretta, and I could drop the knockdowns nine out of 10 times at 200 yards. (I won quite a few free beers that way!)

"I needed a backup gun for Narcotics, so I decided to go with the best, and bought a second Beretta 92F!

"When I became Chief of a small rural community near salt water, I switched to the Stainless 92F, which I dearly love, and it's one of the most beautiful things I've ever seen.

"My final upgrade was to the Stainless 92 Vertec, which maintains the same high standards of all the others, with a few wonderful improvements. I was worried about the change in the grip, but it still points as perfect as ever, and having the light/laser mounted on the gun for building searches is a wonderful feature.

"I've been betting my life on Beretta Pistols every day for over 20 years. I can purchase and carry any pistol in the world. I've shot them all, and tried them all. I'll stick with my Beretta. There was an old saying in the Old West: 'Beware the man with one gun.' Especially if that gun is a Beretta!"

The SWAT Cop

"I've been carrying a 92F since 1987 when my agency's SRT (special reaction team) decided on it as the team's sidearm of choice," Officer Marty Hommel told Beretta. "I have to tell you that I fired thousands of rounds in this pistol, rapid-fire succession with multiple magazine exchanges during a course of fire. I had the barrel hot enough to burn you and never a malfunction. It just seemed to get smoother with age and of course my intimate familiarity over time. Just a fine reliable pistol and I'm still 'totin' it."

The IPSC Shooter

Robert Engh e-mailed Beretta, "As anyone on Beretta Forum knows I've been shooting IPSC (International Practical Shooting Confederation) now for three years. Using my Beretta Elite IIs I have taken 2nd place Nationally in Canada in Production Division (2003), won the British Columbia Production Division Title (2003), and won a number of matches this year as well. I owe a lot of my success to the Elite IIs I shoot, as they fit my hand naturally and point where I want them to without any effort."

The IPSC/IDPA Shooter

J. P. Pohlman submitted the following to the Beretta website. "Three years ago I purchased a used 92FS pistol in 80 to 90 percent condition. Inspired by Ernest Langdon and his 92G series pistol, I planned to 'trick-out' this ordinary 92FS for IDPA (International Defensive Pistol Association) and IPSC shooting. However after shooting it the first time at the range, I decided the pistol was fine just as is. Seeing how it was used there's no telling how many rounds were fired through it before it arrived into my ownership. Yet, I have personally put a bit over 4,000 rounds through it. (I try to keep a close eye on such things.) Thus far I have yet to have a single malfunction of ANY kind! There are not many pistols that can say that."

The list goes on ... and on. You can get updated comments from Beretta's website at www.berettausa.com. Suffice to say that the Beretta name has left a lot of satisfied customers out there.

No pistol is perfect. Each has some idiosyncrasies, even some flaws. But in the great guns, they can be dealt with and compensated for. This book will show you how.

Endnotes

(1) Sweeney, Patrick, "Modern Law Enforcement Weapons & Tactics," Third Edition, Iola, WI: F+W Publications, 2004, P.103.

(2) *Ibid.*, P. 105.

(3) Law, Richard, "The Fighting Handgun: An Illustrated History from the Flintlock to Automatic Weapons," London: Arms & Armour Press, 1996, Pages 132-133.

Shooting the Beretta

The Beretta points naturally.

The Beretta is a shooter's gun. Those who most appreciate them aren't the collectors, but the shooters.

Pick up a Beretta Model 92. Check that it's empty. After you've done so, work the slide one more time, just for the feel of it. The sensation is like glass running on glass. It's like racking the slide of a pre-war Colt National Match pistol, or like running your finger over a piece of fine crystal. No out-of-the-box semiautomatic pistol has so smooth an action. The Beretta is the standard by which the rest of the industry is judged in this respect.

Bring the Model 92 up into firing position, its muzzle pointed in a safe direction. Check out the sight picture. It's a generous one. The front sight is tall and thick, the rear notch is big and blocky, and as a result, even those with imperfect eyesight can align the sights well. The inexpensive models come with three white dots, which stand out against a black target and help the eye see what it is supposed to see in aiming for a perfect shot.

Stroke the trigger. The double-action pull is smooth. Not the lightest in the industry, not even the smoothest, but smooth enough. It is conducive to the marksman's ideal, a surprise shot break.

If your Model 92 or Model 96 is an F or G series instead of the double-action-only D series, it will go into self-cocking single action mode for every subsequent shot. Cock the hammer to get the feel of that. The single-action pull won't be particularly light, but it will be consistent. There will be a very slight palpable movement – it feels like a little bit of a "roll" – as the trigger comes back before it cleanly releases the cocked hammer. This, too, is helpful in achieving a surprise break, which prevents the shooter from anticipating the shot and pulling the gun off target the instant before the bullet is launched.

You're getting a sense of why shooters appreciate the Beretta. But only a sense. To fully share the experience, we have to head to the range.

On The Firing Line

With ear and eye protection in place and all range safety rules adhered to, it's time for the live-fire Beretta experience. As you would with any auto pistol, grasp the grip frame firmly in your dominant hand. The trigger finger should be up on the frame, completely clear of the trigger guard, and the web of your hand should be all the way up on the back, pressing firmly up against the grip tang. The gun's barrel should be in line with the long bones of your forearm. With the muzzle downrange, we're ready to load.

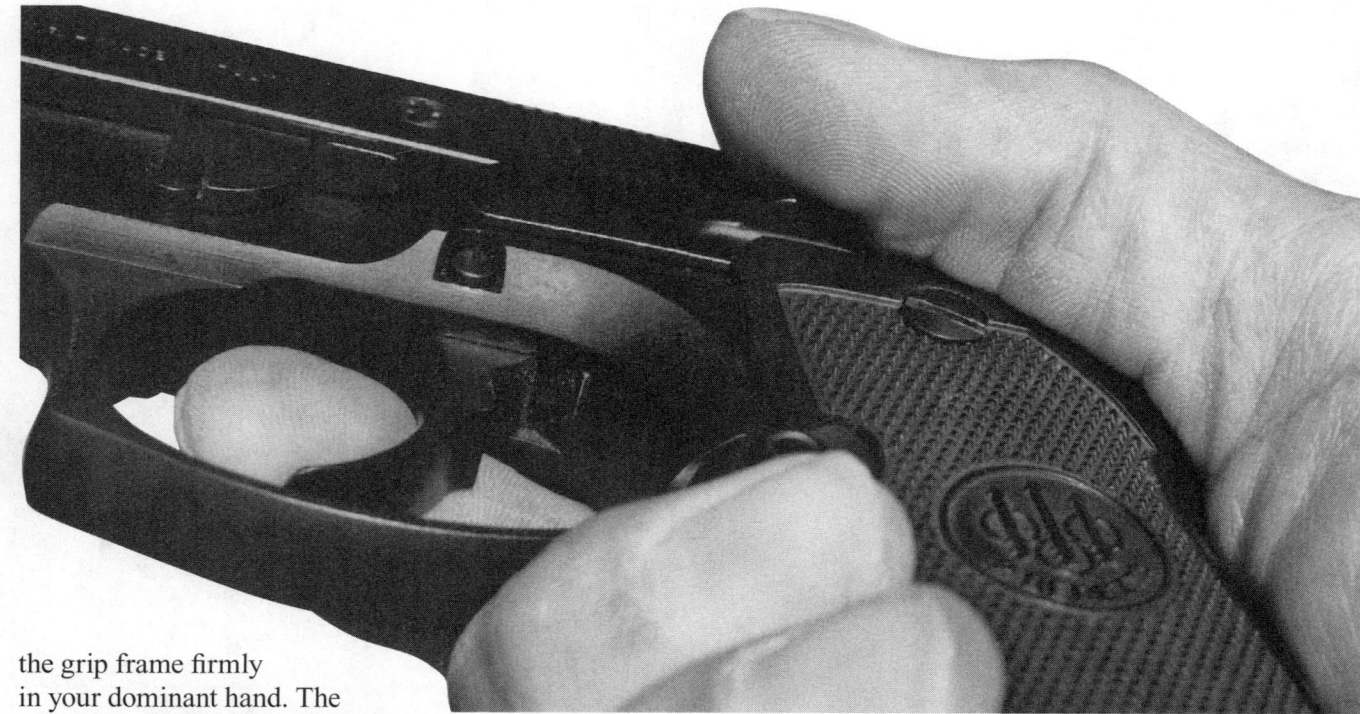

Grasp the magazine with your free hand. Your palm should be under the floorplate, and the topmost round in the cartridge stack should be right above your extended index finger. Bring the magazine to the opening in the butt and slide it in. With one of the double-stack Berettas, you'll notice that the wide opening in the butt combines with the tapered top of the magazine to allow a smooth and fumble-free insertion. It'll work best if you place the flat back of the magazine against the flat back of the magazine chute. Now drive the magazine firmly upward with your palm until you feel it click into place.

It comes with superb sights.

Its manual safety is as easy as any of its type to release at speed reflexively, and perhaps the single easiest.

If the slide is already locked back, you can give it a slight tug and release it to let it fly forward, chambering a round, or you can do the same thing by simply flicking down the slide stop lever with your weak hand.

Let your free hand take a proper supporting grasp. The index finger of the support hand will work best if it's under the trigger guard, not in front of it. Both hands should grasp firmly. Never mind what you've read in gun magazines about one hand applying 40 percent pressure and the other applying 60 percent pressure. That sort of thing constitutes a fine point for target shooters. The Beretta is a defensive pistol, and a pistol used in defense will be used when you're hyper. Grip hard, as you would in a fight; it's the way fighting handguns are designed to be held.

Now take your stance. You can pick from any of several, but execute your stance strongly. Weight should be on the forward foot. Upper body weight should be forward and into the gun. Feet should be at least shoulder-width apart. Always shoot from a position of strength.

Now that you're ready to fire, ease that trigger finger down from the frame and onto the trigger. You'll have more leverage if you can put the last crease on the finger (the palmar surface of the distal joint, if you want to get technical) center on the trigger. If

It has a famously smooth trigger pull. The Beretta is a classic example of a pistol more appreciated by shooters than theoreticians.

the finger doesn't reach that far, you can get by with the pad of the trigger finger, which is generally defined as the center of the whorl of the fingerprint. Now, holding the sights as tightly on target as you can, begin to press the trigger straight back. Let the actual instant of the discharge come as a surprise.

And now, as your Beretta discharges for the first time, there's a surprise for *you*: the pistol's famously light recoil. Across their entire line of semiautomatics, the Berettas are light-kicking guns. Let's digress a moment to examine that point.

The 9mm Beretta is famous in the military and at Camp Perry and on the police firing ranges for its easy kick. Yes, it's a 9mm, but it's a particularly soft-shooting 9mm. Some have theorized that the open top slide splits the recoil impulse into two directions that run back parallel to the barrel, and somehow softens the kick that way. I don't have enough background in physics to determine whether that could be true or not. Certainly, the broad backstrap of the 92's frame distributes the kick into the hand, but even the narrow backstrap of the M-series models seems to come back lightly, so it can't be entirely that. All we know is, a Model 92 is a light-kicking 9mm.

Power up to the Beretta 96 in caliber .40 S&W. This cartridge is notorious for its high slide velocity, relatively high pressure, and snappy recoil. Yet in the Beretta, a 180-grain subsonic .40 caliber round feels about like firing a +P 9mm.

Try the Cougar in any of its four calibers: 9mm Luger, .40 S&W, .357 SIG, and .45 ACP. The rotary breech mechanism really does seem to reduce recoil.

A Cougar 9mm seems, in my hand, to kick slightly less than even a full size Model 92. Part of that may also be that the Cougar's grip frame, being especially designed to allow more of the shooter's hand to wrap around it, gives the shooter more control and more leverage on the pistol, resulting in a sensation of less recoil and less muzzle jump.

In .40, the Cougar is an easy-shooting pistol. There's the good ratio of hand size to grip frame size, and the rotary breech thing. I can't apportion how much the light recoil is attributable to each feature. I can only observe that the Cougar is a particularly soft-shooting .40.

The Cougar in .357 SIG is one of the most controllable guns in its caliber. Spitting the equivalent of a full power .357 Magnum slug from a short-barrel revolver, the 125-grain jacketed hollow-point at 1,350 feet per second produces awesome wounds that tend to stop gunfights with a single solid hit. Its report is startlingly sharp, but its kick in the Beretta feels only like about a .38 Special revolver shot.

The Cougar .45 is very mild in its recoil. I can only presume that the rotating breech performs as advertised. A bunch of us were at the range shooting when I pulled out my Cougar .45 and passed it around. Everyone tried a couple of magazines. Each of us there had other .45s with us. They included Glock, SIG, and numerous 1911 pistols. The unanimous consensus was that with the same ammunition, the Beretta .45 kicked the least of all.

The .22s, of course, have negligible recoil. The Beretta Tomcat has the least recoil of any of the subcompact .32s. We've shot it next to the Seecamp and the Guardian, and there's just no contest. In the .380 caliber, thanks to their size, the Berettas are by far the most controllable guns in that chambering.

End of digression. Suffice to say that light recoil for the caliber is one of the advantages that the Beretta pistol – virtually any modern Beretta pistol – brings to the shooting bench.

Where were we? Ah, yes – we *were* at the shooting bench. Let's keep going. With a strong stance, that light recoil allows you an accelerated pace of accurate fire. You'll quickly get to where you can just about hold a sight picture as the slide comes back from the shot, with the sights staying in line with the target as they ride the slide. This means you can literally race the trigger and, at reasonablly close combat distances, keep every shot where you want it so long as you're bringing that controllable trigger straight back for every shot and not jerking the muzzle off the mark.

The slide locks back, signaling that your pistol is empty. There have been no malfunctions. This is as it should be. The Model 92 is a notoriously jam-free pistol. The Cougars have earned a similar reputation. The Beretta .25 is probably the most reliable gun in its caliber, and no one makes a more reliable .380.

Set down the gun. Confirm that it's clear to go downrange. Now, let's examine the target. If you've done your job as far as holding and squeezing, the shots should be in a nice, tight cluster. Pocket pistol and service pistol alike, Berettas are famous for their accuracy.

You've just learned why the Beretta is a shooter's gun. Its shooting characteristics don't get in the way of good shooting; they enhance good shooting. It's why those who hate the Beretta tend to be internet jockeys who collect often unverifiable beefs about a gun they've rarely if ever shot, and why those who love the Beretta tend to be serious shooters who shoot a lot.

In the end, the latter have more credibility than the former.

Manipulating the Beretta

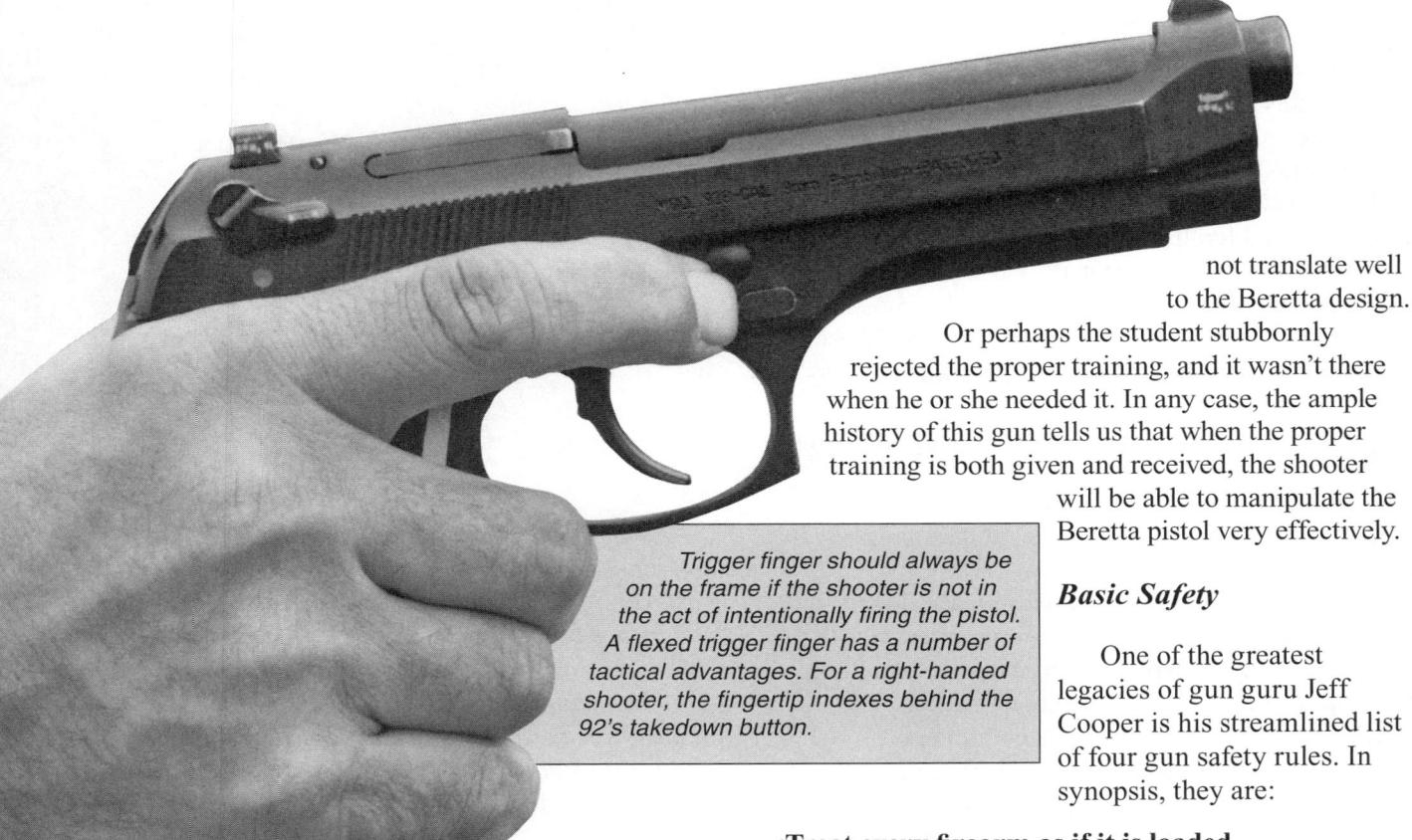

Trigger finger should always be on the frame if the shooter is not in the act of intentionally firing the pistol. A flexed trigger finger has a number of tactical advantages. For a right-handed shooter, the fingertip indexes behind the 92's takedown button.

The U.S. Military Beretta M9 pistol must appear complicated to the novice. After all, there is that bewildering array of levers and buttons. The fact is, though, that it's not particularly difficult to learn to operate and maintain. Field-stripping and reassembly are easy. So is emergency manipulation … *if* the shooter is trained properly. Errors in handling tend to be almost entirely traceable to absence of good training. Perhaps the erroneous shooter did not get any training at all; perhaps he or she got bad training, or training geared for another type of handgun which does not translate well to the Beretta design. Or perhaps the student stubbornly rejected the proper training, and it wasn't there when he or she needed it. In any case, the ample history of this gun tells us that when the proper training is both given and received, the shooter will be able to manipulate the Beretta pistol very effectively.

Basic Safety

One of the greatest legacies of gun guru Jeff Cooper is his streamlined list of four gun safety rules. In synopsis, they are:

- **Treat every firearm as if it is loaded.**
- **Never allow the firearm to point at anything you are not prepared to see destroyed.**
- **Never touch the trigger until you are prepared to fire.**
- **Always be certain of your target and what is behind it.**

Over the years, I've learned to modify Rule Three slightly to make it clearer:

- **Do not let the finger be in the trigger guard unless you are in the act of intentionally firing the weapon.**

For left-handed shooting, the trigger finger indexes on the frame behind the takedown lever. This position is called having the trigger finger "in register."

I say this because many have interpreted Cooper's Rule Three as meaning "On Target, On Trigger; Off Target, Off Trigger." There are problems with that. When the student holds someone at gunpoint, the student *is* literally "on target." If the finger is now on trigger as well, the stage has been set for a tragic unintentional discharge produced by postural disturbance, startle response, or interlimb response. These were defined as the primary causative factors in unintentional discharges many years ago by Dr. Roger Enoka, the first highly credentialed physiologist to directly address the problem.

With that caveat in mind, everyone who ever handles a firearm of any kind should internalize Cooper's four rules.

Handling of defensive firearms breaks down into two categories: *administrative* manipulation and *combat* manipulation. Administrative handling encompasses the routine loading, unloading, checking, etc. of the firearm in a condition of calmness. Combat handling, sometimes called emergency handling, encompasses those techniques the student will use when the firearm must be deployed for its intended defensive purpose. Though most people will only need to perform their combat manipulations in training and skill testing environments, we never know which of our students will be the unfortunate ones who require these skills for real. Therefore, they must be practiced seriously, as if they would have to be called into play to save human life before the day is over.

Let's offer a few tips for handling the Berettas. Remember that every manipulation of the pistol is one more small deposit in your "long term muscle memory account" that will be with you when you have to handle the weapon "on auto pilot" under extreme stress.

Always grasp the weapon's grip frame with the dominant hand, and let the non-dominant hand perform support functions such as exchanging magazines or manipulating the slide. This will reduce "overhandling" and will limit potential for fumbling.

When your gun is drawn, always keep it at least in the lower periphery of your vision, where you can see it without lowering your head. If you cannot see your own drawn gun, you are not in control of the weapon! If an assailant lunges for it from the shadows, his disarming attempt will probably succeed before you can react. If, however, the gun is where you can see it, your eye will also pick up the attack on the gun in time for you to counter it, if you know what to do and are ready to respond.

Keep the operating arm and hand clear of the business end. The tapered front of the slide on the Beretta 92 and 96 seems to invite the support hand to pinch it to push back the slide. Politely decline the invitation. This places the hand too close to the muzzle of what might be a loaded gun. There's a reason the Beretta folks put those slide grooves at the *back* of the slide: working the gun from there keeps the support hand out of harm's way.

Magazine Removal

Modern Beretta service pistols have magazine buttons located on the frame behind the trigger, the location most serious shooters deem optimum. The button is reversible for left-handers. That is, the gun comes from the factory with the button on the left side of the frame, placed for the thumb of the right-handed majority. For the southpaw, an armorer may move it to the right side.

This is an excellent idea. With the button now facing toward the wearer's body, it is protected from bumping against anything that could cause the magazine to prematurely release.

A left-handed shooter can activate a right-handed button with his trigger finger faster than most right-handers can do it with their thumbs. This is also a very safe method, in that it guarantees that the finger is off the trigger at a high-stress moment. If pure speed of reloading was the only concern, the southpaw would do well to leave the button on the left side of the frame, and a rightie might be wise to swap to the right side.

Unfortunately, reloading speed is not the only concern. The danger of something in the wearer's environment bumping against the exposed button and unseating the magazine – a seat belt, a counter-top the officer leans against, whatever – outweighs a fraction of a second increased speed between the 16th and the 17th rounds. If the magazine is accidentally dropped, defensive fire will cease after the *first* shot. Therefore, logic and caution tell us that the right-handed shooter should keep the button on the left side of the frame, and the left-handed shooter should keep it on the right side.

This means that either shooter will follow the usual protocol of pressing the magazine release button with the thumb of the shooting hand when the time

The safe, efficient Israeli Method for operating a Beretta's slide. The frame is grasped in firing hand, finger on frame, and support hand grasps slide as shown …

… he gun hand pushes forward, the support hand pulls back, exerting great force on the gun with minimum effort. Force can be magnified by putting your whole body into the technique …

… and, to chamber a round, the shooter then lets go and allows slide to fly forward. Note that on F-model Berettas, if the safety has been engaged prior, it remains on throughout the procedure and the pistol safely decocks itself. The Israeli technique holds the lever in the position it was in to start.

comes to drop the magazine out of the firearm. The push button magazine release in this location goes back to the pistol of Georg Luger at the turn of the 20th century. The Luger, and the Colt 1911 which followed it and further popularized this magazine release design, were slim-handled pistols with single-stack magazines. The typical Beretta is a double-stack design, necessitating a wider grip frame, which means that those with short thumbs may find the button more difficult to operate.

To better reach the button, the shooter wants to turn his hand on the gun (NOT turn the gun in his hand, which can bring the muzzle to an unsafe direction!) so the grip tang is directly over the proximal joint (base joint) of the index finger. This should extend the thumb's reach and leverage sufficiently to allow it to depress the magazine release button.

If the firing hand thumb still cannot press the button sufficiently to release the magazine, the support hand can come in with a straight thumb and press the button straight in. By hooking the fingers as shown in accompanying photography, the falling magazine can be captured by the fingers.

This is also the most natural way to remove a magazine from a Model 950 or one of the other older-style Berettas whose magazine release button is located toward the lower right corner of the left grip panel.

Some older Berettas, such as the Model 34, have a conventional "European style" butt-heel magazine release catch. The most efficient way to operate one of these is to press the catch to the rear with the ball of the thumb, and use the middle finger to catch the lip of the floorplate and sort of "hook" the magazine out of the pistol.

Locking The Slide Back

Most Beretta pistols have slide lock levers located on the left side of the frame. Those modern Berettas that do not are of tip-up design (Model 86, Model 950, Tomcat), and rather than locking their slide open to clear them, the shooter will activate the tip-up release lever until the barrel pops upward. The chambered cartridge can then be removed with thumb and forefinger, and/or the empty barrel checked and confirmed clear.

There are several ways to operate the slide lock lever to lock the slide open, and the means you choose will depend on range of hand movement, hand size, hand dominance, and similar factors. First, you can simply insert an empty magazine and retract the slide, which will lock open when you release pressure.

When you remove the magazine, the slide will remain to the rear until it is released by a rearward tug, or by a downward pressure on the slide stop lever.

It is more efficient, and probably safer, to lock the slide open without a magazine of any kind in the pistol. If you are right-handed, press upward on the slide stop lever with your right thumb and maintain pressure. With your left hand, retract the slide all the way. Now let it go slightly forward until you feel it stop, and *voila*; the slide is locked open.

If you are left-handed, maintain the upward pressure on the slide stop with your left index finger (it'll probably contact at around the median joint), then use your right hand to retract the slide as above.

If dexterity or range of movement issues do not allow this, the left-handed shooter can grasp the slide with the right hand, placing the right thumb on the left side of the slide and all four fingers on the right side. The grasp should place the right thumb level with where a live cartridge would be in the Beretta's firing chamber. Now, retract the slide with the right hand. The right thumb should now be in proximity to the slide stop lever. Thumb the lever up, ease the slide slightly forward, and it should lock open.

Conventional Slide Operation

To either put a round in the chamber, clear a round out of the chamber, or examine the chamber, the slide will have to be run to the rear. This is variously known as "jacking" the slide, "racking" the slide, "running," the slide, etc. Two primary techniques have evolved over the years. They are known as "American style" and "Israeli style."

The "American" technique goes back to the Colt pistol in the early 20th century. The right-handed shooter grasps the grip-frame with his right hand, and places his left hand palm-down over the top of the slide, with his thumb on the left side of the slide and the four fingers on the right. The left hand then "jacks" the slide in a movement going toward the elbow of the gun arm. The "American" technique has also been called the "overhand" technique, and was dubbed the "straddle" technique by gun expert Dave Spaulding, a term which aptly describes the manner in which the digits of the hand straddle the slide.

This technique causes two concerns, one of which is specific to Beretta-type pistols. First, with any type of gun, it tends to result in the support hand forearm getting dangerously close to the muzzle, and even bringing the gun in to where it is pointed at the shooter's own abdomen in extreme cases. Second, with the Beretta Model 92 style (or S&W, or Ruger, or Walther PPK, or any other autoloader with a wing-shaped, slide-mounted safety) this movement will tend to push the lever down into the "on-safe" position.

What we condition ourselves to do when calm is what we will almost invariably revert to when we are under stress. If we have to clear a defective round in the middle of a firefight and get the gun immediately back up and running, the last thing we want to do is inadvertently on-safe our pistol. Yet this is just what the "straddle" technique is likely to do. My friend and colleague Ken Hackathorn is a Beretta fan, as are many of his students, and he has always used the American technique. He told me that it so often inadvertently on-safed the Beretta, that he had to teach his students a drill that included "work the slide, off safe the pistol again, and prepare to continue firing."

Both of these concerns are effectively eliminated by the second method, the "Israeli style," also known as the "slingshot." As the last nickname describes, the movement mimics the use of a slingshot in that the gun hand holds the weapon pointed straight ahead, while the support hand comes in and pulls the slide to the rear. The support hand's grasp in the Israeli technique is opposite that of the American method, in that the left hand will grab the slide with the thumb on the right and the fingers on the left.

This is commonly done in a sloppy fashion, with only thumb and forefinger in contact with the slide. That's weak, and doing it wrong has given the slingshot method an undeserved reputation as a feeble technique. To do it properly, place the entire weak hand thumb on the slide, from thumbprint to "drumstick," and securely grasp the other side of the slide with all four fingers.

Now, maintaining firm grasp with both hands and of course keeping fingers out of the trigger guard, turn the entire body as if throwing a karate-style reverse punch. That is, the dominant side leg is at the rear, the knee slightly off a full lock. As you push forward on the frame with the dominant hand and pull

Steve Denney demonstrates the Israeli slide operation method from another angle. Note where the term "slingshotting the slide" comes from ...

... as the whole body's force makes slide retraction easy.

back on the slide with the support hand, straighten the rear leg. This drives the strong side hip forward, putting the entire body weight into the technique, and also helping the support hand on the slide to pull backward. In this way, the entire body goes into the movement, making it very powerful.

The Israeli technique tends to keep the muzzle pointed straight ahead, preventing the dangers of the muzzle sweeping the forward arm, the body, or an adjacent shooter as often occurs with the American technique. Moreover, it is "Beretta friendly." The thumb and its drumstick on one side of the slide, and the fingers on the other, tend to pinch the safety lever into the position it was in when the hand came onto the slide. That is, if the movement began with the safety catch in the "fire" position, it will remain in the "fire" position. If it began with the gun on safe, it will stay on safe.

Whenever drawing the slide back, remember that you're not only working against the recoil spring, which is located under the barrel and parallel to it; you're also working against the powerful mainspring in the back of the grip frame, which is holding the hammer down against the slide. If the effort is too much for the given shooter, the hammer can be drawn back to the cocked position by the free hand. (This, of course, will require taking an F-type Beretta off-safe.) This will alleviate the resistance of the mainspring and make it easier to retract the slide.

Confirming Unloaded Status

When checking to make sure a pistol is unloaded, it is always a good idea to check by sight and feel. Peer into the firing chamber to make visually certain that it is empty, and actually look into the magazine well to make sure there is no magazine in place. (Just pressing the magazine release button is no guarantee that the magazine has fallen free of the gun, no matter what type of semi-automatic pistol you might be dealing with.)

To check a semi-automatic pistol by feel, keep the grip frame in the dominant hand and use the little finger of the non-dominant hand, usually the narrowest of the ten digits, as a probe. Actually feel the firing chamber to make certain that it is empty, and actually probe the magazine well to be certain that it is not occupied.

The open slide design of the Beretta 92 and similar pistols is, to my way of thinking, a safety feature. An enclosed slide, when retracted, often creates an overhang in which a live cartridge can "hide" in the firing chamber. This is particularly likely to occur during difficult light conditions: total darkness, for example, or overhead sunlight that creates very deep shadows inside the gun. But even with the open slide, take nothing for granted. Examine by sight and feel.

I do guns for a living. I handle them a lot. Exposure equals risk. One reason I've never injured myself with an inadvertent discharge is that I employ all the many layers of "safety nets" described above. It's sort of like handling a prisoner: you never drop your guard. I don't consider my prisoner safe until he has been strip-searched, cavity searched, and secured in his cell. It's the same way with a pistol. In a "cold range" setting, such as the typical pistol match, in which guns are unloaded unless the shooter is on the

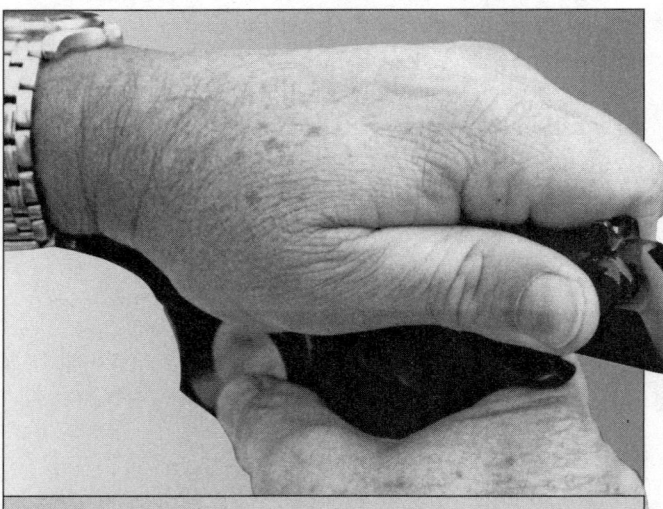

Overhand American-style or "saddle"-style slide operation brings a number of problems …

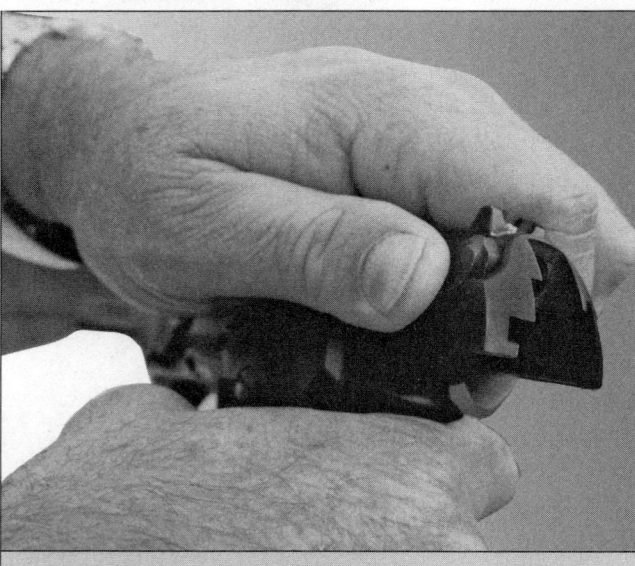

… one of them is that the thumb tends to inadvertently "on-safe" an F-series Beretta.

firing line and has been instructed to load, I use the same protocol. I visually examine the empty firing chamber and the empty magazine well (strip search). I then probe the magazine well and firing chamber with the little finger to confirm that they are empty (cavity search). Finally, I snap the unloaded training gun back in its holster (secured in its cell). It's a simple analogy, and it works.

Confirming Loaded Status

The service pistol, the carry gun, and usually the home defense firearm will be kept loaded. Confirming loaded condition requires a different set of safety protocols than confirming unloaded status. Different jobs, different approaches, each approach tailored for doing that particular job best.

First, on-safe your Beretta if the model in question gives you that option. This adds another safety net to the procedure. Remember, we now *know* we are handling a loaded, potentially lethal weapon: it is all the more important to *keep the fingers away from the trigger, and keep the muzzle pointed in a safe direction!*

Second, release the magazine, maintaining control of the magazine in the non-dominant hand. Sometimes, the magazine's design and the lighting conditions will allow you to confirm the loaded status without even removing it entirely from the grip frame. The eyes may be able to see cartridges in the magazine windows, as those openings in the magazine are called. The hand may be able to tell by feel that the magazine is loaded, although it is a rare practitioner so deft that he can tell the exact number of cartridges by the feel of the magazine.

Once loaded status of the magazine has been confirmed, reinsert it until you feel it lock. Since this is an administrative procedure, rather than an emergency combat procedure it can be done at leisure. Give the magazine a little tug to make sure it is firmly seated in the pistol.

Next, it is critical to check the chamber. Many tragic accidents have occurred over more than a century because careless or ignorant people did not understand that it was the cartridge in the firing chamber, not any of those in the magazine that made a pistol capable of discharging.

Keeping the muzzle in a safe direction and fingers clear of the trigger guard, maintain a firm grasp of the grip frame in the firing hand and retract the slide slightly with the support hand. If the hammer of the pistol is down, the shooter is working against both the mainspring, which holds the hammer firmly against the rear of the frame, and the recoil spring which rides under the barrel and parallel to it. When this resistance is suddenly overcome, the slide can be inadvertently pulled back farther than necessary to check the chamber, with the result that the cartridge flies out of the gun or gets jammed in the mechanism. To keep this from happening, and also to make slide retraction easier, if the pistol is not double-action-only in design the hammer can be cocked. On some models, such as the F-series Beretta fighting pistols, this will put a loaded, cocked, off-safe pistol in the shooter's hand, so particular care is required.

The slide should be retracted just enough to see if there is a round in the chamber. The index finger of the dominant hand, which should have been lying dormant along the frame during this procedure, can now be lifted until its tip enters the chamber area, where it should be able to feel the cartridge casing. We now have both visual and tactile confirmation of a loaded chamber. This is particularly easy – and ambidextrous – with those Berettas that have the open-slide design.

However, an even simpler and more efficient technique exists, though it will

The author recommends against this popular technique for chamber-checking or slide jacking. The hand comes too close to the "business end." It's safer to use grasping grooves at the rear of slide.

Here's a safe, easy way to chamber-check a Beretta with safety and/or decocking levers on the slide. Fingertips take a pincers position on the levers and the thumb is placed on grip tang of this 96G …

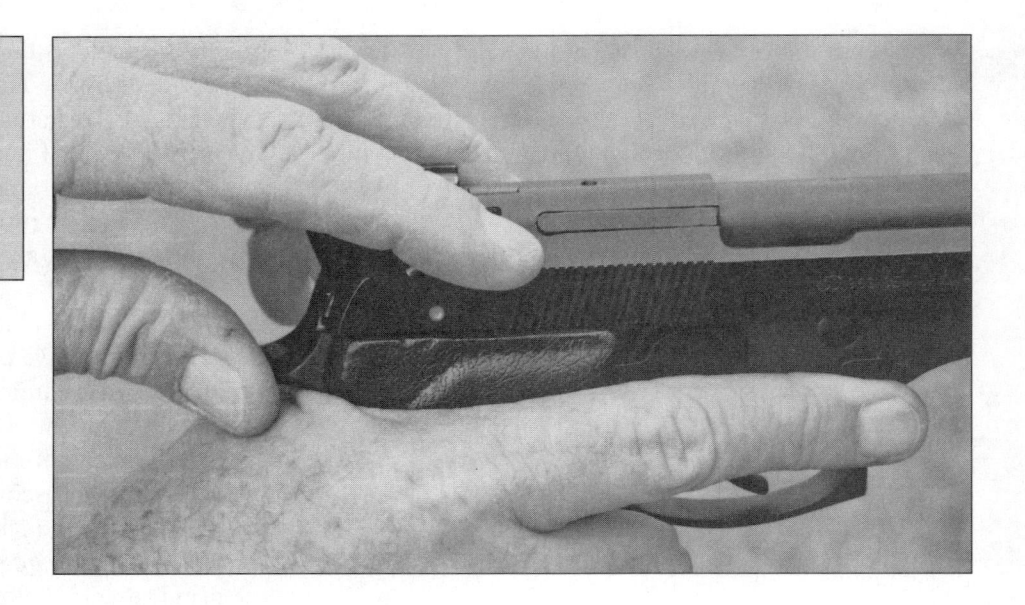

… the digits squeeze, exerting force to the rear. Note that even on decocker-only G series, the levers are forced down into the "safe" position …

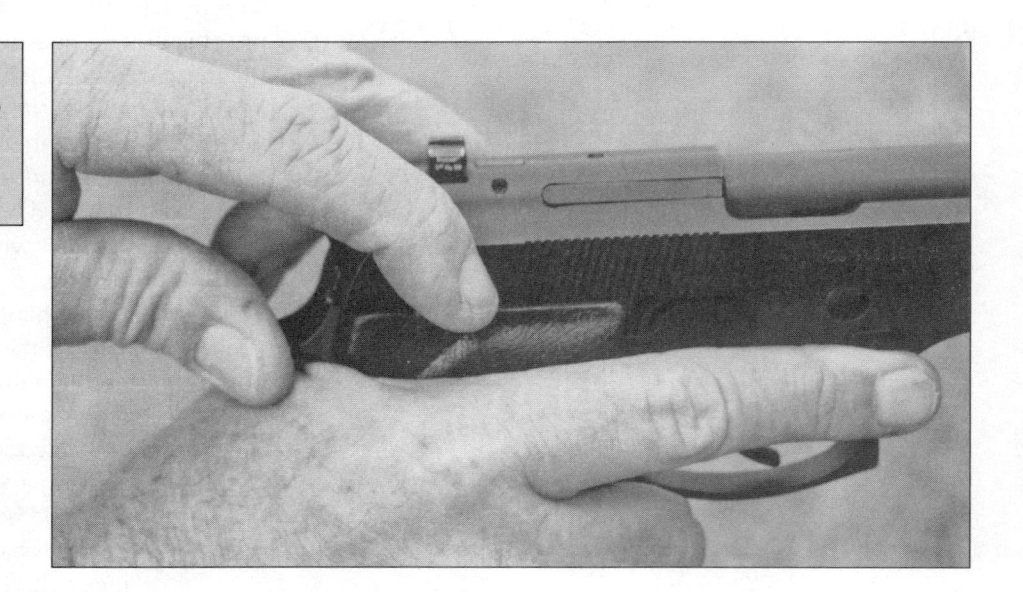

… and slide is easily retracted far enough to check chamber, which in this case is empty.

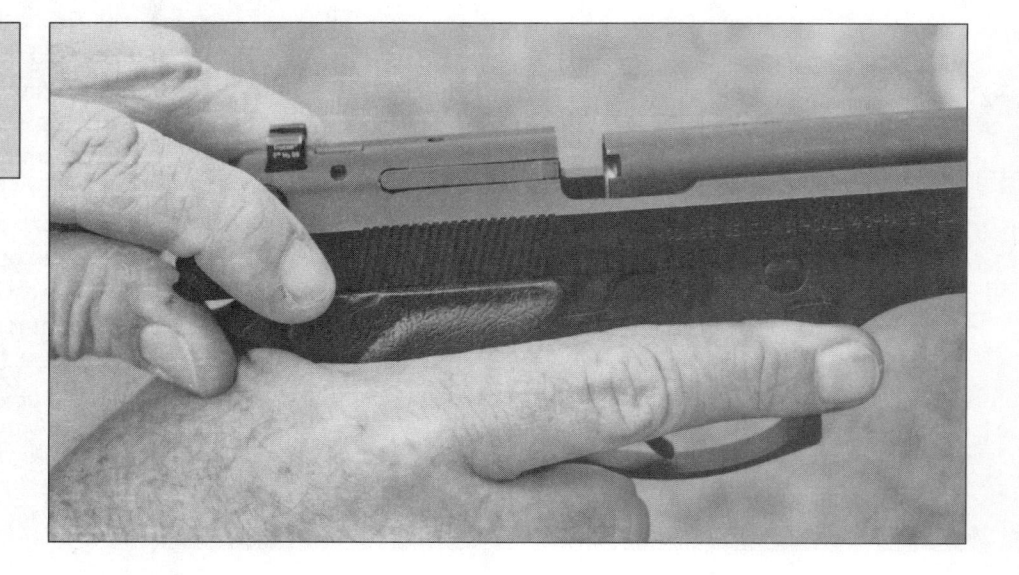

only work with those pistols which have ambidextrous slide-mounted safety/decocking levers – F and G series Model 92, 96, and Cougar pistols, in the Beretta line, or the BDA .380 produced by Beretta for Browning. Keep the pistol in the dominant hand, grasped around the grip frame, trigger finger on frame. Bring the support hand in from behind. Curl the middle finger and index finger of the support hand like hooks and use them to press the slide-mounted levers down and then pull to the rear, while the support thumb braces on the grip tang as shown in the photos. Even a G series 92, 96, or Cougar will in effect be "on safe" while the fingers are holding the levers in this position. Pushing toward the muzzle with the thumb and pulling toward the rear with the middle and index fingers of the supporting hand, a minimal effort will overcome both mainspring and recoil spring resistance and allow the slide to be retracted to where the chamber can be observed. This method will also work with S&W, Ruger, and other pistols that share the design feature of ambidextrous slide-mounted safety/decock levers.

NOTE: Some Beretta pistols have loaded chamber indicators. On the 92 or 96, for example, the extractor performs this function, standing slightly outward from the slide when the extractor is locked around a cartridge rim. This allows another verification of loaded chamber by sight and feel. However, this writer and Beretta USA and the publisher *all* believe that one should never trust any mechanical safety to the exclusion of human examination of the weapon. This is a long-standing tenet of firearms safety. By all means check the loaded chamber indicator, but do not let that be the sole determinant of whether or not there is a round in the chamber.

Finally, remember that a loaded chamber check does not necessarily determine that the cartridge in the chamber is a live round in perfect order. A spent casing, or a dud round with a dead primer will mimic a live round in terms of appearance, feel, and activation of a loaded chamber indicator.

Safely Holstering

Loaded guns are normally carried in holsters. A number of accidental discharges have historically occurred when the shooter was drawing the loaded gun, or reholstering it. In the Pacific Northwest, one of my colleagues at another well-known firearms school was teaching a class when a female officer shot herself in the leg with a Beretta 92. She was wearing a skeletonized belt-slide holster in a position that rode too high for a comfortable draw on a female's body.

As she awkwardly drew, the front sight snagged on the opening at the bottom of the sparely-cut holster. Her finger had gone prematurely to the trigger guard, and she was carrying the 92 off-safe. As her hand continued to tug mightily at the trapped gun, the sympathetic nature of the muscles in her hand and arm caused her trigger finger to contract, firing the pistol while it was still in the holster and inflicting the wound in her leg.

Accidental discharges occur in holstering as well. I was retained as expert witness for the defense of one of the nation's largest holster-makers after they were sued by a deputy sheriff who shot himself in the leg while wearing one of their duty rigs. He had been using all department-issue gear: Beretta 92F pistol, Winchester 147-grain subsonic JHP ammunition, and the holster in question, a level II security rig designed by the sheriff's department and manufactured exclusively for them.

On the day in question, he had to shoot a vicious pit bull. It took several rounds of the low-velocity 9mm ammunition to stop the dog, and when the time came to holster his weapon, the deputy was understandably quite shaken. He had been taught to decock and leave the lever down in the on-safe position after firing, once the danger was over, but he failed to do this. He had been taught to take his finger off the trigger and out of the trigger guard in those circumstances, but he failed to do that too.

With the hammer still cocked, the pistol of course still off-safe, *and his finger still on the trigger,* he proceeded to thrust the pistol firmly into the holster. The holster had been designed to cover the trigger guard for obvious safety reasons, so before the pistol was seated, the trigger finger hit the edge of the holster. This, of course, stopped the finger in place, but his movement continued and the Beretta kept going, forcing the now-single action trigger against the finger. BANG! The pistol discharged, sending a bullet into his leg.

The holster had been designed with an open front, so officers who had habituated to a push-forward movement with their old breakfront revolver holsters before the Beretta was adopted could use the same movement with the new auto pistols. The open front of the holster, coupled with the reliable open top slide design of the Beretta, allowed the 92F to cycle in the holster, cocking itself as it chambered a fresh round.

Under pressure, stressed-out people tend to perform the same ineffective things in a sometimes-endless loop. Now not only flustered but wounded by a self-inflicted bullet, the officer tried to shove the pistol into the holster *again!* BANG! The pistol discharged a second time, pumping yet another bullet through the holster and into his own leg. Fortunately, at about this point he figured out what was going on, got control of himself, and stopped shooting himself to pieces.

Was this unfortunate? Certainly. Was it the fault of the holster? Not at all, and that's why I was comfortable speaking in the holster-maker's defense.

Proper use of the holster will prevent accidental discharges! The trigger finger should be inserted into the trigger guard only *after* the draw. Indeed, if the user simply follows the amplified version of Jeff Cooper's Rule Three cited earlier in this chapter – *the finger should not be in the trigger guard unless the shooter intends to immediately fire* – accidental shooting during the draw will be eliminated.

For holstering, I have taught for more than 20 years a technique that has proven effective in preventing unintentional discharges during this process. First, *the trigger finger should be outside the trigger guard.* This has the added advantage of "pointing" the gun into the scabbard and making the holstering process smoother. The trigger finger should feel the leather or plastic of the holster beneath its fingerprint, an additional felt index that assures that the finger is not going to snag the trigger. Finally, *the thumb should be on the hammer of the pistol, holding it in place.* If the pistol is a cocked and locked Billennium or 950 series, the thumb holds the hammer back, and if it feels the hammer coming forward it can stop the movement and thus prevent an accidental discharge in the holster. If the pistol is a double-action, exposed-hammer design such as the Model 92 or Model 96 series, the thumb holds the properly decocked hammer down. If something has interdicted the trigger, the thumb will feel the hammer begin to rise and can stop all movement, while the shooter analyzes what is going on and rectifies the situation.

One concern with striker-fired pistols, such as the .22 caliber Beretta Neos, is that there is no hammer that can be controlled by the thumb during the holstering process. Therefore, it is all the more critical that the shooter holster the weapon carefully. While this writer generally prefers to holster by feel for tactical reasons (i.e., not having to take the eyes off the danger zone in front of the shooter), I will make a point of glancing down when holstering a striker-fired pistol to assure that no poorly sized safety strap, no twig caught on the shirt or holster while rolling on the ground, is going to interdict the trigger and cause my loaded pistol to fire while I'm inserting it into the holster.

Safe Storage

Obviously, when the gun is not on our person, it should be secured where unauthorized personnel cannot reach it. I am familiar with a number of lawsuits against a number of firearms manufacturers – yes, including Beretta – that grew out of tragic accidental shootings. In some, the allegation was that the pistol in question fired in an unauthorized idiot's hands because it did not have a manual safety. In some others, the fool who pulled the trigger while the gun was pointed at an unoffending human did so because he did not realize that the magazine being out did not mean that there was not still a live round in the chamber. In these, the plaintiffs' allegation was that the gun was unsafe because it did not have a magazine disconnector safety.

I've turned down offers to speak as an expert witness for such plaintiffs, and have accepted the request of defense counsel to speak on their behalf as an expert. The reason is that in all the above cases, the proximate cause – the legal term for "the real reason it happened" – was that someone left a loaded gun, or an unloaded gun in proximity to ammunition, where an unauthorized person could reach it.

Gun safes, lock boxes, and gun locks exist in abundance. It is the gun owner's responsibility to take advantage of this and make certain that at all times, any firearm is secure from the hands of those who might do something stupid, or intentionally dangerous, with it. The firearm, in essence being an extended-range drill, can be considered a power tool. In this, safe storage and competency of users are as critical with firearms as with any other power tool in this industrialized and supposedly advanced society.

Drawing the Beretta

The defensive pistol is primarily a reactive weapon. Swift, certain, decisive draw of this instrument is one of the absolutely critical skills at arms.

Drawing technique has to be tailored to the gun, the wearer, and the wardrobe. Degrees of concealment will affect speed of draw in an almost directly inverse relationship, that is, the more deeply the pistol is concealed the longer it will take to draw and bring the pistol to bear.

Some techniques will work better than others. For many years in the old days, experts taught the "scoop draw" in which the gun hand described a semi-circular pattern of constant movement which never came to a dead stop, but instead "scooped" the gun out of the holster along the way. The only Beretta this will work with is a Stampede single-action revolver, and then only if it's drawn from an open-top cowboy holster. The scoop draw was developed for use with revolvers and open-top holsters, and is not efficient with any other gun/scabbard combination.

As shown in the accompanying photos, the rounded shape of a revolver's grip frame naturally allows the fingers to scoop the frontstrap at the beginning of the draw, allowing the rest of the hand to close firmly on the gun somewhat later in the process. Because the hand comes to the gun from below the grip-frame, the thumb is perfectly situated to slide into position to cock the large, forward-sitting hammer of a single-action revolver such as the Stampede. The hand can be in constant movement from the beginning of the draw to the release of the shot.

All other Berettas are semiautomatics. They have flatter grip shapes, each with a tang at the top rear. The grip tang may have a slight curve going over the back of the firing hand. Hitting this spot exactly right is extremely difficult when coming up to the gun in a scoop draw. Moreover, the modern holster used for duty is likely to have some sort of securing device, and almost all of these are more easily operated by a hand coming down on the gun from above than coming up to the gun from below. This is why the scoop draw is not particularly well suited to modern-design guns and holsters. It's why they're better drawn in a more modern two-step method.

The Two-Step Draw

Even in the single, hopefully uninterrupted movement of a scoop draw, getting a gun out of a holster is actually a two-phase process. The first step is *access*. This is where the hand makes its way to the gun, takes a draw-to-fire grasp, and releases whatever securing mechanisms may anchor the firearm in the holster. It is the more complex of the two steps, and by far the most dependent on fine-motor coordination and skill. The second step is *presentation*. This is where the hand brings the gun out of the holster and either on target, or into whatever "ready" position the user has chosen. This is more of a simple, raw, gross motor skill and is therefore the easiest part to learn, though it can certainly be refined for greater speed, certainty, and efficiency.

While both steps take place in any draw, the difference between them is much more distinct with modern guns. The draw must be adapted to a secured holster versus a simple open-top with no restraining devices. It must be further adapted if there is a manual safety to release. Some users – most Israelis, for instance, and most U.S. Army personnel issued the Beretta – may even have to jack an initial round from the magazine into the empty firing chamber before the first shot can be fired. Subtle techniques of the draw may also change between draw to a one-handed position versus draw to a two-handed firing stance.

Strong-Side Hip Draw

Begin by getting the hand above the gun. Now, bring it down onto the backstrap of the pistol with the web of the hand high into the grip tang. Keeping the index finger clear and "disarticulated" – acting separately – let the other three fingers wrap firmly around the grip frame. The upper edge of the middle finger should be in contact with the bottom of the trigger guard.

It is at this point that the thumb presses against the paddle to release the safety strap on a thumb-break holster. Depending on the type of holster, other security devices may have to be released, such as the second strap on the most popular type of police security rig, which is popped with the tip of the middle finger as the hand takes its grasp, simultaneous with the thumb's release of the first strap. Some holsters will require a downward push, a rearward tug, or a forward shove to release from a securing inner niche, while others may require the shooter to twist the butt slightly to clear an internal locking niche.

Now, the regular draw can commence. (We'll discuss manipulation of the safety catch later). The most efficient draw will be a "rock and lock," in which as soon as the muzzle has cleared the forward part of the holster, the muzzle is rocked upward parallel to the ground and in line with the target the shooter is facing. This allows the gun to be fired with effect as soon as the muzzle clears holster in case the target is a fast-closing threat. The gun is now pushed forward to the target, rising until the sights or at least the top of the pistol are in line with the shooter's eyes. If the shooter is drawing to a two-handed stance, the support hand should come in from behind the muzzle as the gun is being pushed forward toward the target.

Safety Lever Manipulation

Not every Beretta pistol comes with a manual safety lever, but some do. Taking that lever from its "on safe" position to "off safe" is of course a necessary part of the draw. However, not all Beretta pistols have manual safety levers that work in the same direction, nor are all of them carried "on safe." Therefore, some conditional branching is required. Let's look at it design by design.

The Slide-Mounted Safety Lever, as on the Beretta 92F series, renders the gun inoperative when the lever is down, and ready to fire when the lever is up and parallel with the gun's barrel. Many shooters and instructors find this more awkward than with frame-mounted safeties, which lie lower in relation to the shooter's thumb and typically work in the opposite directions. As noted in the chapter *Manipulating the Beretta*, the safety catch on the slide can be popped off with a straight thrust of the thumb at a .45 degree upward angle toward the ejection port. If hand size and shape permit, this can be accomplished with a downward sweep of the thumb that activates the spring

Left: Steve Denney demonstrates a hip draw from concealment. Support hand blades at front of body, to ward off close threats and keep that hand out of the gun's path, as strong hand's fingertips clear back the vest ...

Center: ... the hand now sweeps to the gun, coming down on top. With fingertips touching the body, the edge of hand automatically clears the vest ...

Right: ... with the web of the hand at the grip tang and the trigger finger straight, the draw of Beretta begins ...

assist in the mechanism and pops the lever upward.

Remember that a safety strap over the back of the hammer will impede access of the shooter's thumb to the area of the safety until the gun is coming up and out of the holster. Because I often wear thumb-breaks, I've conditioned myself to wait until the draw is underway before I release the safety. I've watched myself doing it on tape, and appear to be popping the safety about the time the muzzle is starting to come up on target in the "rock and lock" phase of the draw. Doing it this way gives you almost universal adaptability to the different types of holsters you may wear.

If the holster is *always* going to be an open-top – and if the safety lever is not blocked by a piece of leather designed to protect the gun's slide from your sweaty body, and your soft skin from the hard metal – the safety can be "popped" while the gun is still in the leather. If we are dealing with a double-action pistol, it is safe to be carried with the lever in the "fire" position the whole time anyway, so it's equally safe to push the lever to that point while the gun is still in the holster.

Some prefer not to take the safety catch "off" until the gun is on target *and* the intention to immediately fire has been formulated. I can respect that. It extends the manual safety's "proprietary nature to the user" feature into the time the gun is drawn, in case a violent opponent disarms the user of his drawn gun. However, personally, I see the "on-safe" gun as insurance against a disarm while the pistol is holstered. Once I've drawn it, I want the gun "turned on." With a long, heavy, double-action pull to help ward off unintentional discharge, I'm comfortable with it being off-safe once it has been drawn.

The Frame-Mounted Safety Lever found on some Berettas needs to be operated differently, for sometimes obvious and sometimes less obvious reasons. Beretta's own .22, .25, and .32 pocket pistols of the current generation, and their .380s, have the safety catch mounted on the frame where it would be on the old 1911 style. Up is "safe," and down is "fire." There are certain advantages to this style.

Because the flexor muscles of the hand are stronger than the extensor muscles, and because the frame-mounted safety rides lower on the gun and therefore closer to the thumb, most authorities believe that this type of "safety catch" is inherently easier to reach than the slide-mounted type.

Because the thumb curls down when this type of lever is disengaged, there is less likelihood that either thumb will ride the slide stop and cause the slide to fail to lock back when the gun runs empty.

However, there are some other considerations. The slide-mounted lever of an F-series 92 or Cougar can be flicked to "fire" in the holster because these are double-action pistols. One is not drawing a cocked, off-safe gun. This is not necessarily the case with the Berettas that have frame-mounted safeties.

Many of the double-action Berettas with frame-

Left: ... the "rock and lock" phase occurs, with the muzzle coming up as soon as it clears leather, the trigger finger still clear of the guard. The 92F's safety comes off at this point ...

Center: ... the gun is already on target as the hands meet. Now, a forward thrust ...

Right: ... carries Steve into the firing stance.

mounted safeties can optionally be carried cocked and locked. Some *have* to be carried cocked and locked when there is a round in the chamber: the 950 series of pocket pistols, for example, or the Billennium variation of the Model 92. That is because these are single-action pistols. If one thumbs off the safety when the drawing hand takes its grasp on a still-holstered gun, the shooter is drawing a cocked, off-safe pistol that only requires a light touch on the trigger to make it discharge. Most of us consider that manifestly unsafe.

Therefore, with this style of Beretta, the safety catch should not be released until the gun is on target. It would be tempting to say, "Don't worry about the safety with the double-action versions," but that would beg the issue. Habits developed with a Model 86 set for double-action will translate to the Beretta that the owner has inserted cocked and locked into the holster. Thus, it is better to get into the habit of always leaving this style of Beretta on-safe until firing, not just drawing, is required.

In addition to this habituation factor, there is a role model factor. Each of us is the role model for fellow shooters, brother and sister officers, etc. who may be on the firing line with us and may look to us as an example of what they should be doing. Many years ago, I was present on the Trail Glades public shooting range outside Miami, Florida. A gentleman with a Taurus PT92 9mm pistol, which apparently was new to him, was shooting at a position adjacent to a more experienced handgunner who that day was shooting a Beretta 92. Now, those two guns look a great deal alike, as well they should since the Taurus was cloned from earlier model Berettas when first produced under license in Brazil. The Taurus on the line that day was an older model, whose hammer had to be lowered by hand to achieve the double-action position.

However, the Taurus shooter noticed that the Beretta shooter next to him was decocking and firing his first shot double-action, every time he loaded the gun. Quickly thumbing the decocking lever, the Beretta man appeared to the newcomer to be decocking the gun in a flicker of movement, which was indeed the case. The new shooter with the Taurus asked the old hand with the Beretta, "How do you do that?"

Apparently not expecting to be in teaching mode that day, the shooter with the Beretta didn't verbally explain the operation of his gun. He just cocked the hammer, then flicked the decocking lever of the 92

Top: At a combat match, Ayoob draws on target when the range officer behind him activates the timer …

Middle: … and shoots that target, spins and shoots a second on the flank with his 92G …

Bottom: … and comes to low ready, finger in register, to look for other threats before decocking.

rapidly. It appeared to the Taurus shooter that the man had pulled the trigger to lower the hammer.

The Taurus man then swung his loaded, cocked Taurus downward and pulled the trigger.

BANG! The pistol predictably discharged, sending a 9mm bullet through his own foot.

I can't really blame the shooter with the Beretta. He had come to the range to work on his own skills, and was not prepared to teach anything to newcomers. Without much thinking about it, he had just quickly demonstrated, not realizing that quick demonstrations don't show nearly as much as slow demonstrations accompanied by verbal explanation. I don't think anyone can blame him for the accident the Taurus shooter inflicted upon himself. Nor can one blame the Taurus or its design. In the end, it was the new shooter with the Brazilian pistol who had failed to meet the common-sense obligation to learn about his weapon if he didn't understand it.

Still, this incident points up the fact that the role model factor needs to be considered when we adopt a "manual of arms" for any given firearm.

Cross-Draw

When the handgun is carried on the hip opposite the dominant hand, butt forward, it is said to be in a cross-draw position. This style of carry has fallen increasingly out of favor in past decades, but has seen

Upper: Only draw when it's safe to do so. At an IDPA match in Jacksonville, FL, the author starts facing uprange at a "mailbox" ...

Lower: ... on the signal, he spins behind the mailbox for cover, only now reaching for the Langdon Beretta in aSparks IWB holster so he doesn't "cross" spectators and range staff ...

Lower right: ... and only then shoots the targets. Concealing garments normally required by IDPA were waived because of extreme heat at this match, which Ayoob won with the Beretta 9mm.

a small return to popularity in two areas. One is wear by females, and the other is wear while seated.

The concealment holsters that ride high on or behind the strong side hip were developed by and for males. Females have proportionally shorter torsos, and higher and wider hips; on them, the same holsters force the gun butt painfully into the ribs and carry so high that the wearer needs to be double-jointed to draw smoothly. However, these problems disappear when the same gun is carried cross-draw. While men have trouble reaching a cross-draw holster that is far enough back to be concealed by an open coat, women don't: their narrower torso and proportionally longer and more limber arms are now an advantage instead of a disadvantage.

When carjacking became the hot-button *crime du jour,* handgunners looked for quicker ways to reach their weapons while seat-belted behind a steering wheel. An answer put forth by some holster makers was a cross-draw that carried the pistol on a shallow, almost horizontal angle at the belt, just to the weak side of the navel or sometimes directly over the lap. The "counter carjack" holster tended to be much like the brassiere holster in that a lot of people bought them, but few wore them more than once because they were impractical. The gun was clearly visible to any passerby walking on the sidewalk or seated in a higher vehicle. It became glaringly obvious when the driver stepped out of the car, and it was a hassle to remove it at such moments.

Finally, the cross-draw holster is something of an orthopedic gun-carrying device for those shooters who have limited range of movement in their dominant side shoulder. It requires less rotation of the shoulder and can be easier to reach. One well-known gun expert always carries cross-draw because he is handicapped by severe arthritis in his strong-side shoulder.

Cross-draw fell from favor because it presented the gun butt to a hostile person facing the wearer, and because the arc of movement of the across-the-body draw could endanger a companion on the firing line located to the shooter's weak side. Both of these shortcomings can be overcome by simply angling the body so the holster side of the pelvis is pointed toward the target or threat. Now, pulling the gun straight back out of the holster in a "rock and lock" movement gets your Beretta on target quickly, and leaves the weak side arm in position to block any frontal attack to the gun, without the gun swinging past a coach behind you or a fellow shooter standing next to you on the firing line.

If you use an F-type Beretta, bear in mind that the across-the-body reach required for cross-draw can make it more difficult for the thumb to reach the slide-mounted safety until the gun is actually in hand and out of the holster.

Shoulder Holster Draw

Like the cross-draw, the shoulder holster has fallen some from its past popularity, but not so much. The shoulder holster – particularly the true shoulder *rig,* as defined decades ago by Richard Gallagher's Jackass Shoulder System – offers certain advantages. With the holstered gun hanging under the non-dominant arm and with spare magazines, handcuffs, perhaps even a small flashlight and clipped-on knife on the other side, the shoulder system balances nicely. By simply shrugging into the figure-8 harness, the wearer instantly dons everything he or she needs. Thus, the shoulder system is popular with those investigators who don't like to wear their gear unless they think they're actually going to need it. It's also a handy thing to have by the bed, ready to slip on if the burglar alarm goes off.

Draw is similar to the cross-draw, since in either case the shooter is reaching across his or her torso. Again, blade the holster side of the body toward the threat. Raise the weak side arm, as shown in the photos. This puts the arm in position to block or parry a close-range physical assault, and also clears the arm out of the path of the gun so you don't cross your own brachial artery with a loaded pistol under high stress. As with the cross-draw, this is done with a straight pull out of the holster across the chest, followed by a thrust of the gun toward the target.

The oldest style of shoulder holster carries the pistol with its barrel parallel to the length of the torso, muzzle down and butt up and forward. Old holster manuals show the gun being ripped down and out through the front of the holster. This, we know now, is weak and inefficient. The draw works better if the body is bladed and the butt is jerked across the chest, the gun rocked and locked onto the target, and then thrust toward the threat.

Chic Gaylord, holster maven and quick-draw champion of the 1950s and 1960s, always said that a horizontal shoulder holster, which carried the gun with its barrel dead parallel to the ground, was the fastest because its arc of movement from leather to target was the shortest. Upon review, he was right. The trouble is, unless you have great chest depth, you need a handgun of short overall length to carry discreetly at this angle. This means most of us will be limited to the more compact Berettas.

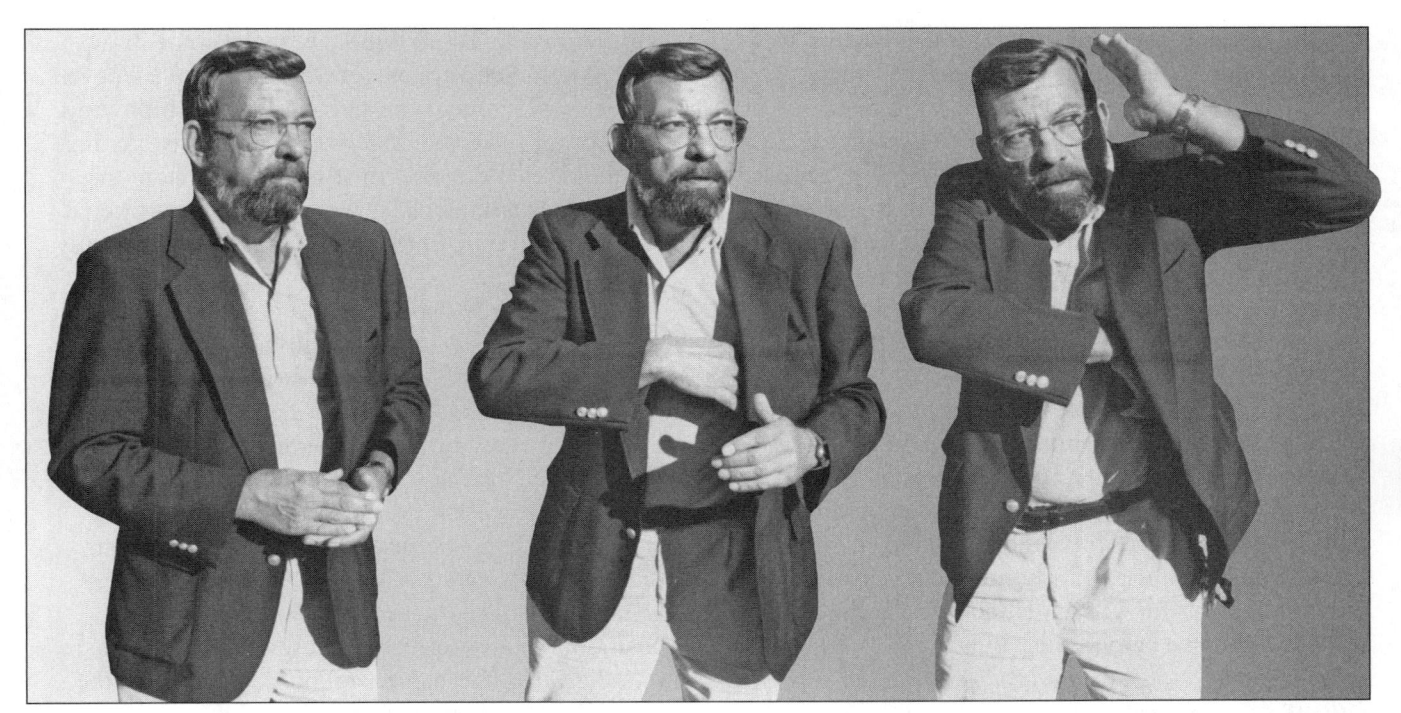

Upper left: Ayoob demonstrates the shoulder holster draw. The shooter will probably start facing the threat …

Upper center: … so the body needs to quarter back, taking a step to the rear with the strong-side leg, as the gun hand "spears" under the blazer toward X15 shoulder holster …

Upper right: … the non-dominant arm rises in a Najiola block to ward off a close threat, and to keep the gun from crossing the arm, as the gun hand achieves access and takes its drawing grasp …

Lower left: … movement straight across the chest is the fastest draw, and keeps the gun downrange. The support arm is still up, and with the finger still out of the guard …

Lower center: … the gun hand thrusts the Beretta 8045 Cougar toward the target and disengages the safety. The support hand is now coming down, from behind the muzzle …

Lower right: … to take a two-hand hold. When the decision to fire is made, the trigger finger takes the firing position.

Upside-down or semi-upside-down holsters are quite popular. Their downside is that they carry the gun butt farther from the reaching hand than either of the other two types of shoulder holster. The long reach may make it more difficult to access a safety catch during the early stages of the draw. Since most shoulder holsters except the first type will have thumb-break safety straps that go over the hammer, the reach of the thumb to the activating lever is further delayed. Do not wear a holster that secures the gun with a strap that goes under the grip tang. The web of the hand will trap the strap there, stalling the draw. For a broad-chested person to draw from a semi-upside down shoulder holster, it may be necessary to perform a version of the scoop draw in which the three lower fingers of the hand catch the front-strap of the grip-frame and pull it outward, into the hollow of the palm. Hunching the shoulders forward will also help in this situation.

Fanny Pack Draw

In warm weather, a belt pouch sometimes offers the most discreet form of concealed carry for a pistol as large as a full-size service Beretta. The downside of this carry is that it is slow. A long, gross motor movement is required to open the pouch before the drawing hand can reach in to achieve access. This is most efficiently done with the weak hand ripping open the fanny pack, and the strong hand making the draw. Take care to get the weak hand out of the way of the muzzle immediately once it has opened the pack. About half of your drawing practice from the fanny pack should be in this mode. The other half should be done strong-hand-only, with the free hand up in a blocking or parrying position, which may be necessary to ward off a close-range threat. Somewhere in there should come at least a little bit of practice in weak-hand-only draw from the fanny pack, in case the dominant arm is injured early in an encounter.

Ankle Holster Draw

You need a small pistol for an ankle holster. The only time I've ever seen anyone draw a full-size Beretta 92 from an ankle rig was in the movie *Kindergarten Cop,* and the guy making the draw was Arnold Schwarzenegger. Now, in real life, even a guy Schwarzenegger's size would need billowing bell-bottoms to make that work. It's clear watching the movie that the only time he actually wore the humongous ankle holster was in the scenes when it was being strapped on or the big pistol was actually being drawn.

European-made pocket auto pistols have tight working tolerances, tighter than the military-spec Beretta 92. An ankle gun gets covered with a fine film of dust and grit within its first day of wear, because it is only inches above the ground and every step is kicking that stuff up. You want to be cleaning such a gun daily or at least every few days.

The ankle holster is at its most efficient when the shooter is seated or supine (on his back) when he needs to make the draw. From the standing position, the most effective draw I've found is to go into the Cover Crouch position I developed for the StressFire™ shooting system. The feet go wide apart, the soles flat, the knees bent to a 90-degree angle. The torso is suspended with equal weight on each leg. To work an ankle holster, position the rig so the butt of the gun is to the rear, on the inside of the ankle of the non-gun-hand-side leg. Reach down with the weak hand and grab a fistful of trouser material and pull it upward, *before* you begin to bend the knees. Once a knee bends, trouser material is held taut at the knee and you can't pull up any more fabric below that point. Now drop into the cover crouch and execute the draw. As you reach your gun hand to the holstered weapon, swing the thumb up to clear any remaining remnant of cuff. Now, once the gun clears, you can fire from the Cover Crouch position, or if time permits, stand and assume your favorite upright shooting stance.

With ankle rigs, as with other holsters, remember that you *don't* want a safety strap that secures over the back of the grip frame, since the web of the drawing hand can trap the strap against the gun and prevent the draw from being completed. Be sure the strap is adjusted to hold the pistol snugly; the hammer spurs on most Beretta pocket pistols are very small, and don't give the strap a whole lot of surface upon which to secure.

Mastering the Beretta

In previous chapters, we've touched upon the basic skills of manipulating the Beretta pistol: loading it, unloading it, holstering it, drawing it, safely shooting it. Now, let's progress to some of the subtleties that will help you to truly master the gun. For the most part, we'll be addressing the 92 series, but the same things will, by and large, be true for all Beretta semiautomatic pistols. Indeed, many of these techniques will work generically with most semi-automatic pistols.

The Fundamentals

I've won my share of matches, some of them with Beretta pistols, and have learned a lot more from people who've won a lot more and a lot bigger matches than I. All are in agreement on one point: Certain key things are nothing less than foundational to good shooting. Before you go to the fine points, you have to master the basics.

Grip: Get the web of the hand up high into the grip tang. This does a number of good things. It minimizes the gun's leverage to jump its muzzle up

In the author's firing grasp of Beretta the dominant thumb is positioned to verify the off-safe condition; the support hand index finger is wedged beneath trigger guard to cam the muzzle upward. The web of the hand is high into the backstrap of the Model 92.

as the pistol recoils in your hand. It minimizes any tendency of the grip frame to shift in your grasp. It helps the gun to function better, because it tends to hold the frame still and give the moving slide a firm abutment against which to work as the pistol cycles.

As noted in the earlier chapter, keep the trigger finger clear of the trigger guard unless you are in the act of intentionally firing the weapon. The other three fingers should be firmly grasping the pistol. I'm a big fan of the "crush grip," in which you grasp as hard as you can. Ignore any minor tremor this may produce: you may shake in the moment of truth you are training for, so you may as well get used to it now. Habituating a firm grip minimizes the chance of you losing control of the gun if it

A 9mm Beretta's light recoil aids fast shooting. The spent casing is just above the gun, but the muzzle is in line for the next head shot.

The Gun Digest Book of Beretta Pistols

261

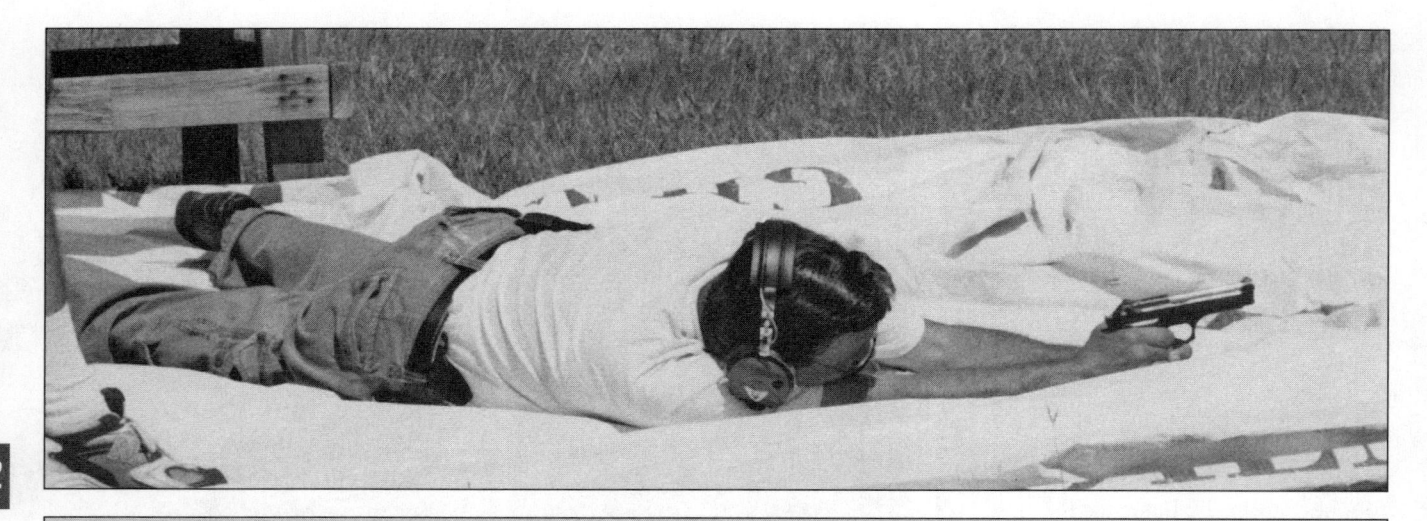

Solid rollover prone lets the shooter take advantage of the Beretta's high order of accuracy; here, Ayoob wins a match in Jacksonville. The target is at about 25 yards.

is struck or grabbed by surprise. It seems to also reduce the sensation of felt recoil.

Perhaps most important, though, is that the hard grasp is the only practical cure for "milking" the pistol. Old-time marksmanship instructors developed that term to explain the handgunner who sympathetically tightens all his fingers when his index finger moves the trigger to the rear. It's not an amateur thing, it's a human thing. When one finger moves, the rest of them tend to move reflexively, a fact of human physiology known as "interlimb response." This is why we keep the finger out of the guard until we're in the act of intentionally firing the pistol. Once we are intentionally firing, however, that sympathetic tightening of the other fingers tends to move the shot off target. By keeping a hard grasp with all but the trigger finger, which is "disarticulated" so you can run it separately, you cure that movement that moves the shot.

Stance: Make sure you have a strong and balanced stance. For slow fire, you can probably shoot standing on one foot (I've done it for demonstration purposes), or for that matter, hanging upside down from a chandelier. However, to be able to deliver rapid, accurate shots, your body needs a strong foundation. Whether firing one-handed or two-, the body should have a pyramidal base, a triangle with depth. It should be balanced front and back, and laterally.

I discussed all this in much greater depth when I wrote *The Gun Digest Book of Combat Handgunnery,* 5th Edition, published by Krause in 2002. For brief review, however, the primary effective two-handed stances are the classic Weaver, the Chapman, and the Isosceles.

Classic Weaver, inspired by Jack Weaver and promulgated by Jeff Cooper, has the torso fairly upright with both elbows bent. The feet are in a boxer's stance, shoulder width apart. The firing arm is bent slightly at the elbow, the support arm is bent sharply, and the elbow of the support arm points straight down. The gun hand pushes forward and the support hand pulls back, with equal and opposite pressure. This isometric pressure is the key to controlling recoil.

Ray Chapman's stance, which the great champion described as a modified Weaver, has the shooter in the same boxer's stance as above, but perhaps slightly wider. The forward leg is distinctly flexed. The gun arm is locked at all joints, straight out, and the forward arm is bent at the elbow as in the classic Weaver. The support hand pulls the locked gun arm tightly into its shoulder socket. Chapman always emphasized that the shoulder should be at least slightly forward of the hip to get effective recoil control with this technique.

The Isosceles stance, *when properly executed,* can be extremely strong. The arms are locked straight out at the target, with the chest parallel to the target; arms and chest form the triangle from which the technique derives its name. For decades, old-fashioned instructors taught it with the legs also forming an Isosceles triangle, parallel to the target. This gave no stability at all in rapid fire as the shoulder tended to rock backward upon recoil; indeed, many shooters would cantilever the shoulders backward even before firing, just to keep their balance. To make Isosceles work, use a modern version like that taught in StressFire™, in which the forward leg is well ahead and sharply bent, and the rear leg flexed and digging the foot into the ground to drive the body forward.

The shoulders should be aggressively forward of the hips, and the feet should be a good distance apart laterally as well as front to back, creating the most effective pyramidal base possible.

All these are two-handed firing positions. For a one-hand stance in something slow, like NRA bull's-eye competition, you want a relaxed stance. Feet are still about shoulder-width apart. However, in a two-hand stance you generally want the weak side foot forward, but in one-handed shooting, you'll be stronger and better balanced if the forward foot is the one on the same side as the gun hand. The bull's-eye target shooter will keep the torso bolt upright, perhaps leaning slightly forward in timed fire (five shots in 20 seconds) or rapid fire (five shots in 10 seconds).

In combat shooting, however, the goal is more like five shots in *one* second, literally 10 times faster than a bull's-eye match. This means a stronger stance is necessary, especially if only one hand is available to control the pistol.

Take a crush grip on your Beretta. With your feet more than shoulder's width apart laterally, place your strong side foot about one natural step forward. Bring the gun up with your dominant arm and lock it straight out. If you can, bring your free hand up in a fist level with its corresponding pectoral muscle, palm up, and squeeze it hard. This will give a sympathetic tightening of all the muscles in the upper body turret and add strength to your firing hand. (Hands, like fingers, are sympathetic. When one hand squeezes, the other wants to squeeze too. Similarly, the gun hand won't be able to exert maximum grasping force unless the other hand is "crushing" along with it, even if it's not at the gun to help.)

The forward leg should be sharply flexed. Pointing the forward toe toward the target helps most shooters align their bodies. The rear leg should be very slightly bent at the knee, with the foot pressing into the ground as if crushing out a cigarette butt. This helps to drive body force forward. Body weight should be primarily on the forward leg, and the shoulder should be aggressively forward of the hip.

Some find it stronger to tilt the gun very slightly toward the weak side, no more than 15 to 45 degrees. This also helps to align the gun with the opposite eye, if the shooter is cross dominant, that is, firing right handed but with left master eye or vice versa.

Sight Alignment

I tell my students that they should approach defensive shooting like fighter pilots, with a progression that goes from "enemy fighter identified" to "lock missiles on target" to necessary adaptation and follow-up to what happens after those missiles are launched. The "lock missiles on target" part, at any distance much beyond arm's length, means somehow aiming the gun.

Point shooting versus aimed fire is one of those debates that seems to come up every generation – virtually always being resolved with a return to some degree of aimed fire – and it's too broad a topic to enter in a book devoted to a certain kind of handgun. For more discussion on this, in full depth, I would refer you

The Beretta 92 is not sensitive to an unlocked wrist, a good thing when the shooter has to fire from an awkward position, as when tasked with a hostage rescue shot from a difficult angle in a Jacksonville IDPA match.

to that fifth edition of *Combat Handgunnery*.

Note that "aiming" does not necessarily require a perfect, traditional sight alignment, but past 7 yards or so, that's what you want. At close range, a very coarse aim of simply seeing the gun superimposed over the spot you want to hit may be good enough. By 7 yards, especially if you want a heart or brain shot, the sights themselves need to be in some sort of alignment. I use what I called a "StressPoint Index" some 25 years ago when I developed it; when world IPSC champion Todd Jarrett rediscovered it some years later, he dubbed it "shooting out of the notch," and I think his term is more descriptive. The front sight sitting *above* the rear sight, but without any barrel or slide visible in between, will deliver that heart shot out to 7 yards, though as range goes beyond that the shot will tend to go high.

Beyond 7 yards I suggest the conventional sight picture. The front sight is nestled in the notch of the rear sight. Front and rear sights are dead level across the top, with an equal amount of light on either side of the front post. Now, *focus hard on the front sight*.

This sounds so simple, but is so hard to do. Yet, every iron-sight handgun expert will tell you, this is the key to hitting what you are aiming at. Simple is not necessarily easy, but it works.

To refine this further, focus on the very top edge of the front sight. John Skaggs, who took over management of the Chapman Academy from Ray Chapman after Ray retired, taught this fine point and demonstrated why it worked. Firing offhand from 50 yards with the pistol he always taught with, a Beretta 92F, John would group his shots with deadly accuracy.

Most Beretta pistols come with three white dots inset into the sights, two in the back and one in the front. If light conditions don't let you take a conventional sight picture, go to the dots. It is not so precise a sight picture, but using the dots can be the difference between a good sight picture, or no sight picture at all.

Remember that since the dots are below the top edges of the sights, a three-dot sight picture is lower to the bore than a conventional sight picture. This means that if your pistol was sighted in with the conventional "post-in-notch" sight picture, you may find your shots grouping slightly high when you aim via the three dots.

One reason I have Trijicon night sights on so many of my Berettas is that while there's no better sight for night shooting, these have a metal capsule around the tritium element that forms a silvery circle in daylight.

Pure quick-draw is easy with the ergonomic Beretta. At powder-burn range, Ayoob wins a match with an 0.80 second reaction, draw, and shot with Langdon 92G.

If time permits and the danger zone has been scoped out, using the wall for support gives more accuracy. Ayoob has found this particular grasp to provide the strongest hold and best accuracy. Note that in PPC competition ...

... the left hand must control the gun on left side of barricade. The pistol is DAO 9mm Beretta traded in by Indianapolis PD.

This gives a much better three-dot sight picture than a trio of painted white dots.

Some Berettas have been produced with the sights painted in the Von Stavenhagen pattern, in which there is a vertical white bar centered under the rear notch, and a white dot on the front sight. It is aligned by "dotting the i" with the rear bar forming the body of the letter and the white circle up front comprising the dot. I don't find it quite as precise to align, especially in terms of elevation, as the three dots, but you may literally see things differently.

Sight Picture

Sight *alignment* is getting the front sight properly in line with the rear. Sight *picture* is what occurs when that sight alignment is superimposed over the portion of the target you want to hit.

Bull's-eye shooters for more than a century advocated the six o'clock sight picture, in which the black circle of the target appears to balance atop the front sight. The sights, of course, have to be adjusted so the shot will go high from point of aim and spot into the center, or eye, of that black "bull." Today, many bull's-eye shooters advocate a center hold with iron sights, and that is certainly what you want with a defensive pistol. If you have to take a precise shot, you want to see exactly where that bullet is going to go.

The ideal is to have the gun sighted so that at about 25 yards, the bullet hole will appear just on top of the front sight when you return from recoil to the original sight picture.

Trigger Press

Call it "trigger squeeze," "trigger press," "trigger roll," or whatever you want: they all mean the same thing. When the shooter intentionally fires the gun, the trigger is brought straight back as if it was pulling a tiny car along the top of the slide from the front sight to the rear. The movement must be smooth, even, and uninterrupted. The actual split instant at which the shot "breaks" should come as a surprise to keep the shooter from jerking the gun in anticipation of the blast and kick.

Beretta pistols tend to come with pretty good trigger pulls. They may be heavy compared to some other brands – 5 to 7 pounds for the single-action pull on a cocked Model 92 is typical – but they are *smooth in movement,* and that's what makes them controllable.

In days of old, target shooters with target pistols that had light, easy triggers recommended using just the tip of the finger on the trigger. The theory was that this was the most sensitive part of the finger and would therefore give the most precise movement. These two things do not necessarily correlate. Moving a piece of metal a fraction of an inch against 5 to 7 pounds of resistance is not what most of us would call precise, especially when it is done at very high speed, as in combat shooting.

Going from the tip to the pad, best defined as the spot on the finger where you find the whorl of the fingerprint, is stronger and gives slightly more leverage. It is not, however, a huge improvement. Unfortunately, the use of the finger or the pad was standard marksmanship doctrine at the time pistols from the Beretta 92 to the Glock were conceptualized and engineered. Fortunately, they were designed to be shot this way, and can be shot this way very well even by short-fingered people if their fingers are strong enough.

For the best high-speed shooting in single-action mode, and particularly in double-action mode, I have found that the distal joint of the trigger finger is the best contact point. It provides a quantum improvement in finger leverage against a heavy trigger pull. It takes a large hand with long fingers to do this on a Beretta 92, but it's easier on the smaller guns. The improved trigger reach afforded by the short-reach trigger option on the 92 and 96 models, and by the design parameters of later Berettas such as the Vertec and the Cougar series, help the shooter with average hands reach that "sweet spot" with the palmar crease of the distal joint placed on the trigger. Old-time revolver shooters who fired double-action-only called that sweet spot on the trigger finger "the power crease."

In 2004, I attended the Small Arms Firing School at Camp Perry, Ohio, conducted by the finest shooters of the armed forces concurrent with the National Championships of the bull's-eye handgun sport. I was pleasantly surprised to see that the distal joint trigger finger placement was now endorsed as an option within military pistol team doctrine, and was indeed the choice of some of the champions.

In fast, sustained shooting, it is critical to master the re-setting of the trigger. On a fighting pistol like the Beretta as opposed to a fine-tuned target pistol, the trigger will continue forward for a distance past the point where the sear re-sets. This is intentional on the part of the designers, and the purpose is to leave enough "slop" in the mechanism that dirt cannot block the trigger return action in an emergency.

In this critical element of trigger manipulation, I've taken a middle ground. On one side are amateurs who jerk their startled finger off the trigger as soon as the pistol discharges. Now they have to bring flesh back to metal, re-establish contact, and start the process all over again. When they try to do it very quickly, the trigger is impacted rather than pressed, which knocks the muzzle off target. This is called "trigger slap."

There are a handful of absolute master shooters like the great multiple-time world champion Robbie Leatham, who at high-speed fire with what might be called a "controlled trigger slap." This is not a viable option for most of us for two reasons. First, Robbie uses a pistol that is set up with literally a 1-pound trigger pull, which moves over a very short distance and comes to a carefully adjusted stop as soon as the shot is fired. Most of us have fighting pistols that just don't work that way. Second, this technique, even with the lightest and shortest trigger pull imaginable, requires the tremendous

Ayoob performs a tactical reload with a Model 92 behind cover in an IDPA match. Technique is one originally developed by Jeff Cooper.

Left: Beretta's smoothness lends itself to sequential fire. The PPC drill begins with a draw ...

Middle: ... six shots are facilitated by the smoothness of DAO Beretta mechanism ...

Right: ... a speed reload is made easier with a curled down firing thumb that doesn't override the slide lock lever ...

dexterity of an accomplished master who fires some 50,000 or more live rounds per year. Someone like, oh, Rob Leatham. Do you or I fit that profile? I know I don't.

On the opposite end of the trigger pull theory scale are those who propound "riding the sear" or "riding the link." At the instant when the sear mechanism resets and the pistol can fire again, but before the trigger has completed its whole forward return movement, the shooter will be able to feel a tiny "click" or "tick." The theory goes that if the shooter stops forward trigger movement when his click is felt and then resumes trigger press, there is less trigger travel and therefore less time between shots.

This theory, I submit, is a classic example of what happens when a time and motion study does not take biomechanics into account. The theory itself is perfectly sound in the pure mechanical sense. Under stress, however, we experience vasoconstriction. That is, our blood flow is redirected from the extremities into major muscle groups and internal organs. Vasoconstriction is what has happened, via another mechanism, when you fall asleep lying on your arm and when you wake up, your hand has "gone to sleep." What the hands experience under stress is a microcosm of that, but sufficient to absolutely ruin fine motor dexterity. This means that under stress we probably won't be able to feel that tiny tick. Off the top of my head, I can recall only one man who was able to "ride the link" during an actual gunfight.

What's more likely to happen instead is that, since the hand's flexor muscles are stronger than its extensor muscles, the vasoconstricted finger won't return the trigger far enough forward to re-set before the finger starts pulling back again. Since the trigger has not reset, the shot will not fire.

In matches, I have seen this happen to great shooters like Mickey Fowler and Mike Plaxco, in their prime and shooting customized 1911 pistols with very short re-sets. Most fighting handguns have longer pulls than that, particularly double-action-only weapons, and the longer the reset the more likely a "short-stroke" of the trigger is to occur, leaving the shooter desperately pulling the trigger of a gun that will not function. In a match, it can cost you a championship. In a gunfight, it can cost you your life.

Let's look at two examples. In Indiana, a police department converted its 92G (double-action first-shot) Beretta pistols to 92D (double-action-only) format. I have been given to understand that they were not retrained with the new mechanism. One officer got into a shootout that was caught on a video camera, and pulled the trigger desperately. Sometimes the pistol discharged and sometimes it didn't. Finally, he got enough 147-grain subsonic 9mm JHP rounds into his attacker and won the gunfight.

Review of the tape showed that each time the Beretta failed to fire, the shooter had failed to return the trigger to its double-action reset point. Rather than acknowledge a training problem, the department simply switched to a different kind of gun – in .40 caliber, which was also easier than acknowledging

Below: ... six more shots; note the spent casing above the pistol but the 9mm Model 92 is already coming back to center. Total time allowed is 20 seconds ...

Right: ... and the Beretta 92's attributes let you turn in scores like this: 120-12X out of 120 possible.

that they had not made the best possible choice in 9mm ammo, but that's a topic for another time.

In Ohio, a courageous female trooper got into a shootout with a gunman who ambushed her with a .44 Magnum slug in the chest. The bullet stopped on her Second Chance vest. As she returned fire with her department-issue Beretta 96D, she perceived her gun to not have fired when she pulled the trigger. Thinking it jammed, she unloaded, reloaded, and shot some more, killing her antagonist. When the gun was examined, no artifact of a jam, such as a damaged cartridge, was found and the gun operated perfectly. Beretta believes that she simply failed to return the trigger all the way forward. She told me she was too busy fighting for her life to analyze the malfunction and doesn't know exactly what happened, only that the gun stopped shooting and she reflexively did what she was trained to do upon such an occasion. The department blamed the gun and switched to a different brand of DAO .40.

Thus we see the dangers on the two ends of the trigger pull theory spectrum. Let the finger come all the way off the trigger, and you get miss-producing trigger slap. Try to ride the link, and you set the stage for a human error-induced failure to fire. This is why I suggest a middle ground, and the middle ground is this:

Maintain a trigger weld, but let the trigger come all the way forward until it stops. By not taking the finger off the trigger, you have kept impact out of the equation on the next trigger pull and helped minimize the danger of an errant shot. However, by letting the trigger come all the way forward until it stops – something that even a vasoconstricted finger can feel and pass on to the brain – you have guaranteed resetting the trigger and *having* a next shot to fire immediately.

This will work with all Beretta triggers.

Speed Reloads

The speed reload is also known as the combat reload or the emergency reload, and as those names imply, it is a technique intended to get a reloaded and ready pistol into the practitioner's hand at maximum speed in a combat emergency when he or she has run out of ammo and still needs to shoot.

We have covered administrative loading in an earlier chapter, and there we have also covered the subtleties of ejecting a spent magazine. In a speed reload, that technique is applied swiftly and smoothly, remembering that the smoothness is the key to the swiftness.

Before we eject the magazine in the gun, we should have our support hand on a fresh magazine. "You play like you practice," said the late Ron Risner when he was debriefed after his superb performance in the notorious FBI firefight in Florida in 1986. What he meant was the universal understanding of combat trainers and combat veterans alike: when we go "auto pilot" in an extreme emergency, we will do what we have become conditioned to do.

On the range, we always seem to have another loaded magazine on our belt. This won't be the case if we've just shoved our Beretta into the waistband to walk down to the corner store for the proverbial quart of milk, or have grabbed the bedside Beretta when awakened by the burglar alarm going off. There may not *be* a spare magazine in the usual spot, and you don't want to automatically jettison a magazine that may have a few rounds left in it until your free hand has already taken a firm grasp on a fully charged one.

As the support hand grasps the spare mag firmly, with thumb and middle finger holding tight and index finger down along the front of the mag, the firing hand now ejects the spent magazine. Ideally, on its way up the new one should pass the falling old one.

Now that index finger does the job it's named for and indexes the fresh magazine into the magazine well. On a double-stack Beretta this is made easy by the wedge effect of the narrow top of the magazine going into the wide opening at the butt of the gun, but some competition shooters open it up even more, a feature Beretta itself incorporated into its Vertec design. At entry, let the flat back of the magazine touch the flat back of the mag well: it's

Exemplar drill at an LFI course. Students learn correct trigger pull by feeling it. Coach's hands overlie those of the shooter and coach's finger pulls finger and trigger of student. The drill goes back to early USMC training doctrine.

the biggest and therefore the easiest and fastest index point. Now continue a firm upward push with the palm of the hand until the magazine locks into place.

At this point, if the pistol is at slide-lock, pressing downward on the slide release lever most easily and quickly returns the slide forward. For a right-handed shooter, this can be done with either thumb but it's better to reach with the left one. The reason is, under stress we can do things out of sequence. Since the right hand remains on the gun throughout the reload, there is the possibility that if the right thumb is habituated to drop the slide, it will do so prematurely and close the slide on an empty chamber. But if we wait for the left hand to get there, that can't happen, and it's just as quick.

The left-handed shooter will find that as the right hand slaps the magazine in, the right hand's fingertips are already approaching the slide stop lever from underneath. Just let the fingers keep moving upward like a karate man's spear hand, and press forcibly down. One of those fingertips will release the slide stop for you, and the hand just pivots swiftly and naturally back into firing position.

Former state and Midwestern regional IDPA champion Dave Maglio carries a Beretta 92F on duty as a full time deputy sheriff, and he's a southpaw. He reloads his Beretta (or any other auto pistol) with just ungodly speed using this technique.

Some feel that reaching up with the whole hand and tugging the slide back and then letting it go is a better way to complete a speed reload. Their theory is that pressing down a lever is a fine motor skill that will desert us under stress. I have never heard them explain how a spear hand (lefty) or curled down thumb (righty) is "fine motor." It's not as if we're talking about threading a needle or something. And if pressing a lever that releases the slide is impossible under pressure, how do these theorists expect to press the lever that releases the shot … the lever known as "the trigger"?

Bear in mind, however, that you want to be ready to use that free hand to jack the slide if you're a right-handed shooter whose thumb, like mine, always seems to ride the slide stop of the pistol and keep it from locking the gun open when it's empty. This is not unique to the Beretta 92; I've seen it happen with the SIG-Sauer and other pistols. It's not necessarily a design flaw, just an incompatibility of shooting technique with a certain design element. I shoot with my thumbs where they are because when firing double-action auto pistols, I long ago became habituated to thrusting my thumb upward on an angle that would off-safe the pistol and continue to verify that it was off safe. When this habitual grasp is applied to a SIG-Sauer or a Beretta 92 or 96, it overrides the slide stop.

By simply shooting with the thumb curled

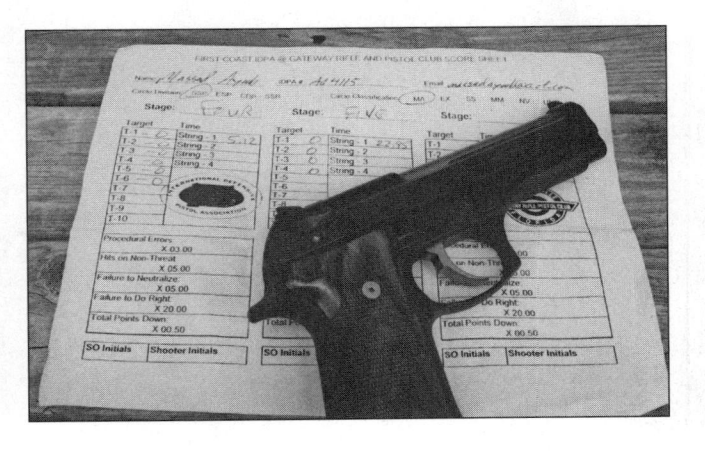

Unloading a Beretta with the mag release on grip panel is quick and easy. The support hand comes up under butt and the thumb presses the release button, dropping the Tomcat's magazine into the palm.

Left: Combined quality of Beretta manufacturing and Langdon gunsmithing pays off. Score sheets show Ayoob's winning score …
Right: … is zero points down for all five stages of IDPA match.

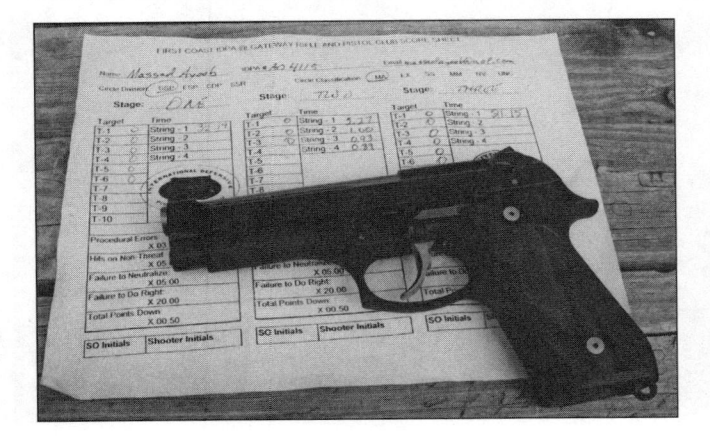

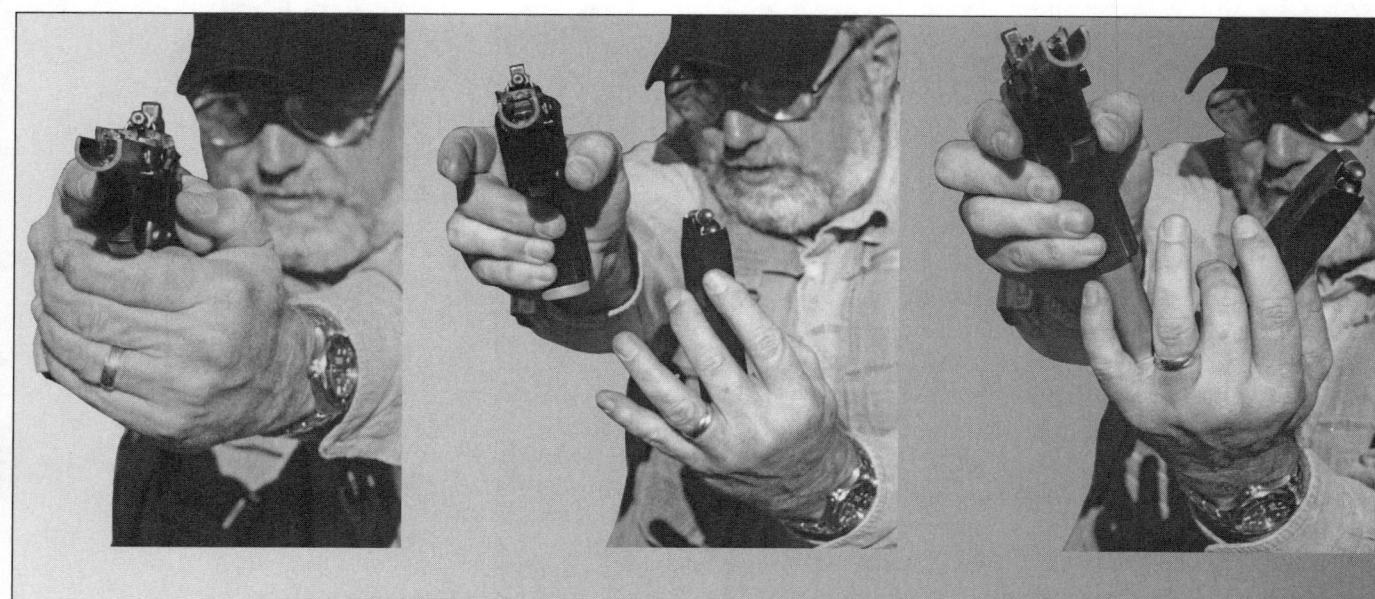

Above left: Steve Denney demonstrates a max speed tactical reload with Beretta 92. The gun's slide has been removed to allow safe viewing from the front…

Above middle: … as hand with fresh mag approaches the pistol, he rotates the butt toward his palm…

Above right: … and ejects the partial mag, which stops on his palm. Note the positions of his little and ring fingers …

Left: … which now grab the partial mag, pulling it out of the gun …

Below left: … clearing the way for a fresh mag to be slammed home. The partial hangs from the last two fingers …

Below middle: … and remains there as his hand returns to a strong shooting grasp …

Below right: … and the depleted mag can be put away as shown at a time of the shooter's choosing.

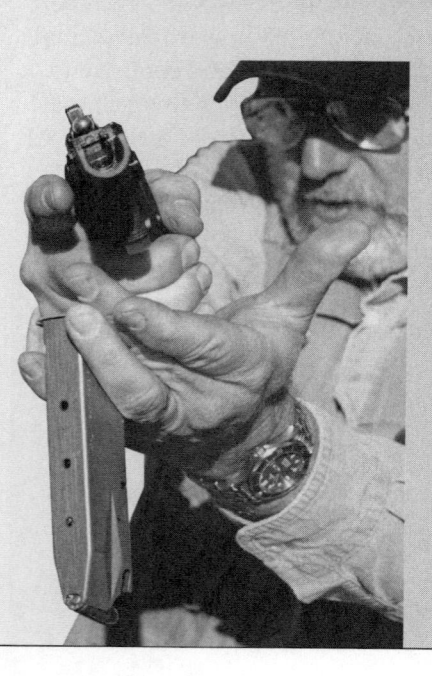

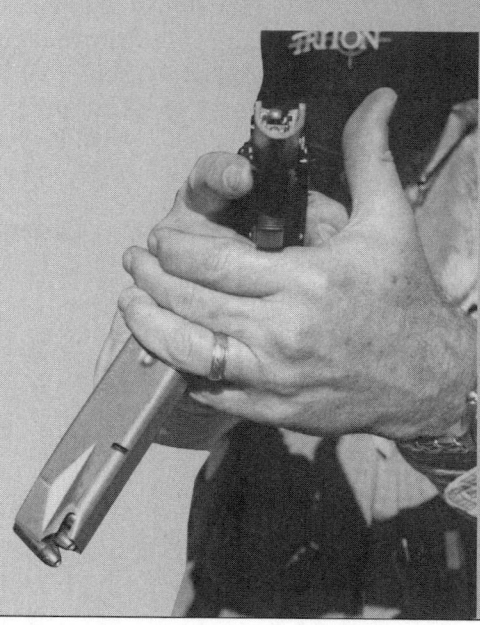

down out of the way, this can be avoided. That is the way I would shoot if I had to start over again, and was using my 92G or 96D. Neither of those models has a manual safety, so there is no need for a high right thumb to begin with.

Tactical Reloads

This is another concept discussed in much greater depth in the fifth edition of *Combat Handgunnery*. Suffice to say that its purpose is to retrieve the remaining ammo from a partially depleted magazine, while at the same time inserting a full magazine into the pistol to bring it back up to full cartridge capacity.

Let's start by saying that in the tac-load, you're juggling two magazines and a loaded pistol. This is a dexterity-intensive activity and, therefore, a fumble-prone one. *It is imperative that the finger be out of the trigger guard and the muzzle in a safe direction at all times during these procedures!* It is also a good idea to decock a traditional double-action pistol, or engage the safety of a single-action like the Beretta Billennium or a selective double/single-action like the Tomcat, while performing these techniques.

Let's look at perhaps four different protocols for the tactical reload, or tac-load, all of which will work with modern Beretta fighting pistols. Each has strengths and weaknesses.

Reload with retention. The term comes from IDPA, and they call it "reload with retention" because it is so slow that it grates on the sensibilities to call it "tactical." However, it is the easiest technique in the group to learn, which gives it some value. Also, an IDPA shooter may find himself at a match where the judges use old rules, in which a shooter could not leave position until the retained magazine had been put away. This is what the reload with retention was developed for.

Remove the magazine with the dominant hand. Thrust it into a pocket. (Not a shirt pocket, forbidden by IDPA rules on the valid theory that when you bend over, the spare magazine is likely to fall out of that location.) Now draw a fresh magazine. Insert it into your pistol. Carry on.

That simple. That easy to learn.

Unfortunately, also, that *slow*. There is an inordinate amount of time in which the magazine is out of the gun. In a life-threatening emergency, you would be holding a single-shot pistol. If your gun was a modern Beretta .380 with a magazine disconnector safety, you wouldn't even be able to fire the single shot in the chamber. This is why I really don't care for this technique.

Maximum speed tac-load. This is the one I practice for real. If I've had to fire enough shots that a reload is a good idea, the situation is dangerous enough that I want a fully loaded pistol in my hand as soon as possible. Moreover, there is always the possibility that the proverbial "lull in the action" that allows the tactical reload may have been caused by an opponent smart enough to play possum and wait for a good opportunity. When he hears me doing a tactical reload, it will sound very much like some poor schmuck with an empty gun trying desperately to reload, and will be an excellent cue for him to suddenly rise up and attack. If that happens, I want to be holding a fully loaded weapon, and I want it to be in the strongest fighting grasp possible.

That is the purpose of this technique, which goes like this:

The support hand grabs the spare mag and approaches the gun as if to do a speed reload. The gun hand then turns the pistol's butt slightly toward the free hand. The support hand palm comes under the butt, and the firing hand releases the magazine, the floorplate of which catches in the palm. The ring finger and little finger of the support hand then encircle the depleted magazine and pull it out of the gun. The support hand rotates slightly and slaps in the fresh mag.

Now, with the depleted mag still protruding from between the two bottom fingers, the support hand takes its two-hand firing position as the shooter covers and scans the danger zone. If danger has indeed arisen, he is fully capable of dealing with it. Once satisfied, the spare magazine can be inserted into a pocket while the pistol is held with the firing hand.

This technique's advantages are that it gives the shooter a fully loaded gun faster than any other technique, and that it finishes with the hands in the strongest possible position to immediately renew firing while still maintaining control of the depleted mag. Downsides? It is more complicated and takes longer to learn.

I don't use this for IDPA shooting anymore, since that sport generally requires movement immediately after the tactical reload, and a magazine held by ring and little fingers is too hard to put into a pocket while moving. Such movement, however, is unlikely after a real-world tactical reload.

This technique works beautifully with most Beretta pistols, since their magazines are so designed that their floorplates create a stopping point as they slip down between those two fingers, making the technique smooth and positive. It works less well with thin magazines whose floorplates are flush with the magazine bodies on the sides: factory 1911 magazines, for example. Also, very small fingers and very large magazines may be incompatible with this technique.

Universal tac-load. Pioneered by Jeff Cooper and standardized by Clint Smith and other great modern masters, this technique seems to be the one best suited to a broad range of hand sizes vis-à-vis magazine sizes. It works like this:

The support hand snatches the fresh magazine and brings it up to the gun as if to carry out a speed reload. As the gun is reached, the index finger slides off the front of the magazine and to its side, the side away from the gun, leaving the index finger and thumb free to receive the depleted mag. Bringing the hand under the pistol, eject with the dominant hand, catching the depleted magazine between thumb and forefinger. Rotate the hand and shove in the fresh magazine, rolling the fingers forward so they don't block a positive seating.

If danger is feared, the support hand can return to its position in a firing grasp, the three bottom fingers reinforcing the firing hand while the index finger and thumb still hold the spare magazine. If this is not necessary, the depleted mag is in a very firmly held position and ready to be quickly put away.

Disadvantages: It's complicated, and slightly less effective for two-hand shooting than the max-speed tac-load above. Advantages: It is very adaptable to different hand and magazine sizes. It works better for sudden, unexpected shooting than anything but the max-speed version. It is very fast for getting the magazine into the pocket even if you are moving.

This is the technique I now use in IDPA. I used the max-speed in the early days when all the rules said was that you had to maintain control of the spare mag. Then, they changed the rules to where you couldn't shoot with a mag in one hand, and further, to where the partial mag had to be stowed before you could move. This gave the "reload with retention" the edge for match-winning speed.

However, current rules say the tactical reload is complete when the full mag locks into the gun, allowing you to put the spare mag in the pocket as you run. This gives you the fastest technique of the conventional tactical reloads for this type of competition. Because it is so user friendly, if I had only time to teach one tactical reload technique for self-defense, it would be this one.

Weasel tac-load. Current IDPA rules (as of late December 2004) allow any tac-load technique that is within "the spirit of the game." Says the manual, "To be in the 'spirit' of the stage, the shooter must retain the magazine in one of the following ways PRIOR to the firing of the first shot after a tactical load: pants pocket, vest pocket, jacket pocket, waistband or magazine pouch. Using specially designed pockets, shirt pockets or holding the magazine in the hand or teeth is NOT permitted."[1]

Now, I've been telling my students for years that I teach them more weaselcraft than pistolcraft. Pistolcraft as the term is now used was pioneered by men like Jeff Cooper and Ray Chapman. They are big and strong. I

Above left: Steve Denney demonstrates a speed reload. The Model 92F has run empty to slide-lock …
Above second from left: … when Steve feels his hand hit the spare magazine, his thumb ejects the empty one …
Above second from right: … he inserts the fresh magazine as shown…
Above right … and, thumbing down the slide stop lever to chamber next round, flows back into two-hand firing hold.

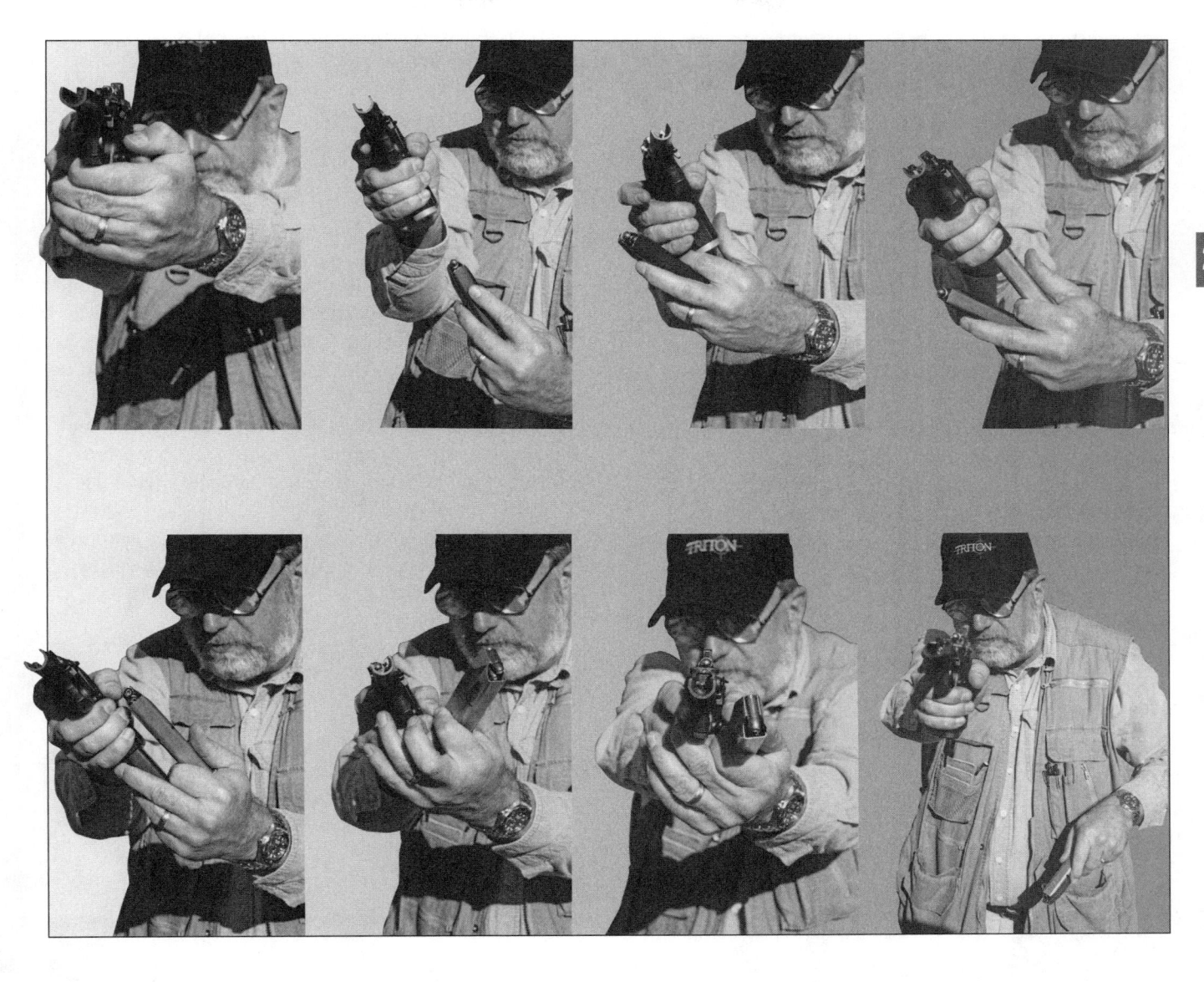

Above left: Steve Denney demonstrates the "universal" tac-load the author recommends. The Beretta would be decocked at this point …

Above second from left: … a fresh magazine is brought to the gun as if for a speed reload …

Above second from right: … but at the last moment the index finger moves so the fresh mag is between it and the middle finger, leaving the thumb and forefinger free …

Above right: … to pull the partially depleted magazine out of the Beretta 92. Now …

Below left: … the hand rotates to push the fresh mag into the grip frame. Fingers must roll clear to avoid blocking …

Below second from left: … as the fresh mag is thrust home. The partial mag is retained in the support hand …

Below second from right: … allowing emergency fire in this two-hand hold if necessary …

Below right: … and the technique finishes as the depleted magazine is secured, with the now fully reloaded Beretta ready on target. Jeff Cooper originally developed this technique.

am little and weak. I teach weaselcraft: how to sneak up on the threat before it sneaks up on you.

Lacking the speed of the leopard and the strength of the bear, in practical shooting competition I have to fall back on the cunning of the weasel. The Chapmans and Leathams of the world are deft and dextrous men. I, on the other hand, require unlimited time and occasionally an owner's manual to change a light bulb. Therefore, I try to out-think a problem rather than out-race or overpower it.

Thus, the weasel tac-load. It works as follows:

The gun hand brings the pistol back to the body, muzzle straight in front and downrange of course, as the support hand in mirror image goes to the magazine on the weak side hip. *If the wearer has a jacket or vest with big, unflapped pockets,* the butt can be positioned over the pocket and the magazine release button then pushed. The depleted magazine falls directly into the pocket. If the butt is angled slightly toward the body, this helps to guide the falling magazine into its intended repository.

While this is happening, the other hand is grabbing the fresh magazine. Now the hands move forward and execute a conventional speed reload, and the thing is done.

Within the rules? Yes. One foot on the rule book and the other on a banana peel? Maybe. Something to practice for the street? NO, because you can't guarantee you'll be wearing a suitable garment, and we do indeed "play like we practice."

I'm stuck in Master class, shooting against Rob Leatham and Ernest Langdon and their peers of the IDPA world. I need every shortcut I can get in a match. That's what this special purpose technique is for. Remember, "use the specific tool for the specific job."

Shooting From Awkward Positions

The more difficult the shooting problem the more an ergonomic pistol like the Beretta helps you solve it. Let's look at some examples from the practical shooting competition world, which is intended to replicate for training purposes the real world of gunfighting.

You won't always have your ideal shooting position. You might have to shoot from under a low overhang, with your head bent so far forward and your body so jack-knifed that you can't lock either arm *or* take a proper Weaver stance. This will accelerate recoil, and will make it more likely that your pistol will jam. When I do this with a Beretta 92, it works fine, because of the gun's light recoil and the fact that it is not particularly sensitive to unlocked wrists. Ditto the Cougar series, whose rotary breech gives them soft recoil for their calibers, 9mm to .40 to .357 SIG and .45 ACP.

The same is true of real-world situations in which the arm cannot lock due to an injury that occurred during, or perhaps long before, the encounter. The M9/M92 pistol is famous for its ability to function even if the shooter's wrist is unlocked. That is not true of most auto pistols, even the Model 92's .40 caliber twin, the Model 96.

> Left: Ayoob struggles to keep a straight face as he demonstrates his Weasel tac-load. With his finger clear of the trigger, both hands pull in toward his body. The muzzle is of course straight downrange …
>
> Middle: … as the left hand reaches for a fresh mag as the right indexes inside of the wrist against the rib cage …
>
> Right: … which positions the Beretta for ejection to drop the pistol's magazine into the open side pocket of vest …

Lighting may be imperfect, and the action fast. Tears or blood or foreign matter in your eyes may impair your vision. You may have lost your eyeglasses or contacts and desperately need the visual correction. In these circumstances, the big, blocky sights of the Beretta service pistols come into their own.

For many years, I made a point of shooting now and again without my eyeglasses. Then came April 11, 1986, and the terrible gun battle between FBI and the armed robbers in Florida from which we learned so much. Ben Grogan, an officer survival instructor, FBI SWAT Team member, and perhaps the best shot on the scene, was among those killed. For all his skills and training, he was extremely myopic, and he lost his eyeglasses in the car crash that immediately preceded the firefight. He fired many shots with his 9mm service pistol (not a Beretta) and never hit anything. His last words before he was shot to death were, "Where is everyone?"

After that, I made a point of shooting one qualification and one match a year "blind," with only plain shooting glasses. The first time I shot a perfect score that way was with a box-stock Beretta 92. The reason: I could *see* those humongous Beretta sights even with my fuzzy uncorrected vision.

Speed and tactical reloads? As noted above, the tapered magazine and wide mag well of the double-stack Beretta make it easier. The reversible magazine release button is handy for southpaws, too.

Left: ... seen here in close-up.
Middle: The fresh magazine is then speed-loaded ...
Right: ... and the shooter gets back to business. This is strictly a match technique, not for the street!

The occasional long-range shot may come your way, in a match or on the street. The Beretta's accuracy and shootability comes into its own there. Many years ago in the Northwest, a soldier went berserk with a personally owned weapon and began shooting people on post. The terror ended when an MP killed him with a head-shot, fired from his standard-issue Beretta M9 pistol at a range of more than 50 yards.

Shooting while moving? Let the hips go back a little bit, keep the knees flexed, and let the feet sort of glide. This turns the joints into shock absorbers that help keep the gun arm from bouncing with each step.

Barricade shooting, or shooting from behind cover, requires different techniques for different situations. If it starts as a search, you want to be well back from the wall; if you're close enough to use the wall for support, you're close enough for an unseen foe on the other side to grab your gun and begin a disarming attempt. If, however, you're under fire and have already scoped out the danger zone and determined that there are no gun grabbers by the cover, go ahead and get close to the barricade. It's simple geometry: the barricade is between you and the identified threat. The farther you are behind your cover, the less distance your opponent has to move laterally to get an easy shot at you. Conversely, the closer you are to the cover, the more difficult it is for him to outflank you, because he must move much farther.

If you are close enough to use the barricade for support, there are multiple ways to do that, too. If you want good accuracy with high speed and don't mind risking a little more exposure – let's say you're leaning out for a rescue shot as opposed to a personal-defense shot – no technique is better than Ray Chapman's. Take a two-hand hold and place the back of your hand on the barricade's outer edge. Come up on the ball of the opposite foot, the left foot if you're shooting around the right side or vice versa, for balance. The back of the hand will ride up and down the wall, giving you very fast recovery time. If it's the support hand making contact, use the metacarpal surface, the backs of the hands. If it's the firing hand, however, the tendons here would move and push both hands and gun outward as you pull the trigger, so use the knuckles. If the surface is rough, it may abrade your hand, but that's a small price for a good score and an infinitesimally small price to save a life.

If you want maximum cover and can afford to slow down your rate of fire slightly, let the knuckles of the support hand touch the side of the wall that faces you. The knuckles of index and middle fingers should be in contact. I find that putting the support hand's thumb on the wall adds some stability. This is as rock-solid a hold as you can get on the barricade for a good precision hit, and it pulls you deep inside the cover for maximum protection. The downside is that it can cause a little more felt recoil and more muzzle rise, slowing your rate of accurate rapid fire somewhat. It also requires you to fire with the left hand controlling the gun on the left side of the wall, and with the right hand on the right side. Not many people are comfortable with ambidextrous shooting, but for those who are, it is a skill so valuable as to be worth the effort to attain.

Famed NYPD Stakeout Squad gunfighter and PPC champion Jim Cirillo developed an alternative that keeps the gun in the dominant hand on either side but still affords good cover. Use the technique described immediately prior on your strong-hand side of the barricade. For shooting around the weak hand side, turn your Beretta 45 degrees outward from the barricade, come up in a classic Weaver stance, and let the knuckles of the weak hand touch the barricade. You can use that squared front of a 92/96 trigger guard to press against the barricade, but recoil may bounce it out of position on the first shot. I find it almost as stable and much faster for follow-up shots to let the *bottom* edge of my Beretta's trigger guard touch that outer edge of the barricade.

The Beretta works very well for barricade shooting. Its positive feeding keeps it from binding if the slide accidentally touches the wall while the pistol is cycling. The open top of the 92/96 series guns minimizes chances of a spent casing being trapped in the slide because the ejection side of the pistol was too close to the barricade.

The Bottom Line

When left to their own devices, a disproportionate number of champion shooters choose the Beretta 92. I've watched the Beretta M9 bark in the hands of six-time national bull's-eye champion Brian Zins in the Distinguished event at the national championships at Camp Perry. I've watched former World IPSC Champion Ray Chapman win the Missouri State Championship with his Beretta 92-SB (he thought the squared trigger guard of the later 92s was ugly). I've watched Ernest Langdon win a National IDPA championship with his Beretta 92G.

When the stakes are higher than national championship titles, the Beretta comes through, too. I've lost count of the men – and women – I've debriefed who owe their lives to the Beretta's ability to shoot straight and fast for them when they stood at the edge of death and looked down into the abyss.

The Beretta is an eminently shootable gun, and a hugely dependable one, in most of its incarnations. That's why I'm comfortable recommending it.

Hell, it's why I was comfortable taking the assignment to write this book.

Endnotes

(1)International Defensive Pistol Association Official Rule Book and Club Affiliation Manual, Effective 5-2-01, pages 32-33.

The Beretta in the Training Environment

This writer's job description is currently full-time trainer, part time cop, and part-time writer. One of the things I bring to the table to write *The Gun Digest Book of Beretta Pistols* is the experience of seeing about 10,000 rounds a week go downrange from all manner of handguns. That teaches you quickly what works and what doesn't work in terms of shooting machines.

I've had the opportunity to see the Beretta in this intensive testing environment from both sides; as an instructor and a student. Both have left me more impressed with the Beretta Model 92 pistol.

I change guns every teaching cycle to stay current with what's out there. But some things have changed over time. I make reference to Thunder Ranch, which is, alas, no more, but Clint Smith and his wonderful wife Heidi teach now at his School of Arms in Oregon. I sincerely hope this new school will prove to be an even greater chapter in the epoch of excellent training he has so long afforded his students. It was a pleasure teaching classes for him at Thunder Ranch, and it was a greater pleasure taking classes from him and his excellent crew.

Most "gun tests" are done primarily on the range or in the shop. The gun is often fired more for accuracy then for ergonomics, sometimes from

The gun should be light and comfortable. The instructor shouldn't be leaving lethal weapons in unattended motel rooms, and will probably end up carrying the gun 24/7. Here, a Beretta 92FS is visible in Ayoob's IWB holster as he gives a lecture on defending deadly force cases.

The Beretta takes down en bloc, making it easy and convenient to strip down to the frame for teaching purposes, so students can see the technique from the front without being crossed with an actual gun. Here, Ayoob demonstrates the Jeff Cooper version of tactical reload with stripped Beretta 92FS at Firearms Academy of Seattle.

a machine rest. Then it's torn apart on the bench to inspect for subtleties of mechanical detail.

All this is well and good. Indeed, in my opinion at least, it's all a necessary part of the picture. However, for the consumer who will use a defensive firearm "for real," the test has to go farther.

How well does it fit the hand? Are the controls ergonomically placed? Is it, in the current parlance, "user friendly?" Does its inherent mechanical accuracy translate to practical accuracy, or in other words, can a person shoot it anywhere near as well as its potential in the machine rest indicates?

One excellent way to test for these factors is to teach with the gun. Some instructors pick one favorite handgun and make it their trademark. Others teach different classes with different guns, to stay current with the various firearms their students might be using. I fall into the latter group.

I've often taught with the Beretta. The one I'll discuss in now is a Model 92 FS. It's a good tool for the task. Let's look at how an instructor's needs might be a predictor of an armed citizen's or a police officer's requirements.

The Reliability Factor

The instructor's gun has to work. If you taught automobile maintenance at a trade school and your own car kept breaking down, where would your credibility be with your students? It's the same at "gun school." A handgun that doesn't run 100 percent reflects badly on the instructor.

In the field—cop or soldier, bodyguard or armed citizen—a pistol that malfunctions can cause something much worse than embarrassment. I believe the term I'm groping for is "death."

This particular Beretta 92FS has had thousands of rounds through it since I won it at an ASLET seminar some years ago. It was among the Berettas my older daughter and I took to Thunder Ranch a couple of years ago. In almost 4,000 rounds of 9mm Black Hills ammo between us on that occasion, the only malfunction occurred when a cartridge I had damaged and negligently allowed back into my ammo supply failed to feed. A quick snap on the slide cleared the stoppage and solved the problem.

I've lent it to several students as a loaner gun. Each fired their allotment of 500 rounds, cleaned it, gave it back, and went on their way. The gun never malfunctioned. In fact, to the best of my knowledge, this particular handgun has never jammed, except for the one damaged round I stupidly fed it.

Will this be true of all Berettas? Nothing is 100 percent, but that said, both military and the police sectors agree that after many thousands of rounds, Beretta 92 series pistols continue to work.

There has been the occasional complaint on the 96 series, which is the 92 format in caliber .40 Smith & Wesson. I have one, in 96D Centurion, that works great and has never missed a lick. Every Border Patrolman I've discussed it with has commented on the extreme reliability of the 96D issued by their agency, using .40 caliber 155-grain high-velocity hollow-points. However, Border Patrol issues the Brigadier version, which has a heavier-duty slide that may be better suited to the rigors of the .40 S&W round, with its high pressure and quick-spiking pressure peak.

Still, most of my Berettas are in 9mm. My friend and mentor Ray Chapman, the first world champion of the combat pistol, noted that handguns tend to work best in the caliber for which they were originally designed. I have seen little in my career to make me want to argue that point. The big Beretta was designed originally for the 9mm cartridge.

Reliability to bet your life on? No doubt about it. Not only am I carrying one at this moment, but the pistol I usually have at bedside for protection of my wife and family is another Beretta 9mm.

Convenience

A gun isn't a sometime thing for a serious firearms instructor. You wear it all the time. I put mine on my hip when I get dressed in the morning, and take it off when I go to bed at night. It's balanced somewhat by the weight of two spare 15-round magazines on my opposite side.

Though it looks and feels big, the Beretta is light for its size, thanks to its aluminum alloy frame. For the 16 rounds it holds, it's remarkably efficient. That's especially true since Beretta warrants the gun to handle the hot +P and +P+ ammunition. A 115-grain JHP 9mm bullet in the 1,300 foot per second (fps) range delivers more energy than the typical factory loaded 110-grain .357 Magnum hollow-point. The 15-round magazines aren't that tough or that expensive to come by, because the Beretta has long been so popular in this country that there are literally millions of those magazines in circulation.

The Beretta easily passes my test for comfortable portability. In any of my several inside-the-waistband holsters for it—Greg Kramer, Ted Blocker, Mitch Rosen, Galco, and Blade-Tech—I can hide the pistol under an untucked shirt that's one size larger than I would normally wear. I'm not a big guy.

The concerned armed citizen, the plainclothes

officer, or the overburdened safety personnel working in uniform also appreciate the constant daily portability of the Beretta pistol.

Accuracy Considered

The professional wants an accurate handgun. It makes an instructor look good. For the practitioner in the field, when a cunning opponent has taken good cover at a considerable distance, accuracy is the key to neutralizing him.

Beretta duty pistols are famous for their accuracy. A friend of mine who teaches at a statewide police academy has noted that among the officers who have their choice of gun, the ones who shoot in competition are disproportionately likely to carry the Beretta Model 92. Accuracy is their stated reason. Among the current crop of 9mm service pistols, only the SIGARMS guns are likely to beat the Beretta, and then not by much. I generally find these guns will shoot between 2 and 3 inches from the bench at 25 yards with good ammunition.

This gun delivers all the accuracy I need. On the second day of an instructor's course, this pistol put five rounds into exactly 2 inches from offhand (Isosceles stance) in front of the class. The distance was 25 yards, and the ammo was ordinary Winchester 115-grain training ball. That kind of performance earns the instructor credibility in what he is teaching, and a gun that delivers it is therefore an important tool of the instructor's trade.

At 50 yards from prone, I got frisky on the trigger and jerked the last of a five-shot group. The first four rounds of Winchester 147-grain subsonic OSM (Olin Super Match) had gone into about 3 inches from the solid on-the-ground position. The called flier almost doubled the spread, but that was my fault, not the pistol's. I noticed also that the group went a bit left. The following day, I aimed the fixed sights where the B-27 silhouette's

Being a popular gun, the Beretta has spawned numerous "non-gun clones." Here, ace police survival and deadly force instructor Jeff Chudwin, a police chief in Illinois, uses a "counterfeit Beretta" to safely demonstrate in front of the class during a lecture at ILEETA, the International Law Enforcement Educators and Trainers Association.

earlobe would be, and was rewarded with five head hits. The distance was 50 yards, the ammo was Winchester's same, accurate 147-grain OSM hollow-point, and I was pleased.

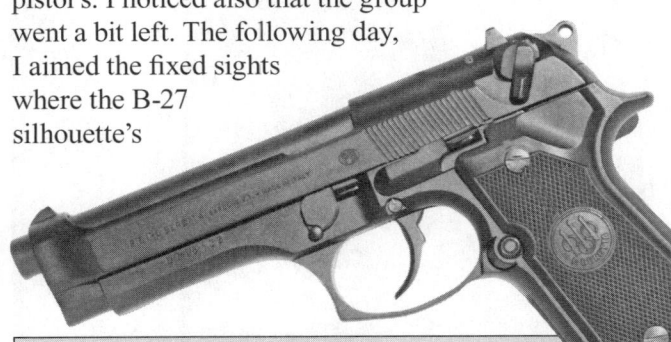

This Beretta has drift-adjustable sights, with three white dots. Out to 10 yards, it shoots where it looks. At 25 yards I have to hold at three o'clock in the 10-ring to hit the letter "X" in the center, and that translates to the hold-off mentioned above at 50 yards. Nonetheless, any pistol that comes out of the box delivering 50-yard head shots is giving you all the accuracy you need to trust your life to.

Fixed sights being slightly off is something I've been seeing more and more lately. I've worked with enough different proven guns to assure myself it isn't just a matter of change in my aging eyes. Others have noted the same sad industry trend, which by no means is limited to Beretta's products.

The Beretta 92 began its splendid record for reliability and performance in the training environment before it proved itself on the street and in battle. The training range has become the predictor of performance in the field.

Frequency of Repair

The Beretta got an undeserved bad rap as a fragile gun over the years. Some said it could be fired by tugging on the outside trigger linkage. I never saw anyone actually make that happen, even deliberately.

There were some early problems with a few slides separating. These were traced eventually to a couple of different things. One was some NATO-spec ammo that was generating almost 50,000 pounds per square inch (psi) pressure levels. That would have broken any other 9mm pistol, too. Another factor was experimental sound suppressor work. The weight of the "silencer" hanging off the Beretta's muzzle interferes with the normal action of the locking blocks, leading to broken blocks and/or stress cracks in the slide.

I've seen most every gun out there break. All tools are weakened by wear and tear. Overall, I've found that Beretta large-frame pistols, particularly the blue as opposed to the stainless, are extremely reliable with a very low breakage rate.

This pistol has been on me for six days with no cleaning. There is no hint of rust. The Bruniton finish wears extremely well. The anodizing on the blue Beretta's frame does tend to wear off when carried constantly, especially when in an exposed duty holster. Nothing underneath corrodes, though. Personally, I think that worn grip look is kind of "salty." Its seasons the gun and makes it look like the owner's been around. Gives it character, sort of.

Berettas are more forgiving than most pistols when it comes to neglect of cleaning and lubrication. Mine has gone weeks at a time of shooting/training without attention. When time comes to clean one, it's among the easiest. Some have suggested that it's too easy to take down and can be ripped apart by an attacker, but that's bogus. It could be done, but would take several times as long as tearing a whole, functional handgun of any kind from your grasp if you didn't know weapon retention. One thing I like about the design as an instructor is that I can quickly pull the barrel/slide assembly off the frame and stuff it in my pocket without fear of losing any small parts. This lets me use just the frame to safely demonstrate certain things to the class that are best seen from a "downrange view," such as the various grasps and reloading techniques.

Ease of Manipulation

Berettas have smooth triggers both double- and single-action. Not necessarily the smoothest or lightest in the industry, but very, very good. The gun I am carrying is straight "out of the box," and I'd guess its trigger pull at about 13 pounds double-action and 6 to 7 single. That's a bit heavy by most people's standards. Personally, I don't mind a heavy trigger. It forces me to hold the gun harder, and in defensive handgun use, I think that is a good thing.

This particular gun is the standard Model 92FS, with an ambidextrous slide-mounted lever that performs double duty as a decocking lever and a manual safety. I have lost count of the number of cases I've seen where the good guy's gun was taken by the bad guy, the bad guy pulled the trigger on the good guy, and nothing happened because the gun was "on safe" and the bad guy couldn't figure it out in time. Some of those guns were Beretta 92FS. In fact, one West Coast Law Enforcement Agency that issues the 92F and mandates that it be carried on safe now has four policemen whose lives were saved by this practice.

Being lightly spring-loaded, the Beretta 92 has what may be the easiest operating slide-mounted thumb safety of any double-action service autoloader.

The instructor's sidearm should be able to deliver a perfect score on demand to demonstrate to students. Author's 9mm Beretta, drawn from an Uncle Mike's police duty rig, has just easily done so.

Mine snaps off 100 percent of the time as I draw and bring it up on target. Some have chosen not to carry a pistol with a safety engaged because they aren't sure they can reliably manipulate the lever when they need the gun to fire. If the ease of operation of the Beretta lever allows them to carry "on safe," that in itself could save their lives one day.

Many still don't care for the idea of a safety catch engaged. Beretta understands that and provides for it. If you like everything else about the 92F, you can consider the 92G. Produced originally for the French national police and adopted since by some police agencies in the United States, the "G" series (for "Gendarmerie," I'm told) replaces the safety/decock lever with a dedicated, spring-loaded part that works as a decocker only.

If I was going to carry a 92F off safe, I'd trade it in for the 92G. (Ditto the .40 caliber 96F versus the 96G.) This is because the spring-loaded lever of the "G" gun can't accidentally get knocked into the on safe position like the "F" gun, when the shooter isn't habituated to flick the lever in the right direction. Be advised, however, the strongly spring-loaded lever of the 92G requires distinctly more force to manipulate than the "push down, push up" lever of the standard 92F.

Another option is the "slick slide," the double-action-only "D" series gun. My 92D and 96D pistols don't need any slide-mounted levers at all, and therefore, don't have any. They also fire double-action-only (DAO) and boast streamlined spurless hammers.

I shoot the "G" or "D" Beretta the way I shoot a SIG, a GLOCK, or a revolver. The thumb of the firing hand is curled down for a maximum strength grab that also keeps the digit out of the way of the working parts. On a 92F, I shoot with the thumb thrust up at about 45 degrees to guarantee that the thumb safety finishes in the "fire" position. However, this causes the thumb to ride the slide release lever and deactivate it. This means that if I've shot the gun dry, the slide will remain closed and I'll have to "jack" it as part of the reloading process. I can accept that.

Fit of the gun can be allowed for. People with small hands find the reach to the Beretta's trigger a long one. The firm now has a short-reach trigger that can be ordered from the factory or retrofitted by a Beretta armorer. It makes the gun much easier to shoot in the average or smaller size hand.

I've taught with each of the above guns. Because I like the "proprietary nature to the user" feature of the manual safety, the "F" series pistol is the one I'm most likely to choose for my own use.

I find the gun very ergonomic. An instructor needs that. If he fumbles with his gun, he loses credibility, and his ability to transmit life-saving information starts going down the chute. But the practitioner needs that, too. As noted above, what can

Upper: The instructor's weapon should work in worst-case scenarios. Here the author uses a stock Beretta 92 to demonstrate shooting from disadvantaged positions to an LFI-II class. The gun needs to work if you're down on your side firing one-handed ...

Middle: ... two handed ...

Lower: ...or from a weakened position with unlocked joints.

be embarrassing for the instructor can be deadly for the practitioner.

Accessories and Custom Features

Pachmayr, Hogue, and others make aftermarket grips for the Berettas. It gives the individual the best range of choice to fit his or her hands. The instructor wants something that makes the gun a natural extension of the hand, so as best to show the students how to do their best. The practitioner needs exactly the same thing to maximize speed or accurate response in a life or death situation.

Any number of night sights are available for Berettas. Three of my 92s wear Trijicons, including the one I keep in the bedroom.

There are also several choices in attachable "white light" units, which make a lot of sense for the tactically trained person executing a building search. My favorite is the powerful, ergonomic SureFire unit. I have one attached to that bedside Beretta.

For those who demand the ultimate in accuracy, at least two fine aftermarket barrels are available. Be cautioned, however: both need to be fitted to the gun, and it works best if the firm that makes the barrels does the installation. After all, they have the most experience. Irv Stone III promises that if his company does the installation, his Bar-Sto barrel will fire a 10-shot group from your Beretta 92 affixed to his Ransom machine rest that will measure between 1 and 1.25 inches at 25 yards. I have a Jarvis barrel in a 92FS. Bill Jarvis installed it himself, and it delivers around an inch at 75 feet. This is a 6-inch barrel, and the part that protrudes beyond the slide was Mag-Na-Ported by Ken Kelley. This reduces the already mild recoil of the 92 still further. Coupled with the weight of the Sure-Fire light underneath, that gun with +P+ ammo feels as if you're shooting a .380.

Many customers prefer finishes that aren't in the Beretta catalog. My colleague Mike Izumi likes electroless nickel for his 92s. Others like Walt Birdsong's Black-T, or the sturdy and attractive coatings applied by Robbie Barkman at Robar or Bob Cogan at Accurate Plating and Weaponry.

Some practitioners want an action hone. For many years, the Beretta I taught with was a 92FC Compact fine-tuned by Jim Horan. My older daughter used it to win High Woman honors at the National Tactical Invitational. It's her gun now. Bill Jarvis did a fine action job on my "bedroom Beretta." Teddy Jacobson at "Actions by T" does a very good job, too.

If you want a lighter Beretta trigger, you can replace the full-size gun's mainspring with one from a 1911 pistol. It seems to work fine in terms of reliability. It will, however, void your warranty. So will custom work, but a good custom pistolsmith will "warrant" his own stuff.

The jury may still be out on the tactical application of laser sights on defensive handguns, but I don't think there's any question that they are extremely useful for instructors. I always have one or another LaserGrip-equipped handgun with me when I'm teaching. It allows me to get multiple points across to the students quickly and easily. I like the LaserGrip, produced by Crimson Trace, on the Beretta, but I'd rather have it on my 92G or one of my slick-slides than on an "F" series gun. The reason is that on the latter, I use the slide lever as a safety catch, and in ambidextrous shooting the laser module on the Crimson Trace unit gets a little bit in the way between my left thumb and the safety lever.

Does that translate to the street? Crimson Trace has numerous letters on file from satisfied users who swear that the laser dot's presence intimidated a potentially violent opponent and kept a dangerous encounter from escalating into a killing situation. Will that work for you? There are no guarantees, but the concept is like the gun itself: it's better to have it and not need it, than to need it and not have it.

Bottom Line

The Beretta 92 helps me teach. It also protects me. If it did not do both, I would not be carrying it in either capacity.

Berettas In Training At Thunder Ranch

The death of Deb Smith at Thunder Ranch in October 1997 brought sadness to the entire tactical firearms training community. We all knew that she and her husband, the legendary Vietnam vet and SWAT cop Clint Smith, had bonded for life like wolves and that she had been a prime mover behind Clint's fabulous Thunder Ranch facility. It was Deb who made things work behind the scenes while Clint and his crack staff were on the ranges and in the simulator teaching their always-full classes how to stay alive in violent encounters.

When each of us who knew them got the news, we paused over memories of this good woman. Mine brought me back to Thunder Ranch, where the previous spring I had gone through the advanced handgun program with my older daughter, Cat.

Both of us used Beretta pistols. My daughter had the distinction of breaking three custom 1911 pistols in a row the previous year, in her debut at Second Chance. She had muttered at me, "A good father would have given me revolvers." At Lethal Force Institute, she had noted that Beretta pistols were the most reliable of all the many weapons the students brought, and they had become the autoloaders she most trusted. I couldn't blame her. I had heard the same sentiments about the Beretta 92 stated by the famed master gunsmith and pistol champion Bill Wilson, and master tactician and firearms instructor Ken Hackathorn, both of whom were to shoot Beretta 92 pistols at the inaugural International Defensive Pistol Association national championships a few months down the road.

Since we were traveling together and studying together, it made sense for us to use similar guns. Ammo, magazines, and leather would be interchangeable. We arranged for 4,000 rounds round of Black Hills remanufactured "blue box" training ammo, 115-grain 9mm FMJ, to be shipped to the Texas facility. I packed several Beretta 92s so we'd have spares.

Fabulous Facility, Terrific Trainers

For my daughter, a graduate of Chapman Academy Advanced and LFI-I through III, Thunder Ranch was another step in her training curriculum. She had won her first pistol match against adult men at age 11, and a couple weeks after her 19th birthday had come in High Woman at her first major shooting event, the National Tactical Invitation of 1996 at Gunsight Training Center. She was pleased that the class included LAPD SWAT types and many true master shooters.

For me, it was a busman's holiday. I teach this stuff for a living. I learned a long time ago that as soon as you think you know it all, you fossilize and doom yourself to obsolescence sometime in the next five years. Tactical self-defense is an evolving and changing discipline. You can't write it if you don't read, and you can't teach it if you can't learn.

And learn we did, both of us. I'll give you an example. For years I had taught my students to inconspicuously set up full-length mirrors at strategic places in their homes, so they could scan hallways in a search situation without exposing themselves to danger. It hadn't occurred to me that polished metal vases in strategic places could do the same thing, but it had occurred to Clint, who taught it. Mastery is in the detail. The difference between an amateur and a professional is the subtlety of technique. At Thunder Ranch, the staff members are all professionals.

Clint Smith is an excellent teacher. There was no rigid "this is the doctrine" attitude. Every technique was taught for a reason that was carefully and clearly explained. Questions were encouraged. It wasn't, "You have to shoot Weaver." It was, "We found that for most people the Weaver stance works best, and we strongly encourage you to try it thoroughly. But, if something else works better for you and you can do it safely, we have no problem with you doing it that way."

Few instructors can make a rapid-fire verbal delivery work, but Clint Smith is one of them. You enjoy listening to him, and when you enjoy listening to the teacher you learn more from him. Preparatory to discussing alternative techniques or weapons systems, Smith will say, "They're all the same ... but they're all different." At another point he might say, "It's not good and it's not bad, it's just fact," a non-judgmental way of getting his point across without turning off a student who might have been habituated to a dubious "doctrine" somewhere else. When Clint Smith says, "I don't know much about shootin' or fightin' but ..." people listen.

Clint's staff thinks the world of him. The feeling is returned. He gives them plenty of time to teach. Each has his or her personal style, but each is clear, patient, and above all dedicated. This is something that can't be faked over a week of intensive training. Adam Kansanof of NYPD once said, "Your students don't care how much you know until they know how much you care," and this concept is in force at Thunder Ranch. You can see that every single member of the cadre staff is there for the student, not for their own self-aggrandizement or time in the sun.

Clint believes that constant, intensive repetition ingrains long-term muscle memory to make techniques work when they're needed. You shoot a lot at Thunder Ranch. When you're shooting a lot, you simply can't afford guns that jam or break down.

Cat and I were glad that we'd brought the right guns and ammo.

Berettas On The Firing Line

Cat and I, along with the officers from LAPD, were the only ones there with Berettas. Colt and Glock pistols dominated in our 17-student class, along with a sprinkling of SIGs.

As noted, Cat and I ordered 4,000 rounds of Black Hills 9mm reloads. We didn't have much to bring back. Cat's faith in the Beretta was rewarded: in some 1,500 plus rounds, she didn't experience a single malfunction.

I had but one, and it was entirely my own fault. Thunder Ranch makes you practice intensively on clearing malfunctions, which you have to set up: stovepipes (which normally do not occur in nature with the open-slide Beretta 92), extraction failures, failures to fire, etc. In one such set-up clearance drill, I had worked the slide violently enough to damage the brass case mouth on one live round, which I failed to inspect when I picked up live rounds from the ground and pocketed them later. I fed it back into a magazine, and predictably, it failed to chamber. A simple tap-rack cleared the Beretta 92 and had me shooting again in literally one second.

We switched off between different Model 92s just for the heck of it. Cat used primarily a Jim Horan-tuned 92FC Compact. This is her favorite gun, her main weapon at the NTI she'd done so well at. I had used it almost a decade before to teach with at Fort Benning when I certified the Army's first cadre of StressFire instructors after that service absorbed the system I developed into their primary combat pistolcraft doctrine (see Army manual FM23-35). It fits her hand better than any other Beretta. Frankly, that's true of me, too. Like me, she carries on-safe and in the course of her draw uses a thrust of the gun hand thumb to snap the safety catch into the fire position.

In The Tower, the four-story monolith that is like Frankenstein's castle when darkness falls, my "bedside Beretta" was most reassuring. Bill Jarvis had fitted this stainless 92 with one of his match barrels in the 6-inch length, which was then MagNa-Ported on its outside inch. Fitted with Trijicon night sights on top, with a SureFire flashlight mounted to the frame below, and enhanced with the same action job Jarvis gave to famed LAPD national champion John Pride, this gun perked 100 percent and never let me miss a shot or get caught disoriented in the darkness. I keep it by my bed at home. For Thunder Ranch's tactical needs, I wore it in a Safariland thigh holster.

Most of the time, blue full-size Model 92s were my mainstay. I passed each to my kid at some point. One was a 92D, the double-action-only slick slide with Trijicon sights. We old wheelgunners appreciate the long, smooth stroke for each shot. In pure rapid fire it slows you to perhaps four shots per second instead of five, but tactical shooting seldom involves pure rapid fire. It also keeps you from jerking the trigger because you anticipated the "glass rod" break of a single-action pull. Finally, you don't have to think about decocking during a lull in the firing. I like these guns. So did my kid. She used this 92D as backup to good effect at NTI and she shot it well at Thunder Ranch. During one stage she used that one, and I used one of the strange hybrids done at the behest of the Indianapolis Police Department some years ago, a 92G converted to 92D configuration with a now totally vestigial spring loaded slide lever that performed absolutely no function. The gun still shot well, though.

Also brought along was a regular 92G. This is the decocker-only model, double-action-only on the first shot. Its slide lever is spring-loaded, snapping the lever up into the "fire" position as soon as the pistol has been decocked, and not usable as a manual safety. This particular specimen shot exquisitely and its sights were dead-on. Interestingly, it had the heaviest single-action pull of any of our Berettas, and after long strings of tactical exercises it was something of a chore to decock the gun, because the thumb has to exert great pressure to overcome the spring the lever is working against.

A couple of years before, I had won a regular 92F, and it got a good workout at Thunder Ranch. Accurate. Utterly reliable. Good trigger both single- and double-action. To decock, flip down and up, almost effortlessly thanks to the ergonomic design of the safety/decock lever. This is the most popular Beretta by far—police, civilian, and of course military in its M9 designation—and it still works superbly well. I always had it in the holster on-safe, and always had the safety off by the time the front sight was on target, using the same manipulation as my daughter, the thrust of the firing hand thumb upward toward the ejection port.

We tried a number of different holsters. Cat gravitated toward Ted Blocker leather, the DA-2 outside-the-belt scabbard and the LFI Concealment Rig inside the waistband. I found myself using the Safariland on the thigh for the flashlight-mounted gun, and for most of the shooting a Kydex inside-the-waistband rig by Tim Wegner of Blade-Tech, whose product is what you have to beat these days if you're entering the Kydex holster market. We both found the Blade-Tech double magazine carrier to be ideal: secure retention even in the most awkward situations of rolling on the ground and shooting, yet the magazines came instantly to hand and gun when you intentionally reached for them.

The pistols and ammo worked superbly. Beretta 92s will generally keep most ammo in 2.5 inches or less at 25 yards. The fixed sights are generally registered for direct point of aim/point of impact, a rarity worthy of note. In the close range basic drills, our Berettas tended to put every Black Hills bullet into one ragged hole. At the end of the course, in side-bet shooting, we were generally able to cut the rubber bands that held up the heads of the 7-yard targets. That's a bit of a trick with pointy 9mm ball, but the gun/ammo combination allowed us to do it.

Tactical Lessons

You're working as partners. One of you is low on ammo. She yells, "Cover," and you swing between your target and hers, taking either or both as necessary if they turn and engage you while she's reloading. "Clear," she yells when her fully loaded pistol is back up, and you take your turn. Clint Smith's cadre emphasizes learning to work together and communicate when you fight together, to back each other up truly instead of merely duplicating one another's efforts. It's part of the whole well-thought out Thunder Ranch approach to survival strategy.

A written exam is part of the final day's schedule. This puts documentation on record that shows the student knew certain things had to be done in certain situations. Thunder Ranch is the only school other than Lethal Force Institute now doing this, and it showed me that Smith and his team have thought out the realities of a graduate actually having to use deadly force in self-defense and stand accountable for it.

The Terminator and other simulators are used to excellent advantage to teach stress control and lessons of tactical movement and building search. Smith wisely and repeatedly emphasizes, "You don't do a building search because you want to. You do a building search only when you have to."

There is much emphasis on low-light shooting. Bill McLennan, the legendary San Antonio street cop and firearms instructor, presented flashlight/weapon coordination as well as I've ever seen it done. Optional techniques included the Harries, the Chapman, the Ayoob, and the Rogers methods, as well as the old FBI technique. All were tried on the line in the dark, and the students were then allowed to use whichever suited them and their equipment the best when they went into the unforgiving live-fire simulators.

One of my favorite simulators at Thunder Ranch is the advancing targets. You have to move backward as they come at you. I personally feel lateral movement would be tactically more sound, but I don't know of any way to teach it safely on a firing line and neither does Clint. Moving backward may be necessary if you've been "canalized" by the opponent's assault, and it well illustrates how quickly the opponent can close with you and kill you with a contact weapon, something Smith's friend and contemporary Dennis Tueller taught us all back in 1983. Sometimes, the instructor running the attacking targets will make it keep coming until he sees that you've gone to plan B or plan C after a few hits in the chest have failed. I was pleased to see that Thunder Ranch teaches the same three target zones I've long recommended at Lethal Force Institute: the center chest (shut off the fuel pump), the pelvis (smash the vehicle's chassis and it will stop moving forward), and deep brain (short circuit the computer and you turn off everything).

While the advancing targets were my favorite from an instructor's standpoint, my daughter and I agreed that for each of us; the most personally demanding was the night assault on The Tower. This four-story monolith looms over the flat Texas hill country, and for this particular exercise, you start some distance away from its base, on the ground. On a signal, you have to run forward and climb a narrow ladder to the top, then "clear the building" from inside out, top to bottom, dealing with all manner of hostile, no-shoot, and hostage targets.

For me, it was a personal coming to terms with something that has long haunted me, the fear of heights that I've had for as long as I can remember. Well into my 20s I would get vertigo—the physical symptoms of pounding heart, dizziness, loss of balance, and a sense of impending unconsciousness—when looking down from great heights. In my late 20s, I cured it with "shock therapy" by strapping myself at the open door of a Cessna and photographing skydivers as they dropped, hanging out over thousands of feet held only by the strap as the pilot banked sharply to give me the camera angle. After that, I still didn't like heights, but figured I could deal with them.

At Thunder Ranch, I experienced a relapse. The rungs of the steel ladder on the outer wall of The Tower are only a couple of inches out from the wall, and I had to turn my surgeon-tuned knee outward to gain purchase with the balls of my feet. By the second floor I was experiencing full-blown vertigo. By the third, I locked onto the wall.

Clint Smith proved what a good man and compassionate instructor he is. He too overcomes a fear of heights every time he scales the wall to demonstrate technique to his students. He reached over the top and told me to come up, not looking up or down. I couldn't do that—it was tactical simulation, and staring at the wall without looking upward would have violated the spirit of the exercise. I had to look up, and for us vertigo victims, looking up the sheer incline is at least as bad as looking down. I finally split the difference.

I was in real danger of passing out, and if I did I would land on the equally compassionate and encouraging Bill McLennan, who was directly below me. It wouldn't do either of us, let alone Thunder Ranch, any good. I asked myself if I'd keep going if my kid was in trouble up there, and the logical side of my brain said, "Yeah, you would, but she ain't." I gained the third floor and snapped to Clint, "Hell with it. I'm going in here. I'll go downward." I knew that with Clint above me, it wouldn't be safe to do the top floor live fire from the inside upward.

I did OK from there, but was cursing myself for cowardice. I was to spend the next several weeks going to high places, staring down and up, and trying to recondition myself to cope with the vertigo. But the point is, that relapse was waiting to happen, and I was able to catch it in time at Thunder Ranch, and that's the kind of thing Clint and his people are there to do for their students.

I then watched my daughter do the same exercise. Her lithe 19-year-old frame scooted up the side of the Tower like a bat scuttling up the side of Castle Dracula. Cat then cleared the building from the inside out, using a SureFire 6P flashlight and a Trijicon-sighted Beretta 92D, in just under three minutes counting her start time from the ground level outside the structure. It was the record time for the class, and every shot she made was perfect. It was an error-free performance.

The kid and I decided later that given a tall building problem, she would go up the outside and I would stand on the ground, refilling magazines and tossing them back up. On graduation day, Clint Smith spoke of Cat's "tactical magnificence" when the certificates were handed out. Her dad's hat size expanded by about a factor of three.

At the End of the Week

The Berettas performed superbly. The Black Hills ammo performed superbly. I had expected no less.

The Thunder Ranch people also performed superbly, and since it was my second time on the premises, that too, was no surprise. Lethal Force Institute recommends Thunder Ranch to its graduates. One is a threat management school, the other is a tactical shooting school, and the two disciplines don't compete against each other so much as they complement one another.

The fabled $3.2 million Thunder Ranch was everything you'd heard it to be. It was Disney World for people like us. But the training is not about the hardware nearly so much as it's about the software. I didn't go to Thunder Ranch for the facility so much as I went there for the quality of training provided by Clint and his staff.

Training is the first environment in which any weapon is tested. It is there that problems of reliability, human engineering, and safety will show up first. The Beretta was tested deeply in training before it was tested in battle or police combat. The fact that it performed superbly in the former predicted that it would perform superbly in the latter … and the gun certainly did that.

La Finé

In Italian, "la fine" (lah FEE-nay) means "the end." This is *la fine* for *The Gun Digest Book of Beretta Pistols,* but certainly not for Beretta or the pistols themselves.

The head of the Beretta family today is Cavalier Ugo Beretta, to my knowledge the only nobleman who leads a gun company. This is in keeping with the gentlemanly way the corporate entity Pietro Beretta has dealt with the often vicious and unwarranted criticism leveled against it and its product.

I think the foregoing chapters will show that I am no flack for Beretta. When something was wrong with the product, I said so. But the fact remains that certain Berettas are at the head of the crowded firearms pack.

No handgun in history has been so exhaustively tested and proven as the Beretta Model 92. At this date, it rules bull's-eye Distinguished competition, and is one of the guns to beat in IDPA competition.

It is no longer first in sales to U.S. police. As noted, LAPD may be switching to Glock on their next mass departmental handgun purchase. Now under the umbrella of Homeland Security, which approves only HK and SIG pistols, when INS came due to retire their old Berettas they went to the SIG-Sauer. Utah State Patrol has traded its Cougars for Glocks. A law enforcement agency's changing of gun brands does not necessarily mean that there was something wrong with the first one.

Civilians still appreciate the Beretta, and I still meet gun dealers who find the Model 92 their single best selling firearm. The Beretta is, of course, the dominant handgun presence in the Iraq and Afghanistan conflicts at this writing. It is likely to remain the primary duty handgun of the U.S. Armed Services for some time to come. All it will take for complaints related to it to be cleared up will be the purchase of proper magazines, and a stroke of the pen at the Pentagon to sign the order that allows hollow-point ammunition to be issued. The Geneva and Hague accords only require ball ammunition for declared international warfare, and the Judge Advocate General's office has already determined that JHP ammo is perfectly acceptable for counter-terrorist use.

As this book goes to the publisher, Beretta is only a few weeks out from introducing their newest pistol, the PX4 Storm. I'm told there are four prototypes in the country at this writing, all at the factory. The gun resembles the Cougar, with updated features like integral flashlight rail and hand adjustment inserts on the backstrap. In addition to the F, G, and D styles, there will be a fourth: "Type C" is described as "Constant action, spurless hammer," and sounds as if it is intended to compete against the Glock, HK LEM, and SIG DAK firing systems.

I wish Beretta luck with it. I hope it does not go the way of the Model 9000. Beretta has brought us many fine, modern pistols. The best of the vest-pocket .25s. The superb Model 92, destined to be a timeless classic, still really "the shape of Beretta" as most visualize it now. The unique Model 86, perhaps the best "orthopedic pistol" for those with weak or crippled hands.

Beretta has the longest history in firearms manufacturing, and one of the most distinguished. They will continue to make fine and classic firearms that protect this nation at home and abroad, fine and classic firearms that free Americans will use to protect their own homes and loved ones.